MW01234972

Information Systems Outsourcing

Third edition

Rudy Hirschheim • Armin Heinzl
Jens Dibbern

Editors

Information Systems Outsourcing

Enduring Themes, Global Challenges, and Process Opportunities

Third edition

 Springer

Editors
Prof. Dr. Rudy Hirschheim
E. J. Ourso College of Business
Louisiana State University
Baton Rouge, LA 70803
USA
rudy@lsu.edu

Prof. Dr. Armin Heinzl
Universität Mannheim
Lehrstuhl für ABWL und
Wirtschaftsinformatik
L 15, 1-6 - Raum 515/516
68131 Mannheim
Germany
heinzl@uni-mannheim.de

Dr. Jens Dibbern
Universität Mannheim
Lehrstuhl für ABWL und
Wirtschaftsinformatik
L 15, 1-6 - Raum 511
68131 Mannheim
Germany
dibbern@uni-mannheim.de

ISBN: 978-3-540-88850-5   e-ISBN: 978-3-540-88851-2

DOI: 10.1007/978-3-540-88851-2

Library of Congress Control Number: 2008940967

Cover design: WMX Design GmbH, Heidelberg, Germany

Printed on acid-free paper

springer.com

Preface

Three years have passed since the second edition of this book was published. The field of IT outsourcing continues to grow in practice as well as in academia and draws further attention in both domains. Aspects of traditional outsourcing (Part II) have remained pronounced but are becoming more mature. While outsourcing determinants are still important, they are now of less interest to researchers. Relationship management (Chap. 1) and capability management (Chap. 2) continue to be of interest; so too are outsourcing outcomes (Chap. 3) and, as a new focus, innovation aspects (Chap. 4). These are motivating more and more research activities, complementing the lifecycle of traditional outsourcing. We note significant growth in the field of IT offshoring (Part II). In our third edition, we offer research results on offshoring patterns and trends (Chap. 5), the crucial aspect of knowledge sharing (Chap. 6), vibrant examples for offshoring dynamics (Chap. 7), and some new contributions on the determinants of offshoring success (Chap. 8). The last part of our book investigates the field of business process outsourcing (Part III). In this section, issues such as standardization, process outsourcing to India and deinstitutionalization patterns in the health-care sector are presented.

Given these new subjects, we believe that *Enduring Themes, Global Challenges, and Process Opportunities* is an appropriate subtitle for this third edition of the monograph. Again, we have thoughtfully compiled contemporary outsourcing research as a primer and a platform for scientific discourse. The third edition is both an update of the second edition and a summary of the *Third International Conference on Outsourcing of Information Services* held in 2007 at Heidelberg, Germany. It will serve as a contemporary basis for further interactions and discussions in the rich field of IT outsourcing. The book will be of interest to academics and students in the field of Information Systems as well as to corporate executives and professionals who seek a more profound analysis and understanding of the underlying factors and mechanisms of outsourcing.

We thank all the authors for their contributions and cooperation. It has been a pleasure to work with you. Our deepest gratitude goes to Jessica Winkler for organizing the third ICOIS. We also thank Martin Eberle, Iris Raquet, and Nina Jaeger, who supported us in indexing, formatting, and editing this book. While we are very grateful to the authors of the chapters of the book, we take responsibility for the content and any errors. We hope the third edition is as instructive and valuable as the first two editions.

Baton Rouge, LA, USA   Rudy Hirschheim
Mannheim, Germany   Armin Heinzl
Mannheim, Germany   Jens Dibbern

Contents

Contributors

Benoit A. Aubert
HEC Montréal and CIRANO, 2020 University, 25th floor, Montréal,
Canada H3A 2A5, benoit.aubert@hec.ca

Michael Barrett
University Reader in Information Technology and Innovation,
Judge Business School, University of Cambridge, UK

Guillaume Beaurivage
HEC Montréal (graduate student), 3000 chemin de la Côte Sainte-Catherine,
Montréal, Canada H3T 2A7
guillaume.beaurivage@hec.ca

Daniel Beimborn
Chair of Information Systems and Services, University of Bamberg,
Feldkirchenstr. 21, 96045 Bamberg, Germany
beimborn@is-bamberg.de

Erran Carmel
Kogod School of Business, American University, Washington DC, USA
carmel@american.edu

T. Rachel Chung
209 Mervis Hall, Katz Graduate School of Business, University of Pittsburgh,
Pennsylvania, USA
tchung@katz.pitt.edu

Anne-Marie Croteau
John Molson School of Business, Concordia University, 1455 de Maisonneuve
Blvd. West, Montréal, Canada H3G 1M8
anne-marie.croteau@concordia.ca

Wendy L. Currie
Warwick Business School, University of Warwick, Coventry CV4 7AL, UK
wendy.currie@wbs.ac.uk

Jason Dedrick
Personal Computing Industry Center, University of California, Irvine, USA
jdedrick@uci.edu

Jens Dibbern
Department of General Management and Information Systems, University of
Mannheim, Schloss, S 135, 68131 Mannheim, Germany
dibbern@uni-mannheim.de

Julie Fisher
Monash University, Caulfield East, Melbourne 3145, Australia
julie.fisher@infotech.monash.edu.au

Tim Goles
Texas A&M International University, 5201 University Boulevard, Laredo,
Texas 78041, USA
tgoles@acm.org

Jahyun Goo
Information Technology and Operations Management, The College of Business,
Florida Atlantic University, 777 Glades Road, Boca Raton, FL 33431-0991, USA
jgoo@fau.edu

Anandasivam Gopal
Robert H. Smith School of Business, University of Maryland, College Park, MD
20742, USA
agopal@rhsmith.umd.edu

Rajesri Govindaraju
Bandung Institute of Technology, Industrial Engineering Department, Bandung,
Indonesia
rajesri_g@mail.ti.itb.ac.id

Stephen Hawk
University of Wisconsin-Parkside, 900 Wood Road, Kenosha, WI 53141, USA
hawks@uwp.edu

Armin Heinzl
Department of General Management and Information Systems, University of
Mannheim, Schloss 219/220, 68131 Mannheim, Germany
heinzl@uni-mannheim.de

Rudy Hirschheim
E. J. Ourso College of Business, Louisiana State University, Baton Rouge,
LA 70803, USA

Jayarama Holla
Indian Institute of Management Bangalore, Bannerghatta Road, Bangalore
560076, India
jayaramh05@iimb.ernet.in

Minh Q. Huynh
Management Department, Southeastern Louisiana University, SLU 10350,
Hammond, LA 70402, USA
Minh.Huynh@selu.edu

Vidya V. Iyer
College of Business Administration, University of Missouri-St. Louis, 8001
Natural Bridge Road, St. Louis, MO 63121-4499, USA
Vidya.iyer@umsl.edu

Robert Jacobs
Monash University, Melbourne 3039, Australia
r.jacobs@bigpond.net.au

Bandula Jayatilaka
Assistant Professor, School of Management, P.O. Box 6000, Binghamton,
NY 13902-6000, USA
jbandula@binghamton.edu

Kate M. Kaiser
College of Business, Marquette University, P.O. Box 1881, Milwaukee
WI 53201, USA
kate.kaiser@mu.edu

Björn Kijl
University of Twente, School of Management and Governance, Enschede,
The Netherlands
b.kijl@utwente.nl

William R. King
222 Mervis Hall, Katz Graduate School of Business, University of Pittsburgh,
Pennsylvania, USA
billking@katz.pitt.edu

Gerhard F. Knolmayer
Institute of Information Systems, University of Bern, Engehaldenstrasse 8,
CH 3012 Bern, Switzerland
gerhard.knolmayer@iwi.unibe.ch

Wolfgang Koenig
Institute of Information Systems, E-Finance Lab, Johann Wolfgang Goethe
University, Mertonstraße 17, 60054 Frankfurt am Main, Germany
wkoenig@wiwi.uni-frankfurt.de

Balaji R. Koka
W. P. Care School of Business, Arizona State University, PO Box 874 006,
Tempe, AZ 85287, USA
balaji.koka@asu.edu

Julia Kotlarsky
ORIS Group, Warwick Business School, Coventry CV4 7AL, UK
Julia.kotlarsky@wbs.ac.uk

Kenneth L. Kraemer
Personal Computing Industry Center, University of California, Irvine, 5251
California Avenue, Suite 250, Irvine, CA 92697-4650, USA
kkraemer@uci.edu

S. Krishna
Indian Institute of Management Bangalore, Bannerghatta Road,
Bangalore – 560076, India
skrishna@iimb.ernet.in

Mary C. Lacity
Professor of Information Systems, University of Missouri-St. Louis,
One University Boulevard, St. Louis, MO 63121, USA
Mary.Lacity@umsl.edu

Jae-Nam Lee
Korea University Business School, Anam-Dong 5 Ga, Seongbuk-Gu,
Seoul 136-701, Korea
isjnlee@korea.ac.kr

Eivor Oborn
Department of BioSurgery and Surgical Technology,
Imperial College London, UK

Ilan Oshri
Rotterdam School of Management, Burg. Oudlaan 50, P.O. Box 1738,
Rotterdam 3000DR, The Netherlands
ioshri@rsm.nl

Kevan Penter
Curtin Business School, GPO Box U1987, Perth WA, 6845, Australia

Graham Pervan
Curtin Business School, GPO Box U1987, Perth WA, 6845, Australia
g.pervan@curtin.edu.au

Peter Reynolds
Department of Information Systems, The University of Melbourne,
111 Barry Street, Carlton, VIC 3010, Australia
p.reynolds@unimelb.edu.au

Suzanne Rivard
HEC Montréal and CIRANO, 3000 chemin de la Côte Sainte-Catherine,
Montréal, Canada H3T 2A7
suzanne.rivard@hec.ca

Joseph W. Rottman
College of Business Administration, University of Missouri-St. Louis, 8001
Natural Bridge Road, St. Louis MO 63121-4499, USA
Rottman@umsl.edu

Anne C. Rouse
Deakin Business School, Deakin University, Melbourne, Australia
anne.rouse@deakin.edu.au

Prasad S. Rudramuniyaiah
University of Missouri-St. Louis, College of Business, One University Boulevard,
St. Louis, MO 63121, USA,
Psrwf4@umsl.edu

Kathy S. Schwaig
Kennesaw State University, Michael J. Coles College of Business, 1000 Chastain
Road, Kennesaw, GA 30144-5591, USA
kschwaig@kennesaw.edu

Detmar Straub
Georgia State University, J. Mack Robinson College of Business, Box 4015,
Atlanta, GA 30302-4015, USA
dstraub@gsu.edu

Reza Torkzadeh
4505 Maryland Parkway, Department of MIS, University of Nevada,
Las Vegas, NV, USA
reza.torkzadeh@unlv.edu

Paul van Fenema
Netherlands Defence Academy, P.O. Box 90002, Breda 4800 DR,
The Netherlands
pfenema@gmail.com

Arjen Wassenaar
Emeritus Professor, University of Twente , School of Management & Governance,
Enschede, The Netherlands
d.a.wassenaar@planet.nl

Peter Weill
MIT, Sloan School of Management, 3 Cambridge Center NE20-336,
Cambridge, MA 02142, USA
pweill@mit.edu

Tim Weitzel
Chair of Information Systems and Services, University of Bamberg,
Feldkirchenstr. 21, 96045 Bamberg, Germany
weitzel@is-bamberg.de

Leslie Willcocks
Information Systems and Innovation Group, Department of Management,
London School of Economics and Political Science, Houghton Street,
London WC2A 2AE, UK
l.p.willcocks@lse.ac.uk

Fabian S. Willi
Vereinsweg 4, CH 3012 Bern, Switzerland
fabian.willi@gmail.com

Jessica K. Winkler
Department of General Management and Information Systems, University of
Mannheim, Schloss, 134, 68131 Mannheim, Germany
winkler@uni-mannheim.de

Kim Wuellenweber
Institute of Information Systems, E-Finance Lab, Johann Wolfgang Goethe
University, Mertonstraße 17, 60054 Frankfurt am Main, Germany
wuellenweber@wiwi.uni-frankfurt.de

Part I
Overview

Outsourcing in a Global Economy: Traditional Information Technology Outsourcing, Offshore Outsourcing, and Business Process Outsourcing

Rudy Hirschheim and Jens Dibbern

1 Introduction

The notion of outsourcing – making arrangements with an external entity for the provision of goods or services to supplement or replace internal efforts – has been around for centuries. Kakabadse and Kakabadse (2002) track one of the earliest occurrences of outsourcing to the ancient Roman Empire, where tax collection was outsourced. In the early years of American history, the production of wagon covers was outsourced to Scotland, where they used raw material imported from India in the production process (Kelly 2002). Outsourcing remained popular in the manufacturing sector, with part of the assembling in many industries being sub-contracted to other organizations and locations where the work could be done more efficiently and cheaply (Vaze, 2005). Commenting on this unstoppable trend, Pastin and Harrison (1974) wrote that such outsourcing of manufacturing functions was creating a new form of organization which they termed the "hollow corporation" (i.e., an organization that designs and distributes, but does not produce anything). They note that such an organizational form would require considerable changes in the way organizations were managed. While they limited their research to the role of management in the hollow corporation, they comment on the substantial (and unpleasant) social and economic changes that the outsourcing of manufacturing was causing.

It was not long before the idea of outsourcing was applied to the procurement of information technology (IT) services also. While the current wave of IT outsourcing can be traced back to EDS' deal with Blue Cross in the early sixties, it was the landmark Kodak deal in 1989 that won acceptance for IT outsourcing as a strategic tool. Many large and small outsourcing deals were inked in the years that followed. From its beginnings as a cost-cutting tool, IT outsourcing has evolved into an integral component of a firm's overall information systems strategy (Linder, 2004). Still, reducing costs is an idea that never loses its appeal, and the opportunity to meet the IT demands of the organization with a less-expensive but well-trained labor pool has led organizations to look past their national borders, at locations both far and near, for such resources. Recent statistics vouch for the continued acceptance and popularity of IT outsourcing as well as this trend towards outsourcing to different global locations. A Gartner study conducted in 2004 placed global IT

R. Hirschheim et al. (eds), *Information Systems Outsourcing,*
© Springer-Verlag Berlin Heidelberg 2009

outsourcing at $176.8 billion in 2003, and suggested that it would grow to $253.1 billion in 2008 (Souza et al., 2004). A recent IDC Report noted that the IT service market has now reached $746 billion (Fogarty, 2008). While outsourcing has grown beyond the domain of IT embodying decisions such as where and how to source IT to a much wider set of business functions, IT outsourcing still leads the pack with 67% of all global outsourcing deals in 2004 being related to IT (Pruitt, 2004). This inexorable trend towards outsourcing and offshoring brings unique sets of challenges to all parties involved. Western organizations have to walk a tightrope between the savings and efficiencies that offshoring could provide and the adverse reactions from a society increasingly disenchanted by the job displacement and loss that outsourcing brings.

2   IT Outsourcing Motivation and History

Although organizations outsource IT for many reasons, the growth of IT outsourcing can be attributed to two primary phenomena: (1) a focus on core competencies and (2) a lack of understanding of IT value (Lacity, Hirschheim, & Willcocks, 1994). First, motivated by the belief that sustainable competitive advantage can only be achieved through a focus on core competencies, the management of organizations have chosen to concentrate on what an organization does better than anyone else while outsourcing the rest. As a result of this focus strategy, IT came under scrutiny. The IT function has been viewed as a non-core activity in organizations; further, senior executives believe that IT vendors possess economies of scale and technical expertise to provide IT services more efficiently than internal IT departments. Second, the growth in outsourcing may also be due to a lack of clear understanding of the value delivered by IT (Lacity & Hirschheim, 1993a, b). Though senior executives view IT as essential to the functioning of the organization, it is viewed as a cost that needs to be minimized. Believing that outsourcing will help meet the IT needs of the organization less expensively, organizations have chosen to outsource. Interestingly, some researchers (e.g., Hirschheim & Lacity, 2000) have found that outsourcing has not always yielded the benefits that organizations had hoped for. This has led to numerous normative strategy proposals to help organizations achieve success (Cullen, Seddon, Willcocks, 2005; Lacity & Hirschheim 1993a, b; Linder 2004).

Initially, when organizations looked to external sources for the provision of IT services, the vendor provided a single basic function to the customer, exemplified by facilities management arrangements where the vendor assumed operational control over the customer's technology assets, typically a data center. The agreement between Blue Cross and Electronic Data Systems (EDS) in 1963 for the handling of Blue Cross' data processing services was different from such previous 'facilities management' contracts. EDS took over the responsibility for Blue Cross's IT people extending the scope of the agreement beyond the use of third parties to supplement a company's IT services. EDS's client base grew to include customers such as Frito-Lay and General Motors in the seventies, and Continental Airlines, First City Bank and Enron in the eighties. Other players entered the outsourcing arena as well, the most noteworthy of those being the ISSC division of IBM. ISSC's deal with Kodak in 1989 heralded the arrival of the IT outsourcing mega-deal and legitimized the role of outsourcing for IT. Following the success of the Kodak deal, well-known companies around the world quickly followed suit – General Dynamics, Xerox, and McDonnell Douglas in the U.S.; Lufthansa and Deutsche Bank in Germany; Rolls Royce and British Aerospace in Britain; KF Group in Sweden; Canada Post in Canada; Telstra, LendLease, and the Commonwealth Bank of Australia in Australia; and ABN Amro in the Netherlands (Dibbern, Goles, Hirschheim, & Jayatilaka, 2004).

IT outsourcing has evolved from sole-sourcing and total sourcing arrangements of yester-years where one vendor provides all IT services to its client to complex arrangements involving multiple vendors and multiple clients (Clemons, Hitt, & Snir, 2000; Gallivan & Oh, 1999). According to Mears and Bednarz (2005) companies are also outsourcing on a much more selective basis than ever before. The tools and resources available today make it easier for IT executives to manage their IT portfolio and achieve the economies they need without outsourcing everything. (Of course a key challenge is determining what pieces of the IT portfolio to outsource and what to keep internally.) Outsourcing also now embraces significant partnerships and alliances, referred to as co-sourcing arrangements, where client and vendor share risk and reward. These co-sourcing arrangements build on the competencies of the client and vendor to meet the client's IT needs. Kaiser and Hawk (2004) provide recommendations to organizations considering co-sourcing arrangements with offshore vendors. They note that organizations should avoid total dependency on the vendor by maintaining their IT competencies in-house.

IT outsourcing – as it was practiced through the turn of this past century – was primarily domestic outsourcing. While it had considerable impact on the way organizations structured and managed their IT, and to some extent, redefined the roles of IT managers, the impacts were largely limited to the client and vendor firms' boundaries with the possible exception of the creation of some new intermediary organizations (e.g., outsourcing consulting firms). Domestic IT outsourcing barely created a stir in the public press perhaps because no one foresaw that the outsourcing of a critical knowledge-work function (i.e., IT) might have more dramatic effects if these tasks could be performed not domestically but globally. In some way this is surprising because most international firms were hiring numerous foreign IT people, and importing people from places like the Philippines, India, etc. on staff augmentation contracts. Indeed, according to Sheshabalaya (2004) and Friedman (2005), major changes were already taking place in IT in the late 1980s and throughout the 1990s in the US but went unnoticed, mostly because of the dot.com boom and Y2K remediation needs.

3   Offshore Outsourcing

A prominent change in the outsourcing arena is the growth in offshore outsourcing (Lacity & Willcocks, 2001; Morstead & Blount, 2003; Robinson & Kalakota, 2004). Driven by the pressures of globalization and the ensuing need to address opportunities and threats from global competition, companies are increasingly looking at less-expensive resources available in offshore locations. And these less expensive resources are readily available in countries like India, China and the Philippines.

An outsourcing arrangement is considered 'offshore outsourcing' when the responsibility for management and delivery of information technology services is delegated to a vendor who is located in a different country from that of the client (Sabherwal, 1999). While the three well-known countries in the offshore outsourcing arena (the so-called three I's) are India, Israel, and Ireland (Carmel, 2003a, b), near-shore providers in Canada and Mexico are also popular among U.S. clients just as eastern Europe has become a prime near-shore option for central European countries, because of geographic and cultural proximity. Some clients find the near-shore scenario more attractive because these locations facilitate continuous monitoring (Rao, 2004). China is also quickly gaining popularity because of its low labor costs.

As in domestic outsourcing, a primary driver of offshore outsourcing is the continued pressure organizations face to cut costs associated with IT while maintaining and improving processes (McFarlan, 1995; Nicholson & Sahay, 2001; Rajkumar & Dawley, 1998). The time differences between the client and the offshore vendor locations create extended work days which can contribute to increased IT productivity. With efficient distribution of work between the client and vendor locations, projects can theoretically be finished faster (Apte, 1990; Carmel & Agarwal, 2001; Carmel & Agarwal, 2002; Morstead & Blount, 2003; Rajkumar & Dawley, 1998; Ramanujan & Lou, 1997).

Organizations also turn to offshore outsourcing because of the lack of IT resources to perform required tasks. Faced with the lack of trained professionals, organizations look to foreign shores to gain access to knowledgeable IT personnel and valuable IT assets (Apte et al., 1997; Morstead & Blount, 2003; Rottman & Lacity, 2004; Sahay, Nicholson, & Krishna, 2003; Terdiman, 2002). Offshore vendors typically have well-trained IT personnel with the requisite technical knowledge and skills. These vendors have also recognized the need to train their staff not only in the latest technologies, but also in management and communication skills and have established numerous world-class facilities to do so (Khan, Currie, Weerakkody, & Desai, 2003). Such technical expertise and qualifications of the staff make these vendor firms very attractive to clients, since clients look to outsource activities that involve high level of technical skills (Aubert, Patry, & Rivard, 2004).

In addition, offshore vendors have obtained certifications to prove their ability to execute and deliver quality work. These certifications assure the client organizations that the vendor is following quality practices in the management of the project and are important in gaining the client's trust and developing the client-vendor relationship (Heeks & Nicholson, 2004). Vendors aim to align their practices with standards in different areas including software development processes (e.g., CMM), workforce management (e.g., PeopleCMM), and security (e.g., ISO 17779)

(Hirschheim, George, & Wong, 2004). Qu and Brockelhurst (2003) find that client organizations pay particular attention to these certifications in the vendor evaluation and selection process. However, Coward (2003) comments that while large organizations look towards certifications for quality assurance and success in offshore projects, small and medium enterprises focus on personal connections in the selection of vendors.

Finally, as in domestic outsourcing, the bandwagon effect (Lacity & Hirschheim 1993a; 1995) comes into play in offshore outsourcing as well. The sheer fact that these offshore choices are available and that other organizations are taking advantage of these options prompt other organizations to consider offshore outsourcing (Carmel & Agarwal, 2001; Carmel & Agarwal, 2002; Gopal, Mukhopadhyay, & Krishnan, 2002; Overby, 2003; Qu and Brocklehurst, 2003). With such drivers, offshore outsourcing is growing at a faster rate in many more countries than domestic outsourcing. For example, while outsourcing within the United States is growing at a rate of 10–15% annually, offshore outsourcing is growing at a rate higher than 20% (EBusiness Strategies, 2004). A MetaGroup report predicts that by 2009, an average organization will be sending 60% of its applications work offshore (Hirschheim & George, 2007).

Offshore arrangements come in a variety of flavors to match the client's desire for ownership and control: conventional offshore outsourcing arrangements, joint ventures, build-operate-transfer arrangements, and captive centers. These arrangements span the continuum from complete hand-over of the project to an offshore vendor in conventional offshore outsourcing arrangements to establishing a captive center in the foreign country. While the client usually has a low to medium level of control on the operation and delivery services in conventional offshore outsourcing, the client retains full ownership and control of the assets, personnel, management and operations of a captive center. Such captive center arrangements are not strictly outsourcing arrangements, since in outsourcing the responsibility for the management of the IT services is handed off to an external vendor. These captive center arrangements fit under the umbrella of "offshoring" (Robinson & Kalakota, 2004). In joint ventures and build-operate-transfer arrangements, the client is able to take advantage of the vendor's knowledge of the local market, while retaining a certain amount of control. Such shared ownership can reduce the risk of offshore outsourcing. A build-operate-transfer is an arrangement where a domestic client contracts with an offshore vendor to set up an offshore center, with the goal of taking over the ownership and management of the center once it is established (Anthes, 1993; Khan et al., 2003; Kumar & Willcocks, 1996; Morstead & Blount, 2003).

A related development has been the offshore outsourcing of IT-enabled services and business processes. Many offshore IT vendors have produced offshoots to manage business process outsourcing (BPO) deals. Examples are Wipro's Spectramind and Infosys' Progeon. The BPO market is making giant strides; it is estimated that the offshore BPO market will grow at a rate of 79% annually to reach a size of $24.2 billion, while the offshore IT outsourcing market is expected to grow at a rate of 43% to $56 billion by the end of 2008 (EBusiness Strategies, 2004). Currently, IT outsourcing dominates offshore outsourcing and BPO, but this is likely to change in the future.

4 Motivation for the Third Edition

When we produced the first edition of the book *Information Systems Outsourcing in the New Economy: Enduring Themes, Emergent Patterns and Future Directions* in 2002, the motivation rested on the need to take stock of a field which had been around for about 10 years. Since then a paper was published which offered a good overview of the field (Dibbern et al., 2004). But because it was a paper, it could not do justice to the depth and breadth of the outsourcing landscape which includes the more recent development of offshore outsourcing. To this end, the second edition was developed. In this follow-up edition, that came out in 2006, we reproduced a number of what we consider more 'classic' papers in the field and supplemented them with a large number of new contributions, in particular on the topic IT offshoring. This new direction was reflected by the subtitle: *Enduring Themes, New Perspectives and Global Challenges*.

This third edition, now includes a completely new collection of papers on the topic of information systems outsourcing. Similar to the first edition, the contributions of the third edition are based on an international conference that we held for the third time involving key researchers from around the world with a proven track record in the field of Information Systems Outsourcing. As such, this new book is based on the research presented by the participants attending the 3rd International Conference on Outsourcing of Information Services (www.ICOIS.de) which was held in Heidelberg, Germany, May 29 to 30, 2007. We believe this new edition offers an excellent roadmap of the IT outsourcing academic literature, highlighting what has been learned so far and how the work fits together under a common umbrella.

5 Book Structure and Outline

To provide such a common umbrella we categorized the papers included in this book under three major topics that are related to one another. And we have divided the book into four parts: (1) Overview, (2) Traditional IT Outsourcing, (3) IT Offshoring, and (4) Business Process Outsourcing. The structure of the book is illustrated in Fig. 1.

In Part 1 of the book (this chapter), we attempt to offer a roadmap of IT outsourcing which hopefully helps the reader to separate the forest from the trees, so to speak. It provides an overview of the area which can act as the foundation for the papers included in this volume. The sum of the papers represents a microcosm of the IT outsourcing research field at large. It is hoped that the synthesis provided in

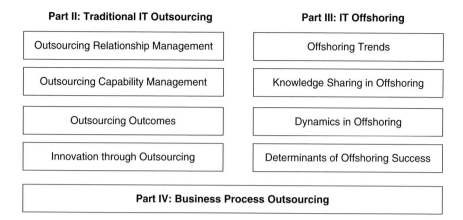

Fig. 1 Book structure

this book is an important contribution – especially for the academic readership – in identifying research gaps, reflecting upon critical research issues, and showing potential paths for future research in IT outsourcing.

5.1   Part II: Traditional IT Outsourcing

The second part of the book contains papers which are concerned with the traditional form of IT outsourcing, where an organization decides to outsource part or all of its IS function to one or more external service providers. The issues raised in these papers are of general appeal. They are not necessarily limited to the domestic context or even to the IT context. In our two previous editions we framed these traditional IT outsourcing issues under the umbrella of "Basic IT outsourcing life cycle" covering the key problem domains along the process of making the sourcing decision, arranging and managing the outsourcing relationship, and changing or renewing the relationship based on a recurrent evaluation of the outcome of the relationship. The focus of this third edition will be on the implementation of the outsourcing decision and its re-evaluation rather than the initial decision. The determinants of the sourcing decision have been widely researched (see Dibbern et al., 2004)[1] and accordingly it is of little surprise that the primary attention of studies concerned with

---

[1] It is to be noted, though, that some key theoretical challenges such as inter-theoretical linkages and the question of generalizability across countries, IS functions, or industries continue to be important issues for future research (Dibbern 2004). Moreover, the outsourcing decision as a process is still heavily under-researched (Dibbern et al. 2004).

traditional IT outsourcing has shifted towards the later stages in the outsourcing life cycle asking questions such as how to outsource efficiently and effectively.

When implementing an outsourcing decision, there are various challenges facing both client and vendor. This book focuses on four of these challenges including (1) the management of the relationship between client and vendor, (2) the management of the capabilities (both at the client and the vendor side), (3) the determination of success or failure, and (4) the more specific consideration of innovation as one often neglected issue in outsourcing deals.

5.1.1   Outsourcing Relationship Management

Past research has clearly shown that one of the key success factors of an outsourcing arrangement is the proper formation and management of the relationship between client and vendor. In general, the outsourcing relationship can be broken down into two constituent elements: "(a) the formal contract that specifies the task requirements and obligations of each party in written form, and (b) the psychological contract (Sabherwal 1999) that is based on the parties' mutual beliefs and attitudes" (Dibbern et al., 2004, p. 51).

Goo provides one of the first studies that explicitly considers the duality and interplay between elements of the psychological and formal contract. More specifically, he argue that the formal contract, reflected by various service level agreements (SLA), provides the foundation for relational governance, reflected by trust and commitment in the relationship between client and vendor. This view is empirically tested based on data from firms in South Korea yielding new insights into the interplay between formal and informal aspects of the outsourcing relationship.

Lee, Huynh, and Hirschheim set the focus on the psychological contract, by examining more closely the constituent parts of mutual trust and how trust may improve knowledge sharing between client and vendor personnel as a primary prerequisite for successful outsourcing arrangements. One of the unique features of this study is the recognition of both the vendor and the client side which is included in the empirical comparison. This paper thus examines outsourcing success from both perspectives. Moreover, the authors add a temporal dimension to the phenomenon by distinguishing between initial and current trust in outsourcing relationships.

5.1.2   Outsourcing Capability Management

Given the strong importance that relational governance together with the proper arrangement and management of the formal contract play for successful outsourcing, the next question to ask is who should be responsible for these management tasks at both client and vendor side and which capabilities are required from the people involved. Answers to these questions are provided by the next two studies.

Reynolds and Willcocks set the focus on the capabilities needed by the client organization. They provide an in-depth longitudinal analysis of the outsourcing arrangement from Commonwealth Bank (Australia) which entered into a ten-year joint venture with Electronic Data Systems (EDS) in 1997, later on evolving more into a multi-sourcing arrangement. By analyzing the role of nine key capabilities ranging from informed buying to contract monitoring as well as hands-on capabilities such as architecture planning and design, they are able to show how these capabilities evolve and are required to be adapted over time due to changes in the organization's requirements and environment conditions. Important implications are derived about organizational mechanisms available to senior executives for developing these capabilities within their organization over time.

Goles, Hawk, and Kaiser on the other hand, are studying IT outsourcing capabilities from the vendor side and also make comparisons to the client side. More specifically, they examine the particular skill sets that are required by IT-firms now and in the future. Their study is rare in that it takes a vendor perspective as well as in the detail in which the skills of IT professionals are analyzed. Also illuminating is the comparison of required skill sets from the perspective of IT firms and non-IT firms. These differences have implications for the design and implementation of the different possible roles for client and vendor firms.

5.1.3   Outsourcing Outcomes

One of the key motivations to study outsourcing relationship and capability management more extensively has been the observation of considerable variation in the success of IT outsourcing arrangements.

Rouse, in her paper, has taken a closer look at the variation of IT outsourcing success and indeed speaks of an IT outsourcing paradox reflecting the fact that the practice of IT outsourcing has steadily grown worldwide, while at the same time the expected benefits from outsourcing are often not achieved. Based on a review of past research, including evidence from her own research, she substantiates the existence of this paradox and seeks to explain it. Interestingly, the majority of her reasoning is concerned with the initial sourcing decision, which according to her analysis, is often based on vague business cases, neglect of various trade-offs in outsourcing objectives, and few attempts to consider future changes. Moreover, difficulties in performance measurement and path dependencies that make it difficult to reverse outsourcing decisions often amount to continued unsatisfactory outsourcing decisions. These issues clearly point at research gaps in the current literature on IS outsourcing success.

Past research may in fact have overly relied on fighting against the symptoms of ill outsourcing relationships rather than critically reflecting upon the conditions for and constraints against more fundamental changes in an organization's sourcing arrangements. Such a view would certainly require a more longitudinal perspective on outsourcing arrangements. Such a view is provided in the next paper.

Fisher, Hirschheim, and Jacobs explicitly recognize temporal dynamics in outsourcing relationships. By analyzing the outsourcing endeavor of a single Australian firm at three different points in time over a period of 9 years, they are able to show how changes in the objectives associated with outsourcing lead to different responses in the management of the outsourcing relationship.

This raises interesting questions in terms of outsourcing flexibility. Can we really speak of outsourcing success if a vendor perfectly meets a client's prior expectations, as specified in the contract, but is unable to adjust to changing client requirements? One way to abstract from the initial IS related objectives of an IS outsourcing arrangement (as specified in the contract) as well as from the outsourcing relationship as the unit of analysis, is to examine higher level outcome variables, such as the impact of IT outsourcing on firm performance or on market value of a firm. This is taken up by the next two studies.

Straub, Weill, and Schwaig examine how IS outsourcing is related to overall firm performance. Unlike other prior research that examined the direct impact of the degree of IS outsourcing on firm performance, they argue that the impact of IT outsourcing on firm performance depends on the alignment between the outsourcing decision and the strategic role that is attributed to an organization's IS function. More specifically, they argue that outsourcing reduces the level of control over the IT resource and accordingly needs to be aligned with the strategic IS objectives. This view is empirically examined with an international set of empirical data on outsourcing contracts.

Willi and Knolmayer take a higher level perspective by examining stock market reactions to outsourcing announcements and events. Their results - based on a literature review and their own study on the link between IT outsourcing and stock market reactions - provide a number of important implications. From a theoretical point of view, it appears necessary to consider potential moderation effects of industry differences and cultural differences more closely in future studies. For example, the risk propensity of a country may well be reflected in the shareholders response to outsourcing events, i.e., whether such events are viewed in a positive or negative way. One interesting observation from previous research is also that it seems to matter greatly which kinds of objectives are communicated in the event of an outsourcing announcement. For example, it was shown that strategic objectives were more positively related with positive stock market reactions than efficiency objectives.

This latter argument is related to the next issue of the role of innovation in IS outsourcing relationships.

5.1.4 Innovation Through Outsourcing

The role of innovation can be viewed from different angles in IS outsourcing. On the one hand, IT outsourcing may itself be viewed as a form of organizational innovation (Loh & Venkatraman, 1992), which likely has important implications on the willingness of firms to enter into such innovative endeavors. On the other hand, innovation may be viewed as one of the objectives in the sourcing decision itself. For example, an organization may strive to increase its innovative capabilities through outsourcing or it may decide against outsourcing because it sees its innovativeness endangered. Moreover, innovation may occur at different levels, e.g., at the technology level it may be necessary for an organization to keep up with the latest information technologies; or, at the business process level, an organization may strive for enabling new business processes. Moreover, the IT sourcing decision may even be linked to the innovativeness of an organization's products and services.

Aubert, Beaurivage, Croteau, and Rivard take up the first of these perspectives. They examine how the IS sourcing decision is influenced by the strategic profile of a firm separated into three types: prospectors, analyzers, and defenders (based on Miles & Snow, 1978). One of the key differentiators between these three strategy types is the propensity towards innovation of a firm. For example, the typical prospector company focuses on new product and service development and innovation to meet new and changing customer needs and generate new demands. Based on multiple case studies the authors come up with a number of interesting implications on how the generalization of the link between strategy type and degree of outsourcing of a firm is influenced by the type of IS function that is being examined. As such, some differences between IT operations and maintenance outsourcing are highlighted.

Wassenaar, Govindaraju, and Kijl take a more general conceptual approach on the issue of innovation in IT outsourcing. They argue that innovation can occur both in terms of contextual changes, mostly reflecting the client side, and in terms of solution changes, mostly being the responsibility of the vendor. However, the interplay between the problem context and the problem solution domain suggests an interrelated innovation process between client and vendor (interaction domain). The authors provide a number of instrumental recommendations on how such an interaction domain can be established for enabling constant innovation in IT outsourcing relationships.

Jayatilaka examines the enabling forces for the delivery of product and service innovations by the vendor, which may in part stem from process and administrative innovations at both the client and the vendor side. He argues that the contractual arrangements and the relationship between client and vendor play a mediating role in the development of innovations in IT outsourcing arrangements. The results from the analysis of four outsourcing cases show that in the majority of cases the vendor is the key source of innovations based on cumulative effects of learning. However, the costs of innovations may not be neglected calling for future research on possible trade-off effects of innovation in IT outsourcing contracts.

5.2 Part III: IT Offshoring

The third part of the book contains papers that are concerned with the increasing practice of IT offshoring.

5.2.1 Offshoring Trend

This part begins with two papers that examine the offshoring trend from two different perspectives: trends in the market, and trends in research.

Dedrick and Kraemer provide insights into the evolution of offshoring in the PC industry. This is interesting because in many ways the developments in the hardware industry can be conceived as a forerunner of the IT services industry. For example, the authors show how the type of work that was offshored in the PC industry has shifted from work in the later production phases, such as operations (i.e., pure manufacturing), to the more innovate, creative, and intellectually challenging tasks, such as development and design. Similar developments may be expected in the IT services sector. This has important implications for the IT industry and the competitiveness of particular firms in the industry. Companies are forced to adjust to the new opportunities in the division of labor across the globe and to develop new roles, such as those of systems or components integrators in order to stay competitive in the market.

King, Torkzadeh, and Chung seek to provide an overview of the status quo in IT outsourcing research by analyzing the content of a subset of research papers made up by the submissions to a special issue of the journal *Management Information systems Quarterly* (MISQ) for which the first two authors served as guest editors.[2] The review of papers reveals some intriguing findings about the breath of current research reflected by the range of research objectives, methodological aspects, and theoretical foundations. Based on this overview, researchers may be able to identify potential open spots in the IT offshoring research landscape.

The next papers have a specific research focus in IT offshoring and certainly contribute to filling the open spots as identified by *King, Torkzadeh, and Chung*.

5.2.2 Knowledge Sharing in Offshoring

The first two papers are concerned with the issue of knowledge sharing in IT offshoring. As can be inferred from the study by *Lee, Huynh, and Hirschheim* in the chapter on *Relationship Management*, knowledge sharing also plays an important role in domestic outsourcing, however, the additional boundaries between client and vendor, which are created through offshoring, such as geographical distance, differences in national culture, or language barriers, pose additional challenges to the knowledge transfer processes between client and vendor (See also Cha, Pingry, & Thatcher, 2008; Dibbern, Winkler, & Heinzl, 2008; Leonardi & Bailey 2008).

Oshri, Kotlarsky, and van Fenema focus specifically on how knowledge transfer between client and offshore vendor personnel can be improved through a combination

---

[2] This Special Issue of *MISQ* appeared in June 2008, containing 9 research papers on IT offshoring. 43 of the submitted papers were considered in the review.

of codification and personalization mechanisms, which together form a so called "transactive memory" in globally distributed teams. The study provides empirical evidence from two projects from an Indian vendor, where services were delivered to two European banks. The two cases show how personalized and codified knowledge directories are used in conjunction for enabling knowledge transfer. Specifically, the processes of coding, storing and retrieving knowledge were examined for both enabling codification and personalization knowledge transfer processes. The findings have important implications for emergent theorizing on the interplay between codification and personalization mechanisms as known from the knowledge management literature (Alavi & Leidner 2001) and how to balance and combine these mechanisms in the context of IT offshoring projects.

Barrett and Oborn examine knowledge sharing in a special constellation, where an insurance conglomerate in a developing country (Jamaica) decided to insource the development of a new insurance system to a newly founded IT spin-off after the system specifications had been done with the help of an external consultancy company. The situation in this case is unique because due to labour shortages in Jamaica a significant portion of the IT staff was hired from India and indeed took the lead in the internal IT group of the insurance conglomerate. Drawing on theoretical lenses of knowledge transfer and communities-of-practice, the case study provides insights into the enablers and barriers to knowledge sharing in an environment that is characterized by cultural differences as well as the general boundary between expertise in the business domain and the IT domain.

5.2.3 Dynamics in Offshoring

As indicated by the previously discussed papers by *Dedrick and Kraemer* as well as *Barret and Oborn*, offshoring is no static phenomenon. In fact it is evolving over time both on an industry level, signalled by changes in the distribution of IS tasks worldwide, as well as on a firm or project level indicated by changes within particular sourcing arrangements over time. The dynamic nature of IT offshoring on different levels of abstraction and how to respond to these dynamics is the shared subject of the next three papers.

Carmel, Dedrick, and Kraemer begin their analysis by taking a firm level perspective. They examine the key determinants of IT offshoring by confronting factors that may lead companies to pull offshore as opposed to staying onshore. To this end, they conducted multiple case studies among Indian, Chinese, and U.S. firms to examine how these pull/stay factors are related to the key activities of the software development life cycles and to what extend they indeed explain why a company stays onshore or pulls offshore. They then continue to transfer their results to more of an evolutionary perspective that predicts shifts in the onshore/offshore distribution of software life cycle activities over time.

Lacity, Iyer, and Rudramuniyaiah concentrate their analysis on one particular dynamic in offshore projects that is often neglected: the high level of employee turnover. Based on expert interviews with Indian IS professionals they seek to identify the main reasons for turnover intentions. They find some interesting offshore specific features that call for a number of adaptations of factors and relationships that were found to be of relevance in previous research studies in the context of traditional non-offshore settings.

Krishna and Holla by noting the dynamics in offshore outsourcing call for a stronger recognition of improvisation as one potential response to the changing requirements and challenges of IT offshoring. As such, they take the perspective of offshore vendors studying two cases of IT firms that founded an offshore development centre in India. Their theoretical focus is on studying the key enabling and deterring factors of an offshore center's ability to improvise. The findings point to the importance of culture (organizational and local context), leadership style, and balance between planned Vs. situated action.

5.2.4 Determinants of Offshoring Success

While knowledge sharing and the understanding of practices for managing offshore dynamics are certainly important aspects in the achievement of offshore success – either from the perspective of client or vendor organizations – the next three studies have more explicitly studied the determinants of IT offshoring success.

Rottman and Lacity examine how certain situational factors are related to the success of offshore outsourcing projects. The study makes an important contribution to a better understanding of offshore outsourcing success factors by identifying two categories of situational factors that explain variations in the success of offshored IS projects. The authors note that the characteristics of the client, such as its former social ties with domestic outsourcing vendors, its organizational culture, and its project management processes and expectations can have an impact on the relationship with the offshore vendor and, thereby, impact the success of the project. But they also note that specific project properties, such as the size of the vendor, the duration of the contract, the value of the contract, or the type of the IS function that is offshored, can also influence offshore outsourcing success.

Winkler, Dibbern, and Heinzl examine the impact of cultural differences between Germany and India on the success of software development projects that were offshored to Indian vendors by German client organizations. A number of cultural themes were identified that are related to established cultural dimensions as distinguished in different norms and values of cultural groups. These cultural differences are found to impact established outsourcing success factors such as mutual trust, cooperation, avoidance of conflicts, and vendor performance.

Gopal and Koka empirically examined the driving factors of service quality of offshore software development projects. They gathered data from 100 offshore projects of a single vendor through a survey. The results show that project properties, such as requirements uncertainty, as well as vendor characteristics, such as experiences, have a significant effect on service quality. However, the effect of these dimensions is moderated by the type of contract. This highlights the importance of aligning contractual arrangements with situational factors, such as project properties and the attributes of the client and vendor personnel, for increasing the benefits from IT offshoring.

5.3   Part IV: Business Process Outsourcing

The final three papers are not exclusively concerned with the sourcing of IT products and services, but expand the perspective to include entire business processes. As such, they certainly contain a number of conceptual overlaps with studies on IT sourcing, however, the shift in focus from IT to business processes implies some unique features that deserve a focused analysis paving the way for potential future studies. Such studies could elaborate on the differences and possible interplay between the sourcing of IT services and products and that of entire business processes.

Wuellenweber, König, Beimborn, and Weitzel focus on typical transaction processes in the banking industry and the factors that may lead to higher level of successes when outsourcing such business processes. Special attention is given to the role of standardization as a key determinant of BPO success. Drawing on economic theories and relational exchange theory they test three alternative explanations for the impact of standardization on BPO success.

The results show some intriguing parallels to the study of success factors in IT offshoring by *Gopal and Koka*. Both studies highlight that the reduction of uncertainty about the tasks being outsourced (standardization may actually be viewed as form of uncertainty reduction in requirements within the task domain) is a key prerequisite for successful outsourcing. This actually reflects the results of early studies in IT outsourcing which made similar claims in terms of "outsourcing readiness" (Lacity & Hirschheim 1993a; Lacity *et al.* 1995). To develop this thought further the question is raised to what extent different forms of outsourcing, such as traditional IT outsourcing, offshoring, and BPO, actually differ in the underlying problem domain and hence their theoretical understanding. There clearly is a common denominator in terms of a general outsourcing theory as also assumed by *Gopal and Koka* in their conclusion. One promising starting point for studying the interplay of the theoretical foundations for new outsourcing phenomena, such as offshore outsourcing, application service providing, and business process outsourcing may be to study how will these phenomena can be explained by existing theories of traditional IT outsourcing (Dibbern, 2004, p. 6).

Penter and Pervan examine the BPO arrangements of two small-to-medium sized companies in Australia. One of the unique features of this study is that contrary to the study by *Wüllenweber et al.* who looked at secondary transaction processes of banks, these two Australian companies offshored to India primary business processes which were part of their core business. In one case, it was debt collection, which was the main business of that company; and in the other case, it was equity analysis from a company whose core business was portfolio management services. Interestingly, however, both companies chose to establish a captive center rather than handing over process execution to an external vendor in India. The establishment of captive centers brings about unique challenges of coordination and leadership in the offshore country. These challenges are highlighted in the case analysis together with an analysis of the key drivers of the captive center decision in both cases.

Currie closes this book with a paper that actually somewhat abstracts from the key problem domains in outsourcing. It shows that the decision of who should deliver IT services or perform business processes becomes somewhat irrelevant or at least less critical if the key question of what is to be delivered or performed is not solved at all among the various stakeholders of an organization (including internal and external authorities).

This is exemplified by the case of the UK healthcare sector which is represented by the National Health Service (NHS) organization aiming at offering free health-care at the point of delivery to all citizens of the UK. This public health care system was highly inefficient and ineffective and accordingly government decided to move from professional dominance within local health care organizations to the use of more market-based governance mechanisms. As part of this strategic move, an IT programme was established that aimed at increasing efficiency and effectiveness of the health care system through large IT investments. As such, a nationwide electronic patient database together with the development and implementation of a national patient booking system was established and realized with the help of large scale IT outsourcing contracts. However, the patient booking system turned out to be "not just another public sector IT project, but a large-scale innovation and change program designed to alter the working practices of clinicians, managers and other NHS staff." This business process change programme caused tremendous difficulties in the acceptance of the new system.

The case shows how the success of the introduction of IT innovations is heavily influenced by institutionalization mechanisms. IT sourcing issues reside in the background in such scenarios. This has important implications for the evaluation of IT outsourcing success in the face of large IT projects that include fundamental innovations in business processes.

6   Conclusions

In reading the various chapters in this book, we reflected upon what we know and what we don't know about the field. Although the third edition of the book did much to document the latest international research results on IT outsourcing, off-shoring, and BPO, numerous interesting questions remain. For example, do we need more of a general theory (or pool of theories to start with) of outsourcing, where the differences between certain types of outsourcing are integrated as variables (e.g., moderators) rather than treated as separate phenomena? How will organizations determine the optimal mix of outsourcing and insourcing of their business processes and IT functions across the globe and how can globally distributed services be managed appropriately? How will it differ between different organizations in different industries in different countries? Will organizations tire of outsourcing and decide to bring IT back in-house? How will organizational politics and institutional forces influence outsourcing – especially global outsourcing - decisions and their management now and in the future? How should the IS discipline respond to these challenges (*cf.* Hirschheim *et al.* 2007). We have tried to articulate some of these important questions but there are many more. Hopefully this book will help motivate individuals to either begin research in the field or continue engaging in outsourcing research. Much has been done, but there is still much more to be done. We hope the reader enjoys the papers in this volume. Happy reading!

References

Alavi, M., & Leidner, D. E. (2001). Review: Knowledge management and knowledge management systems: conceptual foundations and research issues. *MIS Quarterly 25*(1), 107–136.

Anthes, G. (1993). In depth; not made in the USA. In: *Computerworld.*

Apte, U. (1990). Global outsourcing of information systems and processing services. *Information Society, 7*(4), 287–303.

Apte, U. M., Sobol, M. G., Hanaoka, S., Shimada, T., Saarinen, T., Salmela, T., & Vepsalainen, A. P. J. (1997). Is outsourcing practices in the USA, Japan and Finland: A comparative study. *Journal of Information Technology, 12,* 289–304

Aubert, B. A., Patry, M., & Rivard, S. (2004). A transaction cost model of IT outsourcing. *Information and Management, 41*(7), 921–932.

Carmel, E. (2003a). The new software exporting Nations: Success factors. *Electronic Journal of Information Systems in Developing Countries, 13*(4), 1–12.

Carmel, E. (2003b). Taxonomy of new software exporting nations. *Electronic Journal of Information Systems in Developing Countries, 13*(2), 1–6.

Carmel, E., & Agarwal, R. (2001). Tactical approaches for alleviating distance in global software development. *IEEE Software, 18*(2), 22–29.

Carmel, E., & Agarwal, R. (2002). The maturation of offshore sourcing of information technology work. *MIS Quarterly Executive, 1*(2), 65–78.

Cha, H. S., Pingry, D. E., & Thatcher, M. E. (2008). Managing the knowledge supply chain: An organizational learning model of information technology offshore outsourcing. *MIS Quarterly, 32*(2), 281–306.

Clemons, E. K., Hitt, L. M., & Snir, E. M. (2000) "A Risk Analysis Framework For IT Outsourcing. Working Paper, The Wharton School, University of Pennsylvania, Philadelphia

Cullen, S., Seddon, P., & Willcocks, L. (2005). Managing outsourcing: The lifecycle imperative. *MIS Quarterly Executive, 4*(1), 229–246.

Dibbern, J. (2004). *The sourcing of application software services: empirical evidence of cultural, industry and functional differences.* Berlin: Springer.

Dibbern, J., Goles, T., Hirschheim, R. A., & Jayatilaka, B. (2004). Information systems outsourcing: A survey and analysis of the literature. *The DATA BASE for Advances in Information Systems, 35*(4), 6–102.

Dibbern, J., Winkler, J., & Heinzl, A. (2008). Explaining variations in client extra costs between software projects offshored to India. *MIS Quarterly, 32*(2), 333–366.

EBusiness Strategies (2004) *Offshoring Statistics – Dollar Size, Job Loss, and Market Potential.*

Fogarty, K. (2008). The state of outsourcing IT. In: *Baseline Magazine, May 20,* 2008.

Friedman, T. (2005). *The World is flat: A brief history of the twenty-first century.* New York, Farrar, Straus & Giroux.

Gallivan, M. J., & Oh, W. (1999). Analyzing IT outsourcing relationships as alliances among multiple clients and vendors. In: *Annual International Conference on System Sciences*. IEEE, Hawaii, 1999.

Gopal, A., Mukhopadhyay, T., & Krishnan, M. S. (2002). The role of software processes and communication in offshore software development. *Communications of the ACM, 45*(4), 193–200.

Heeks, R., & Nicholson, B. (2004). Software export success factors and strategies in follower nations. *Competition and Change, 8*(3), 267–303.

Hirschheim, R., George, B., & Wong, S. (2004). Information technology outsourcing: the move towards offshoring. *Indian Journal of Economics and Business*, Fall, 103–123.

Hirschheim, R., & George, B. (2007). Three waves of information technology outsourcing. In A. Huizing & E. de Vries (Eds.), *Information management: Setting the scene* (pp. 175–190). Amsterdam: Elsevier.

Hirschheim, R. A., & Lacity, M. C. (2000). The myths and realities of information technology insourcing. *Communications of the ACM, 43*(2), 99–107.

Hirschheim, R., Loebeckke, C., Newman, M., & Valor, J. (2007). The implications of offshoring on the is discipline: Where perception meets reality. *Communications of the Association for Information System, 20(51)*, 824–835.

Kaiser, K., & Hawk, S. (2004). Evolution of offshore software development: from outsourcing to co-sourcing. *MISQ Executive, 3*(3), 69–81.

Kakabadse, A., & Kakabadse, N. (2002). Trends in outsourcing: contrasting USA and Europe. European Management Journal, 20(2), 189–198.

Kelly, T. (2002) *A brief history of outsourcing. Global envision*. Available at http://www.globalenvision.org

Khan, N., Currie, W. L., Weerakkody, V., & Desai, B. (2003). Evaluating offshore IT outsourcing in India: supplier and customer scenarios. In: *Annual Hawaii International Conference on System Sciences*. Big Island, Hawaii.

Kumar, K., & Willcocks, L. (1996). Offshore outsourcing: a country too far? *Proceedings of the 4th European Conference on Information Systems* (pp. 1309–1325).

Lacity, M. C., & Hirschheim, R. A. (1993a). The information systems outsourcing Bandwagon. *Sloan Management Review, 35*(1), 73–86.

Lacity, M. C., & Hirschheim, R. A. (1993b). *Information systems outsourcing: myths, metaphors, and realities* (pp. xiv, 273). Chichester: Wiley.

Lacity, M. C., & Hirschheim, R. A. (1995). *Beyond the information systems outsourcing bandwagon: the insourcing response* (pp. xxi, 237). Chichester: Wiley.

Lacity, M. C. Hirschheim, R. A., & Willcocks, L. P. (1994). "Realizing outsourcing expectations: incredible promise, credible outcomes. *Journal of Information Systems Management, 11*(4), 7–18.

Lacity, M. C., & Willcocks, L. P. (2001). *Global information technology outsourcing: In search of business advantage*. Chichester: Wiley.

Lacity, M. C., Willcocks, L. P., & Feeny, D. F. (1995). IT outsourcing: maximize flexibility and control. *Harvard Business Review, 73*(3), 84–93.

Leonardi, P. M., & Bailey, D. E. (2008). Transformational technologies and the creation of new work practices: making implicit knowledge explicit in task-based offshoring. *MIS Quartely, 32*(2), 411–436.

Linder, J. (2004) *Outsourcing for radical change*. New York: AMACOM.

Loh, L., & Venkatraman, N. (1992). Diffusion of information technology outsourcing: influence sources and the Kodak effect. *Information Systems Research, 3*(4), 334–358.

McFarlan, F. W. (1995). Information-enabled organization transformation and outsourcing. In: W. König (Ed.), *WIRTSCHAFTSINFORMATIK '95: Wettbewerbsfähigkeit, Innovation, Wirtschaftlichkeit* (pp. 3–23). Heidelberg: Springer.

Mears, J., & Bednarz, A. (2005). Take it all outsourcing on the wane. May 30, 2005.

Miles, R., & Snow, C. (1978). *Organizational strategy, structure and process*. New York: McGraw-Hill.

Morstead, S., & Blount, G. (2003). *Offshore ready: strategies to plan & profit from offshore IT-enabled services*. ISANI Group.

Nicholson, B., & Sahay, S. (2001). Some political and cultural implications of the globalisation of software development: case experience from UK and India. *Information and Organisation, 11*(1), 25–43.

Overby, S. (2003). The hidden costs of offshore outsourcing. CIO Magazine.

Pastin, M., & Harrison, J. (1974). Social responsibility in the Hollow corporation. *Business & Society Review*, 54.

Pruitt, S. (2004). Survey: 275,000 telecom jobs to go offshore by 2008. In: *Computerworld*.

Qu, Z., & Brocklehurst, M. (2003). What will it take for China to become a competitive force in offshore outsourcing? An analysis of the role of transaction costs in supplier selection. *Journal of Information Technology, 18*, 53–67.

Rajkumar, T. M., & Dawley, D. L. (1998). Problems and issues in offshore development of software. In: L. P. Willcocks, & M. C. Lacity (Eds.), *Strategic Sourcing of Information Systems*. New York: Wiley.

Ramanujan, S., & Lou, H. (1997). Outsourcing maintenance operations to off-shore vendors: some lessons from the field. *Journal of Global Information Management 5*(2), 5–15.

Rao, M. T. (2004). Key issues for global IT sourcing: country and individual factors. *Information Systems Management,* (Summer), *21*(3), 16–21.

Robinson, M., & Kalakota, R. (2004). *Offshore outsourcing: business models, ROI and best Practices*. New York, Milvar Press, 2004.

Rottman, J. W., & Lacity, M. C. (2004). Twenty practices for offshore sourcing. *MIS Quarterly Executive, 3*(3), 117–130.

Sabherwal, R. (1999). The role of trust in outsourced IS development projects. *Communications of the ACM, 42*(2), 80–86.

Sahay, S., Nicholson, B., & Krishna, S. (2003). *Global IT outsourcing*. Cambridge: Cambridge University Press.

Sheshabalaya, A. (2004). *Rising elephant: the growing clash with India over white collar jobs and its challenge to America and the World*. Monroe, ME: Common Courage Press.

Souza, R. D., Goodness, E., Young, A., Silliman, R., & Caldwell, B. M. (2004) IT outsourcing market forecast: Worldwide, 2002–2007. *Gartner Research*.

Terdiman, R. (2002) Offshore outsourcing can achieve more than cost savings. *Note number: CS-16-3520, Gartner Research*.

Vaze, S. (2005). The politics (and economics) of outsourcing. *Express computer*.

Part II
Traditional IT Outsourcing

Chapter 1
Outsourcing Relationship Management

Promoting Trust and Relationship Commitment through Service Level Agreements in IT Outsourcing Relationship

Jahyun Goo

1 Introduction

As business organizations are moving to become agile and responsive to a dynamically changing business environment, firms increasingly employ Information Technology (IT) outsourcing to support strategic IT decisions that lead to sophisticated forms of business process outsourcing (Mani, Barua, & Whinston, 2006), offshore outsourcing (Rottman and Lacity 2004) and capability outsourcing[1] (Gottfredson, Puryear, & Phillips, 2005). As organizations outsource more and more of their IT operations, the skill sets that manage the relationship between the service recipient (SR) and the service provider (SP) becomes new strategic asset (DiRomualdo & Gurbaxani, 1998). Most recent outsourcing practices put more emphasis on managing the outsourcing relationship and on nurturing a high level of trust and commitment during the course of the relationship (Datz 2003). As in marriages or friendships based on trust and commitment, however, not all outsourcing relationships work well. The participants may find themselves wishing they had planned better in addition to exclusively relying on trust and commitment. As the overall relationship deteriorates the results will be higher costs, operational disruption and lost business opportunities (Goolsby, 2002). It is expected that an outsourcing relationship would fail to achieve both parties' desired results if it is not organized and managed well from the outset. Thus, greater understanding of how to manage IT outsourcing relationships that create and sustain strategic value for the client firm is required. The paper attempts to improve the specifications of IT outsourcing management solutions by exploring the complementarity between two governance modes in the interorganizational relationship (IOR) literature.

---

[1] Capability sourcing emphasizes that every activity in the value chain is a potential candidate for externalization. This new view of how to organize business functions sees each firm as a function-based company, a provider of a set of knowledge- and information-intensive functions alone that drive competitive advantage in its industry (Gottfredson et al. 2005).

R. Hirschheim et al. (eds), *Information Systems Outsourcing,*
© Springer-Verlag Berlin Heidelberg 2009

While prior research on IOR has suggested two distinct modes of governance: *formal controls* (written contracts, management-initiated mechanisms designed to guide behavior toward desired objectives) and *relational governance* (unwritten, practice-based mechanisms designed to influence interorganizational behavior) in managing IOR, existing literatures on IT outsourcing relationship have leaned toward the latter (Lee, Huynh, Kwok, & Pi, 2003). This stream of research views formal contracts as a more costly substitute for relational governance (Dyer & Singh, 1998; Gulati, 1995; Uzzi, 1997). Contrary to this substitution position, economics and strategic management literature empirically showed that contracts and relational governance function as complements (Baker, Gibbons, & Murphy, 1994; Poppo & Zenger, 2002). In practice, it is widely observed that an increasing range of outsourcing activities is organized through complex contracts (Fitzgerald & Willcocks, 1994; Kern, Willcocks, & Heck, 2002; Saunders, Gebelt, & Hu, 1997) although many studies have found that IT outsourcing arrangements employ various relational governance mechanisms to communicate the success of outsourcing relationships (Grover, Cheon, & Teng, 1996; Koh, Ang, & Straub, 2004; Lee & Kim, 1999). This could be understood with the emerging research that effective collaboration between firms requires alignment of both *interests* and *actions* between them (Gulati, Lawrence, & Puranam, 2005; Mani et al. 2006). The formal contract masks how structured controls address opportunism concerns of relational uncertainty and is thus enacted to provide an administrative architecture within which the partnership proceeds (Gulati & Singh, 1998). While the contract attempts to align incentives and interests in the relationship, it might prove insufficient in aligning the actions of participant firms. Relational governance addresses how the contract is actually used in the outsourcing relationship to facilitate information exchange between the SR and the SP to promote both a shared understanding of the task environment and how mutual adjustments will be accomplished to align actions. Thus, this suggests that exchanges be guided through well-structured relationship-based agreements that protects relationship-specific assets and that is shaped by relational governance to ensure success of IT outsourcing relationship (Poppo & Zenger, 2002; Ring & Van de Ven, 1994; Zaheer & Venkatraman, 1995; Zucker, 1986).

While some recent studies have shown that contracts could be used to effectively manage various dimensions of relational exchange in IT outsourcing (Mani et al. 2006; Mayer & Argyres, 2004; Vaast & Levina, 2006), there has been relatively little understanding of how contracts could build and improve relationship quality in the outsourcing arrangements. Given the positive association between relationship quality and IT outsourcing success (Grover et al., 1996; Lee & Kim, 1999), identifying contractual provisions that might foster favorable relational attributes should fill a current gap in the IT outsourcing literature. Thus, this study attempts to reconcile two governance modes (often considered as substitutes) by exploring the complementarity of service level agreements (SLA) in the development of relational governance in IT outsourcing arrangements (cf, Poppo & Zenger, 2002; Sabherwal, 1999). From a literature review on relational governance, the Morgan and Hunt (1994) model of commitment-trust was adapted to this research setting, thereby providing a model that explored the possibility that a well structured service level agreements (SLA) could foster the relational governance in IT outsourcing engagements.

2 Trust and Commitment in Relational Governance

The centrality of the relationship has led researchers to identify attributes that must exist to ensure successful relational exchange (Dwyer, Schurr, & Oh, 1987; Ganesan, 1994; Goles & Chin, 2002; Heide & Miner, 1992; Kern & Willcocks, 2002; Lambe, Spekman, & Hunt, 2000; McEvily, Perrone, & Zaheer, 2003; Morgan & Hunt, 1994; Wilson, 1995; Zaheer &Venkatraman, 1995). Significant research effort has also been directed to explaining how these necessary relationship attributes are developed. In this regard, Morgan and Hunt (1994) theorized that trust and relationship commitment play key mediating roles in the process of relationship development. Figure 1 presents the Morgan and Hunt (1994) model of relationship marketing. They believe that when both trust and relationship commitment - not just one or the other - are present, they produce outcomes that promote efficiency, productivity, and effectiveness. Shown in Fig. 1, they posit that (1) relationship termination costs and relationship benefits directly influence commitment, (2) shared values directly influence both commitment and trust, and (3) communication and opportunistic behavior directly influence trust (and, through trust, indirectly influence commitment).

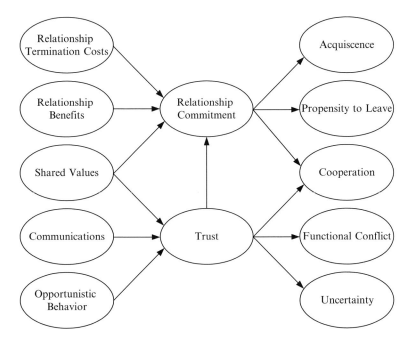

Fig. 1 The trust and commitment theory of relational marketing (Morgan and Hunt 1994)

Although, as components of the relationship development process, relationship commitment and trust are, per se, highly desirable "qualitative outcomes" (Mohr & Nevin, 1990), they posit five additional qualitative outcomes. First, acquiescence and propensity to leave directly flow from relationship commitment. Second, functional conflict and uncertainty are the direct results of trust. Third, cooperation arises directly from both relationship commitment and trust. They theorized that these outcomes promote relationship success.

Trust and relationship commitment have also been found as key factors in the context of managing IT outsourcing relationships (Choudhury & Sabherwal, 2003; Sabherwal, 1999) wherein two organizations need to cooperate toward sometimes ambiguous outcomes involving the exchange of invisible assets (Itami, 1987) as compared to definable outcomes over the exchange of tangible assets. Although these two attributes can exist at the outset among partners who have had prior transactional relationships or social ties (Galaskiewicz & Shatin, 1985), many interorganizational relationships in today's corporate environment are formed among parties who are initially unfamiliar with each other. This situation requires "initial trust" because parties have not worked together long enough to develop an interaction history (McKnight, Cummings, & Chervany, 1998). Initial trust situations are becoming more common because the number of temporary task teams and project engagements (i.e., outsourcing) is increasingly becoming more common (Meyerson, Weick, & Kramer, 1996). In such a case, trust and relationship commitment in interorganizational relationships might begin with legal recourse such as contracts and promises (McKnight et al., 1998; Shapiro, 1987; Zucker, 1986). This developmental process is consistent with the premise of institutional trust that views the formal contracting as an initial trust building mechanism in inter-organizational trust (Gefen et al., 2006; McKnight et al. 1998; Zucker 1986). This informs the research question we address in this paper: how can contracts be used to foster attributes of relational governance that mediate success of IT outsourcing engagements?

Consistent with the commitment-trust theory (Morgan & Hunt, 1994), we argue that the presence of trust and relationship commitment is central to success-ful IT outsourcing relationship although other contextual factors contribute to the success or failure of IT outsourcing management. In addition, this study incorpo-rates the two governance perspectives and proposes that formal contracts promote the development of relational governance in IT outsourcing arrangements (Poppo & Zenger, 2002). Specifically, this study posits that a well-developed and well-specified SLA may actually promote trusting exchange relationships and the relationship commitment in IT outsourcing engagements. We believe that this complementary relationship between formal contracts and relational governance is reciprocal, that is, as trust and relationship commitment in relational govern-ance could generate SLA refinements they further support greater relational exchanges (Poppo & Zenger, 2002; Ring & Van de Ven, 1994). However, in this study we focus on the direction from SLA as formal contracts to trust and com-mitment as key relational attributes in order to examine how specific clauses of a contract may be related to the development of relational governance and their impact on qualitative relationship outcomes.

3 SLA: Formal Contract in IT Outsourcing Arrangements

We define an SLA as a formal written agreement developed jointly between SR and SP that specifies a product or service to be provided at a certain level so as to meet business objectives. Once the overall outsourcing deal is negotiated by lawyers, SLA are added as an addendum to the contract and contain project-specific terms and conditions which provide a specific way to manage outsourcing relationships. In practice, practitioners often claim that the key to managing successful IT outsourcing relationships is related to the quality of the SLAs terms (Mingay & Govekar, 2002) because governance of IT outsourcing relationships should deal with the perspective of both parties and thus it is widely observed that an increasing range of exchange activities is governed by well-structured SLA (Karten, 2004; Mani et al. 2006; Singleton, McLean, Altman, 1988). Prior studies have indicated that SLA help to ensure that the early, more vulnerable stages of exchange are managed successfully (Singleton et al., 1988).

Recently Goo, Kim, and Cho (2006) and Goo, Kishore, and Rao (2004) identified the structure of eleven contractual issues in SLAs that could be important in managing IT outsourcing relationships. Through conceptual and statistical validation, they categorized contractual elements into three areas, *change management, governance, and foundation characteristics*[2]. *Foundation characteristics* in SLAs deal with the ground rules for future exchanges (Stone, 2001). This builds a spirit of agreement and ownership of the functional exchange among those entities who are involved with its development (Singleton et al., 1988). This also helps decision makers who actually deal with contracts to understand and share the intent of the creation of the relationship. It sets clear standards of conduct by defining what the SR and SP are obligated to deliver and at what cost (Ring & Van de Ven, 1994). *Governance characteristics* provide a way to harmonize the relationship through a clear statement of measurements, the communication channel and method, conflict arbitration, and penalty and rewards. A way to ensure that the relationship remains on course is to continually assess the value that the relationship is creating for the various stakeholders (Bendor-Samuel, 1999). *Change management characteristics* address uncertainty (e.g., clauses for agreeing to agree). Because the IT environment evolves rapidly and business conditions often require a fast response by SPs to deliver new services or modify current services, a change management plan is a critical dimension in SLAs. These ensure that the SP will deliver valuable inputs to the SR and strengthen the SR/SP relationship when constructing contractual and service level definitions that are unrealistic in situations of increasing uncertainty (Scardino, 2001). Thus, each characteristic refers to a set of inter-related formal contract clauses reflecting substantive goals or themes to be realized. Using Goo et al.'s

---

[2] In this study, we use the term SLA characteristic to refer to a formal contract clause. We do this because actual clauses may differ in different SLAs. While a particular clause may not be explicitly specified in a particular SLA, the essence of that clause may still be present in the SLA. Thus, we use the term characteristic rather than the term clause.

(2006) operational constructs for the structure of SLA, this study examines the effects of specific contractual elements (as antecedents) on the cultivation of trust and relationship commitment (as key relational attributes of relational governance), and assesses their influence on the qualitative outcomes in IT outsourcing. These relationships are discussed in the following section.

4   Model and Hypotheses

Like any other relational exchange, we argue that cooperative behaviors that are the basis for companion working spirit in IT outsourcing arrangements are emanated from psychological attributes such as trust and commitment (Koh, Tay, & Ang, 1999). In this paper, following Morgan and Hunt (1994), relationship commitment is conceptualized in terms of the SR's perception on parties' intention to stay in the relationship and willingness to put in effort to maintain the relationship. While the SR's relationship commitment could arise as early as the selection of the SP, the SP's relationship commitment becomes formalized with the signing of the contract in outsourcing practice. Relationship commitment of one party increases as the perception of the other party's commitment increases (Anderson & Weitz, 1992). Morgan and Hunt (1994) suggest that relationship commitment depends on relationship benefits, termination costs, shared values and trust. We believe that SLA contract clauses encode these precursors and thus reinforce the commitment of both parties to the relationship in the context of IT outsourcing. The Morgan and Hunt's conceptualization of trust, having been developed for a customer–company relationship, was seen as too transactional (Gabarino & Johnson, 1999) and thus not adopted. Instead, the measure of trust was based on a conceptualization of McKnight et al. (1998), reflecting the SR's expectation that the SP will fulfill the requirements specified in the SLAs in future actions. In essence, all precursors of trust in Morgan and Hunt model are based on socio-cognitive learning theories (Heider, 1958), which assume that individuals are rational and learn from the past. Individuals interact, experience and observe the actions of a relationship partner (e.g., how they have communicated, whether they have kept commitments or been honest etc.) and use these perceptions to develop a view of how the partner will act in the future (i.e., their trust in the partner).

These relational attributes could be nurtured over time through joint development of SLA as well as ongoing exchanges guided by the elements of SLA. For example, outsourcing relationships generally begin with negotiations over joint expectations, risk and trust through formal bargaining or informal sense making (Ring & Van de Ven, 1994). Then the SR and the SP reach an agreement on the obligations and rules for future action in the relationship. At this point, the terms and governance structure of the relationship are established and codified in a formal relationship-based contract as a commitment to the engagements (Mayer & Argyres, 2004; Vaast & Levina, 2006) and informally understood in a "psychological contract" during the contracting process (Koh et al., 2004). The parties might then use their perceptions to develop

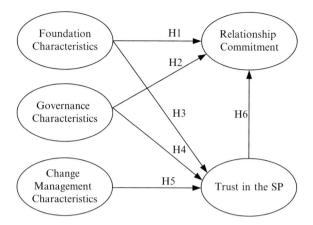

Fig. 2 Research model: trust and commitment theory of IT outsourcing relationship

a view of how the partner will act in the future (i.e., their trust in the partner). Shown in Fig. 2, therefore, we posit that (1) foundation characteristics (reflecting the relationship benefits and shared values as in Morgan and Hunt model) and governance characteristics (reflecting the relationship termination costs and communication flow as in Morgan and Hunt Model) directly and positively influence both commitment and trust, (2) change management characteristics (specifying to mitigate opportunistic behavior originated from requirement uncertainty) directly and positively influence trust (and, through trust, indirectly influence commitment), and (3) trust directly and positively influences commitment.

In addition to trust, relationship commitment, and their antecedents, the Morgan and Hunt's (1994) model also has several outcome variables. For the reasons of simplicity and focus, this paper excludes consideration of the outcome variables, which are left as suggestions for further research later. At this stage we shall concentrate only on the SLA as antecedents of trust and relationship commitment in IT outsourcing arrangements.

4.1 *Precursors of Trust and Relationship Commitment: SLA Characteristics*

Foundation characteristics. Three contractual elements in SLAs comprise foundation characteristics. *Service level objectives* consist of short statements about key principles and agreements between the parties that will drive value extraction from the execution of the contract. The *process ownership plan* includes the formal identification of key process owners, which might be accompanied by definitions of roles and responsibilities so that the SR and SP process owners, as well as both supporting organizations, understand the scope of the process owners' authority to plan, manage and evolve services. *Service level contents* specify what services will be delivered by the SP, how often and to what extent those services will be required, and when and where they are required. The target service levels need to be specified by and coordinated with the process owners identified.

The SLA elements related to foundation characteristics can increase the parties' relationship commitment in many ways. As the organizational commitment literature (Anderson & Weitz 1992; Gundlach, Achrol, & Mentzer, 1995; Jap & Ganesan, 2000; Morgan & Hunt, 1994) suggests, when the SR and the SP share values they indeed will be more committed to their relationships. SLA provisions reflecting foundation characteristics strive to implement partners' mutual goals by sharing common expectations and capabilities. For example, foundation characteristics specify common goals and general commitment, and set clear standards of conduct by defining roles and responsibilities of the parties involved in the outsourcing arrangement. This reinforces the perception that both parties' intentions to remain in the relationship prevail, which thereby, reflects the relationship's consistency (Anderson & Weitz, 1989).

In addition, being more knowledgeable about each other's business allows parties to more effectively cooperate and, for the SP, to carry out services that the SR depends upon. The cultivation of these mutually beneficial IORs can be "institutionalized" through foundation characteristics that encourage a mindset of continuous commitment to the relationship (McKnight et al. 1998). Moreover, since the intention of the relationship is defined in the SLA, the objectives that initially motivated the creation of the relationship are at least partially understood and shared by the decision makers and other individuals who inherit the responsibility for carrying out the terms of the SLA (Koh et al. 2004; Ring & Van de Ven, 1994) thus making the relationship stable over time. Therefore:

H1: Foundation characteristics of the SLA positively influence relationship commitment of both parties to IT outsourcing relationships.

Shared values, that is the extent to which partners have common beliefs about what behaviors, goals, and policies are important and appropriate, are a direct precursor of both trust and relationship commitment (Dwyer et al. 1987; Heide & John, 1992; Morgan & Hunt, 1994). Elements under foundation characteristics including *service level objectives*, the *process ownership plan*, and s*ervice level contents* are explicating common beliefs between outsourcing partners, which reinforce a spirit of agreement among those involved with their development. Joint development of expectations about the deliverables should result in tighter coupling among parties. This, in turn, should reinforce a sense of structural assurance and situational normality which positively inform trusting beliefs (McKnight et al. 1998). Furthermore, SLA identification of process ownership and level of service to be delivered formalizes the roles and the responsibilities of the SP and SR which also reinforces trust in the outsourcing relationships (Ang & Slaughter, 2001; Sabherwal, 1999). Finally, trust will emerge when the outsourcing relationship are characterized by bilateral convergence of interests (Kumar, Scheer, & Steenkamp, 1995). Contractual elements of foundation characteristics provide ground for building and sustaining trusting beliefs of the SR, where their interest convergence with those of the SP can be assured. Therefore:

H2: Foundation characteristics of the SLA positively influence trust of SR in SP.

Governance characteristics. The contractual elements underlying governance characteristics provide a way to maintain the relationships through a clear statement of the measurements, conflict arbitration, penalty and rewards, exit policy, and communication plan. The *communication plan* ensures communication flow between the two parties. The documented communication standards and processes facilitate the extent and consistency of knowledge exchange between the two parties. The *measurement charter* includes how, when, and by whom the relationship between the SR and SP will be measured. This specifies tactical measures of service performance, as well as metrics that enable the IT unit to manage components necessary for meeting the goals of outsourcing relationships. The *conflict arbitration plan* states the parameters for involving a third party in discussions between the SR and SP, timetables for resolving issues between the SR and SP, process descriptions to determine how the parties interact, and the practices and conduct rules required to preserve the independence of the independent advisor. The *enforcement plan* states the parties' negotiated incentives and penalties, and incorporates options to add or subtract work from the SP based on performance.

SLA provisions underlying governance characteristics build commitment in the IT outsourcing relationship. First, the *communication plan* plays an important role in sustaining mutual benefits by ensuring information sharing that may be useful to both parties and fostering confidence in the continuity of the relationship (Mohr & Nevin, 1990). Second, the *enforcement plan* supports the motivation to continue a relationship because it requires the parties to take into account the legal and economic consequences of violating explicit terms of the contract. The prospect of termination costs leads the parties to view the relationship as important and reinforce commitment (Jap & Ganesan, 2000). For example, when the SP makes relationship-specific investments in the relationship, the enforcement plan codifies the penalties associated with opportunistic behaviors or termination without due cause to protect the SP's investment. When the SP perceives that its investments are secured because of the terms of the plan, the SP becomes more committed to the relationship. The SP's commitment, in turn, increases the SR's perception of the SP's commitment, increasing the SR's commitment (Anderson & Weitz, 1992). Third, because parties that agree to deliver desired benefits will be highly valued, firms will commit themselves to establishing, developing, and maintaining relationships with such partners. The *measurement charter* sets the benchmarks and assesses whether the SP is meeting the target performance and accomplishing stipulated terms in the SLA to ensure that the relationship remains on course (Susarla, Barua, & Whinston, 2003). The measurement charter might also reduce the uncertainty about behaviors and outcomes by providing formal rules and procedures to govern the relationship. The clear guidelines specifying the rights and obligations of both parties improve coordination and increase both parties' commitment. Therefore:

*H3: Governance characteristics of the SLA positively influence relationship com-
mitment of both parties to IT outsourcing relationships.*

Contractual elements under *governance characteristics* commonly set and
assess the relationship benefits and value that the relationship is generating for the
stakeholders to ensure that the relationship remains on course. Trusting beliefs in
IT outsourcing relationships is largely associated with creating confidence of the
SR in the SP as a result of that party's ability to meet the target performance and
accomplish the stipulated terms in the SLA (Kern & Willcocks, 2002). For example, the enforcement plan serves as "carrot and stick" to ensure that the SP satisfies
the provisions in the SLA. The SR's belief in the SP's benevolence is supported if
the SR perceives that the SLA states appropriate incentives and penalties based on
performance (Snir, 2000). When the outsourcing exchange is bounded by such SLA
safeguards, the SR is encouraged to believe that the SP is trustworthy. In addition,
a mutually agreed method of conflict resolution engenders feelings of procedural
justice between the two parties. These perceptions encourage positive beliefs about
the SP's integrity by suggesting that there can be harmonious outcomes to conflict
resolution. This trusting belief may introduce greater flexibility in the future interactions. Such leeway will tend to reduce the scope, intensity, and frequency of
opportunistic behavior of the SP, which in turn, will lead to mutual trusting beliefs
(Zaheer, McEvily, & Perrone, 1998). Moreover, specifying communication processes such as the frequency, relevance and timeliness of interactions facilitates
consistent knowledge exchange (Morgan & Hunt, 1994) which, in turn, reinforces
positive SR perceptions about the faithfulness of the SP (Deutsch, 1973). An integrative method of governing the exchanges specified in the SLA should lead to the
development of trusting beliefs of the SR in the SP. Therefore:

H4: Governance characteristics of the SLA positively influence trust of SR in SP.

Change management characteristics. TCE of contracting prescribes that IORs
incorporate mechanisms that facilitate joint adaptation to problems raised from
unforeseeable changes into the contract. Mayer and Argyres (2004) found that
changes to the structure of contracts were made to reflect learning over time. Most
notably contract modifications involved inclusion of planning for contingencies, as
well as processes for incorporating feedback. Thus the purpose of change management elements in SLAs is to establish ground rules and procedures for dealing with
future contingencies. Because IT environments evolve rapidly and business conditions often require fast response from the SP to modify current services or deliver
new services, change management characteristics attempt to provide access to such
capabilities. These characteristics also seek to ensure that the SP continues to
deliver valuable input to the SR and that the SR/SP relationship remains close even
when precise specification of services and service levels may not be possible in
situations of high uncertainty.

Four contractual elements underlie change management characteristics. The
future demand management plan specifies the processes that will be used by the SR
and SP to define requirements, prioritize initiatives, prepare and approve schedules,

and manage the implementation of new or modified services. The *anticipated change plan* ensures that the right processes, people and tools are in place to enable the SR and SP to stay on top of changes and ensure effective decision-making. The *innovation plan* identifies the structure and processes for introducing new innovations and is synchronized with enforcement plans such as penalties or incentives to be effective. The *feedback plan* documents the feedback processes and provides the road map for efficient adjustments by identifying all affected areas and resources.

Specifically, change management characteristics in the SLA help the SR to build trust in the SP by serving as repositories for knowledge about how to govern future collaborations (Mayer & Argyres, 2004). The *change management* elements including the *future demand management plan*, the *anticipated change plan*, and so on provide the ground rules and procedures for future contingencies, which should lead to desired outcomes if followed. These plans are open-ended provisions that detail contingency plans and reflect the expectations that both parties will be willing to adapt as circumstances change, which reinforces mutual perceptions of benevolence (Mani et al. 2006). For example, the plans in the SLA provide a sense of fairness with respect to how the parties will handle unexpected future contingencies. These plans seek to ensure that the SP will continue to deliver valuable inputs to the SR and that the relationship will remain close even though service level delineations may be unrealistic in situations of greater uncertainty. The provisions in the SLA support a sense of situational normality implying that the SP in the contingent situation will act normally and can be trusted. Therefore:

H5: Change management characteristics of the SLA positively influence trust of the SR in the SP.

Trust. Trust is defined as trusting beliefs in other party and in this study it refers to the SR's beliefs about the favorable characteristics of the SP such as benevolence and integrity/honesty. Trusting beliefs are distinct from trusting intentions, which is the willingness to depend on the SP. The trusting beliefs definition reflects the SR's expectation that the SP will fulfill the requirements specified in the SLAs in future actions. Trust is a necessary condition for relational governance (McKnight et al., 1998; Morgan & Hunt 1994; Zaheer et al., 1998), and arises from various sources.

Trust, in widely varying levels, is a trait that is embedded in every exchange relationship. Greater trust leads to the commitment of interorganizational relationships (Morgan & Hunt, 1994; Zaheer et al., 1998). Relationships imbued with trust are often valued as "the cornerstone of the strategic partnership" and parties will desire to commit themselves to such relationships (McEvily et al., 2003). In essence, once exchange partners are granted 'trustworthy' status, they are expected to behave in a trustworthy fashion in the future. Social exchange theory supports this causal relationship through the principle of generalized reciprocity, which holds that the SR trusts whenever the SP has been trusted in prior exchanges and defects in response to defection (Lambe et al., 2000). Economists also emphasize that rational, calculative trust, particularly with respect to expectations of future exchanges, prompt trust in the present (Heide & Miner 1992; McKnight et al., 1998). Therefore, to succeed in reciprocity strategies, SP and SR are motivated to place sufficient value on future returns (inputs) or on a sufficiently long "shadow of the future" (durability). SR's perceptions and its SP's intent to trust in the relationship reflect the relationship's stability. Therefore:

H6: Trust positively influences commitment of both parties to IT outsourcing relationships.

5   Research Methodology

5.1   Data Collection

The current study utilized a "key informants" methodology for data collection, a method that relies on a selected set of members to provide information about a social setting (Venkatraman, 1989). In survey research, targeted respondents assume the role of a key informant and provide information on an aggregated unit of analysis (a single contract in this study) by reporting on group or organizational properties rather than personal attitudes and perceptions. For this study, it was important to identify organizations that actively engaged in IT outsourcing using SLAs with an IT vendor and to identify respondents within those organizations who were responsible for and most knowledgeable about the arrangement. Therefore, pre-recruiting calls were made to IT professionals on the attendee list of a national outsourcing conference in South Korea. This list provided an initial sampling frame of potential respondents. It was determined that executives (i.e., Presidents, CIO/Vice Presidents, Directors/Assistant Vice-Presidents, IT Managers, Contract Officers, Heads of IT Sourcing Teams) appeared to be the most appropriate sources of organizational information regarding IT sourcing decisions. The sampling frame was reduced by eliminating individuals whose firms had not been involved in any IT outsourcing engagement within the past five years. One hundred fifty professionals from the revised list agreed to participate in the survey or directed us to key informants involved in IT outsourcing arrangements using SLAs. E-mails containing the URL for the web-based online survey instrument were sent to 150 key informants in SRs. Of the 150 participants who agreed, 92 (61.3%) completed responses.

To assess potential threats of nonresponse bias, the respondent and nonrespondent firms were compared with respect to sales and the number of employees. No significant differences were found at the significance level of 0.05. Further, the distribution of responses across industries was examined. While the manufacturing industry was found to be slightly over represented and the public/government sector was slightly under represented, the sample included numerous cases from a variety of industries (Table 1). Demographic information about the respondents showed that about 46.8% were senior IT executives and 41% were IT managers. Although some preliminary steps were taken to ensure appropriate selection of key informants, a formal check was administered as part of the questionnaire (Kumar, Stern, & Anderson, 1993). Specifically, two items regarding key informant quality were used to assess

Table 1 Demographic characteristics of respondents (N = 92)

Characteristics	Frequency	Percentage	Mean	Std. Dev.
Titles of Respondents				
President	2	2.2		
CIO/Vice president	11	12.0		
Director/Asstt. Vice President	30	32.6		
IT Manager	38	41.3		
Other	7	7.6		
Not Mentioned	4	4.3		
Respondents' Knowledge regarding current SL4s	–	–	5.60	1.04
Respondents' Involveinentin Outsourcing	–	–	5.80	1.08

the informant's knowledge about the SLA chosen and his or her involvement with IT outsourcing arrangements on a seven-point scale. The mean score for informant quality for each item was 5.60 (SD = 1.04) and 5.80 (SD = 1.08) out of 7, respectively, indicating that respondents chosen were appropriate and thus all responses were retained.

5.2   Operationalization of Constructs

All constructs in the survey were measured using multi-item scales with seven-point Likert rating systems. A conscientious effort was made to adapt existing measures validated from prior studies for the latent constructs in this research. Thirty-three items were directly adopted from Goo et al. (2006, 2004) to measure the extent to which provisions of the eleven elements were addressed in the SLAs (Appendix A).

Trust measures were based on Zaheer et al.'s (1998) conceptualization of SR's perceptions of SP's goodness, which is similar to benevolence beliefs. Three items were adapted from scales used capture SR trust in the SP (Lee & Kim, 1999). The scales were found to be reliable (Cronbach's alpha = .81). Commitment measures the willingness of the parties to exert effort and devote resources in order to sustain an ongoing relationship (Fontenot & Wilson, 1997). The two items loaded on a single factor with a high internal consistency (Cronbach's alpha = .89). Three items for measuring acquiescence (Cronbach's alpha = .81) are adapted from existing scales (Goles & Chin, 2002; Heide & John, 1992). Relationship durability were operationalized to measure a desire to continue a relationship because of positive affect toward the partner (Kumar et al. 1995; Meyer and Allen 1984) with acceptable reliability (Cronbach's alpha = .77). To measure cooperation (Cronbach's alpha = .74), we adapted the three scales developed by Anderson and Narus (Anderson & Narus, 1990). Harmonious conflict resolution was measured using three items adapted from the existing scale (Frazier & Rody, 1991; Robey, Farrow, & Franz, 1989). Three items were adapted from Heide and John (1992) to measure active information exchange. Appendix B shows the measurement items used for research variables.

5.3   Data Analysis and Results

The assessment and estimation of the structural model was conducted using the statistical technique of partial least squares (PLS). This technique is especially suited for this study because it allows latent constructs to be modeled as formative or reflective indicators. Reflective constructs are formed with the indicators directed in an outward fashion from the latent variable items representing the effects of the construct under study and, therefore, "reflect" the construct of interest. All first-order constructs as well as IT outsourcing success constructs in this study are reflective. In contrast, a formative construct is formed with the indicators directed in an inward fashion toward the latent variable if the indicators are conceptualized as the aggregation of variables that in combination lead to the formation of the latent variable. Thus formative indicators are often used to construct super ordinate constructs where the individual indicators are weighed according to their relative importance in forming the construct (Chin, 1998a). In our model, three SLA characteristics were assessed as formative constructs, where eleven SLA elements (i.e., first order constructs) served as indicators of the second order constructs. Consistent with the view of Goo et al. (2006), the theoretical justification for this modeling is that it was anticipated that the elements were not necessarily correlated with each other. However, sets of different elements could be aggregated to visualize the same underlying characteristics. For example, the presence of governance characteristics is the result of a collection of legal provisions involving multiple contractual elements in the SLA. But the fact that governance characteristics exist does not necessarily ensure that a communication plan exists, and vice versa.

Each one of the constructs in the structural model exhibited convergent validity and discriminant validity. Convergent validity is adequate when constructs have an Average Variance Extracted (AVE) of at least 0.5 and when items load highly (loading > 0.5) on their associated factors as well. Table 2 shows that the reflective measures have significant loadings that are much higher than the suggested threshold.

For satisfactory discriminant validity, the square root of the AVE should be greater than the variance shared between the target construct and other constructs in the model (Chin, 1998a). These items also demonstrated satisfactory convergent and discriminant validity (Table 3).

Having validated the measurement model, the next step was testing the hypothesized relationships among various latent constructs in the PLS structural model. To determine the estimation, two rules were followed. First, heuristics on sample size in the PLS literature suggests a rule of thumb of using 10 cases per predictor, whereby the overall sample size is 10 times the largest of two possibilities: (1) the block with the largest number of formative indicators (i.e., the largest so-called measurement equation) or (2) the dependent variable with the largest number of independent variables impacting it (i.e., the largest so-called structural equation) (Chin, 1998b). Our sample size of 92 exceeded the recommended minimum of 30 (for the relationship commitment construct), which was adequate for model testing. Second, we performed a *reactive* Monte Carlo analysis such as the popular bootstrap approach (Chin, 1998b; Wold, 1982) in which the performance of an estimator of

Table 2 The assessment of the measurement models: Evidence of convergent validity

Constructs	# of Items	Composite Reliability[a]	Average Variance Extracted	Loadings (t-Statistics)[b]
Service level objectives	3	0,87	0,69	0.83 (19.01), 0.84 (17.33), 0.81 (12.47)
Process owner-ship plan	3	0,92	0,80	0.94 (62.93), 0.89 (32.61), 0.85 (22.68)
Service level contents	3	0,91	0,77	0.90 (50.49), 0.89 (35.26), 0.83 (20.31)
Future demand mgmt plan	3	0,93	0,81	0.89 (35.81), 0.90 (37.28), 0.91 (39.86)
Anticipated change plan	3	0,92	0,80	0.90 (42.75), 0.89 (29.37), 0.90 (35.02)
Innovation plan	3	0,90	0,75	0.75 (8.94), 0.90 (37.87), 0.92 (52.41)
Feedback plan	3	0,94	0,84	0.90 (43.50), 0.91 (19.15), 0.93 (52.56)
Communication plan	3	0,93	0,81	0.88 (29.53), 0.91 (29.34), 0.91 (43.10)
Measurement charter	3	0,93	0,82	0.90 (37.49), 0.89 (33.16), 0.92 (35.83)
Conflict arbitra-tion charter	3	0,89	0,73	0.82 (14.18), 0.84 (28.00), 0.90 (28.37)
Enforcement plan	3	0,91	0,76	0.87 (28.70), 0.91 (36.34), 0.84 (14.77)
Commitment	2	0,94	0,90	0.95 (76.08), 0.94 (79.00)
SR trust in SP	3	0,89	0,72	0.79 (16.65), 0.86 (25.83), 0.89 (46.33)

[a]The composite reliability scores were calculated with the formula prescribed by Fornell and Larcker (1981).
[b]$p < .001$

interest is judged by studying its parameter and standard error bias relative to repeated random samples drawn with replacement from the original observed sample data. A bootstrapping procedure with resampling of 500 subsamples was used to determine the statistical significance of the parameter estimates. Based on the results of this procedure, the structural model was assessed examining the magnitude, statistical significance of the path coefficients, and R^2 in the structural model. A summary of these results is presented in Fig. 3.

Foundation, governance, and change management characteristics contributed positively and significantly to the development of trust ($\beta = 0.393$, $p < 0.01$; $\beta = 0.293$, $p < 0.01$; and $\beta = 0.145$, $p < 0.1$, respectively), supporting hypotheses 2, 4, and 5. Similarly, foundation characteristics, governance characteristics, and trust contributed positively and significantly to commitment ($\beta = 0.242$, $p < 0.05$; $\beta = 0.241$, $p < 0.05$; and $\beta = 0.351$, $p < 0.01$, respectively), supporting hypotheses 1, 3 and 6. Thirty percent (30%) of the variances in trust was explained by formal structural assurance (i.e., the three characteristics of the SLA). About half of the variance (49%) in relationship commitment was explained by the effects of both

Table 3 Correlations of latent variables and evidence for discriminant validity

	SLO	POP	SLC	FDMP	ACP	IP	FP	CP	MC	EP	T
SLO	**0.83**										
POP	0.51	**0.89**									
SLC	0.60	0.68	**0.88**								
FDMP	−0.39	−0.61	−0.56	**0.90**							
ACP	−0.35	−0.56	−0.40	0.75	**0.90**						
IP	−0.36	−0.41	−0.37	0.66	0.75	**0.86**					
FP	−0.45	−0.48	−0.47	0.69	0.55	0.60	**0.91**				
CP	0.48	0.58	0.56	−0.56	−0.47	−0.46	−0.68	**0.90**			
MC	0.54	0.56	0.68	−0.61	−0.38	−0.49	−0.67	0.68	**0.91**		
EP	0.31	0.45	0.45	−0.33	−0.23	−0.26	−0.15	0.37	0.28	**0.87**	
T	0.44	0.43	0.46	−0.21	−0.22	−0.27	−0.36	0.41	0.47	0.20	**0.85**

Note: Bolded diagonal elements are the square root of average variance extracted (AVE)
These values should exceed the inter-construct correlations (off-diagonal elements) for adequate discriminant validity.
Index:
SLO = Service Level Objective; PO = Process Ownership; SL = Service Level Contents; FDMP = Future Demand Mgmt Plan; AC = Anticipated Change Plan; IP = Innovation Plan; FP = Feedback Plan; CP = Communication Plan; MC = Measurement Charter, EP = Enforcement Plan; RC = Relationship Commitment; T = SR Trust in SP

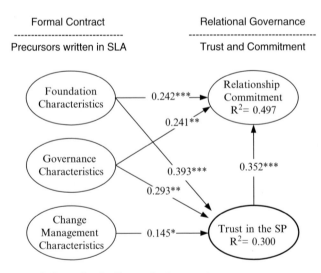

*   indicate the significance level at p< .1
** indicate the significance level at p< .05
*** indicate the significance level at p< .01

Fig. 3 Results

structural assurance such as governance and foundation characteristics and the relational attribute of trust. Overall, the results provide strong support for the model predicting the importance of using SLA characteristics to cultivate key relational attributes, trust and relationship commitment.

6 Discussion and Implications

Three characteristics of SLAs (i.e., foundation, governance, and change management characteristics) were significantly related to trust and relational commitment. Specifically, foundation and governance SLA characteristics, reflecting the parties' expected relationship benefits, shared values, and termination costs, encouraged economic actors to depart from pure economic motives and make social investments that carry strong expectations of relationship commitment (Granovetter, 1985). While the results of this study are consistent with the notion that a relational attribute of trust is significantly related to commitment in the IT outsourcing relationship, a formal contract of well-structured SLA are also critical in making the "shadow of the future" (Heide & Miner, 1992; Jap & Ganesan, 2000) by safeguarding future exchanges in the IT outsourcing relationship.

The association between three SLA characteristics and SR trust in SP is interesting. The results further showed that the three SLA characteristics, which reflect precursors of trust such as shared values, communication, and lack of opportunistic behavior, positively influenced the formation of trust in the interorganizational relationships. This suggests that "secured" precursors of trust contained in written SLA elements reflect a state of relational "embeddedness" (Lee, Miranda, & Kim, 2004; Uzzi, 1997) between SRs and SPs in which outsourcing exchanges are improved through economies of time, integrative agreements, improvements in allocative efficiency, and complex adaptation. Consistent with the literature, trusting beliefs in the context of IT outsourcing relationships appears formed largely with cognitive cues (Sitkin & Pablo, 1992) based on interactions and institutional support (Zucker, 1986) such as formal SLA. According to Morgan and Hunt (1994), trust is dependent on three variables: shared values, communication and opportunistic behavior. This assumes that the SR and the SP interact within the framework of provisions specified in that SLA. Thus, experience and observations of the SP's actions (e.g., how they have communicated, whether they have kept commitments or been honest, etc.) informs perceptions about how the SP will act in the future (i.e., SR's trust in the SP). In addition, the SR seems to believe that the necessary impersonal structures are in place to enable the SP to act in anticipation of a successful future endeavor. Institution-based trust often considered as an initial trust building mechanism in organizational relationships particularly in new work relationships such as outsourcing (McKnight et al., 1998). Structural assurance is likely to induce the trusting beliefs of SR in the SP in this study because an SLA provides security about the arrangement and supports the SR's beliefs about the maintenance and integrity of future exchanges with the SP.

Thus, for researcher this research contributes of the growing evidence that effective institutional structures engender trust in impersonal contexts of IT use (e.g., Gefen et al., 2006; Pavlou & Gefen, 2004). This study reinforces the importance of institution based trust as an initial trust building mechanism in the context of IT outsourcing. As trust is more essential between strangers than when parties interact repeatedly (Ho & Weigelt, 2005; La Porta, Lopez-de-Silanes, Shleifer, & Vishny, 1997), the role of initial trust building in IT outsourcing has become increasingly important because the number of new task teams in IT outsourcing arrangements continues to increase. For example, institutional trust is especially salient in IT-enabled outsourcing activities such as application service and offshore outsourcing where there is often minimal prior interaction and individuals often interact with new or unknown entities under the aegis of structural assurance. Based on field surveys among individuals responsible for IT outsourcing engagements, the study found support for specific forms of structural assurance in building interorganizational trust and commitment. Future research should test the effect of structural assurance and situational normality (the perception that the environment is in order, the situation is normal, appropriate, well-ordered, and favorable for assuring a transaction) on initial institutional trust building in various interorganizational relationships.

This study also provides practitioners with a strategy for structuring SLAs to appropriately manage outsourcing relationships during the life of the contract. In many cases, organizations lack well-developed SLAs that can be used to effectively gauge and manage relationships and activities associated with IT outsourcing (Fitzgerald & Willcocks, 1994; Karten, 2004). In other words, SLAs are often developed with little guidance resulting in missing essential elements. For example, SLAs contain clauses dealing with only the most rudimentary service elements and metrics and ignore important issues pertaining to governance (including communication mechanisms, joint decision making mechanisms, and conflict management) as well as those pertaining to past experience and the client's changing business needs. Underspecified SLAs, therefore, ignore the intangible benefits that can be derived from them related to building effective SP-SR relationships (Kern et al., 2002). This study identified eleven contractual elements categorized into three substantive dimensions including foundation, change management, and governance characteristics. Practitioners should find the contractual elements associated with these characteristics a useful tool for rationalizing and refining SLA elements. These characteristics might not only provide a parsimonious structure for developing SLAs but also render meaningful insights regarding which characteristics of SLA are particularly effective for enhancing specific relational attributes. Thus, managers may customize their SLAs within the diverse contexts of outsourcing arrangements by composing the different sets of the elements in SLAs. In other words, an SLA with emphases on different characteristics could nurture different relationships. For example, SLAs that emphasizes both clan control-based foundation characteristics and behavior-based change management characteristics could be structured to effectively foster relationships that facilitate the development of relationship-specific systems and applications over the years. Implementing relationship-specific systems and applications demand trust between both parties to lure the SP into undertaking risk-inherent relationship-specific investments.

One implication of the study's results is the recommendation to establish well-structured SLAs at the initiation of the engagement. While some outsourcing engagements are largely based on mutual trust without written terms of the arrangement due to the difficulty of anticipating or specifying all possible contingencies, the results of this study suggest that employing well structured SLAs are important for ensuring IT outsourcing success. These SLAs not only supply a "safety net" in lieu of exclusive reliance on trust, but also serve to build social elements such as trust and commitment. As Fitzgerald and Willcocks (1994) have noted, partnership issues in IT outsourcing must be considered in conjunction with the contractual arrangements. This is consistent with Sabherwal's (1999) recommendation to balance structural control and trust to improve performance in outsourced IS development projects in light of his observation that excessive focus on either structure or trust hurts performance.

7   Limitations and Future Research Directions

The first limitation is the cross-sectional design employed. In any model in which causality is suggested, longitudinal studies provide strong inferences. The model developed and tested here could benefit from being tested in a longitudinal design. Such a research setting could also allow a study to consider the reverse effect of relational governance on contract refinements. One would expect that initial engagements with a new partner would be characterized by amount of trust and a maximum effort to ensure formal governance. Trust over time may reduce formal governance mechanisms and these changes may lead to higher success. Future research ought to examine the reverse relationship through a longitudinal study to better understand the virtuous (vicious) cycle of outsourcing relationships in nature (Sabherwal, 1999).

The study utilized a single respondent for each outsourcing contract. This introduced potential concerns associated with the common methods variance. However, given the factual nature of the items used to assess a majority of the constructs, the possibility of common method bias problem was minimal (Podsakoff, MacKenzie, Lee, & Podsakoff, 2003). We also performed Harman's single factor test by loading all of the items in this study into an exploratory factor analysis. The results generated a large number of factors with one factor accounting for 18% of covariance among the measures at maximum, evidence that there is not a substantial amount of common method variance present.

Another limitation of this study lies the one-sided focus of the interorganizational relationship. While our model is based on at least some degree of accuracy as perceptions about one partner's commitment are influenced by the other partner's actual commitment because both partners presumably reveal their true perceptions, intentions, and actions to each other during interactions over time (Anderson & Weitz, 1992), this paper approaches from the SR side of the SR-SP dyad only, which did not directly examine the quality of the relationship from the SP's side. An analysis of the relationship between SLA and trust and commitment and their relational outcomes from the SP's perspective would be important for better under-standing high-quality relationships over time. Had the paper investigated the perspectives of both the SR and SP, the contribution would have been greater.

Another potential limitation concerns the nature of the sample utilized in this analysis. The survey in this study was aimed at organizations that implemented IT outsourcing through SLAs, and senior executives with vested interest in SLA outcomes. Although the sampling frame has been widely used in IS research and contains organizations which likely participate in the activity of interest, no claim of external validity for this study's findings can be made. While the sample shows good representation of firms by size and industry, these findings can only be gen-eralized to the firms within the sampling frame. These firms were most interested in IT outsourcing because of their current or past involvement. In addition, the sample was limited to Korean domestic organizations which were selected from the attendee list of an outsourcing conference. We anticipate that there could be systematic differ-ences between countries in drafting contracts or SLAs. Therefore, generalizing the observed structure of SLA to organizations of other nations or beyond the sampling frame may be problematic and thus requires caution.

8 Contributions and Conclusion

The contribution of this study is in two fold. First, the paper shifts our focus from the major stream of IT outsourcing research (focusing on relationship quality only) to how to foster and manage the attributes of partnership relationships that promote relationship quality. Many of the studies that have been conducted on IT outsourcing relationships examine partnership factors that influence IT outsourcing effective-ness and do not provide insight into how to cultivate those factors to garner success in IT outsourcing arrangements. As an extension of past studies which emphasize the importance of the contract (Kern & Willcocks, 2002; Saunders et al., 1997), we view SLAs as the foundation of the outsourcing relationship and the road map for outsourcing success. This paper applied the commitment-trust theory of relationship marketing to IT outsourcing arrangements and extended the theory by examining the role of formal contracts as potential precursors of trust and commitment. The findings indicate that the formal SLA elements are related to the development of trust and commitment in IT outsourcing engagements, which plays a mediating role in enlarging self-enforcing range of relational governance, five relational outcomes in this study (Klein, 1996).

Second, it contributes to the emerging research stream of research on IOR gov-ernance (Gefen et al., 2006; Gulati et al., 2005; Mani et al., 2006; Poppo & Zenger, 2002) by providing a bridge between formal contracts and relational governance, which were usually investigated separately. It is true that the preponderance of empirical work has focused mainly on social mechanisms that foster trust and com-mitment, where formal mechanisms have been regarded as a signal of distrust (Bernheim & Whinston, 1998; Ghoshal & Moran, 1996; Macaulay, 1963). This study assessed the relationship between formal contracts (i.e., SLA characteristics) and relational governance (i.e., trust and commitment) In the context of IT outsourcing, the results clearly show the complementary relationship between two governing modes, specifically a positive effect of well-structured SLA on the formation of cooperative relationships from the SR's perspective. Overall, three characteristics of SLAs contribute to the development of trust and commitment.

In conclusion, the intent of this study was to understand how formal contractual characteristics contributed to developing relational attributes such as trust and relationship commitment in IT outsourcing practices. Using cross-sectional data, the results indicated that well-structured SLAs play an important role in cultivating favorable relationships in the course of outsourcing engagements, which, in turn, are related to successful relational outcomes of IT outsourcing. Therefore, this study suggests that firms strategically use SLA to successfully manage IT outsourcing relationship (Aubert, Dussault, Patry, & Rivard, 1999; Mayer & Argyres, 2004).

Appendix A Operationalization of SLA measurements

Constructs	Items
Sevice Level Objectives	To what extent are the following statements addressed for specifying service level objectives? 1. A statement of the SR's management and organizational structure expectations at the end of the contract, once the relationship is fully operational 2. A statement of innovation expectations and capabilities of the Service Provider 3. A statement of the Service Recipient's (SR) business objectives from the service
Process Ownership Plan	To what extent are the following statements addressed for specifying process ownership? 1. Statement of process ownership roles and responsibilities 2. Inventory of processes that are required to manage the agreements between the SR and SP 3. Inventory of processes directly affected by the services included in the agreements
Service Level Contents	To what extent are the following statements addressed for specifying service level/quality? 1. A statement of the key business measurements required by the SR 2. Established service-level/quality targets 3. A general description of the service required, major categories of services, and specific service elements
Future Demand Management Plan	To what extent are the following statements addressed for specifying the process dealing with future demands? 1. Processes for scheduling, costing and modifying agreements with new demand 2. The processes used to obtain end-user feedback on the SP's delivery of services that are provisioned to meet new demand 3. The processes that the SR and SP will use to prioritize changes and modify the volume, type, or level of service to match evolving user requirements

(continued)

Appendix A (continued)

Constructs	Items
Anticipated Change management Plan	To what extent are the following statements addressed for specifying anticipated changes in the course of relationship? 1. Relevant technology, business and industry drivers for change 2. Roles, responsibilities and decision-making procedures of the SR and SP for each category of change 3. Clear definitions of the key categories of change (i.e., predetermined change such as charges for volume changes, computer updates.)
Innovation Plan	To what extent are the following statements addressed for planning of innovation? 1. Process for innovation, including implementation and prioritization 2. Process for business improvement and technology advancements (e.g., scope improvement and technology refreshes/upgrades) 3. Innovation incentive (reward) programs
Feedback Plan	To what extent are the following statements specified and addressed for guiding the feedback and the sequences of the measurements? 1. Statement of how changes will be implemented based on measurement results 2. The road map for an efficient feedback on the identified drawbacks 3. Prioritization methodology for current tasks and feedbacks
Communication Plan	To what extent are the following statements specified and addressed for ensuring communication flow? 1. Statement of the communication policy 2. Organizational reporting structure 3. Identified communication initiatives/initiative owners and recipients for various communication initiatives
Measurement Charter	To what extent are the following statements specified and addressed for determining how well the services are provided? 1. Statement of measurement methodology 2. Definition of what is to be measured (e.g., price and service benchmarking clause, customer satisfaction, contract and relationship alignment.) 3. Definition of processes to periodically measure the defined categories
Conflict Arbitration Charter	To what extent are the following statements specified and addressed for facilitating dialog and trust to work out possible conflicts? 1. A statement of the parameters for involving the third party in discussions between the SR and SP 2. A schedule for regular interactions between the parties, and timetables for resolving issues between the SR and SP 3. A statement of the practices and conduct rules required to preserve the independence of the independent advisor
Enforcement Plan	To what extent are the following statements addressed for enforcing the service agreements? 1. Penalty definitions and formula 2. Conditions under which termination may occur 3. Statement of exit responsibilities

Appendix B Measurement Items for research variables

	Items
Trust (Cronbach's alpha = .81)	The SP makes beneficial decisions to us under any circumstances.
	The SP is sincere at all times.
	The SP has always provided us a completely truthful picture of the relevant IT services.
Relationship Commitment (Cronbach's alpha = .89)	Both parties are highly committed to the relationship.
	Both parties are willing to commit resources to sustain the relationship.
Acquiscence (Cronbach's alpha = .81)	Both parties in the relationship are willing to accommodate each other as conditions change.
	If we requested it, SP would be willing to make further investment to support our needs.
	We are willing to put more effort and investment in building our business relationship with SP.
Relationship Durability (Cronbach's alpha = .77)	Even if they could, SP would not drop our organization as a service recipient (client) because they like being associated with us.
	We want to remain a customer to SP because we genuinely enjoy our relationship with them.
	The continuation of a relationship with this SP is very important to us.
Cooperation (Cronbach's alpha = .74)	We are apt to be very conscientious, responsive, and resourceful to maintain a cooperative relationship with this provider.
	Problems that arise in the course of this relationship are treated by the parties as joint rather than individual responsibilities.
	The parties in this relationship do not mind owing each other favor.
Harmonious Conflict Resolution (Cronbach's alpha = .85)	Disagreements between both parties in the relationship are almost always successfully resolved.
	Differences of opinion were resolved to the mutual satisfaction of conflicting parties.
	The discussions I have with this SP's personnel on areas of disagreement increase the effectiveness and strength of our relationship.
Active Information Change (Cronbach's alpha = .76)	In this relationship, it is expected that any information that might help the other party will be provided to them.
	It is expected that the parties will provide proprietary information if it can help the other party.
	It is expected that we keep each other informed about events or changes that may affect the other party.

References

Anderson, E., & Weitz, B. (1989). Determinants of continuity in conventional industrial channel dyads. *Marketing Science, 8*(4), 310–323

Anderson, E., & Weitz, B. (1992). The use of pledges to build and sustain commitment in distributional channels. *Journal of Marketing Research, 29*, 18–34

Anderson, J. C., & Narus, J. A. (1990). A model of distributor firm and manufacturer firm working partnerships. *Journal of Marketing 54*(1), 42–58

Ang, S., & Slaughter, S. A. (2001). Work outcomes and job design for contract versus permanent information systems professionals on software development teams. *MIS Quarterly 25*(3), 321.

Aubert, B. A., Dussault, S., Patry, M., & Rivard, S. (1999). Managing the risk of IT outsourcing. In: *Proceedings of the 32nd Hawaii International Conference on System Sciences*, Maui, Hawaii.

Baker, G., Gibbons, R., & Murphy, K. J. (1994). Subjective performance measures in optimal incentive contracts. *The Quarterly Journal of Economics, 109*(4), 1125–1156.

Bendor-Samuel, P. (1999). Crafting a better outsourcing contract. *White Paper*. Everest Group.

Bernheim, B. D., & Whinston, M. D. (1998). Incomplete contracts and strategic ambiguity. *The American Economic Review, 88*(4), 902–932.

Chin, W. W. (1988a). Issues and opinion on structural equation modeling. *MIS Quarterly, 22*(1), vii–xvi.

Chin, W. W. (1988b). The partial least squares approach to structural equation modeling. In: G. A. Marcoulides (Ed.), *Modern methods for business research* (pp. 295–336.). Mahwah, NJ: Lawrence Erlbaum Associates.

Choudhury, V., & Sabherwal, R. (2003). Portfolios of control in outsourced software development project. *Information Systems Research, 14*(3), 291–341.

Datz, T. (1973). Merrill Lynch's billion Dollar Bet. *CIO*, September 15, 2003.

Deutsch, M. (1973) *The resolution of conflict: constructive and destructive processes*. New Haven: Yale University Press.

DiRomualdo, A., & Gurbaxani, V. (1998). Strategic intent for IT outsourcing. *Sloan Management Review, 39*(4), 67–80.

Dwyer, F. R., Schurr, P. H., & Oh, S. (1987). Developing buyer-seller relationships. *Journal of Marketing, 51*(2), 11–27.

Dyer, J. H., & Singh, H. (1998). The relational view: cooperative strategy and sources of interorganizational competitive advantage. *Academy of Management Review, 23*(4), 660–679.

Fitzgerald, G., & Willcocks, L. (1994). Contracts and partnerships in the outsourcing of IS. In: *Proceedings of the 15th international conference on information systems* (pp. 91–98).

Fontenot, R. J., & Wilson, E. J. (1997). Relational exchange: a review of selected models for a prediction matrix of relationship activities. *Journal of Business Research, 39*(1), 5–12.

Frazier, G. L., & Rody, R. C. (1991). The use of influence strategies in interfirm relationships in industrial product channels. *Journal of Marketing, 55*(1), 52–69.

Gabarino, E., & Johnson, M. S. (1999). The different roles of satisfaction, trust, and commitment in customer relationships. *Journal of Marketing, 63*, 70–87.

Galaskiewicz, J., & Shatin, D. (1985). Leadership and networking among neighborhood human service organizations. *Administrative Science Quarterly, 26*, 434–448.

Ganesan, S. (1994). Determinants of long-term orientation in buyer-seller relationships. *Journal of Marketing, 58*(2), 1–19.

Gefen, D., Pavlou, P., Benbasat, I., McKnight, H., Stewart, K., Straub, D. W. (2006). ICIS panel summary: should institutional trust matter in information systems research? *Communications of the Association for Information Systems, 17*, 205–222.

Ghoshal, S., & Moran, P. (1996). Bad for practice: a critique of the transaction cost theory. *Academy of Management Review, 21*(1), 13–47.

Goles, T., & Chin, W. W. (2002). Relational exchange theory and IS outsourcing: developing a scale to measure relationship factors. In: R. Hirschheim, A. Heinzl, & J. Dibbern (Eds.), *Information systems outsourcing in the new economy*. Berlin: Springer

Goo, J., Kim, D., & Cho, B. (2006). Structure of service level agreements (SLA) in IT outsourcing: the construct and its measurement. In: *Proceedings of the12th Americas conference on information systems (AMCIS)* (pp 3222–3232). Acapulco, Mexico.

Goo, J., Kishore, R., & Rao, H. R. (2004). Management of information technology outsourcing relationships: the role of service level agreements. In: *Proceedings of the 25th International Conference on Information Systems (ICIS)* (pp. 325–338). Washington DC.

Goolsby, K. (2002). "Growing beyond illusions: guidelines for changing and improving outsourcing relationships. White Paper Outsourcing Center.

Gottfredson, M., Puryear, R., & Phillips, S. (2005). Strategic sourcing: from periphery to the core. *Harvard Business Review, 83*(2), 132–140.

Granovetter, M. (1985). Economic action and social structure. *American Journal of Sociology, 91*(3), 481–510.

Grover, V., Cheon, M. J., & Teng, J. T. C. (1996). The effect of service quality and partnership on the outsourcing of information systems functions. *Journal of Management Information Systems, 12*(4), 89–116.

Gulati, R. (1995). Does familiarity breed trust? The implications of repeated ties for contractual choices in alliances. In: *Academy of Management Journal, 38*(1), 85–112.

Gulati, R., Lawrence, P. R., & Puranam, P. (2005). "Adaptation in vertical relationships: beyond incentive conflict. *Strategic Management Journal, 26*(5), 415–440.

Gulati, R., & Singh, H. (1998). The architecture of cooperation: managing coordination costs and appropriation concerns in strategic alliances. *Administrative Science Quarterly, 43*(4), 781–809.

Gundlach, G. T., Achrol, R. S., & Mentzer, J. T. (1995). The structure of commitment in exchange. *Journal of Marketing, 59*(1), 78–93.

Heide, J. B., & John, G. (1992). Do norms matter in marketing relationships? *Journal of Marketing, 56*(2), 32–45.

Heide, J. B., & Miner, A. S. (1992). The shadow of the future: effects of anticipated interaction and frequency of contact on buyer-seller cooperation. *Academy of Management Journal, 35*(2), 265–291.

Heider, F. (2005). *The psychology of interpersonal relations*. Hillside, NJ: Erlbaum.

Ho, T.-H., & Weigelt, K. (2005). Trust building among strangers. *Management Science, 51*(4), 519–530.

Itami, H. (1987) *Mobilizing invisible assets*. Cambridge: Harvard University Press.

Jap, S. D., & Ganesan, S. (2000). Control mechanisms and the relationship life cycle: implications for safeguarding specific investments and developing commitment. *Journal of Marketing Research, 37*(2), 227–245.

Karten, N. (2004). With service level agreements, less is more. *Information Systems Management, 21*(4), 43–44.

Kern, T., & Willcocks, L. (2002). Exploring relationships in information technology outsourcing: the interaction approach. *European Journal of Information Systems, 11*(1), 3–19.

Kern, T., Willcocks, L. P., & Heck, E. V. (2002). The winner's curse in IT outsourcing: strategies for avoiding relational trauma. *California Management Review, 44*(2), 47

Klein, B. (1996). Why hold-ups occur: the self-enforcing range of contractual relationships. *Economic Inquiry, 34*(3), 444–463.

Koh, C., Ang, S., & Straub, D. W. (2004). IT outsourcing success: a psychological contract perspective. *Information Systems Research, 15*(4), 356–373.

Koh, C., Tay, C., & Ang, S. (1999). Managing vendor-client expectations in IT outsourcing: a psychological contract perspective. In: *Proceedings of the Twenties International Conference on Information Systems (ICIS)*. Charlotte, North Carolina.

Kumar, N., Scheer, L. K., & Steenkamp, J. -B. E. M. (1995). The effects of perceived interdependence on dealer attitudes. *Journal of Marketing Research, 32*(3), 348–356.

Kumar, N., Stern, L. N., & Anderson, J. C. (1993). Conducting interorganizational research using key informants. *Academy of Management Journal, 36*(6), 1633–1651.

La Porta, R., Lopez-de-Silanes, F., Shleifer, A., & Vishny, R. W. (1997). Trust in large organizations. *The American Economic Review, 87*(2), 333–338.

52   J. Goo

Lambe, C. J., Spekman, R., & Hunt, S. D. (2000). Interimistic relational exchange: conceptualization and propositional development. *Journal of the Academy of Marketing Science, 28*(2), 212–225.

Lee, J. -N., & Kim, Y. -G. (1999). Effect of partnership quality on IS outsourcing: conceptual framework and empirical validation. *Journal of Management Information Systems, 15*(4), 29–61.

Lee, J. -N., Huynh, M. Q., Kwok, R. C. -W., & Pi, S. -M. (2003). IT outsourcing evolution: its past, present, and future. *Communications of the ACM, 46*(5), 84–89.

Lee, J. -N., Miranda, S. M., & Kim, Y. -M. (2004). IT outsourcing strategies: universalistic, contingency, and configurational explanations of success. *Information Systems Research, 15*(2), 110–131.

Macaulay, S. (1963). Non-contractual relations in business: a preliminary study. *American Sociological Review, 28*, 55–67.

Mani, D., Barua, A., & Whinston, A. B. (2006). Successfully governing business process outsourcing relationships. *MIS Quarterly Executive, 5*(1), 15–29.

Mayer, K. J., & Argyres, N. S. (2004). Learning to contract: evidence from the personal computer industry. *Organization Science, 15*(4), 394–410.

McEvily, B., Perrone, V., & Zaheer, A. (2003). Trust as an organizing principle. *Organization Science, 14*(1), 91–105.

McKnight, D. H., Cummings, L. L., & Chervany, N. L. (1998). Initial trust formation in new organizational relationships. *Academy of Management Review, 23*(3), 473–490.

Meyer, J. P., & Allen, N. J. (1984). Testing the "Side-Bet Theory" of organizational commitment: some methodological considerations. *Journal of Applied Psychology, 69*(3), 372–378.

Meyerson, D., Weick, K. E., & Kramer, R. M. (1996). Swift trust and temporary groups. In: R. M. Kramer, & T. R. Tyler (Eds.), *Trust in organizations: frontiers of theory and research* (pp. 166–195). Thousand Oaks, CA: Sage.

Mingay, S., & Govekar, M. (2002). ITIL's service-level management strength is in integration. TG-15–3491, Gartner Group.

Mohr, J., & Nevin, J. R. (1990). Communication strategies in marketing channels: a theoretical perspective. *Journal of Marketing, 54*(4), 36–51.

Morgan, R. M., & Hunt, S. D. (1994). The commitment-trust theory of relationship marketing. *Journal of Marketing, 58*(3), 20–39.

Pavlou, P. A., & Gefen, D. (2004). Building effective online marketplaces with institution-based trust. *Information Systems Research, 15*(1), 37–59.

Podsakoff, P. M., MacKenzie, S. B., Lee, J. -Y., & Podsakoff, N.P. (2003) Common method biases in behavioral research: a critical review of the literature and recommended remedies. *Journal of Applied Psychology, 88*(5), 879–903.

Poppo, L., & Zenger, T. (2002). "Do Formal Contracts and Relational Governance Function as Substitutes or Complements?" *Strategic Management Journal* (23:8), 2002, pp. 707–725.

Ring, P., & Van de Ven, A. (1994). "Developmental Processes of Cooperative Interorganizational Relationships," *Academy of Management Review* (19:1), 1994, pp. 90–118.

Robey, D., Farrow, D.L., & Franz, C.R. (1989). "Group Process and Conflict in System Development," *Management Science* (35:10), 1989, pp. 1172–1191.

Rottman, J.W., & Lacity, M.C. (2004). "Twenty Practices for Offshore Sourcing," *MIS Quarterly Executive* (3:3), 2004, pp. 117–130.

Sabherwal, R. (1999). "The Role of Trust in Outsourced IS Development Projects," *Communications of the ACM* (42:2), 1999, pp. 80–86.

Saunders, C., Gebelt, M., & Hu, Q. (1997). "Achieving success in information systems outsourcing," *California Management Review* (39:2), 1997, pp. 63–79.

Scardino, L. (2001). "IT Services Contracts - Demand Management Plan," COM-14-3264, Gartner Group, 2001.

Shapiro, S.P. (1987). "The Social Control of Impersonal Trust," *American Journal of Sociology* (93:3), 1987, pp. 623–658.

Singleton, J.P., McLean, E.R., Altman, E.N. (1998). "Measuring Information Systems Performance: Experience with the Management by Results System at Security Pacific Bank," *MIS Quarterly* (12:2), 1988, pp. 325–337.

Sitkin, S. B., & Pablo, A.L. (1992). "Reconceptualizing the Determinants of Risk Behavior," *Academy of Management Review* (17), 1992, pp. 9–38.

Snir, E.M. (2000). Economics of Information Technology Outsourcing and Markets," Unpublished Doctoral Dissertation, The Wharton School, University of Pennsylvania, 2000.

Stone, L. (2001). "Beyond T&Cs: What Must Be Included in Services Contracts," AV-14-3036, Gartner Group, 2001.

Susarla, A., Barua, A., & Whinston, A.B. (2003). "Understanding the Service Component of Application Service Provision: An Empirical Analysis of Satisfaction with ASP Services," *MIS Quarterly* (27:1), 2003, pp. 91–123.

Uzzi, B. (1997). "Social Structure and Competition in Interfirm Networks: The Paradox of Embeddedness," *Administrative Science Quarterly* (42:1), 1997, pp. 35–67.

Vaast, E., & Levina, N. (2006). "Multiple Faces of Codification: Organizational Redesign in an IT Organization," *Organization Science* (17:2), 2006, pp. 190–201.

Venkatraman, N. (1989). "Strategic Orientation of Business Enterprises: The Construct, Dimensionality, and Measurement," *Management Science* (35:8), 1989, pp. 942–962.

Wilson, D.T. (1995). "An Integrated Model of Buyer-Seller Relationships," *Journal of the Academy of Marketing Science* (23:4), 1995, pp. 335–345.

Wold, H. (1982). "Soft Modeling: Intermediate Between Traditional Model Building and Data Analysis," *Mathematical Statistics* (6), 1982, pp. 333–346.

Zaheer, A., McEvily, B., & Perrone, V. (1998). "Does Trust Matter? Exploring the Effects of Interorganizational and Interpersonal Trust on Performance," *Organization Science* (9:2), 1998, pp. 141–160.

Zaheer, A., & Venkatraman, N. (1995). "Relational Governance as an Interorganizational Strategy: An Empirical Test of the Role of Trust in Economic Exchange," *Strategic Management Journal* (16:5), 1995, pp. 373–392.

Zucker, L. G. (1986). Production of trust: institutional sources of economic structure, 1840–1920. In: *Research in Organizational Behavior*, B. M. S. a. L. L. Cummings (ed.) 8, JAI, Greenwich, Conn, 1986, pp. 53–111.

Exploring the Role of Initial Trust, Initial Distrust, and Trust through Knowledge Sharing in IT Outsourcing: From a Service Receiver's Perspective[1]

Jae-Nam Lee, Minh Q. Huynh, and Rudy Hirschheim

1 Introduction

According to the International Data Corporation, the worldwide outsourcing market size is estimated to rise from $100 billion in 1998 to $152 billion by 2005, with an annual growth rate of 12.2% (Dibbern, Goles, Hirschheim, & Jayatilaka, 2004). Despite a new wave of billion dollars contracts, hardly anyone can attest a successful return in outsourcing investments with certainty. One of the difficulties for this uncertainty is due to the complexity inherently built in an outsourcing relationship. How can this relationship be untangled when it is based on overwhelmingly complex contract? Yet, even with a very detailed contract, it is not possible to spell out every rule and condition. As observed, the interactions between the clients and their service providers often go beyond rules, agreements, and exceptions. They also rest on intangible factors that could not be easily captured in the contract such as trust and interdependency (cf. Goles, 2001). Hence, rather than relying on a rigid contract, there is an interest in seeking and building flexibility in an outsourcing relationship where trust plays a significant role. According to the social exchange literature, trust is one of the most desired qualities in any close relationship (Mayer & Davis, 1995; Moorman, Deshpande, & Zaltman, 1993). Accordingly, trust plays a critical role in the development of long-term relationship and in facilitating exchange relationship. Without trust, organizations will cooperate with their service providers only under a system of formal and legal rules.

In recent years, "partner" based outsourcing has emerged as a major strategic alternative in information systems management. In this study, we posit that trust may serve as a critical success factor for the "partner" based outsourcing because it could allow the parties in outsourcing the ability to effectively manage their relationship. This creates a real opportunity when the parties involved may benefit from

---

[1] The authors would like to thank the organizers and participants of the 3rd International Conference on Outsourcing of Information Services (ICOIS 2007) for their helpful feedbacks on this paper. This work was supported by the Korea Research Foundation Grant funded by the Korean Government (MOEHRD, Basic Research Promotion Fund) (KRF-2007-332-B00113).

the synergy and interdependence as well as sharing of critical information derived from a relationship based on trust. Recent studies stress that the most critical time for a successful interorganizational relationship is at the beginning of their relationships. Trust has been considered as a central aspect of a successful outsourcing from the beginning of outsourcing relationship to the end. A great deal of interest in trust has been described, but there has been little in the way of strong theoretical models to aid in understanding the role of trust, the antecedents of trust, and the consequences of trust in outsourcing relationship. Such a deficiency motivates us to undertake this study.

Our paper represents one of the forefront efforts to conceptualise and validate a theoretical model of trust in the context of outsourcing relationship. The proposed model in this study is based on an integrative model of organizational trust developed by Mayer, David, & Schoorman, (1985). Then, the hypothesized model is then tested empirically using data collected from customer organizations in Korea. Research questions addressed in this study include: *(1) what is the role of mutual trust in outsourcing relationship?; (2) how can the mutual trust be nurtured?;* and *(3) what are consequents of the mutual trust?* With the premise that the most critical time for successful interorganizational relationship is at the beginning of the interaction, this study tries to answer above three questions.

Our paper is organized into six sections. Following the introduction is a section on theoretical background. In this section, we developed an integrated trust model in the outsourcing context based on the past literature and proposed our research hypotheses. In section three, we describe our research methodology. Section four presents our analysis and results. It is followed by the discussion of the study and concluded with the highlight of the paper's contribution, its implications as well as the future research direction.

2 Theoretical Development

2.1 Integrative Model of Organizational Trust

As shown from the literature, trust has been considered essential in many business activities because it enables the parties involved in a relationship to form appropriate and positive expectation with one another (Anderson & Narus, 1990; Gefen, 2002; Mohr & Spekman, 1994). The previous studies have shown that trust indeed determines the nature of many buyer–seller relationships (Dwyer, Schurr, & Oh, 1987; Heide & John. 1990), working partnerships in marketing area (Moorman et al., 1993; Morgan & Hunt, 1994), and strategic alliances in management area (Lewis & Weigert, 1985; Yoshino & Rangan, 1995). Hence, the literature suggest that trust is an important component of many social and business relationships because it helps shape the nature of the interactions and expectations between parties.

Although the importance of trust had been recognized, there has been a lack of obvious differentiation among factors that contribute to trust, trust itself, and outcomes of trust. To overcome the problems and enhance the existing knowledge of trust, Mayer et al. (1995) proposed an integrative model based on a dyad of trustor and trustee by clarifying the role of risk in a trust-based relationship, as shown in Fig. 1. This model is widely used in the relationship literature to study consumer behaviour in Internet (e.g., Gefen, 2002; Jarvenpaa & Tractinsky, 1999), and relationship management (e.g., Mayer & Davis, 1999).

According to the model, the differentiations between factors that cause trust, trust itself, and outcomes of trust are critical and can be done as follows. First, trust is defined as the willingness of a party to be vulnerable to the actions of another party based on the definition of the previous literature (Boss, 1978; Gambetta, 1988). Second, the trust is in turn influenced by a trustor's propensity to trust, the trustor's perceived characteristics of a trustee (e.g., trustworthiness of trustee based on his/her integrity, benevolence, and ability). Third, the trust leads to actual risk taking in a relationship since behavioral trust is the assuming of risk (Sitkin & Pabio, 1992). Finally, the desired outcome results from the result of risk taking. The model assumes that the decision to trust is influenced by the trustor's initial perception, trust (e.g., willingness to assume risk) and trusting behaviours (e.g., actually assuming risk) are fundamentally different, and taking a risk leads to a positive or unfavourable outcome in a given context.

Since there is a scarcity of research on trust in an outsourcing relationship, this study tries to provide a better understanding of the notion of trust by applying and adopting the Mayer et al.'s model to the context of IT outsourcing as show in Fig. 2 below. In the next section, we are going to elaborate on each of the construct in this model and explain their relationship in the context of outsourcing.

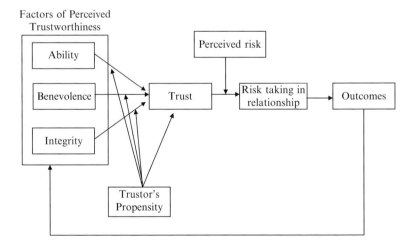

Fig. 1 Integrative model of organizational trust (Adopted from Mayer et al. 1995)

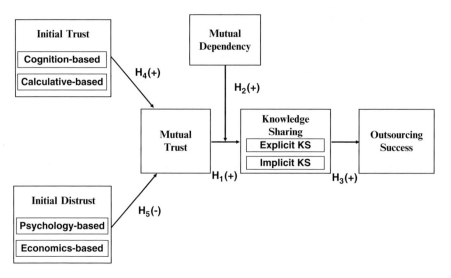

Fig. 2 An outsourcing relationship trust model

2.2   The Importance of Mutual Trust in Outsourcing Relationship

Trust, a feature of relationship quality, has been conceptualized as the firm's belief that the other company will perform actions that will result in positive outcomes for the firm, and will not take unexpected actions that would result in negative outcomes for the firm (Gulati, 1995; Mayer & Davis, 1995). Morgan and Hunt (1994) describe trust as "existing when one party has confidence in an exchange partner's reliability and integrity." This definition highlights the important of confidence in the relationship. Moorman et al. (1993) define trust as "a willingness to rely on an exchange partner in whom one has confidence". They argue that willingness is a critical facet of trust's conceptualization because if one believes that a partner is trustworthy without being willing to rely on that partner, trust is limited. In summary, trust can be conceptualized as two dimensions, confidence and willingness (Gulati, 1995).

This conceptualization is based on optimistic expectations that the other person or persons will protect the rights of all involved (Hosmer, 1995). An expectation about an exchange partner is an important part of this conceptualization. In other words, it is the expectation that commitments undertaken by another party will be fulfilled, especially in relationships where the trust party lacks control over the trusted party but must still depend on it (Fukuyama, 1995; Rotter, 1971). Therefore, trust is essential in many relationship activities, especially those where the service or product cannot be evaluated immediately (Fukuyama, 1995), and where rules and regulations are not enough to predict the behavior of other parties and to reduce the relationship complexity (Gefen, 2002; Luhmann, 1979).

Trust in outsourcing relationship is very similar to above conceptualization because, as in other relationships, the interaction between the client and the service provider in IT outsourcing often goes beyond the rules, agreements, and exceptions specified in a legal contract. There are always trust-related elements that are intangible and not easily captured in a contract. Relationships based on a formal contract and rooted in mutual trust give rise to stronger bonds between clients and their service providers (Klepper, 1994; Sabherwal, 1999). In many cases, organizations seek to create flexible relationships with their service providers after they have identified the limitations of legal contracts. There is also evidence that outsourcing projects in the 1990s increasingly shifted from contractual to trust-based relationships (Willcocks & Kern, 1998). Consequently, forming effective relationships based on mutual trust might be a key predictor of future outsourcing success (Lee, Minh, Kwok, & Pi, 2003).

The role of trust in IT outsourcing was highlighted by Sabherwal (1999) and Lee and Kim (1999). According to Sabherwal (1999), trust leads participants to work together rather than seek ways to deflect blame, and the balance between trust (i.e., psychological contract which consists of unwritten and largely unspoken sets of congruent expectations) and formal written contract is critical. Lee and Kim (1999) emphasize that trust is a basic component to classify a relationship type into transaction style and partnership style, and evolving through mutually satisfying interactions and increasing confidence in relationship. So, trust is considered as a major component of relationship quality, which directly affects the degree of outsourcing success.

However, it is not assumed that the trust-based relationship always leads to the best results in outsourcing relationships. Instead, we believe that trust is a necessary but not necessarily a sufficient condition for outsourcing success. For instance, when the outsourcing objective is cost reduction but the vendor cannot meet this objective, the outcome of such outsourcing cannot be called a success even if their relationship is trust-based. Therefore, a better understanding of trust in outsourcing relationship is crucial to have a successful outsourcing project. This is the reason why we explore the source, role, and outcome of trust in outsourcing relationship.

2.3 Trust Consequents

2.3.1 Knowledge Sharing as Risk taking in Relationship

A factor that is critical in leading to a successful outsourcing is the ability of parties involved to share and exchange knowledge. Since organizational knowledge is inherently created and resides with individuals (Nonaka & Takeuchi, 1995), the challenges are how to change individual into organizational knowledge and to integrate and manage organizational knowledge so that it results in successful performance. Since organizational knowledge is usually distributed within an organization and organizational products or services generally require multiple knowledge (or collective knowledge), organizations need to integrate the knowledge to produce new products or services, or to improve business performance (Brown & Duguid, 1998). The key to overcome these challenges is on knowledge sharing. Individual knowledge should be shared among organizational members. Many organizational managers focus their managerial efforts on this organizational sharing of individual knowledge.

Though organizational knowledge is created within an organization, it can also be acquired externally (Badaracco, 1991). Recently, there are more and more organizations that form strategic alliance in order to learn from their partners and develop new competencies. (e.g., Simonin, 1999). According Nelson and Cooprider (1996), trust exerts a major impact in relationships between organizational groups as well as inter-organizational groups. Their study identifies mutual trust among the determinants of shared knowledge. The development of mutual trust leading to shared knowledge is an ongoing phenomenon. Repeated intergroup exchanges of information generate trust, which lead to increased communications and eventually facilitate sharing of knowledge (Anderson & Narus, 1990).

In the outsourcing context, knowledge sharing is not just a simple shared reality between groups in the case of IS performance. Because of the nature in a trust-based relationship, both the client organization and the service provider are coupled in an intimate interaction. There is a high degree of interdependency and vulnerability. Hence, knowledge sharing involves an element of risk taking. The effectiveness of knowledge sharing is related to the willingness for parties involved to take risks by opening up to each other. Thus, the higher level of perceived mutual trust between the client and the service provider organizations are in their relationship, the more willingness for risk taking the client and the service provider organizations have in their knowledge sharing.

For purpose of this study, we frame knowledge sharing as activities of transferring or disseminating knowledge from one person, group or organization to another. This conceptualization of knowledge sharing broadly includes both tacit and explicit knowledge. To make more concrete and new definitions of tacit and explicit knowledge, we introduce the concept of knowledge representativeness (Polanyi, 1996) – the degree to which knowledge can be expressed in verbal, symbolic or written form. That is, we consider the representativeness of knowledge to be a continuum. According to this rationale, tacit knowledge is defined as knowledge that cannot be expressed in verbal, symbolic and written form while explicit knowledge is knowledge that exists in symbolic or written form. Then, implicit knowledge is knowledge that can be expressed in verbal, symbolic or written form, but not yet expressed. Since tacit knowledge is hard to formalize and communicate, this study focuses mainly on explicit and implicit knowledge sharing between the service receiver and provider. Based on above premise, we propose the following hypothesis.

H1: The mutual trust will be positively related to the degree of knowledge sharing.

2.3.2 Mutual Dependency as Perceived Risk

In a joint project, organizational groups are often dependent upon each other. Similarly, in an outsourcing relationship, groups have to work together to achieve the interorganizational goals. This interdependence creates the sphere of mutual dependency. While trust limits the need for formally written contract or structure by reducing the perceived need to guard against opportunistic behavior, exclusive mutual dependency is dangerous (Sabherwal, 1999). Even if the parties may be confident in each other's trustworthiness, they also may be uncertainty how much they rely on each other.

While the degree of interdependency is varied between the service provider and client organizations, it is clear that propensity by itself is not insufficient to account for the association between mutual trust and knowledge sharing. To address this variance, we introduce another construct – mutual dependency as perceived risk. Mutual dependency between organizations results from a relationship in which participating parties perceive mutual benefits and share the risks from their interactions (Bensaou & Venkatraman, 1995; Emerson, 1962; Mohr & Spekman, 1994). Such dependency is determined by the organization's perception of its dependency on its partner in relation to the partner's dependency on it (Anderson & Narus, 1984). When the size of the exchange increases and the importance of the exchange is recognized, the level of mutual dependency is high (Heide & John, 1990).

In such a case, participating parties usually see their partners as the best alternative for sources of exchange. According to Lee and Kim (1999), the higher the degree of mutual dependency is likely to result in the higher quality of relationship. In an outsourcing context, we posit that the higher the mutual dependency between the service provider and client organizations, the more likely they would share their knowledge. Subsequently, the stronger the level of mutual dependency, the stronger the relationship between mutual trust and knowledge sharing. We hypothesize that:

H2: The relationship between mutual trust and knowledge sharing will be moderated by the degree of mutual dependency.

2.3.3 Outsourcing Success

The success of outsourcing can manifest in several different ways. Generally, success may be reflected by the degree to which predefined objectives are realized. In most outsourcing cases, outsourcing objectives relate to the strategic, economic and technological benefits. Then the success of outsourcing should be assessed in terms of attainment of these benefits (Loh & Venkatraman, 1992). Outsourcing relationship based on mutual trust can create a competitive advantage through the strategic sharing of organizations' key information and knowledge (Konsynski & McFarlan, 1990). Closer relationships result from more frequent and more relevant information and knowledge exchanges among high performance partners (Lam, 1997). By sharing knowledge between the client and the service provider, they are able to sustain a more effective outsourcing relationship over time. Therefore, the absence of knowledge sharing is a critical factor in a dysfunctional inter-organizational dynamics, whereas the presence of such a shared perception may lead to better outsourcing performance. Therefore, this study hypothesizes that:

H3: The knowledge sharing will be positively related to the outcome of outsourcing.

2.4   Antecedents of Trust

As shown in literature, trust plays a critical role in the development of long-term relationship and in facilitating exchange relationship. This type of committed and long-term relationship is perceived as a dynamic process as the parties mutually demonstrate their trustworthiness through specific sequential interactions. If trust is indeed a dynamic process, then it should be considered as a process-oriented concept rather than an outcome-oriented concept or an input-oriented concept (Lee & Kim, 1999). While interorganizatonal trust is dynamic, a propensity to trust is perceived to be a stable within-organization factor that will affect the likelihood the organization will trust. This propensity is rooted in the organizational culture and value. Based on what Mayer et al.'s proposed model of trust (1995), we distinct trust and initial trust as two separate entities. At the organizational level, trust is a set of expectations shared by all those in an exchange (Zucker, 1986), while initial trust is the general willingness to trust others prior to data on that particular party being available. Initial trust between parties is not based on any kind of prior experience with each other. Rather, it is based on an individual or institutional cue that enables one person or party to trust another without firsthand knowledge.

According to the differentiation above, we define the notion of initial trust as one party's disposition to believe based on the economic and cognitive cues that the other party would fulfill the commitment and behave in a predictable way. In outsourcing relationship, interaction between client and its service providers is commonplace. Such a situation involves initial trust. Since they have not worked together enough to develop an interaction history, initial trust situations occur naturally.

Ajzen (1988) explains evidence that beliefs and intentions tend to stay consistent. If one is likely to have initial trust toward the other, they are likely to have a successful relationship with consistent trustworthiness from the beginning to the end. Some researchers for cognitive consistency have found evidence that related beliefs tend to stay consistent with each other because people keep their various cognitions reconciled (Abelson et al., 1968). When parties first meet, already-formed initial trust will encourage a high level of trust beliefs and intentions. Over time, the relationship between parties will be reciprocal and will reach equilibrium. Although the level of initial trust can be lower (Worchel, 1979) or higher (Zand, 1972) as time passes and conditions change, we generally expect to find relatively consistent level of initial trust in forming and developing organizational relationships.

According to McKnight, Cummings, and Chervany (1998), there are five research streams to explain how initial trust forms: (1) calculative-based; (2) knowledge-based; (3) personality-based; (4) institution-based; and (5) cognition-based. Calculative-based trust researchers theorize that individuals make trust choices based on rationally derived costs and benefits (Lewick and Bunker 1995). In this study, we chose two research streams – calculative-based and cognition-based – as a basis to conceptualize initial trust, even though each of other three streams can be adopted for initial trust. Knowledge-based trust assumes that the parties have firsthand knowledge of each other. However, the concept of initial trust in this study does not include any interaction history and focuses on second-hand knowledge such as reputation as a categorization process (McKnight et al. 1998). Personality and institution-based trust are not appropriate for this study because of their totally different point of view. Based on above explanation and classification, we formulate the following hypothesis.

H4: Initial trust will be positively related to the level of mutual trust in an outsourcing arrangement.

The distinction between trust and distrust is less complicated than that of trust and initial trust. Our justification is drawn from Lewick and Bunker (1995) and McKnight and Chervany (2001)'s works. Going back to the context of Rotter's definition of trust, trust is characterized as confident positive expectations from one partner toward the other partners. According to Lewick and Bunker (1995), distrust can be viewed as confident negative expectations toward other partners. Unlike Lewick and Bunker's view of distrust as the opposite of trust, McKnight and Chervany (2001) insisted that distrust is not synonymous with low levels of trust. This is mainly because trust and distrust typically separate and appear to have somewhat different determinants and consequences. Having low trust in a vendor may indicate that one does not want to do business with this firm, whereas to have disposition to distrust in a vendor means that one is suspicious of the vendors' intention.

Though many researchers described that trust is crucial in interorganizational relationships, interestingly few researchers brought up the notion of distrust in organizational relationship. In this study, we specifically examine the role of initial distrust in an outsourcing relationship. Our definition of initial distrust is one party's disposition to believe based on the economic and cognitive cues that the other party may not fulfill the commitment or behavior in a predictable way. Similar to initial trust, we posit that initial distrust is an important construct in outsourcing. Applying McKnight and Chervany (2001)'s interpretation, we adopted two subconstructs for disposition to initial distrust: the first one based on the psychology perspective is the suspicion of humanity by which one assumes others are not usually honest, benevolent, competent, and predictable (Wrightsman, 1991); and the second one related to the economic perspective is the distrusting stance by which one assumes that he/she will achieve better outcomes by dealing with people even though these people are not well-meaning and reliable (Riker, 1971).

The basic assumption is that initial distrust can be considered as the absence of such safeguards against risks of bad relationship. Thus, if a party's prior beliefs are negative, cognitive biases that prefer conservatism generally will sustain negative intensions and behaviors (Fazio & Zanna, 1981). Consequently, over time, the negative belief will compound and adversely affect the mutual trust and then the knowledge sharing and eventually the outcome of the relationship. Thus, our next hypothesis is the following.

H5: Initial distrust will be negatively related to the level of mutual trust in an outsourcing arrangement.

3   Research Methodology

In this study, a field survey method was adopted with a confirmatory analysis approach from the service receiver's perspective.

3.1   *Measures*

After developing the research framework, we conducted a series of personal interviews with IT outsourcing professionals to assess the external validity of the model. We then developed a questionnaire based on the previous literature and the comments gathered from the interviews. To develop the measurement, we relied on the multiple-item method and hence assigned each item on a five-point Likert scale. Whenever it is appropriate, we adapted the existing measures to our research context (e.g., knowledge sharing (Lee, 2001) and outsourcing success (Grover, Cheon, & Teng, 1996)). In some cases, we converted the definitions of the constructs into a questionnaire format (e.g., initial trust and initial distrust).

An initial version of the survey instrument was subsequently refined through extensive pretesting with seven academics who have significant expertise in the area of outsourcing. The instrument was further pilot tested with ten service receivers in Korea. We interviewed a representative in charge of the firm's IT operations in each service receiver. The multiple phases of instrument development resulted in a significant degree of refinement and restructuring of the survey instrument (Nunnally, 1978). Our survey instrument is available upon request.

3.2   *Sample and Data Collection*

The data were obtained from a field survey of service receivers. The primary source of the sampling frame for service receivers was a list of the 1,000 large firms reported in the *Maeil Business Newspaper* in Korea as of year 2003. Then, these firms were checked in the Book of Listed Firms published by the Korea Stock Exchange to obtain the name of the IS executive in each firm. Finally, the survey questionnaire was mailed to 970 corporate-level top IS executives of the service receiver's firms.

In order to increase the response rate, Dillman's Total Design Method (1991) had been applied. A postcard follow-up was conducted one week after the original mailing and the same questionnaire was mailed again four weeks after the original mailing. After the three rounds of solicitation, a total of 285 service receivers responded to the survey representing a response rate of about 29%. Most of the respondents provided the name and address of the vendor representative who was most knowledgeable about the relationship. 86 out of 285 responses did not provide their vendor information, while 36 responses were discarded due to incomplete data. Finally, 163 responses could be used for the second survey for the service provider. Among respondents, a large number of the responses came from the manufacturing (25.2%), construction (22.7%), and banking and finance (20.2%). Of the 163 companies, 54 firms had total sales of 1 billion dollars or more. The average outsourcing period was about 3.5 years (S.D. = 1.52).

4   Analysis and Results

4.1   Analysis Method

This study selected a confirmatory approach using Partial Least Squares (PLS). Although one of advantages in adopting the PLS method is to test the measurement model and structural model at the same time, this study decided to adopt a two-step analysis approach in which the measurement model was first estimated, much like the factor analysis, and then the measurement model was fixed in the second stage when the structural model was estimated (Anderson & Gerbing, 1988; Hair et al. 1995). The rationale for this approach is to ensure that our results on the structural relationship come from accurate and desirable representation of the reliability of the indicators in the measurement model.

4.2   Measurement Model

To validate our measurement model, three types of validity were assessed: content validity, convergent validity and discriminant validity of the instrument. First, content validity refers to the comprehensiveness of the items used to create a scale. It is established by ensuring the consistency between the measurement items and extant literature, by interviewing senior practitioners and pilot-testing the instrument. Second, convergent validity was assessed by looking at the composite reliability and the average variance extracted from the measures (Hair, Anderson, Tatham, & Black, 1995). Table 1 shows that the average variances extracted by our

Table 1 Results of PLS confirmatory factor analysis

Construct	Item	CR/AVE[a]	Loading	t-value
Cognition-based initial trust	COIT1	0.949/0.823	0.887	51.069
	COIT2		0.964	214.440
	COIT3		0.805	24.273
	COIT4		0.964	214.439
Calculative-based initial trust	CAIT1	0.884/0.718	0.771	8.375
	CAIT2		0.889	9.718
	CAIT3		0.877	9.736
Psychology-based initial distrust	PSID1	0.906/0.707	0.895	9.876
	PSID2		0.882	9.775
	PSID3		0.743	8.015
	PSID4		0.834	9.614
Economics-based initial distrust	ECID1	0.863/0.677	0.773	8.963
	ECID2		0.882	9.818
	ECID3		0.810	9.183
Mutual trust	MT1	0.871/0.632	0.702	12.815
	MT2		0.763	17.294
	MT3		0.758	14.188
	MT4		0.620	9.053
	MT5		0.764	17.294
	MT6		0.758	14.188
Explicit knowledge sharing	EKS1	0.932/0.775	0.888	9.837
	EKS2		0.862	9.710
	EKS3		0.856	9.690
	EKS4		0.913	9.881
Implicit knowledge sharing	IKS1	0.866/0.684	0.767	8.699
	IKS2		0.881	9.734
	IKS3		0.829	9.401
Mutual dependency	MD1	0.957/0.816	0.920	11.525
	MD2		0.879	15.834
	MD3		0.919	11.524
	MD4		0.879	15.834
	MD5		0.920	11.522
Outsourcing success	OS1	0.920/0.664	0.692	14.944
	OS2		0.771	23.003
	OS3		0.750	20.423
	OS4		0.738	10.183
	OS5		0.735	15.458
	OS6		0.780	25.210
	OS7		0.812	31.741
	OS8		0.756	20.263
	OS9		0.807	30.827

[a] CR stands for Composite Reliability and AVE is Average Variance Extracted

measures were very satisfactory at 0.632 or above. In addition, Table 2 exhibits the loadings and t-values of the measures in our research model. All measures are significant on their path loadings at the level of 0.01. Finally, the discriminant validity

Table 2 Correlations between constructs

Construct	1	2	3	4	5	6	7	8	9
Cognition-based initial trust	0.907								
Calculative-based initial trust	0.333	0.847							
Psychology-based initial distrust	0.237	0.092	0.841						
Economics-based initial distrust	0.265	0.206	0.366	0.823					
Mutual trust	0.375	0.317	0.055	0.306	0.795				
Explicit know. sharing	0.389	0.344	0.155	0.501	0.553	0.880			
Implicit know. sharing	0.281	0.291	−0.091	0.334	0.610	0.584	0.827		
Mutual dependency	0.314	0.135	0.157	0.122	0.236	0.201	0.147	0.903	
Outsourcing success	0.363	0.300	0.183	0.391	0.477	0.462	0.423	0.242	0.815

The shade numbers in the diagonal row are square roots of the average variance extracted.

of our instrument was verified by looking at the square root of the average variance extracted. The result revealed that the square root of the average variance extracted for each construct on models is greater than the correlations between it and all other constructs. Also, the results of the inter-construct correlations exhibited that each construct shared larger variance with its own measures than with other measures. Overall, these results explain that the measurement models are strongly supported by the gathered data and ready for further analysis.

We then checked multicollinearity of the measurement model. Multicollinearity may potentially exist among the independent variables. Table 2 displays the correlations among all variables. These correlations plus the result from VIF suggest that multicollinearity is not a serious problem for the proposed model from the service receiver's perspectives, particularly when the purpose of the analysis is to make inferences on the response function or the prediction of new observations (Neter, Wasserman, & Kutner, 1985), which is the case in this study.

4.3   Structural Model

The results of the analysis of the structural models are summarized in Fig. 3. Tests of significance of all paths were performed using the bootstrap resampling procedure. As shown in the figure, among five hypothesized paths, three are found significant at the level of 0.01.

4.3.1   Mutual trust

A service receiver's perception of initial trust was found to be significantly related to the mutual trust ($\beta = 0.418$; $t = 6.127$; $p < 0.01$). Hence, H4 was supported.

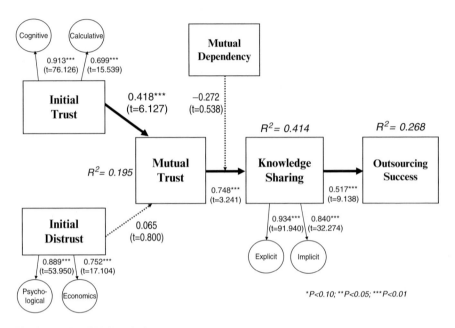

Fig. 3 Results of PLS analysis

However, initial distrust was not found to be significantly related to the service receiver's perception of mutual trust; H5 was not supported. The testing results of both H4 and H5 indicate that mutual trust is more likely shaped by its initial trust of a service provider and not its initial distrust.

In other words, the more positive a service receiver's disposition to believe based on the economic and cognitive cues that its service provider is a trustworthy partner, the stronger its perception of mutual trust with its service provider becomes.

4.3.2 Knowledge Sharing

As hypothesized, the results show that mutual trust has a significant impact on the degree of knowledge sharing between the service receiver and its provider ($\beta = 0.748$; $t = 3.241$; $p < 0.01$), supporting H1. This means that when a service receiver has confidence in its service provider, it is more willing to engage in activities of explicit and implicit knowledge sharing. Contrary to previous studies (e.g., Bensaou & Venkatraman, 1995), mutual dependency didn't have significant effect on the relationship between mutual trust and knowledge sharing. This suggests that when engaged in an outsourcing arrangement, a service receiver may already presume its dependency on its service provider. Hence, it is a mutual trust rather than mutual dependency that plays a significant role in the process of knowledge sharing.

4.3.3 Outsourcing Success

As expected, the degree that a service receiver engages in knowledge sharing with its service provider is significantly associated with the outsourcing success. That is, the higher the degree of explicit and implicit knowledge sharing taken by a service receiver, the greater the attainment of the strategic, economic, and technological outsourcing benefits, supporting H3.

5 Discussion

By applying an integrative model of organizational trust to the context of outsourcing relationship, this study has explained the importance of initial trust, mutual trust, and knowledge sharing for the success of outsourcing. The results from this study partially support the proposed framework. Two major factors – mutual trust and knowledge sharing - influence the outsourcing success. Similarly, both the mutual dependency and initial distrust were found to be insignificant, while initial trust contributes to strengthen the mutual trust.

Specifically, the finding of this study first shows that knowledge sharing is perceived to be a critical success factor in outsourcing relationship, which is consistent with the existing literature (e.g., Lam, 1997). The result of H3 suggests that the perception of outsourcing success is determined by the extent to which both service receiver and provider share their explicit and implicit knowledge with one another. The evidence indicates that knowledge sharing plays an important role for the attainment of outsourcing strategic, economic, and technological benefits. Furthermore, explicit knowledge sharing appears to be a more effective way for outsourcing success than implicit knowledge sharing. Explicit knowledge is easier to understand and share with other organizations than implicit knowledge that is yet not expressed.

Second, mutual trust is found to be significantly affected by the initial trust. Hence, the initial disposition that one believes in the other's ability, expertise, and credibility is very crucial in the emergence of mutual trust (Nelson & Cooprider, 1996). Moreover, once it is established and developed, mutual trust also focuses not only on specific actions or behaviors but also on the motives and intentions of the exchange partner (Rempel et al., 1995). As a result, mutual trust increases the confidence in which the exchange parties have for one another in performing the tasks and achieving the common goals. Then, it reduces the uncertainty in the relationship and in turn contributes to the process of knowledge sharing. With mutual trust, both parties believe that no one is taking advantage of the others and walk away from the project in the event of unanticipated contingencies. The results suggest that mutual trust can provide a conducive environment where knowledge can be freely flown and shared between a service receiver and provider. It is an ingredient that fosters cooperation and partnership.

Third, since the dynamic nature of trust provides the need for identifying and assessing its antecedents, this study introduces two relevant antecedents, initial trust and initial distrust. According to the test result, there is no significant negative effect of initial distrust on their perception of mutual trust, contrary to what we expected (Fishbein & Ajzen, 1975; Ajzen, 1988). One possible explanation is that, unlike the initial trust, the initial distrust is often emerged from the experience or exposure to specific negative actions or behaviors. This implies an existing or previous relationship among the parties involved. Thus, in the absence of working history, the parties involved are less likely to develop initial distrust for one another. With respect to the initial trust, the service receiver considers initial trust to be as a significant factor in its perception of mutual trust. This credibility is based on the extent to which a service receiver believes that a certain provider has the required expertise to perform the job successfully (Lindskold, 1978).

The analysis of initial trust and initial distrust provides a mechanism to examine the relationship between mutual trust and knowledge sharing at a deeper level. By recognizing and including initial trust and initial distrust, it is possible to derive three possible cases. In the first case, initial trust and distrust assume to have minimal impact because the mutual trust may already be formed. In the second case, the knowledge sharing process involves no previous relationship. In this situation, the initial trust plays a dominant role in shaping the sequent development of mutual trust and knowledge sharing. In the final case, the knowledge sharing process involves the case where one party or both parties has some distrust on the other or on one another. In this case, the initial distrust has an interesting impact on the evolving relationship between both parties.

Finally, regarding the mutual dependency, previous studies suggest that it is an influencing factor on both trust and knowledge sharing (e.g., Bensaou & Venkatraman, 1995). While Lee and Kim (1999) reported that the degree of mutual dependency affects the quality of outsourcing relationship, this study shows non-significant effect of mutual dependency on knowledge sharing. It is possible that when both the service receiver and provider have developed a mutual trust, they are more inclined to perceive that their knowledge sharing is not driven by the degree of mutual dependency but in large part by the level of trust with one another. In a tightly coupling relationship, the feeling of mutual trust among the parties is much stronger and prevalent than that of mutual dependency. This in turn is a good effect because mutual trust provides much more effective environment for knowledge sharing than mutual dependency.

6   Conclusion

Although a great deal of interest in trust has been explored in previous studies, there has been little in the way of strong theoretical models to aid in understanding the role of trust, the antecedents of trust, and the consequences of trust in outsourcing relationship. Filling this deficiency in the outsourcing literature marks one of the potential contributions of this study. Our research is associated with the introduction of new concepts to the study of outsourcing relationship. These concepts are initial trust and initial distrust. This study shows that both initial trust and initial distrust are significant determinants of knowledge sharing and outsourcing success. It implies the need to provide opportunities for these qualities to be developed. Internally, by defining knowledge sharing as an appreciation between the service receiver and provider for the technologies and processes that influence their mutual performance, both should be provided opportunities to socially interact and communicate about their work. Externally, by having positive reputation and impression between the service receiver and provider in market, both should be provided opportunities to believe and be believed each other when they start a project. These opportunities could lead to improved outsourcing performance by providing a greater belief and commitment and understanding and appreciation of the constraints and environment of each other.

There are some limitations associated with this study. First, while the tests of the research framework provide partial support for the hypotheses, the nature of our cross-sectional design study limits our ability to eliminate the confound effects and also other possible causes. Another limitation is that the results of this study may include some bias since the sample was restricted to Korea. Although we tried to remove the distinctiveness of the Korean outsourcing context, replication of this study is needed to fine-tune the analysis in a more extensive geographical area. Furthermore, the sample size is relatively small. This may lead to self-selection bias and also cause the instability of the parameter estimates.

From a managerial perspective, it is important to know the significant role of knowledge sharing in determining the success of IT outsourcing initiatives. Fostering a productive environment for knowledge sharing is one of the critical successful factors for outsourcing relationship in general and for partnership-oriented outsourcing in particular. Outsourcing based on the premise of knowledge sharing would help to draw both the receiver and the provider together on seeing a shared vision and achieving a common goal. Being sensitive and aware of the presence of initial trust and initial distrust is critical especially for the service receiver, because it may provide managers with many subtle cues for selection and evaluation of the right service provider. Putting an effort to build strong initial trust would be a stepping stone for the successful outcome of their outsourcing relationship.

References

Abelson, R. P., Aronson, E., McGuire, W. J., Newcomb, T. M., Ronsenberg, M. J., & Tannenbaum, P. H. (1968). *Theories of cognitive consistency: a sourcebook*. Chicago: Rand-McNally.

Ajzen, I. (1988). *Attitudes, personality and behavior*. Chicago: Dorsey Press.

Anderson, J. C. & Gerbing, D. W. (1988). Structural equation modeling in practice: a review and recommended two-step approach. *Psychological Bulletin, 103*(3), 411–423.

Anderson, J. C. & Narus, J. A. (1984). A model of distributor's perspective of distributor-manufacturer working relationships. *Journal of Marketing, 48*, 62–74.

Anderson, J. C., & Narus, J. A. (1990). A model of distributor firm and manufacturer firm working part-nerships. *Journal of Marketing, 54*(1), 42–59.

Badaracco, J. L. (1991). *The knowledge link*. Boston, MA: Harvard Business School Press.

Bensaou, M., & Venkatraman, N. (1995). Configurations of interorganizational relationships: a comparison between U.S. and Japanese automakers. *Management Science, 41*(9), 1471–1492.

Boss, R. W. (1978). Trust and managerial problem solving revisited. *Group and Organization Studies, 3*, 331–342.

Dibbern, J., Goles, T., Hirschheim, R., & Jayatilaka, B. (2004). Information systems outsourcing: a survey and analysis of the literature. *The DATA BASE for Advances in Information Systems, 35*(4), 6–102.

Dillman, D. A. (1991). The design and administration of mail survey. *Annual Review of Sociology, 17*, 225–249.

Dwyer, F. R., Schurr, P. H., & Oh, S. (1987). Developing buyer-seller relationships. *Journal of Marketing, 51*, 11–27.

Emerson, R. M. (1962). Power dependence relationship. *American Sociological Review, 27*, 31–41.

Fazio, R. H., & Zanna, M. P. (1981). Direct experience and attitude-behavior consistency. In: L. Berkowitz (Ed.), *Advances in experimental social psychology* (pp. 162–202). New York: Academic.

Fishbein, M., & Ajzen, I. (1975). *Belief, attitude, intention and behavior: an introduction to theory and research*. Reading, MA: Addison-Wesley.

Fukuyama, F. (1995). *Trust: the social virtues and the creation of prosperity*. New York: The Free Press.

Gambetta, D. (1988). *Trust: the making and breaking of cooperative relationships*. Oxford: Basil Blackwell.

Gefen, D. (2002). Reflections on the dimensions of trust and trustworthiness among online consumers. *The DATA BASE for Advances in Information Systems, 33*(3), 38–53.

Goles, T. (2001). *The impact of the client/vendor relationship on outsourcing success*. Unpublished PhD Dissertation, University of Houston.

Grover, V., Cheon, M. J., & Teng, J. T. C. (1996). The effect of service quality and partnership on the outsourcing of information systems functions. *Journal of Management Information System, 12*(4), 89–116.

Gulati, R. (1995). Does familiarity breed trust? The implications of repeated ties for contractual choice in alliances. *Academy of Management Journal, 38*(1), 85–112.

Hair, J. F., Anderson, R. E., Tatham, R. L., & Black, W. C. (1995). *Multivariate data analysis with readings* (4th ed.). New York: Prentice Hall.

Heide, J. B., & John, G. (1990). Alliances in industrial purchasing: the determinants of joint action in buyer-supplier relationships. *Journal of Marketing Research, 27*, 24–36.

Hosmer, L. T. (1995). Trust: the connecting link between organizational theory and philosophical ethics. *Academy of Management Review, 20*(2), 379–403.

Jarvenpaa, S., & Tractinsky, N. (1999). Consumer trust in an internet store: a cross-cultural validation. *Journal of Computer-Mediated Communication, 5*(2), 1–34.

Klepper, R. J. (1994). Outsourcing relationships. In: M.Khosrowpour, (Ed.), *Managing Information Technology Investment with Outsourcing* (pp. 218–243). Harrisburg, PA: IDEA Group Publishing.

Konsynski, B. R., & McFarlan, F. W. (1990). Information partnerships-shared data, shared scale. *Harvard Business Review, 68*(5), 114–120.

Lam, A. (1997). Embedded firms, embedded knowledge: problems of collaboration and knowledge transfer in global cooperative ventures. *Organization Studies, 18*(6), 973–996.

Lee, J. N., Minh, H. Q., Kwok R. C., & Pi, S. M. (2003). IT outsourcing evolution: its past, present, and future. *Communications of the ACM, 46*(5), 84–89.

Lee, J. N. (2001). The impact of knowledge sharing, organizational capability and partnership quality on IS outsourcing success. *Information and Management, 38*(5), 323–335.

Lee, J. N., & Kim, Y. G. (1999). Effect of partnership quality on IT outsourcing success: conceptual framework and empirical validation. *Journal of Management Information Systems, 15*(4), 29–61.

Lewick, R. J., & Bunker, B. B. (1995). Trust in relationships: a model of trust development and decline. In: B. B. Bunker, & J. Z. Rubin (Eds.), *Conflict, cooperation and justice* (pp. 133–173). SanFrancisco: Jossey-Bass

Lewis, J. D., & Weigert, A. J. (1985). Social atomism, holism, and trust. *The Sociological Quarterly, 26*, 455–471.

Lindskold, S. (1978). Trust development, the grit proposal, and the effects of conciliatory acts on conflict and cooperation. *Psychological Bulletin, 85*(4), 772–793.

Loh, L., & Venkatraman, N. (1992). Determinants of information technology outsourcing: a cross sectional analysis. *Journal of Management Information Systems, 9*(1), 7–24.

Luhmann, N. (1979). *Trust and power*. New York: Wiley.

Mayer, R. C., & Davis, J. H. (1999). The effect of the performance appraisal system on trust in management: a field quasi-experiment. *Journal of Applied Psychology, 84*(1), 123–136.

Mayer, R. C., David, J., Schoorman, F. (1995). An integrative model of organizational trust. *Academy of Management Review, 20*(3), 709–734.

McKinght, D. H., & Chervany, N. L. (2001). While trust is cool and collected, distrust is fiery frenzied: a model of distrust concepts. In: *Proceeding of the Seventh Americas Conference on Information Systems* (pp. 883–888). Boston, MA.

McKnight, D. H., Cummings, L. L., & Chervany, N. L. (1998). Initial trust formation in new organizational relationship. *Academy of Management Review, 23*(3), 473–490.

Mohr, J., & Spekman, R. (1994). Characteristics of partnership success: partnership attributes, communication, behavior, and conflict resolution techniques. *Strategic Management Journal, 15*, 135–152.

Moorman, C., Deshpande, R., & Zaltman, G. (1993). Factors affecting trust in market research relationships. *Journal of Marketing, 57*, 81–101.

Morgan, R. M., & Hunt, S. D. (1994). The commitment-trust theory of relationship marketing. *Journal of Marketing, 58*, 20–38.

Nelson, K. M., & Cooprider, J. G. (1996). The contribution of shared knowledge to IS group performance. *MIS Quarterly, 20*, 409–434.

Neter, J., Wasserman, W., & Kutner, M. H. (1985). *Applied liner statistical model* (2nd ed.). Illinois: Irwin.

Nonaka, I., & Takeuchi, H. (1995). *The knowledge-creating company*. New York: Oxford University Press.

Nunnally, J. C. (1978). *Psychometric theory*. New York: McGraw-Hill.

Polanyi, M. (1966). *The tacit dimension*. New York: Bantam Doubleday and Company.

Rempel, J., Holmes, K., & Zanna, M. (1995). Trust in close relationships. *Journal of Personality and Social Psychology, 49*(1), 95–112.

Riker, W. H. (1971). The nature of trust. In: J. T. Tedeschi (Ed.), *Perspectives on Social Power* (pp 63–81). Chicago: Aldine Publishing Company.

Rotter, J. B. (1971). Generalized experiences for interpersonal trust. *American Psychologist, 26*(5), 443–452.

Sabherwal, R. (1999). The role of trust in outsourced is development projects. *Communications of the ACM, 42*(2), 80–86.

Simonin, B. L. (1999). Ambiguity and the process of knowledge transfer in strategic alliances. *Strategic Management Journal, 20*, 595–623.

Sitkin, S. B., & Pabio, A. L. (1992). Reconceptualizing the determinants of risk behavior. *Academy Management Review, 17*, 9–38.

Willcocks, L. P., & Kern, T. (1998). IT outsourcing as strategic partnering: the case of the UK Inland revenue. *European Journal of Information Systems, 7*, 29–45.

Worchel, P. (1979). Trust and distrust. In: W. G. Austin, & S. Worchel (Eds.), *The social psychology of intergroup relations* (pp. 174–187). Brooks, Monterey, CA.

Wrightsman, L. S. (1991). Interpersonal trust and attitudes toward human nature. In J. P. Robinson, P. R. Shaver, & L. S. Wrightsman (Eds.), Measures of personality and social psychological attitudes: Vol.1. Measures of social psychological attitudes (pp 373–412), San Diego, CA: Academic.

Yoshino, M. Y., & Rangan, U. S. (1995). Strategic alliances: an entrepreneurial approach to glo-
    balization. Boston, MA: Harvard Business School Press.
Zand, D. E. (1972). Trust and managerial problem solving. *Administrative Science Quarterly, 17*,
    229–239.
Zucker, D. E. (1986). Production of trust: institutional sources of economic structure. In: B. M.
    Staw, & L. L. Cummings (Eds.), *Research in organizational behavior* (pp. 53–111). Gerrnwich,
    CT: JAI Press.

Chapter 2
Outsourcing Capability Management

Building and Integrating Core IT Capabilities in Alignment with the Business: Lessons from the Commonwealth Bank 1997–2007

Peter Reynolds and Leslie Willcocks

1 Introduction: Why Core IT Capabilities?

A key issue facing senior executives is to what extent IT should be outsourced, if at all. By implication, this issue includes identification of the core capabilities that should be retained to provide the organization with sustainable competitive advantage. From the late 1990s, there has been increased executive focus on internal IT capabilities and where to draw the line – in light of a history of mixed outsourcing outcomes. Even more recently, with growing acceptance of the need for internal IT core capabilities, the issue has included the mechanisms for developing, nurturing, maintaining and evolving these capabilities.

We define a capability as a distinctive set of human-based skills, orientations, attitudes, motivations and behaviors that transform resources into specific business activities. Collections of capabilities, in turn, create high-level strategic competencies that positively influence business performance. The importance of such capabilities is established in three related bodies of literature. The first, grounded in microeconomic strategy, is the *resource-based view of the firm* (RBV), which argues that an organization's performance depends on the organization's ability to acquire, deploy and maintain a set of advantageous resources or assets (for more detail see Wernerfelt, 1984; Barney, 1991; Amit & Schoemaker, 1993). The second, which extends RBV, is the *capability-based perspective,* popularized through Prahalad & Hamel's landmark 1990 HBR article on core competencies, focuses on intangible resources, suggesting that an organization is a learning or 'smart', organization that builds and deploys assets, capabilities and skills in order to achieve strategic goals.[1] Third is a related stream of research that has focused on

---

[1] It has been argued that an organization, can only be effective at a few core activities. The organization should concentrate on developing these core capabilities to world class levels. Anything else should be eliminated, minimized or outsourced. Further work in this area examines the dynamic nature of these competencies and the ability to adapt and innovate by identifying, building and leveraging new competencies. Others have worked from this foundation to develop a coherent theory of competence-based management (for more detail see Hamel & Heene, 1994). This ability is itself a competence, a meta-competence referred to as dynamic capability (for more detail see Teece, Pisano, & Shuen, 1997).

R. Hirschheim et al. (eds), *Information Systems Outsourcing,*
© Springer-Verlag Berlin Heidelberg 2009

knowledge as a key enabling organizational capability Furthermore, its relationship to competence is critical: *"Knowledge defines and is embedded in the competencies of a company"* (Mohrman, Finegold, & Klien, 2002).

Moving the focus to core IT capabilities, multiple strands of research have been undertaken during the 1993–2007 period. The IT work is represented in Feeny and Willcocks (1998) and in Willcocks and Lacity (2007). Additional BPO research can be pursued in Feeny, Willcocks and Lacity (2005), Hindle, Willcocks, Feeny, and Lacity (2003), Lacity, Willcocks, and Feeny (2003), Willcocks and Feeny (2005), and in Willcocks, Feeny, and Olson (2006). We found organizations converge on a core capabilities strategy from two different directions. Some organizations started, sometimes up to 15 years ago, with the premise that IT should be outsourced, leaving the question: what, if any, capability should be built in-house to manage the vendor and its strategic direction? By contrast, other organizations started with the premise that IT represented an important strategic resource, leaving the question: what internal capabilities do we need to ensure continual exploitation? Bringing these together, we found that high performing IT functions are managed by a residual team of highly capable, demand-led, and strategy-focused people. Senior executives in these organizations view their IT as performing "strategic", "governance" or "intelligent customer" roles. Essentially, this view emphasizes full in-house involvement for upstream activities (particularly governance and strategy) and a 'procure and diligently manage' role for downstream activities (such as infrastructure, service management, and support).

2 Revisiting the Feeny–Willcocks Framework

The Feeny and Willcocks (1998) framework synthesized the findings into four strategic inter-related competencies (business, technology, sourcing and governance), and nine capabilities for high performing IT functions (see Fig. 1):

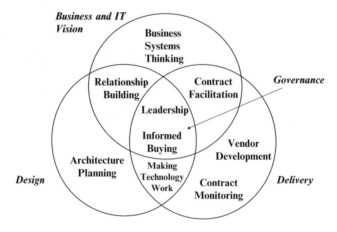

Fig. 1 The core IT capabilities framework (adapted from Feeny & Willcocks, 1998)

Table 1 Nine core IS capabilities

Capability	Code	Description
Leadership	(L)	Integrates the IT effort with business purpose and activity
Informed buying	(IB)	Manages the IT sourcing strategy to meet the needs of the business
Business systems thinking	(BST)	Ensures that IT capabilities are envisioned in every business process
Relationship building	(RB)	Gets the business constructively engaged in operational IT issues
Contract facilitation	(CF)	Ensures the success of existing contracts for external IT services
Architecture planning and design	(AP)	Creates the coherent blueprint for a technical platform that responds to present and future needs
Vendor development	(VD)	Identifies the potential added value from IT service suppliers
Contract monitoring	(CM)	Protects the business's contractual position present and future.
Making technology work	(MTW)	Rapidly trouble-shoots problems which are being disowned by others across the technical supply chain

1. The business competency is concerned with the elicitation and delivery of business requirements.
2. The technical competency is concerned with ensuring that the business has access to the technical capability it needs.
3. The sourcing competence encompasses understanding and use of the internal and external IT and business services markets.
4. The governance competence involves oversight, governance and coordination of IT activities relative to the organization as a whole.

Nine capabilities make the four competencies dynamic and fully operational (see Table 1). These capabilities populate seven spaces in Fig. 1. Their placement in these spaces represents the relative contribution of a specific capability to the four competencies. Each capability has varying requirements for business, inter-personal and technical skills.

Previous advisory and casework provides insights into the challenges to be expected in implementing the nine core capabilities. These will be pursued in the Commonwealth Bank case below.

3   Core IT Capability Challenges Explored in Practice

3.1   Building Core IT Capabilities

Core IT capabilities identify the individual competencies and capabilities required by organizations for high performing IT functions. Further, they identify the relationships between these capabilities and the skills required (technical, business and/or inter-personal). Here we examine the practical challenges for building these capabilities within an organization:

- *How to address the strategic business and IT challenges faced by the organization?* What are the IT expectations of the business? What is the state of the relationship between IT and the business, and IT and suppliers? What are the relationships between different IT functions internally?
- *What capabilities should be built first?* Building all capabilities at once is difficult. What are the immediate and longer-term business problems needing to be solved?
- *Where should specific capabilities be located - within the IT organization (central IT group or business unit IT group) or within the business?*
- *What are the organizational mechanisms available to senior executives to build these capabilities?* How will capabilities be reflected in the organizational structure? What are the necessary processes? What cultural changes are required? Which mechanisms should be used and at what time? (See also Willcocks, Reynolds, & Feeny, 2007)

3.2 Integrating Core IT Capabilities

The integration of core IT capabilities deals with how capabilities are brought together to solve an organization's problems. Multiple competencies may be required to solve an organizational problem. What are the formal and informal processes needed to harness capabilities for strategic advantage?

- *How will the necessary core IT capabilities be integrated to solve individual problems[2]?* How are individuals provided the necessary authority, scope and/or autonomy to exercise the capabilities across the organization as part of a high performing team? How are team and individual roles and responsibilities defined?
- *How will the necessary core IT capabilities be integrated with business capabilities, such project management, and change management?* While project and change management capabilities do not appear as a core retained capability in Fig. 1. In dynamic business environments, the emphasis has shifted from hierarchical, function based, organizations toward task and project-based ways of operating. The assumption here is that project management skills will be spread throughout such organizations. Project management must be an organization-wide core capability, and not the preserve of one function or department. However, research into IT outsourcing and BPO arrangements frequently reveals organization wide project management capability as patchy at best. Yet,

---

[2] In contrast to the more traditional skills found in IT functions, our work suggests organizations need to place a much greater emphasis on business skills and business orientation in nearly all the capabilities, develop significantly 'soft' skills across all the capabilities; attract, develop, and retain high performers; and employ enough people to cover sufficiently all nine capabilities.

outsourcing can involve immense organizational, human resource and technological changes that require strong project management skills. Should these rest
within the internal function or in the supplier, if they are not available from
within the wider organization?

3.3 Aligning Core IT Capabilities with the Business

As the business changes, so do the requirements of IT and the capabilities required
to service the business. A different emphasis and focus is required on different
capabilities depending on the business demand and maturity.

- *What capabilities will need to change as the organization changes business
  direction, priorities and matures?* As we will see in the CBA case below, the
  organizational focus moves from managing IT suppliers, through managing IT
  across the group, to enabling IT-enabled business transformation.

The case that follows, throws light on all these challenges and how they can be
resolved. It also poses new issues while revealing the power of building core IT
capabilities for succeeding in dynamic business contexts. The case documents the
development of CBA's IT capabilities, based on the Feeny–Willcocks model, in
four stages over a ten-year period covering 1997–2007.[3] By early 2007, with a new
CEO and CIO, IT capabilities had become unified across the group but new challenges had emerged. At each stage, we examine how internal capabilities were
realigned to meet new, different, business challenges.

4 The Commonwealth Bank Case: 1997 to 2007

4.1 Business Context and IT Sourcing History

The CBA was established in 1911. It also served as the country's Reserve Bank
until 1959. The Bank completed its privatization process in 1996. At the present
date, it provides a full range of banking services to retail, commercial, corporate
and institutional clients. It has over 9 million customers and more than 35,000 fulltime equivalent staff. The bank operates the largest financial services distribution
network in Australia serviced by more than 1,000 branches, 3,800 agencies, 3,200

---

[3] This case has been assembled through over 80 interviews during four time periods: January 2001,
August 2001, August 2003 and August 2005. In addition the first co-author continued to interview
throughout 2006–7, while working on a major project at CBA. Respondents included senior executives, the CIO and direct reports and other IT managers as appropriate. In addition we were provided
access to organizational announcements and reviewed external market information and reports.

ATMs, more than 135,000 EFTPOS terminals and internet banking services to more that 2.5 million customers. In 2006, CBA was rated in the top 25 banks in the world by capitalization (all figures for 2006; Commonwealth Bank Australia Annual Reports, 1997–2006).

On 10 October 1997, CBA entered into a ten-year $US3.8bn single-source joint venture with Electronic Data Systems (EDS), taking a 35% stake in its local operation to form EDS Australia. Internally, it retained a group of 35 IT staff to manage the contract and maintain control of its strategic IT direction. This function reported to the head of the shared services business unit. Of the 35, four dealt with service delivery from EDS, including enterprise processing services, end user computing, telecoms and applications. Another six dealt with relationship management and liaison with the four business divisions. Another eight looked after contract management and IT finance and the remainder looked after IT strategy and information management.

By early 2000, the two-year transition to new vendor arrangements was completed and good progress had been made on the outsourcing objectives of controlling costs and improving service levels. CBA achieved its objectives in relation to IT cost reduction. Costs as a proportion of non-interest expense were reduced from 16.3% in 1998 to 15.5% (according to CBA Head of Technology, Operations & Procurement; Scrimshaw, 2002). Total service outages were reduced by over a third and the critical 'Severity 1 errors' reduced by a factor more than double this.

After nearly 3 years, however, many of the internal IT staff had moved on, including the CIO. At the same time, CBA was undergoing significant changes following the announcement of a $US8bn merger with Colonial Bank, and was taking its first steps towards multi-sourcing with the appointment of a specialized telecommunications provider – Telecom New Zealand (TCNZ). Moreover, the business was restructuring around individual business units to service different customer segments as shown in Fig. 2.

	Retail Banking Services	Premium Financial Services	Investment & Insurance Services	Institutional and Business Services
Customer Group	Personal banking customers, Small business banking customers	Premium clients including professionals and business	Agents, Brokers, Financial Advisers	Institutional, Corporate, Commercial business customers
Channels	Branch, Ezy-Banking, ATM, EFTPOS, Phone, On-line, Mortgage brokers	Relationship managers, Business centres, Phone, On-line.	Agents, Branches, Brokers, Financial Advisers, Premium investment centres Direct Dealerships	Relationship managers, Business centres
Support functions	Financial & Risk Management Group Human Resources Group Strategic Development **Technology Services**			

Fig. 2 CBA post-2001: customer centric model

The new CIO, Bob McKinnon, a career business professional, had a finance background and was previously CEO of State Street's operations in Australia. By the time he took up his appointment in August 2000, it was clear that there were significant relationship pressures between and within the individual business units, IT functions and vendors (see Fig. 3). There was poor coordination of IT needs between business units resulting in a loss of scale and integration. There was a lack of IT governance across the central IT team and the new business unit IT functions that had evolved, or had been acquired through the merger with Colonial. Finally, there was tension between the multiple vendors concerning boundary and demarcation disputes. Consequently, the benefits of the IT outsourcing and of IT to the business were under threat. As described by one respondent:

> "… being distracted by Y2K and other bank integrations, we basically had no capability to manage service performance or the performance of the service providers, in terms of their obligations as we had established them" (CBA service delivery executive)

Recognizing the need to strengthen Group Technology, McKinnon looked for best practice models for managing large scale IT outsourcing deals. This led to a conscious adoption of a core IT capabilities model in 2001.

An initial assessment of the CBA by the second author against the model (see Fig. 4) showed that the strongest internal IT capabilities sat within the Contract Management function. The relationship was being driven from a contractual standpoint without the necessary contract facilitation or informed buying capabilities. It was also damaging any vendor development capability. Whilst a relationship management team was ostensive there to build the relationship between the central IT function and the business, their focus was being dragged into contractual disputes creating a void in relationship building and business systems thinking. The limited number of retained staff who understood the complexity of the existing systems, combined with the small number of architects, left the bank with a deficit of making

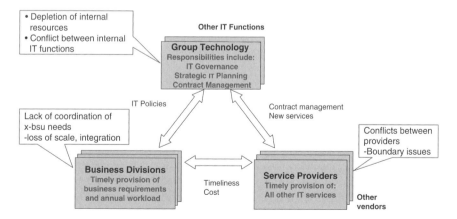

Fig. 3 CBA IT – Relationships under pressure

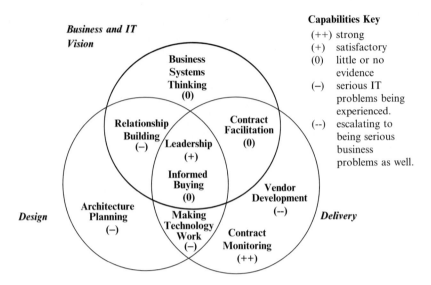

Fig. 4 Initial assessment of CBA IT capabilities, January 2001

technology work and architecture planning and capabilities. Leadership, however, was seen as strong with a new sense of drive and urgency driving the need to rebuild the Bank's internal capabilities.

The Bank also had pockets of internal project delivery capability (providing mixed success) that still needed to work with EDS, who now managed the Bank's broader IT environment, to integrate any new solutions into production. There were no formal engagement or management protocols to get predictable delivery results.

4.2   Stage 1: Building IT Capabilities in the Central IT Team 2001–2002

McKinnon's first step was to ensure the efficient and effective delivery of IT from the vendors. A new structure was put in place that focused resources around three functions: architecture planning (to define what the Bank needed), service delivery (how services were delivered) and informed buying (who they were obtained from). Business systems thinking remained as a function that was seen to be the primary responsibility of the business units, liaising with the architecture planning and service delivery teams. McKinnon espoused the desired high performance culture, including being a small team of high caliber people (around 50), a centre of IT excellence and leadership that attracted and retained the right people. This was to be achieved through:

- An open, flexible workplace
- Challenging career opportunities
- A focus on personal development
- Competitive (above median) remuneration
- Clear roles, responsibilities and accountabilities
- Good people attracting good people

Additional resources were recruited to fill in the structure including a new head of service delivery, appointed in November 2001. He quickly recognized the need to work with the service provider every day to have oversight and input to fundamental IT management areas. A two-step process of building internal capability was implemented. Step 1 was oriented to around day-to-day service performance:

> "I employed three or four really capable and experienced operations management 'thugs' and I put them on-site with the service provider on the basis that if I was going to be accountable for the outcome in some way, I needed to have some oversight of the input, but do that in a way that did not compromise the service provider (CBA service delivery executive)."

Step 2 was more commercially focused to appoint service delivery managers that understood what CBA was buying and to ensure that the bank was getting the services as prescribed by the contract and value for money for new services. People with a depth of commercial and technology experience were recruited into these roles. They provided an internal capability to understand the long-term design implications of what was being done, the commercial consequences of the technologies that were being deployed, the potential behavioral implications of the commercial contracts put in place, and to run benchmarking to give an understanding of value.

To build the relationship between the business and service delivery (contract facilitation), a new direct report to the CIO was appointed, an ex-partner from a 'top five' consultancy firm, to head relationship management and build a demand management capability. This role was internally focused, working with the business units to help them articulate what they wanted; understand what else was being done and how to get best business value from IT.

> "So before I took over, no-one actually managed the demand and looking for consolidation, prioritization, efficiency, all those type of things. It was all about an order-taking point of view… I had to change what they were doing, I had to take them up the food chain to be genuinely relationship managing, rather than just being the person you call when you want a new PC; the need was to take an holistic view" (CBA relationship management executive)

The Head of Architecture Planning/CTO built the Architecture Planning team up to around a dozen people, mostly from external recruits and including a chief architect recruited from a competitor Bank. An exception was the head of IT security, who was recruited from the internal audit team. The team was organized into: enterprise IT architecture, business systems planning and IT security.

A separate Value-Add team was formed to enact the informed buying and vendor development capabilities. This initially focused on the second biennial major contract review updating services and preparing for future contract renewals. As the responsibilities of this small group grew, this capability was eventually absorbed into the service delivery structure. Extracting any value-added services from the current suppliers was forgone in substitute for developing a new contract with improved incentives and alignment to bank goals.[4]

Building on the appointment of people to enact the selected core IT capabilities, CBA recognized the need to formally define their roles and responsibilities. Towards the end of 2001, new roles and responsibilities were defined across Group Technology. Responsibilities were assigned in such a way that no individual was expected to have to more that 2 (maximum 3) core IT capabilities to perform their role.

The process followed was:

Step 1: Definition of a list of desired outcomes and activities based on the agreed role of central IT, and the desired capabilities as per the Core IT Capabilities model.[5]

Step 2: Mapping of activities to functional groups based on core capabilities required to perform its activities. A design target was set for each functional area to have no more than three required capabilities to perform each function. This was based on observations that people are unlikely to demonstrate a full competency in more that one or two capabilities.

Step 3: Rationalization of functional groups based on combining groups that aspired to similar outcomes and required similar core capabilities.

Step 4: (Re)allocation of these new functional groups to individual CIO Direct reports.

IT governance and leadership skills were seen as a requirement of all managers. Business systems thinking remained a function that was seen to be the primary responsibility of the business units, liaising with the Architecture Planning and Relationship Management teams. The resulting structure is shown in detail in Fig. 5.

The new role of Head of Project Management was filled by an external resource with strong project management background and training, including a PhD related to project management. He recognized that the Bank relied on the supplier for much of its project delivery resources and management, with only supra-level supervision from the Bank. The supplier had access to many delivery methodologies – most too complicated for the Bank's needs A program, ZIP, was set up as an 'across Bank-EDS engagement process for projects'.

> "By engaging all interested parties it had the advantage that the bank and its suppliers had a common framework to run projects with a good governance, high predictability to get better repeatable and consistent results with a lower degree of risk of failure (CBA project management executive)."

A summary of the challenges facing CBA in Stage 1 is presented in Table 2.

---

[4] Interestingly, this group was later strengthened and broken out again as a direct report of the CIO as the strategic focus moved to implement the sourcing strategy in preparation for the 10-year deal renewal

[5] To illustrate, when the outsourcing was entered into in 1997, it identified 38 activities for GT. 31 of these, or around 80%, related to the delivery of IT services: With and expanded set of 75 activities to support all core IT capabilities, these represented only 40% of activities.

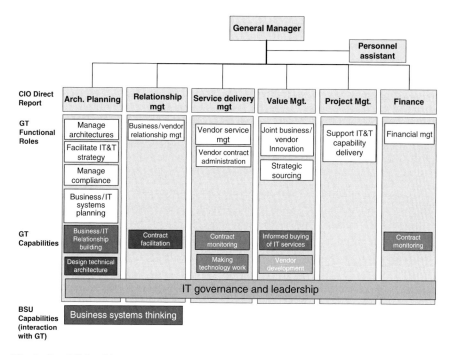

Fig. 5 Capabilities drive new structure

Table 2 Summary of Stage 1: building core IT capabilities in the central team

Challenges	Stage 1: Building Core IT Capabilities in the Central Team
Business context	• Business strategy focus on cost and service
	• Recent merger to build Insurance and Investment market share and focus
	• Move to customer-centric business model
IT context	• 10 yr single-source outsourcing deal, contract driven
	• Loss of intellectual property around IT
	• Beginnings of moving to multi-sourcing
IT organizational model	• Centralized, outsourced model
	• CIO reporting to head of one of the business units
Capabilities focus	• CF and CM (within the Service Delivery function) and AP
Capabilities location	• Model implemented in central IT group
	• BST assumed to be a 'business capability'
Capabilities mechanisms/ levers	• New processes for managing vendors and demand from the business
	• Architecture reviews on new investments against IT strategy
	• Some consolidation in central IT structure
Integration of capabilities	• Limited: role of central IT was to oversee service provider delivery to the business
	• Capabilities grouped under two main functions: AP and SD – little interaction
	• PM capabilities focused on engagement with EDS
Alignment with the business	• Focus on service level and cost efficiencies
	• Looking to protect and leverage outsourcing benefits

4.3 Stage 2: Extending Capabilities for Managing IT across the Group

McKinnon's second focus was to extend the Core Capabilities model across all IT functions within CBA, including IT functions in business units, to foster the business systems thinking and relationship building skills. This required establishing effective governance of IT across the group, including those IT functions acquired from Colonial, and those that had emerged in existing business units or subsidiaries, to fill capability gaps.

A first action was to establish a monthly Executive Technology Committee (ETC), chaired by the CEO and attended by each group executive and the CIO. The ETC role was to agree IT&T strategy, track progress, and resolve cross-organizational strategic IT&T issues. One of the first agreements of the ETC was a set of IT principles that provided consistent guidelines for the way IT should be managed in CBA (Fig. 6).

Under the sponsorship of the ETC, three cornerstone strategies were developed to address the capabilities required by CBA to enable its corporate business strategy. Each of the strategies was oriented around specific competencies. The IT&T Strategy was facilitated across the business unit heads to develop a consistent view of the technical capabilities needed to compete in the 3–5 year timeframe. The twenty technical capabilities defined included items such as the ability to have the single view of a customer, consistent content and interface standards and a single authentication and authorization capability. The IT&T capabilities then shaped the enterprise architecture and supporting IT policies, processes and standards to guide the way the systems were built.

The IT&T sourcing strategy integrated much of the learning from the first three years of managing the IT&T agreements to present a staged plan of activities in

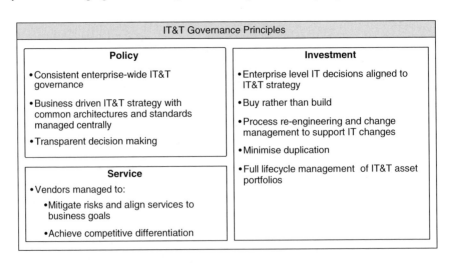

Fig. 6 Group-wide IT&T principles critical to focus change

preparation for 2005/6 contract renewal. The IT&T management model provided a framework for decision-making and process development across the Bank. This aimed at balancing individual business unit needs with group-wide scale and leverage to ensure optimum value from technology investments.

The central IT group was made responsible for decisions on strategy, architecture and policy as well as recommendations related to all service elements for core infrastructure. Business unit IT functions were made responsible for consolidating their business systems functionality requirements, implementation planning, design, vendor selection and delivery management of IT-based business projects (Fig. 7).

The value of a stronger IT management was soon recognized by the CEO, who appointed McKinnon as a direct report mid-2002, appointing him as part of the bank's Executive Committee (EXCO) soon thereafter. This then removed the need for a separate Executive Technology Committee.

The next review conducted by the authors in August 2003 highlighted the influx of new IT resources into Group Technology. These resources were noted as 'capabilities by recruitment'. The review identified that there was yet to be a framework embedded in the key HR processes of appraisal and targeted development for nurturing internal capabilities once inside the bank.

The review also noted the need across the business units for broader educational processes linked to specific business/IT problems as they arise. While the awareness of the framework was there at a business unit level, how the capabilities could be harnessed to resolve problems was less clear. Recognizing the different needs and levels of maturity of the business units, the review recommended addressing this one business unit at a time.

A summary of the challenges facing CBA in the Stage 2 is presented in Table 3.

4.4   Stage 3: A Focus on Delivery: 2004–2006

In September 2003, the CEO decided to accelerate the business change and announced a $US1.2bn cultural transformation program over 2½ years. The 'Which new Bank' (WnB) program focused on excelling in customer service through engaged people who are supported by simple processes (Fig. 8). A coordinated set of some 120 projects was assembled, with an IT investment of over $US500m, to accelerate the delivery of the enterprise architecture.

> "Getting the architecture capabilities and through that process putting in place an IT strategy that people can buy into and start building towards was a really important breakthrough. That really helped the articulation of what, in an IT sense' needed to happen in order to get the 'Which new Bank' process going' " (CBA Group CIO – Bob McKinnon)

Delivery of the many business projects required CBA to rapidly extend its internal delivery capabilities, from its initial focus on IT architecture and IT service delivery in the central IT group, to business systems thinking, project management and change management in the business units (in accordance with the management model).

Service element		Core infrastructure			Business system capability		
		ETC	Group IT	Business	ETC	Group IT	Business
Strategy, architecture and policy	Policy, implementation approach, delivery accountability and enterprise solution architecture	●	■	◀	●	■	◀
	Enterprise roadmap	●	■	◀	●	■	◀
Demand management	Consolidated business requirements and implementation planning	●	■	◀		◀	■ ●
	Consolidated infrastructure requirements and implementation planning	●	■	◀		■ ●	◀
Service development	Business system design, vendor selection for development (Incl. Front-end integration) and delivery management for business system development	●	■	◀		◀	■ ●
	Infrastructure solution design, vendor selection for infrastructure delivery and back-end integration and delivery management for infrastructure solutions	●	■	◀		◀ ●	■
Supply management	Vendor contract and performance management for systems development (Incl. Front-end integration) and infrastructure acquisition	●	■	◀		◀	■ ●
	Vendor contract and performance management for infrastructure operation and back-end integration	●	■	◀		◀ ●	■
Service delivery	Service level definition	●	■	◀		◀	■ ●

Fig. 7 Group-wide IT&T governance (developed based on Weill and Ross (2004)

Table 3 Summary of Stage 2: Extending core IS capabilities across the group

Challenges	Stage 2: Extending Core IS capabilities across the group
Business context	• Individual customer segment business strategies (multi-business organizational form) • Different pace/priorities of individual business unites
IT context	• Focus on core IS strategies and governance processes • Engagement with senior business heads
IT organizational model	• Federal, outsourced model. • Formalized divisional IT functions • CIO reporting to head of one of the business units
Capabilities focus	• Processes – governance, IT investment reviews, policies and procedures
Capabilities location	• SD and AP in central business units • BST and RB defined to be in business unites (although little development) • PM still expected to be performed by EDS, although stronger business accountability was recognized
Capabilities mechanisms/levers	• New governance processes distinguishing 'core infrastructure' and 'business systems'
Integration of capabilities	• Limited: role of central IT continued to be to oversee service provider delivery to the business
Alignment with the business	• Balancing business unit flexibility and group-wide scale • Optimum value from IT investments

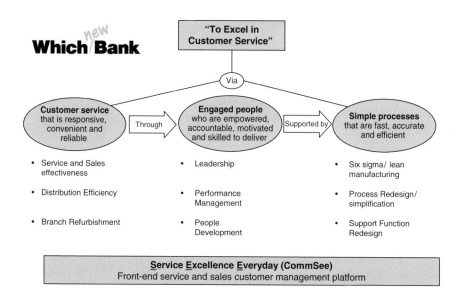

Fig. 8 WNB transformation underpinned by new sales and service platform (adapted from which new Bank update, CEO, 24 May 2005)

The cornerstone of WNB was a new customer management platform, CommSee. Its purpose was to provide consistent customer information and processes to customer-facing staff in any location. This critical project ($US200 m) would deliver major components of the enterprise architecture by integrating all of the different channels (e.g. branch, call centre, and internet), providing a consistent SOA access to back-end systems and providing role-based access to applications.

This project represented a significant technical challenge. Similar to most financial services organizations, the Bank's systems had evolved separately for different products, channels (e.g. branch, call centre, and internet), and business unit. In addition, the project faced many management challenges. The development team was required work across all business units to gather and agree on requirements, adjust processes, decommission existing systems, and capture benefits. Accordingly, in addition to the technology stakeholders, the project had numerous business stakeholders whose support was necessary for a successful outcome.

Faced with an ambitious timetable and the need to have the CommSee platform in place to support other components of WnB, the CEO made the decision to leverage an existing system developed by an internal team from CBA's innovative on-line stockbroking subsidiary. This internal team of approximately 60 people brought new capabilities to the broader bank with had a track record of rapid delivery using a combination of decoupling projects into independent components, prototyping, and iterative development. With the strong support from the CEO, the CommSee team rapidly implemented a pilot in Tasmania by February 2004 and scaled up its team to approximately 500 IT staff by mid-2004, culminating in nearly 800 IT staff by the end of the project.

The central IT team moved to strengthen its governance role, around IT project delivery, beyond the initial process efforts of the ZIP program. This included IT portfolio, program and project management. Portfolio management looked at all the asset classes of IT, trying to understand how both collectively and individually they added value to the organization. The program office coordinated IT projects across the Bank to defined appropriate project standards.

> "We created a project office in group technology under the portfolio management area as well… So we have to define end to end how any project with an IT&T component should be managed in the Bank and how that must interface with what we do from an enterprise perspective when it comes to project management." (CBA IT governance executive)

At the same time, Technology Services had to build its own project management capability for its responsibilities for the delivery of all IT infrastructure projects across the bank (desktop services, telecommunications, etc) and the common IT systems that now fell under the management of Enterprise Solutions in Technology Services. This included management of the Bank's traditional infrastructure as well as shared information systems such as the core customer information repository and group data warehouse.

In May 2004, McKinnon, recognizing the rapid growth of IT staff across the group and need to maintain effective control, moved to formally centralize IT so that all IT would report into the Group CIO, rather than individual business unit heads. This process resulted in the nomination of 'Business Unit CIO' positions for each divisions. However, based, in part, on the focus on WnB delivery and lack of delivery capabilities in Technology Services, an argument was accepted for the IT staff delivering CommSee to remain separate. This effectively resulted in two large IT groups in the CBA.

Our final assessment in January 2005 highlighted the massive dual task of managing $1.2bn per annum IT expenditure and the additional $700m WnB expenditure on IT over 2½ years. The service delivery function was stable, with focus moving to the implementation of the new sourcing strategy. The role of central IT group had been expanded to consolidate demand and deliver some of the key infrastructure projects. The architecture planning team had ensured a set of enterprise-wide architectures, policies and standards to ensure project alignment to the IT&T blueprint. The WnB program had delivered the opportunity to introduce new IT capabilities, which in turn created new business opportunities.

> "If you line up [all of the priorities of the executive committee], there is a huge correlation between the priorities of the IT strategy of 18 months ago and what's actually happening (CBA Group CIO – Bob McKinnon)."

The assessment, however, highlighted the need for more internal capabilities while also planning for a revised sourcing strategy to reflect the changing market and internal arrangements. This presented new challenges to extend the internal capabilities to design and integrate solutions delivered from multiple internal and external parties:

> "As the technology supply market has shifted over the last few years, there are more specialized applications providers and we've probably got two or three contracted for any major project. There is a need for a layer that can put all that together in a way that delivers the business outcome to which we aspire (CBA service delivery executive)."

A summary of the challenges facing CBA in Stage 3 is presented in Table 4.

4.5 Stage 4: Unification of Core IT Capabilities

By August 2005, The CEO was able to announce that the WnB program was making significant progress and shortly thereafter retire. Following the appointment of the new CEO, Ralph Norris, McKinnon announced his departure and a new CIO, Michael Harte, was appointed commencing April 2006. Harte has a career as an IT professional and was formerly CIO of PNC Financial services in the USA.

Harte's initial review highlighted that the technology teams had a great deal to be proud of and stated his belief that the Bank is one of a few financial services organizations globally to have seriously invested in technology and proven its capability to deliver it. However, it was clear that there was a significant gulf splitting the central and divisional IT groups.

Table 4 Summary of Stage 3: A focus on delivery

Challenges	Stage 3: A Focus on delivery
Business context	• $US1.2bn business transformation • Over 100 individual business projects and 20 cross- divisional initiatives
IT context	• $US500 m IT investment spread across business • Growing IT functions in business units, central IT focused on IT governance and supplier management • Focus on delivery
IT organizational model	• Federal, outsourced model. Internal capability leveraged and built upon • Some business unit CIOs established reporting to Group CIO • Group CIO Reporting to the CEO
Capabilities focus	• BST and RB • PM and change management
Capabilities location	• SD and AP in central business units • BST and RB in business units • Delivery by a combination of multiple internal teams and multiple service providers
Capabilities mechanisms/ levers	• Project management/program office processes • Business case/architectural review processes
Integration of capabilities	• role of central IT to oversee service provider delivery to the business as well as some IT infrastructure projects • Projects established with business unit project managers, change managers and internal IS delivery capabilities
Alignment with the business	• Supporting delivery in such a way that to deliver stated projects benefits and also built future IT&T capabilities

To integrate the teams, Harte announced a new business unit led structure (Fig. 9) with all IT functions reporting to the central IT group, renamed, Enterprise Services. This structure focused on its alignment to business units, with the primary focus on each of the business unit CIOs and business systems thinking capabilities. The business unit CIOs were supported by a single enterprise IT solutions group (from the former Enterprise Systems, CommSee and Colonial groups) and Enterprise Operations group (formerly the service delivery group). With only a single solution delivery group, the architecture planning was relocated within enterprise IT solutions. Two additional CIO support functions were also maintained, one around governance (including finance) and the other around project execution (from the CommSee change management team).

A new set of challenges faced Harte as he focused on "getting the best value from technology investments by leveraging the capabilities and standardizing technology offerings". With focused execution becoming the hallmark of CBA's technology organization, the new set of technology challenges included:

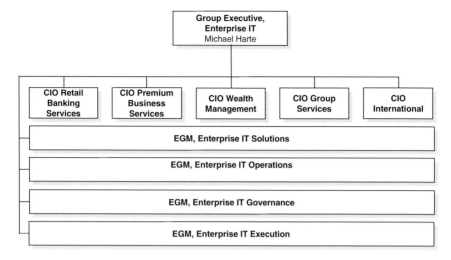

Fig. 9 Unification

Table 5 Summary of Stage 4: Unification

Challenges	Stage 4: Unification
Business context	• Focus on service excellence
	• Focus on leveraging/optimizing IT investments
IT context	• New CIO with a mandate for centralized management of IT
	• Multiple internal and external service providers
IT organizational model	• Centralized, with SBU aligned business unit CIOs.
	• Multisourced (including insourced)
Capabilities focus	• All
	• Building IB and VD skills as 10year deal expires
Capabilities location	• BST and RB with business unit CIOs
	• Delivery in central IT team
	• PM and CM in central IT team
Capabilities mechanisms/levers	• Structure: Centralization
	• Culture: Service orientation
Integration of capabilities	• All core IS capabilities under one management
	• IT delivery integrated within business projects
Alignment with the business	• Getting the best value from technology investments by leveraging the capabilities and standardizing technology offerings

- Providing a group-wide leadership model of IT
- Leveraging IT capabilities and expertise to revitalize systems
- Implementing smarter sourcing; and
- Continuing to develop lean and efficient processes.

A summary of the challenges facing CBA in Stage 4 is presented in Table 5.

5   Analysis of the Case

The CBA case provides a powerful illustration of the implementation of the Feeny–Willcocks model. The observations of the authors at each of the three individual assessments in time during the case have already been shared in the case discussion. This section discusses the CBA's implementation of the Core Capabilities model, what it tells us about the model and how to build and integrate capabilities with the business.

While every organization's implementation is likely to start from a different point and follow a different process, the CBA case provides an interesting reference point, displaying the advantages of using an established framework, and pointing to some of the key challenges to be managed.

In examining the dynamics of capabilities over time, we use an evolutionary growth model developed from research by David Feeny (1997) (further elaborated in Willcocks & Lacity, 2007, p. 94). Figure 9 shows how an organization may start with very questionable ability to manage IT. Feeny found that such organizations typically need to evolve to a 'service delivery' stage, marked by a CIO with the skills to focus the IT group on developing technical service capabilities and delivering on IT promises to the business. Once technical and service competences are in place, a reorientation phase becomes possible. This will see a CIO and the IT team become more business-focused, while the business executives and units will need to become more pro-active in managing IT for strategic business purpose. Once reorientation has been accomplished, the new challenge is reorganization - devolving IT responsibility to the business units, integrating CIO effort with business strategy and the top team, and streamlining the IT function further into a core IS capabilities high performance model. Figure 10 summarizes the path an organization can take to evolving its IS capabilities and maturing its overall ability to manage and source IT strategically.

CBA's first stage, service delivery, started with the convergence of thinking around a single, shared, capabilities model. The Feeny–Willcocks model provided a framework to evaluate the current state and articulate where they would like to be to the senior business executives, internal IT staff and businesses units. In a resource-constrained world, the framework can help build the case for more resources to manage IT by explaining the capabilities and competencies to be built. It also helps signal to the existing IT function that a new way of working, based on high performance teaming has arrived. Being able to take accountability for and provide transparency of the delivery of services, this marked the first stage of growth, focusing on improving service delivery and re-establishing internal CBA accountabilities:

> "many of the deals done in the 1990s actually gave the responsibility for monitoring and reporting of supply performance to the supplier. And I didn't ask my children to fill in their own report card last year, (CBA service delivery executive)."

The adoption of the core capabilities model within the central IT group demonstrates an example of top-down structuring, starting with CIO direct reports,

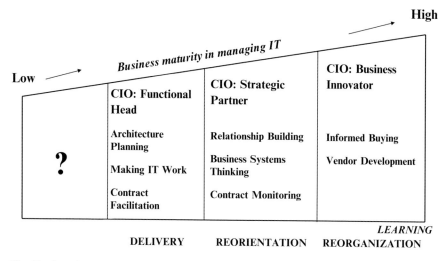

Fig. 10   Growth stages for the business, CIO and the IT function

although there are likely to be other approaches. The CBA case reinforces the HR challenges indicated by other research cases and presented earlier in this paper. When starting from a small base, there is often not the depth to draw upon for new appointments. 'capabilities by recruitment' is the order of the day. However, as demonstrated by the CBA case, as the organization matures, staff can be brought in from other areas within the organization, and business units and subsidiaries provide a ripe source of new capabilities.

The CBA then formalized roles and responsibilities for each capability area in line with agreed IT operating model and governance responsibilities. CBA demonstrated an approach for maintaining a reasonable number of capabilities (no more than three) that any individual appointee is expected to display. This helped with simplifying recruitment where there was a clear expectation of the capabilities and skills required. An additional key consideration in the mix of an individual's capabilities was the selection of short-term or long-term orientation.[6]

In the second stage, reorientation, CBA extended its core IS capabilities to more effectively manage IT across the organization. This required corresponding changes of the IT organizational model, IT governance and structure. The challenges are well covered in the case. The key here was the need to develop

---

[6] For example, the establishment of separate Service Delivery and Architecture planning capabilities reflect extremes of focuses from day-to-day and 3–5 year planning.

complementary capabilities in the business units (i.e. BST and RB) rather than overlapping capabilities, roles and responsibilities. The separation within the governance model of core infrastructure (with decision authority held by the central IT group) and business systems accountabilities (with decision authority held by the business units) went a long way to achieving this, as did the eventual creation of business unit CIO roles. However, the operational and service functions that these existing teams were initially set up to perform meant that it was often difficult to release their previous responsibilities and work they did themselves and reorient themselves to fit in the new framework and capabilities now expected to be leveraged from the central IT team.

The final stage, reorientation, required all core IT capabilities to work together, as well as integrate with business capabilities to deliver IT-based strategic change. The rapid acceleration of delivery around WnB provides a critical event to examine the integration required of capabilities.

First, the WnB program required significant strengthening of BST and RB capabilities in the business units. These capabilities provide the ability to translate business processes and problems into technical solutions in accordance with the organization's architectures. These must still be delivered in the context of the organizational governance arrangements and the services provided by external IT service providers. This required strong coordination by the architecture group and service delivery functions in the centre team.

At the same time, implementing the systems across their business units required significant strengthening of project management and change management functions. The CBA case sees these capabilities germinating from business unit IT functions and subsidiaries and built internally as well as added to with multiple suppliers. These became part of the business unit team alongside core IT capabilities.

The final major integration challenge came from the need to coordinate multiple internal and external IT suppliers. In contrast with a single-source model, where generally the supplier takes the integration risk to ensure all components come together to a working solution, the multi-sourcing model can result in a transfer of integration risk back to the organization. This integration requires strong knowledge of existing systems and architecture (MTW) to both define requirements and integrate the resulting solution. As recognized by CBA' Group CIO:

> "If you outsource your intellectual Property and your capability, you lose the ability to do the integration role, because you don't understand, in an operational sense, the way your systems are configured or, in an applications sense, the way they are built." (CBA Group CIO – Bob McKinnon)

Finally, as we see in the CBA, core IT capabilities need to be developed in context and in concert with the business and IT strategy, IT structure, IT governance and IT sourcing strategy. For example, the focus of what capabilities are most important, the architecture that is being built to, the structure of the IT organization in relation to the overall organization, and how decisions rights are allocated.

The CBA experience and that of other case studies has been that capabilities are evolved in a semi-structured order as the business and IT matures along the stages of growth. Here we highlight the business catalysts for the transition to each stage. The first stage was driven by cost and service, which required improved management of IT suppliers and demand from the business (primary focus on CF and AP). The second stage was driven by the need to coordinate, leverage and achieve economies of scale across the group. The third stage focused to deliver a major program of work. The final stage, now being addressed by Michael Harte is how to capture the value from strategic sourcing – leveraging both his internal capabilities and multiple suppliers (primary focus on IB and VD).

6   Learning Points and Conclusion

The CBA case, and others we have studied (in particular see Willcocks & Feeny, 2005; Willcocks, Feeny, & Olson, 2006; Willcocks & Lacity, 2007, Chap. 3), provides insight into how the core capabilities can be applied, their relevance, the challenges arising, and how these were handled. Here, we reflect on what can be learned from implementing the Feeny–Willcocks core capabilities framework.

6.1   Building Core is Capabilities

How to address the strategic business and IT challenges faced by the organization? Organizations need to ensure they develop the long-term strategic core capabilities of the model rather than being drawn into fire-fighting and focusing only on the shorter-term capabilities in our model. Problems develop when any of the core IS capabilities are not suitably staffed, but there is a tendency in the first few years to neglect the capabilities with longer time horizons (e.g. BST, RB and AP) thus building up important issues further down the line.

Getting innovation and business value-added from outsourcing, needs organized, pro-active, in-house core capabilities being applied to the task. CBA basically gave this away to focus on immediate issues and pulled back to a supplier-customer model to focus on a new sourcing model that provided the appropriate incentives and selection of partners.

- *What capabilities should be built first?* Particularly endorsed was the Feeny model of IT organizations passing through Delivery, Reorientation and Reorganization phases (see Fig. 9; Feeny & Ross, 2000). Core capabilities focusing on service and delivery competences are developed in the delivery phase; more business – focused capabilities in the reorientation phase; with the fully-fledged model being applied only in the reorganization phase. CBA was poorly placed for internal capabilities from the start of its deal with EDS, yet by 2006 was able to reconfigure its structure and capabilities with minimal external appointments thereby protecting its intellectual property. The focus then moved to dynamic capability to develop new capabilities as business needs and direct changed.

- *Where should specific capabilities be located - within the IT organization (central IT group or business unit IT group) or within the business?* We see organizations such as CBA focusing on building IS capabilities in the central IT team first. In the early stages of growth, the focus on service delivery from external IT suppliers requires centralized contract management and facilitation. New capabilities are introduced in the central team to provide greater visibility and accountability of services delivered from the supplier, often with angst over a new, more proactive, demanding role of the internal IT function:

> "We found that having a capability that can drive a vendor to be successful is really important. Interestingly enough, [the supplier] has been co-operative in the process and in hindsight, while they kicked and screamed a bit as we put much closer supervision around those services, they would publicly say today that they are a better service provider because we were a better customer (CBA Group CIO – Bob McKinnon)."

The implementation of core IT capabilities across the broader organization was not a smooth ride either, as control was debated between business unit and central IT functions. This highlighted the importance of strong senior executive leadership and an effective IT governance model that is bought-into by all areas of the business. At the same time, however, business units need to be confident that the release control of functions does not represent an operational risk to the business where capabilities have not yet been proven.

- *What are the organizational mechanisms available to senior executives to build these capabilities?* We see three mechanisms available to senior executives for evolving capabilities: process, culture and structure. For those organizations requiring additional resources, we see executives recruiting, developing and/or acquiring from other parts of the organization. To transform resources into IS capabilities we see CBA developing: (1) processes to define the governance, in particular the decision-rights across the organization, and how capabilities can be applied to solve individual problems; (2) the IT structure, along with associated roles and responsibilities, to focus these resources to specific capabilities and addresses specific organizational challenges; and (3) culture, which provides a powerful tool to focus the efforts and development of the IT function as well as repositioning the role of IT within the organization.

6.2   Integrating Core IT Capabilities

• *How will the necessary Core IT Capabilities be integrated to solve individual problems?* Issues of core capability development and succession emerged to ensure high performance individuals formed into a high performing team. Problems emerge from smaller teams with lots of high performers. The concept of high performance teaming is about getting things done by the team – not individual areas of capabilities. CBA suffered from this when it allocated processes to the CIO direct reports, hence the problem solving process often started with a focus on accountability, rather than how capabilities could be applied to fix a problem.

The case supports the earlier 1998 finding that high performers with distinctive skills, capabilities, orientations need to be appointed. The case also indicated what was only supposed in 1998 – that there would be major challenges getting organizations to develop HR policies in the areas of recruitment, pay, motivation and retention to support the different, high performance, team-based, core capabilities modes of operating.

• *How will the necessary Core IT Capabilities be integrated with business capabilities, such project management, and change management?* Business system projects need to be structured that include both IT and business capabilities. The traditional reliance on 'IT project and business implementation' (where IT hands over to the business for implementation) or 'IT project and Business project' (where two project or subproject mangers are appointed – one from the business and one from IT) reinforce the segregation of the business and IT capabilities needed to be brought together to delivery IT-based business transformation. We see the emergence of IT-based business projects that are business-led defined by a clear business outcomes. A powerful approach is for the projects to either contain or leverage available business and IS resources. These resources must then be brought together to deliver the business solution in accordance with the enterprise architecture and desired capabilities.

6.3   Aligning Core IT Capabilities with the Business

• *Which capabilities will need to change as the organization changes business direction, priorities and matures?* Our framework is better applied as a dynamic process rather than as an instant fix. We determine in our analysis of the stages of growth that organizations tend to go through a similar order of capability development. We have also identified three mechanisms that help develop the capabilities at each stage: process, structure and culture. The challenge then for CIOs, is how to evolve through the stages of growth to reach the reorientation of 'business innovator'. Answering this challenge requires careful management across IT capabilities in coordination with IT strategy development, IT organizational structure, IT governance and IT structure.

The key challenge in Stage 1 is to establish service delivery credibility and control. This requires having the capabilities to manage external IT suppliers as well as being able to implement the necessary mechanisms (process, structure or culture) across the internal IT and business functions to manage demand.

The key challenge in Stage 2 is to add value to the business as a strategic partner in their delivery of IT-based business change. This requires a strong understanding of businesses objectives, an aligned IT strategy and clear governance on IT decision making across the organization.

Finally, the challenge in Phase 3 is to leverage the internal capabilities to bring innovation to the business. This includes a clear strategic sourcing model to leveraging external IS capabilities through the external IT sourcing market to help shape business strategies and initiatives.

References

Amit, R., & Schoemaker, P. (1993). Strategic assets and organizational rents. *Strategic Managamenet Journal, 14*, 33–46.

Feeny, D. (1997). The five year learning of ten IT directors. In L. Willcocks, D. Feeny, & G. Islei (Eds.), Managing IT as a strategic resource. Maidenhead: McGraw Hill.

Feeny, D., & Ross, J. (2000). The evolving role of the CIO. In R. Zmud (Ed.), Framing the domains of IS management research: glimping the future through the past. Cicinnati: Pinnaflex.

Feeny, D., & Willcocks, L. (1998). Core IS capabilities for exploiting information technology. *Sloan Management Review, 39*(3), 9–21.

Feeny, D., Willcocks, L., & Lacity, M. (2005). Taking the measure of outsourcing providers. *Sloan Management Review, 46*(3), 41–48.

Hindle, J., Willcocks, L., Feeny, D., & Lacity, M. (2003). Value-added outsourcing at Lloyds and BAE systems. *Knowledge Management Review, 6*(4), 28–31.

Lacity, M., Willcocks, L., & Feeny, D. (2003). Transforming a back office function: lessons from BAE systems' enterprise partnership. *MIS Quarterly Executive, 2*(2), 86–103.

Mohrman, S., Finegold, D., & Klien, J. (2002). Designing the knowledge enterprise: beyond programs and tools. *Organizational Dynamics, 30*(2), 134–150.

Scrimshaw, R. (2002) Strategic considerations for IT outsourcing. Salomon Smith Barney, The 2002 Australian Banking Conference, 6 March 2002.

Teece, D. J., Pisano, G., & Shuen, A. (1997). Dyanmics capabilities and straegic management. *Strategic Management Journal, 19*(7), 509–533.

Wernerfelt, B. (1984). A Resource-based view of the firm. *Strategic Management Journal, 5*(2), 171–180.

Wernerfelt, B. (1995). The resource-based view of the Firm: ten years after. *Strategic Management Journal, 16*(3), 171–174.

Which new Bank update, CEO, 24 May 2005.

Willcocks, L., & Feeny, D. (2005). Implementing core IS capabilities at Dupont. Information. *Systems Management Journal.*

Willcocks, L., Feeny, D. (2006). IT outsourcing and retained IS capabilities: challenges and lessons. Information Systems Management, 23(1), pp. 49–56.

Willcocks, L., & Lacity, M. (2007). Global sourcing of business and IT services. London: Palgrave Macmillan, Basingstoke.

Willcocks, Reynolds, & Feeny, (2007). Evolving capabilities to leverage the external IT services market. *MIS Quarterly Executive*, 6(3), 127–145.

Information Technology Workforce Skills: The Software and IT Services Provider Perspective[1]

Tim Goles, Stephen Hawk, and Kate M. Kaiser

1 Why Study the Information Technology Workforce?

The business environment continues to evolve at a dizzying pace. Advances in technology, emergence of new business practices, and shifting social and geopolitical circumstances have combined to create a 'brave new IT world' for organizations. This has raised a host of intriguing challenges for managers and researchers alike. This paper explores one of those challenges: acquiring skilled information technology (IT) professionals. More specifically, it examines the current and future employee skill sets desired by IT software and service provider firms. We focus on providers as a follow-up to previous studies on non-IT firms[2] (Abraham et al., 2006; Zwieg et al., 2006) and because of the projected growth of these organizations as a result of increased demand for technology solutions and outsourcing.

Before proceeding further, a note on the terminology used in this paper will be helpful. While it is not the intent of this paper to provide definitive meanings for the following terms, it will be beneficial to ensure that key concepts are interpreted similarly by the readers, and in accordance with the authors' intent. We define "Information Technology" (IT) as a field about the analysis, design, development, implementation, support, and management of computer-based information systems, composed of software, hardware, people, procedures, and data (Davis and Olson, 1985). Although the terms skills, capabilities, and competencies are often used interchangeably, we differentiate between them as follows. The term "skills" is defined as proficiency in a specific tool or method. It is the most basic level in a hierarchy of proficiencies. We view capabilities as the proficiency to adapt skills to broad sets of activities, and competencies as aggregates of capabilities (Abraham et al., 2006; Gallon, Stillman, & Coates, 1995). For this study, we will organize related skills into categories.

---

[1] This paper previously appeared as: Goles, T., Hawk, S. and Kaiser, K. M. "Information technology workforce skills: The software and IT services provider perspective", Information Systems Frontiers (10) 2008, pp 179–194. The current version appears with permission of Springer, the publisher of ISF.

[2] "Non-IT firms" are defined as those whose primary business is the production of goods or services other than IT products or services (Abraham et al., 2006).

R. Hirschheim et al. (eds), *Information Systems Outsourcing,*
© Springer-Verlag Berlin Heidelberg 2009

The use of IT service provider firms, commonly referred to by the generic term 'outsourcing,' is by now a well-accepted means for organizations to meet some or all of their IT needs. More recently, the traditional model of outsourcing has evolved to include offshore outsourcing, a global practice whereby professionals who provide IS services are located in different parts of the world from the firm that uses those services. In either case, the underlying concept is the same. One firm contracts with another for the provision of some or all of its IT functions. We refer to those requiring the services as non-IT, or client, firms whose primary business is the production of goods or services other than IT products or services (Abraham et al., 2006).

Client firms and their service providers have different missions. Thus, it seems reasonable to expect that they will require employees with different skill sets. This leads to a series of questions:

1. What skills do client organizations seek in their employees regarding the utilization of IT?
2. What skills do IT software and service providers seek in their employees regarding their IT service offerings?
3. Are there any differences in desired skills between client organizations and IT providers?

To address these questions, the Society for Information Management (SIM), an association of senior IT executives, consultants, and academics, recently sponsored a multi-year study of the IT workforce. In an exploratory study, a team of over twenty international U.S. and European researchers interviewed senior IT executives of client firms regarding their current and future workforce trends and skill requirements, effectively answering the first question (Zwieg et al., 2006). The purpose of this paper is to address the second and third questions by replicating and extending that previous research. This paper focuses on a complementary sample of IT provider firms for purposes of determining what skills IT providers seek in their employees, and identifying any differences between these skills and the skills desired by client firms.

This paper proceeds as follows. In the next section prior research into the IT workforce is reviewed. Then, a series of hypotheses is developed. They are tested using data gathered from senior managers and executives of IT providers. The results are presented, followed by a discussion of the findings, including implications for managers and researchers.

2   Prior Research

There is a lengthy history of studies that confirm IT workforce issues as a key concern of practitioners. An ongoing series of focus groups involving senior IT managers have explored staffing issues since 1990 (McKeen & Smith, 1995; 1996; 2003; Smith & McKeen, 2006). Another series of studies has consistently identified the workforce as one of the top issues facing IT executives since 1980 (Ball & Harris, 1982; Dickson, Leitheiser, Wetherbe, & Nechis, 1984; Brancheau & Wetherbe, 1987; Niederman, Brancheau, & Wetherbe, 1991; Brancheau, Janz, & Wetherbe, 1996; Luftman & McLean, 2004; Luftman, 2005, Luftman, Kempaiah, & Nash, 2006). One outgrowth of managers' interest in this topic is the development of a large body of research investigating the IT workforce.

A prominent stream in IT workforce research is identifying and classifying skill requirements for IT professionals (Ang & Slaughter, 2000). Generally speaking, prior research in this area has resulted in two broad categories of skills; technical, and non-technical. Technical skills basically consist of those skills specific to the IT field, including but not limited to knowledge and competencies associated with hardware, systems and application software, and telecommunications (Cash, Yoong, & Huff, 2004). The definition of non-technical skills is less precise, but generally includes (1) business skills (e.g., knowledge of the organization's structure, strategy, processes, and culture, and the ability to understand the business environment) (Cash et al., 2004; Lee, Trauth, & Farwell, 1995); (2) management skills (for the most part, the ability to perform some variation of the traditional management activities of planning, leading, organizing, and controlling) (Lee et al., 1995; Igbaria, Greenhaus, & Parasuraman, 1991); and (3) interpersonal skills (sometimes referred to as soft skills, these consist of such things as ability to communicate, ability to work in teams, relationship building skills, and leadership) (Cappel, 2001/2002; Cash et al., 2004; Lee et al., 1995; Litecky, Arnett, & Prabhakar, 2004).

There are two themes underlying prior research on IT workforce skills. First is the notion that advances in technology and developments in the business environment have driven changes in desired skill sets of IT professionals. For example, one study found that the emergence of e-commerce and subsequent changes in business models led to changes in the skills required of IT professionals (Cash et al., 2004). Another study found that, as technology progresses, employers look for IT employees to have an expanding number and variety of skills (Gallivan, Truex Iii, & Kvasny, 2004).

The second theme is that practically all the prior research on IT workforce skills has examined the topic from the perspective of the individual employee; that is, what skills are necessary for an individual to have a successful IT career (Lash & Sein, 1995; Lee et al., 1995; Lee, 2005). There is scant research focusing on what individual skills organizations seek in their employees. It should be noted that this is distinct from research into what organizational capabilities and competencies are necessary for a firm to be successful. Organizational capabilities arise from a combination of many factors, including the firm's strategy, structure, technology base, and employee skill sets.

Drawing from these two themes, this paper extends previous research by investigating the specific skills sought by firms, from the organizational perspective. It does so in the context of a specific type of organization – IT service providers. Thus, this paper ventures into a hitherto under-researched area which is becoming more central since the market volumes have been and will be steadily increasing.

What little research there has been in this area delivers a consistent message – there are differences in the skills sought by IS providers and client firms (Levina, Xin, & Yang, 2003; Slaughter & Ang, 1996).

Software and IT service providers tend to employ professionals with skills that can be leveraged to develop IS products and services applicable to multiple organizations; in other words, technically-oriented skills. For non-IT firms, retaining such skills internally is not critical, and may in fact be counter-productive in the face of a dynamic technical environment and an era of globalization (Slaughter & Ang, 1996).

Different internal labor market strategies[3] are applied to different types of IT jobs. In general, a craft strategy is employed for technical jobs. Viewed from this perspective, technical positions are associated with skills that are non-organization specific (that is, they can be easily transferred from one organization to another). They tend to be filled by individuals hired from outside the firm. Conversely, an industrial strategy is utilized for non-technical jobs. Seen in this light, these types of jobs are organization-specific. They are typically occupied by individuals who have been with the firm long enough to acquire high levels of organization-specific knowledge and experience (Ang & Slaughter, 2004). Applying this to provider and client firms suggests that providers will seek technical skills, while clients will prefer non-technical skills.

Recent research findings complement this view. Skills which are perceived as critical for client firms should be retained in-house, as opposed to acquiring them in the market place. They are weighted towards skills that specifically contribute to the core mission of the firm. This includes such business-centric skills as industry knowledge, functional area process knowledge, and business process re-engineering knowledge. Skills that bridge business and technology, such as project management and systems analysis proficiencies were also considered important to be kept in-house. Conversely, skills that are more general and more technology-centric, such as programming, systems testing, and desktop support, were seen as most likely to be outsourced (Zwieg et al., 2006).

Conceptually, identifying and classifying critical IT capabilities may be done in several ways (Lee et al., 1995). One approach is to elicit specific skills from knowledgeable respondents. Then, using statistical techniques such as factor analysis, the skills can be grouped into empirically derived categories (e.g., Igbaria et al., 1991). However, prior research has noted the fluctuation of desired skill sets over time (Gallivan et al., 2004; Litecky et al., 2004). Based on this temporal variance, other scholars who have researched desired skill sets both at a fixed point in time and then projected into a future period - similar to this paper - have deemed the factor analysis approach not appropriate for this purpose (Lee et al., 1995).

A second approach is to use a theoretical foundation to define a priori the skill sets. One example of this approach is the categorization of skills according to the

---

[3] Internal labor market strategies consist of the organization's practices, policies, and procedures that govern employee hiring training, and retention (Kerr, 1954; Osterman, 1984).

theoretical constructs of organizational and functional learning (e.g., Nelson et al., 1991). Another example is the use of the career anchor model to identify skills that shape an individual IT professional's career (e.g., Ginzberg & Baroudi, 1988; Lash & Sein, 1995; Josefek & Kauffman, 2003). From our perspective, however, there are two drawbacks to using a theoretical foundation to define the skill sets a priori. First, theoretically-based IT workforce research does not focus on identifying and categorizing skills per se, but rather on the relevance of those skills to a given problem domain, typically in the context of the individual professional's career. Second, the research has been conducted from the individual professional's perspective, not the organizational perspective. This paper's objective is to identify desired skills from the organization's perspective. Hence this approach is not suitable for our purposes.

A third approach groups skills into categories based on criteria to which respondents – in this case IS managers – can easily relate (Cappel, 2001/2002; Cash et al., 2004; Lee et al., 1995). Some researchers favor this approach "because of its content validity, conceptual simplicity, and the ease of relating our findings to… management" (Lee et al., 1995, p. 321). This approach was deemed most appropriate for our purposes, in that it adds an element of relevance to the research that practitioners can appreciate. It also allows us to directly compare our results from IT service providers to results from client firms.

3 Skills Categorization

For this study, we drew heavily on the list of skills used by Zwieg et al. (2006). We validated the categories used to group the skills through comparisons with prior studies, feedback from practitioners, and review by an expert panel[4]. The skills are more generic than specific, based on the fact that some specific skills identified in previous studies are rare today (e.g., microcomputer operating system skills), and some common current specific skills did not exist when early studies were conducted (e.g., Web development skills). For example, one of the technical skills identified in this study is "programming," as opposed to skills associated with a specific language such as Fortran or Java. See Table 1 for a list of the particular skills used in this study.

Consistent with previous studies, there is a *technical* category that emphasizes skills specific to the IT field (Cash et al., 2004), such as systems development life cycle skills (systems analysis, systems design, programming, and systems testing). In response to concerns voiced by senior IT managers and executives, this category includes security and business continuity skills, along with IT architecture skills (Luftman, 2005; Smith & McKeen, 2006). Also included are basic support skills

---

[4] The panel consisted of a subset of the research team. There were six international IT academics and one IT practitioner with primary research interests and experience in IT human resources.

Table 1 IT workforce skills by type

Technical	Project Management
Systems analysis	Project planning/budgeting/scheduling
Systems design	Project risk management
Programming	Negotiation
System testing	Project leadership
Database design/management	User relationship management
Data warehousing	Project integration/Program management
IT architecture/standards	Working with virtual teams
Voice/Data telecommunications	Working globally
Operating systems	Capability maturity model utilization
Server hosting	
Security	Sourcing – managing customers
Mainframe/Legacy	Customer/Product/Service strategy
Operations	Customer selection or qualification
Continuity/Disaster recovery	Contracting and legal
Desktop support/Helpdesk	Managing customer relationships
Business Domain	Sourcing – Managing Suppliers
Industry knowledge	Sourcing strategy
Company specific knowledge	Third-party provider selection
Functional area process knowledge	Contracting and legal
Business process design/Re-engineering	Managing third-party providers
Change mgmt/Org. readiness	
Managing stakeholder expectations	
Communication	

such as operations, telecommunications, desktop support/helpdesk, and server hosting. Finally, fundamentals such as operating system, database, and mainframe/legacy skills are also included.

A second category consists of skills relevant to various aspects of the *business domain*, such as relating to the general business environment (industry knowledge), understanding the organization's strategy and structure, and the ability to integrate technology with business needs (functional area process knowledge; business process design/re-engineering). Of particular relevance to IT service providers are skills related to managing stakeholder expectations, managing change, and communicating. Joseph, Ang, & Slaughter, (2006) predicted a curvilinear relationship of firm-specific training and experience with turnover. Applying this finding to our research, one would expect that mid-level IT professionals have more firm-specific training and experience such as business domain skills.

A significant activity undertaken by IT service providers – arguably *the* most significant activity – is managing projects. Projects are integral to IT service providers, ranging from large and complex software package development and implementation to performing routine upgrades to simple customer support systems. As such, it is critical that employees of IT service providers possess a wide range of *project management* skills. Paramount among these is the basic ability to plan, budget, and schedule projects. These are key in any project, of course, but difficulties with schedule and budget management have been identified as the most likely problems to arise in outsourced projects (Taylor, 2006). Thus, these skills are highly valued by service providers.

Risk management is generally acknowledged to be a critical success factor for software projects (Barki, Rivard, & Talbot, 2001). Consequently, IT service provider employees must have the skills necessary to identify and mitigate project risks (Taylor, 2006). One factor contributing to project risk is that service provider firms are often engaged in projects spanning multiple locations and organizations. In today's global business environment, additional issues related to language and culture can compound the challenges of managing across time, distance, and organizational divides. Clearly skills associated with working globally, and working with virtual teams, are essential.

The Capability Maturity Model (CMM) is often used as a tool to assess a service provider's software development capability. Many service providers have adopted the CMM in order to compete on a global scale, and prize employees with CMM skills.

Projects rarely stand alone. Whether a project is truly enterprise or not, skills which encompass the ability to integrate projects are in more demand today than in the past. Entry-level IT professionals may be focused on one or few projects. As they progress in their career, they inevitably become involved in multiple projects. Skills associated with coordinating multiple projects, or program management skills, become more valuable as employees advance beyond the entry level.

Tying the bundle of project management skills together is the project manager or leader. A recent study has confirmed that project leadership skills are associated with IT project success (Sumner, Bock, & Giamartino, 2006). Thus project leadership skills are highly desirable in IT service provider employees.

Skills particular to providers are those that focus on their clients. While one may argue that all IT professionals serve clients, software and service providers depend solely on customer organizations for their livelihood. In contrast, the relationship between an organization's IS function and its internal customers is not as precarious. The customer-facing skills we investigated involve how the provider firm determines its strategies, selects and qualifies its target markets, and manages the resulting relationship (Karmarkar, 2004). The complexity of engagements requires contracting and legal knowledge (Lee, 1996). The importance of nurturing sourcing relationships has brought new positions of relationship managers in both client and provider firms (Overby, 2006). From the service provider's perspective, customer relationship management skills play a key role in client satisfaction (Levina and Ross (2003).

Although client firms expect providers to fill their skill shortages, in order to secure or retain an engagement service providers may also need to turn to other providers as the source of work for either their internal needs, or more importantly to satisfy their clients (Feeny, Lacity, & Willcocks, 2005). IT providers need skills to determine their own strategy for sourcing, along with determining their criteria for selecting vendors. They have the same contracting and legal needs of their clients when the shoe is on the other foot to finalize and monitor contracts with their own providers. They also require employees with the skills to manage those third-party providers.

To summarize, the skills used in this study, and their categorization, essentially duplicates the ones used by Zwieg et al. (2006). They were validated by reviewing prior research and soliciting feedback from practitioners and academics. This facilitates a direct comparison between IT service providers (the focus of this study) and client firms (the focus of the Zwieg et al. study).

4   Research Methodology

The research team developed a Web-based survey derived from Zwieg et al. (2006) and customized it for provider firms. Participants were solicited from the Society for Information Management membership, researcher contacts, and various organizations focused on outsourcing. An effort was made to broaden the sample to include global representation. Having made a contact in the organization, one of the research team and the contact would determine who in the firm determines human resource strategy. It could be a vice president of human resources, a practice manager, or a chief executive officer. Upon securing permission from these individuals, they were e-mailed a unique identifier and the URL for an online survey. Data collection for this paper ran from October 2006 to April 2007.

There were some differences in how responses were obtained when comparing the use of the Web-based survey in the current study with the personal interviews conducted as part of the Zwieg et al. (2006) study. One difference was the inclusion of three items related to management of the internal IT function in the first study, and the inclusion of four items related to customer-facing capabilities in the second study. Internal IT management was not a relevant issue in the second study and hence these items were not included. Likewise, customer-facing capabilities did not come up in the first study (although user relationship capabilities did). Otherwise, the capabilities included in the first study and the second study were the same.

Perhaps the most important difference in data collection is that the first study used open-ended questions to identify capabilities that were critical and to identify capabilities that were sought in entry and mid-level hires. Respondents were not given a list of specific capabilities to respond to. Instead, interviewers used a key that identified 38 capabilities to code the open-ended answer by checking capabilities mentioned. The Web-based survey, however, provided respondents with a list of all capabilities, grouped according to the five skill categories discussed earlier. Without the prompting provided by the list of capabilities, respondents in the first study tended to identify a fewer number of capabilities as being critical or sought when hiring. An additional difference between the two studies is that the time frame for comparison in the first study was from 2005 to 2008, while it was 2006 to 2009 in the current study. In both studies, however, a three-year time horizon was used when asking about current versus future needs.

The survey included three sections that asked questions about the 38 capabilities. The first section asked respondents about the capabilities their organizations need to maintain. The second and third sections asked respondents to indicate the capabilities they desired in entry level and mid level employees, respectively.

The first section asked three different questions about each capability:

1. Is the capability considered critical currently?
2. Will the capability become critical for its employees over the next three years?
3. Will the capability decline in importance over the next three years?

While responses to each question were summarized separately, these questions were also used in determining whether a capability would be critical in the future. If a capability was critical today, it was considered to be critical in the future, unless it declined in importance. If a capability was not critical today, it was considered to be critical in the future when a respondent indicated that it would emerge as a critical capability.

Results were computed by counting how many times respondents checked a response to a question and dividing this total by the sample size to yield a percentage. This procedure was applied to the different questions for each of the capabilities. To determine the leading capabilities for each of the questions, we selected the 10 highest percentages and included ties when two or more capabilities tied for at the 10th position.

As stated previously, this study is a replication and extension of an earlier exploratory study (Zwieg et al., 2006). The exploratory nature and research design of that study does not lend itself to formal hypotheses development. However, the results of that study, combined with the prior research discussed in Section 2 of this paper, lead to certain expectations, which we have presented as a series of propositions. These are discussed in the following paragraphs, and then evaluated using data from a sample of IT service providers.

Although there are many reasons why firms outsource, the two primary drivers are economic (to reduce expenses) and strategic (to focus on core competencies) (Dibbern, Goles, Hirschheim, & Jayatilaka, 2004). Therefore, in order to be successful, an IT service provider must be able to either (1) generate economies of scale by leveraging employee skills to support multiple customers (e.g., generic programming, server hosting, telecommunications), (2) work closely with a specific customer or industry to meet more focused needs, or (3) do both.

The expertise necessary for service providers to offer a broad range of general IT services to multiple customers is based on technical skills specific to the IT industry. It is reasonable to presume that an IT service provider firm will expect its employees to possess these skills. In fact, basic technical skills are often used as a threshold or filtering device to separate desirable prospective employees from undesirable ones, especially at the entry level (Litecky et al., 2004). Furthermore, there is a movement by non-IT firms towards outsourcing non-core or technical skills, while retaining core or business-oriented skills in-house (Slaughter & Ang, 1996; Zwieg et al., 2006), adding to the demand by service providers for technical skills. Moreover, while basic technical skills serve as entry-level credentials, over time, IT employees are expected to master additional technical skills (Gallivan et al., 2004). This leads to the first two propositions.

P1: For entry-level employees, IT service provider firms will have more demand for technical skills than client firms.

P2: For mid-level employees, IT service provider firms will have more demand for technical skills than client firms.

Technical skills by themselves are not sufficient for service provider firms to survive and prosper. Service providers also must work with their customers in applying those technical skills in a business context. This involves such customer-centric activities as analyzing user requirements and developing new processes or systems (e.g., systems analysis, systems design, business process design/re-engineering), participating in project teams (e.g., project management, teamwork), and understanding the customer's business environment (e.g., industry knowledge, company specific knowledge, functional area knowledge). While it is desirable for all the service provider's employees to have these capabilities, it is arguably more important for mid-level employees to possess them to a greater extent than entry-level employees, because mid-level employees generally have more interaction with customer employees. Thus, we can deduce proposition 3:

P3: For IT service provider firms, customer-centric capabilities are in greater demand for mid-level employees than for entry-level employees.

We received 104 responses to the survey. Seventy percent of the sample came from North American firms, five percent from firms in Western Europe, and the remainder from offshore locations such as India, Russia, Eastern Europe and Asia. Average firm size in term of full time equivalent employees was 5,466. More than 61% of the firms, however, had fewer than 1,000 employees. Sixty-seven percent of the firms had less than $500 Million USD revenue during the last fiscal year, 18% had revenue between $500 million and $3 billion USD, and the remaining 15% of the firms earned more than $3 billion USD. Seventy-six percent of the respondents were senior or executive level managers, with almost all of the rest (22%) being at the middle management level.

5   Results

5.1   IT Service Provider Firms

Table 2 shows IT firms' top ten highest ranked capabilities considered critical today. Table 2 also shows the capabilities the respondents thought would be most critical in the future. The skills are arranged by rank order for critical skills today. The first column shows the rank order based on the percent of firms that chose that skill. The second column shows the percentage of respondents that considered them

Table 2 Highest ranked skills for IT firms -present and future

Rank Today	Percent Today	Type	Skill	Rank 2009	Percent 2009
1	79	Project management	Project planning/budgeting/ scheduling	4	84
2	78	Business domain	Industry knowledge	1	88
3	77	Business domain	Functional area knowledge	5	83
4	77	Sourcing–customer	Managing customer relationships	10-tie	79
5	75	Project management	Project leadership	2	87
6	73	Business domain	Communication	7	81
7	70	Technical	Systems analysis	10-tie	79
8	69	Technical	Systems design		
9	69	Business domain	Company specific knowledge		
10	69	Project management	User relationship management	6	83
		Project management	Project risk management	3	86
		Technical	IT architecture/standards	8	80
		Project management	Working with virtual teams	9	80
		Business domain	BPR	10-tie	79
		Sourcing–Customer	Managing customer relationships	10-tie	79

critical. The third and fourth columns indicate the skill category, and the particular skill. The fifth and sixth columns indicate how participants projected what skills would be critical over the next three years. Although the order of the top 10 skills changes somewhat, there are few differences between the skills considered critical today and those considered critical in the future, with the exception of more skills included in the future due to ties in the rankings.

The skills primarily include business domain and project management capabilities. Only one technical skill is included during both time periods: systems analysis. This skill, albeit categorized as technical, also requires elements of business domain and client-facing skills. One technical skill – system design, another skill with business domain and client facing overtones – appears in the 'today' skills, but not in the future skills. A different technical skill, IT architecture and standards, is present in the future skills list.

For 2009 there are few projected changes in the general make-up of desired skills. Business domain and project management skills still predominate, although there is a trend towards more project management capabilities, such as project risk management and project planning, budgeting and scheduling. Other additions include working with virtual teams, along with IT architecture and standards.

Furthermore, it is interesting to note the IT firms' lowest ranked skills, both current and future (see Table 3). Technical skills predominate in both time periods, indicating that these types of skills are not considered critical by our respondents. This is somewhat surprising, given that the respondents are all from IT service providers, whom one might naturally expect to value technical skills.

Table 4 presents the entry-level skills desired by IT provider firms. These show less technical skills than expected. The lower percentages in this table compared to Tables 2 and 5 can be interpreted two ways. One, it could be that a number of our responding firms do not hire at the entry-level. Two, there could be a greater variation in entry-level skills desired by the responding firms than in skills considered critical (Table 2) or skills desired in mid-level employees (Table 5).

The results for desired mid-level skills in provider firms are shown in Table 5. There is a greater emphasis on project management and business domain skills. Even the technical skills included reflect a shift away from primarily technical capabilities and towards more customer-facing skills. This provides support for proposition 3.

Table 3 Lowest ranked skills for IT firms – present and future

Rank Today	Percent Today	Type	Skill	Rank 2009	Percent 2009
1	48	Sourcing–Vendor	Managing third party providers		
2	47	Technical	Continuity/Disaster recovery		
3	47	Sourcing–Vendor	Contracting and legal	2	63
4	44	Project Management	CMM utilization	3	59
5	43	Technical	Voice/Data telecommunications	1	63
6	40	Technical	Desktop support/Help desk	7	46
7	37	Technical	Operations	8	43
8	36	Technical	Operating systems	9	38
9	33	Technical	Server hosting	6	46
10	32	Technical	Mainframe/Legacy	10	27
		Sourcing–Customer	Contracting and legal	4	59
		Technical	Programming	5	49

Table 4 Entry-level skills desired by IT firms

Rank	Type	Skill	Percent
1	Technical	Programming	59
2	Business domain	Communication	57
3	Technical	System testing	55
4	Business domain	Functional area knowledge	47
5	Projectmanagement	Project planning/budgeting/scheduling	46
6	Business domain	Industry knowledge	44
7	Project Management	User relationship management	43
8	Project Management	Working with virtual teams	43
9	Technical	Systems analysis	42
10	Technical	Desktop support/Help desk	41

We also asked IT provider firms to tell us what skills were emerging or becoming increasingly important. Table 6 shows the top ranked ones. The top two ranked emerging skills clearly show an emphasis on a global model of development, indicating an expectation that offshoring in some form will continue to play a significant role in IT service delivery in the foreseeable future.

Finally, we asked IT provider firms what skills were declining in importance because they will become irrelevant, automated, or outsourced to other IT firms. Most of these declining skills shown in Table 7 are in the technical category. Nine of the ten skills declining in importance are also among the capabilities that received low rankings for being critical now and in the future (see Table 3). This suggests that these skills are increasingly becoming commoditized. They may be necessary to an IT service provider firm, in the same sense that electricity is, but they are not viewed as providing competitive advantage.

Table 5 Mid-level skills desired by IT firms

Rank	Type	Skill	Percent
1	Project Management	Project Planning/budgeting/scheduling	78
2	Project Management	Project leadership	76
3	Business domain	Industry knowledge	74
4	Business domain	Functional area knowledge	74
5	Project Management	User relationship management	73
6	Project Management	Project risk mgmt	71
7	Business Domain	Communication	68
8	Technical	Systems analysis	66
9	Technical	Systems design	66
10 (tie)	Project Management	Working with virtual teams	63
10 (tie)	Technical	IT architecture/standards	63
10 (tie)	Project management	Negotiation	63

Table 6 Skills emerging in importance/becoming more critical

Type	Skill	Percent
Project management	Working with virtual teams	64
Project management	Working globally	63
Technical	IT architecture/standards	59
Business domain	Industry knowledge	56
Sourcing – Vendor	Managing third party providers	56
Business domain	Change management	55
Business domain	BPR	54
Business domain	Communication	53
Technical	Security	51
Project management	User relationship	51

Table 7 Skills declining in importance

Type	Skill	Percent
Technical	Mainframe/Legacy	40
Technical	Programming	35
Technical	Operating systems	24
Technical	Desktop support/Help desk	24
Technical	Server hosting	22
Technical	Operations	18
Technical	System testing	15
Project Management	CMM utilization	14
Technical	Voice/Data telecommunications	13
Sourcing – customer	Contracting and legal	9

5.2 Comparison of IT Firms and Non-IT Firms

Table 8 contains the results for skills from the current study on IT firms and comparable results for client firms from the prior study (Zwieg et al., 2006) on critical skills for the future, entry-level, and mid-level skills[5].

Comparing the rankings of IT firms with the highest-ranked skills for client firms indicates that, overall, IT organizations perceive no more need for technical capabilities than their clients.

With regard to new hires, the comparison reveals that, while both types of firms rank programming and system testing highly, client firms tend to be much more interested in technical skills than the firms to which they outsource. Provider firms place much greater emphasis on project management skills, and rank business domain capabilities higher, than do client firms. This indicates that the first proposition is not supported.

For mid-level hires, interestingly, these results are very similar to those of client firms. Although the exact rankings differ somewhat, both types of firms agree on nine of the top ten desired skills. This indicates that there is virtually no difference in the skills desired by IT and client firms for mid-level employees. Thus proposition 2 is not supported.

6 Discussion

The results are consistent across the three analyses of skills: overall critical skills, entry-level, and mid-level. In all of these, for IT provider firms, technical skills are not as important as other types of skills. They rank the lowest as a group of skills in comparison to the groups of business domain, project management, and sourcing

---

[5] Please note that the original study of client firms asked the respondents to list desired skills, while the survey of IT firms presented respondents with a list of skills derived from the original study. This may account for some of the differences in results.

Table 8   Desired skills for IT firms and non-IT firms: percentage of respondents

Type	Skill	Critical 2009 IT firms	Critical 2008 Client firms	Entry-Level IT firms	Entry-Level Client firms	Mid-Level IT firms	Mid-Level Client firms
Technical	Systems analysis	79	66	59	44	78	48
	Systems design	76	63	42	33	76	45
	Programming	49	37	55	48	71	28
	System testing	68	36	36	35	66	23
	Database design/Management	68	51	57	23	73	20
	IT architecture standards	80	58	41	25	66	33
	Voice/Data telecommunications	63	27	19	27	74	14
	Operating systems	38	27	34	19	63	16
	Server hosting	46	23	38	13	74	11
	Security	76	51	44	13	63	17
	Mainframe/Legacy	27	24	31	10	68	11
	Operations	43	28	47	15	62	13
	Continuity/Disaster recovery	69	30	43	13	63	14
	Desktop support/Help desk	46	25	28	27	62	13
Business domain	Industry knowledge	88	65	46	19	56	44
	Company specific knowledge	78	69	33	8	58	25
	Functional area knowledge	83	72	24	17	56	42
	BPR	79	66	23	6	52	33
	Charge management	76	59	18	6	53	20
	Manage stakeholder expectations	77	58	19	13	62	25
	Communication	81	54	43	29	52	36
Project management	Project plan/Budget/scheduling	84	76	37	13	44	56
	Project risk mgmt	86	64	30	4	41	52
	Negotiation	75	58	25	8	30	44
	Project leadership	87	65	40	8	33	55
	User relationship management	83	57	30	15	31	48
	Work with virtual teams	80	51	35	8	26	39
	Working globally	76	47	35	4	25	36
	CMM utilization	59	30	30	2	38	20
Sourcing – Vendor	Sourcing strategy	66	51	38	2	59	11
	Third party provider selection	68	49	28	2	49	11
	Contracting and legal	63	46	26	2	43	11
	Managing third party providers	70	59	22	2	38	16

capabilities. This is counterintuitive, given that one would reasonably expect firms whose core business is providing IT products or services to attach a high degree of importance to skills that are fundamental to doing so. Upon reflection, however, it

may be that our respondents, who are senior managers and executives, view technical skills as necessary to achieving their mission, but not critical in the sense that
those skills lead to a competitive advantage. In other words, basic technical skills
such as the ability to program are essential, but do not differentiate one firm from
another in the same sense that project management or business domain skills do.
Thus, they may be perceived as a necessary but non sufficient condition.

The findings are also consistent with research on client firms (Zwieg et al., 2006).
Again, this is somewhat surprising because in that study client firms indicated that
they would primarily seek technical skills from their providers. In fact, six of the top
eight skills identified as critical to keep in-house by client firms are also in the top ten
critical skills identified by provider firms. Project management capabilities predominate. Reflecting on this finding leads to the implication that the provider firms are
more interested in higher-level IT work (e.g., systems integration) than 'commodity'
work such as programming and basic development. This reinforces the growing perception that many offshore firms desire to move up the value chain beyond programming. They see their future in the higher level work. Furthermore, most of the
offshore outsourcers now have US and European locations, making virtual teamwork
skills even more important. Domestic provider firms with offshore locations are also
quickly learning to appreciate skills necessary for working virtually.

Respondents had mixed views about programming skills. Approximately as many
firms designated it as a critical skill as those that designated it as a skill declining in
value. One interpretation of this is that some of the organizations may specialize in the
higher level analysis and design rather than basic development work (e.g., programming
and systems testing) because they believe it will be more lucrative. These firms may
outsource the programming they need to complete projects for clients. In addition,
some domestic providers may feel threatened that offshore firms are moving up the
value chain. Consequently, they are responding by honing their expertise in higher
level areas rather than compete with development work where offshore organizations
have a labor arbitrage advantage and a growing reputation.

The types of skills IT provider firms desire for entry-level employees are more
diverse than those desired by client firms, which are primarily technical. One
possible interpretation of this disparity is that client firms view entry-level positions
as a training ground or place to prove one's worth more so than IT firms. Another
possibility is that the emphasis on client-facing or customer-centric skills for
provider firms implies that these organizations expect their employees to be able to
work well with customers from day one. In fact, many domestic consulting firms
now do take new hires to client sites soon after their orientation and training are
completed, even if they have formal training programs.

At the mid-level, the demand for project management capabilities is no surprise.
Project management is a necessity for the bulk of sourcing engagements, and may
involve managing clients' employees on teams. The increasing emphasis on certifications and project management experience is apparent in job listings. Managing
virtual teams is an acquired skill. Client firms would naturally look to their sources
for more expertise in this capability than they might have in house. The high ranking
of IT architecture and standards reflects the pervasiveness recently of frameworks

such as the Information Technology Infrastructure Library (ITIL – a widely accepted formal approach to IT service management) and Control Objectives for Information and related Technology (COBIT – a framework of best practices for IT control and management).

Comparing mid-level needs of client and provider companies shows few differences. They are almost identical. This may be heartening to a generation that has little organizational loyalty. They not only can easily change jobs but they could easily transfer from a client firm to a provider firm and vice versa multiple times during their career. These career choices present more options to the individual.

Two skills are highly valued by IT firms, appearing in the top ten skills across the board (highest ranked capabilities present, future, entry-level, mid-level, and emerging in importance). Both of these are from the business domain category; industry knowledge, and communication. The importance of industry knowledge could stem from two sources. One, some providers' strategy is to target specialized vertical markets where industry knowledge is valuable (i.e., niche differentiation). Two, providers in general seek to achieve economies of scale. Hiring employees knowledgeable in a particular industry is one way to leverage the firm's knowledge base. As for communication skills, they are fundamental and vital to several other desired skills from the other categories, including systems analysis (technical), working on projects and with teams (project management), and managing customer relations (sourcing – managing customers)

A global world is more reflected in the provider firms than the client firms. This could be due to the number of offshore organizations in the sample and the preponderance of domestic firms that have captive centers in global locations. This may explain the high ranking of sourcing capabilities such as managing third-party providers. It appears that many of the outsourcing firms also outsource to other outsourcers and that skills related to this practice are important enough to appear in the higher ranked capabilities.

The importance of security is rising and shown as an important skill for organizations offering IT services. Occurrences of change management, business process re-engineering, and IT architecture and standards are not surprising because these issues are important aspects of implementing IT to support the value chain outside the organization (e.g., Enterprise Resource Planning and Customer Relationship Management systems), as well as recent developments such as Service Oriented Architecture, Net 2.0, and the Information Technology Infrastructure Library (ITIL). They may also signal intentions on the part of IT service providers to move up the value chain from programming to involvement in the full set of development activities, and for partnering with client organizations on larger-scale initiatives involving multiple application areas where these capabilities would be critical.

The percentages for skills considered to be declining in importance (Table 7) were lower than the percentages for skills considered to be increasing in importance (Table 6). This finding reinforces the conclusion of Gallivan et al. (2004) who found that as technology evolves and new technologies emerge, employers expect their employees to add more and more skills to their repertoire, while maintaining the skills they already possess.

The lowest ranked skills for the future are mostly technical (Table 3). The occurrence of contracting and legal skills, and CMM utilization skills in this group could indicate that these are not an issue for most organizations. The CMM is perceived by some as a marketing tool rather than a true strategic differentiator, perhaps because CMM adherence is beginning to permeate the workforce. Mainframe legacy skills appeared as the lowest ranked skill, both present and future. This could portend unfortunate future consequences, given the pending baby-boomer retirements. It may be that sourcing firms do not see this market as lucrative, perceiving the mainframe as dead. Or if they do see it as lucrative market, they may be doubtful that they can service it, given there are few people with these skills, many of whom are nearing retirement, while the younger generation is not being trained in mainframe skills. The overall implication of this study – that IS provider firms value business-oriented skills more than technical ones – was somewhat unexpected. Upon further reflection, we now believe this should not have come as a surprise. Years of research have indicated that non-technical skills are more valuable to internal IT departments than technical skills. The fact that the IS 'department' now resides outside the organization should not diminish the value of those skills. In fact, recent research has suggested that IS providers should possess a collection of core capabilities based on technical and non-technical skill sets (Feeny et al., 2005). Thus future researchers should feel comfortable in extending past studies on internal IS skills and capabilities to the sourcing realm.

One of the largest concerns of IT management is being able to hire and retain valuable talent. With fewer people in the workforce pipeline and impending baby-boomer retirements, coupled with increasing demand for technology, managers will have more difficulty acquiring needed skills. The similarity of what client companies and IT industry companies want in their skills portfolio means that competition for talent will be across these two types of firms more so than in the past when client firms sought technical skills from their providers. The implication for individual career development is that one can easily move back and forth from a client organization to a provider with no hazards to career growth or limiting opportunities.

Although client firms said they wanted technical skills in their entry-level professionals, provider firms were less concerned about these capabilities for their entry-level professionals. Because of this the provider companies may have an easier road grooming their entry-level candidates to become business analysts and project managers than their clients will. This may very well add more impetus to the outsourcing/offshoring movement, and quite possibly lead to a self-fulfilling prophecy whereby a steady growing number of IT jobs move from client firms to service providers.

Research needs to study these trends longitudinally to monitor changes. A different appro ach is to measure at the individual level rather than at the organizational unit of analysis.

When considering these results some limitations of the study should be kept in mind. First, the data for this paper was collected between October 2006 and April 2007. A second round of data collection is ongoing at the time of writing. Thus, while we expect the additional data to confirm the findings reported in this paper, at this point they must be considered preliminary.

Secondly, the time frame difference between the first phase and the second phase should also be noted. The 2005 data collection was performed during a time when the job market was beginning to revive from a recession. While skill needs were changing during that period, one can imagine that those skill needs may be changing even more rapidly in the next 18 months when the second phase data collection occurred.

A third limitation of the comparisons of the two data sets is that the first phase had few global locations outside of the United States, while the second data set collected from IT service providers had much more international representation.

Finally, the methodology used in this paper is a comparison of rank-ordered lists. We acknowledge that this is not a sophisticated statistical analysis technique. We do, however, believe that it accurately reflects basic truths and trends.

The implications for individuals, hiring firms, and institutions of higher education are clear. Individuals should acquire a set of diverse skills that include not only technical ones, but business-related and 'soft' skills as well. Organizations must be aware of pending shortages of and competition for well-rounded and qualified individuals, and implement training and retention programs to attract and retain capable employees. Colleges and universities must make curriculum changes to better prepare students for this new reality. Finally, the IT industry as a whole must communicate the message to the world at large that there are and will continue to be rewarding career opportunities for IT professionals.

7   Summary

The research describes fundamental shifts in the nature of capabilities and skills of IT professionals. Although IT professionals have been highly valued for their technical expertise, business acumen and the ability to manage projects are essential not only for IT professionals in non-IT firms but also for those professionals whom they contract for services to enhance their staffing. These characteristics are in demand at mid-level careers and increasingly for entry-level hires. Organizations will need to groom IT professionals to develop these skills and to work with educational institutions to convey the importance of the changing skill needs.

References

Abraham, T., Beath, C., Bullen, C., Gallagher, K., Goles, T., Kaiser, K., & Simon, J. (2006). IT workforce trends: implications for IS programs. *Communications of the Association for Information Systems (CAIS), 17*(3), 1147–1170. (Article 50).

Ang, S., & Slaughter, S. (2000). The missing context of information technology personnel: a review and future directions for research. In: R. Zmud (Ed.), *Framing the domains of IT management: projecting the future through the Past* (pp. 305–327). Cincinnati: Pinnaflex Education Resources.

Ang, S., & Slaughter, S. (2004). Turnover of information technology professionals: the effects of internal labor market strategies. *The DATA BASE for Advances in Information Systems, 35*(3), 11–27.

Ball, L., & Harris, R. (1982). SIM members: a membership analysis. *MIS Quarterly, 6*(1), 19–38.

Barki, H., Rivard, S., & Talbot, J. (2001). An integrative contingency model of software project risk management. *Journal of Management Information Systems, 17*(4), 37–69.

Brancheau, J. C., Janz, B. D., & Wetherbe, J. C. (1996). Key issues in information systems management: 1994–1995 SIM Delphi results. *MIS Quarterly, 20*(2), 225–242.

Brancheau, J. C., & Wetherbe, J. C. (1987). Information systems management issues in the 1990s. *MIS Quarterly, 11*(1), 135–159.

Cappel, J. J. (2001/2002). Entry-level IS job skills: a survey of employers. *Journal of Computer Information Systems, 42*(2), 76–82.

Cash, E., Yoong, P., & Huff, S. (2004). The impact of E-Commerce on the role of IS professionals. *The DATA BASE for Advances in Information Systems, 3*(3), 50–63.

Davis, G. B., & Olson, M. (1985). Management information systems: conceptual foundations, structure, and development. New York: McGraw-Hill.

Dickson, G. W., Leitheiser, R. L., Wetherbe, J. C., & Nechis, M. (1984). Key information systems issues for the 1980s. *MIS Quarterly, 8*(3), 135–159.

Dibbern, J., Goles, T., Hirschheim, R., & Jayatilaka, B. (2004). Information systems outsourcing: a survey and analysis of the literature. *The DATA BASE for Advances in Information Systems, 35*(4), 6–102.

Feeny, D, Lacity, M., & Willcocks, L. P. (2005). Taking the measure of outsourcing providers. *Sloan Management Review, 46*(3), 41–48.

Gallivan, M. J., Truex Iii, D. P., & Kvasny, L. (2004). Changing patterns in IT skill sets 1988–2003: a content analysis of classified advertising. *The DATA BASE for Advances in Information Systems, 35*(3), 64–87.

Gallon, M., Stillman, H. M., & Coates, D. (1995). Putting core competency thinking into practice. *Research Technology Management, 38*(3), 20–29.

Ginzberg, M. J., & Baroudi, J. J. (1988). MIS careers – a theoretical perspective. *Communications of the ACM, 31*(5), 586–594.

Igbaria, M., Greenhaus, J., & Parasuraman, S. (1991). Career orientations of MIS employees: an empirical analysis. *MIS Quarterly, 15*(2), 151–169.

Josefek, R. A., & Kauffman, R. J. (2003). Nearing the threshhold: an economics approach to pressure on information systems professionals to separate from their employer. *MIS Quarterly, 20*(1), 87–122.

Joseph, D., Ang, S., & Slaughter, S. (2006). Examining the role of general and firm-specific human capital in predicting IT professionals' turnover behaviors. In: K. M. Kaiser, & T. Ryan (Eds.), In: *Proceedings of the 2006 ACM SIGMIS CPR conference on computer personnel research: forty four years of computer personnel research: achievements, challenges and the future* (pp. 120–122).

Karmarkar, U. (2004). Will you survive the services revolution? *Harvard Business Review, 82*(6), 100–107.

Kerr, C. (1954). The balkinization of labor markets. In: E. W. Bakke (Ed.), *Labor mobility and economic opportunity* (pp. 92–110). Cambridge, MA: MIT.

Lash, P. B., & Sein, M. K. (1995). Career paths in a changing IS environment: a theoretical perspective. In: *Proceedings of the ACM special interest group in computer personnel research (SIGCPR)* (pp. 117–130). Nashville, TN.

Lee, C. K. (2005). Transferability of skills over the IT career path. In: *Proceedings of the ACM special interest group in computer personnel research (SIGCPR)* (pp. 85–93). Atlanta, GA., 85–93.

Lee, M. K. O. (1996). IT outsourcing contracts: practical issues for management. *Industrial Management & Data Systems, 96*(1), 15–20.

Lee, D. M. S., Trauth, E. M., & Farwell, D. (1995). Critical skills and knowledge requirements of IS professionals: a joint academic/industry investigation. *MIS Quarterly, 19*(3), 313–340.

Levina, N., & Ross, J. W. (2003). From the vendor's perspective: exploring the value proposition in information technology outsourcing. *MIS Quarterly, 27*(3), 331–364.

Levina, N., Xin, M., & Yang, S. (2003). Understanding IT workforce structure in IT vs. Non-IT firms: implications to IT outsourcing. In: *Proceedings of the International Conference on Information Systems.* December 2003.

Litecky, C. R., Arnett, K. P., & Prabhakar, B. (2004). The paradox of soft skills versus technical skills in IS hiring. *Journal of Computer Information Systems, 45*(1), 69–76.

Luftman, J. (2005). Key issues for IT executives 2004. *MIS Quarterly Executive, 4*(2), 269–285.

Luftman, J., & Mclean, E. (2004). Key issues for IT executives. *MIS Quarterly Executive, 3*(2), 89–104.

Luftman, J., Kempaiah, R., & Nash, E. (2006). Key Issues for IT executives. *MIS Quarterly Executive, 5*(2), 27–45.

Mckeen, J. D., Smith, H. A. (1995). The future of IS: looking ahead to the year 2000. IT Management Forum, 5(1). School of Business, Queen's University, Kingston, Canada, K7L 3N6.

Mckeen, J. D., & Smith, H. A. (1996). *Management challenges in IS: successful strategies and appropriate action.* England: Wiley.

Mckeen, J. D., & Smith, H. A. (2003). *Making IT happen: critical issues in managing technology.* New York: Wiley.

Niederman, F., Brancheau, J. C., & Wetherbe, J. C. (1991). Information systems management issues in the 1990s. *MIS Quarterly, 15*(4), 474–499.

Nelson, R. R. (1991). Educational needs as perceived by IS and end-user personnel: a survey of knowledge and skill requirements. *MIS Quarterly, 15*(4), 502–525.

Osterman, P. (1984). Internal labor markets. Cambridge, MA: MIT.

Overby, S. (2006). The new IT department: the top three positions you need. CIO Magazine, http://www.cio.com/archive/010106/soc_staffing.html, last viewed March 28, 2007.

Slaughter, S., & Ang, S. (1996). Employment outsourcing in information systems. *Communications of the ACM, 39*(7), 47–55.

Smith, H. A., & Mckeen, J. D. (2006). ÍT in 2010: the next frontier. *MIS Quarterly Executive, 5*(3), 125–136.

Sumner, M., Bock, D., & Giamartino, G. (2006). Exploring the linkage between the characteristics of IT project leaders and project success. *Information Systems Management, 23*(4), 43–49.

Taylor, H. (2006). Critical risks in outsourced IT projects: the intractable and the unforeseen. *Communications of the ACM, 49*(11), 74–79.

Zwieg, P., Kaiser, K., Beath, C., Bullen, C., Gallagher, K., Goles, T., Howland, J., Simon, J., Abbot, P., Abraham, T., Carmel, E., Evaristo, R., Hawk, S., Lacity, M., Gallivan, M., Kelly, S., Mooney, J., Ranganathan, C., Rottman, J., Ryan, T., & Wion, R. (2006). The information technology workforce: trends and implications 2005–2008. *MIS Quarterly Executive, 5*(2), 47–54.

Chapter 3
Outsourcing Outcomes

Is There an "Information Technology Outsourcing Paradox"?

Anne C. Rouse

1 Introduction

This paper examines an apparent paradox: given the increasing adoption of out-sourced IT service delivery, why has the academic literature been unable to confirm widespread satisfaction with the strategy? Instead it has come to be seen as almost axiomatic that outsourcing IT *must* be perceived as beneficial by purchaser firms – after all, why would organizations engage in this practice if it did not produce corporate benefits? Yet there is a growing body of evidence collected by both consultants and researchers that significant numbers of outsourcing arrangements are quite unsatisfactory (e.g., Aubert, Patry, & Rivard 1999; Bernard 2005; Gartner 2002; Ozanne 2000; Rouse & Corbitt 2003b).

Trade and academic claims of a range of benefits have fuelled the worldwide adoption of IT outsourcing. Certainly, outsourcing has the *potential* for a number of benefits in addition to, and sometimes instead of, cost savings. These include enhanced business flexibility: access to skills; or to new or better technologies; increased capacity to concentrate on core business; enhanced managerial control; and financial restructuring benefits (such as converting capital to operating expenses (Lacity & Willcocks 2001). But in this chapter the evidence on which such claims are based is unpacked, and it will be shown that while in some cases substantial benefits accrue from IT outsourcing, the strategy can also lead to a number of negative outcomes. The most common of these is a failure to deliver the benefits that were the primary reason for engaging in the activity in the first place. Because of the significant disruption and expense caused when outsourc-ing is entered into, this fundamental failure means that funds and management attention are diverted from other more fruitful business strategies, often for considerable periods.

The continued growth of a strategy whose theoretical benefits have largely not been confirmed is puzzling, and has been labelled in this chapter the "IT outsourcing paradox." This paradox is based on an apparent "disconnect" between the growing level of outsourcing activity in the community and the empirical evidence about how decision makers engaged in outsourcing actually evaluated outsourcing's

R. Hirschheim et al. (eds), *Information Systems Outsourcing,*
© Springer-Verlag Berlin Heidelberg 2009

success when surveyed. This growth is made up of existing outsourcing firms that continue and possibly expand their arrangements, plus new outsourcing arrangements in firms that had not previously experienced IT outsourcing. The latter group, having no experience of outsourcing, are likely to be particularly influenced by "myths" circulating in the IS community (Lacity & Hirschheim 1993).

The chapter describes and illustrates the existence of the paradox, then goes on to suggest explanations that are drawn from a body of qualitative and quantitative studies conducted between 1997 and 2007. The chapter concludes by urging corporate decision makers to be more sceptical about claimed benefits of outsourcing, to scrutinize the business care for IT outsourcing carefully, and to recognize that many benefits come with associated trade-offs.

2   A Theoretical Model of Outsourcing Success

Much of IT outsourcing research has been concerned with what motivates firms to outsource (or not outsource) rather than with the success of the strategy (Dibbern, Goles, Hirschheim, & Jayatilaka 2004). In this form of research the dependent variable is whether or not firms choose to adopt outsourcing. However, it is much easier, and quicker, for firms to outsource their IT than to reverse that decision (Rouse & Corbitt 2006). So it is quite possible for firms to be engaged in for some time, or even increase their use of, "unsuccessful" outsourcing.

Another body of IT outsourcing research has concentrated on practices and structures for managing outsourcing arrangements (Dibbern et al. 2004). This research raises the question of "How do we know that such practices will lead to *better* outsourcing?" It is here that the body of literature is problematic, because most of the claims that recommended practices are beneficial to firms rely large on plausible illustrations, rather than on systematic evidence. Furthermore, the issue of a reliable indicator of long-term outsourcing "success" has not been resolved. As a consequence, despite widespread agreement about certain propositions (such as "multiple vendor" or selective outsourcing is more successful), these propositions are rarely tested. Consequently, there is no generally agreed "theory of outsourcing" grounded in a body of strong, disconfirmatory research. Instead, the discipline relies largely on theoretical propositions taken from exploratory case studies, or from theories coming from cognate disciplines (such as economics or marketing).

The most widely cited body of theory for explaining outsourcing "success" is drawn from *transaction cost economics* (TCE). This theory sees the decision to outsource in terms of the relative cost of alternative strategies. TCE's contribution (cf. Williamson 1979, 1981) was to recognize that market-based cost savings depend on two forms of costs: *production costs* (the costs of actually delivering the IT services) and market-related *transaction costs* (the additional costs associated with finding, negotiating with, and managing the work of a vendor). Another form of transaction cost is the "switching cost" incurred if arrangement proves unsatisfactory. However, because switching costs are potential rather than actual, they are sometimes left out of discussions of outsourcing transaction costs.

TCE predicts that production costs will usually be reduced by outsourcing because of market forces (provided there are a sufficient number of vendors competing in the marketplace). However, it also predicts that transaction costs will usually rise with outsourcing, sometimes substantially (Ang & Straub 1998). "Cost savings" will only result if the decreased production costs are not outweighed by the purchaser's additional transaction costs, and if economies of scale or scope are passed onto the purchaser by the vendor.

While TCE sheds light on the economic aspects of outsourcing, another theory illuminates judgments made by senior decision makers about the success of an outsourcing arrangement. *Services marketing theory* is concerned with the notions of service quality, customer value and customer satisfaction, and their relationship with repeat purchase. An important proposition, known as the "disconfirmation hypothesis" (Oliver 1980), is concerned with how services (such as outsourcing) are judged by organizational decision makers. According to this theory, a decision maker unconsciously compares the experiences of the services against his/her expectations. Where this is positive, perceptions of quality and value will be positive, but where expectations are not met, and a "gap" exists, service quality, satisfaction and value perceptions will be reduced (Cronin & Taylor 1994; Lee, Lee, & Yoo 2000; Spreng & MacKoy 1996). Whether actual measures of the expectation–experience gaps are appropriate is long debated (Cronin & Taylor) as there is evidence that this approach introduces psychometric problems. Simpler measures of overall performance are argued to be more reliable measures of the gap (Cronin & Taylor; Lee et al.). These still reflect the underlying disconfirmation hypothesis. While services marketing theory originated in the study of direct consumers, it has more recently been applied to business to business service arrangements.

Business-to-business service marketing theory predicts that where decision makers' expectations about the benefits of outsourcing are confirmed by actual experience, they are likely to be satisfied with the arrangement. They are also likely to experience a positive relationship with the vendor, to report that the arrangement is valuable (i.e., worth the costs), and as a consequence they will intend to repurchase the vendor's services at the end of the contract (Patterson & Spreng 1997). Conversely where expectations are not met (i.e., expectations are *disconfirmed*), decision makers are likely to experience dissatisfaction, report poor overall value, experience a worsening relationship with the vendor, and have an intention to quit the vendor, if this is possible (Oliver 1980; Patterson & Spreng 1997; Patterson, Johnson, & Spreng 1997). Services marketing theory also explains how it is possible for decision makers to have high levels of dissatisfaction, and a low "intention to continue" even though the firm does continue with the arrangement, because of an absence of other providers for example, or because of high switching costs.

Figure 1 is a model of the managerial evaluations and decision making associated with IT outsourcing. This illustrates that continuation of an IT outsourcing arrangement is largely dependent on whether, overall, organizational decision makers are satisfied with the arrangement and receive value for money. In the marketing literature,

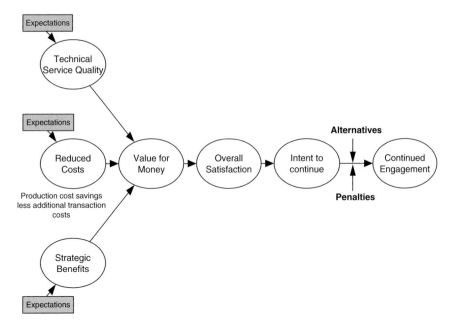

Fig. 1 A theoretical model of outsourcing success (adapted from Rouse 2002)

it is generally acknowledged that satisfaction is determined by the *net* perceptions of value, i.e., all benefits less all "sacrifices," or downsides (Patterson & Spreng 1997). Satisfaction in turn depends on the expected benefits of outsourcing being achieved, and these have been grouped into three clusters in Fig. 1.

The first benefit cluster is *technical service quality* which in service quality literature (Gronroos 1984, 1998) relates to the quality of the services the provider is contracted to supply, the "service" in the "fee for service" arrangement. The use of the term "technical" does not relate specifically to technology, rather to the particular services the purchaser expects to obtain from the vendor, which in the case of IT outsourcing includes delivery of systems, information, technology, and support. The service quality literature differentiates "technical" service quality from "functional" service quality, which is the way services are delivered. However, senior organizational decision makers, who may not have firsthand experience of service delivery.

In the IT outsourcing domain technical service quality would embrace both the technology and skills supplied by the vendor. This would also be reflected in the services and performance criteria described in the service level agreement that normally accompanies an outsourcing arrangement. This dimension is a more general conception than the "technology benefits" identified in earlier analysis of outsourcing benefits by Grover, Cheon, and Teng (1996).

The second benefit cluster (reduced costs) relates to cost savings compared with the costs of providing services in-house. This dimension reflects the major economic argument for outsourcing – that in the longer term the organization will reduce IT costs if it outsources its IT services (Domberger 1998). As a consequence, the firm can redirect financial resources to alternative uses, or alternatively, reap the savings as profits.

The third benefit cluster relates to the strategic benefits often sought from IT outsourcing. These include increased IT competence (or capability), increased business flexibility, and the ability to redirect managerial attention to focus on core business as a result of outsourcing IT services.

In Fig. 1, these benefits predict the overall evaluation of the relative costs and benefits of the strategy to the purchaser firm (value for money) and, consequently, overall IT outsourcing satisfaction and thus intention to continue. As with technical service quality, perceptions of reduced costs and strategic benefits would be compared with decision-makers' expectations. These expectations are often fuelled by pronouncements in the press and trade literature (Lacity & Hirschheim 1993), many of which come directly, or indirectly, from outsourcing vendors.

Figure 1 also illustrates that whether or not "intention to continue" actually leads to a firm continuing with that particular arrangement is influenced by two important elements: whether there are alternative suppliers to move to, and the existence of penalties (or switching costs) for moving. As will be discussed below, these can form powerful disincentives to move even when satisfaction and perceived value for money are quite low. In addition, since business to business purchasing rarely involves only one decision maker, the evaluations made by other decision makers within the firm would also influence the extent to which an informant's "intention to continue" was translated into actual changes in the sourcing arrangements for a particular firm.

The analytical framework shown in Fig. 1 will be used to structure the discussion of evidence about outsourcing success and, later, to propose reasons for a disconnect between evaluations of success (the left hand of the model) and the increasing adoption (and continuation) of IT outsourcing arrangements (right hand of the model).

3   Research Undertaken

This chapter is based on a body of interrelated research into IT outsourcing that has been conducted over the period 1997–2007 by Rouse, and Rouse and Corbitt:

- A longitudinal study into three substantial IT outsourcing arrangements carried out (and later abandoned) by the Australian Federal Government (Rouse and Corbitt 2003a)
- A quantitative survey of 240 medium to large IT outsourcing purchasing firms in the public and private sector. Aspects of this survey have been reported in Seddon, Cullen, Willcocks, Rouse, and Reilly (2001); Seddon, Cullen, and Willcocks (2007); Rouse, Corbitt, and Aubert (2001); Rouse (2002); and Rouse and Corbitt (2003b)

- A series of 16 focus groups with 51 informants from both large IT outsourcing purchasing organizations, and international IT outsourcing vendors (Rouse 2002; Rouse & Corbitt 2006)
- Four additional case studies including a study of a New Zealand based outsourcing vendor's response to Indian competition (discussed in Rouse and Watson 2005); two BPO outsourcing cases (reported in Rouse & Corbitt 2006); and an IT outsourcing case conducted in 2007
- An ongoing review of the IT outsourcing literature, supplemented by reanalysis of quantitative data published in the Information Systems literature between 1997 and 2007; and
- A meta analysis of published surveys of IT outsourcing outcomes (Rouse & Corbitt 2007)

4   Evidence for the Existence of an Outsourcing Paradox

While there is substantial industry data documenting the growth of IT outsourcing (coming from firms such as Dun and Bradstreet, IDC and Gartner), in the academic literature empirical evidence of the success or failure of IT outsourcing as a general strategy is surprisingly difficult to obtain. This is because the majority of those academic studies that have explored outsourcing success, and the firm behaviors that lead to it, have involved singular cases that may or may not be representative. In addition, many case studies have taken place early into an initial outsourcing arrangement, when firms are reporting their hopes and wishes for an arrangement, rather than what actually resulted.

Outsourcing as a business strategy typically lasts for years, if not decades, because once entered into, outsourcing is only terminated when services are rein-sourced or discontinued. Instead, typically, the nature of particular outsourcing arrangements will change over time as contracts evolve, and, sometimes, purchasers move from vendor to vendor seeking better outcomes. According to Lacity and Hirschheim (1993) purchaser experiences in the early years (including cost savings observed) are not necessarily continued into the later years of an arrangement, when vendors often seek to recoup profits lost in the earlier period, and when purchasers are substantially more dependent on the vendor than earlier. Despite the fact that initial "honeymoon" reports by purchasers may not reflect longer term outcomes, there have been few longitudinal cases. Only a handful of the reported case studies have been revisited by researchers, though where they have (Kodak, Xerox, and BP Exploration are examples) later studies have often revealed greater complexity, and far less positive outcomes, than the earlier optimistic descriptions of these cases (Kern & Willcocks 2001; Strassman 2000).

The case studies that have been revisited suggest that negative outcomes occur relatively frequently. Lacity and Willcocks (1998, p. 372) reported that of 41 outsourcing cases they had studied several years earlier, 9 (22%) did not achieve expected cost savings. In a further 10 (24%) of their cases the firms could not determine cost outcomes (p. 368)[1], leaving only 21 (51%) cases where expected cost savings were achieved. In a later nonrandom survey, Lacity and Willcocks (2001) reported that only 53% of respondents obtained savings, with only 31% reporting "significant" savings. Saunders and Gebelt (1997) reported that only 13 (38%) of the cases they studied produced cost savings, the other cases either could (or would) not report savings, or failed to obtain savings. In another longitudinal study, Aubert et al. (1999) reported that 49% of their cases reported costs increased with outsourcing over time.

When cost outcomes are considered in single point case study research, the reported outcomes are in some ways suspect. This is because most case study accounts of savings are based on extrapolations made when the contract was begun, rather than after-the-fact measurements – as few organizations conduct formal audits of actual savings. This issue can be overcome by large scale surveys, where it can be expected that the pool of response will, as a group, sample firms at various stages in the outsourcing lifecycle. However, there has been limited generalizable survey research into outsourcing outcomes (Dibbern et al. 2004). Most samples have been unrepresentative, or too small (less than 100 responses) to produce reliable estimates of success rates. The majority have used "costs saved" as the measure of success (labelled "reduced costs" in Fig. 1). However, surveys using cost as a success measure have generally failed to control for changes in the quantity or quality of services, and few have considered transaction costs and switching costs.

Even when production cost savings alone are considered, there are mixed findings about outsourcing success. The Australian Industry Commission (1996) reviewed 203 international studies of government outsourcing and concluded that the extent of savings varied widely, and that there was evidence of cost increases in a number of cases. When reviewing quantitative studies of government outsourcing using statistical meta-analysis, Hodge (2000) established that some types of services (generally simple services) achieved much better production cost savings than others. In the areas of garbage collection, cleaning and maintenance services, he found evidence for substantial production cost savings (of between 19 and 30%). However, Hodge found limited research into the cost outcomes for complex services (like IT), and in the few he found to analyse, cost estimates ranged from an 8% saving to a 24% increase. This contrasts with anecdotal accounts of 20–30% savings quoted by outsourcing proponents.

In another study of 7,500 government outsourcing contracts published by CTC (1999), Domberger, a strong proponent of outsourcing, found similar outcomes, reporting an average increase in production costs of 8.6% when IT services were outsourced. Seddon et al. (2001) reporting on a survey of 235 public and private sector firms found that only 7% reported substantial cost savings, and only a minority (42%) reported any cost savings at all.

Rouse and Corbitt (2007) initially attempted a statistical meta analysis of cost savings from IT services outsourcing, but had to abandon the attempt after concluding

---

[1] The authors studied 46 outsourcing cases, but for 5 of these it was too early to determine cost outcomes (p. 368).

that virtually no appropriate data had been gathered despite 15 years of academic study. Their analysis of 13 surveys of IT outsourcing success conducted since 1994 revealed that "none of the surveys [that reported cost outcomes] explicitly asked purchasers to report both production savings and transaction cost" (p. 6). As a consequence, the little evidence gathered by academics about outsourcing cost outcomes is based largely on opinions about the level of *production cost savings* expected to be made. Rouse and Corbitt also identified that, with the exception of the analyses done on the Seddon et al. data (Rouse 2002), there had been no statistical reports of the outcomes of other facets of outsourcing success included in Fig. 1 – technical service quality, strategic benefits, value for money, or satisfaction. In part this may be because statistical studies that have measured nonfinancial outcomes have largely focused on the relationship between outsourcing benefits and other predictors or outcomes, and so have not reported the level of achievement of the benefits sought.

On the basis of their meta analysis, Rouse and Corbitt (2007) concluded that the evidence for the general "success" of IT outsourcing arrangements is, at best, equivocal. What little statistical evidence exists fails to confirm that substantial production cost savings are widely experienced, and suggests that at best, production cost savings are likely to be low (less than around 12% of the contract cost, before transaction and management costs are considered). Unexpected cost increases, on the other hand, occur often (Seddon et al. 2001). The proposition that external sourcing leads to *net economic benefits* (once transaction costs are included) cannot be tested with the existing relatively-poor evidence base. However, since it appears that even production cost savings of any substance are uncommon, net savings are unlikely.

Rouse and Corbitt's analysis highlights another aspect of the "IT outsour-cing paradox." As outsourcing of IT has been widely adopted and is extensively studied, this raises the question – why has the discipline been unable to confirm that the theoretical benefits are commonly experienced? In part, this is because few academics have studied this aspect of outsourcing. While there are obvious difficulties associated with studying experiences across a large number of firms, these are not insurmountable, and a mature discipline should be seeking to confirm as well as posit theory. Yet many academic studies into outsourcing ignore this issue, beginning their discussion of outsourcing with a statement that outsourcing typically leads to a range of benefits. While it is certain that benefits have *sometimes* been obtained by *some* firms, the evidence that such benefits are "typical," and are not offset by other negative aspects of outsour-cing is not yet available.

5   Explanations for the IT Outsourcing Paradox

In the rest of this chapter circumstances that might contribute to this "outsourcing paradox" are described, drawn largely from the qualitative research conducted by Rouse and Rouse and Corbitt (cited above).

5.1   The Business Case for Outsourcing is Generally Poorly Developed

Based on the notion of expectations-actual gap discussed above, one likely reason that purchasers might be dissatisfied with their IT outsourcing arrangements is that their original business case is poorly developed, and over-optimistic. Rouse and Corbitt (2003a) reported on the audit of three large government outsourcing arrangements. In these, the Australian Auditor General reported substantial flaws in the business cases that determined that outsourcing should be adopted, despite purchasers' reliance on advice from several leading international outsourcing consultancies. According to the audit, flaws in accounting for the economic life of equipment, and in classifying the level of risk retained by the purchasers meant that the projected savings on which the decision was made would only eventuate in one of the three arrangements. Even there, on the basis of an audit of savings in the first year of operation (when savings are likely to be highest) changes to business demands had reduced expected savings (calculated in the business case to be around 26%) by more than half. As a result of this finding, Rouse (2002) began scrutinizing what was included in the "business case" arguments that led to sourcing decisions in the firms she was studying.

Rouse's (2002) focus group informants revealed that in their business cases, few of the represented firms included initial transaction costs, or the switching costs they would incur unless they continued with the incumbent vendor. This meant that these outsourcing projects were substantially under-budgeted, providing a strong disincentive to change vendors, due to the considerable costs involved. Her case studies and focus groups also revealed that the more contracts and vendors that were involved (both of which increase with "selective" or "best of breed" outsourcing) the less likely was it that transaction costs would be taken into account in the original costing models, in part because it was difficult to account for and attribute these costs.

Rouse's informants also revealed that virtually no purchasing firms were including risk exposure costs in their business case models. Risk exposure costs are allowances for foreseeable risks that are calculated by multiplying the impact of the risk (i.e., the negative consequence) by the probability (Aubert, Patry, & Rivard 1998; Boehm 1991). For example, if there was a one in three chance that variations would be needed to meet business changes, at a potential cost of $2 million, the risk exposure for this is $666,000. Logically, this cost should be offset against potential benefits, but in practice this was not done. Rouse's and Rouse and Corbitt's research revealed that few cases explicitly planned for scenarios where the expected savings (usually expected to be around 15–20%) did not eventuate. Instead, it was implicitly assumed that the projected costs/benefits for the outsourcing case, as well as those for the internal "counterfactual" case, had 100% probability.

It is worth noting that as a group, the firms studied by Rouse and Corbitt were some of the largest and most successful firms operating in Australia, with access to substantial levels of expert international advice. Yet the focus groups and case studies echoed the findings made in the late 1990s by Ang and Straub (1998) that those who chose to outsource focused mainly on the projected production cost savings. Although firm analyses did make allowances for ongoing management costs, the business cases for the organizations studied by Rouse (2002) and Rouse and Corbitt (2003a) did not focus at all on other transaction costs, particularly initial market-exploration and contracting costs (which were substantial, in some cases millions of dollars) or on switching costs.

Considered as a whole, the business cases observed by Rouse (2002), while complex and adhering to good industry practice, still had substantial limitations, and led in most cases to considerable over-optimism about likely benefits, and about the effort (and costs) needed to ensure these benefits were realized. Rouse was struck by the extent to which, in general, vendor and purchaser firms were working hard to overcome these difficulties so as to make the arrangements work, but they were substantially handicapped by poor initial business cases, which predicted benefits (and lack of risks) that could never be obtained in real life. The contextual quantitative data gathered by Rouse and Corbitt (2003b) revealed that expected benefits (including financial, strategic and technological benefits) did not meet original expectations in *most* firms, and that this gap accounted for the high level of dissatisfaction expressed amongst both public and private sector firms involved in IT outsourcing (Rouse 2006).

5.2 Many Firms Fail to Recognize that Outsourcing Involves Trade-Offs

Another finding from Rouse, and Rouse and Corbitt's qualitative research was that many organizations failed to initially identify that outsourcing decisions usually involve substantial trade-offs. When these unexpected trade-offs were eventually recognized in purchasing firms, this contributed to high levels of dissatisfaction. Few of the firms studied in either their case studies or the focus groups were particularly inefficient in their use of IT, as most were medium to large, successful, well-established firms that had, before outsourcing, access to high levels of IT skills. As a result of their generally high levels of efficiency, their IT outsourcing did not reap the savings observed in some of the earlier ITO case studies (eg those studied by Lacity and Hirschheim 1995). As those authors highlighted, outsourcing savings were in reality not the result of outsourcing per se, but of improved IT management strategies (such as rationalizing of data centres, or reductions in end-user demand due to more tightly controlled access to services). It is generally only very inefficient firms (like some described in Lacity and Hirschheim 1993) that are not confronted with outsourcing trade-offs (Maital 1994).

As a group, the purchaser firms studied by Rouse (2002) did not expect, and so did not think through, likely trade offs. They did not appreciate the dynamic nature of their business, and so expectations about the level of major business changes (and consequent changes that would need to take place in their IT delivery) were inaccurate. This was the case even for changes that would occur within 12–36 months of entering into their outsourcing arrangements. The business changes they were confronted with had IT implications that went beyond the level of flexibility allowed within the contracts, which catered for variations in service demand only within a relatively narrow range. As a consequence of business-driven changes, large-scale changes in the contracted services were required, triggering major variations at a time when the vendor was in a position to charge substantial fees (given the absence of alternatives to the purchaser). In effect while in the longer term (provided a firm had budgeted for substantial switching costs) outsourcing might lead to greater business flexibility, in the shorter term business flexibility was obtained by the purchaser firms only at a significant increase in IT charges.

Most purchaser informants studied by Rouse and Corbitt also underestimated the idiosyncratic nature of their organization's requirements, and were generally initially surprised to find that "industry best practice" provided a service that was less customized to their requirements than they needed. Studied purchaser firms as a general rule had overestimated their ability to rely on industry-standard "vanilla" services because they did not recognize that what they perceived as "vanilla" (within what, it eventually became clear, was a relatively sophisticated and demanding subcommunity of firms) was substantially different from the "vanilla" services other customers required of these vendors. These firms thus failed to recognize how much of their unique business requirements would have to be traded off to obtain cost savings.

On the basis of her studies, Rouse (2002) observed that "trade-off-less" outsourcing, while frequently implied by vendors and proponents of outsourcing, almost never occurs outside those firms that were in such major financial trouble (eg Xerox, Kodak); without an internal capability (such as new business start-ups) or so poorly managed (some of Lacity and Hirschheim's cases) that they had no choice *but* to outsource.

5.3   Firms Don't Think Through What Happens After Outsourcing is Entered Into

One of the most striking issues observed by Rouse and Corbitt was that few firms believed at the time of contracting that their outsourcing arrangements would fall apart, or that their vendor might go out of business, be taken over, or in other ways change substantially. This belief occurred despite trade reports suggesting that firms are forced to renegotiate contracts, and to change vendors, frequently (eg Bernard 2005; Ozanne 2000). Because of this belief many of the cases studied tended to treat their outsourcing arrangement as occurring in perpetuity, without planning for (and costing) any changeover to an alternative vendor, or back in-house. When they discovered that this expectation was not met, their levels of dissatisfaction increased substantially.

While the more sophisticated purchasing firms studied *had* included terms in their contract related to vendor responsibilities during changeover to an alternative vendor, several did not. And at a meeting of one of the more sophisticated firms studied for her thesis (2002) – GOVAFF – senior management revealed to Rouse that although they had included detailed contract clauses related to changeover, it would still be possible for an uncooperative "ousted" vendor to extend the changeover process (and so increase switching costs) substantially. Like TRANSPORT1, GOVAFF did decide to break its initial contract apart, contracting with a number of vendors, though the net costs (incorporating production cost savings plus additional transaction costs) were likely to increase as a result of this strategy.

As with other firms studied by Rouse, the switching costs that would be incurred if GOVAFF's arrangement was moved to an alternative vendor were not included in the original "business case" (or financial argument) for outsourcing. Had the foreseeable risk associated with GOVAFF's potential switching costs been incorporated into the business case, it is likely that the savings made by the firm (approximately 12% in the first year of operation) would have been compromised by these switching costs, and by the additional transaction costs incurred when the contract was broken up amongst multiple vendors. Including likely switching costs in the outsourcing business case will tend to make the "don't outsource" option more attractive, which is probably why they are left out of so many outsourcing business cases. Yet the unavailability of budgeted funds for switching costs can force purchasing firm to continue for long periods with an unsatisfactory arrangement, and at a macro level, contribute to the IT outsourcing paradox.

5.4 Assessing Firm and Vendor Performance is Difficult in Practice

Another finding obtained by Rouse and Corbitt from their qualitative studies was that few organizations formally revisited the analyses and projections made when they made the decision to outsource, and to choose their vendor. This helps fuel unrealistic positive expectations in the wider community, and so contributes on a macro scale to over-optimistic beliefs about the likelihood and magnitude of benefits from outsourcing. These in turn contribute to high ":expectations-actual" gaps, and hence dissatisfaction.

The publicly audited cases these authors reported in Rouse and Corbitt (2003a) were unusual because projections were reviewed and reevaluated, yet the cost of this audit was over $AU500,000. Such sums act to deter firms from formally reviewing their outsourcing experiences. Few other follow-up studies have appeared in the academic literature, though one exception is that by Kern and Blois (2002) of the BP Exploration case, which was initially promoted with such a fanfare in the Harvard Business Review. It too proved far less successful when reviewed several years into the arrangement.

Rouse's (2002) discussions with focus group and case study informants revealed that there are many forces encouraging firms not to question their initial decision, including political forces – the original decision might be seen as inadequate and call into question the judgements of decision-makers – and practical – any announcement that the expectations weren't actually met might have stock market repercussions. Furthermore, the financial and managerial costs of a review of the decision would be substantial. Since the lead times to change vendors are so long (usually several years) few firms studied by Rouse had any other options but continuing with their arrangements in the medium to long term, so any formal review would serve only to add tension to the existing arrangement with little additional benefit. The lack of formal reviews (or publication of the findings of internal reviews) serves to hide from decision makers how often outsourcing arrangements fail to meet initial optimistic expectations.

There are also problems with using benchmarking to determine whether outsourcing arrangements are indeed providing expected benefits. One perhaps surprising finding (reported in Rouse 2005) was that although benchmarking was associated with more positive outcomes when tested statistically, the practical difficulties and costs of benchmarking are substantial, while the outcomes are not particularly helpful in determining if the arrangement is still achieving expectations. Rouse (2002) was given the opportunity to study in detail a benchmarking exercise conducted for one large outsourcing contract over a period of 8 months by a leading international benchmarking specialist firm. The formal benchmarks supplied by the specialist indicated that the vendor (who had commissioned the benchmarking exercise to meet contractual requirements) was highly efficient compared to firms operating overseas. Yet the purchaser had evidence from other sources that in the local market the vendor was charging about 50% above the "going rate" for labor. The major source of the benchmarked savings was not the vendor's efficiency, but the relative cheapness of IT labor in Australia at that time, which was not necessarily reflected in currency comparisons.

An unexpected consequence of the practical difficulties of determining what the outcomes of outsourcing IT are is that much of our discipline's "common wisdom" is based on projections made by decision makers about what they initially *thought* (and hoped) would happen, rather than an objective after-the-fact evaluation of what did happen. The majority of academic outsourcing cases where outcomes were assessed (such as those reported by Lacity and Willcocks in 1998) were conducted relatively early in the outsourcing arrangements. For Lacity and Willcocks' cases, the outcomes were largely unrevised by the authors when compared with reports in Lacity's original thesis (1992) and the authors' earlier 1995 paper (Lacity, Willcocks, & Feeny 1995), probably reflecting the informants' inability (or unwillingness) to revisit outcomes at a later date. In several other cases reported in the academic literature (including the South Australian Government, the Commonwealth Bank, The UK Inland Revenue, and BP Exploration) the initial arrangement discussed in early academic case studies was later radically changed (usually because of substantial problems) meaning that few opportunities for revisiting outcomes against the original expectations were possible (Kern & Willcocks 2001; Lacity & Willcocks 2001).

5.5 Many IT Outsourcing Decisions are in Practice Difficult to Reverse (Hysteresis Effects)

One major contribution to the "IT outsourcing paradox" is the lag between recognizing an expectations-actual gap and being able to discontinue the unsatisfactory outsourcing arrangement. Furthermore, although outsourcing is presented in the trade literature as a reversible decision, case studies and focus groups conducted by the author show that, for other than simple, commodity-like IT outsourcing arrangements, the possibility of being "locked into" an unsatisfactory relationship is surprisingly high. In several cases studied by Rouse and Rouse and Corbitt, vendor informants stated that the original outsourcing arrangement had been "underbid" (i.e., the vendor had deliberately quoted a price that did not permit them sufficient profit), in order to gain a toehold in that market. When expected growth in contracts did not eventuate, some of these vendors withdrew from the local market leaving few, or no, alternative bidders. Several purchasing firms Rouse followed up over the period 2002–2007, had problems attracting alternative bidders (other than the incumbent) when their contract was finally reoffered for tender.

In one of these, TRANSPORT1, the author observed first-hand the firm's attempts to benchmark the performance of its vendor, and the subsequent discovery that it was being charged inflated prices (compared to local market rates). However, in this case senior management were so unwilling to go through the disruption and expense they had incurred when the IT outsourcing arrangement was initially entered into that they deferred for more than 3 years the retendering process. This was despite knowing their vendor's charges were excessive. Eventually the single-vendor outsourcing arrangement was split into a number of smaller contracts with a range of different providers. While a few residual services remained with the incumbent, and other services (desktop and Helpdesk) were reinsourced, most services were shared amongst three other bidders. In effect this meant the purchasing firm had to take back the role of "prime contractor" which increased transaction costs substantially, particularly the costs of negotiating and coordinating when problems fell "between providers." An even more problematic outcome occurred with another of the cases studied by Rouse (2002) GOVAFF2. This long-standing contract was relet in 2006, but the incumbent vendor was the only bidder. In both cases the public pronouncements were highly positive, describing how the purchasers had adopted "higher quality" "niche" (i.e., selective) outsourcing (TRANSPORT1) or had obtained "very competitive" terms (GOVAFF2). But according to informants, beneath these pronouncements the firms involved were confronted with substantially higher costs overall than had they not decided to outsource in the first place.

As an illustration of the magnitude of costs involved, in another case studied later by the author (TELCOM2) an informant reported that on becoming aware that their services were now charged at substantially higher than market rates the firm explored the possibility of reinsourcing. The feasibility study revealed that the likely once-off cost to reinsource would be in the realm of $AU3.7 million, however the firm expected to save $4.8 million pa of the $9.5 million pa contract by bringing desktop and helpdesk services back in-house. This $3.7 cost would be incurred on top of the ongoing outsourcing charges for many months, as the contract would need to be continued until the new internal IT-delivery group was reestablished. This organization was in a position to pay this high reinsourcing premium, but many firms are not. In the case of GOVAFF2, the scope of the activities that had been outsourced, and the length of period the outsourcing arrangements had lasted (14 years) meant that the option of reinsourcing was not practically possible, as they had lost the capabilities to manage a reinsourced function.

In all three cases cited above, where purchasers perceived they were "locked into" their vendor arrangements, their privately expressed levels of satisfaction were low, even though this is quite at odds with the picture presented to the public through newspaper and vendor announcements.

6 Conclusions

This chapter has highlighted that while according to a range of trade and economic reports outsourcing of IT has continued to grow, the evidence that IT outsourcing's attractive promise is experienced by the majority of purchasers is relatively scarce. The implications for decision makers, and for academics studying outsourcing is that it cannot be assumed that just because a firm is still engaged with a vendor, the arrangement is satisfactory. According to the survey conducted by Rouse and Corbitt (2003b) almost two thirds of firms were either dissatisfied or equivocal about the benefits they receive from outsourcing, while only a minority were satisfied with the value for money they obtained from their arrangement. According to Lacity and Hirschheim (1993), this situation is likely to increase over time, so the longer firms are involved in an arrangement the less likely that the arrangement will be experienced as satisfactory. Lee and Kim (1999) also observed this phenomenon when they statistically tested the relationship between contract length and outsourcing partnership quality – they had expected instead that longer serving arrangements would lead to more positive "partnership" indicators. The so-called "hysteresis effect," where firms find it much easier to get into the outsourced state than to reverse this by reinsourcing (Rouse & Corbitt 2006) is also likely to lead to more examples of continuing outsourcing without concomitant levels of satisfaction.

This situation has implications for both purchasers and vendors. From the vendors' point of view, the danger is that without high levels of satisfaction with the arrangement, purchasers will churn contracts within a pool of vendors. This increases both vendor and purchaser transaction costs, and reduces the longer term benefits that come from an effective vendor–client relationship. Using the model presented in Fig. 1, a key leverage point vendors should attempt to address is the level of unmeetable expectations they create, particularly expectations that outsourcing does not need to involve substantial trade-offs. Vendors can be seen attempting this in trade literature suggests that outsourcing should not be entered into just to "save money" but rather to obtain strategic and technology benefits, or to free up resources so that firms can concentrate on their core business. Unfortunately, at this stage the evidence that such benefits are themselves obtained without trade-offs is slim, while the evidence that we do have about these benefits is that they, like cost savings, are experienced only by a minority (Rouse & Corbitt 2003b). Perhaps it is time for vendors to "come clean" by acknowledging that making outsourcing work effectively is probably much harder, and more expensive, than most purchasers expect.

Another implication of the findings presented here is that purchasers need to substantially improve the analyses they do before entering into outsourcing arrangements, particularly the financial "business case" that supports (or does not) the externally sourced option. By doing so, decision makers should go into an IT outsourcing arrangement with more realistic expectations, and so be less susceptible to high levels of disconfirmation (and a consequent reduction in satisfaction) when actual experiences do not meet expectations. If purchasers' expectations are more realistic, satisfaction levels should rise above those reported in academic and trade reports, and the "outsourcing paradox" phenomenon of high levels if nonsatisfaction (i.e., dissatisfaction or equivocality) occurring at the same time as high levels of outsourcing growth, may be ameliorated.

The evidence presented in this chapter also has some salutary lessons for those contemplating new variants of outsourcing that are now being popularized in the trade press, including business process outsourcing (BPO); "software as a service" (or "application service provider") outsourcing, and offshore outsourcing. Each of these variants is following the pattern established with the growth of IT outsourcing in the late 1980s and early 1990s. The benefits are being "talked up" by vendors and consultants, and these phenomena are now going through what Gartner Consulting has described as the "hype" phase of their "Speed of Hype:" model (Gartner Group 1999). While undoubtedly, like IT outsourcing, these strategies have potential benefits, they too are likely to have unacknowledged trade-offs, and risks, and many decisions to adopt these forms of outsourcing will probably be based on poorly-thought-through business cases. Decision makers who are contemplating these new forms of outsourcing would do well to check whether the explanatory factors discussed above might not apply in their case too.

References

Ang S., & Straub, D. W. (1998). Production and transaction economies and IS outsourcing: a study of the US banking industry. *MIS Quarterly, 22*(4), 535–552.

Aubert, B, Patry, M, & Rivard, S. (1998). Assessing the risk of IT outsourcing. 31st Annual Hawaii International Conference on Systems Sciences (HICSS), Big Island of Hawaii, HI, Jan 6–9, pp. 685–692.

Aubert, B., Patry, M., & Rivard, S. (1999). L'impartation des services informatique au Canada: Une comparaison 1993–1997 (Outsourcing of IT services in Canada: a Comparison 1993 – 1997). In M. Poitevin (Ed.), *Impartition: Fondements et analyses (Outsourcing: Foundations and Analyses)* (pp. 202–220). Montreal, Canada: University of Laval Press.

Bernard, A. (2005). *Renegotiating IT outsourcing contracts*. CIO Update. www.cioupdate.com/reserach/article.php/3501026, (Accessed 13 April 2006).

Boehm, B. (1991). Software risk management: principles and practices. *IEEE Software, (Jan)*, 32–41.

Cronin, J. J. & Taylor, S. A. (1994). SERVPERF versus SERVQUAL: reconciling performance-based and perceptions-minus-expectations measurement of service quality. *Journal of Marketing, 58*, 125–131.

CTC (1999). *Government outsourcing: what has been learnt?* Sydney, Australia: CTC Consultants.

Dibbern J., Goles, T., Hirschheim, R. & Jayatilaka, B. (2004). Information systems outsourcing: a survey and analysis of the literature. *The DATA BASE for Advances in Information Systems, 35*(4), 6–102.

Domberger, S. (1998). *The contracting organization: a strategic guide to outsourcing*. Oxford, UK: Oxford University Press.

Gartner Group (1999). *When to leap on the Hype cycle*. Decision Framework DF-08–6751, 1999. www3.gartner.com. (Accessed 12 Jan 2003).

Gartner Group (2002). *Outsourcing information technology*. www.gartner.com (Accessed 13 Oct 2002).

Gronroos C. (1984). A service quality model and its marketing implications. *European Journal of Marketing, 18*, 36–44.

Gronroos C. (1998). Marketing services: the case of the missing product. *Journal of Business and Industrial Marketing, 13 (4–5)*, 322–338.

Grover, V., Cheon, M. J., & Teng, J. T. C. (1996). The effect of service quality and partnership on the outsourcing of information systems functions. *Journal of Management Information Systems, 12*(4), 89–116.

Hodge, G. A. (2000). *Privatization: an international review of performance*. Boulder, Colorado: Westview.

Kern, T., & Blois, K. (2002). Norm development in outsourcing relationships. *Journal of Information Technology, 17*(1), 33–42

Kern T., & Willcocks, L. P. (2001). The relationship advantage: information technologies, management and sourcing. Oxford: Oxford University Press.

Lacity, M. C. (1992). An interpretive investigation of the information systems outsourcing phenomenon. Unpublished doctoral dissertation, University of Houston, Texas, USA.

Lacity, M. C., & Hirschheim, R. (1993). Information systems outsourcing: myths, metaphors and realities. Chichester, England: Wiley.

Lacity, M. C., & Hirschheim, R. (1995). Beyond the information systems outsourcing bandwagon: the insourcing response. New York: Wiley.

Lacity, M. C., & Willcocks, L. P. (1998). An empirical investigation of information technology sourcing practices: lessons from experience. *MIS Quarterly, 22*(3), 363–408.

Lacity, M. C., &Willcocks, L. P. (2001). *Global information technology outsourcing: in search of business advantage*. New York: Jossey-Bass.

Lacity, M. C., Willcocks, L. P., & Feeny, D. F. (1995). Information technology outsourcing: maximising flexibility and control. *Harvard Business Review, (May-June)*, 84–93.

Lee, J.-N., & Kim, Y.-M. (1999). Effect of partnership quality on IS outsourcing success: conceptual framework and empirical validation. *Journal of Management Information Systems 15*(4), 29–61.

Lee, H., Lee, Y., & Yoo, D. (2000). The determinants of perceived service quality and its relationship with satisfaction. *Journal of Services Marketing, 14*(3), 217–231

Maital, S. (1994). *Executive economics*. New York: Free Press.

Oliver, R. L. (1980). A cognitive model of the antecedents and consequences of satisfaction decisions. *Journal of Marketing Research, 17*, 460–469.

Ozanne, M. R. (2000). *Barometer of global outsourcing: the millennium outlook*. Dun and Bradstreet Report, http://www.dnbcollections.com/outsourcing/bar1.htm Released February 29, 2000. (Accessed 12 March 2001).

Patterson, P. G., & Spreng, R. A. (1997). Modelling the relationship between perceived value, satisfaction and repurchase intentions in a business-to-business context: an empirical examination. *International Journal of Service Industry Management, 8*(5), 414–434.

Patterson, P. G., Johnson, L. W., & Spreng, R. A. (1997). Modeling the determinants of customer satisfaction for business-to-business professional services. *Journal of the Academy of Marketing Science, 25*(1), 4–17.

Rouse, A. C. (2002). *Information technology outsourcing revisited: success factors and risks.* Unpublished doctoral dissertation. University of Melbourne, Victoria, Australia.

Rouse, A. C. (2005). The role of benchmarking and service level agreement (SLA) practices in IT outsourcing success. *Proceedings of 9th pacific asia conference on information systems (PACIS)*, Bangkok, Thailand, July 7–10.

Rouse, A. C., & Corbitt, B. J. (2003a). The Australian government's abandoned infrastructure outsourcing program: what can be learned? *Australian Journal of Information Systems, 10*(2), 81–90.

Rouse, A. C., & Corbitt, B. J. (2003b). Revisiting IT outsourcing risks: analysis of a survey of Australia's top 1000 organizations. *Proceedings of 14th Australasian Conference on Information Systems 2003, delivering IT and e-Business value in networked environments* (pp. 1–11), School of Management Information Systems, Edith Cowan University, Perth, Western Australia

Rouse, A. C., & Corbitt, B. J. (2006). Business process outsourcing. In R. Hirschheim, A. Heinzl & J. Dibbern (Eds.), *Information systems outsourcing: enduring themes, new perspectives and global challenges*, 2nd Edn. Berlin: Springer.

Rouse, A. C., & Corbitt, B. J. (2007).Understanding information systems outsourcing success and risks through the lens of cognitive biases. *Proceedings of the fifteenth European conference on information systems (ECIS)*, St Gallen, Switzerland, June 7–9.

Rouse, A. C., & Watson, D. J. (2005). Cyberfraud and identity theft. *Monash Business Review, 1*(2), 30–33.

Rouse, A. C., Corbitt, R., & Aubert, B. (2001). Perspectives on IT outsourcing success: covariance structure modeling of a survey of outsourcing in Australia. *Proceedings of the Ninth European Conference on Information Systems (ECIS)*, Bled, Slovenia, June 27–29.

Saunders, C., Gebelt, M., & Hu, Q. A. (1997). Achieving success in information systems outsourcing. *California Management Review, 39*(2), 63–79.

Seddon, P., Cullen, S., Willcocks, L. P., Rouse, A. C., & Reilly, C. (2001). *Report on information technology outsourcing practices in Australia, 2000.* Version 1, October. Melbourne: Department of Information Systems, University of Melbourne. (Available from Department).

Seddon, P., Cullen, S., & Willcocks, L. P. (2007). Does Domberger's theory of 'the contracting organization' explain why organizations outsource IT and the levels of satisfaction achieved? *European Journal of Information Systems, 16*, 237–253.

Spreng, R. A., & Mackoy, R. D. (1996). An empirical examination of a model of perceived service quality and satisfaction. *Journal of Retailing, 72*(2), 201–214.

Strassman, P. A. (2000). The xerox tragedy. *Computerworld*, 6 Nov.

Williamson, O. E. (1979). Transaction cost economics: the governance of contractual relationships. *Journal of Law and Economics, 22*, 233–261.

Williamson, O. E. (1981). The economics of organization: the transaction cost approach. *American Journal of Sociology, 87*, 548–577.

A Story of IT Outsourcing
from Early Experience to Maturity

Julie Fisher, Rudy Hirschheim, and Robert Jacobs

1   Introduction

Commenting on the continuing growth of IT outsourcing, King (2004) argues that "The sourcing issue is among the top five agenda items for IT executives, as the amount of such outsourcing grows, its impact on the economies of companies and nations increases and political controversy over the consequent jobs lost to offshore outsourcing heightens". By 2009, it is predicted that IT outsourcing expenditure will exceed $260 billion (Tan & Sia 2006).

For the purposes of this chapter we have adopted the definition of outsourcing and selective sourcing used by Hirschheim and Lacity (2006). IS outsourcing is where an organization outsources at least 80% of their budget to a third-party provider. Selective sourcing is where an organization uses third-party vendors for some of the IT functions but still retains a substantial IT department.

Over, at least the last 20 years, the outsourcing of IT services and functions as a business option has been relatively commonplace (McFarlan & Nolan 1995; Earl 1996; Lee, Huynh, Kwok, & Pi 2003). Outsourcing as a research interest has also been growing with numerous studies reported and papers written (Dibbern, Goles, Hirschheim, & Jayatilaka 2004). Gonzalez, Gasco, and Llopis (2006) note that the use of the term 'outsourcing' in published papers "can be traced back to the 1990s". Lee et al. (2003) suggest early research in the area focused on acquisition of IT commodities, with later research examining the motivation for outsourcing. More recently the results of outsourcing decisions has been a research focus (Lee et al.). Gonzalez et al. analysed outsourcing publications from 1988 to 2005, this included an analysis of topics. Reasons for outsourcing accounted for more than 13% of papers published and success factors accounted for almost 4% of published papers. This chapter presents a case study of one large corporation, Alpha, over a 9-year period. Alpha was the first large corporation in Australia to extensively outsource their IT function. We explore both the reasons for outsourcing and success factors from the perspective Alpha's experience and reflect on how the company matured in its approach to outsourcing over the period.

R. Hirschheim et al. (eds), *Information Systems Outsourcing,*
© Springer-Verlag Berlin Heidelberg 2009

2   Rationales for Outsourcing

The reasons why companies outsource their IT function are many and varied. As mentioned above, there has been significant research conducted on why companies take the decision to outsource. We have therefore limited the following discussion to key authors and significant papers published. We acknowledge that there are many other papers and authors worthy of consideration however we believe the following are representative of the main issues broadly discussed in the literature. The key reasons discussed in the literature therefore are:

1. Companies are looking for cost reduction and efficiencies in IT. "IS improvement" (DiRomualdo & Gurbaxani 1998) is one of the most reported reasons for outsourcing (McFarlan & Nolan 1995; Baldwin, Irani, & Love 2001). Smith and McKeen (2004) describe what they call "Outsourcing for operational efficiency". This involves outsourcing some of the more 'utility' functions of IT, with a clear objective of saving money through reductions in staff and other resources (Lacity & Hirschheim 1993).
2. The use of outsourcing to strategically improve business performance or "Business Impact", a term used by DiRomualdo and Gurbaxani (1998) to describe looking to the IT marketplace for state-of-the-art skills that are not currently available within the organization. "Its primary goal is deploying IT to significantly improve critical aspects of business performance". (DiRomualdo & Gurbaxani). "Outsourcing for strategic impact" is describe as using outsourcing for "whole business processes that are not considered business critical" (Smith & McKeen 2004). Enabling he company to focus on its core business.
3. Outsourcing for "Commercial exploitation". Smith and McKeen (2004) use the term "Outsourcing for tactical support". The aim is to increase the availability and numbers of IT staff "to achieve flexibility and responsiveness" (Smith & McKeen). The outsourcing organization keeps the mature systems running while the company embarks on the development of new systems using existing staff. It can also provide the organization with an opportunity to access new technology (Baldwin et al. 2001).
4. Outsourcing is sometimes adopted to get rid of a problem area. If companies cannot manage a particular function they may look to another organization to take over that function. McFarlan and Nolan (1995) describe this as "elimination of an internal irritant", suggesting that this is often due to tensions between IT management and the users. Jayatilaka's (2006) research supports this as well. Risk mitigation is included in this, where companies, for example, outsource potential risks associated with complex technology (Baldwin et al. 2001).
5. The 'Bandwagon effect', is where companies adopt outsourcing because it is seen as common practice so therefore must be good (Lacity & Hirschheim 1993; Jayatilaka 2006).

3 Outsourcing Success Factors

Factors that are important for an outsourcing arrangement to be successful are also reported in the literature but not as extensively as the reasons for outsourcing. Again we have elected to keep the discussion to those issues that could be regarded as those most frequently reported high-level factors contributing to successful outsourcing. These are:

1. Selecting carefully what is to be outsourced and what will be managed in-house. The term coined by Lacity, Willicocks, and Feeny (1996) to describe this was 'selective outsourcing'. They raised this issue as far back as 11 years ago and more recent research reported by Poppo and Lacity (2006) confirms that this continues to be an important success factor.

2. The length of the contract. Shorter contracts, it is suggested, are more likely to lead to successful outsourcing arrangements (Lacity et al. 1996; Smith & McKeen 2004). This is supported by Barthelemy and Geyer (2004) who argue from their research that long term contracts are a risk because they are hard to handle given changing technology and business needs. Research by Lee, Miranda, and Kim (2004) however did not support this, suggesting that longer contracts were more successful. This they argue is because there is improved financial predictability and initial setup costs are spread over the time of the contract.

3. The need for detailed contracts that are well thought out and have some level of flexibility (Lacity & Willcocks 2000; Beaumont & Costa 2002; Kern & Willicocks 2002). Research by Gellings and Wullenweber (2006) found an important link between the contract and outsourcing success particularly in relation to risk mitigation. The inclusion of clauses relating to the employment of appropriate IT technical expertise is important (DiRomualdo & Gurbaxani 1998) as is monitoring the contract to ensure quality of service and post contract management (Lacity & Willcocks 2000; Baldwin et al. 2001).

4. Both business and IT executives need to be involved in the outsourcing decision making process (Smith & McKeen 2004). Baldwin et al. (2001) suggest that this includes strong commitment from senior company executives for the outsourcing arrangements. In order to achieve "Business Impact", DiRomualdo and Gurbaxani (1998) argue that there must be an understanding of the link between the business and IT, recognizing that different skills are needed from each area. This is supported by research conducted by Lacity and Willcocks (2000); Poppo and Lacity (2006) also raise this as an issue.

5. Understanding and managing all the costs involved. This firstly involves being able to identify those outsourcing costs that are often hidden. Such costs are an issue particularly in relation to costs associated with managing the outsourcing contract, which are often not fully anticipated. (Kern & Willicocks 2002; Ho, Ang, & Straub 2003). Secondly, it involves ensuring the pricing structure is appropriate. (Lacity et al. 1996). It is important to "create a highly competitive vendor selection process" (DiRomualdo & Gurbaxani 1998) This is particularly

important where the outsourcing is a joint venture. "For these deals to succeed they must contain adequate incentives for each party to share costs and risks over the course of the relationship" (DiRomualdo & Gurbaxani).

6. The relationships that are developed between the business and the outsourcing company impact on outsourcing success (Baldwin et al. 2001; Kishore, Rao, Nam, Rajagopalan, & Chaudhury 2003; Poppo & Lacity 2006). The management of the internal relationships that are likely to change as a result of the decision to outsource are also an issue. (Ho et al. 2003) Ho et al suggest this is a problem both internally and externally, where previous subordinates become external contractors and the relationship changes but not necessarily in the mind of the business manager. Choudhury and Sabherwal (2003) argue the need for "client managers to pay adequate attention to the control of outsourced projects, right from the start." Their research found that where systems development was outsourced, it was important for the business to monitor progress of the outsourcing arrangements closely. Managing the relationships also extends to managing staff within the organization who may be resistant to the change to outsourcing (Lacity & Willcocks 2000).

7. Retention of essential skills and staff. There is an argument that organizations need to be careful to ensure that they do not outsource people who are key to the organization (Lacity & Willcocks 2000; Baldwin et al. 2001). Companies may outsource to get new IT skills, but if, in so doing, they give all their internal IT skills to the vendor, they are left with no-one internally to manage or plan for future IT. It can be a dire mistake for a company to assume an outsource vendor would take care of strategic IT planning, since this is a business responsibility.

Table 1 presents a summary of the key reasons for outsourcing and the most commonly reported outsourcing success factors reported in the literature.

Table 1 Summary of outsourcing decision-making and success factors

Rationales for outsourcing	
1. Cost reduction and efficiency	4. Divest the company of a difficult problem area
2. Improvements in business performance	
3. Commercial exploitation of outsource provider capability	5. Following the lead of others

Success factors	
1. Careful selection of functions to be outsourced	5. Understanding and management of costs
2. Length of the contract	6. Management of relationships both internal and external
3. Development of detailed contracts with some flexibility built in	
4. Involvement of senior business people and IT executives in the outsourcing decision	7. Skills to be retained and careful selection of people

4   IT Outsourcing Maturity

There is limited discussion in the literature relating to outsourcing maturity. Gottschalk and Solli-Saether (2006) propose a maturity model detailing three stages: the Cost stage, where the organization is concerned with the cost and the economic benefit outsourcing might bring; the Resource Stage, where the organization looks for access to alternative resources from vendors and resources for innovation; and the final stage, the Partnership Stage, where alliances are built and there are economic exchanges among partners. Gottschalk and Solli-Saether conclude that "the stages of growth are sequential in nature, occur as a hierarchical progression that is not easily reversed, and involve a broad range of organizational activities and structures".

Five stages of IT outsourcing maturity are identified by Olayele and Wabash (2004). In the first stage the organization makes a decision not to outsource. Stage two sees an ad hoc approach to outsourcing with cost as the major driver. In stage three, management makes a decision to more seriously pursue outsourcing as an option. In the fourth stage the company matures in its approach to outsourcing and management roles and responsibilities are identified and developed. In the final stage the organization matures in its outsourcing arrangements with all the partners involved successfully working together.

Carmel and Agarwal (2002) identify four stages for offshore IT sourcing. In the first stage the organization engages in domestic outsourcing arrangements, followed in the second stage by some limited offshore outsourcing. In the third stage more work is sent offshore and finally in the fourth stage, the organization engages offshore partners for core IT work.

Outsourcing is today a standard business practice, most large Australian companies outsource at least some of their IT function. Australian research found 57% of companies outsourced some work functions (Beaumont & Costa 2002), with larger organizations more likely to engage in outsourcing than smaller firms. In a later paper based on the same research Beaumont and Sohal (2004) report that 65% of Australian organizations surveyed believe outsourcing will become increasingly important to their business operations. This chapter describes the outsourcing experience of one large corporation – which we will call Alpha – over a 9-year period beginning in 1997 through to 2006.

5   Research Method and Data Analysis

This chapter presents an in-depth interpretive case study describing the IT and outsourcing arrangements of a large Australian telecommunications company, Alpha. This is consistent with the methodological research approach frequently used in outsourcing research. An analysis of the literature by (Gonzalez et al. 2006) found that case studies are the second most frequently used method to gather data, the first being field studies. Recent outsourcing case studies reported in some of the top journals and books include: research conducted by Baldwin et al. (2001) which investigated the outsourcing arrangements in a large bank in the UK; Kishore et al. (2003) present four case studies in their paper; Hirschheim and Lacity (2000) use case studies to describe insourcing archetypes; research by Oshri, Kotlarsky, and Willcocks (2007) describes a single case study involving Tata; Choudhury and Sabherwal (2003) examine outsourced software development projects involving five case studies.

Walsham (1995) notes that: "It can be argued that there is a need for much more work from an interpretive stance in the future, since human interpretations concerning computer-based information systems are of central importance to the practice of IS, and thus to the investigations carried out by IS researchers". Given the importance of the field of outsourcing and the fact that the very nature of the area is people focused, interpretive research is therefore appropriate. Moreover, according to Walsham, creating a theoretical framework of previous research is important, Table 1 presents the theoretical framework used here. It provided the lens to explore how Alpha as a large organization, approached outsourcing from a decision making perspective and the extent to which the identified success factors were relevant in this case.

The selection of Alpha for the case study was based on the following:

- Alpha at the time was one of Australia's largest corporations
- Alpha was amongst the first large Australian companies to extensively outsource their IT function
- Data for the period 1997 – 2006 was available from key individuals in Alpha.

5.1   Data Collection and Analysis

Data for this case study was gathered over time via interviews with a number of senior people within Alpha who were responsible for the decisions and management of the outsourcing arrangements. The interviews did not include lower-level managers or employees as the focus was on the high level company decision making. One of the authors was the National Sourcing Manager for Alpha and a member of the commercial group responsible for managing the relationships with the contract companies. His involvement began in 1997, and from 2000 to 2003 he played a major role. Walsham (2006) argues that this is an appropriate approach but one to be undertaken with caution as it can result in compromises. Specifically the organization does not want to be portrayed negatively. The dilemma for the researcher is therefore how to remain truthful in such a situation. Walsham however sees this as more shades of grey rather than black and white and makes the comment more as a caution for researchers. In our case the National Sourcing Manager sought independent comment on the material. The case study material was reviewed by and augmented through interviews with other Alpha managers who were involved in the outsourcing project during this period. These included: the Director of Corporate Services; the contract manager responsible for the outsource service provider, Delta corporation; and, the contract negotiator for other outsource service providers, Sigma and Epsilon. Further, the responsible relationship manager within Sigma also reviewed the case study material and provided what could be considered an independent review of the reported material. The key data is derived from the National Sourcing Manager's experience from 2000 to 2003. Other interviewees however, from Alpha, provided material on the early outsourcing activity. Further interviews with key people involved, were also conducted in 2005 and 2006. This resulted in a 9 year historical/interpretive case study of Alpha's experience with outsourcing.

Walsham (1995) identifies three issues critical for interpretive case studies. One is the researcher's role; for this case, one researcher was a participant observer. As noted by Walsham this allowed the researchers an inside view of the target organization. However, the risk to the research is a biased view. To address this, interviews were conducted with a range of other important players, described above, both within Alpha and the vendor organizations. Summary documents were circulated to people in all organizations for feedback.

The data analysis was guided by the key issues derived from the literature identified in Table 1; the rationale for outsourcing and factors contributing to success. Additionally, there are three distinct phases of outsourcing maturity identified in this case study. Each phrase is described in terms of how Alpha reflected on, and revised their outsourcing arrangements and thus illustrates how the company's outsourcing approach has matured over the period.

6 Background of Alpha Corporation – Government Monopoly to Private Company

Alpha is a large telecommunications corporation with a dominant market share and with 80 years experience providing essential utility services. Once a government owned monopoly, Alpha was transformed from an engineering/technology driven department to a commercial corporation.

In this transition period, the internal service functions were reorganized and centralized, including accounting and training services, fleet management, engineering construction, warehousing, information technology, property and accommodation. Full costing and transfer pricing of these services was implemented. Reviews of each function were carried out to compare the internal cost with external market prices in order to determine whether the function should continue to be provided internally, or be outsourced to the external market. The internal services units were given a 2 year moratorium period of protection from external competition whilst internal efficiencies were sought.

Alpha lost its monopoly when direct competition was introduced by the government as part of general market reforms in the early 1990s. This placed immediate pressure on Alpha's profitability, since the new competitors were new 'greenfield' start-up companies and had inherently lower costs than Alpha. In particular, Alpha had much higher fixed costs than its new competitors. International benchmarking of Alpha's costs was, although arguable, also unfavourable. The pressures on Alpha to reduce costs became irresistible when a partial privatization occurred in the late 1990s, and the market began determining the share price in large part based on the success of Alpha's drive for cost competitiveness.

Alpha was an early user of large scale computing for its engineering and billing needs, and the IT service function evolved in-house, from managing the earliest 'data processing' systems, to operation of a full scale modern corporate platform with three large data centres for mainframe computer systems. All IT functions were performed, including application development and maintenance, and data centre operations. A full range of large scale applications was implemented, including billing, financials, operations workforce management, service and fault management, and customer activation. IT was one of the last functions to be centralized, and at its peak, in the early 1990s, the internal IT group numbered more than 3,000 staff and contractors. When business units required systems work to be done they engaged the internal IT group.

Alpha has now progressively moved most of the internal service functions to external providers. Outsourcing has been a business practice in Alpha for more than 15 years, as it responded to the pressures of cost reduction and market performance expectations. This chapter however, describes only where the outsourcing focus was on IT.

7   The First Foray into Outsourcing (1995–2000)

Alpha began its foray into IT outsourcing in 1995, when the debate regarding privatization was taking place. This involved a proposal, developed at executive level, for a major multinational IT services provider, Delta Corporation (Delta), to provide outsourced IT services for Alpha. Alpha was one of the first large corporations in Australia to significantly outsource their IT function. It was also the first IT outsourcing contract Delta entered into in Australia. Poppo and Lacity (2006) note that "Prior to 1992, most organizations insourced the majority of their information technology, and thus lacked the skills to evaluate outsourcing, craft optimal contracts, or manage suppliers". The market they note was not mature.

In 1997, Delta began providing outsourced IT services for Alpha. It was a large and complex transaction, encompassing IT services, data centre operations and facility management, and also included an agreement for joint business development between Delta and Alpha. Not all IT work was included: major business functions, the financial/ERP systems and the Billing systems, were excluded. Approximately 70% of Alpha's IT budget, around $500 M per annum, was outsourced.

The contract was complex due to the large number of staff involved, and took almost 2 years to complete. The final form of the agreement was reached with optimism and high expectation, and with the investment community looking on, as at the time the contract was negotiated, there was no mature outsourcing industry in Australia. A new Joint Venture legal entity (JV) was formed between Alpha, Delta, and another of Delta's corporate customers to deliver the services. Delta held a significant majority stake in the JV. The JV arrangement suited both Alpha and Delta for commercial reasons. Both Alpha and Delta wanted to reduce their commercial risk, and it was expected that the new company would become a major player in providing outsourcing services and other commercial activities in the region.

The essential elements of the deal were:

- About 2,800 staff and contractors were transferred from Alpha to the Delta JV together with key assets (equipment, licences, data centres) required for provision of the services.
- There was guaranteed minimum revenue to the JV – reflecting the scale of the commitment made with the transfer of staff and assets. There were also working cash flow obligations by Alpha – in effect a pre purchase of services – on a pay now, argue later, basis.
- All data centre operations (Ops) and most of Alpha's applications development and maintenance (AD&M) services were outsourced. In value terms, the Ops and AD&M were about 50:50.
- There was agreement for annual productivity improvements to be delivered by Delta.
- The term was 10 years, with significant costs for early termination.
- The outsourced scope included architecture and design functions.
- Pricing was set against Alpha's 1997 baseline, with commitments by the JV to productivity and efficiency benchmarks included. Productivity was based on Function Point counts and measured as Cost/Function Point.
- Application Maintenance was fixed price against the historical baseline, with defined services, and guaranteed productivity improvements of 10–15% pa, in line with historic IT Industry experience.
- Data centre services had a formula for productivity improvements, but also price escalation for growth in the scale of the applications.

Some restructuring of Alpha's IT organization was necessary as part of the implementation. There was significant turnover of Alpha and Delta's senior IT managers at the time of the deal including the CIO who initiated the Delta discussions. Similarly, the Delta personnel who had negotiated the contract handed over to new managers, and moved on. Accountability for ongoing management therefore passed to new executives in both companies.

7.1 Outcomes of the First Foray into Outsourcing

Seeds of future difficulties were sown in the JV structure, and with Delta having the balance of influence. The JV agreement became a major distraction and difficulty in the relationship between Alpha and Delta as each partly came to manage their differing, conflicting, commercial objectives: cost reduction by Alpha, margin growth for Delta. Alpha found itself heavily dependent on Delta for the provision of services and expertise for approximately half of its business applications.

The details of the engagement process and the pricing approach also led to cost and quality control issues for Alpha. Software enhancement/development was ordered with a conventional quote and acceptance process. If a business unit required any systems work to be done they engaged the internal IT group who then engaged Delta.

Although the contract was flexible and allowed almost any pricing arrangement, in practice the work ordering process favoured time and materials pricing to Alpha, based on a scale of hourly rates for agreed IT staff competencies. In practice, no software development was done at fixed price, and consequently Alpha carried all project cost variance risk.

Since implementation of the contract in 1997, Alpha and Delta have renegotiated key aspects of the outsourcing agreement at about 2 yearly intervals. The immediate workload under the contract included changes and enhancement to applications for Year 2000 readiness, closely followed by implementation of a new goods and services tax regime. This meant that the volume of work was much higher than expected – by about a third, and the agreed hourly labour rates were too high, with over-recovery of fixed costs. In 1999, when the contract had been in place for 2 years, there were difficult negotiations regarding new pricing. At this time Delta also had difficulty in meeting the contracted productivity commitments, and faced large reimbursement to Alpha. Agreement was reached for general (and deep) price reductions, structured as discounts at invoice level, when billing exceeded certain threshold levels. This helped Delta meet its productivity obligations by lowering the effective cost per Function Point (rather than by actually increasing labour productivity). This pricing arrangement worked fine initially, however, work volumes eventually reduced to around the threshold level, at which point Alpha ordered work unnecessarily to ensure volume discounts were maintained.

The mainframe data centre operations part of the contract worked well – it was well understood and well benchmarked. However, management processes for the then newer technology midrange Unix-based systems were not so well defined, and the initial pricing agreement was formula based with disk capacity as a price determinant. By year 3 of the agreement, technology change and low costs of disk storage made this pricing clearly and increasingly uncompetitive for Alpha, but profitable for Delta.

Alpha recognized from this first experience of outsourcing, that there were difficulties with the JV arrangements. Under market pressure to conclude the outsourcing deal Alpha conceded too much control of the commercial situation and had very little leverage to change the balance of influence with Delta. The outsourcing was too deep (strategic functions including system architecture and high level design were outsourced), and, at the time, there was no existing market for the outsourced services and so a single negotiation with Delta had been entered into.

8   Consolidation of IT Outsourcing Arrangements (2000–2002)

In the second phase of outsourcing, having learned from the first phase we see a consolidation in Alpha's approach. Alpha negotiated shorter term 5-year outsourcing contracts with other outsource providers, and brought IT architecture back in-house. Alpha also sought to renegotiate contract arrangements with Delta, but was unsuccessful.

In 2000, Alpha decided – for further cost reduction reasons – to outsource all the IT systems not previously outsourced to Delta. This coincided with a major reorganization of Alpha's IT function, to move from centralized IT investment and budgeting decisions, and centralized IT delivery, to a 'federated' governance model, with IT investment decisions, work ordering and delivery controlled by the sponsoring business units. A limited tender process was used, with a commercial arrangement based on wider North American experience, including:

- Customer controlled Service Levels, linked with an 'at risk' percentage of fees
- Industry Benchmarking of productivity for AD&M
- Scope of services changed to exclude architecture
- Shorter, 5 year term contracts
- Volume based pricing with quarterly forecasts of minimum work level

The scope of work outsourced included all the components that were excluded from the initial outsourcing to Delta, including the billing systems and the ERP systems. It also included work such as system maintenance in the engineering area not covered in the Delta agreement.

There were changes to Alpha's internal accounting procedures whereby business units were now responsible for budgets and were accountable for ordering and accepting of work. This led to a change in the role of the IT function within Alpha, to now cover only infrastructure, strategy, and standards.

In early 2001 Alpha's remaining IT portfolio was successfully outsourced after detailed tender and contract negotiation with another company, Epsilon. Epsilon was an established IT outsourcing provider, with other large outsource contracts. For the tender, Epsilon formed an alliance with Sigma Consulting in order to offer expertise and continuity of service for Alpha's financial/ERP environment. This approach was successful and a detailed service contract was negotiated with the Epsilon/Sigma alliance. In the final stages of negotiation the tender was split, and two identical contracts were signed, with Epsilon taking the outsourced billing work, including about 300 staff from Alpha, and Sigma taking the ERP and SAP outsourced work, involving about 100 staff. Sigma consulting had a number of other support contracts, however the contract with Alpha was the largest.

8.1   Outcomes of the Consolidation Phase

In summary, as Alpha consolidated its approach to outsourcing, Alpha found that the 5-year contracts were effective. However new issues surfaced relating to the skills the outsourcing companies were able to provide and their ability, at times, to meet the needs of Alpha.

Delta was unsuccessful in their bid for more work under the new contractual arrangements. Alpha and Delta also undertook renegotiation of their agreement at this time, to make it operationally consistent, and to address business disquiet over cost and performance quality. This negotiation failed, as Alpha had very little leverage, and Delta had no incentive to modify the existing terms and conditions, or to forego guaranteed contract revenues.

Negotiation continued, however, to establish the new work order engagement process, and to resolve issues with the formula based calculation of fees for mid-range data centre operations. This was not resolved until early 2003, when a comprehensive agreement was reached with Delta on the dissolution of the JV arrangements and the guaranteed revenues.

In the meantime there was continuing general dissatisfaction within Alpha with the cost and quality of work by Delta. Work was given to other suppliers, where the revenue guarantee permitted, including Indian based companies, who seemed to perform very well and were demonstrably much cheaper than Delta.

The subsequent approach of the two suppliers, Epsilon and Sigma, to the relationship with Alpha and the management of the outsource service delivery was quite different:

- Epsilon set up a classical 'factory' service operation, staying strictly within the agreed contracted scope of managing the Billing systems. This in itself was a substantial workload, involving about 200 staff. Epsilon took no proactive position on development of new billing strategies or facilities for Alpha, to the point of not tendering when such work was offered.
- Sigma saw the outsource relationship as a leverage opportunity to sell other services into Alpha. Sigma actively sought additional work, and quickly had added Alpha's middleware platform and the Siebel call centre platform to the scope of their outsource contract. Sigma was also successful in a systems integration proposal for delivery of an internet billing (transaction rating) platform. At the end of the second year of the contract, Sigma had as much work in dollar value terms from the new scope as from the initial ERP outsource scope.

Problems arose with the decision by Sigma to take on more work:

- The middleware platform was technically unstable. It was in a growth phase and had become mission critical to Alpha. As the implementation grew in scale there were evident problems with the architectural design. These led to operational problems requiring skills beyond the scope of the outsourced services.
- The Siebel platform was also not technically stable: there had been a fragmented implementation with different versions, and poor standardization, however the technology was reasonably well understood and skilled people were available in the market. The performance of the platform was also strongly dependent on interfaced telephony platforms managed separately by Alpha. When service quality problems became evident, it was generally attributed within Alpha management to Sigma's performance, even though many of the technical issues were within the related telephony systems managed by Alpha.

- The billing platform implementation work had been won with the support of skilled Sigma staff from North America. Even though this was ultimately a successful project, there was split accountability between Alpha and Sigma for the early key deliverables, and project delays at that time added to the impression within Alpha of poor performance by Sigma.

The common issue in all new work that Sigma took on was Alpha's expectation that the work would be performed under the terms of the outsource agreement, particularly at the outsource contract daily rates. In fact, higher rates were agreed for the initial new works, but these reverted to the contract rates over time (about 2 years). Nonetheless, the new work came at a cost to Sigma – there was a general market shortage of skilled resources for both the middleware platform and the new billing platform, and attracting these resources was at rates far in excess of the contract rates. The end result was that the new work was short-staffed and suffered from insufficient resources with the deep technical skills required of such large and complex systems. Alpha business units were not satisfied, and blamed Sigma.

9   Maturity of IT Outsourcing – Alpha Goes Offshore (2003–2006)

With the experience of the initial foray and consolidation phases and with refined outsourcing arrangements in place, Alpha was more mature in its approach to outsourcing and was well positioned to consider the way forward when offshore outsource opportunities arose. The JV agreement with Delta was dissolved in 2003, 2 years early. It entailed a complex negotiation process, including any consequential obligations for minimum work levels.

A new CIO at Alpha provided strong executive sponsorship to move IT work offshore. Previously company policy had not allowed offshore work; however, this policy was changed allowing Alpha to move to a global sourcing model. Early in 2003 on the basis of the issues described above, and the continuing need to reduce costs, Alpha decided to re-tender all of the three outsource agreements. This included considering use of low cost offshore IT services. Delta contracted on the same terms as the other three providers. The incumbent suppliers, all of whom had access to offshore development centres, and two Tier One Indian IT providers were invited to compete for the work. Indian IT companies hade been prospecting into Alpha for some years and there had been positive experience of their service delivery.

At the same time there was a deep reorganization and rationalization of the overall IT function within Alpha, to recentralize and rationalize the architecture and design functions, particularly to bring the architecture and design functions back in-house to Alpha.

Alpha approached the decision to move to a global outsourcing model from the position of having outsourced the key IT systems already. The business rationale for global outsourcing was simply to move to use lower cost IT labour – provided that the transition costs are manageable. There is further rationale of expected improved quality from the tailored processes and stricter methodologies (to Capability Maturity Model 5 (CMM5)) used by the offshore outsourcing companies. The offshore suppliers are specialist outsource providers with large portfolios able to absorb scale risk.

This change has been implemented with contracts, similar to those in the second phase of outsourcing including a 5-year contract term, but with modified scope of services, as above. Sigma declined to bid. Delta and Epsilon bid because each company is a large provider with global outsourcing capability. Two Indian companies also bid. The contracts negotiated with each were essentially similar to those established in the second phase. In particular the conditions included service level management agreements and management of work levels. New suppliers, Indian based, have been engaged, and existing suppliers (including Delta) have also been retained on the basis that they are permitted to use offshore labour, and price accordingly. New engagement processes have been implemented, reflecting both the new Alpha IT organization, and the need to manage the interface to overseas development locations. The overall cost of outsourcing has been reduced substantially because of labour cost reductions.

9.1   Outcomes of the Maturity Phase

The maturity of Alpha's outsourcing arrangements is reflected in the company's willingness and confidence to move to offshore outsourcing. Alpha also restructured its in-house capability and aligned its IT process with what is now global outsourcing practice. It remains to be seen how well outsourcing works in the longer term, as there are some areas of concern:

- There continues to be strong market pressures for cost reduction by Alpha, and as recently as 2006 further redundancies were announced. The offshore companies are currently very profitable, high margin suppliers, and this fact is understood by Alpha. Offshore IT labour prices are expected to rise, and current tax breaks in India have a sunset. There will inevitably be further robust negotiations around price.
- There is an expectation by Alpha that the outsource providers will deliver low cost IT solutions, including new systems, however the onshore services are provided at onshore market rates. There are clear technology trends to the use of off-the-shelf enterprise software, with much lower maintenance effort, but high business process integration effort. This reduces the need for offshore IT labour, weakens the cost justification of the global model, and opens niche competitive opportunity for onshore local IT service providers.
- The impact of cultural differences between Alpha and offshore service providers remains to be seen. Indian companies in particular have access to employees with supposed good English language skills. This creates an initial impression

of cultural alignment, however, the underlying culture and belief systems can be completely alien to Western norms (Nicholson & Sahay 2001; Hirschheim, Loebbecke, Newman, & Valor 2005).

Initial experience by Alpha is that the cost of IT has risen, evidently due to transition costs, and a backlog of demand for systems changes. There has been large scale recruiting of local staff to meet the onshore work load.

10 Alpha's Outsourcing Experiences in Context

Alpha now has mature outsourcing arrangements in place using a global outsourcing model. In early 2005, Alpha corporation appointed a new CEO. Alpha is now moving to a major modernization of its IT platform and systems managed under outsourcing arrangements are being replaced. For this modernization project none of the outsourcing companies has a prime systems delivery role. Alpha has engaged specialist consulting firms to build the new systems, however management of the process remains with Alpha. Specialist consulting companies are responsible for the delivery of new systems. Once the systems are installed the consulting firms have no further involvement, the ongoing support and maintenance is passed to the outsourcing providers.

Table 2 is a timeline providing a snapshot of the key events both prior to outsourcing and after each phase.

As a result of the three phases of outsourcing and the lessons learned, Alpha today has two distinct approaches to managing their IT function.

- Low-level, non-strategic work is outsourced primarily to offshore vendors
- Complex and strategic systems work is managed in-house with specialist consultants. Alpha determines the architecture, selects the platform, manages the business decisions and analysis, with specialist consulting firms building and delivering the systems

Reduction in costs, improved business performance and outsourcing for commercial exploitation were reasons identified in the literature for companies seeking to outsource their IT. In the case of Alpha the key imperative was cost savings.

The first IT outsourcing by Alpha to Delta was an early foray into outsourcing in Australia, and reflected the knowledge of the time. Many aspects of these early outsourcing arrangements were seen as effective but there were issues in particular with systems enhancement. As Alpha's approach to outsourcing consolidated, the key issues experienced with Delta: perceived poor quality work, and poor timeliness were dealt with in the consolidation phase in new contracts. Alpha recognized that the initial outsourcing had been too deep, and hence changed the contract scope. Alpha reached a level of maturity through its experience and was able to move offshore successfully in the third phase.

Table 2 Timeline of Alpha Outsourcing Activities

Date	Activity
Late 1980's	Alpha became a corporation and subject to corporation's law
	Privatization process began
1993	Australian telecommunication's market was deregulated.
1995	Discussions about outsourcing within Alpha began
1st Foray	Partial privatization of Alpha.
Late 1997	JV and outsourcing agreements with Delta signed
1999	Y2K and GST implementation resulted in increased workloads and a recognition that the price points were wrong.
	Delta had difficulty meeting productivity requirements.
	Alpha attempts to renegotiate pricing. Some contact arrangements were successfully renegotiated.
Consolidation 2000	Recognition within Alpha that the pricing was uncompetitive in particular given a drop in hardware prices.
	Alpha pursued cost reductions with Delta unsuccessfully.
2001	New, 5-year contracts, put out to tender and Epsilon and Sigma were the successful bidders.
	New contracts excluded architecture but the rest of the systems work was included.
	Restructuring within Alpha resulted in a drop in work orders for IT services.
Maturity 2003	JV dissolved.
	Offshore work approved.
	All contracts were re-tendered with Epsilon and Delta (including Indian offshore partners), and Indian outsource providers bidding successfully. Sigma did not bid.
	All architecture and design functions brought back in-house
2005	Alpha appoints a new CEO.
	Major modernization of systems start but prime supply and delivery role kept in-house
2007	Modernization of systems continues

In the following, we look at the effectiveness of Alpha's outsourcing experience as discussed through each of the outsourcing phases. The seven key factors identified in Table 1 are used to describe the experience.

1. *Careful selection of functionss to be outsourced*

At the time of agreement there was little experience and no existing market for outsourced IT services in Australia (a single negotiation with Delta occurred). Alpha outsourced all functions in the first foray (architecture, design, building, testing and implementation) and two thirds of applications and business functionality. The mainframe data centre operations were well defined and this part of the contract worked well. However, Alpha included strategic functions including the high level and strategic functions of systems architecture and high level design, and systems design in the scope of the outsourcing. This had several effects:

- Alpha lost key skilled staff, transferred to Delta, and eventually to other clients of Delta
- Alpha lost control of the scope of work required for system changes
- Lock-in of Alpha to Delta, or to other suppliers chosen by Delta, and to the selection of technology preferred or owned by Delta
- The result of Alpha outsourcing too deeply, was the loss of important IT knowledge and capability

The systems outsourced in the consolidation phase were those that had not been previously outsourced, and scope/depth reflected the outcome of the first initial experience. Two major systems were included in the second outsourcing arrangements: the Billing and ERP/financial systems. These were outsourced for cost saving reasons but there was recognition of the need to control architecture design decisions and strategic development of these functions. One particular issue that was addressed in the consolidation phase was to bring back in-house, decisions relating to selection of software and hardware. This gave Alpha more control of lock-in to architecture and software owned by the outsource provider.

The third phase highlights Alpha's maturity as the company further consolidates what it was prepared to outsource. As Alpha reached this level of maturity, it recognized that building of new strategic systems should not be outsourced.

2. *Length of the contract*

The initial JV construct with Delta was used for two reasons: to offset the risk to Delta in taking on the employer liabilities associated with staff transferred from Alpha, and, to create a vehicle for future joint business development. Alpha further committed quite high minimum revenue levels to the JV for the 10 year duration of the contract, on a take-or-pay basis. This created a barrier to renegotiation, since Delta had no reason to forgo the guaranteed revenue stream, and, with majority control of the JV, Delta simply and rationally refused to discuss any changes that impacted on this revenue.

Delta and Alpha are both large corporations who expected to exist, and to do business together, well into the future and at least for 10 years. The contract included detailed price and productivity agreements aimed at keeping the deal competitive and effective for such a long period, however, these agreement terms proved inadequate and unmanageable in practice, and Alpha was limited in any negotiation by the penalties for early termination of the contract.

Alpha learned from this and in the consolidation phase 5-year contracts were negotiated with Sigma and Epsilon. The 5-year contracts were seen to be successful and therefore, Alpha signed similar length contracts with offshore vendors.

3. *Development of detailed contracts with some flexibility built in*

The first foray saw an outsourcing agreement between Alpha and Delta reached under market pressure to conclude the outsourcing deal. This resulted in Alpha conceding too much control of the commercial situation and Alpha then had little leverage to change the balance of influence with Delta. With business cycles of 3–5 years, and ongoing technology change operating in similar cycles, it is unlikely that any service contract will be appropriate after 5 years, let alone 10 years. Renegotiation of the outsource contract on a 2–3 year cycle should have been anticipated, under conditions whereby each party had the option to walk away, and have the services re-tendered to other suppliers in the marketplace. The contract with Delta did not include balanced conditions for termination, and transition to another supplier.

Alpha was unable to renegotiate the contract with Delta in the consolidation phase. Delta had no incentive to modify the contract, with its guaranteed minimum ordering levels, and there was little Alpha could do. Alpha would have preferred to divert work elsewhere but the inflexibility of the agreement and Delta's uncompromising commercial position meant this was impossible.

The arrangements with Sigma and Epsilon however were different. The contracts were much more flexible in the way work levels could be increased or reduced. There were no minimum work levels or guarantees but there were limitations on the rate of change. From Alpha's perspective the second phase contractual arrangements were successful and therefore contracts with offshore partners were similar.

A particular issue did arise with additional scope of work taken on by Sigma. The expectation by Alpha was that the work would be performed under the terms of the outsource agreement, particularly at the outsource contract daily rates. The work involving the middleware platform, and the Siebel platform was new and technically complex. Higher rates were agreed for the initial new works, but these reverted to the contract rates over time. The new work came at a cost to Sigma; there was a general market shortage of skilled resources for both the middleware platform and the new billing platform, and these resources had to be obtained at rates far in excess of the outsource contract rates. The end result was that the new work was short-staffed and suffered from insufficient skilled resources (i.e. lack of staff with the deep technical skills required of such large and complex systems). Although Alpha had flexibility, problems arose because of the difficulties Sigma faced.

4. *Involvement of senior business people and IT executives in the outsourcing decision*

Despite high level agreement and support for the outsourcing arrangements, there was not a significant level of involvement by the business side of Alpha in defining the scope and structure of the first outsourcing foray. The result was that at the working levels, some areas in Alpha were happy with Delta's performance, however, at senior business management level there were stories of delays and rework by Delta. The impact of the limited involvement of senior business people was that in Alpha's view the service level metrics were not representative of business priorities: for example, they measured component level delivery, but did not drive timely delivery of overall business solutions; there was no service level agreement for levels of rework, or quality of code written. However, under the terms of the contract, service levels could not be modified without agreement by Delta who had no reason to agree to stricter performance measures.

The consolidation phase and then maturity phase saw Alpha address these contractual problems by adopting international best practice for developing service level agreements. The new agreements were designed to be adapted, as Alpha's business priorities changed, and to deliver business functionality.

5. *Understanding and management of costs*

Alpha initially underestimated the staff resources and the effort required to manage and administer the agreement. Once the agreement was signed, and the negotiators had left, the haggling began, and continued, over interpretation of agreement terms, documentation particularly the scope of work included in the fixed price agreement, and the work carried out at additional cost to Alpha. There was pressure within Alpha to track and manage to minimize cost, while Delta was logically managing to meet revenue targets.

Cost and service management by both parties was a factor contributing to poor delivery under the agreement. For example: Delta consistently used disproportionate numbers of low level personnel (recent graduates, base level IT staff) to fulfil the contract. There was very low engagement of higher grade personnel (such as designers, architects, and experienced project managers). The factors driving this behaviour were:

- Alpha made almost exclusive use of hourly rate charging for delivery of enhancement services by Delta, rather than using fixed price, or outcome based service delivery.
- The high dollar value of the contract and the visibility of the monthly invoice payments made proposals by Delta to supply personnel at higher price competency levels unacceptable to Alpha.
- Delta was meeting performance service levels under the letter of the contract. Delta's response to cost scrutiny by Alpha was to maximize the use of low cost personnel.

Monthly cost control of hourly charges, rather than use of outcome based payment for services, contributed to the underlying skewed resource profile, and to poor service delivery. Alpha accepted delivery risk it could not control and was not able to manage.

Alpha's business units were given budget accountability as part of the outsourcing consolidation phase. The business units were much more discerning when buying direct from service providers and so more frugal when required to pay for every piece of work commissioned. When the business units became accountable, with hindsight, it was not therefore surprising that Alpha discovered that the volume of work ordered dropped by about one third. It seems that the IT teams had in the past created much of their own work. During the maturity phase a more rational approach to managing cost took hold.

6. *Management of relationships both internal and external*

Alpha initially underestimated the effort needed to manage the outsource agreement with Delta. There was tension between Alpha's objectives of cost control, and Delta's need for revenue. This contributed to a general view within Alpha management that Delta's performance was high cost and low quality, although Delta consistently met the service level metrics agreed in the contract.

As Alpha consolidated and matured in the approach to outsourcing they ensured they had more control of service quality due to the more effective Service Level procedures and measures. Following the second, consolidation phase, particularly where budgeting and ordering arrangements were consolidated under business unit control, Alpha achieved improved commercial balance in the outsource relationships. Notwithstanding, issues arose from differing expectations in the relationship with Sigma, as noted above.

7. *Skills to be retained and careful selection of people*

The decisions by Alpha regarding which IT staff would be outsourced was determined by the decision of what scope and functions were to be outsourced. Alpha initially elected to include strategic IT functions in the scope of outsourcing to Delta and lost key skilled staff. With the loss of key expertise Alpha was dependent on Delta for the provision of services and expertise for almost half of its business applications. Staff involved with the billing and financial systems were selected on the same basis, although the depth of functions outsourced was less. However, some functions that went to Delta as a result of the first phase, for example, the IT architecture functions, were re-established in-house by Alpha as the outsourcing arrangements were consolidated, with recruitment of necessary skilled staff. As Alpha's outsourcing approach matured there were no further significant staff movements Alpha had already made all the major staffing decisions.

10.1   Additional Success Factors

As seen above, the seven key success factors identified in the literature also came through as issues in the Alpha case. But in addition to these seven, five additional factors were identified as important yet not given much attention in the literature.

1. *Type of outsourcing partner arrangement*

The linkage of the outsourcing contract to joint business development created tension within Alpha between the IT cost centre, and sales revenue. The overall net value of the deal to Alpha is difficult to determine, as a normal sales partnering agreement may have had the same effect. Linking the purchase of a business input – IT services – with product sales/revenue was problematic. There was an underlying conflict of interest between the two parties contracted together for low cost inputs and high margin sales.

Alpha's contract with Delta included the transition costs and other ongoing outsourcing liabilities in an engineered financial construct which included price premiums, revenue guarantees and unrelated obligations such as joint business activities. Once the outsource agreement was in place, and the negotiators gone, the rationale behind the pricing was forgotten when the contract was put to market price scrutiny by the incoming accountable managers. Alpha may have been better off paying out the staff termination costs at once, or over a short period of time, and with no contracted compensating conditions such as minimum revenue levels over the term of the agreement.

2. *Outsourcing vendor capabilities*

Sigma was keen to expand their business and take on more work with Alpha. The initial contract with Sigma was to provide simple outsourcing work for the ERP/financials system. Sigma however sought to extend this to applications that were at the time new and immature: middleware, and the CRM platform. Although the new scope of work was close to Sigma's core consulting competencies, it included new systems which were not entirely stable, and still subject to significant functional change. This was a high risk strategy because such work required highly skilled IT professional staff to manage and implement the systems. Sigma had difficulty providing the resources and skills to meet the demand and at the price point negotiated in the outsourcing agreement. The arrangement eventually failed as Sigma ran into problems of time, cost and quality. A more mature Alpha ensured that the outsourcing companies in future arrangements had the capability to carry out the work contracted to them.

3. *Changing business environment*

Both Epsilon and Sigma ran into immediate problems with the outsource relationship for an unexpected reason. The level of business (the "baseline" of activity) which was used in the tender for costing and pricing by Epsilon and Sigma, was the pre-existing staffing within Alpha. When Alpha implemented its new decentralized IT accountabilities for ordering IT services, there was significantly lower demand for services. The volume of work ordered dropped by about one third.

Alpha had agreed minimum revenue levels for Epsilon and Sigma in view of the staff commitments taken on by each company, but these only applied in the short term, and both suppliers were overstaffed. There was pressure on the suppliers to control costs due to this, leading to staff reductions through redundancies, and the use of lower cost, low level personnel. This caused service and quality issues, and led to dissatisfaction with the outsource suppliers by Alpha's business units, similar to their experience with Delta.

Outsourcing was a relatively new business for Sigma, and Alpha was the dominant customer. When Alpha reduced the level of work orders Sigma was initially better off, having expanded its scope of work into the new platforms (see above) and this compensated for the reduction in the ordering of services. However, the significant fall in demand for ERP services left Sigma with high numbers of staff unable to be re-deployed. This left Sigma heavily exposed to the loss of scale, in both financial and client relationship terms.

For Alpha the off-shore phase was driven by the continuing need for low cost services. Outsourcing offshore will remain a viable business option while Indian labour costs are low and the Indian government continues the current policy of offering taxation breaks.

4. *Managing service demand*

Alpha's business units were given budget accountability as part of the consolidation phase, and became more discerning in ordering new work. The contracts were negotiated based on historical work levels so when the levels of orders dropped, both Sigma and Epsilon were overstaffed, and lost money. The underlying demand for services was not understood by Alpha; demand was much less than expected, and this caused dysfunctional behaviour by the outsource providers. From Alpha's viewpoint the cost reduction objectives had been met and exceeded but this was not so much from price reduction it was from the reduced demand for services. This situation required significant management, including relationship management, by all parties. No one was really happy.

The contract agreement provided for changes in work demand, but Alpha potentially had to pay penalties for lower levels of work. Managing costs in this situation was complex for Alpha: it required ensuring sufficient work was being ordered from each of Sigma and Epsilon to avoid penalties, and at the same time ensuring the work was needed.

5. *Managing new systems work outside the contract*

As an outcome of the initial outsourcing to Delta, Alpha's response to perceived poor quality and high cost was to avoid giving new systems development work to Delta, preferring to tender into the external systems integration market. Accordingly, Delta's competitors developed niche capability to compete and beat Delta for the higher margin new systems development work. Delta won very few tenders for new systems work in the period from 1997 to 2003.

Alpha got this part of the Delta relationship right. Outsourcing is low margin delivery of low risk, high volume IT commodity services such as applications enhancement and maintenance. For delivery of new systems, a risk managed project construct should be used, and the costs will be greater: higher grade personnel are required, at higher cost, and there will be a price premium for risk. Alpha used competitive processes (tendering) to select suppliers and to negotiate delivery terms for new systems development. Such processes are essential to achieve a balance of outcomes (particularly the management and pricing of the risk) between customer and service provider.

11   Alpha's Outsourcing Maturity

Alpha's outsourcing journey began in 1997 with the first contract and JV arrangements with Delta. The first phase of outsourcing saw 70% of the IT budget outsourced to Delta. In the current phase of maturity it is estimated that around 20% of Alpha's IT budget is for internal IT resources.

It can be seen with each phase of outsourcing that Alpha, reflecting on the outcomes, has learnt and matured in their approach. Although over this time, Alpha has not fundamentally changed its rationale for outsourcing, the factors that have impacted on the success of the arrangements did change, reflecting how the company matured.

11.1   Rationale for Outsourcing

Table 3 identifies against each outsourcing phase the rationale for outsourcing at that time. A tick indicates a rationale relevant to Alpha.

Table 3 highlights that in the case of Alpha Corporation, the decision to outsource was primarily for cost reduction and efficiency reasons. Alpha however was also aware of what their international competitors were doing initially, and then later, with the move to offshore service provision, so they were to some extent following the lead of others. In Alpha's first outsourcing foray there is evidence that improvement to business performance was also an objective, although as Alpha matured in their approach this became a lesser objective.

11.2   Success Factors

Table 4 describes the success factors identified in the literature and other success factors emerging from the Alpha case study. A tick indicates this was a success factor for Alpha in this phase. A cross indicates that this was a problem for Alpha. Neither a cross nor a tick means that the item was not relevant. Where there is a tick and a cross it means that for one of the outsourcing partners it was successful but not for the other (D – Delta, S – Sigma, E – Epsilon).

Table 4 illustrates the extent to which Alpha matured in its approach to outsourcing over the 9-year period. It should be noted that given no changes could be made to the Delta contract, the lessons Alpha learnt in the first phase of outsourcing are reflected in Table 4, in the new contracts struck (with Sigma and Epsilon). Most of the identified success factors were not met in the first foray whereas by the third phase Alpha had largely addressed these concerns.

Table 3 Analysis of the Alpha case study against current thinking relating to rationales for outsourcing

Rationales for outsourcing	1st Foray	Consolidate	Maturity
Cost reduction and efficiency	✓	✓	✓
Improvements in business performance	✓		
Commercial exploitation of outsourcing provider capability	✓		
Divest the company of a problem			
Following the lead of others	✓		✓

Table 4 Analysis of the Alpha case study and success factors

Success factors	1st Foray	Consolidate	Maturity
Careful selection of functions to be outsourced was made.	X	✓	✓
Sufficient involvement of both business and IT executives in the outsourcing decision making process.	X	X	✓
Understood and managed all costs.	X	✓	✓
Contract length appropriate.	X	✓ X D	✓
Contracts had high level of detail and flexibility.	✓	✓	✓
Outsourcing relationships within the o rganization and the outsourcing vendor were well managed.	X	X	
Skills to be retained and careful selection of people.	X	✓	
Additional outsourcing success factors			
Effective and balanced outsourcing partner arrangement	X	✓	✓
Outsourcing vendor capabilities	✓	✓ X S	
Changing business environment		X	✓
Managing service demand	X	✓ X S	✓
Managing new systems work outside the contract	✓	✓	✓

Figure 1 illustrates from the perspective of the level of complexity of the work and the extent to which the work was strategic, how Alpha matured in their approach to outsourcing.

Alpha's experience confirms that risk and accountability should not be outsourced. Fig. 1 illustrates that initially Delta was given work and responsibility that although was not highly complex it was strategic. Alpha recognized that this was not appropriate in the second phase and the new agreements were for work that was not as complex nor as strategic. Sigma on the other hand did bid and was successful for more complex work within Alpha, but as was mentioned, this was not successful. The lesson that Alpha has learnt is that outsourcing is a business strategy suited to low-risk established business activity, performed in bulk at low cost. Complex tasks such as the integration of new systems require different skill sets and financial arrangements. Alpha has therefore moved to a model of selective outsourcing for strategic systems delivery work.

11.3   *Reflections on Outsourcing Maturity at Alpha*

In describing their IT outsourcing maturity model Gottschalk and Solli-Saether (2006) conclude "As an outsourcing relationship matures, the maturity model suggests that performance measures develop beyond cost minimization and operational efficiency into business productivity and technology innovation, and further

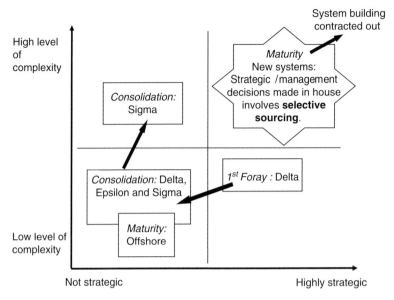

High level of complexity

Low level of complexity

Consolidation: Sigma

Maturity
New systems:
Strategic /management
decisions made in house
involves **selective sourcing**.

System building contracted out

Consolidation: Delta, Epsilon and Sigma

Maturity: Offshore

1st *Foray* : Delta

Not strategic   Highly strategic

Fig. 1 Summary of Alpha's outsourcing

into business benefits and achievement of mutual goals for client and vendor". This has not been the case for Alpha Corporation – cost minimization has continued to be the major driver. This is consistent with the work reported by Carmel and Agarwal (2002) who argue that companies focus strongly on costs in the third stage of maturity for offshore IT outsourcing.

Olayele and Wabash (2004) argue that the second stage of outsourcing maturity involves organizations "taking the baby steps" and approaching outsourcing in an ad hoc way. Again this was not the case at Alpha. The first foray into outsourcing by Alpha involved more than 70% of Alpha's IT budget with work outsourced to Delta, although it was recognized that the outsourcing was too deep and some functions were brought back in-house.

For Alpha, the experience has shown that outsourcing is about buying routine IT services in bulk, at low prices. Part of the learning and maturity process for Alpha has been to understand the limitations of outsourcing. Alpha found that innovation and leading-edge development services were beyond the reasonable scope of the IT services outsourcing arrangements. The experience has been that typically such development services require specialist, strategic expertise that is priced in the market at much higher prices than could be provided within the outsourcing agreement. This was part of Alpha's bitter experience in the second phase when Sigma stepped out of a strict outsourcing relationship and found itself caught between the expectations of Alpha and the market realities of the costs of services it had undertaken to provide. This is in contrast to Carmel and Agarwal (2002) who argue that offshore companies are used "to increase business innovation, third technology innovation, develop new products, gain access to new markets, and grow globally".

In Alpha's current systems renewal project these high-end services and project deliverables are not part of the scope of an outsourcing service provider. They are part of separate contracts with specialist systems integrators, and at much higher, market, prices. At the end of the systems renewal project, the systems will be transitioned to outsource service providers for longer term maintenance and support.

Other lessons that Alpha learnt as the outsourcing arrangements matured were that contract length was a critical factor. Locking in arrangements for 10 years reduced Alpha's leverage and flexibility to achieve cost savings from technology change, from internal changes within the company, and from changing business environment. From Alpha's perspective, business productivity and technology innovation were not measurably improved as the outsourcing arrangements matured.

12   Conclusions

In the period from 1997 Alpha Corporation has learned, reflected and matured in its approach to outsourcing. It has now addressed most of the early issues and has been able to successfully move outsourcing work offshore. This is consistent with the maturity model reported by Carmel and Agarwal (2002) who suggest that organizational maturity in outsourcing operations is an important factor in offshore outsourcing success. The Alpha case study therefore provides some insight of how one large organization has reached the point it has in terms of outsourcing.

Outsourcing is widely seen as a key business strategy and is increasingly being used in IT. Of the three key reasons for outsourcing identified in the literature, described in Table 1, *cost reduction* was the key driver of Alpha's outsourcing decisions. But as the case of Alpha shows, even experienced, large corporations where IT is critical to their success, have difficulties in achieving successful outsourcing, particularly in the early stages. The standard seven factors commonly thought to be necessary for success were insufficient for Alpha. Indeed, five other factors were necessary. Thus the key success factors identified in the literature are necessary but not sufficient conditions for success. To this list, we would add Alpha's five factors. While we cannot guarantee that these twelve factors will lead to outsourcing success in all cases, we believe these new factors offer a more complete range of issues which organizations will need to consider for achieving outsourcing success.

Although these twelve success factors should help organizations better understand outsourcing, we would like to conclude with what we believe to be the critical issue, viz. carefully selecting what is to be outsourced. For a function to be successfully outsourced, it must be:

- Not excessively complex nor strategically critical to the business
- Well understood and under management control before outsourcing
- Available in an external competitive market at a competitive price

Whilst these rules seem obvious, it is surprising how often they are violated in practice. Many organizations outsource parts of the IT portfolio which are strategic, assuming that vendors are 'partners' who would share their business strategy, IT expertise, and offer IT strategic direction to the client. Such 'partnering' has typically been problematic as the Alpha case shows (e.g. the JV). For a business function to be successfully outsourced we believe it has to be routinely performed, and be a non-core, non-strategic function, for which there are external companies that can perform the function better through specialization, or cheaper, through economies of scale and portfolio effects. For example, service functions such as infrastructure that can be moved to a 'factory' delivery model, are classic outsourcing candidate functions.

References

Baldwin, L., Irani, Z., & Love, P. E. D. (2001). Outsourcing information systems: drawing lessons from the banking case study. *European Journal of Information Systems, 10*, 15–24.

Barthelemy, J., & Geyer, D. (2004). The determinants of total IT outsourcing: an empirical investigation of French and German firms. *The Journal of Computer Information Systems, 44*(3), 91–97.

Beaumont, M., & Costa, C. (2002). Information technology outsourcing in Australia. *Information Resources Management Journal, 15*(3), 14–30.

Beaumont, N., & Sohal, A. (2004). Outsourcing in Australia. *International Journal of Operations and Production Management, 24*(7), 688–700.

Carmel, E., & Agarwal, R. (2002). The maturation of offshore sourcing of information technology work. *MIS Quarterly Executive, 1*(2), 65–77.

Choudhury, V., & Sabherwal, R. (2003). Portfolios of control in outsourced software development projects. *Information Systems Research, 14*(3), 291–314.

Dibbern, J., Goles, T., Hirschheim, R., & Jayatilaka, B. (2004). Information systems outsourcing: a survey and analysis of the literature. *Database, 35*(5), 6–102.

Diromualdo, A., & Gurbaxani, V. (1998). Strategic intent for IT outsourcing. *Sloan Management Review, 39*(4), 67–81.

Earl, M. (1996). The risks of outsourcing IT. *Sloan Management Review, 37*(3), 26–32.

Gellings, C., & Wullenweber, K. (2006). Successfully implementing IT outsourcing strategy in German banks: the role of contract design and risk analysis. *Proceedings of the European Conference on Information Systems 2006*, Gotenberg, Sweden.

Gonzalez, R., Gasco, J., & Llopis, J. (2006). Information systems outsourcing: a literature analysis. *Information and Management, 43*, 821–834.

Gottschalk, P., & Solli-Saether, H. (2006). Maturity model for IT outsourcing relationships. *Industrial Management and Data Systems, 106*(2), 200–212.

Hirschheim, R., & Lacity, M. (2000). The myths and realities of information technology insourcing. *Communications of the ACM, 43*(2), 99–107.

Hirschheim, R., & Lacity, M. (2006). Four stories of information systems insourcing. In R. Hirschheim, A. Heinzl, & J. Dibbern (Eds.), *Information systems outsourcing: enduring themes, new perspectives and global challenges* (pp. 303–346). Berlin: Springer.

Hirschheim, R., Loebbecke, C., Newman, M., & Valor, J. (2005). Offshoring and its implications for the information systems discipline. In D. Avison, & D. Galletta (Eds.), *Proceedings of the 26th International Conference on Information Systems* (pp 1003–1018), Las Vegas, Dec. 12–14.

Ho, V., Ang, S., & Straub, D. (2003). When subordinates become IT contractors: persistent managerial expectations in IT outsourcing. *Information Systems Research, 14*(1), 66–125.

Jayatilaka, B. (2006). IT sourcing as a dynamic phenomena: forming an institutional theory perspective. In R. Hirschheim, A. Heinzl, & J. Dibbern (Eds.), *Information systems outsourcing: enduring themes, new perspectives and global challenges* (pp. 103–134), Berlin: Springer.

Kern, T., & Willicocks, L. (2002). Exploring relationships in information technology outsourcing: interaction approach. *European Journal of Information Systems, 11*, 3–19.

King, W. (2004). Outsourcing and the future of IT. *Information Systems, 21*(4), 83–84.

Kishore, R., Rao, H., Nam, K., Rajagopalan, S., & Chaudhury, A. (2003). A relationship perspective on IT outsourcing. *Communications of the ACM, 46*(12), 87–92.

Lacity, M., & Hirschheim, R. (1993). The information systems bandwagon. *Sloan Management Review, 35*(1), 73–86.

Lacity, M., & Willcocks, L. (2000). Survey of IT outsourcing experiences in US and UK organizations. *Journal of Global Information Management, 8*(2), 5039.

Lacity, M., Willicocks, L., & Feeny, D. (1996). The value of selective IT sourcing. *Sloan Management Review, 37*(3), 13–25.

Lee, J., Huynh, M., Kwok, P., & Pi, S. (2003). IT outsourcing evolution – past, present and future. *Communications of the ACM, 46*(5), 84–89.

Lee, J., Miranda, S., & Kim, Y. (2004). IT outsourcing strategies: universalistic, contingency, and consideration all explanations of success. *Information Systems Research, 15*(2), 110–131.

McFarlan, W., & Nolan, R. (1995). How to manage an IT outsourcing alliance. *Sloan Management Review, 36*(2), 9–23.

Nicholson, B., & Sahay, S. (2001). Some political and cultural issues in the globalisation of software development: case experience from Britain and India. *Information and Organization, 11*(1), 25–43.

Olayele, A., & Wabash, S. (2004). IT outsourcing maturity model. *Proceedings of the European Conference on Information Systems*, Turku, Finland.

Oshri, I., Kotlarsky, J., & Willcocks, L. (2007). Managing disbursed expertise in IT offshore outsourcing: lessons from TATA consultancy services. *MIS Quarterly Executive, 6*(2), 53–65.

Poppo, L., & Lacity, M. (2006). The normative value of transaction cost economics: what managers have learned about TCE principles in the IT context. In R. Hirschheim, A. Heinzl, & J. Dibbern (Eds.), *Information systems outsourcing: enduring themes, new perspectives and global challenges* (pp. 259–282). Berlin: Springer.

Smith, H., & McKeen, J. (2004). Developments in practice XIV: IT sourcing – how far can you go? *Communications of the Association for Information Systems, 14*, 508–520.

Tan, C., & Sia, S. (2006). Managing flexibility in outsourcing. *Journal of the Association for Information Systems, 7*(4), 179–206.

Walsham, G. (1995). Interpretive case studies in IS research: nature and method. *European Journal of Information Systems, 4*(2), 74–81.

Walsham, G. (2006). Doing interpretive research. *European Journal of Information Systems, 15*, 320–330.

Strategic Dependence on the IT Resource and Outsourcing: A Test of the Strategic Control Model[1,2]

Detmar Straub, Peter Weill, and Kathy S. Schwaig

1 Introduction

When managers outsource all or part of IT, the motivation is to create business value for the firm. One means of creating business value is by achieving dramatic cost savings through outsourcing; another is through decisions that lead to strategic control of IT resources. In the former, IT outsourcing returns profits to the firm by taking advantage of economies in the marketplace. Theoretically, IT vendors/outsourcers drive down the costs of production and technical expertise by spreading these expenses over a large client base; accordingly, their customers are able to benefit indirectly from these *economies of scale* through attractive pricing of IT products and services by vendors (Dibbern, Goles, Hirschheim, & Jayatilaka 2004).

Strategic control is the second avenue for value creation. Managers who identify IT resources that are critical to their firm's operations and to its strategic direction are theoretically better able to manage those resources if the firm maintains control over them. By divesting themselves of activities that are not strategic, they can capitalize on superior design, marketing, production, inbound logistics, or distribution capabilities. Thus, organizations that outsource IT activities that are not strategic can concentrate energies on distinctive resources that are directly related to value creation for the firm. The notion of strategic control of the IT resource has strong theoretical underpinnings in resource dependency theory (Pfeffer & Salancik 2003).

While both the cost savings and strategic control lines of reasoning have solid theoretical bases, nearly all of the research to date on IT sourcing has posited and/or tested economic and financial models, i.e., has stressed cost, rather than positing strategic control models. The current study seeks to fill this gap in the IT outsourcing research portfolio by proposing and testing a Strategic Control Model.

---

[2] This paper previously appeared as: Straub, D., Weill, P. and Schwaig, K. S. "Strategic dependence on the IT resource and outsourcing: A test of the strategic control model", Information Systems Frontiers (10) 2008, pp 195-210. The current version appears with permission of Springer, the publisher of ISF.

R. Hirschheim et al. (eds), *Information Systems Outsourcing,*
© Springer-Verlag Berlin Heidelberg 2009

The notion of resource dependency is central to RDT and to the current study. Specifically, a resource dependency is created any time a firm relies on an external entity for a resource needed by the firm. The more critical the resource is to the firm, the more serious is the dependency. This thesis posits, therefore, that, overall, when organizations depend on external entities for IT resources critical to their survival, they yield control and ultimately jeopardize firm performance.

The results of this study offer insights for researchers and managerial guidelines regarding whether and how managers control the IT resource. When making such critical decisions, strategic control proves to be a good explanation for how the most effective managers outsource IT and how the firm reaps downstream benefits from their control decisions.

2   Theoretical and Conceptual Background

2.1   *Resource Dependency Theory*

Resource Dependency Theory (RDT) examines organizational decision making in light of the impact of the environment on the organization. RDT recognizes that the key to organizational survival is the ability to acquire and maintain resources (Pfeffer & Salancik 2003). An organization must be open to its environment due to its dependence on that environment to obtain critical resources such as personnel, information, raw materials and technology. Resource acquisition may be problematic and unpredictable. To guarantee the flow of resources, therefore, a firm will adapt to changes in its environment that impact the flow of resources to the firm. Adaptation is not passive, however, but rather a strategic choice to cope with pressure in the environment (De Wit & Verhoeven 2000). Successful organizations, therefore, attempt to minimize their dependence on or increase their influence over organizations in their environment (Birkinshaw, Toulan, &Arnold 2001; Grover, Cheon, & Teng 1994; Teng, Cheon, & Grover 1995).

Although organizations are constrained by their dependency on their environment, opportunities exist to pursue organizational interest (Pfeffer & Salancik 2003). Firms can negotiate their positions within these constraints. RDT recognizes that organizational strategy focuses not only on products and customers but also on the suppliers and other entities in the environment that impact the flow of resources to the firm. Organizations thereby interact dynamically as they act strategically to manage their resource dependency on other firms (Pfeffer & Salancik).

Given the preceding discussion of RDT, an important research question emerges: *To what extent does the degree of dependency that results from outsourcing various IT resources affect firm performance?* The ultimate decision that organizations make is based upon the degree of control desired for a given IT resource. According to RDT, firms will choose to own, nurture, have exclusive access to, and thus *control* strategic resources that will lead to improved competitiveness. Conversely, it is not necessary for firms to own and *control* those assets that are not strategic and integral to their distinctive competence.

2.2 *Information Technology Outsourcing and RDT*

Prior studies indicate that outsourcing is a strategic arrangement for a firm (Insinga & Werle 2000; Lacity & Hirschheim 1993). At its core, RDT argues that no firm can exclusively rely on its own resources to survive. The effectiveness of a firm, therefore, is related to its ability to acquire needed resources from external vendors.

RDT argues that organizations will engage in a strategic decision making process when deciding whether or not to acquire critical resources from external entities (Pfeffer & Salancik 2003). Important resources will be retained in-house while less important resources will be outsourced. Implicit in the outsourcing deal will be a dependent relationship that will have to be negotiated and constructed. According to Pfeffer and Salancik this dependence is determined by three resource dimensions: importance, discretion and substitutability for that resource. Important resources are those critical to the survival of the firm. Discretion is the ability of the firm to control resource availability. Finally, substitutability refers to the availability of alternative sources for obtaining the resource. By assessing all three factors with respect to a given IT resource, a firm can determine the degree of dependence associated with outsourcing a specific resource and make the decision according to the degree of control the firm is willing to relinquish.

Importance of the IT resource is probably the most researched of the three factors affecting the firm's dependence. IT resources are playing an increasingly critical role in organizations. Much has been written about the strategic role of the IT resource in organizations (Brynjolfsson & Hitt 1996; Clemons & Row 1991; Sethi & King 1994) and studies have found a relationship between IT and sustained competitive advantage (Clemons 1991; Clemons & Row). With respect to discretion, firms attempt to minimize dependency on external entities through negotiation and contracts. In addition, many IT resources in firms are idiosyncratic to the business and not easily duplicated. Hence, few or no substitutes exist for those IT resources that have a great deal of specificity to the firm. While discretion and substitutability are important factors, we have chosen to focus on and operationalize the importance factor.

Lacity and Willcocks (2001) analyzed hundreds of case studies and determined that the decision to outsource critical IT applications increased the firm's dependency on the external entity. The resultant dependency is enough to deter the firm from transferring control via an outsourcing deal. Similarly Kern and Willcocks (2002) analyzed several outsourcing relationships and concluded that too much dependence on vendor's performance is risky.

Traditionally, core IT applications are recommended for in house control (Lacity & Hirschheim 1993). Research suggests that core competencies are what make an organization "unique" in its competitiveness (Quinn & Hilmer 1994). It is the knowledge that the organization has gained of its own processes (Prahalad &

Hamel 1990) that allows it to compete with the best in the world (Quinn & Hilmer). An organization that possesses a core competency can integrate core technologies and governance processes, realizing price-performance ratios and customer service levels that exceed those of its competitors (Prahalad 1993). Core technologies are a critical enabler of this capability (Prahalad). To compete globally, firms need to ask whether external control of a function will improve its ability to perform an activity at a level comparable with the best of breed (Drtina 1994).

2.3   Control of the IT Resource

Although the issue of IT as a strategic resource has been discussed widely in IS studies, little previous research has empirically examined the effect of a resource-dependency perspective on sourcing decisions (Dibbern et al. 2004). Prior research using transaction cost analysis (Ang & Straub 1998; Beier 1989; Grover, Cheon, & Teng 1996; Nam, Rajagopalan, Rao, & Chaudhury 1996; Schary & Coakley 1991) has studied the impact of asset specificity on external procurement. While Grover et al. (1994) and Teng et al. (1995) used RDT as a theory base for studying the impact of resource gaps and strategic role of IS on the IS outsourcing decision, the wider implications of resource dependency through IS outsourcing on firm performance were not examined. Whereas case study evidence suggests that managers think value is created in the IT function through strategic focus on core competencies (Lacity, Hirschheim, & Willcocks 1994), more quantitative evidence is needed to support this qualitative work in order to better understand the relationships between views about IT as a strategic resource and the control of IT functions.

Reasoning from transaction cost and agency theories, for example, Ang (1993) discusses the role of agents of the firm and agents of the outsourcing vendor and how the nature of the relationship leads to different kinds and different intensities of control. Part of this control is related to the contract that binds the organizations, but part is built into the management decision to give up control over assets.

The basic argument in Ang's work is that the degree of outsourcing depends on which agent has control over the activity. When one agent is completely responsible for an activity, then her conceptualization argues that this would be a case of either "total outsourcing" to outsiders or "total insourcing" to insiders. In the former situation, the firm has lost nearly all control of the asset. In the latter, the firm retains total control. But monitoring by one of the agents of the firm would indicate a higher level of firm control decisions whereas providing information or other inputs to the outsourcer, without extensive monitoring, would represent less control.

Based on RDT and consistent with other researchers, we conceptualize the notion of control of the IT resource as a continuum (see Fig. 1). One end of the continuum occurs when the firm yields control of all of its IT resources resulting in the greatest dependency on the external environment. In this case the firm is engaged in "Total Outsourcing." Conversely, the decision to control all IT resources may be said to be a "Total Insourcing" decision. The extent of control of the IT resource, therefore, represents a set of decisions regarding which resources are to

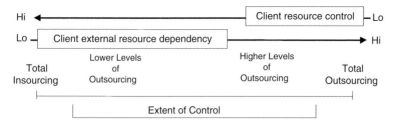

Fig. 1 Continuum of control of the IT resource

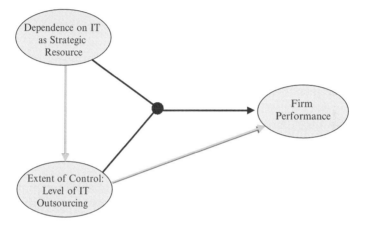

Fig. 2 The Strategic control model (SCM). *NB*: The *solid dot* represents a moderated path tested by H1. The *grayed paths* are part of the SCM but are not tested in this paper

be retained and which are not. We refer to this as *Extent of Control*. This notion is conceptually close to what Lacity and Willocks (1998) call "selective" outsourcing.[3]

2.4   *Research Model and Hypotheses*

The Strategic Control Model (SCM; Fig. 2) expresses causal relationships in the context of resource dependency.

The model indicates that when firms depend on external entities for resources critical to their survival, they yield control. IT functions that are viewed as important and, thereby, strategic are more likely to be controlled internally. IT functions that are less strategic are more likely to be outsourced to some extent. Our contention is

---

[3]Lacity and colleagues use the term "selective outsourcing" in apposition to total outsourcing or insourcing, which is why "Extent of Outsourcing" appears within these two extremes in Figure 1. Our argument is a selective outsourcing argument in that firms that abjure total outsourcing are making decisions about not outsourcing what are viewed as strategic resources, which allows them more control over their core assets.

that the effects of IT as a strategic resource on performance will depend on *where* the resource is controlled. The more strategic the resource, the more the need to control that resource internally. The less strategic the resource, the less the need to control that resource internally. When a "match" exists (Venkatraman 1989) between how strategic a resource is and where that resource is located, higher performance should ensue. Where such a match is not observed, lower levels of performance should be expected. SCM argues, therefore, that extent of control moderates the effect of strategic IT resources on performance (H_1).

3   Study Hypotheses

3.1   Detailing of Hypotheses

When organizations depend on external entities for resources critical to their survival, they yield control. Yielding control of highly dependent resources leads to lower performance. Based on the Strategic Control Model, we test the following:

H_1: Extent of control negatively moderates the relationship between strategic dependence on IT resources and firm performance.

The conventional graphical model showing this set of relationships is Model A (see Fig. 3a). Directionality is a measurement issue as to which direction the variables move to show stronger effects. Extent of Control in this study is being measured as higher when a firm outsources. Therefore, as this number goes higher (and dependence is also high), the firm performance declines. This is why we expect a negative coefficient.

From a resource dependency perspective, management must direct the acquisition and deployment of resources, and thereby, control resources to optimize performance and obtain organizational goals. RDT stresses the need for firms to capitalize on their unique assets and to develop management strategies to exploit the advantages from strategically positioned resources.

A full testing of the moderating effect calls for a comparison with the direct effect of strategic dependence on the IT resource on performance (Chin, Marcolin, & Newsted 2003; Sharma, Durand, & Gur-Arie 1981). A direct effect is not

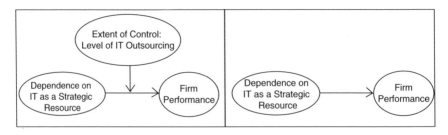

Fig. 3   (**a**) Model A (**b**) Model B

expected to add significantly to the explained variance and is examined specifically to see if the posited moderation is the most powerful explanation of performance. Formally, H_2 is:

H_2 *A model linking the moderator extent of control X resource dependence to performance will have statistically higher explained variance than a model linking only resource dependence to performance.*

What is being tested in H_2, in effect, is the difference in explained variance between Model A and Model B.

3.2 Design, Sampling, and Measures

To assess the hypotheses, 54 business units (BUs) in 27 firms were investigated. Since outsourcing and firm performance were measured at the BU level, our N for testing was 54. See Appendix A for a list of international firms chosen to represent a breadth of industry deployment of IT as a strategic asset; this sample also represented a breadth of outsourcing experiences, as can be seen in Table 1. These firms were headquartered in seven countries (USA, Canada, Malaysia, Singapore, Australia, UK and Switzerland) in the financial, retail and manufacturing industries. These three industries are at the forefront of change in industry structure due to the

Table 1 Constructs and measure

Construct, source, and nature	Code	Description of measure
Dependence on IT as a Strategic Resource:	RESOURCE1	% of strategic IT investment in prior year
Objective Measures (CE; formative)	RESOURCE2	% of strategic IT investment – average % change over previous 5 years
Dependence on IT as a Strategic Resource:	RESOURCE3	The extent that BU managers consider IT in their strategic decision-making
Subjective Measures (CIO; reflective)	RESOURCE4	The extent that IT infrastructure has a role in BU decision-making
	RESOURCE5	Senior managers see IT as providing competitive advantage
	RESOURCE6	IT enables new business strategies
Extent of Control of IT Resource:	CONTROL1	Average of rankings of the extent to which IT is outsourced by the BUs in each of 15 functional areas
Level of Outsourcing (BU IT mgrs.; formative)	CONTROL2	% of IT investment spent on services outside the firm– average % change over past 5 years
	CONTROL3	% of IT investment spent on services outside the firm over last 2 years
Firm Performance:	PERF1-2	Profits per employee ($)
Business Units	PERF3	Pricing against competitors (index)
(CE and BU IT mgrs.; formative)	PERF4	Return on assets

combination of technological innovation and the accelerated pace of globalization (Bradley, Housman, & Nolan 1993). They also provide a contrast in their strategic use of information and information technology (Cash, McFarlan, McKenney, & Applegate 1992; Porter & Millar 1985). Data were collected both at the firm and business unit (BU) levels. The firm level provides insight into the strategic role of IT in the organization. The business unit level allows us to examine the outsourcing decision at the point closest to the outsourcing experience.

In order to focus on BU outsourcing of IT in complex and representative settings, the firms selected met the following criteria:

1. Comprised of at least two autonomously managed BUs with a distinct set of products or customers;
2. Were in the top five in their industry by market share in their region;
3. Recorded data on historical IT investment, IT outsourcing and performance which could be made available to the researchers; and
4. As a group of firms, offered a broadly based international perspective.

To implement the study internationally, a research team collected data from universities located in or near the country of the firm's headquarters (see "Acknowledgments" for list of research partners). The researchers met to refine the concepts and methods for the study and then used the same data collection procedures.

Appendix B shows the instrument that was used to collect data (Table 1 below is a shorthand version) and details of the research method, including the justification of measures employed.

3.3 Descriptive Statistics

As can be seen from Table 2, the variables demonstrate reasonable dispersion, none suffering from a floor or ceiling effect. This distribution suggests that the data is conducive for further statistical testing.

Firms varied in the level of their strategic IT investment from 0 to 70% of their portfolios, and the average deltas varied from a 100% decrease to 75% increase. Clearly, all firms were engaged in making decisions about which IT functions to outsource in that no firm or business unit in the study completely outsourced all of their IT activities. As a percentage of IT investment, the 5 year average of IT outsourcing varied from 0 to 50%, averaging 8.6%. The average delta increase over that time was 3.9%, moreover, which suggests that firms were gradually outsourcing more and more of their IT services over time.

3.4 Data Analysis

The frequency distributions for CONTROL1 indicate that the sample group did not have cases of total outsourcing. Fortunately, there is dispersion on the CONTROL

Table 2 Descriptive Statistics from Study [*NM = not meaningful]

Construct	Scale items/ code	(Rank) Mean	S.D.	Range	Max	Min
Dependency on IT as a strategic	RESOURCE1	26.88	23.11	NM*	70	0
Resource: objective measures	RESOURCE2	1.78	27.37	NM	75	−100
Dependency on IT as a strategic resource: subjective measures	RESOURCE3	2.85	1.53	1–5	5	1
	RESOURCE4	4.00	1.21	1–5	5	2
	RESOURCE5	3.89	1.42	1–5	5	1
	RESOURCE6	3.72	1.32	1–5	5	1
Extent of control of IT resource	CONTROL1	1.47	NM	1–3	2.13	1.0
	CONTROL2	3.70	22.07	NM	63.36	−33.15
	CONTROL3	8.44	12.18	NM	50.00	0
Performance	PERF1	94,109	12,216	NM	55,3000	0
	PERF2	54,048	8,531	NM	44,6760	0
	PERF3	79.07	45.17	NM	126.2	0
	PERF4	12.22	20.94	NM	110.43	−23.24

variables, although it is equally clear that no firms were engaged in total outsourcing. This means that a straightforward PLS analysis can be performed on the CONTROL variables without transforming them to match the conceptualization of Extent of Control in Fig. 2. In this case, higher levels of internal control should moderate IT as a strategic resource and this moderation should lead directly to higher performance.

Partial Least Squares (PLS) was used to analyze the variables and relationships posited for explaining the IT outsourcing environment. Table 3 is a snapshot of the overall results of hypothesis testing.[4] While the distinction between formative and reflective indicators is still ambiguous in the methodological literature (Diamantopoulos & Winklhofer 2001), we are convinced that the constructs of Extent of Control and Firm Performance are formative and thus treated them in that way. Dependence on IT is a multidimensional construct with both formative and reflective aspects and was modeled in the PLS runs as such (Petter, Straub, & Rai 2007).

Sample size was sufficient for PLS analysis (Gefen, Straub, & Boudreau 2000). The path coefficients, their T-statistics, and the explained variance for the models are shown in Fig. 3. The model to test H_1 explains circa 49% of the variance in the latent dependent variable.

In the test of H_1, the coefficient linking BU-level IT resources moderated by extent of control of those resources with performance was statistically significant.

---

[4] These results will be examined further in the discussion section.

Table 3 Overall results of study hypothesis testing

H_x	Hypothesis	PLS statistics (Formative)	Support?
H_1	Extent of control moderates the relationship between a strategic dependence on IT resources and firm performance (Model$_1$).	Coeff = –0.702	Yes
		T = 3.95	
		R^2 = 0.487	
H_2	A model linking the moderator extent of control X resource dependence to performance will have statistically higher explained variance than a model linking only resource dependence to performance.	Model A	Yes
		R^2 = 0.487	
		Model B	
		R^2 = 0.281	

This result supports H_1 (formative coefficient = –0.702; p-value <. 05; R^2 = 0.487). The finding suggests that firms that invest in IT as a strategic asset are less likely to outsource, and supports the proposition that strategic or core competencies should be retained within the organization and not be outsourced (Prahalad 1993).

3.5   H2 Comparative Model Analysis

To examine the moderation issue further, a PLS run was performed that linked only the dependence on IT as a strategic resource with performance. In this way we are able to compare a model (Model B) that links our resource dependence variable directly to performance with the moderation acting alone (Model A). The test is a pseudo-F test, which in both the case of the formative and reflective interpretation are highly significant (p<.05). Effect sizes (f^2) are calculated as $(R^2_{Model\ 1} - R^2_{Model2})/(1 - R^2_{Model2})$ (Chin et al. 2003; Mathieson, Peacock, & Chin 2001). Multiplying f^2 by (n–k-1), where n is the sample size and k is the number of independent variables (IVs), yields a pseudo-F test for the change in R^2 with 1 and n–k degrees of freedom (Mathieson et al. 2001). According to Cohen (1988), an effect size of 0.02 is small, 0.15 is medium, and 0.35 is large. In our case, the effect size difference is medium, indicating that the models are markedly different in terms of their ability to explain the variance in the dependent variable. In short, the SCM is validated by this model comparison.

4   Discussion, Implications, and Limitations

The analysis uncovered numerous exciting findings about control over IT resources and the effects of IT outsourcing. The strategic control model, a major contention of the research, was supported in the hypotheses. Firms that invest at significant levels in strategic systems are sensitive to when they should retain control of core assets (Lacity 1995). This has major implications for the concept of strategic fit.

C-level executives are responsible for recognizing which assets the firm is dependent on for its competitive advantages and to nurture these core assets. This fitting of strategy to firm performance is one of the most important jobs of a C-level manager. Not to recognize the strategic nature of this choice is tantamount to allowing the firm to drift and to only randomly capitalize on what has or can make it a success. Outsourcing too much or outsourcing the wrong assets represents a failure of strategic fit.

This is one of the first studies that examines under which circumstances outsourcing will contribute to relatively better firm performance. As such, our focus is set on the role of fit between the strategic role of IS assets within a firm and its sourcing strategy as a key enabler for higher firm performance.

Sustaining an IT-enabled competitive advantage requires continuous innovation, environmental scanning and a corporate mindset that understands the strategic use of IT. Such an environment is difficult to cultivate when control over a strategic asset is handed over to an integrator or service provider.

Whether managers view IT as a strategic resource or not, the outsourcing decision is almost certainly not an indiscriminate one. There is evidence in the study that selective sourcing decisions lead to higher performance and that there are adverse consequences involved in ignoring the connection between viewing IT as a strategic resource and selectively outsourcing it. Higher levels of performance uncovered in this study include: (1) larger profits per employee and (2) higher ROA. PERF3, increased competitiveness or comparative pricing against competitors, did not load significantly (see Appendix B), but the other performance measures did. These significant effects are last in a value chain that begins by arguing that strategic choices about sourcing IT eventually impact the firm's bottom line.

Grounded in resource dependency theory, the strategic control model expresses these relationships in a parsimonious fashion. In this study, the model received sufficient support to justify further research in this vein. In short, it appears that firms that selectively outsource IT and take advantage of these competitive opportunities will be justified in their investment decision. A significant business payoff awaits firms that can successfully manage selective outsourcing.

Managers and researchers alike need to consider the implications of these findings. For scholars, it is important to note that the strategic control hypothesis received support through both the objective and subjective measures, but that the theoretical framework does needs further work in construct specification and testing of subjective measures and alternate measures of performance.

Of course, all research has limitations and there are some that need to be noted in the present study and addressed in future work. Whereas the quality of the data was generally excellent and 14 observations per business unit assessing the outsourcing activity (CONTROL1) added richness to our measures, further studies in differing settings and locales are always in order and part of the process of normal science.

Measurement issues lie at the heart of solid research and, although most of the measures in the instrument performed reasonably well, further work in this vein can refine and hone the approach. It would be useful, for example, to have accompanying subjective and objective measures for even more of the variables in the data set. This would help to rule out methods bias and to conclude that the effects observed are not artifactual. Instrumentation of the attitudes toward IT as a strategic asset needs to be revisited.

Given that the present study represents a departure from the usual outsourcing theory bases of transaction cost and incomplete contracting (Ang & Straub 1998; Lacity & Hirscheim 1993; Richmond, Seidmann, & Whinston 1992a, b), we feel that RDT has proven itself to be a useful lens for formulating theoretical propositions related to the outsourcing decision.

Practitioners should recognize that deciding which IT resources are strategic is a crucial phase in the overall systems integration process. Noncore assets can be taken over by outsourcers with no loss of *strategic control*. On the other hand, retaining IT assets that are strategic will enable the firm to remain competitive and better capable of responding to future technological uncertainty.

This study raises interesting questions about the worldwide trend of increasing IT outsourcing. For example, some governments (e.g., Federal Government of Australia)[5] have mandated market testing for outsourcing all IT investments, often combining several departments in the outsourcing contract (e.g., Taxation and Health) to achieve a stronger bargaining position. In contrast to this approach, the results of this study strongly support a selective approach to outsourcing based on strategic control of key IT assets and the core competencies of the organization. Strategic control should be the ultimate purpose of outsourcing, rather than any arbitrary attribution of value to IT outsourcing in its own right. Managers in the position to influence key outsourcing decisions should think about the need to strategically control each IT activity and make their decisions accordingly.

Acknowledgments We wish to acknowledge researchers who contributed to the collection of insights and data for this research:

- Marianne Broadbent, Edward W Kelley and Partners Pty Ltd (formally with Gartner and University of Melbourne)
- Carey Butler, Monash University, Australia
- John Henderson and Christine Lentz, Boston University
- Jeff Sampler, Oxford University
- Ali Farhoomand, Hong Kong University
- Peter Keen, Keen Education
- Jack Rockart, Jeanne Ross, Massachusetts Institute of Technology
- Judith Quillard, IBM
- Neo Boon Siong National University of Singapore and Christina Soh, Nanyang Technological University, Singapore

---

[5] See www.aph.gov. au for details of a Federal Australian Government inquiry into IT outsourcing.

Appendix A

Annotated Instrument Items

[CONSTRUCT: DEPENDENCE ON IT AS A STRATEGIC RESOURCE: OBJECTIVE MEASURES (RESOURCE1 AND RESOURCE2)]

Levels of Investment in I/T Infrastructure

The following questions relate to the level of investments in I/T in the corporate I/S function and the BUSINESS UNITs. Please be as accurate as you can. If you don't have the information, please provide your best estimation and mark the estimate with a star (*).

In completing these questions, please use the FIRM's or BUSINESS UNIT's reporting year. For example, if the last month of your reporting year is September, for Year 1 you would report for the year ended September Year.

Corporate I/T Investment

In answering the following questions, please consider I/T Infrastructure as:

the base foundation of I/T capability budgeted for and provided by the I/S function and shared across multiple BUSINESS UNITs. The I/T capability includes both the technical and managerial expertise required to provide reliable services.

1. Of the corporate I/T investment identified in Question 3, what percentage would you classify as I/T Infrastructure ?

Year 1	Year 2	Year 3	Year 4	Year 5	Year 6
_____%	_____%	_____%	_____%	_____%	_____%

2. Of the corporate I/T investment in Year 6 *that is not infrastructure*, estimate the percentage which was to:

   (1) Cut operating costs – e.g., reduce costs of preparing and sending invoices –%
   (2) Increase or protect your sales (or market share) by providing new (or –% improved) customer service or products. This type of investment generally positions the firm in the marketplace (e.g.: Create competitive advantage by significantly reducing the delivery time of your services by placing order entry links in your customer's offices) [RESOURCE1]
   (3) Provide information. This would include information for control, _____% communication, accounting, managing quality, EIS, MIS, etc.

3. Please estimate this breakdown in previous years.

	Year 1	Year 2	Year 3	Year 4	Year 5
(1) Cut Costs	____%	____%	____%	____%	____%
(2) Gain Sales [RESOURCE2]	____%	____%	____%	____%	____%
(3) Provide Information	____%	____%	____%	____%	____%

[CONSTRUCT: DEPENDENCE ON IT AS A STRATEGIC RESOURCE: SUBJECTIVE MEASURES (RESOURCE3 THROUGH RESOURCE6)]

Decisions about I/T Infrastructure Investments

I/T Infrastructure refers to the base foundation of I/T capability budgeted for and provided by the I/S function and shared across multiple BUSINESS UNITS. The I/T capability includes both the technical and managerial expertise required to provide reliable services.

The following questions relate to the way decisions are made about I/T Infrastructure investments. Please CIRCLE the number that best describes your FIRM.

RESOURCE3. In forming business strategies, the BUSINESS UNIT (BU) considers the capabilities of the I/T Infrastructure.

1	2	3	4	5
Never	Sometimes in some BUs	Sometimes in All BUs	Often in most BUs	Always in All BUs

RESOURCE4. In justifying Infrastructure investments, the flexibility to quickly meet future, but as yet unspecified, BUSINESS UNIT strategies is valued.

1	2	3	4	5
Never	Rarely	Sometimes	Usually	Always

RESOURCE5. Senior managers of the FIRM perceive a flexible I/T Infrastructure as providing a competitive advantage.

1	2	3	4	5
Strongly Disagree	Disagree	Neutral	Agree	Strongly Agree

RESOURCE6. In meetings between senior I/T managers and senior BUSINESS UNIT managers, the most important topic is the capabilities of I/T to enable new business strategies.

1	2	3	4	5
Never	Rarely	Sometimes	Usually	Always

[CONSTRUCT: EXTENT OF CONTROL OF THE IT RESOURCE (CONTROL1, CONTROL2, AND CONTROL3)]

Management of IT Activities

This question seeks to identify various types of responsibility and input for different I/T related activities throughout the FIRM. There are four groups indicated: the Corporate I/S group, the Business I/S group, Business Unit Line Managers and any organizations external to the firm. For each of the activities listed (Items 1–15), please indicate the level of management responsibility and input for each of the four groups using the following symbols:

R = Responsible for this activity   M = Monitor this activity
I = Provide Input for this activity   N = No involvement at all in this activity

Each box should have one of the letters (R,I,M,N) entered into it. For a particular activity there may be dual responsibility (or perhaps input). Thus a letter can be used more than once for an activity.

	Corporate IS group	Business IS group	Line manager	Organization external to the firms
1. IT planning				
2. Operations				
3. Systems development				
4. Systems maintenance				
5. Overall architecture				

Establishing technological standards for the organization in order to ensure compatibility (e.g.: only UNIX). Within the architecture, who has the responsibility for:

6. Data				
7. Hardware				
8. Applications				
9. Communications				

10. Security

11. Infra structure

12. Technology
    Transfer

Introducing existing technologies into the firm:

13. Human
    Resource
    Management

14. Training in the
    use of IT

15. Research and
    development
    (development of
    new technology)

[CONTROL1. This measure was a mean rank of the codings of each of the 15 IT activities in the above scale.]

CONTROL2. Of the business unit IT investment identified earlier in Question 3, what percentage is spent on services provided outside the firm ?

Year 1	Year 2	Year 3	Year 4	Year 5	Year 6
_____%	_____%	_____%	_____%	_____%	_____%

[CONTROL3. Average of last 2 years of the data collected in CONTROL2.]
[CONSTRUCT: PERFORMANCE (PERF1 – PERF4)]
BUSINESS UNIT Financial Performance
The following questions refer to the financial performance of this BUSINESS UNIT.

PERF1&2. Please report this BU's revenue for the past 5 years. If a bank, please define revenues as NET INTEREST INCOME (after INTEREST PAID) plus OTHER OPERATING INCOME

Year 1	Year 2	Year 3	Year 4	Year 5
$M_____	$M_____	$M_____	$M_____	$M_____

PERF1. Please report this BU's expenses (including cost of goods sold) for the past five years.

Year 1	Year 2	Year 3	Year 4	Year 5
$M_____	$M_____	$M_____	$M_____	$M_____

PERF2. Please report this BU's cost of goods sold for the past 5 years

Year 1	Year 2	Year 3	Year 4	Year 5
$M_____	$M_____	$M_____	$M_____	$M_____

PERF3. For each year, please indicate how your pricing of products compared to your three largest competitors. For example, if this BU's prices averaged 10% above those of the three largest competitors, then 110% is reported for each year.

Year 1	Year 2	Year 3	Year 4	Year 5
_100_%	_____%	_____%	_____%	_____%

PERF4. Please report your Return on Assets (ROA) for the past 4 years. ROA is calculated by dividing (i.e., profit) before interest and tax (EBIT) by total assets.

Year 1	Year 2	Year 3	Year 4
_____	_____	_____	_____

Appendix B

Research Methods

B1.0   Data Collection

To adequately address the issues raised in the current study requires a study design that collects data from multiple respondents, thereby achieving independence of sources and reducing the likelihood of systematic bias. Data were collected via interviews, the completion of response forms by participants, analysis of organizational documentation (e.g., memos, internal reports) and notes of presentations made by executive managers about recent strategy and technology developments.

In each firm there were a minimum of four participants, some interviewed on multiple occasions. The four participants were the Chief Information Officer (CIO), IS executives from at least two different business units, and a corporate executive (CE) who was able to provide a strategic perspective across the firm as a whole. This person was the CEO, the Chief Financial Officer, Chief Operating Officer, or the Director of Strategy. In each firm, the CIO was interviewed about IS arrangements and the decision-making process relating to both business and IT strategy and the extent of IT outsourcing. Four different response forms were distributed to participants. When these were completed and returned, interviews were held with each IT manager, including the CIO and the BU manager to explore the issues in more depth and to ensure that consistent definitions of constructs were used in the data collection. Excerpts from these interviews appear later in the paper.

To ensure independence of variables, data on IT investment was gathered through different sources. The subjective view of IT as a strategic resource was provided by the CIO while objective IT investment data and performance data were gathered primarily from the CE and his/her staff, the one exception being IT investment in competitive systems, as described below. IT managers from the respective business units provided data on the nature and degree of outsourcing in the BUs. Some of these measurements called for judgments whereas others were more oriented toward accounting-type data. Performance data was also gathered from two sources: the CE and the BU information technology managers and then checked for inter rater reliability.

B2.0   Measures

B2.1   Dependence on IT as a Strategic Resource: Objective Measures

To capture the firm's dependence on IT as a strategic resource, we chose first to use objective measures of the percentage of the IT budget that was considered strategic. To achieve consistency across the sample we provided respondents with a simple definition of strategic IT based on the work of Clemons (1991), Ives and Learmonth (1984), and Porter and Millar (1985). CIOs were asked to provide the percentage of the IT budget over the past 5 years that was invested to:

> '…increase or protect your sales (or market share) by providing new (or improved) customer service or products. This type of investment generally positions the firm in the marketplace (e.g., creates competitive advantage by significantly reducing the delivery time of your services by placing order entry links in your customer's offices).'

Besides RESOURCE1, data on actual firm actions included the calculation of both a 5-year average and an average year-to-year percentage change in assessments of IT as a strategic resource (RESOURCE2).

B2.2   Dependence on IT as a Strategic Resource: Subjective Measures

The goal of this set of measures (RESOURCE3 – RESOURCE6) was to capture the CIO's belief of the extent to which managers (both senior managers and BU managers) saw IT as a strategic resource. We asked the CIO to consider his or her dealings with senior business managers and answer four items. The items measured factors such as whether BU managers considered IT when they formed business strategies or whether they viewed a flexible IT infrastructure as strategic. Scores from the four, five-point Likert scales were used to measure IT as a strategic resource, with higher scores indicating IT was a highly strategic resource. The measures tap into arguments that a focus on IT lowers dependency on others' IT resources which will, in turn, lead to advantages. The measures, positioned at a molar level of abstraction, are omnibus measures. See Appendix B for the relevant instrument items.

B2.3 Extent of Control of IT Resource: Subjective Measures

To capture the extent to which managers decided to give up control of IT resources to outsourcers, we queried managers about fifteen typical IS activities (CONTROL1). The control perspective on IT outsourcing has been conceptualized by Ang (1994) and validated in Ang and Straub (1998). In psychometric tests in the latter study, the researchers found that measures of the control of IT as a resource (not necessarily a strategic resource) correlated highly with an applications-oriented perspective and an operations-oriented perspective. Since validation is always "egalitarian and symmetrical" (Campbell 1960, p. 548), their cross-methods validation suggests that a control-oriented perspective captures the essence of the construct of IT outsourcing (Ang & Straub 1998).

Using Ang's theoretical perspectives (1994, 1993), the instrumentation measured the shift in control from internal to external service providers for each of fifteen IT resources. Participants filled in the matrix entitled "Management of IT Activities" in Appendix B. The list of IT activities on the research instrument was similar to that used in the validated Ang and Straub field study (1998) and Smith, Stoddard, and Applegate case study (1987); it also aligned well with activities identified in the IT services work of Weill and Broadbent (1998).

The four groups responsible for sourcing are indicated in Table 4 below, which presents an example of how a respondent may have filled out the form. Levels of control were denoted by the respondents as "R" if the group was responsible for an activity, "M" if the group monitored the activity, "I" if the group provided input, and "N" if there was no involvement.

The coding of these levels of control for each activity was a straightforward ordinal scaling, varying from 1 to 4. If the matrix data indicated that control was entirely internal, the IT activity was coded "1." In cases where the outsourcer was being monitored by the client firm, the decision was coded as "2." If control was shared with the external provider but only input was provided by the firms' agents, then it was coded "3." If control was entirely in the hands of the outsourcer, then the coding was a "4."

An example might help to explain how this coding was performed. If the codes "M" or "R" was denoted for *any* of the inside agents (IS corporate, business unit, or line manager) *and* the outsider ("organization external to the firm") role

Table 4 Coding categories for construct: control of IT functions/services

Corporate IS group	Business IS group	Line manager	Organization external to the firms
I	I		R
R = Responsible for this activity		M = Monitor this activity = Monitor this activity	
I = Provide input for this activity		N = No involvement at all in this activity	

was coded "R" as being responsible for the activity, IT planning was coded as a 2. The reasonable assumption here is that the firm is attempting to control this activity by either monitoring it or sharing in the delivery of the service. If the outsider is responsible for the activity (coded as "R") and one or more of the firm agents is providing input (coded as "I"), then the firm is exerting less influence over the delivery of the service. This lower level of control was classified as "3," therefore.

B2.4   Extent of Control of IT Resource: Objective Measures

An objective surrogate for control over the IT resource is the extent to which a firm outsources IT. Two objective measures were also used. The first, CONTROL2, was gathered at the corporate level. It is a financial measure where the outsourcing budget is expressed as a percentage of the firm's total IS budget for that year. Five years of data were collected allowing the calculation of both a 5-year average (CONTROL2) and an average year-to-year percentage change in outsourcing (CONTROL3). Similar approaches were used in Loh and Venkatraman (1992) and Grover et al. (1996).

The second objective variable, CONTROL3, was the percentage of IT invest-ment spent on services outside the firm. Averaged over the last 5 years, CONTROL3 measured the delta or change in percentage of IT investment outside the firm.

B2.5   Business Unit Performance

The construct "Performance" is used extensively in organizational and information systems research. A broad range of quantitative performance measures are often employed by researchers, including measures of profit such as return on assets (ROA) (Floyd & Woolridge 1990; Hitt & Brynjolfsson 1996), return on net worth (Cron & Sobol 1983), expenses as a ratio of income (Bender 1986; Harris & Katz 1991), and the ratio of operating profit to revenue (Markus & Soh 1993). These measures of profitability are lagging measures (i.e., accounting end-of-period measures). Kaplan and Norton (1992) recommend a balance of leading (i.e., meas-ures of performance that predict lagging measures) and lagging measures to capture performance. We chose 3 measures that provide a balance of leading and lagging measures that also relate well with the theoretical issues we are expostulating. They tap into: (1) labor productivity, (2) competitiveness, and (3) return on assets.

First, profit per employee (PERF1-2) was chosen as a measure of labor produc-tivity (Weill 1992) as it is likely to be sensitive to the level of outsourcing used. The first of the measures included cost of goods sold (COGS) and all other expenses. The second was COGS alone. Two other firm-level measures were used, namely, an index of competitiveness of the firm compared to its industry (PERF3). This was assessed by the chief officer of the business unit. Finally, a standard return on assets (ROA) measure (PERF4). All of these measures should reflect higher performance if the firm does not outsource more strategic assets than the SCM argues it should. See Appendix B for instrument items and elaboration.

B3.0   Instrument Validation

Many of the measures employed to test the SCM are likely formative rather than reflective (Gerbing & Anderson 1988; Petter et al. 2007) in that the types of measurement and the scales being employed were radically different for most measures and constructs. For example, the construct "firm performance" was measured by two profitability per employee figures and two items tapping into competitiveness and asset utilization. While each of these very different measures "forms" the construct of firm performance, they likely do not "reflect" it (Campbell 1960; Chin 1998; Cohen, Cohen, Teresi, Marchi, & Velez 1990; Diamantopoulos & Winklhofer 2001; Fornell & Bookstein 1982; Fornell & Larcker 1981; Petter et al. 2007; Thompson, Barclay, & Higgins 1995) in the sense that our four questions with similar low to high semantic anchors do "reflect" the perception of the CIO on whether IT is viewed as a strategic resource.

One indication of whether statistical tests favor a formative or reflective handling is to examine their assumptions. Reliability tests such as Cronbach's α make the assumption that scales are relatively similar in the meaning of the scale values; if not, the α statistic rapidly becomes meaningless. Constructs that rely on formative measures call for structural equation modeling (SEM) techniques such as Partial Least Squares (PLS) or LISREL, and PLS, in particular, can model the latent construct whether it is reflective or formative (Gefen et al. 2000).The other advantage of using PLS analysis is that the measurement error is being modeled, and it is, therefore, possible to use all measures even when their contribution is calculated as being small or modest.[6]

Given the choice of measures in the present study, we engaged in several different forms of analysis to examine the psychometric properties of the instrument. Cronbach's α assesses the reliability of the reflective measures. Significance of PLS loadings or weights indicate acceptable construct validity. The relevant PLS loadings/weights are presented in Table 5.

The occasionally insignificant loading/weight in Table 5 is not a surprise, given that some of the measures are formative (Edwards & Bagozzi 2000). The reflective

---

[6] Particularly because we had numerous formative latent constructs in the SCM, we adopted a holistic data analysis approach with measurement and structural models being run simultaneously. That is, no confirmatory factor analysis preceded the structural model to "cleanse" the scales. A holistic analysis grants high conceptual integrity in the latent constructs. Holistic analysis retains the meaning of each construct, which is drawn from both its measurement items and the other latent variables (Bagozzi 1984).

Table 5 Loadings/weightings from PLS Run

Construct	Item	PLS loading or weight	T
Dependence on IT as strategic resource (Objective; formative)	RESOURCE1	0.9464	7.6849[*]
	RESOURCE2	0.6580	1.7191
Dependence on IT as strategic resource (Subjective; reflective)	RESOURCE5	0.9194	1.9704[*]
	RESOURCE6	0.7558	1.9871[*]
	RESOURCE4	0.5280	2.7585[*]
	RESOURCE3	0.4837	3.1304[*]
Firm performance (formative)	PERF1	0.8758	13.5146[*]
	PERF2	0.7094	4.8963[*]
	PERF4	0.4613	2.7507[*]
	PERF3	0.3282	1.5997

subjective measures (no. 2 in Table 5) should have loaded well, and, indeed, they all load significantly, at α protection level of 0.05, which reinforces the interpretation that the instrument has some convergent validity.

According to Petter et al. (2007), an instrument with formative constructs demonstrates construct validity when the weights are significant, as these generally are. In addition to these tests, the Cronbach's α for the subjective view of IT as a strategic resource was 0.920, which is acceptable by Nunnally and Bernstein's rule of thumb (1994). Therefore, our interpretation of these loadings/weightings is that whereas the measures are not perfect, they are sufficiently valid for purposes of further testing. They are also acceptable because we are adopting a holistic analytical approach, which means that no attempts have been made to "cleanse" the constructs and reduce the *a priori* measurement error in the entire instrument (Bagozzi 1984). Measurement error is accounted for in the statistical technique, but not removed. If we find significance under these harsher statistical conditions, then the findings may be interpreted to be even more robust than otherwise.

We used Goodhue, Lewis, and Thompson (2007) summated approach to running our moderations. There are trade-offs between this approach and Chin et al.'s product-indicator approach (2003) and we felt that the greater parsimony of the former warranted its use here.

References

Ang, S. (1994). Toward conceptual clarity of outsourcing. In B. C. Glasson et al. (Eds.), *Business process reengineering: information systems opportunities and challenges* (pp. 113–126). North-Holland: Elsevier.

Ang, S., & Straub, D. W. (1998). Production and transaction economies and IS outsourcing: a study of the U.S. banking industry. *MIS Quarterly, 22*(4), 535–552.

Bagozzi, R. P. (1984). A prospectus for theory construction in marketing. *Journal of Marketing, 48*, 11–29.

Beier, F. J. (1989). Transportation contracts and the experience effect: a framework for future research. *Journal of Business Logistics, 10*(2), 73–89.

Bender, D. H. (1986). Financial impact of information processing. *Journal of Management Information Systems, 3*(2), 22–32.

Birkinshaw, J., Toulan, O., & Arnold, D. (2001). Global account management in multinational corporations: theory and evidence. *Journal of International Business Studies, 32*(2), 231–248.

Bradley, S. P., Housman, J. A., & Nolan, R. L. (1993). Globalization and Technology, In S. P. Bradley, J. A. Housman, R. L. Nolan (Eds.), Globalization, technology, and competition: the fusion of computers and telecommunications in the 1990s (pp. 3–32). Boston: Harvard Business School Press.

Brynjolfsson, E., & Hitt, L. (1996). Paradox lost? Firm-level evidence on the returns to information systems spending. *Management Science, 42*(4), 541–559.

Campbell, D. T. (1960). Recommendations for APA test standards regarding construct, trait, discriminant validity. *American Psychologist, 15*, 546–553.

Cash, J. I., McFarlan, F. W., McKenney, J. L., & Applegate, L. M. (1992). Corporate information systems management: text and cases. Burr Ridge, Illinois: Irwin.

Chin, W. W. (1998). The partial least squares approach to structural equation modeling. In G. A. Marcoulides (Ed.), *Modern methods for business research* (pp. 295–336). Mahwah, NJ: Lawrence Erlbaum.

Chin, W. W., Marcolin, B. L., & Newsted, P. R. (2003). A partial least squares latent variable modeling approach for measuring interaction effects: results from a monte carlo simulation study and an electronic-mail emotion/adoption study. *Information Systems Research, 14*(2), 189–217.

Clemons, E. K. (1991). Evaluation of strategic investments in information technology. *Communications of the ACM, 34*, 1 24–36.

Clemons, E. K., & Row, M. C. (1991). Sustaining IT advantage: the role of structural differences. *MIS Quarterly, 15*, 275–292.

Cohen, J. (1988). Statistical power analysis for the behavioral sciences, 2nd edn. Hillsdale, NJ: Erlbaum.

Cohen, P., Cohen, J., Teresi, J., Marchi, M., & Velez, C. N. (1990). Problems in the measurement of latent variables in structural equation causal models. *Applied Psychological Measurement, 14*, 183–196.

Cron, W. L., & Sobol, M. G. (1983). The relationship between computerization and performance: a strategy for maximizing the benefits of computerization. *Journal of Information Management, 6*, 171–181.

De Wit, K., & Verhoeven, J. C. (2000). Stakeholder in universities and colleges in flanders. *European Journal of Education, 35*(4), 421–437.

Diamantopoulos, A., & Winklhofer, H. M. (2001). Index construction with formative indicators: an alternative to scale development. *Journal of Marketing Research, 38*(2), 269–277.

Dibbern, J., Goles, T., Hirschheim, R., & Jayatilaka, B. (2004). Information systems outsourcing: a survey and analysis of the literature. *The DATA BASE for Advances in Information Systems, 35*(4), 6–102.

Drtina, R. E. (1994). The outsourcing decision. *Management Accounting, 75*(9), 56–62.

Edwards, E. A., & Bagozzi, R. (2000). On the nature and direction of relationships between constructs and measures. *Psychological Methods, 5*(2), 155–174.

Floyd, S. W., & Woolridge, B. (1990). Path analysis of the relationship between competitive strategy, information technology, and financial performance. *Journal of Management Information Systems*, 47–64.

Fornell, C. R., & Bookstein, F. L. (1982). Two structural equation models: LISREL and PLS applied to consumer exit-voice theory. *Journal of Marketing Research, 19*(4), 440–452.

Fornell, C., & Larcker, D. (1981). Evaluating structural equation models with unobservable variables and measurement error. *Journal of Marketing Research, 18*, 39–50.

Gefen, D., Straub, D., & Boudreau, M.-C. (2000). Structural equation modeling and regression: guidelines for research practice. *Communications of AIS, 7*(7), 1–78.

Gerbing, D. W., & Anderson, J. C. (1988). An updated paradigm for scale development incorporating unidimensionality and its assessment. *Journal of Marketing Research, 25*, 186–192.

Goodhue, D., Lewis, W., & Thompson, R. (2007). Statistical power in analyzing interaction effects: questioning the advantage of PLS with product indicators. *Information Systems Research, 18*(2), 211–227.

Grover, V., Cheon, M. J., & Teng, J. T. C. (1994). An evaluation of the impact of corporate strategy and the role of information technology on IS functional outsourcing. *European Journal of Information Systems, 3*(3), 179–190.

Grover, V., Cheon, M. J., & Teng, J. T. C. (1996). The effect of service quality and partnership on the outsourcing of information systems functions. *Journal of Management Information Systems, 12*(4), 89–116.

Harris, S. E., & Katz, J. L. (1991). Organizational performance and information technology investment intensity in the insurance industry. *Organization Science, 2*(3), 263–295.

Hitt, L. M., & Brynjolfsson, E. (1996). Productivity, business profitability, and consumer surplus: three different measures of information technology value. *MIS Quarterly, 20*(2), 121–142.

Ives, B., & Learmonth, G. (1984). The information system as a competitive weapon. *Communications of the ACM, 27*(12), 1193–1201.

Insinga, R. C., & Werle, M. J. (2000). Linking outsourcing to business strategy. *Academy of Management Executive, 14*(4), 59–61.

Kaplan, R., & Norton, D. (1992). The balanced scorecard – measures that drive performance. *Harvard Business Review, 70*, 71–79.

Kern, T., & Willcocks, L. P. (2002). Service provision and the net: risky application sourcing? In Hirschheim, R., Heinzl, A., & Dibbern, J. (Eds.), *Information systems outsourcing: enduring themes, emergent patterns, and future directions*. Heidelberg: Springer.

Lacity, M., & Hirschheim, R. (1993). Information systems outsourcing myths, metaphors, and realities. New York: Wiley.

Lacity, M. (1995). IT outsourcing: maximize flexibility and control. *Harvard Business Review,* 84–93.

Lacity, M., Hirschheim, R., & Willcocks, L. P. (1994). Realizing outsourcing expectations. *Information Systems Management, 11*(4), 7–18.

Lacity, M. C., & Willcocks, L. P. (1998). An empirical investigation of information technology sourcing practices: lessons from experience. *MIS Quarterly, 22*, 363–408.

Lacity, M. C., Willcocks, L. P., & Feeny, D. F. (1996). The value of selective IT sourcing. *Sloan Management Review, 37*(3), 13–25.

Lacity, M. C., & Willcocks, L. P. (2001). Global information technology outsourcing: in search of business advantage. Chicester, UK: Wiley.

Loh, L., & Venkatraman, N. (1992). Diffusion of information technology outsourcing: influence sources and the Kodak effect. *Information Systems Research, 3*(4), 334–378.

Markus, L. M., & Soh, C. (1993). Banking on information technology: converting IT spending into firm performance. In R. D. Banker, R. J. Kauffman, & M. A. Mahmood (Eds.), *Strategic and economic impacts of information technology investment: perspectives on organizational growth and competitive advantage* (pp. 364–392). Middletown, PA: Idea Group.

Mathieson, K., Peacock, E., & Chin, W. W. (2001). Extending the technology acceptance model: the influence of perceived user resources. *The DATA BASE for Advances in Information Systems, 32*(3), 86–112.

Nam, K. S., Rajagopalan, H., Rao, R., & Chaudhury, A. (1996). A two-level investigation of information systems outsourcing. *Communications of the ACM, 39*(7), 36–44.

Nunnally, J. C., & Bernstein, I. H. (1994). *Psychometric theory*. McGraw-Hill: New York.

Petter, S., Straub, D., & Rai, A. (2007). Specifying formative constructs in IS research. *MIS Quarterly, 31*(4), 623–656.

Pfeffer, J., & Salancik, G. R. (2003). *The external control of organizations: a resource dependency perspective*. Chicago, IL: Stanford University Press (Originally published: New York: Harper & Row, 1978).

Porter, M. E., & Millar, V. E. (1985). How information gives you a competitive advantage. *Harvard Business Review,* 149–160.

Prahalad, C. K. (1993). The role of core competencies in the corporation. *Research-Technology Management, 36*(6), 40–47.

Prahalad, C. K., & Hamel, G. (1990). The core competence of the corporation. *Harvard Business Review, 68*(3), 79–91.

Quinn, J. B., & Hilmer, F. G. (1994). Strategic outsourcing. *Sloan Management Review, 35*(4), 43–55.

Richmond, W. B., Seidmann, A., & Whinston, A. B. (1992a). Incomplete contracting issues in information systems development outsourcing. *Decision Support Systems, 8*(5), 459–477.

Richmond, W. B., Seidmann, A., & Whinston, A. B. (1992b). Contract theory and information technology outsourcing. *Decision Support Systems, 8*(5), 459–477.

Schary, P. B., & Coakley, J. (1991). Logistics organization and the information system. *International Journal of Logistics Management, 2*(2), 22–29.

Sethi, V., & King, W. (1994). Development of measures to access the extent to which an information technology application provides competitive advantage. *Management Science, 40*(12), 1601–1627.

Sharma, S., Durand, R. M., & Gur-Arie, O. (1981). Identification and analysis of moderator variables. *Journal of Marketing Research, 18,* 291–299.

Smith, H. J., Stoddard, D., & Applegate, L. (1987). Manufacturers hanover: the new organization A, B and C (9–189-051). London, UK: Harvard Business School Press.

Teng, J. T. C., Cheon, M. J., & Grover, V. (1995). Decisions to outsource information systems functions: testing a strategy-theoretic discrepancy model. *Decision Sciences, 26*(1), 75–103.

Thompson, R., Barclay, D. W., & Higgins, C. A. (1995). The partial least squares approach to causal modeling: personal computer adoption and use as an illustration. *Technology Studies: Special Issue on Research Methodology, 2*(2), 284–324.

Venkatraman, N. (1989). The concept of fit in strategy research: toward verbal and statistical correspondence. *Academy of Management Review, 13*(3), 423–444.

Weill, P. (1992). The relationship between investment in information technology and firm performance: a study of the valve manufacturing sector. *Information Systems Research, 3*(4), 307–333.

Weill, P., & Broadbent, M. (1998). *Leveraging the new infrastructure: how market leaders capitalise on information technology*. Cambridge, MA: Harvard Business School Press.

The Effects of Outsourcing Announcements on Market Values of Swiss Firms: An Event Study

Fabian S. Willi and Gerhard F. Knolmayer

1 Introduction

The potential benefits of IT outsourcing are discussed very controversially. For determining the cost effects, cost data for providing the IT services internally must be available. However, this data is often not disposable in the necessary level of detail. For instance, the IT costs emerging in the business departments are typically not well documented. Furthermore, the value propositions of outsourced IT services such as higher quality customer service, streamlined business processes, and better and earlier information about IT innovations are difficult to quantify.

A main paradigm of economists is that efficient markets provide correct valuations. Therefore, it seems appropriate to evaluate the external view on IT outsourcing by observing changes in stock prices after outsourcing announcements. If rational investors value both the tangible and intangible effects of IT outsourcing, a change in stock price should reflect the contribution of the outsourcing engagement to the firm's value. And the paradigm presumes that the market's evaluation will be more correct than individual computations.

Since 2000 a few event studies on the effects of announcing the outsourcing of IT systems were published. We summarize the results of these studies and replicate them for outsourcing decisions of Swiss companies.

2 Event Studies

2.1 Methodology

Event studies have been used primarily in Finance and Accounting to measure the impact of an announcement or another event on the share price and, thus, on the market value of the affected company. First event studies go back to the 1930s (MacKinlay, 1997); however, the methodology usually applied today was deve-loped by Fama, Fisher, Jensen, and Roll (1969) and extended by Brown and Warner (1980, 1985). Typical news considered in event studies concern financial reporting, mergers and

R. Hirschheim et al. (eds), *Information Systems Outsourcing,*
© Springer-Verlag Berlin Heidelberg 2009

acquisitions, issues of new shares, dividend announcements, and macroeconomic data. With respect to IT, event studies were carried out for instance to evaluate IT investments (Dos Santos, Pfeffers, & Mauer, 1993; Im, Dow, & Grover, 2001), establishing CIO positions (Chatterjee, Richardson, & Zmud, 2001), ERP system implementations (Hayes, Hunton, & Reck, 2001; Ranganathan & Samarah, 2001), E-commerce systems (Subramani & Walden, 2001), or IT outsourcing announcements (cf. Sect. 2.2).

The idea behind event studies is to attribute an abnormal return, defined as the difference between the actual return and the expected normal return that would have occurred without the event, to the new information. Event studies basically assume that due to an at least semi-strong form of market efficiency the stock prices reflect all public available information immediately (McWilliams & Siegel, 1997).

The abnormal return, attributed to the event, is computed as (MacKinlay, 1997)

$$AR_{it} = R_{it} - E(R_{it} \mid X_t) \tag{1}$$

where AR_{it}, Abnormal return for stock i and period t; R_{it}, Actual return for stock i and period t; $E(R_{it} \mid X_t)$, Normal (expected) return for stock i and period t; X_t, Conditioning information for the normal return model.

Equation (1) indicates that the abnormal return is determined individually for each firm's stock in the sample and for a certain time period, the so-called event window. To calculate the abnormal return, a normal return has to be computed which would have been expected without the occurrence of the event. Several methods for estimating the normal return have been proposed. They may be loosely distinguished as economic and statistical approaches. The Capital Asset Pricing Model is often used for event studies that follow the economic approach. Statistical methods can be grouped into mean-adjusted methods, market-adjusted methods, and market models (Dyckman, Philbrick, & Stephan, 1984). Based on a comparison of these four approaches, Cable and Holland (1999) recommend the market model, where the return of a market index is used as computational basis (X_t), as most suited for estimating normal returns in event studies. This model implies a linear dependency between the stock return of a company and the corresponding market return expressed by the regression equation (MacKinlay, 1997)

$$R_{it} = \alpha_i + \beta_i R_{mt} + \varepsilon_{it} \tag{2}$$

where $E(\varepsilon_{it}) = 0$ and $\text{var}(\varepsilon_{it}) = \sigma_{\varepsilon_i}^2$; R_{it}, Return on stock i in period t; R_{mt}, Return on market index in period t; α_i, Intercept; β_i, Slope coefficient; ε_{it}, Disturbance term in period t.

By substituting the estimated coefficients of (2) in (1), the abnormal return can be computed as

$$AR_{it} = R_{it} - \hat{R}_{it} = R_{it} - \left(\hat{\alpha}_i + \hat{\beta}_i R_{mt} \right) \tag{3}$$

where $\hat{R}_{it}$ is the expected return of security i during the event window and $\hat{\alpha}_i$ and $\hat{\beta}_i$ are the ordinary least squares (OLS) parameter estimates obtained from the regression of R_{it} on R_{mt} using historical returns over the time period t, the estimation window. In other words, the abnormal return is the disturbance term of the market model, calculated on an out-of-sample basis.

To express the market effect of a portfolio of firms affected by the event of interest, the individual firm-specific abnormal returns are aggregated for each day t within the event window:

$$\overline{AR_t} = \frac{1}{N} \sum_{i=1}^{N} AR_{it} \tag{4}$$

The average abnormal return $\overline{AR_t}$ may be computed for different sample sizes (e.g., industries) where N indicates the number of firms included. To derive a measure for the market impact over the event window or a certain interval within the event window (t_1, t_2), the average abnormal returns are aggregated over time as

$$\overline{CAR_{(t_1,t_2)}} = \sum_{t=t_i}^{t_2} \overline{AR_t} \tag{5}$$

Finally, the values of the cumulative average abnormal returns $\overline{CAR_{(t_1,t_2)}}$ are tested for statistical significance. In this study we apply two-tailed tests for significance levels 10%, 5%, and 1%, following the recommendations of MacKinlay (1997).

Event studies require decisions on the lengths of the event windows and of the estimation windows. In earlier times the knowledge about certain events may have been spread via press news typically 1 day after their announcements. Today intermediaries such as PRNewswire and Businesswire distribute press releases via the Internet and make information available to all potential market actors almost in real-time. Therefore, 2 days are often recommended as appropriate for the length of the event window, including the day of the event and the following day (Peterson, 1989; MacKinlay, 1997). However, some actors inside the reporting company may spread their insider knowledge, resulting in information leakage and rumours. It may therefore be appropriate to open the event window a few days before the announcement, particularly if many people know about the (potential) event. This holds especially for new outsourcing contracts because in the evaluation process of different service providers many people recognize that a company is considering an outsourcing deal. However, if the event window chosen is too large, confounding effects may bias the analysis. In our study we computed cumulative abnormal returns (CAR) as well for a maximum event window of 31 days [−10, +20] as for selected shorter intervals, e.g., [0, +1], [−1,0] or [−1, +1].

The estimation window typically lies before the event window. It should not overlap with the event window to avoid distortion of the regression parameters. Estimation windows between 100 and 300 days are commonly used (Peterson, 1989). Furthermore, a time buffer between the end of the estimation window and the beginning of the event window may be appropriate (Gewald & Gellrich, 2007). Considering these suggestions, we selected an estimation window of 250 trading days which closes 10 days before the event window.

2.2 Event Studies on Effects of Outsourcing Announcements

Among others, shares are priced based upon the discounted free cash flow a company is expected to generate and the effect outsourcing may have on generating free cash flow. Therefore, outsourcing should positively affect company valuations if companies communicate to investors how they will use the financial benefits expected from outsourcing.

The first event study on IT outsourcing was probably done by Loh and Venkatraman (1992); unfortunately their working paper is no longer accessible. Since 2000, results of several event studies on the effects of outsourcing decisions were published. In the seminal survey paper by Dibbern, Goles, Hirschheim, and Jayatilaka (2004) these empirical studies have not been considered. Table 1 describes their main properties and results for selected event windows.

Table 1 Event studies on effects of outsourcing announcements

Source	Time interval of study	Region and type of contracts analyzed	Sample sizes	Event windows	Cumulative abnormal returns (%)
Hayes et al. (2000)	(1990–1997)	USA; IT outsourcing	76[a]	[0, +1]	0.35[n.a.]
Peak et al. (2002)	(1988–1993)	USA; Large-firm IS/ IT outsourcing	64[a]	[−1, +1]	0.40
				[+2, +45]	4.90[***]
				[−45, +45]	6.41[**]
Farag and Krishnan (2003)	(1994–2001)	USA; IT outsourcing	172[a]	[0]	0.43[n.a.]
				[0, +9]	1.72[n.a]
Juma'h and Wood (2003)	(1991–1997)	UK; Business service outsourcing	83[a]	[−5, 0]	1.04[**]
				[−20,0]	2.58[**]
Friedrich and Gellrich (2004)	(2000–2003)	Worldwide; Financial services industry	105[b]	[−1, +1]	−0.40
			117[c]	[−1, +1]	−0.04
Oh and Gallivan (2004)	(1998–2001)	USA; IT outsourcing	97[a]	[0, +1]	0.65[*]
Beasley et al. (2005)	(1996–2003)	USA; IT outsourcing	103[a]	[−1, 0]	−0.20[n.a.]
Gao (2005)	(1990–2003)	USA	475[a]	[−1, +1]	0.07
			932[d]	[−1, +1]	1.51[***]
Gellrich and Gewald (2005)	(1997–2004)	Worldwide; Financial services industry	122[a]	[−1, +1]	−0.68[**]
			144[d]	[−1, +1]	0.20
Agrawal et al. (2006)	(1999–2002)	USA; e-business	65[a,e]	[−1, +1]	−1.75[***]
			31[a,f]	[−1, +1]	2.05[***]
Oh et al. (2006)	(1995–2003)	USA; IT outsourcing	192[a]	[0, +1]	0.54[**]
				[−1, +1]	0.47[*]

(continued)

Table 1 (continued)

Source	Time interval of study	Region and type of contracts analyzed	Sample sizes	Event windows	Cumulative abnormal returns (%)
Gewald and Gellrich (2007)	(1998–2004)	Worldwide; Financial services industry	138[a]	[−1, +1]	−0.50**
			164[d]	[−1, +1]	−0.12

*, **, *** denote statistical significance at 10, 5, and 1% levels. *n.a.* statistical significance not reported

[a]Results for contract-granting firms (clients)

[b]Results for contract-granting firms (clients)

[c]Results for outsourcing service providers (vendors)

[d]Results for outsourcing service providers (vendors)

[e]Results for non-commercial intent

[f]Results for commercial exploitation intent

Hayes, Hunton, and Reck (2000) were the first who applied modern event study methodology to outsourcing announcements. Among others, they found that due to information asymmetry the effect is greater for smaller firms which are less covered by analysts than large companies and in cases where the outsourcing announcements are less anticipated. In supplemental analyses they showed that the market values of service industry firms were more positively affected when compared to non-service industry firms.

Peak, Windsor, and Conover (2002) analyzed outsourcing transactions of large firms with gross revenues greater than 500 million USD. Their findings were that IS/IT outsourcing has a value-neutral effect on the firm's stock price around the announcement day (event windows [−1,0] and [−1, +1]) whereas in the long-run significant positive abnormal returns can be identified. Furthermore, the abnormal returns were positive and significant for financially weak firms and those announcing cost reductions or vendor expertise as main reasons for outsourcing.

Farag and Krishnan (2003) classified outsourcing contracts in two main categories, namely strategic projects and non-strategic, cost-cutting projects. Contrary to Peak et al. (2002) their results indicated a negative market reaction for outsourcing projects aiming at cost reduction. Strategic projects showed significant positive abnormal returns, especially for "IT-related firms."

Juma'h and Wood (2003) discussed the effects of different event windows and specific contract characteristics. They found that the abnormal return is higher for companies reporting a new outsourcing contract than those prolonging an outsourcing relationship. Furthermore, the effect is described to be larger for multinationals than for domestic companies.

Friedrich and Gellrich (2004) restricted their research to the financial services sector. They analyzed the impact of outsourcing deals on both the market values of contract-granting firms and of outsourcing service providers. Since negative abnormal returns resulted for most of their event windows, they concluded that on average the capital market does not seem to reward outsourcing announcements.

Many studies on IT outsourcing not only address the benefits but also its potential risks (cf. Aubert B.A., Patry, & Rivard, 1998; Earl, 1996; Kremic, Tukel, & Rom, 2006; Lacity & Hirschheim, 1995; Osei-Bryson & Ngwenyama, 2006; Rottmann & Lacity, 2004). Oh and Gallivan (2004) employed the event study methodology to empirically assess how capital markets evaluate the risks resulting from transaction-specific factors (asset specificity, contract size and duration, and performance monitoring). They found that investors perceive larger outsourcing contracts and those involving firm-specific assets as riskier, resulting in negative abnormal returns.

The study of Beasley, Bradford, and Pagach (2005) extends the work published by Hayes et al. (2000) by examining a larger sample of IS outsourcing announcements and by covering a more recent time interval. Controlling for firm size and industry, they analyzed which financial variables (liquidity, leverage, efficiency, and growth) may result in abnormal returns. Their findings indicate that abnormal returns are significantly higher for more efficient firms (measured by total asset turnover) and, contrary to Hayes et al., also for larger firms.

Similar to Friedrich and Gellrich (2004), Gao (2005) investigated the outsourcing announcement effects on firm values separately for client and vendor firms. No significant value changes for the full sample of client firms were found, whereas on average vendor firms experienced significant positive abnormal returns. Hence, the signing of a new outsourcing contract seems to be rewarded by an increase in the vendor's stock price and, according to Gao, this increase is positively related to the contract value.

In addition to the overall effect of outsourcing announcements, Gellrich and Gewald (2005) analyzed the influence of several factors on the abnormal returns. They found that outsourcers benefit significantly from large deals and that long contracts are negatively related to abnormal returns. However, results of a later study by the same authors partially contradict these results (Gewald & Gellrich, 2007).

Agrawal, Kishore, and Rao (2006) focused on outsourcing of e-business projects. They showed that the purpose of outsourcing (commercial vs. non-commercial exploitation strategic intent) is very relevant for the abnormal return. "… the CARs for non-commercial intents were negative, indicating that markets punished firms for investing in E-business outsourcing projects without commercial intent" (Agrawal et al., p. 868).

Oh, Gallivan, and Kim (2006) tested several hypotheses about investors' perception of transactional risks associated with IT outsourcing. In accordance with Oh and Gallivan (2004) their findings support the negative relationship between investors' reactions and contract size as well as asset specificity of the outsourcing deal. Furthermore, they find that abnormal returns are positively influenced by large vendor size and negatively if high difficulties in monitoring the vendor's perfor-mance are assumed.

The research interest of Gewald and Gellrich (2007) focused again on the financial services industry with special emphasis to the perceived contract's inherent risks (deal size and duration, contract complexity and strategic focus, service provider experience and financial reliability). On average, slightly negative CAR for most event windows were detected. The cross-sectional regression analysis delivers statistically significant values for only two of six risk factors: investors seem to associate smaller outsourcing transactions as well as transactions of strategic core activities with a lower level of risk.

2.3 Related Studies

A few publications which are not or only partly based on event study methodology also investigate the effect of outsourcing announcements on the market value of contract-granting firms. These studies are summarized in Table 2.

Glassmann (2000) explored the market reaction to announcements of mega IT outsourcing deals, defined as deals in which the contract value is $\geq 2\%$ of the company's market value prior to the announcement. The sample's median contract size was 1 billion USD. He defined the excess return as difference between the stock returns of each company and the market index. Positive excess returns were observed for 17 companies, 7 were negative and 3 companies were about break-even. On average a cumulative abnormal return of 5.7% resulted, indicating that mega deals are very positively rewarded by the capital market.

The research of Albright (2003) is inspired by Glassmann (2000) and uses the same approach for a larger sample. His findings provide similar evidence: outsourcing announcements of mega deals positively influence the firms' market value. Both studies do not discuss the statistical significance of their results.

In the following we primarily compare our results to the study published by LogicaCMG in 2005 which received much public attention. The first part of this study investigates the correlation between the announcement of an outsourcing deal and a company's market valuation 1 month after the announcement. Companies having announced an outsourcing deal perform on average 1.7% higher in the stock market benchmarked against others in their sector that did not announce such deals. Companies that outsource outperform peers in five out of seven sectors. In some sectors, companies are realizing an 11% increase in share value. The second part of the study uses the results to forecast the economic impact on corporate values from outsourcing: If UK companies were to increase outsourcing by 52% until 2010, over 17.3 billion USD in additional stock market value would be created (LogicaCMG, 2005).

Table 2 Additional studies on effects of outsourcing announcements

Source	Time interval of study	Region and type of contracts analyzed	Sample sizes	Event windows	Cumulative abnormal returns [%]
Glassmann (2000)	(1993–1999)	Worldwide; IT mega deals	27	[−40, +40]	5.70[n.a.]
Albright (2003)	(1993–2002)	Worldwide; Mega deals	45	[−40, +40]	3.50[n.a.]
LogicaCMG (2005)	(2000–2005)	UK	?	[0, +20]	1.70[n.a.]

n.a. statistical significance not reported

3   Empirical Study for Switzerland

Until recently, no event study on the effects of outsourcing announcements on corporate values was available for Swiss companies. A first study was conducted by Willi F. S. (2006). In this study a company was defined as a "Swiss company" if its headquarter is located in Switzerland. Due to the rather small number of cases all types of outsourcing contracts announced were analyzed; however, all but two concern the outsourcing of IT systems.

3.1   Data about Outsourcing Announcements

No data base about outsourcing contracts of Swiss companies exists. Therefore outsourcing deals had to be detected by primary research. The following sources were checked to find announcements of outsourcing contracts:

- On the websites and archives of 26 providers of outsourcing services we detected 73 news releases about outsourcing contracts. Information was handpicked from globally acting companies like Accenture, ACS, Atos Origin, BT, Capgemini, CSC, EDS, HP, IBM, Siemens, and T-Systems and also from local Swiss outsourcing providers like Bedag Informatik and Swisscom IT Services.
- By scanning the news pages of companies included in the Swiss Market Index (SMI) and selected companies of the broader Swiss Performance Index (SPI) we detected 10 additional outsourcing announcements.
- We also accessed the Factiva database from Dow Jones, a collection of more than 10,000 sources including The Wall Street Journal, the Financial Times, Dow Jones and Reuters newswires and the Associated Press, as well as Reuters Fundamentals and D&B company profiles. Established Swiss newspapers such as the Neue Zürcher Zeitung and Finanz und Wirtschaft were also scanned in detail. This search delivered 11 extra announcements.
- 26 additional announcements were detected by reading electronic newsletters (e.g., published by Active Sourcing AG (http://www.active-sourcing.com/)), bulletin boards, and Google alerts.

In summary we detected 120 outsourcing announcements.

Several criteria were used to define a data basis which is well suited for our event study. We excluded:

- Five cases for which the exact timing of the announcement was not available
- 66 announcements of companies not publicly traded on the SWX Swiss Exchange
- One case in which confounding effects were obvious because the company (Sia Abrasives) announced the outsourcing contract simultaneously with financial data and a dividend increase

- Eight announcements prior to the year 2000. These announcements were eliminated because many electronic archives do not cover these periods. Outsourcing
  was not very common in Switzerland in these days, and particularly to allow for
  a better comparison with the results published by LogicaCMG

In total, only 40 events from 25 companies remained after these adjustments of the
data set; 38 of them pertain to IT outsourcing. Unfortunately, in the majority of
cases the duration of the contracts and their financial volumes have not been
announced.

3.2 Industry Clusters

The Swiss Exchange (SWX) assigns companies considered in the SPI to industries
according to the Industry Classification Benchmark. Figure 1 shows the industries
to which the 40 cases included in our database belong to.

The financial services industry is predominant in our data set about outsourcing
relationships; this is in accordance with other studies about the outsourcing market
in Switzerland (Pierre Audoin Consultants, 2006; Regniet, 2006).

3.3 Results

Figure 2 describes the abnormal returns on the day of the outsourcing announcements. The Swiss capital market seems to react to outsourcing announcements,
even if the effect is not very large: in 25 of 40 cases the abnormal return lies

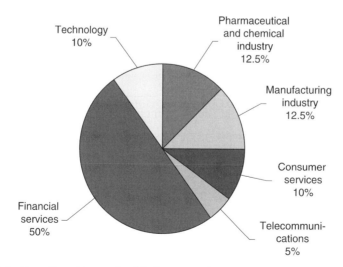

Fig. 1 Industries reflected in sample of Swiss outsourcing companies

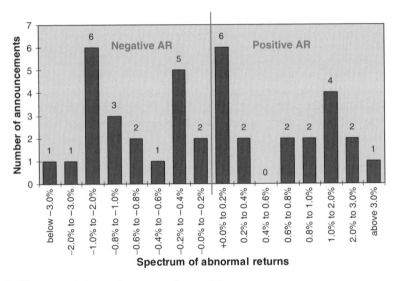

Fig. 2 Histogram of abnormal returns on the event day

between −1% and +1%, in 35 cases between −2% and +2%. The number of negative and positive market reactions is almost equal (21 and 19 cases) and the average abnormal return is close to 0%. Thus, not only potential benefits but also potential risks of outsourcing seem to influence the reactions of the market participants. We conclude that investors also evaluate contract-specific determinants of an outsourcing deal.

For event windows of 2 and 3 days, positive cumulative average abnormal returns of 0.48% (for the event window [0, +1]) and 0.65% [0, +2] were found. These values do not differ significantly from 0%. However, Oh and Gallivan (2004) and Oh et al. (2006) find similar and significant positive abnormal returns for an event window (0, +1]; this property may result from their larger sample sizes.

Our results differ remarkably within the maximum event window considered; however, no clear trend exists. The largest average abnormal return +0.59% is obtained for day [+12] whilst for the rather close day [+18] the most negative abnormal return (−0.67%) is found (Fig. 3). The bars in Fig. 3 indicate the daily average abnormal returns and the line the cumulative average abnormal returns for all cases considered.

In the next step we split the sample into 19 outsourcing announcements concerning (larger) SMI companies and 21 announcements of (smaller) companies considered in the SPI but not in the SMI. The results indicate that the SMI shares react stronger and more positively to an outsourcing announcement (Table 3). One possible explanation for the (partially significant) results is that companies in the SMI are more in the focus of investors and analysts and, therefore, also their announcements receive more attention. This result contradicts data published by Hayes et al. (2000) which show statistically significant positive abnormal returns for small firms but not for large companies.

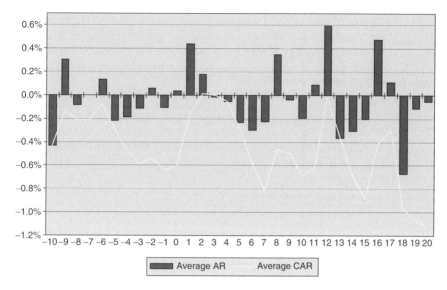

Fig. 3 Development of the average (cumulative) abnormal returns over the event window [−10, +20]

Table 3 Cumulative abnormal returns (in %) for selected event windows

| Companies | Event windows | | | | | |
	[−1, +1]	[0, +1]	[0, +2]	[0, +3]	[0, +4]	[0, +5]
19 deals of SMI companies	−0.10	0.55	1.00	1.53*	1.77*	1.33
21 deals of SPI companies	0.80	0.41	0.34	−0.17	−0.49	−0.53

*, **, *** denote statistical significance at 10, 5, and 1% levels

If the analysis is differentiated for the industries shown in Fig. 1, mostly small sub-samples result. For event windows [0, +1] and [0, +2] we find positive CAR for manufacturing, financial services, and technology industries; negative values are obtained for consumer services, telecommunications, and pharmaceutical and chemical industries. However, only the positive abnormal return (0.65% for the event window [0, +1]) for the financial services industry is statistically significant (at 10% level); the result is influenced by the fact that this sub-sample is comparatively large (20 cases). The largest positive value of 8.29% is obtained for the manufacturing industry and an event window [0, +4]; this result is heavily affected by the mega deal between ABB and IBM in 2003.

A comparison between the results of the LogicaCMG study and our results is not easy: The methodology used in the LogicaCMG study is not clearly described and also the sample size is missing. The effect is measured 1 month (!) after the announcement. With respect to the assumption of efficient markets and their fast information processing mechanisms and with the high danger of confounding effects this event window [0, +20] does not seem to be appropriate. No information about statistical significance of the LogicaCMG results is available. With these reservations we find that LogicaCMG reports a positive cumulative abnormal return of 1.7%, whereas for the Swiss companies we find a negative cumulative abnormal return of −0.49% for the identical event window. In both cases positive CAR exist in the manufacturing industry and negative values in the financial services and telecommunications industries. The differences may indicate that the public opinion about outsourcing and its economic effects is more positive in the UK than in Switzerland, and, probably, in continental Europe in general. Risk-averse Swiss investors (Hall, 1999) may be more impressed by the risks associated with organizational changes and resulting dependencies than by their potential benefits due to economies of scale and higher proficiency.

4   Conclusions

Our review of previous event studies and related studies reveals that the data estimating the effects of outsourcing announcements on the firm's market value is ambiguous and to some extent contradictory. Although precise comparisons of the reported CAR are impeded by different event windows and lacking data about statistical significance, it can be stated that they considerably differ both in their sign and size. We conclude that investors rather evaluate the contract-specific determinants of an individual outsourcing deal than attributing an overall value-creating or value-destroying impact to outsourcing announcements. Many properties affect potential benefits and risks of outsourcing (Mertens & Knolmayer G.F., 1998) and, thus, may influence the decisions of the investors. While findings for the factors "firm size," "contract size," and "cost reduction" are quite contradictory, it seems that the capital market reacts favourably to outsourcing projects characterized by strategic intents. Therefore one could assume that an announcement of a strategically motivated outsourcing will result in an increase of the firm's market value, which is typically a major goal of CEOs. Furthermore, if resources like a data centre are sold to a service provider, the revenue will typically exceed the book values of these resources. In contract negotiations there may be some pressure on service providers to offer very favourable conditions in the near future; later on, when the CEO may have moved on, the financial conditions may become less attractive for the outsourcing company.

When looking at the highly promoted LogicaCMG data, CEOs may see it as an additional and maybe very convincing argument for outsourcing IT systems. LogicaCMG argues that CEOs and shareholders can gain much by realizing outsourcing contracts and announcing them in a spectacular way. However, most scientific research does not show substantial positive effects of outsourcing announcements. This also holds for the first event study on outsourcing decisions of Swiss companies which is described in Sect. 3 of this paper. In summary, CEOs should not base their outsourcing decisions too strongly on "consultancy research" and should be reluctant in assuming that they can push up the market value remarkably by announcing outsourcing contracts.

References

Agrawal, M., Kishore, R., & Rao, H. R. (2006). Market reactions to E-business outsourcing announcements: An event study. *Information & Management, 43*(7), 861–873.

Albright, C. (2003). *Outsourcing for outsized gains: Lessons from the best and biggest deals.* New York: Marakon Associates Research.

Aubert, B. A., Patry, M., & Rivard, S. (1998). Assessing the risk of IT outsourcing. In *Proceedings of the 31st Hawaii international conference on system sciences* (pp. 685–692). Los Alamitos: Computer Society Press.

Beasley, M. S., Bradford, M., & Pagach, D. (2005). *Security price reaction to IS outsourcing announcements.* Raleigh: Working Paper, Department of Accounting, North Carolina State University.

Brown, S. J., & Warner, J. B. (1980). Measuring security price performance. *Journal of Financial Economics, 8*(3), 205–258.

Brown, S. J., & Warner, J. B. (1985). Using daily stock returns: The case of event studies. *Journal of Financial Economics, 14*(1), 3–31.

Cable, J., & Holland, K. (1999). Modelling normal returns in event studies: A model-selection approach and pilot study. *The European Journal of Finance, 5*(4), 331–341.

Chatterjee, D., Richardson, V. J., & Zmud, R. W. (2001). Examining the shareholder wealth effects of announcements of newly created CIO positions. *MIS Quarterly, 25*(1), 43–70.

Dibbern, J., Goles, T., Hirschheim, R., & Jayatilaka, B. (2004). Information systems outsourcing: A survey and analysis of the literature. *The DATA BASE for Advances in Information Systems, 35*(4), 6–102.

Dos Santos, B. L., Pfeffers, K., & Mauer, D. C. (1993). The impact of information technology investment announcements on the market value of the firm. *Information Systems Research, 4*(1), 1–23.

Dyckman, T., Philbrick, D., & Stephan, J. (1984). A comparison of event study methodologies using daily stock returns: A simulation approach. *Journal of Accounting Research, 22*(Suppl), 1–30.

Earl, M. J. (1996). The risks of outsourcing IT. *Sloan Management Review, 37*(3), 26–32.

Fama, E. F., Fisher, L., Jensen, M. C., & Roll, R. (1969). The adjustment of stock prices to new information. *International Economic Review, 10*(1), 1–21.

Farag, N. I., & Krishnan, M. S. (2003). The market value of IT outsourcing investment announcements: An event-study analysis. In D. Galletta & J. Ross (Eds.), *Proceedings of the north Americas conference on information systems* (pp. 1623–1629). Atlanta: Association for Information Systems.

Friedrich, L., & Gellrich, T. (2004). Capital market reaction to outsourcing in the financial services industry. Working Paper, E-Finance Lab, Frankfurt am Main. http://www.uni-tuebingen.de/dgf/program/CPaper73.pdf.

Gao, N. (2005). *Firm value: Market reaction to corporate outsourcing transactions.* Pittsburgh: Seminar Paper, University of Pittsburgh.

Gellrich, T., & Gewald, H. (2005). Sourcing, risk and the financial market. In D. Bartmann et al. (Eds.), *Proceedings of the thirteenth European conference on information systems, Regensburg.* http://csrc.lse.ac.uk/asp/aspecis/20050061.pdf.

Gewald, H., & Gellrich, T. (2007). The impact of perceived risk on the capital market's reaction to outsourcing announcements. *Information Technology and Management, 8*(4), 279–296.

Glassmann, D. (2000). *IT outsourcing and shareholder value.* New York: EVAluation, Stern Steward Research. http://www.sternstewart.com/research/studies2.aspx?ID=1054.

Hall, W. (1999). Switzerland: Slow to join the bandwagon. Financial Times Survey 1999-12-02. http://specials.ft.com/ln/ftsurveys/industry/sc7906.htm.

Hayes, D. C., Hunton, J. E., & Reck, J. L. (2000). Information systems outsourcing announcements: Investigating the impact on the market value of contract-granting firms. *Journal of Information Systems, 14*(2), 109–125.

Hayes, D. C., Hunton, J. E., & Reck, J. L. (2001). Market reactions to ERP implementation announcements. *Journal of Information Systems, 15*(1), 3–18.

Im, K. S., Dow, K. E., & Grover, V. (2001). Research report: A reexamination of IT investment and the market value of the firm – An event study methodology. *Information Systems Research, 12*(1), 103–117.

Juma'h, A. H., & Wood, D. (2003). The price sensitivity of business service outsourcing announcements by UK companies. *International Journal of Information Technology & Decision Making, 2*(1), 161–180.

Kremic, T., Tukel, O. I., & Rom, W. O. (2006). Outsourcing decision support: A survey of benefits, risks, and decision factors. *Supply Chain Management, 11*(6), 467–82.

Lacity, M. C., & Hirschheim, R. (1995). *Beyond the information system outsourcing bandwagon.* Chichester: Wiley.

Logicacmg. (2005). *Outsourcing for corporate value: Accelerating growth through outsourcing.* London: White Paper. http://www.logicacmg.com/pSecured/admin/countries/_app/assets/outsourcingcv-752005.pdf

Loh, L., & Venkatraman, N. (1992). *Stock market reaction to information technology outsourcing: An event study.* MIT Working Paper No. 3499-92BPS. Cambridge: Massachusetts Institute of Technology.

MacKinlay, A. C. (1997). Event studies in economics and finance. *Journal of Economic Literature, 35*(1), 13–39.

Mcwilliams, A., & Siegel, D. (1997). Event studies in management research: Theoretical and empirical issues. *Academy of Management Journal, 40*(3), 626–657.

Mertens, P., & Knolmayer, G. (1998). *Organisation der Informationsverarbeitung, Grundlagen – Aufbau – Arbeitsteilung,* 3rd edn. Wiesbaden: Gabler.

Oh, W., & Gallivan, M. J. (2004). An empirical assessment of transaction risks of IT outsourcing arrangements: An event study. *Proceedings of the 37th Hawaii international conference on system sciences* (p. 251 plus CD-Rom). Los Alamitos: Computer Society Press.

Oh, W., Gallivan, M. J., & Kim, J. W. (2006). The market's perception of the transactional risks of information technology outsourcing announcements. *Journal of Management Information Systems, 22*(4), 271–303.

Osei-Bryson, K.-M., & Ngwenyama, O. K. (2006). Managing risks in information systems outsourcing: An approach to analyzing outsourcing risks and structuring incentive contracts. *European Journal of Operational Research, 174*(1), 245–264.

Peak, D., Windsor, & Conover, J. (2002). Risks and effects of IS/IT outsourcing: A securities market assessment. *Journal of Information Technology Cases and Applications, 4*(1), 6–33.

Peterson, P. P. (1989). Event studies: A review of issues and methodology. *Quarterly Journal of Business and Economics, 28*(3), 36–66.

Pierre Audoin Consultants. (2006). Outsourcing in der Schweiz - kaum mehr lukrativ? Press Release, München. http://www.pac-online.com/pictures/Germany/press/2006/Schweiz_AM.pdf

Ranganathan, C., & Samarah, I. (2001). Enterprise resource planning systems and firm value: An event study analysis. *Proceedings of the twenty-second international conference on information systems* (pp. 157–158). Atlanta: Association for Information Systems.

Regniet, S. (2006). Quo vadis outsourcing-Markt Schweiz? Netzguide IT management/outsourcing (pp. 8–9). Basel: Netzmedien.

Rottmann, J., & Lacity, M. (2004). Offshore sourcing: Twenty practices for swift learning, risk mitigation, supplier management, cost control, and quality assurance. *MISQ Executive, 3*(3), 117–130.

Subramani, M., & Walden, E. (2001). The impact of E-commerce announcements on market values of firms. *Information Systems Research, 12*(2), 135–154.

Willi, F. S. (2006). Die Marktwirkung von Outsourcing-Ankündigungen: Eine Event-Studie im Schweizer Kapitalmarkt. Master Thesis, Institute of Information Systems, University of Bern.

Chapter 4
Innovation Through Outsourcing

Firm Strategic Profile and IT Outsourcing[*]

**Benoit A. Aubert, Guillaume Beaurivage,
Anne-Marie Croteau, and Suzanne Rivard**

1 Introduction

The objective of this paper is to examine the relationship between business strategy and the level and nature of information technology (IT) outsourcing behaviors. Past research in IT outsourcing has mainly focused on the role of the transaction itself in explaining outsourcing decisions, without investigating the influence of strategic characteristics of the organization. The few studies looking at the strategic profile of organizations led to inconclusive results when looking at the direct effect of strategic characteristics of organizations on outsourcing decisions. When observing organizations, one cannot avoid noticing that organizations of similar size and dealing in the same markets sometimes make very different decisions with respect to IT outsourcing. Because major organizational decisions are likely to reflect a firm's business strategy, it is anticipated that the decisions to outsource IT activities will be influenced by the business strategy.

The IT outsourcing phenomenon has been expanding during the past decade, and this growth is likely to continue (Pati & Desai, 2005; Young & Scardino, 2006). An important strand of research has examined the outsourcing decision using transaction costs theory.

Asset specificity has received a lot of attention from researchers (Williamson, 1985). The role of asset specificity has been supported by studies in many fields: auto parts (Monteverde & Teece, 1982), aerospace (Masten, 1984), and aluminum (Hennart, 1988). However, results were ambiguous in the IT field (Aubert B.A, Patry, & Rivard, 2004; Nam, Rajagopalan, Rao, & Chaudhury, 1996). Measurement and uncertainty were also studied in information systems. Empirical studies showed that uncertainty played a key part in the choice of a governance mode. These studies also supported the proposition that the measurability of the transactions strongly

---

[*] This paper previously appeared as: Aubert, B. A., Beaurivage, G., Croteau, A.-M., & Rivard, S. (2008). Firm strategic profile and IT outsourcing. *Information Systems Frontiers, 10,* 129–143. The current version appears with permission of Springer, the publisher of ISF.

increases the probability of outsourcing decisions by reducing the cost of using market mechanisms (Aubert B.A. et al., 2004; Poppo & Zenger, 1998).

Studies relying on transaction costs, while providing several insights on the organization behavior, have ignored some intrinsic properties of the organizations. The transaction costs model only considers the characteristics of the transaction itself. It does not take into account, for instance, any preferences of the managers or intent from the organization. While ignoring these differences did not prevent transaction costs theory to explain outsourcing patterns, taking into account these unique organizational properties would increase our understanding of IT outsourcing. A similar concern arises with the resource-based view. Its analysis remains more focused at the resource level, not at the organization level, although it considers the historical path of the organization and the configuration it generated (Barney, 1999).

Business strategy is one key organizational element that distinguishes one organization from another. It corresponds to the outcome of decisions made to guide an organization with respect to its environment, structure, and processes that influence its organizational performance. In other words, it represents the means taken by an organization to reach its goals. Teng, Cheon, and Grover (1995) measured the strategic orientation of firms, using the Miles and Snow typology, and did not find any relationship between the strategic type and the use of outsourcing. The same authors (in Grover, Cheon, & Teng, 1994) also looked at the moderating effect of strategic type on the relationship between gaps in IS resources and outsourcing and found some significant results, suggesting that there is a moderating effect. At the same time, a significant body of literature in information system has been devoted to the study of strategic alignment, notably alignment with the structure (see for example Bergeron, Raymond, and Rivard (2004). Given that outsourcing is a key decision about structure (Williamson, 1985), it is perplexing that the relationship between strategy and outsourcing has not been established more convincingly. These results are intriguing and call for additional investigation.

This study revisits how different strategic profiles make different use of IT outsourcing. It could be described as an extension to the previous studies according to the definitions of Berthon, Pitt, Weing, and Carr (2002). It mainly differs from Grover et al. (1994) and Teng et al. (1995) in two ways. First, the activities examined are different. The two studies done in the mid-nineties looked at five large groups: application development, systems operations, telecommunications, end-user support, and system planning. This study focuses on IS operations (including telecommunications) but details the activities with finer granularity than previous studies, establishing differences among the activities included in each group. The second difference lies in the measure of the strategic types. Most studies, both in information systems and strategy, rely on self-typing. The studies on strategy and outsourcing used these self-typing strategies. The current study also offers an innovative way to operationalize the strategic profile of the organization, using secondary data (from financial databases). This information is reported to regulatory agencies and deemed reliable. There is a possibility that biases were introduced in self-typing methods. These biases would be avoided using public financial data. Therefore, this study would be a method and context extension of past studies.

This extension leads to significant results (which were not visible in past studies). Results show significant influence of strategic type on outsourcing, namely that prospectors and analyzers are more aggressive in their use of outsourcing for IT operations. The separation of maintenance and operational activities also proved useful. These two activities do not appear to be managed in the same manner. By focusing on the governance of each activity instead of using the percentage of budget allocated to outsourcing, the differences between the activities were recognized.

2   Strategic Types of Organizations

2.1   Miles and Snow's Typology

Approaches to identifying a business strategy can be textual, multivariate, or typological (Hambrick, 1980). The typological approach is recognized as creating a better understanding of the strategic reality of an organization, since all types of business strategies are viewed as having particular characteristics but a common strategic orientation. While several typologies have been proposed by Ansoff and Stewart (1967), Freeman (1974), Miles and Snow (1978), or Porter (1980), the most frequently used in empirical research is Miles and Snow's (Smith, Guthrie, & Chen, 1989; Zahra & Pearce, 1990), which has been quoted more than 1,100 times (ISI Web of Knowledge, 1989–2007). This typology has successfully been used in research for more than a quarter century (Croteau & Bergeron, 2001; Jusoh, Ibrahim, & Zaimuddin, 2006; Sabherwal & Chan, 2001; Snow & Hrebiniak, 1980; Tavakolian, 1989).

Miles and Snow's typology reflects a complex view of organizational and environmental processes, as well as the attributes of product, market, technology, organizational structure, and management characteristics (Smith et al., 1989). The principal strength of this typology is the simultaneous consideration of the structure and processes necessary for the realization of a given type of business strategy.

Miles and Snow's typology defines four types of business strategies: prospector, analyzer, defender, and reactor. Firms choose one type rather than another according to their perception of their environment. The first three types are expected to enhance organizational performance and share a continuum where the prospector strategy is at one end, the defender at the other, and the analyzer strategy stands in the middle. The reactor strategy is excluded from the continuum since it represents an organization having no specific strategy identified, which is likely to impede organizational performance. Some performance variations among the four strategic types have been observed depending upon the industry, the sample size, or other organizational constructs. Generally, it was found that prospectors, analyzers and defenders are all performing and outperform reactors (Conant, Mokwa, & Wood, 1987; Smith et al., 1989; Snow & Hrebiniak, 1980).

Organizations that have a prospector strategy try to reach the largest market possible. They repeatedly make efforts to innovate and continuously search for new product/market opportunities. As the creators of change in their market, prospectors stress innovation and invest heavily in product R&D and environmental scanning. They usually seek for flexibility and prefer a decentralized organizational structure. However, prospectors are not very efficient in their operations due to their strong concern with flexibility and innovativeness.

At the opposite, organizations that adopt a defender strategy have a restricted market. They emphasize the efficiency of their production operations, the excellence of their products, the quality of their services, and their lower prices. They have a stable and narrow niche product/market in their industry. Focusing on the efficiency of their current operations, they deploy a centralized functional structure which facilitates the offer of high-quality and standard products or services at low prices. They mainly invest in their core and most efficient technologies. However, since defenders rarely search outside their domain for new opportunities, they almost never make major adjustments in their technology, structure, or methods of operation.

Organizations that have implemented the analyzer strategy share both prospector and defender characteristics, but in moderation. They try to be the first to introduce new products, yet remain in second place with certain products for which they offer a good quality/price ratio. With the strengths of the above two types, they operate in a stable domain of core products and seek new product/market opportunities at the same time, in order to maximize growth opportunities and minimize risk. They watch their competitors much closely for changes and innovations, and rapidly follow the prospectors who quickly introduce competitive products. They also copy the defenders characteristics when it comes to their stable domains by fostering routines and efficiency of their core operations. Overall, analyzers adopt a matrix organizational structure and deal with the challenge of simultaneously handling such conflicting demands of efficiency and innovation.

Finally, organizations supporting the reactor strategy do not have the capacity to take over new opportunities or maintain markets already acquired. They are the most unstable organizations among the four types. They do not respond consistently or effectively to the change and uncertainty of their environment due to the lack of strategy or misalignment between their strategy and their structure. Their incapacity to appropriately perceive the environmental change results in poor performance.

2.2 Linking Strategy and IT Activities

An IT activity might be managed very differently depending on the strategic type of an organization. Previous research has indeed found that each type of business strategy has a different portfolio of IT activities compared to the other ones (Croteau & Bergeron, 2001). For example, it was found that prospectors use IT applications to enhance their market flexibility and make quick strategic decisions. Defenders implement IT applications to create operational efficiencies (Tan, 1997). They also improve their business performance by giving a strategic role to the IT department, maintaining an open IT architecture, conducting strategic scanning, and constantly evaluating their information systems' performance (Croteau & Bergeron, 2001). Analyzers use IT applications to conduct strategic scanning, and, therefore, improve their comprehension of the other organizations' behavior (Croteau & Bergeron, 2001; Croteau, Raymond, & Bergeron, 2001; Sabherwal & Chan, 2001).

Taking into account the strategic type of the organization can enable a finer analysis of outsourcing. While common wisdom has often suggested that strategic activities should be kept inside the firm, research has avoided the analysis of outsourcing taking into account specific strategic characteristics of the organization. Activities were deemed comparable from one organization to another. While this approach is not false, it may be improved.

2.3 Linking Strategy and IT Outsourcing

This study explores whether there is a link between an organization's strategic type and its use of IT outsourcing. More specifically, it investigates how strategic types in Miles and Snow's typology can be related to the level of IT outsourcing activities deployed by an organization and its organizational performance. As mentioned earlier, past research on this relationship was not conclusive (Teng et al., 1995). This research takes a different approach in the measurement of strategy by using secondary data, such as financial information disclosed and annual reports, rather than mailed questionnaires to analyze the strategy.

When examining the possible linkages between strategic type and IT outsourcing, we can formulate the following hypotheses:

H_1: Prospectors will have a higher usage of IT outsourcing than defenders
H_2: Prospectors will have a higher usage of IT outsourcing than analyzers
H_3: Analyzers will have a higher usage of IT outsourcing than defenders

The justification for these hypotheses can be found in the description provided in Miles and Snow (1978), especially when considering the adaptive cycle describing how organizations adjust to their environment. This cycle includes three elements: the entrepreneurial problem, when the choice of a given strategy is made, the engineering problem, which demands a specific portfolio of technologies and capabilities, and finally the administrative problem, which involves the choice of structure and process that would influence the future entrepreneurial problem. The authors saw these three problems as a cycle.

When looking at how defenders, prospectors, and analyzers address these problems, many differences emerge. When solving the entrepreneurial problem, Miles and Snow (1978) argue that defenders will grow cautiously and incrementally, while prospectors will grow in spurts. This would suggest that defenders can establish an internal governance for IT activities since the volume of activity will be continuous and would occupy an internal workforce continuously. At the opposite, the prospectors would face important fluctuations. One way to face fluctuating demand would be to rely on outside help. Similarly, the environment scan of the defenders would be limited. These companies would rely on their core capabilities. At the opposite, prospectors would try to introduce change and would be more inclined to work with external partners to broaden their operating arena.

When addressing the engineering problem, defenders will rely on vertical integration and a single core technology while prospectors will tend to use prototyping and use multiple technologies. This also supports our hypotheses. The vertical integration favored by the defenders is directly aligned with the hypotheses. The use of multiple technologies used by the prospectors also suggests support to the hypotheses. Using multiple technologies simultaneously requires a very diverse skill set. It is difficult to maintain such skill set and outside providers are a way to gain access to these skills.

Finally, the administrative problem, as described by Miles and Snow (1978) indicates that tenure in positions would be longer and structure more stable for defenders, while prospectors would experience frequent changes and accept people from the outside more easily than defenders. This also supports our hypotheses. Internal organization would be easier to maintain for defenders than for prospectors.

Another element that supports the hypotheses is the risk profile of each type. The prospector is the risk taker in Miles and Snow's typology. At the opposite, the defender is the risk adverse. Entering into an outsourcing contract entails changes and contractual risks (Aubert B.A., Patry, & Rivard, 2005). Therefore, taking into account the risk-aversion profile associated with the strategic type of the organization would also support the hypotheses. Table 1 summarizes the key elements.

We can hypothesize that defenders, nurturing stability, control, focused activities and longer tenure, will be the most cautious users of IT outsourcing, avoiding the risks associated with outsourcing. Stability in their use of their resources will facilitate the establishment of internal governance (Williamson, 1985). At the opposite, prospectors, being the most prone to change in business volume, seeking flexibility,

Table 1 Main differences between strategic profiles

	Market	Main concern	Structure	Technology used	Risk profile
Prospectors	High fluctuations, growth in spurts	Flexibility, change	Decentralized, shorter tenure	Varied	High risk tolerance
Analyzers	↕	↕	↕	↕	↕
Defenders	Stable	Control	Centralized, longer tenure	Focused	Low risk tolerance

diversity, and adopting a more decentralized (and less stable) structure, will be the highest users of IT outsourcing. Outsourcing would be a suitable response to these fluctuations. Prospectors would also be more tolerant to outsourcing risks. In all cases, analyzers will be between the two groups.

Rockart and Leventer (1979) proposed three distinctive categories of IT activities, which are development, operations and management. Similarly, Tavakolian (1989) identified three major groups of IT activities, i.e. systems development and maintenance, systems operations, and systems administration. Past research in IT outsourcing has looked at IT operations and maintenance activities. Dibbern and Heinzl (2006) found that the most specific activities were the most strategic ones. Aubert B.A. et al. (2004) found that maintenance activities were less specific than IT operations. Therefore, it can be reasonably assumed that maintenance activities are less strategic than IT operations, all other things being equal. It is posited in this paper that different categories of IT activities will be outsourced differently depending on the strategic type of the organization. Operations should be more influenced by strategic type than by maintenance activities.

H_4: *The impact of strategic type on the outsourcing decision will be stronger for IT operations than for maintenance activities*

3   Methodology

This section presents the methodology followed to assess the relationship between the strategic type of an organization and its use of outsourcing. The sample of firms came from an existing database (Aubert B.A. et al., 2004). The outsourcing data are described in Sect. 3.1. The procedure used to classify the firms into one of the three categories (prospectors, analyzers, and defenders) will be described in detail, from Sect. 3.2. It is one of the original contributions of this study.

3.1   Outsourcing Data

The sample was taken from an existing database (Aubert B.A. et al., 2004). This database included data on 200 Canadian firms whose CIO had participated in a survey on IT outsourcing. The database contained the firm's identity, as well as data on whether each of 17 IT activities was outsourced or performed in-house. To be included in the sample of the present study, a firm had to be publicly traded, to ensure that its financial data and annual reports were available. The final sample includes data about 41 firms; their annual revenue varied from 15 million and 15 billion dollars, and they operated in a total of 29 industries.

As described in Aubert B.A. et al. (2004), a survey was conducted to assess the use of outsourcing from Canadian companies. Each company was asked to indicate, for 17 activities (listed in Table 6), if it was doing the activity in-house, using its own employees, or using an outside supplier to perform the activities. Respondents had to select only one of the choices per activity; indicating the main governance mode adopted for each of the 17 activities. For each firm, two IT outsourcing scores were computed. One was the IT operations outsourcing score, the other the IT maintenance outsourcing score. This score was obtained by adding the number of activities of a given type – either operations or maintenance – that were outsourced by the firm, divided by the number of activities. The average of these outsourcing scores was calculated for each of the three strategic types. The analysis will examine both the detailed data and the outsourcing scores.

3.2   Strategic Type

The literature using the typology of Miles and Snow offers several ways to operationalize the constructs. The simplest one was developed by Hambrick (1983) who looked at the number of new products brought to market by the firm. Snow and Hrebiniak (1980) developed a more encompassing measure where four descriptions, one by type, are introduced to the respondent who has to select the most appropriate one to represent the firm. This measure was used in several studies, especially during the 1980s. Segev (1987) used an approach relying on 27 Likert-scale questions. This measure was used more than 80 times in literature (ISI Web of Knowledge, 1989–2005). Finally, Conan et al. (1990) introduced a measure based on the three cycles of adaptation. This measure was also widely used.

All these measures (except the one by Hambrick, 1983) were based on perceptions. Hambrick, while using a very simple indicator (some will argue too simple), had the intuition that the strategy of a firm could be deducted from observable facts. Other authors relied on managers indicating what the intentions of the management team were, or what their perception of the course of action was. These approaches, often relying on self-typing, are vulnerable to "strategic desirability." Managers might describe the strategy they would have liked to follow, or the one they were planning to follow in the future, rather than the one they used to guide their action in the past.

The classification procedure proposed in this paper relies solely on secondary data. It uses the financial information provided by the firm and verified by auditors. It also uses annual reports. In this sense, the procedure is based on hard facts as much as possible. It also takes into account the corporate intention as communicated to the shareholders in the official documents.

Based on literature, it was possible to identify what would be the profiles of each strategic archetype. The measures of Segev (1987) helped to choose the indicators, while those of Conan et al. (1990) were used to identify the relevant elements of the annual reports to consider. A database containing all variables for companies and available years was created. As will be described later, each firm was compared with the other firms in its industry. To do this industry comparison, all the firms in the same industry available in the databases described under the section labeled "Information sources" were used (It was not limited to the firms in the sample).

After the analysis of the financial data was completed, the annual report was examined to understand and validate the elements found in the financial databases. The annual report helped understand the environment in which the organization operated. The indicators used and their expected patterns for each profile are described in the following pages.

3.3   Information Sources

Many sources were used to retrieve the information on each firm:

Stock Guide: This database provides financial data and ratios for the publicly listed Canadian firms.

Mergent Online: This database provides data on active and inactive Canadian and international firms.

Corporate Retriever: This database provides financial data as well as information about the type of activities performed by the firm. It also indicates the business sectors in which a company operates.

Annual Reports: Available for every year and for every public company. In each one, a letter to the stockholders is provided. It shows the picture which higher management tries to convey to the stockholders. Audited financial data served to validate the data obtained from the other databases.

3.4   Indicators

When looking at the secondary data available, several elements were analyzed. First, the financial information was surveyed: beta, debt structure, liquidity ratios, stability of the benefits and payment of dividends. The annual report was then assessed and used to understand some figures. The business volume of the firm, compared with the other players of the industry, also provided information about the strategy of the firm.

The first indicator considered was the beta of the firm. The beta coefficient is a measure of the volatility of the company shares compared to the market volatility. It gives an indication of the level of risk of the firm, as perceived by the market. A firm with a low beta indicates a company less subject to variations than the market average. On the contrary, a higher beta means that the value of the firm varies more than the market. Considering this definition, a defender should have a low beta, usually under one, and under the median of the industry. A prospector should have a high beta, considerably higher than one, and higher than the industry average. An analyzer should have a beta around one, close to the median of the industry.

The debt structure of the firm was analyzed with four financial elements: debt/equity ratio, debt ratio, interest paid per $100 of sales, and intensity of use of long-term assets. This helps understand whether the firm is financed by debt or by equity. A defender will favor stability by having a low debt which will strive toward zero, pay little interest, have low debt/equity ratio. Prospector will show opposite profiles. These firms take risks to generate high yields and use debt to favor expansion (debt ratio over 1). A prospector will show high interest payments per sale. Finally, the analyzer will have a moderate level of debt (around 30% of sales amounts), pay some interests and show a median debt and debt/asset ratios to favor both expansion and stability. Of course, any ratio has to be compared to the industry average for a firm. On its own, the ratio has limited usefulness.

The amounts invested in research and development are another source of information on the strategic type of the organization. The amounts allocated to research and development were taken into account and compared to the industry averages. It is expected that a defender will have lower R&D expenses than a prospector. The analyzer will exhibit R&D expenses close to the industry median.

Sales expenses ratio illustrates the effectiveness of the firm in leading its business activities, and its marketing aggressiveness. Lower expenses, under 60%, will point out a competitive firm, with a lean approach, which is rather associated with a defender. High expenses, above 85%, point out a firm which either experiences difficulty in controlling its expenses or invests aggressively in marketing activities, what would be associated with a prospector. Moderate expenses, between 60% and 85%, will point out to an analyzer. This ratio varies considerably from one industry to another. Again, firms were compared to their industry average. The percentages given are an illustration for the "typical firm."

Concerning liquidity ratio, three financial ratios were considered: cash ratio, current ratio (also called working capital ratio) and EBITDA – to interest coverage ratio. The first one is the amounts in cash or cash equivalents divided by the liabilities; the second one is computed by dividing short-term assets by short-term debt. The last one measures the capacity of the firm to cover its interest payments using its benefits.

Defenders will have high liquidity ratios, providing stability to the firm. A cash ratio of 1.5 and a current ratio above 1 will be considered to be associated with the defender. The EBITDA – to interest coverage ratio will be high, or there will not be interest payments. This analysis will also have to take into account the industry averages. Prospectors will show low liquidity ratios since short-term assets are reinvested continuously to favor expansion of the firm. The analyzer will have liquidity ratios around 1 (or around its industry average).

The stability of the benefits was also considered. Miles and Snow (1978) maintained that each strategic type (prospector, defender and analyzer) will be linked to performance. However, the pattern of profits will differ from one type to another. Three financial indicators were considered: the variation of raw and net benefits and treasury movements generated by the company.

A defender will have a stable pattern of benefits when compared to the average of its industry, while the prospector will show highly variable levels of benefits from one year to another and when compared to the industry. Analyzers will follow the industry average.

The dividends paid on regular shares as well as the remittance of past dividends were analyzed. For defenders, the payment of dividends will be positive and constant since, generally speaking, they will be able to balance their portfolio of activities and pay predictable dividends. For prospectors, the payment of dividends is not part (in general) of their preferences and, as a result, there will be few or punctual payments. Expansion will be favored, which reduces the possibility of dividends. Available resources will be reinvested in the company, not returned to the shareholders. For analyzers, the firm will be generally distributing dividends corresponding to the median of the industry.

Finally, the annual report of the firm has to be considered at three levels, the first two will be for validation of the previous analysis and the last, for analysis as an indicator. First, a validation of key figures was performed to ensure that the data obtained from the various databases was accurate, errors like a difference in the fiscal year or territory was to be detected. Second, some explanation of the numbers could be obtained. For instance, one defender might have surprisingly low liquidity, but we will understand in the annual report that the purchase of a competitor was realized to save the *niche* which will be aligned with the defender's strategy. Third, the section "Letter to the stockholders" allowed an understanding of the strategy which the firm officially claims it is following. A defender will speak about reducing expenses, about focusing on the effectiveness of the firm, about quality, about delivery, or about vertical integration. A prospector will discuss expansion, innovation and strategies to get closer to the customer. An analyzer will seek both types of objectives in moderate manner. This served as an additional indicator.

In summary, the following table shows the categories of indicators used and the expected trends (Table 2).

Table 2 Indicators

Indicator or group of indicators	Defender	Analyzer	Prospector
Beta	Low	Industry average	High
Debt structure	Little or no debt	Industry average	High levels of debt
Research and development	Lower than industry average	Industry average	Higher than industry average
Sales expenses	Low	Median	High
Liquidity ratios	High	Industry average	Low
Stability of the benefits	Very stable	Fluctuates with industry trends	Higher variability than industry
Payments of dividends	High	Industry average	Little, irregular or no dividends
Strategy in the annual report	Cost, effectiveness, quality, delivery, vertical integration	Seek a median strategy	Expansion, innovation, customer

Firms with no coherent pattern, which would not fit in any of the profiles, would be classified as reactors. These firms would react to outside events without a guiding line of conduct. They lack cohesiveness in their responses to the environment and, therefore, a pattern would be impossible to identify for reactors.

3.5 Final Database and Validation

A database comprising the data about the firms in the sample and the firms in their industry was constructed. The firms were coming from 29 industries. Data over 15 years were extracted to adequately understand each industry. This was done to avoid potential exceptional events in a given industry. Once the portrayal of each industry was established, the data from the companies in the sample were compared to their corresponding industry data. A descriptive table was established for each firm in the sample.

In order to validate the classification of the organizations in their appropriate strategic category, two activities were performed. First, the indicators and the expected trends were validated by an academic expert and an accounting expert. Then, once the firms were classified into their respective categories, ten firms were selected for a second evaluation. The accounting expert reclassified the firms and confirmed all but one decision.

3.6 Examples

In order to illustrate how the secondary data were used to identify the strategic types of the organizations, three examples are provided. They are representative of a defender, an analyzer, and a prospector. All the firms in the sample were classified using the same procedure.

3.6.1 Defender

The first example is Cameco, the world's largest supplier of uranium at the time of the study. Cameco has a beta lower than the one of its peers in the industry. Its debt/equity ratio was at 0.17, its debt ratio was at 0.14, and $1.24 of interest was paid per $100 of sales. The intensity of use of long-term assets was at 5.84. Cameco is in a better position than the firms in its industry. Its interest expenses are among the lowest and the debt ratio of the industry is at 0.27. These indicators all suggest a defender.

The research and development in the mining industry is limited (and often centered on finding new mining sites). Half of the firms have no R&D outside the exploration of new sites. Cameco has limited expenses of R&D outside exploration (0.029% of revenues) which would be between analyzer and defender. The sales expenses (0.49) are very low compared to the other firms in the industry (0.76), which is the mark of a defender.

The liquidity ratios also bear the stamp of a defender, with the exception of the cash ratio. The cash ratio is at 0.77. However, the working capital is at 1.96 and the interest coverage ratio is at 19.58 (half of the firms in the industry were showing losses, thus showing negative ratios). The firm is profitable, although profits are variable (but much less than the other firms in its industry). Interestingly, over several years, the profits before taxes of Cameco are more stable than the net profit, which might suggest adjustments in accounting rules. Cameco is very profitable. At the current 12% rate of return, it is actually a low point for several years.

Cameco pays regular dividends (approximately 4% of the gross sales). This is in an industry where less than half of the firms pay any dividends at all. In the annual report, we notice that Cameco relies on very long-term contracts. This emphasizes the stability of the firm. The annual report indicated that contracts were very long term. The firm emphasized its ability to offer stability and low prices for its products, outlining the quality of its assets (mining sites). The majority of the indicators point toward a defender profile (Table 3).

3.6.2   Analyzer

The second example is Alcan, evaluated as an analyzer. Alcan is a leader in the aluminum industry. At the time, it had revenues of $11 billion. Alcan had a beta in the highest quintile of its industry, which indicates that the investors saw the firm as risky. However, its financial structure was more conservative. Its debt ratio was 0.19, the debt/equity ratio was at 0.3, and $1.30 of interest was paid per $100 of sales. The intensity of use of long-term assets was 2.23. In its industry, half of the firms had a debt ratio under 0.2. The average was at 0.27. The interest paid was under the average (3.31). The financial structure leans toward the one of an analyzer in this industry.

The research and development expenses also point toward an analyzer. The average of the industry is slightly over 4% of revenues. Alcan is at 1.85%. However, half of the firms showed near-zero R&D expenses in this industry. Alcan is, therefore, in a middle ground. The sales expenses provide a similar picture. The industry average is at 0.76 and Alcan is at 0.77.

Table 3 Defender

Indicator or group of indicators	Defender	Analyzer	Prospector
Beta	Cameco		
Debt structure	Cameco		
Research and development	Cameco		
Sales expenses	Cameco		
Liquidity ratios	Cameco		
Stability of the benefits	Cameco		
Payments of dividends	Cameco		
Strategy in the annual report	Cameco		

The liquidity ratios also suggest that Alcan is an analyzer. The cash ratio is at 1.39, the working capital ratio is at 2.28, and the interest coverage ratio is at 8.46. Looking at the industry, the cash ratio is above 1, the working capital ratio is around the median (2.12). The interest coverage ratio is high (especially considering that half of the firms in this industry show a negative interest coverage ratio).

The industry shows variable profitability. In fact, the average of the sector shows a loss and the median shows a 5% rate of profit. The variance is very high. Compared to the industry, Alcan shows a stable profit pattern and a 6% margin. This oscillates between a defender and an analyzer. Alcan always paid regular dividends. Only half of the firms in this industry pay dividends. This would lean toward a defender. Finally, the annual report indicates shows that the organization was establishing a risk management program while pursuing expansion through vertical integration. This suggests a carefully managed expansion in areas in which the firm has knowledge and expertise. The following Table 4 summarizes the situation of Alcan.

The overall strategy clearly is one of analyzer. While a few elements would point toward prospectors' or defenders' behavior, Alcan showed a very balanced profile.

3.6.3 Prospector

The company GEAC computer is an example of a prospector. The year before the study, it showed revenues of $190 M. These revenues grew to $366 M the year of the survey and to $629 M the following year. This is an average yearly rate of growth of 180%.

Not surprisingly, the beta is at 1.24, which is over 1 but not extremely high. However, the debt ratios are high. The debt ratio is at 0.63, the debt/capital ratio is at 1.73 (the industry is at 0.38), and $1.72 is paid per $100 of sales. The intensity of use of long-term assets is at 2.45. When looking at the high-growth pattern of the company, it shows that this growth is aggressive and financed through debt. This is the mark of a prospector.

The sales expenses ($69) are above the industry average ($60). The R&D expenses in this industry are usually high (around 20% of sales). GEAC's expenses are lower than those of the other firms (10%) but have doubled (in % of sales) from

Table 4 Analyzer

Indicator or group of indicators	Defender	Analyzer	Prospector
Beta			Alcan
Debt structure		Alcan	
Research and development		Alcan	
Sales expenses		Alcan	
Liquidity ratios		Alcan	
Stability of the benefits	Alcan		
Payments of dividends	Alcan		
Strategy in the annual report		Alcan	

Table 5 Prospector

Indicator or group of indicators	Defender	Analyzer	Prospector
Beta		GEAC	
Debt structure			GEAC
Research and development		GEAC	
Sales expenses			GEAC
Liquidity ratios			GEAC
Stability of the benefits			GEAC
Payments of dividends			GEAC
Strategy in the annual report			GEAC

the previous years. An additional 2% was added the following year. This suggests higher reliance on research and development (moving toward prospector).

The liquidity ratios are low. The cash ratio is at 0.54. The working capital ratio is at 0.57. The interest coverage ratio is negative (−8.82). The firm is in the lower end of its industry distribution on liquidity measures, which is the mark of a prospector.

The firm was not profitable the year of the survey. It posted a loss. The following year, a profit (twice as important as the previous loss) was posted, followed by another year of loss, followed by another profitable year… This pattern shows high variability and is the mark of a prospector. The firm has never paid dividends. The strategy outlined in the annual report reflected a prospector's behavior, insisting on offering a complete solution to its customers and on growth. The firm had just completed an acquisition that tripled its revenues.

The indicators, summarized in Table 5, suggest that the firm has adopted a prospector's strategy. The firm is acquiring other companies in order to complete its offering to its clients.

4 Results

4.1 Strategic Profiles

The 41 firms of the sample were found to include 11 prospectors, 14 analyzers, 13 defenders, and three reactors. Firms showed coherent sets of characteristics that corresponded well to one of the categories. The few deviations are explained in the paragraphs below.

4.1.1 Prospectors

The data on the 11 prospector firms suggested a management that was not very conservative. These firms paid dividends only when they were operating in an industry where all players paid dividends. Even then, the prospectors paid lower dividends than their competitors. There was a high level of coherence among the different indicators for this category of firms. No prospector had a ratio of debt under the average of industry, and none had sales expenses lower than the average of its industry. The liquidity ratios of all firms were considerably lower than the average of their industry. Annual reports introduced a clear picture of a prospector.

4.1.2 Analyzers

Fourteen firms were classified as analyzers. While analyzers can show some degree of behaviors similar to prospectors' or defenders', a majority of their indicators were in the center of the scale. These firms' management was in general conservative. The ratios of the analyzers tended to follow the industry average. Moreover, in the annual reports, these firms talked as much about quality and about competitive prices as they did about innovation and about closeness to the customers. They addressed issues of expansion and management of risks since the analyzers are risk averse. Horizontal or vertical integration was also part of their strategy.

4.1.3 Defenders

Thirteen firms were classified as defenders. This group was not as homogeneous as the two previous ones. These firms had a conservative, rigid management and showed risk aversion. Of course, not all the elements considered were perfectly aligned toward the "defender" category. However, a majority of indicators converged toward the same conclusion. Some facts could explain why some indicators moved away from the typical defender profile.

One firm was more into debt than the average of the industry, while still being a defender. The debt was due to the acquisition of a company in financial difficulties. Five firms had higher sales expenses than the industry average, while having all other indicators toward the defender profile. Two reasons were believed to explain this situation. Firstly, among all analyzed ratios, sales expenses is probably the most controversial since the annual reports do not always include the same types of expenses in this category from one company to the other, even for firms working in the same industry. It seems that accounting rules allow some flexibility to the firms when reporting these expenses. Secondly, some firms incur these expenses to respond to quality norms or certifications, thus increasing the expenses even when it is only to protect access to a market.

Then, four firms had weak liquidity ratios for defenders. In fact, some firms, having very stable income, financial structure funded by equity and stable sale expenses, still had very little liquid assets. It might be due to the fact that it is not necessary to maintain high levels of liquidities to ensure their financial stability since all of the other elements in their environment are stable. Another firm showed a loss. Its industry faced difficult times. Finally, the analysis of the annual reports was mostly in line with the financial data. Four defenders spoke about expansion, what, a priori, would contradict the defender profile. However, expansion is necessary for some defenders, to secure their niche. They have to grow and secure their market.

4.1.4 Reactors

Three firms were classified as reactors. One of the firms recorded no income. This firm seemed to be liquidating its assets or transferring them to another company. Another firm was in severe deficit and trying to straighten its finances before being acquired by foreign investors. Finally, in an industry in full growth, a third firm could not succeed in generating profits. It would be in transition and restructuring before being acquired by foreign investors. These firms were discarded from the sample.

4.2 IT Outsourcing Patterns

For each firm, data were available on whether the firm had outsourced or not each of the 17 IT activities. Table 6 reports the percentage of firms from each category that outsourced a given activity. The results show a pattern generally aligned with

Table 6 Patterns of IT outsourcing

| | Activities | Percentage of firms outsourcing the activity | | | |
		Prospector (n = 11)	Analyzer (n = 14)	Defender (n = 13)	Expected pattern
IT operations	Scheduling of operations	18.18%	14.29%	0.00%	√
	Control of operations	18.18%	21.43%	0.00%	
	Technical support services	45.45%	25.00%	7.69%	√
	Software operation	18.18%	14.29%	7.69%	√
	Operating system operation	27.27%	21.43%	7.69%	√
	CPU operation	27.27%	28.57%	7.69%	
	Operation of client-server systems	9.09%	25.00%	0.00%	
	Operation of telecom software	40.00%	38.46%	25.00%	√
	Printer operation	40.00%	28.57%	7.69%	√
	Disk space management	27.27%	21.43%	0.00%	√
	Data entry	22.22%	7.69%	7.69%	+/−
	Operating system maintenance	45.45%	30.77%	7.69%	√
Maintenance	Hardware maintenance	81.82%	71.43%	92.31%	
	Micro-computer maintenance	54.55%	78.57%	84.62%	
	Network maintenance	54.55%	42.86%	38.46%	√
	Printer maintenance	72.73%	71.43%	84.62%	
	Telecom lines maintenance	81.82%	64.29%	75.00%	

the hypotheses. Indeed, ten of the 17 activities exhibit the expected pattern. Only one of the 17 is opposite to expectation (micro-computer maintenance). The check mark (&surd;) in the right column indicates that the expected pattern was found for the activity.

As expected, prospectors and analyzers have much higher outsourcing scores than the defenders for the operations (activities 1–11). Seven of the 11 activities show the expected pattern for IS operations. Another activity – Data entry – exhibits the expected pattern, although to a lesser extent: while a significantly larger proportion of prospectors than defenders outsourced this activity, the percentage of analyzers and of defenders that outsourced it was the same (hence the +/− indication mark in Table 6).

When looking more closely at the results, it appears that IT operations and maintenance activities are not managed in the same way. First, there is more outsourcing of maintenance activities than of IT operations activities. Second and surprisingly, the outsourcing scores in the maintenance activities are at times higher for defenders than for prospectors and analyzers (although these differences are not significant).

It is important to remain cautious when looking for statistical significance for such a small sample. The analysis of these results is mainly aimed at identifying the most important differences. It is not done to "prove" a result with the idea that it can be generalized.

When comparing analyzers and prospectors using T-tests, these two groups do not show any significant difference. However, when comparing the activity means of defenders with the corresponding means of analyzers and prospectors combined, several activities show significant differences ($p < 0.05$). Several activities are significantly less outsourced by defenders than by both analyzers and prospectors. These activities are shown in Table 7.

For each firm, two IT outsourcing scores were computed. One was the IT operations outsourcing score, the other the IT maintenance outsourcing score. These scores were obtained by adding the number of activities of a given type – either operations or maintenance – that were outsourced by the firm, divided by the number of activities. The average of these outsourcing scores was computed for each of the three strategic types.

Table 7 Significant differences

Activities that are significantly less outsourced by the defenders than by the analyzers and prospectors combined ($p < 0.05$)

1 Scheduling of operations
2 Control of operations
3 Technical support services
7 Operation of client-server systems
9 Printer operation
10 Disk space management
12 Operating system maintenance

Fig. 1 Outsourcing scores

A T-test was conducted and the results indicate that the average IT operations outsourcing score was significantly lower for the defenders than for the prospectors and for the analyzers. No significant difference between the strategic types was found for the IT maintenance outsourcing scores (Fig. 1).

5 Discussion

Two different types of results were obtained, according to the types of IT activities. For IT operations, both H_1 and H_3 were supported. Both prospectors and analyzers relied more on outsourcing for their IT operations than defenders did. H_2 was not supported; there was no significant difference between prospectors and analyzers. For maintenance activities, none of the hypotheses about the influence of strategy on outsourcing profile was supported. Therefore, H_4, stating that the impact of strategic type on the outsourcing decision will be stronger for IT operations than for maintenance activities, was supported.

5.1 *Distinction Between Strategic Profiles*

When comparing the strategic profiles, the immediate observation is the similarities between the outsourcing pattern observed for both prospectors and analyzers. The numbers are extremely close. Defenders showed a different pattern. Their use of outsourcing for IT operations is extremely limited. In a way, this challenges the idea that the continuum applies for all the elements of the strategic profiles. Traditionally, analyzers are always portrayed as a middle ground between the two extremes. However, if analyzers are thought as a combination of prospectors' and defenders' characteristics, maybe outsourcing is one of the prospectors' behaviors that analyzers adopt more readily, at least for IT operations. The results suggest that it might be worthwhile to further investigate this aspect.

"Classical" outsourcing, namely the main data center operations (software, OS, and CPU operations), was used by approximately a quarter of prospectors and analyzers. Almost no defenders used outsourcing for these operations. This pattern is also observable when looking at the management activities. These activities provide another distinction between the outsourcing behavior of the different profiles.

These activities involve the management of the operations. Control and scheduling imply decisions about how and when IT operations are conducted. Support services also imply control activities since they include the activities associated with the introduction of software modifications or new functionalities into production.

None of the defenders had outsourced scheduling or control of operations. Only one had outsourced technical support services. While prospectors and analyzers were not massively outsourcing these activities outsourcing was still present. Almost half of the prospectors had outsourced their technical support services.

The only activity that defenders seemed to outsource within the IT operations was the operation of telecommunication software. Twenty-five percent of the defenders outsourced this activity. This percentage was still lower than the one observed for the other firms, which was around 40%.

All these elements outline the tight control (internal) on operations that defenders keep over their key IS operations. This appears to be an extreme stance. The other two profiles show moderate usage of outsourcing. As will be described in the next section, these differences were not observed for the maintenance activities.

One hypothesis that can be formulated to explain these differences would be linked to the fact that the risk tolerance of prospectors and analyzers is higher than the one of the defenders. Prospectors and analyzers might be more subjected to internal resource gaps (as described by Grover et al., 1994) compensated by the use of outsourcing. Alternatively, they might simply be more tolerant to outsourcing risk, looking for increased flexibility with or without resource gaps. Current data do not provide information to further investigate this aspect.

5.2   Distinction Between IT Operations and Maintenance Activities

As mentioned before, maintenance activities are significantly more outsourced than IT operations. Two possible explanations can be offered to explain these differences. The first one pertains to the more systemic nature of IT operations when compared to maintenance activities. IT operations are more tightly integrated with the organization's activities. Information system operations are processing the information associated with the day-to-day activities of the organization. Sales, purchases, production activities are all included in the list of activities supported by the IS operations. Therefore, these IT operations vary in synch with the company operations. Information system operations probably present similar patterns in variety and volume as the company operations.

On the other hand, maintenance activities are more autonomous than IT operations. Maintenance activities are performed according to a calendar that is not necessarily linked to the operations of the organization. Some maintenance activities are performed at regular time intervals (for instance on equipment) or according to a calendar determined by the vendor (for instance on the operating system). It is unclear, looking at the description of maintenance activities (Ng, See, Gable, &

Chan, 2002) if the maintenance activities are more or less stable in volume and skills required than IS operations. However, these activities are very similar from one organization to another since many tasks are vendor dependent and vendor initiated (Ng et al.). Therefore, the economies of scale available for these activities should be more significant than for IS operations (vendors performing standard tasks for every clients). This could explain why defenders, analyzers, and prospectors all adopt outsourcing patterns that are similar.

As illustrated in Fig. 2, the second explanation relies on the proximity to the core of the organization. IS operations support the core activities of the organization. Maintenance activities are very indirectly linked to the core activities. The maintenance activities are not as specific as IT operations (Aubert B.A. et al., 2004). This would lead us to expect that they are not as strategic as IT operations (Dibbern & Heinzl, 2006). Maintenance activities are further away from the core of the organization than IS operations. This would mean that these activities are too far away from the organizational core to be affected by the strategic orientation of the organization. The choice of governance mode for these activities would be determined primarily by the characteristics of the activities, not by organizational level variables.

5.3 Limitations

Prior to discussing the contributions of this study and suggesting avenues for future research, some limitations of the study must be acknowledged. These limitations mainly concern sample size, measure of the dependent variable, and the variance of characteristics among the activities.

The first limitation is that of the small sample size. Indeed, the fact that each of the four sub-samples included less than 15 firms puts some limitations to the extent of generalization that can be made from this study. Because of data availability, the sample size was limited to 41 organizations. However, detailed information was obtained on each of these firms. The limited sample size prevents the statistical detection of small differences between two strategic types that share some characteristics. It might be why, when considering H_2, no difference was observed

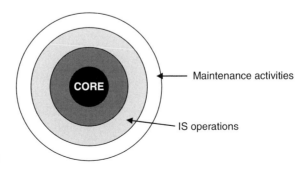

Fig. 2 Distance from the core

between prospectors and analyzers. Although the patterns observed in Table 6 provided some support for H_2, these differences were not significant.

A second limitation is related to the measure of the dependent variable. In this study, respondents were asked to indicate the main governance mode for each of 17 information systems operations activities. It might be argued that such a measure is weak because a firm that outsources a small portion of a given activity – say 10% of its hardware maintenance – would fall in the same category as another firm that does not outsource any of its hardware maintenance activities. Other researchers have alleviated this issue by weighing the importance of outsourcing a given activity relative to the budget of the IS function (Grover et al., 1994 for instance).

The other limitation of the study is the fact that all the IT activities studied were IT operations. It would have been interesting to include software development in order to increase the variety of activities and the diversity of the activity characteristics. Some software development activities might be closer to the core of the organizations. It would have provided additional information about the "closeness to the core" proposition.

6   Contributions and Avenues for Future Research

Notwithstanding the limitations outlined in the previous section, the results indeed support the idea that there is a link between the strategic profile of an organization and the use of outsourcing by the organization. However, this link is not systematically present for all activities. Past research (Teng et al., 1995) had not been able to identify this direct link. By extending the work done in the past and using a different measure of strategic profile, a direct link could be established. The results highlighted the importance of retaining a sufficient level of granularity for the activities considered when studying outsourcing. Aggregated measures of outsourcing might not have revealed the differences observed in the current results.

The other contribution is the measure of strategic profile. While past studies had relied on perceptions of the managers concerning the overall organizational strategy, this study used secondary data, publicly available, to draw the strategic profile of the organization. Using financial information, organizations could be compared to accepted accounting standards as well as to their peers in their industry. This enabled a classification into strategic categories that was devoid from some limitations associated with self-typing (notable social desirability and local perceptions or imperfect knowledge of the organization as a whole, especially in the case of large organizations).

The results suggest several avenues for future research. First, the extension of the study to include software development would be very interesting. One could presume that software development would be closer to the core of the organization than both IS operations and maintenance activities. If it is the case, and if the "distance" from the core is affecting the relationship between the strategic profile of the organization and the outsourcing level, a stronger relationship between software development outsourcing and strategic profile should be expected.

An interesting extension would be to include firm performance in the model. It would be interesting to see if firms that do not follow the outsourcing pattern suggested by the theory perform less than firms adjusting their behavior to the theoretical propositions. A larger sample size would enable the evaluation of a model of fit between strategic profile and outsourcing profile.

The research could also be extended to non-IS activities. By increasing the variety of activities considered, the understanding of the relationship between outsourcing and strategy would be increased. The other avenue suggested by the results is the extension of the study to offshoring. On the one hand, similar results could be expected. On the other hand, since a key advantage argued by practitioners for offshoring is the cost reduction, the offshoring option should be particularly attractive for defenders, who are always trying to find ways to reduce their costs.

References

Ansoff, H. I., & Stewart, J. M. (1967). Strategies for a technology-based business. *Harvard Business Review, 45*(6), 71–83.

Aubert, B. A., Patry, M., & Rivard, S. (2004). A transaction cost model of IT outsourcing. *Information & Management, 41*, 921–932.

Aubert, B. A., Patry, M., & Rivard, S. (2005). Taking stock on IT outsourcing risk. *Database, 36*(4), 9–28.

Barney, J. (1999). How a firm's capabilities affect boundary decisions. *Sloan Management Review, 40*(3), 137–145.

Bergeron, F., Raymond, L., & Rivard, S. (2004). Ideal patterns of strategic alignment and business performance. *Information & Management 41*(8), 1003–1020.

Berthon, P., Pitt, L., Weing, M., & Carr, C. (2002). Potential research space in MIS: A framework for envisioning and evaluating research replication, extension, and generation. *Information Systems Research, 13*(4), 416–427.

Conant, J. S., Mokwa, M. P., & Wood, S. D. (1987). Management styles and marketing strategies: An analysis of HMOs. *Health Care Management Review, 12*(4), 65–75.

Conant, J. S., Mokwa, M. P., & Varadarajan, P. R. (1990). Strategic types, distinctive marketing competencies and organizational performance: A multiple measures-based study. *Strategic Management Journal, 11*(5), 365–383.

Croteau, A.-M., & Bergeron, F. (2001). An information technology trilogy: Business Strategy, technological deployment and organizational performance. *Journal of Strategic Information Systems, 10*(2), 77–99.

Croteau, A.-M., Raymond, L., & Bergeron F. (2001). Comportements stratégiques, choix et gestion des systèmes d'information : contribution à la performance, *Systèmes d'Information et Management, 4*(2), 5–17.

Dibbern, J., & Heinzl, A. (2006). Selective outsourcing of information systems in small and medium sized enterprises, information systems outsourcing – Enduring themes. In R. Hirschheim, A. Heinzl, & J. Dibbern (Eds.), *New perspectives and global challenges* (pp. 70–82, 2nd edn.). Berlin: Springer.

Freeman, C. (1974). *The economics of industrial innovation*. Harmondsworth, England: Penguin.

Grover, V., Cheon, M., & Teng, J. T. C. (1994). An evaluation of the impact of corporate strategy and the role of information technology on IS functional outsourcing. *European Journal of Information System, 3*(3), 179–190.

Hambrick, D. C. (1980). Operationalizing the concept of business-level strategy in research. *The Academy of Management Review, 5*(4), 567–575.

Hambrick, D. C. (1983). Some tests of the effectiveness and functional attributes of miles and snow's strategic types. *Academy of Management Journal, 26*(1), 5–26.

Hennart, J.-F. (1988). Upstream vertical integration in the aluminium and tin industries: A comparative study of the choice between market and intrafirm coordination. *Journal of Economic Behavior & Organization, 9*(3), 281–299.

Jusoh, R., Ibrahim, D. N., & Zainuddin, Y. (2006). Assessing the alignment between business strategy and use of multiple performance measures using interaction approach. *The Business Review, 5*(1), 51–60.

Masten, S. (1984). The organization of production: Evidence from the aerospace industry. *Journal of Law and Economics, 27*(2), 403–418.

Miles, R. E., & Snow, C. C. (1978). *Organizational strategy, structure, and process.* New York: McGraw Hill.

Monteverde, K., & Teece, D. J. (1982). Supplier switching costs and vertical integration in the automobile industry. *The Bell Journal of Economics*, 206–213.

Nam, K., Rajagopalan, S., Rao, H. R., & Chaudhury, A. (1996). A two-level investigation of information systems outsourcing. *Communications of the ACM, 39*(7), 37–44.

Ng, C., See, P., Gable, G., & Chan, T. (2002). An ERP-client benefit-oriented maintenance taxonomy. *The Journal of Systems and Software, 64*, 87–109.

Pati, N., & Desai, M. S. (2005). Conceptualizing strategic issues in information technology outsourcing. *Information Management & Computer Security, 13*(4), 281–296.

Poppo, L., & Zenger, T. (1998). Measurement explanations for make-or-buy decisions in information services. *Strategic Management Journal, 19*(9), 853–877.

Porter, M. E. (1980). *Competitive strategy: Techniques for analyzing industries and competitors.* New York: Free Press.

Rockart, J. F., & Leventer, J. S. (1979). Centralization vs. Decentralization of Information Systems: A Preliminary Model for Decision Making, CISR Working Paper, Sloan School of Management, MIT.

Sabherwal, R., & Chan, Y. E. (2001). Alignment between IT and business strategies: A study of prospectors, analyzers, and defenders. *Information Systems Research, 12*(1), 11–33.

Segev, E. (1987). Strategy, strategy-making, and performance in a business game. *Strategic Management Journal, 8*(6), 565–577.

Smith, K. G., Guthrie, J. P., & Chen, M. J. (1989). Strategy size and performance. *Organizational Studies, 10*(1), 63–81.

Snow, C. C., & Hrebiniak, L. G. (1980). Strategy distinctive competence and organizational performance. *Administrative Science Quarterly, 25*, 317–336.

Tan, F. B. (1997). Strategy type, information technology and performance: A study of executive perceptions, proceedings of the AIS Americas conference, Indianapolis, Indiana. August, 848–850.

Tavakolian, H. (1989). Linking the information technology structure with organizational competitive strategy: A survey. *MIS Quarterly, 13*(3), 309–317.

Teng, J. T. C., Cheon, M. J., & Grover, V. (1995). Decisions to outsourcing information systems functions: Testing a strategy-theoretic discrepancy model. *Decision Sciences, 26*(1), 75–103.

Williamson, O. (1985). *The economic institutions of capitalism.* New York: Free Press.

Young, A., & Scardino, L. (2006). Outsourcing more but enjoying it less: What's the real problem. *Gartner Report.* 7 pp.

Zahra, S. A., & Pearce J. A. II. (1990). Research evidence on the miles-snow typology. *Journal of Management, 16*(4), 751–768.

In Context Outsourcing: Between Solution Making and Context Making

Arjen Wassenaar, Rajesri Govindaraju, and Björn Kijl

1 Introduction

At the end of the nineteenth century a new transport and data infrastructure enabled the shift from small focused companies operating in market based networks towards vertical integrated companies. However during the beginning of the twenty-first century, the ICT infrastructural revolution (Internet, World Wide Web) reversed this shift by outsourcing, breaking up the vertical integrated companies again in market based loosely coupled business networks.

1.1 Infrastructures are Enabling New Industrial Landscapes, Often by Surprise

Before 1850 Dutch rivers were fully out of control and not useful at all as a waterway. At one season transport by ship was impossible because of the water level was too high and the flow too heavy, destroying dikes and inundating the central and lower part of the Netherlands. At the other season transport by ship was impossible because of the sandy banks and low water level. Between 1850 and 1880 Dutch civil engineers innovated the Dutch river system by dredging sandy river branches and by creating new canals as open river branches between the central part of the Netherlands and the North Sea. They created these outlets in the first place to avoid the yearly inundations in the lower part of the Netherlands.

The amazing fact was that within 20 years a few Dutch engineers (from the newly founded Polytechnical School in Delft) were building a new "open Dutch river system" that avoided inundation and enabled transport by ship between Dutch harbours and the emerging German industrial areas. Ironically, this building of new river branches and canals (to the North Sea) was primarily reasoned to avoid inundations. It was not the intention to create a waterway with Germany at all. For this reason a railway connection was planned between Flushing in the southern part of the Netherlands and Germany. Talking about unintended outcomes!

R. Hirschheim et al. (eds), *Information Systems Outsourcing,*
© Springer-Verlag Berlin Heidelberg 2009

Another unexpected outcome of this 'innovation' was the rise of Rotterdam as the central European "transit trade gateway" and the fall of Amsterdam as the "stock trade gateway". What happened? At that time, Amsterdam was already the biggest Dutch harbour for centuries with trade all over the world. Rotterdam had a harbour with just regional significance. So, there was a big difference in mind set between these two Dutch cities. Amsterdam with its rich business aristocrats was the leading city in the Netherlands and dominated the central Dutch government. Their attitude was "be sophisticated, we are the best". Rotterdam, at that time, was just a small regional city and had hardly any influence on the Dutch government. Their attitude was "keep it simple and stupid, we just want to earn money". Therefore Rotterdam made a 'simple' choice for a new "transit harbour concept" based on a value chain with low margins and high volumes. This innovation fits quite well in the open river connection with the North Sea. Amsterdam was following their centuries old tradition and made a 'sophisticated' choice for a "stocking harbour concept" characterised by a value chain based on high margins and low volume. In their mind a "closed North Sea connection" by canal and gates was needed. Their strong lobby overruled the governmental engineers and they got a canal to the North Sea with expensive gates (near a new founded town IJmuiden) financed by the central government. And from that time there was every 30–40 years a discussion for enlarging the IJmuiden gates. Recently, Amsterdam started a lobby for an investment of €800 million again in new gates at IJmuiden, to be paid by the central government of course! On the other side, Rotterdam made the winning choice with their transit harbour innovation concept and open river connection and became one of most important harbours of the world. In line with their 'open' mind for an open connection with the sea they are planning a new harbour in the North Sea. In a global world 'transit harbours' survived and Amsterdam is now a harbour of regional importance. And there is still a difference in mind of Amsterdam and Rotterdam that can be illustrated by the rivalry between their football clubs Ajax and Feyenoord. Ajax Amsterdam pretends to play the most excellent and sophisticated football of the world and Feyenoord Rotterdam has less pretensions and plays for winning by articulating "no words just act for results".

This case shows how new infrastructures are innovations creating quite unintended outcomes and that institutions can be psychic prisons where people become trapped by their own thoughts, ideas and beliefs. Not "the reality" but their interpretation and sense making is decisive for reactions on new developments in, e.g. infrastructures. The innovation context and innovation solution are shaping each other by interaction. The case suggests there are different levels or layers:

- An operational process layer of value chain activities
- A human organizational layer of required human skills and their division of labour
- An institutional coordination, power and conflict resolution structure
- A strategic-cognitive and affective frame

1.2   Two Infrastructural Revolutions?

Chandler (1977) states that in the above mentioned period of 1850–1870 technical breakthroughs in physical transport by rail and ship and data transport by telegraph and telephone were fundamentally changing the (American) industrial landscape. It caused the integration of regional markets into national or even global markets and the concentration of production facilities on a national and global scale. Small, regional oriented companies – mutual connected by regional markets – were merging into big vertical integrated companies. And the new data network enabled a world-wide coordination of these global companies, such as the big, fully integrated oil and automotive companies. Central headquarters were ruling their companies just like European countries were ruling their colonies all over the world. Chandler concluded that at the end of the nineteenth century the market as dominant transaction govern-ance mechanism was replaced by hierarchy in vertical integrated companies. This shift from (external) market towards (internal) hierarchical coordination was strongly facilitated by the breakthrough of the new data infrastructure. So, a new infrastructure was enabling new ways of business and ways of transaction governance and on their turn new ways of business were asking for new improved infrastructures. This first wave in globalisation ended in World War I with a collapse of "colonial empires" and "renationalization" of the economy during the two world wars.

Perhaps a second ICT infrastructure revolution is happening between about 1980–2000. It was prepared in the 1960s and 1970s. King argued in an interesting key note speech for the ICIS conference in Brisbane that this second ICT infrastructure was a "spin off" of the cold war between Russia and US of America. The defence against Russian rockets required early warning systems based on sophisticated information processing power and high speed data communication systems. In my professional life as a system designer during the seventies we experimented with full text retrieval systems, packet switching networks and end user computer terminals for civil applications such as job matching and police intelligence systems. However we failed in that time because of insufficient (central) computer power, unreliable retrieval and network software. Looking back, finally in the nineties there was a breakthrough of reliable standardised retrieval, browser and network technology. This ICT infrastructure revolution (Internet, World Wide Web) reversed the shift in the nineteenth century from small focused companies operating in market based networks towards strong vertical integrated companies. It is because of worldwide outsourcing that vertical integrated companies are now perhaps broken up again into loosely coupled (global) business networks.

1.3   Objective and Structure Paper

Outsourcing refers to the practice of contracting outside a firm to receive some or all of the (IS) services needed by that firm affecting the existing hierarchal transaction governance mechanism and therefore the existing (inter-) organizational structures. Inspired by the rivalry between the two Dutch harbours Amsterdam and Rotterdam, outsourcing will be considered as innovation with partly unattended outcomes caused by the interaction between outsourcing solutions and their organizational context. Our assumption is that the outcomes of outsourcing depend on the interaction between shaping solutions and shaping context. Successful outsourcing is like dancing a tango. This paper aims the development of a theoretical framework elaborated into an instrument in order to embed outsourcing in the organizational and institutional context in a more systematic way. It is structured as follows. The first section places outsourcing in a historical context of doing business and argues that breakthroughs in infrastructures are causing outsourcing and affecting industrial landscapes. The objective and structure of this paper is formulated. The second section presents an overview of the development of outsourcing in theory and practice. In the third section an in context framework is developed as a starting point for the design of an instrument for embedding outsourcing in their context in a more systematic way.

2 Historical Developments in Outsourcing

In the nineties, outsourcing started with a pioneering, initial stage of ad hoc, ICT based outsourcing projects and changed at the end of the nineties in an expanding contagious stage of global business process outsourcing and off shoring. In a new emerging stage companies are integrating their outsourcing activities in their business strategy by restructuring business models and structure.

2.1 The Initial, Pioneering Stage of Outsourcing

Although the term outsourcing came into common parlance in the late 1980s, the concept of contracting-out or farming out for IS services was not new. Outsourcing is the decision taken by an organization to contract out or sell the organizations assets, people, processes and/or activities to a third party supplier which in exchange provides and manages assets and services for monetary returns over an agreed period of time.

Even in the early 1960s, when computers were first introduced to businesses, outsourcing was characterised by the presence of service bureaus that offered application-specific, transaction-processing services to firms. In the late 1980s, however, IS outsourcing took a new turn and outsourcing became an important topic of research. One of the first outsourcing projects by Kodak for example got a lot of research interest. The OUT'93 conference at the University of Twente provided an overview of the latest developments in outsourcing in different countries, such as the USA (Clark and Zmud; Peak; Lacity and Hirschheim; Klepper; Turner and Kambil; Apte and Mason), Belgium (Auwers and Deschoolmeester), the UK

(Willcocks), Switzerland (Griese), Spain (Valor), Finland (Saakjarvi and Saarinen; Ivari), Germany (Heinzl), and the Netherlands (Wassenaar and Thiadens), resulting in taxonomies describing the phenomena of outsourcing. Furthermore, different perspectives on outsourcing were already emerging at this conference; these perspectives would dominate the literature throughout the 1990s. Three dominating perspectives will be discussed.

First, transaction economics perspective focuses on why managers might choose specific contractual modes of governance rather than hierarchies implemented by vertical and horizontal integration. This normative, static-oriented perspective explains the most important determinants of outsourcing, namely the reasons to shift from an internal oriented hierarchy to external oriented market context, but it does not take into account the actual change process of outsourcing (Klepper & Hartog 1992).

Second, strategic and alliance-oriented perspectives consider the roles of organizational resources and capabilities in maintaining and leveraging of core competencies. In these models, popularised by Prahalad and Hamel (1990), excellence in maintaining, growing, and leveraging the process of turning a number of competencies into products and services is what determines the success of firms in an increasingly turbulent and competitive environment. Quinn and Hilmer (1994) therefore introduced the term "strategic outsourcing." They argue that companies have to consider outsourcing in a strategic context and not only as a way to reduce short-term costs. A strategic outsourcing or partnership approach can yield significant additional benefits, such as lower long-term capital investments and leveraging of core competencies. They and others suggest that if firms concentrate on their own unique "core competencies" and strategically outsource those for which the firm has no strategic need in terms of special capabilities, managers can leverage their firms' resources and skills to achieve increased competitiveness (McFarlan & Nolan 1995; Feeny & Willcocks 1998).

Third, political and implementation-oriented perspectives consider outsourcing as a phase-based, decision-making process in a context driven by stakeholders' interest. This research focuses on successful decision-making patterns (Lacity & Hirschheim 1995). In particular, the roles of stakeholders and their interests constitute a central topic of study. What are the objectives of stakeholders (vendors, top management, IT management) in evaluating outsourcing decisions? What problems do stakeholders attempt to solve by outsourcing? Do organizations initiate outsourcing for reasons other than cost efficiency?

2.2   The Expanding, Contagious Stage of Outsourcing

In this stage outsourcing is becoming a common activity in business illustrated by different terms for this phenomenon: business process outsourcing (BPO), IT enabled BPO, captive off shoring, direct off shoring, near shore outsourcing, offshore outsourcing, onshore outsourcing and shared services. In our contribution (Wassenaar & Swagerman 2001) to the second conference in 2001 on outsourcing, we argued that by the end-1990s, the one time outsourcing approach had evolved into a more selective and worldwide sourcing environment (Lacity, Willcocks, & Feeny 1996) enabled by an emerging new IT infrastructural context, such as EDI, Internet, and World Wide Web). They enlarged the range and richness of information exchange among economic actors (Keen 1990; Evans & Wurster 1997). These new electronic pathways could be taken as conduits enabling "dynamic sourcing of IT facilities on the tap worldwide". These improved telecommunications capabilities have opened new opportunities for spreading business operations at locations across all over the world and created new inter-organizational contexts for doing business.

In this stage, structural and architectural design perspectives emerged about virtual organizations (VOs) and dynamic networks incorporating dynamic sourcing (Hoogeweegen 1997; Venkatraman & Henderson 1998; Wassenaar 1999). ICT (out- and insourcing) is becoming so dominant that we argued (Wassenaar & Swagerman 2001) in line with Lucas (1996) that instead of designing a virtual organization and adding ICT later, managers have to use ICT actively in designing new organizational and architectural platforms incorporating outsourcing from the beginning. TomTom, a Dutch company in navigation systems is a good example: their business model is based on radical outsourcing, no product elements are produced "in house". The same is true for a company like BMW, a car maker, which outsourced a lot of its produc-tion activities. Increased complexity of products and services and time based competition have forced companies to share (and outsource) the development and production tasks among several partners. Companies, like TomTom, have to design modular product architectures where interfaces between individual elements are well defined in order to enable (radical) outsourcing. Their core competencies are embodied in architec-tural knowledge. Managers are suggested to redesign their existing business and organizational patterns in new flexible modular product architectures (platforms) and virtual interorganizational structures.

2.3   The Integrating Stage of Outsourcing

At the end of the expanding stage, outsourcing became a general part of successful business operations. So successful, in fact, that many executives pursue outsourcing compulsively – putting everything from finance to R&D on the block without careful evaluation, benchmarking and so on. Cohen and Young (2006) argue that 50% of outsourcing contracts signed during the past 3 years will fail to meet expectations. So, yesterday's ad hoc outsourcing approaches are ineffective in today's complex terrain. Many problems are not primarily related with the external provider but within the company itself and in the shortcomings in sourcing practices: miscom-munication, misalignment, poor governance and lack of coordinated management (Cohen and Young). They are suggesting outsourcing strategy guidelines for tightly linking outsourcing to the overall business strategy and constantly monitoring on "outsourcing value for business".

Beside the more architectural platform perspective, there is (again) emerging a strategic oriented perspective – obvious driven by the consultancy industry – and elaborated in methodology based approaches such as Cohen and Young. They differ from the before mentioned strategic and alliance oriented perspectives (in the pioneering stage) because of their extensive practical approaches to guide managers. Cohen and Young (2006) are suggesting a new (strategic) mind-set and a seven pillar framework for communicating, interacting with and overseeing service relationships both inside and outside the organization. It is based on a linear cycle of strategic management analysis, choice, implementation and evaluation, with a clear beginning and end.

However we concluded (Wassenaar 2002) that if emergence and turbulence rather than stability are taken as the dominant contextual characteristics (often the case in interorganizational settings) strategic (IS) management can no longer be considered as a linear cycle. On the contrary, emergence calls for continuous, iterative, evolutionary, strategic behaviour, often triggered by external events. A new, more eclectic approach of strategic management of interorganizational systems is needed, based on the assumption that organizations are economical rational systems and social communities: often economical managerial choices are not decisive but have to be confirmed by – often social–cultural -individual choices of the members of the community. Therefore change and innovation is an emergent, path dependent and evolutionary process. Ciborra and Lanzara (1991) are reasoning extensively this emerging and evolutionary character of innovation theoretically and practically.

2.4   Conclusions

A. Outsourcing is not anymore an isolated activity: it can be considered as an innovating activity crucial for business performance. The historical development can be summarised in a pioneering, expanding and integrating stage which has a lot of similarities with the early, intermediating and final stages of Cohen and Young (2006). In their framework these stages are corresponding with three types of service deals:

  (1) Efficiency focusing on operational level by lowering costs
  (2) Enhancement focusing on structural level by improving operations performance
  (3) Transformation focusing on strategic level by improving business performance.

B. Most of the companies are now in the integrating stage of global worldwide innovative outsourcing striking at the heart of company's business model and strategy. However, relevant "guiding" theories are missing to support companies in outsourcing. The innovation theory can deliver an important contribution.

C. From a historical perspective, we see the "outsourcing theories" moving from understanding in the pioneering stage towards predicting the future and giving guidelines what to do in practice in the integrating stage. Their practical importance is growing because of the increasing complexity of outsourcing and their increasing impact on all business activities. Therefore outsourcing has to be studied from a more integrated knowledge perspective based on different disciplines such as innovation theory, organizational learning theory and strategic management theory.

D. The dominant characteristics of the outsourcing context are emergence and turbulence rather than stability and therefore, theoretical approaches of outsourcing call for evolutionary models which are open for "spontaneous" interaction between problem solving and problem context.

3 In Context Outsourcing Framework

Outsourcing is theoretically based on the integration of different disciplines, especially innovation theory, IS planning theory and organizational learning which is elaborated in an in context outsourcing framework and reflection instrument.

3.1 Theoretical Foundations

Outsourcing (solutions) are seen as innovations emerging in the interaction between the problem solving domain and the problem context domain by matching problems and solutions and can be characterised as a path dependent, emerging process resulting in – just like a garbage can – often unintended outcomes. This "shifting and drifting" character of innovating is explained by the formative context concept of Ciborra and Lanzara (1991), defined as the set of institutional arrangements and cognitive and affective frameworks that shape the daily practical and argumentative routines of people at work. It comprises both the (often) taken for granted division of labour and the set of unwritten social scripts that tacitly govern the invention of alternative forms of work, their modes of conflict resolution, revision of existent organizational arrangements and even the learning processes carried out by agents when they implement new systems. In our framework the problem context domain encloses – in line with the definition of Ciborra and Lanzara – different layers such as a set of cognitive and affective frames, strategy (making routines), coordination and conflict resolution mechanisms and working process practices. Outsourcing solutions – developed in the problem solving domain – have to fit in the different layers of problem context domain. If not, this formative context is generating spontaneously adapted solutions or even quite new solutions. Ciborra and Lanzara are arguing and illustrating extensively that the interaction between problem solving and (layers of) formative context are causing an emerging shifting and drifting process with often unexpected outcomes. Their conclusion is that successful innovating is both solution making and context making. The discussed theoretical foundations will be consolidated in an in context outsourcing framework based on the EMIOS model (emerging and matching innovations in interorganizational systems) (Wassenaar & Gregor 2001).

3.2   Building Blocks in Context Outsourcing Framework

This in context outsourcing framework, based on the EMIOS model, has three building blocks:

- A problem solving domain as a source unit for developing outsourcing solutions, which has to be transferred too
- A problem context domain as a destination unit for embedding outsourcing solutions in the organizational (problem) context
- An interaction domain with a constellation of involved actors as an interacting unit for matching problems or needs with solutions

The constellation of involved actors encloses owners and/or representatives of the problem context domain, owners and/or representatives of the problem solving domain and finally intermediaries between the two domains. At one side these patterns of activities on each field are creating of conditions for (managerial) processes and creating results or products (artefacts). At the other side the patterns of activities that can be distinguished are reflecting activities for understanding reality (reflecting mode) and intervening activities for changing reality (intervening mode).

The problem solving domain and problem context domain and therefore also the interaction domain are levelled after:

- An operational process layer of value chain activities
- A human organizational layer of required human skills and their division of labour
- An institutional layer of coordination, power and conflict resolution structure
- A strategic layer of cognitive and affective frames

An outsourcing solution can be considered as a set of technology related issues and a set of content related issues. The content of an outsourcing solution can be expressed and evaluated in their impact on the different layers of the context. Mostly the innovation solution has hidden assumptions regarding their problem context. Especially our reflection instrument aims to make explicit their hidden impact (Fig. 1).

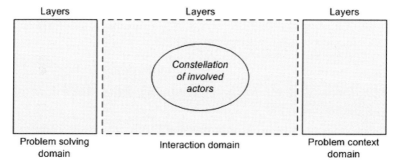

Fig. 1 Building blocks in context outsourcing framework

4   Reflection Instrument

This instrument is based on the developed theoretical framework and can be used for diagnosing and evaluating outsourcing in and between companies. It is flexible and the focus depends on the chosen viewpoint. Starting from this diagnosis/evaluation, the solution or the context can be adapted (by certain interventions). The topics of this instrument are presented in a sequential order which has to be followed.

4.1   Shared Vision on Intended Outcome Outsourcing Innovation

The intended outcome regarding the set of delivered services and the value proposition of outsourcing innovation has to be outlined before realisation in order to tune the expectations of the service provider and customer and other involved actors.

- This *set of delivered services* consists of the exchange of resources between a service provider and a customer. It has to be clear for all involved actors what the outsourcing solution means in terms of delivered services, their components and service levels. Dissonance in expectations is a risk factor.
- The *value category of outsourcing proposition*, which is indicated by the type of business model for effective delivery. It focuses on the type of value delivered and the amount of customization (and therefore on the impact on the customer context). Four different worlds of service delivery and four different business models and related value propositions can be distinguished (Cohen & Young 2006):

  1. Optimization model – paying for business performance (focused on business value and customization)
  2. Creation model – business transaction priced (focused on business value and standardisation)
  3. Management model – fee for service level (focused on operational efficiency and customization)
  4. Access model – pay for usage (focused on operational efficiency and standardisation).

- The value monitoring of the outsourcing proposition encloses an agreed cost–benefit analysis and agreements about a regular update of this analysis during the development and execution of the solution.

4.2   Exploring Impact on the Outsourcing Innovation Context

The outsourcing innovation has to embedded in the innovation context and is therefore interacting on different layers. The exploration of the interaction and impact of the outsourcing innovation and the context can be done by forcing (simulating) a relation between the outsourcing innovation and the innovation context on the distinguished layers. By this effort hidden assumptions of the outsourcing innovation and hidden constraints of the innovation context are made explicit. The results of the exploration can be summarised in a certain *sets of impacts and constraints (on the different levels)*.

4.3 Reshaping the Outsourcing Innovation and the Innovation Context by Balancing the Intended Outcome and Impact on the Innovation Context

The intended outcome and impact of the innovation context are strongly interrelated and have to be balanced for a successful implementation. Lowering the intended outcome (for example by lowering or staging the intended outcomes) can result in less impact on the innovation context and will be easier to implement. The equilibrium can be expressed in an *innovation ambition level*, which gives an indication of the required effort to embed the outsourcing innovation in the context and therefore the required knowledge to bridge the gap between the outsourcing solution domain (service provider) and the innovation context domain (customer organization). This innovation ambition level is mostly a mix of (re)shaping the outsourcing innovation and (re)shaping the innovation context and especially the changes on the distinguished layers.

4.4 The Innovation Strategy

Given an innovation ambition level, an innovation strategy and organizational structure of an innovation system have to be formulated for implementing this ambition level. The *innovation strategy* is a trade off between project and system staging. This means that by incremental strategies the scope of the implemented system (parts) is limited implicating many small short time projects with less failure risk and giving a lot of feed back how to progress. In total strategies systems with a wide scope are realised in a one time radical, big change effort (project). This strategy implicates often a big failure risk requiring a lot of feed forward efforts to avoid uncertainties. So the chosen strategy means a choice for small or big steps in realising outsourcing and has strong consequences for the composition of the *innovation workforce and their expertise*. Especially the balance between (cognitive) transformation skills (mostly experts) and (affective) transfer skills (mostly organizational development) are important for knowledge building and knowledge exchange between involved actors on the solution and the problem context domain.

4.5 The Project Organization

Given an innovation strategy, an appropriate project organization has to be designed for creating and maintaining the interaction patterns between the involved actors shaping the outsourcing innovation solution and the outsourcing innovation context. This project organization is a trade off between external integration (anchoring the project in the involved standing line organization) and the internal integration (assurance of the cohesion and consistence of the project team). It is a balance between external commitment and internal consistency. This project organization is often elaborated with a management system controlling time, costs, quality and report documents.

4.6 Balance Between Ambition Level and Innovation Capabilities

Finally, the intended outcome (4.1), the impact on the outsourcing innovation context (4.2), the innovation strategy (4.4) and the project organization (4.5) have to be balanced with the innovation ambition level and innovation capabilities (4.3) as intermediating variables.

5 Conclusion and Final Remarks

The elaborated instrument is based on the notion that successful outsourcing innovation depends on the fit between innovation solution and innovation context. This fit requires reshaping outsourcing solutions in combination with (re)shaping the innovation context.

In practice, we often see that the level of outsourcing ambitions in companies is relatively high and that the impact of the intended solutions is often being underestimated, whereas the innovation capabilities of companies are being overestimated. In such a context, the reflection instrument as described can have an added value as outsourcing management tool.

References

Ciborra, C., & Lanzara, G. F. (1991). Designing networks in action: formative contexts and post-modern systems development. In R. Clarke & J. Cameron (Eds.), *Managing information technology's organizational impact* (pp. 265–279). Amsterdam: Elsevier Science.

Chandler, A. D. (1977). *The visible hand: The managerial revolution in American enterprise*. Homewood (Illinois): Richard D. Irwin.

Cohen, L, & Young, A. (2006). *Multisourcing, moving beyond outsourcing to achieve growth and agility*. Boston: Harvard Business Press.

Evans, P., &Wurster, T. S. (1997). Strategy and new economics of information. *Harvard Business Review*, September–October, 71–82.

Feeney, D. F., & Willcocks, L. P., (1998). Core IS capabilities for exploiting information technology. *Sloan Management Review, 39*(3), 13–25.

Hoogeweegen, M. R. (1997). *Modular network design: Assessing the impact of EDI.* Rotterdam: Erasmus University Rotterdam.

Keen, P. G. M. (1990). *Shaping the future.* Boston: Harvard Business Press.

Klepper, R., & Hartog, C. (1992). Some determinants of MIS outsourcing behaviour. In *Handbook BIK.* The Netherlands: Samson, Alphen a/d Rijn.

Lacity, M. C., & Hirschheim, R. (1995). *Beyond the information systems outsourcing bandwagon.* Chichester, New York: Wiley.

Lacity, M. C., Willcocks, L. P., & Feeny, D. F. (1996). The value of selective IT sourcing. *Sloan Management Review, 37*(3), 13–25.

Lucas, H. C. (1996). *The T-form organization.* San Francisco: Jossey-Bass.

McFarlan, F. W., & Nolan, R. L. (1995). How to manage an IT outsourcing alliance. *Sloan Management Review, 36*(4), 9–23.

Prahalad, C. K., & Hamel, G. (1990). The core competence of the corporation. *Harvard Business Review*, May–June, 79–91.

Quinn, J. B. & Hilmer, F. G. (1994). Strategic outsourcing. *Sloan Management Review, 35*(4), 73–87.

Venkatraman, N., & Henderson, J. C. (1998). Real strategies for virtual organising. *Sloan Management Review, 40*(1), 33–48.

Wassenaar, D. A. (1999). Understanding and designing virtual organizational forms. *VoNet Newsletter*, 3(1).

Wassenaar, D. A. (2002). *Towards an eclectic approach of Strategic IOS Management – or how to act strategically in a turbulent E-Business Environment.* In Proceedings of the 4th International Conference on Electronic Commerce, October 23–25, Hong Kong.

Wassenaar, D. A., & Gregor, S. (2001). *E-business formulating and forming: New wine in old bottles? Towards an emergent management concept of interorganizational systems (IOS).* In Proceedings of the 9th ECIS Conference: Vol. 2, June 27–29, (pp. 1242–1253), Bled, Slovenia.

Wassenaar, D. A., & Swagerman, D. M. (2001). Transaction platforms as flexible interorganizational systems enabling dynamic sourcing based virtual organizations – the case of m-commerce payment service. Paper presented at Information Systems Outsourcing Conference, Bayreuth.

Reaching Across Organizational Boundaries for New Ideas: Innovation from IT Outsourcing Vendors

Bandula Jayatilaka

1 Introduction

Companies outsource IT either to obtain resources they lack or to obtain IT resources more effectively and efficiently. Vendors are not limited to only providing common solutions. Innovative use of IT resources is critical to the success of organizations, and innovativeness also contributes to competitiveness. However, in outsourcing, more emphasis on cost savings, the need to focus on core competencies and the need to focus on strategic activities overshadows the need for innovativeness. The prescriptions of treating IT outsourcing as a strategic decision (Quinn 1999), outsourcing nonstrategic IT while focusing on internal strategic activities and outsourcing IT for cost savings are sound advice. Vendor innovativeness must complement client activities that are directed towards these more obvious objectives. Although IT outsourcing is often regarded as outsourcing of a nonstrategic resource for cost savings, both vendors and clients gain from vendors' innovations (Quinn 1999, 2000). There are risks such as opportunism involved and it is necessary to have proper contracts and relationship management for obtaining benefits. Despite rapid changes in technologies, focus in academic IT research has been more on cost savings and nonstrategic outsourcing (Dibbern, Goles, Hirschheim, & Jayatilaka 2004). This paper attempts to make a contribution by exploring the organizational and IT factors enabling innovation in outsourced IT.

IT research on innovativeness in outsourcing is scanty. During the early days of IT outsourcing, researchers treated it as an administrative or an organizational innovation where companies rearranged the organizational arrangements for producing IT in a profitable manner (Loh & Venkatraman 1992; Hu, Saunders, & Gebelt 1997). Most of the focus had been on viewing IT outsourcing as a market transaction, which matched the early types of IT outsourcing. IT outsourcing has evolved from facilities management to obtaining IT services (e.g., systems development, data centers) and IT supported services (e.g., Business Process Outsourcing (BPO)). Vendor–customer relationships evolved from managing contracts (Currie & Seltsikas 2001) to more involved relationships where both the vendors and the customers participate in the outsourced activities (Kaiser & Hawk 2004), sometimes referred to as 'co sourcing'. These changes allowed for the discovery of the need for more involvement of the vendors in providing customer specific solutions.

Seeking innovation from IT outsourcing vendors seems to be contradictory to propositions based on the Transaction Cost Economics (TCE). The likelihood of opportunism and seeking nonspecific assets potentially leads to outsourcing of noninnovative commonly available resources (Williamson 1985). This has lead to the suggestion that companies must outsource IT tasks readily available in the market, and obtaining unique solutions from the market will not be cost effective. In non IT outsourcing also, the past practice had been to outsource activities like production, and companies handed over routine or repetitive activities to outside suppliers. In the case of both IT and non IT outsourcing, commonly outsourced activities are the ones vendors are capable of performing without new learning. Hence, it is often assumed that it is unlikely for companies to seek innovative IT solutions from vendors. Seeking innovative IT solutions from vendors is also not complementary to the prescription of outsourcing nonstrategic activities. Now, however, it is not unusual for companies to outsource highly specific activities such as research and development, especially in global markets (Mahnke & Ozcan 2006; Prahalad & Krishnan 2004). This practice has potential strategic value. Some companies seek to outsource nonroutine or nonrepetitive activities, which deviates from past practices. Essentially, some seek new knowledge and innovations from their suppliers or vendors.

Many questions arise when attempting to obtain innovation from outsourcing. Managers have to consider innovation at each phase of outsourcing, i.e., when making the decision to outsource, searching for vendors, negotiating contracts, and implementing and managing the outsourcing relationships. Such considerations are best served by examining the factors that lead to innovation in IT outsourcing environments. In an attempt to find these factors, this paper focuses on two overarching questions: (1) Can IT outsourcing be innovative? (2) If so, what are the critical factors of innovation?

The paper organization is as follows. The next section (Sect. 2) discusses common industry practice as reported by researchers and practitioner publications. This discussion is done to show the somewhat contradictory existent assumptions and practices not supportive of innovation in outsourcing. Section 3 reviews past research on IT outsourcing and innovation. Section 4 discusses factors enabling innovation and innovation across organizational boundaries. Section 5 presents case studies on enabling innovation and inhibiting innovation. Section 6 discusses implications of the research.

2   Industry Practice – Past and Present

Both research and practice has shown a major emphasis on cost savings. The earliest research on determinants of IT outsourcing shows the importance of cost savings. Accordingly researchers also have mostly used transaction cost theory to investigate the antecedents to outsourcing (Dibbern et al. 2004). Comparative cost advantage due to low transaction costs (Ang & Straub 1998; Hancox & Hackney 1999), and the need for cost reduction (Apte et al. 1997; Sobol & Apte 1995) drove IT outsourcing in the early days. The companies that outsourced IT also had a significant cost focus and need for cash (Smith, Mitra, & Narasimhan 1998).

Early research parallels the type of IT outsourcing in which companies handed over their internal IT departments to vendors on facilities management contracts (Currie & Seltsikas 2001). Companies formulated contracts to cut costs and expected the IT services and solutions to follow. Vendors' focus on cost cutting met the demands of the customers for low cost IT services but resulted in poor performances (Hirschheim & Lacity 2000). This became unacceptable to customers and service variations occurred. Emphasis on service levels emerged resulting in service level agreements. Despite the emphasis on service levels, the importance of cost savings and the practice of outsourcing nonstrategic IT remained predominant. However, back sourcing or bringing back the IT in-house also occurred due to reasons such as lack of satisfaction with vendors, rising costs and changing strategic focus. Some companies started seeking innovative IT solutions by expanding their internal IT capabilities, and strategic intents became apparent in outsourcing arrangements (DiRomaualdo & Gurbaxani 1998).

It is a common understanding that the expansion of offshore IT outsourcing activities is due to the availability of low cost skills in other countries. Still the primary need of companies is cost reduction. However, like in domestic outsourcing some companies seek some degree of innovation from vendors. For example, some companies find that IT development projects are more successful when high level specifications yield better outcomes from offshore vendors than when detailed low level specifications are given to them. This implies the necessity for the clients to rely on the solution construction capabilities and some degree of innovativeness of the vendor personnel. Yet, there are no clear indications of companies seeking innovations from offshore outsourcing.

This changing trend indicates the inadequacy of the sole focus on costs or mere service levels, and the necessity for vendors to focus on providing innovative solutions. Just providing low cost IT services will not always be effective. Customer requirements change and new situations warranting new solutions emerge. Supplying new solutions necessitates learning, and the learning must occur both at the vendor and customer organizations. This learning incurs costs. Often both vendors and customers set up the governance of the IT supply agreeing to costs. IT outsourcing occurs within the contractual framework under spending/cost constraints. Within these constraints the vendors have to consider their learning costs. It is necessary to consider other factors influencing innovativeness in IT outsourcing in addition to the learning costs. As a prelude to constructing a conceptual basis for innovation in IT outsourcing the following section reviews the past IT outsourcing research examining the antecedents to IT outsourcing and those deemed relevant to innovation in IT outsourcing.

3   Literature Review – Past IT Outsourcing Research

According to the results from a keyword search for innovation and IT outsourcing, there are no papers in the four major academic IS journals (i.e., EJIS, ISR, JMIS, and MISQ) directly addressing innovation in IT outsourcing (except for two related to economic performance – cf. property rights and value propositions by Levina and Ross (2003)). Researchers have limited their discussions to innovation in business processes and to considering IT outsourcing as an organizational innovation (Hu, Saunders, & Gebelt 1997; Loh & Venkatraman 1992). Hence, I assumed it was prudent to examine three other areas of research containing issues related to innovation. They are the research based on: resources, strategy and transaction costs. Resources are related to innovation because companies search for innovation from vendors due to lack of internal resources, and enabling of innovations needs resources. The resource view was taken by researchers who applied the Resource Based View (Cheon, Grover, & Teng 1995; Poppo & Zenger 1998) and Resource Dependency Theory (1995). Strategy is related to innovation because innovations provide strategic advantage and the researchers taking a strategic perspective have considered IT outsourcing as a means for intensifying internal focus on strategy and core competencies (Smith et al. 1998). Research with TCE as the basis explains the influences of asset specificity, costs and opportunism in outsourcing. While it is easy to associate resource and strategic approaches with innovation, TCE *apparently* contradicts the possibility of obtaining innovative benefits from vendors. According to TCE, asset specificity will make market costs of obtaining specific IT solutions high. Successful IT solutions are outcomes sought from outsourcing.

Researchers have examined success in outsourcing without explicitly examining innovations. However, they have examined some related factors such as resources. Outcomes of IT innovations such as applications systems are unique resources. Depending on the type of contractual agreements, the ability to produce unique solutions can be advantageous to vendors. Nevertheless, researchers have examined the client-side of outsourcing. Research was limited to investigating the role of resource needs and availability in determinants of IT outsourcing. The role of IT in the organization has a moderating effect on the extent of outsourcing and IT outsourcing is a strategic decision (Grover, Cheong, & Teng 1996). In IT outcomes research using Resource Dependency Theory, some activities where innovations matter most, such as applications and systems planning and management, service quality and partnership showed relationships to outsourcing success (Grover et al.). In applications development and maintenance, both service quality and partnership were directly related to outsourcing success. The relationship between nonstrategic IT and outsourcing complements the prescription to outsource nonstrategic IT (Quinn & Hilmer 1994. Strategic IT solutions must be unique for them to provide competitive advantages. This implies that companies, in general, have not sought innovative solutions from their vendors (during the time of the previous research – more than 12 years ago).

Outsourcing of nonstrategic IT need not involve innovative vendors and from the vendor side it will be disadvantageous. When a client company outsources nonstrategic IT, essentially it is not looking for strategic IT from the vendor. Often such outsourcing turns out to be activities vendors already provide to other clients. These are more 'commoditized' IT vendors produce at low (comparatively) costs and clients obtain these IT services through low cost transactions. Outsourcing of strategic IT is looked upon with suspicion due to the possibility of opportunism, and the possibility of diminishing competitive advantages due to a vendor's solutions becoming available to other clients. However, DiRomualdo and Grubaxani (1998) suggest that companies outsource with some strategic intentions, i.e., IS cost reduction and service improvement, business improvement, and creation of commercial ventures. Vendors meet some of these objectives even without innovation. However, very often, the objectives of improvements (business and service) and creation of commercial ventures need innovations.

Innovation is important for vendors, and clients benefit from vendor innovations. If the vendors do not innovate, they would lose the potential to find new clients or continue working with existing clients. Due to changing (IT) technologies and social conditions, it has become essential for vendors to innovate. Suppose the vendors choose to innovate despite the lack of demand for innovation. Then the benefits to the vendor will depend on the costs of innovations and the gains due to information asymmetry. Innovations produce more asset specificity on the vendor side. Based on TCE, more clients seek non specific solutions from the vendors (Poppo & Zenger 1998). In addition, due to asset specificity, vendor opportunism may occur (Williamson 1985). However, both vendors and clients seek cost advantages or cost effectiveness.

The cost advantages or cost effectiveness must encompass innovation costs/ benefits as well. This implies the application of TCE must not be limited to comparisons of transaction and production costs only as done in past IT outsourcing research (Ang & Straub 1998; McLellan, Marcolin, & Beamish 1995; Hancox & Hackney 1999; Slaughter & Ang 1996; Smith et al. 1998). Within the transaction cost economics framework, IT outsourcing researchers have not examined the costs of learning and innovation and the benefits of innovation. Nevertheless, there are several empirical transaction economic studies done in relation to non IT activities (Globerman 1980; Montevede & Teece 1982; Tapon 1989). Innovation in IT is not less critical to success compared to other business activities mainly due to technological changes and accompanying business changes.

Innovations in IT may not be limited to those in Business Process Outsourcing. While looking for lowering costs, eliminating internal production and services does make sense. After some time companies may find needs for making use of new technologies, change the business processes or use IT in different ways to expand the businesses. All of these activities call for innovation and adopting new solutions in such situations may incur costs. To meet the needs for new solutions a company already outsourcing IT will have to back source, find new outsourcing arrangements, or seek new solutions within the existing outsourcing arrangements. The last two options require innovations from the vendors and the first option necessitates innovations by the client.

4   Innovation in IT Outsourcing

Proper organizational, managerial, and individual factors and processes are essential for innovation. When considered as an isolated activity, innovation is people generating and implementing new ideas. In organizational contexts, there are many interacting organizational units and individuals generating new ideas and implementing them. Van de Ven defines the process of innovation as "the development and implementation of ideas by people who over time engage in transactions with others within an institutional context (Van de Ven 1986, p. 591)." In outsourcing, the institutional context consists of the vendor and client organization, and both vendor and client people may be involved in the innovation process.

Through innovation processes new services and products are formed, and it is useful to treat innovation processes and outcomes distinctly. Very often the innovation process occurs at the vendor while the client receives the outcome. However, for some IT activities the innovation process may cross organizational boundaries. For example, a vendor's development of an innovative system will institute business changes in the client organization when implemented. IT researchers have focused on diffusion and adoption (Cooper & Zmud 1990; Lyytinen & Rose 2003), and these are only two stages of innovation (Rogers 1983). Overall, stage models of innovation will be useful when managing a specific activity (Rogers; Zaltman, Duncan, & Holbek 1973). When IT outsourcing consists of multiple activities, a non stage approach will be more appropriate for exploring innovation in IT outsourcing.

Both on vendor and client sides, product/services, related processes and administrative activities are potential targets for innovative change. As shown in Fig. 1, the innovations at these points are related and will be either constrained or

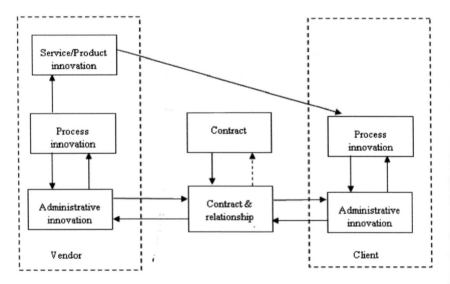

Fig. 1 Vendor Client context for innovation

enabled by the contracts. A vendor can develop new processes to produce its services, and as a result there will be improvements in services provided by the vendor. These improvements due to innovations in the services will positively influence the client's processes. Both the service and process innovations are technical innovations that are influenced by administrative innovations. A vendor might find new approaches to project management, in providing desktop support, in help desk activities, or in operational procedures in data centers. These innovations will help change the vendor's systems/software development, user support activities, and data center operations. All these IT related activities will influence the client's business processes. In BPO, services will be the outcomes of the business process having influences on the client's in-house activities that are interacting with the outsourced business processes. Administrative activities are the activities that support the vendor's primary activities and also result in interactions with clients.

Technical innovations do not occur in isolation from administrative innovations and vendors' administrative innovations also effect client activities to a certain degree. If we follow a dual-core model, the innovations in the administrative activities are separate from the technical activities (Daft 1978). Nevertheless, administrative innovations are not completely separable from technical innovations. Administrative innovations help and enable technical innovations (Daft). For example, changes in structuring of the activities, in human resource management or in budgetary controls may influence technical processes and services. Administrative processes on both sides (vendor and client) act as effective conduits for contract management activities. Innovations in administrative actions enable good contract and relationships management.

Depending on the contract, the vendor or client innovations cause contract changes. Contracts provide structures to the vendor and client outsourcing activities. Although innovations in both vendor and client organizations impact contract and relationships management, these improvements have to occur within the existing contractual agreements. When the contracts impose constraints on vendors' or clients' activities, contractual re negotiations or terminations occur. For example, a vendor re negotiates due to increase demand on their personnel due to client innovations or the client renegotiates due to the vendor not meeting the new expectations. Contracts must be formulated to enable innovations and contracts impose significant influences along with other factors helping innovations.

4.1 Enablers of Innovations

Successful innovation results from deliberate management of individual, structural and organizational elements (Kimberly & Evanisko 1981; Van de Ven 1986). A multilevel analysis is necessary to describe innovation. At the individual level, the personnel and the leadership play pivotal roles. Organizationally, availability of resources and the perceived returns from innovations are important. Structurally, relationships between the vendor and client, and enabling structures within the vendor organization influence the client outcomes. Figure 2 shows the relationships among the factors and innovations. The above mentioned factors are necessary conditions but they are not sufficient. For example, tolerance for risk taking in an organization enables innovations (O'Reilly & Tushman 1997), and a company with no tolerance for risk-taking will not have any or very few incidences of innovations. On the other hand, it is possible to include certain risk related factors with the estimation of returns and personnel and leadership behavior. It is prudent to avoid or mitigate risk in IT outsourcing (Aubert, Dussault, Patry, & Rivard 1999) due to constraints. It will become difficult for the vendors to absorb the returns due to failures. Vendors' success depends on contract continuation with clients, and often failure due to risk taking will result in the vendor losing future prospects. Hence, this paper does not consider risk explicitly (cf. Sitkin & Pablo 1992; Miller, Kets De Vries, & Toulouse 1982 for more on risk).

Resource availability contributes to innovativeness (Amabile, Conti, Coon, Lazenby, & Herron 1996; Nadler & Tushman 1997) and outsourcing vendors are in possession of resources that many client companies or a single client does not possess. The relationship between resource use and innovativeness is not apparent due to

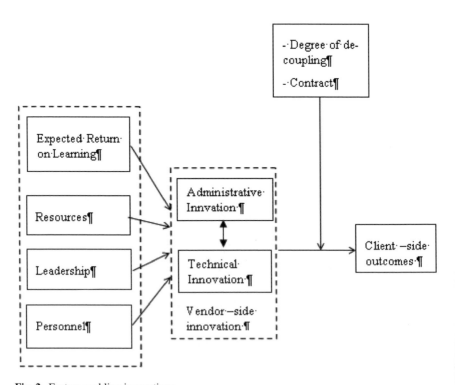

Fig. 2 Factors enabling innovations

non linearity. Not having access to resources contributed significantly to stagnation in some companies, and this can affect innovation even if other factors such as top management support is present (Dougherty & Hardy 1996). Resource availability does not guarantee innovativeness and availability of resources may not always has a positive effect on innovation. Allocation of resources more than required will have a negative effect on innovation. Because of complacency and the security such allocation of funds provides, the need to succeed in innovation may not be felt properly by the employees. Increasing slack or a pool of resources in excess of the minimum necessary to produce a given level of organizational output will increase innovation to a certain extent. Slack and innovation are related in an inverted U-shaped curve showing that increasing slack beyond a certain point results in a decrease in innovation (Nohira & Gulati 1996). Vendor resources and constraints imposed by contracts establish the environment in applying the necessary amounts of resources for innovation. This is different from the argument that vendors do not necessarily have the economy of scale advantage (which is stated as a myth – Lacity & Hirschheim 1993). Resources cannot be separated from economic considerations because there are costs associated with resources.

Cost effectiveness is a critical factor in outsourcing and it may be necessary to forgo cost savings to produce innovative solutions. Cost cutting has been associated with reduction of services (Hirschheim & Lacity 2000) and this also implies inhibition of innovation due to the cost cutting imperative. Ensuring adequate resources for innovations requires monetary funds. While cost savings may not be a major goal when looking for innovations from a vendor, it is necessary to evaluate the costs/ benefits of innovations. Innovations will have a cumulative effect and benefits of an innovation will not be limited to one client or one contract. Innovation done for one client may spawn efficiencies in other clients' work. For example, innovations in systems development project management are applicable to systems development activities for many clients. Some benefits are incremental and some are major. Proper evaluation of the costs and benefits will provide incentives for a vendor to invest in innovations.

Costing of innovations and learning will help the client's evaluation of the vendors. Having innovation contributions as a performance measure gives an incentive for the vendor to become innovative. Although at the individual level extrinsic motivation and monetary rewards do not influence creativity (Cooper & Jayatilaka 2006), at the organizational level linking remunerations to innovativeness will help allocation of resources necessary for innovation related activities. Having adequate resources in the organization will enable individuals to perform their activities without many hindrances. However, having resources alone does not spawn innovations and other individual factors must be present.

Innovations start with attention to new ideas and later developments occur through developing the ideas further, combining with existing knowledge and finally by implementing the developed and assimilated ideas in a useful manner. Often individuals become complacent and tend to dwell on familiar activities. This implies that new idea generation requires triggers that change or threaten the existing circumstances. Threatening or disruptive events cause new idea generation (Schon 1971) but in an organization such generations occur due to expectation failures or due to deliberate actions such as goal setting (Argyris & Schon 1977). Idea generation occurs at the individual level while groups and organizations enable and provide support. The relationship of the new ideas to the whole activity or the organization must be understood and the relationship must emerge for the innovative idea to become a reality.

Such assimilation and integration with existing activities often involves group interactions, dialogues and even political processes (Anderson & Tushman 1991; Murman & Tushman 2001). For example, an IT idea to improve a business process must be related to the present and future business contexts before becoming a reality. The system developed as a result of the idea must have the capability to transform the existing business process. The transformation cannot occur without properly understanding the existing and the future requirements. Starting from the idea generation to implementation individual actions, interactions and social processes enable and facilitate these individual level activities.

In an outsourcing environment, the vendors are working under specific contracts to achieve identified goals and certainty, explicit specifications and contractual constraints often influence the individual behavior. During the first generation of outsourcing, the vendors hired clients' employees to work on the clients' projects. The transfer of employees enabled the vendors to develop knowledge about the customer's business. However, in the long-run companies seek innovations in the systems and the business processes. This necessitates transformation of existing structures and processes while paying attention to idea generation, new learning and acquiring new knowledge. Uncertainties arise and they are necessary for innovation. In addition to idea selection, experimentation must occur. All these must take place within limits that ensure the continuity of the organizational activities and the usefulness of ideas. Leadership plays a critical role in providing an environment of guarded uncertainty and transformative thinking.

At the organizational level, leadership provides stability by obtaining, providing and controlling resources. Leadership provides a stable environment, but for innovations leaders must construct challenges to generate new ideas. Leaders act as a catalyst for new ideas. Essentially the leaders must enable double-loop learning in the organization and in individuals. Leaders must be able to question the existing standards, norms and processes to cause useful dialog resulting in innovations. The transformation of ideas to reality involves social and political processes. This may involve intraorganizational as well as interorganizational communications and activities. Outsourcing vendors will have to engage clients in a dialogue to find triggers for new idea generation and organizational leadership needs to play an important role in enabling interactions with the clients.

Innovations need new knowledge and vendors will have to pursue new knowledge. These pursuits will require scanning the external environment for knowledge and filtering out unnecessary knowledge. With rapid changes in technologies, organizational leadership must be able to provide the required knowledge leadership as well. This will involve either having the appropriate technical skills within or leaders developing the necessary technical knowledge.

Learning and creating knowledge is inadequate, and the necessary changes in the processes must occur effectively. As shown in Fig. 1 (previous section), transformation will occur in both vendor and client organizations. Effective organizational leadership must exist for the transformations to succeed because it is necessary to change organizational behaviors and processes embedded within organizations.

5   Four Cases on Innovation

This section illustrates vendor roles and the factors contributing to innovations in four companies. The data are presented here as exploratory cases aimed at assessing the frameworks presented earlier. They are linked to the factors driving innovation in the vendor, the influences of the contracts/relationships and the outcomes of the innovative efforts.

Using interviews, I collected data from these four client companies and their vendors. The interview data was transcribed and the case narratives were created. Both vendor and client narratives were analyzed looking for incidences of seeking innovation, activities resulting in innovations and the outcomes of innovations. The four client companies are from different industrial sectors and their sizes vary. All four companies have sought either direct innovations or innovative support from their vendors. The companies are named Med Kits, E-Services, Trans-Edge and Global Geo. Table 1 gives summary data on the companies and their respondents.

5.1   Med Supplier

A Med Supplier produces material for medical testing such as testing kits. It has branches and sales offices worldwide. Due to the rapid rate of development in the medical field, medical testing procedures and tests also change frequently. This makes it necessary for Med Supplier to change or improve their products, i.e., laboratory testing material. Med Supplier uses IT heavily in all its activities and has established global connectivity with its distributed locations. Its internal IT department supplies most of the IT and data communications services and web related development activities are done collaboratively by IT and the marketing division. The activities in the company are integrated through an ERP system while some divisions such as R&D, production, marketing, and sales have their domain specific applications. Although the company uses IT heavily in its activities, some groups within the company are not satisfied with the responsiveness of the internal IT department and the services they receive.

Due to frequent changes in the medical field and the associated regulatory changes coming from the FDA, Med Supplier has to develop and produce new products frequently. Activities in the R&D and production divisions are critical to

Table 1 Summary of client and vendor companies

Client	Industry	Client–Interviewees	Out-sourcing	Vendor Interviewees
Global Geo	Petroleum	Senior managers – engineering	Total	Senior IT manager
		– Knowledge engineering		Account expert
		– Marketing Director IT		Contract Manager
E-Servi-ces	Energy	CIO	Total	Senor account expert
		Director IT		IT manager
		Contract manager		IT Manager – E-services account
Med Sup-plies	Medical testing	CIO	Selective	Senior IT manager
		Director production		Account expert
		Senior manager sales		Contract manager
		Senior manager marketing		
		Manager marketing		
		IT support specialist		
Trans Edge	Transpor-tation	CIO	Total	Director marketing relations
		Director IT		
		Contract manager		
				Senior accounts manager
				IT manager
				User specialist

the company and these two divisions are responsible for implementing the emerging change requirements. As a result, the production division is often faced with the need to change their production schedules, methods and processes. The production division found that its frequently changing operations could be easily supported with more innovative and agile systems. However, the production division was not happy with the rigidity and lack of responsiveness from the IT department. They did not accept the solutions offered by the internal IT department. The solution offered was to upgrade the existing software within an ERP structure.

To obtain the service it required, the production division outsourced its IT activities. The production department sought help from an outside vendor who was willing to innovate, and cost savings was not a reason. They by passed the internal IT department and started exploring the market. They succeeded in selecting a vendor who was willing to provide a new solution to them. The vendor has the resources and flexibility to provide a system and support to Med Supplier's production division. According to the agreement, the vendor must support the integration activities when it is necessary to integrate the production systems with the rest of the systems in the company.

These activities needed some degree of customization and innovation. Although Med Supplier's vendor has systems that met the needs of Med Supplier, it had to modify the software to meet the needs effectively. According to Med Supplier's vendor, the following capabilities enabled them to provide the innovative solutions.

- Resources and expertise accumulated in the company by virtue of being an IT supplier in the market
- Flexibility in the organization to deploy the resources and expertise when necessary
- Expert leaders capable of solving problems quickly
- Technical leaders who can also lead the necessary transformations
- Uncertainty created by the client's needs
- Ability to transform its systems and systems development efforts

According to Med Supplier, they could obtain the products and services from the vendor successfully because the contractual agreements were specific about the innovative and changing needs of the production division. Also, the production division handles its own vendor relationship management activities and the internal IT department does not participate. The production division is successful in managing the contract and the relationship to obtain the necessary services and the vendor continues to innovate as required by Med Supplier. Although the innovations can be treated as incremental, both the vendor and the client have succeeded in implementing the innovations.

The role of resource availability and the leadership (transformation and expertise) provided by the vendor is prominent in this case. The uncertain situation could be exploited properly through innovations. Also innovations would not have occurred if the client had not communicated the needs to the vendor and the vendor had not seized the opportunity. While cost was not a major reason for the client, the vendor considered the cost of learning/innovation as a benefit because of the accumulating effect. There is no indication of the long-term cost effectiveness of this outsourcing. However, a later inquiry found that both the client and the vendor have continued with the outsourcing agreement despite Med Supplier changing its ERP system.

5.2 E-Services

E-Services is an energy producer and supplier that found itself in need of innovations. Like other energy companies, E-Services had traditional operations and there was no necessity for innovation because its market was guaranteed through regulations. However deregulation of the energy industry and advances in information and communications technologies found E-Services needing to use IT more innovatively. This meant changing the traditional uses of IT for operational efficiency. They had to use IT strategically to become more competitive in a deregulated market. E-Services outsourced its IT to a vendor prior to deregulation to cut its IT costs.

Within the deregulated environment, the existing outsourcing arrangement did not seem to be giving E-Services the necessary competitive edge. Under the then existent contract, the vendor was responsible for transactions systems, management support systems, accounting systems and other activities such as data center operations, user support and help desk. They were doing maintenance of the application systems and the changes were mostly incremental. There was no need for innovations. The vendor employed the IT personnel of E-Services at the time of the first outsourcing and the vendor was a large vendor who was working with other companies in the industry.

After the deregulation, E-Services sought ways to become competitive and the managers at E-Services wanted to use IT more effectively in their strategies. However, the existing vendor was not capable of meeting the emergent strategic needs. Because of regulations, E-Services had not been exposed to all of the industry activities, and its IT use had been limited to traditional activities. As a result, it did not have the capabilities to map a strategic course appropriately by taking into consideration the IT potentials. The vendor had resources and expertise that could be placed at the disposal of E-Services, but E-Services did not want to align with the vendor.

E-Services renegotiated the IT outsourcing contract with the vendor and requested the vendor to provide innovative strategic input. The contract stipulated the investments that must be made by the vendor for development of innovative IT solutions. They added IT strategic goals to the contract and the payments were tied to attainments of these strategic goals. One of the goals of E-Services was to increase the percentage of investments in strategic IT while relatively reducing the spending on IT operations. An E-Service executive referred to this goal as inversion of the IT spending triangle. Traditionally, the spending on transactional/operational IT is at the base of the triangle and they wanted strategic IT spending to be at the base of the triangle.

Effective implementation of IT and transformation of the E-Service business could not be performed without the participation of the experts and transformational leaders. E-Services did not have the necessary leadership internally. The vendor had to transfer business experts from other locations to provide the necessary expertise and leadership. Both the vendor and the client described the outcome as a win–win situation. E-Services was successful in expanding their strategic IT use with innovations and gained strategic advantages due to the outsourcing arrangement. They were able to enter into new markets as a result of the newly deployed systems. From the vendor point of view the outsourcing arrangement was also successful.

According to the vendor the following factors were present.

- Expertise and business knowledge gained from related activities
- Transformational leadership
- Contractual obligations and stipulations in the contract
- Incentives provided by the agreement
- Availability of resources
- Treating the innovations as an accumulation of knowledge helpful in future activities
- Cost effectiveness of learning through innovations
- Cooperation received from the client allowing the vendor to be innovative

5.3   *Trans Edge*

Trans Edge is a leading company in the transportation sector and has experienced growth despite its industry's trend of stagnation. They seek innovative ways of improving their business activities and claim to be successful in their efforts. According to a manager at Trans Edge, their competitors attempt to mimic or follow the developments at Trans Edge. Their strategy is to focus on providing excellent services to their customers. While focusing on their major strategic goal, they attempt to use IT innovatively. Because of the size of the company, its IT spending was also several hundred million dollars. The company wanted to reduce its IT spending and it adopted the strategy of outsourcing.

They outsourced a major part of their IT activities and the IT director called it a total outsourcing. The company kept only some cutting edge development activities and transferred all the IT employees to the vendor. One reason for transferring their IT employees to the vendor was to ensure that the vendor had the proper expertise and business domain knowledge to perform Trans Edge's IT functions. By having an internal IT department, they wanted to develop the internal skills and expertise to adopt new technologies and develop new systems. Later, these internal IT personnel worked alongside vendor personnel in areas of planning, project management and design.

The vendor played a proactive role in providing effective solutions and IT services to Trans Edge. According to vendor experts, vendor personnel acted as consultants on some IT projects. They were also instrumental in changing the outsourcing arrangements and ensuring that Trans Edge's systems and services were changed with the advances in technologies and changing business process needs. The vendor also hired new account experts (with PhD's) to ensure meeting Trans Edge's requirements. The new experts worked successfully with Trans Edge and met the goals of outsourcing. The vendor developed new systems and effective diffusion of IT had taken place. The IT managers and the Director of IT at Trans Edge were satisfied and happy about the vendor's performance. They achieved the necessary business transformations. However, Trans Edge did not want to depend solely on the vendor and continued using (and maintaining) internal expertise on projects in which they adopted new technologies Trans Edge changed its original objectives of cost cutting only due to the need to use IT effectively.

Unlike the previous two cases, both Trans Edge and the vendor were instrumental in bringing about innovations. According to the vendor, factors associated with the innovations at Trans Edge are:

- Willingness of the vendor to be innovative in order to accumulate learning and expertise
- Use of leaders who are capable of leading the transformation at Trans Edge and provide expertise as consultants
- Resource base of the vendor
- Expectations to have long-term relationships with the vendor
- Expectations to use the learning from the vendor in the future
- Transformational leadership

Trans Edge managers attributed the successful outsourcing to Trans Edge's involvement in the IT activities along with the vendor personnel. Working with the vendors in planning, project management and design have facilitated the innovations and effective use of IT. Although Trans Edge added these factors also as contributors to the innovativeness, Trans Edge managers did not contradict the vendor managers' claims. Trans Edge managers also acknowledged the contributions made by the vendor experts. According to Trans Edge managers, only the transfer of employees to the vendor could not have achieved the success.

5.4 Global Geo

Global Geo is a company in the petroleum industry and has global operations. The company uses IT extensively. To cut costs the company outsourced all of its IT while retaining top level IT managers. Due to a global reorganization, Global Geo started implementing new systems integrating different geographic locations. For example, they implemented a new system integrating communication capabilities such as e-mail for improving collaborations across the different geographical locations. Also managers wanted to use new technologies such as data warehouses and knowledge management systems more extensively. Essentially, Global Geo took initiatives to change the systems in almost all its activities including sales, marketing, production and engineering.

In outsourcing, instead of making its main vendor complacent by guaranteeing the contracts for different IT activities, Global Geo opened projects for bidding. This meant the vendor had to be competitive in order to continue working with the client. The vendor had to meet the cost cutting objectives and provide effective solutions at the same time. However, being the main vendor to Global Geo and having Global Geo as its major client the vendor had to be proactive. The absence of IT personnel in Global Geo made it necessary for the vendor to find effective solutions. Very often the solutions had to be innovative due to emergent needs of the client. Especially in application areas like knowledge management, data mining, financial analysis and supply chain, the vendor had to improve techniques, technologies and systems. The vendor's work was not limited to the operations, applications and tactical levels.

The vendor also had to provide strategy making support to Global Geo. The vendor's experts and top management participated in some strategy making sessions for Global Geo. At the same time, the vendor had to present strategic IT proposals to Global Geo. Global Geo needed to use IT strategically and due to the absence of internal high-level IT experts the vendor's proposals and contributions became valuable to them. However, the vendor's opportunity to participate in the strategy making was not guaranteed. The continuation of the vendor's activities depended on the performance of the vendor and the effectiveness of their support in the strategy making. One of the IT managers referred to this as "earning a seat at the strategy making table." The vendor's activities and proposals had to undergo the strict scrutiny of the business experts and the top management at Global Geo. Global Geo's business managers and experts could reject the proposals and ideas of the vendor and request implementation of their own ideas. One of the business experts at Global Geo showed me a system that was rejected by him and other experts in his area. Also, despite providing input to the strategy making process, the vendor had to go through the bidding process when obtaining new contracts. The bidding process ensured that Global Geo got the best return on their investments.

Global Geo also did not claim ownership of the systems developed by the vendor and the vendor had the right to sell the nonstrategic systems. The vendor advertises and sells several new applications they developed for Global Geo. The vendor's innovations have a cumulative effect because the knowledge gained can be used for further developments. This has not lead to opportunism because the vendor has not undermined the strategic advantages of Global Geo.

Prior to becoming the IT supplier, the vendor's approach to systems development had been mainly technical. They ignored the social aspects of the users, and the developers did not consider user participation important. Due to the needs of Global Geo, the vendor changed its approach. It focused more attention on user participation and gave more consideration to the social aspects of the systems.

The vendor postulated the following as the reasons for their success:

- Providing strategic input to the client
- Attempting to provide innovative solutions
- Cumulative effects of their learning and systems development efforts
- Readiness to compete with other vendors, which creates a certain degree of uncertainty driving innovations
- Efforts to cut costs
- Taking a more participative approach; listening to users
- Willingness of the vendor to change their approaches and technologies

Global Geo managers were happy with the performance of the vendor and they value the success of the vendor in producing systems that can be sold to other clients. There was a dialogical relationship between the vendor and client that created the necessary awareness to become innovative. The dialogue also eliminates the complacency on the part of the vendor.

6 Discussion and Conclusion

There are commonalities as well as some differences in the four cases. The differences could be due to the context of the companies, i.e., some factors more prominently present in some cases than the others. The factors can be summarized as shown in Fig. 2 (discussed earlier). The discussion centers on transaction costs, opportunism, and asset specificity because they are of major concern in outsourcing.

In all four cases, the vendors were innovators for their clients. Except for Trans Edge, the vendors were the only innovators. In Trans Edge, the internal IT departments and the IT managers were maintaining the innovative capabilities. They had long-term objectives of using internal IT innovatively. The vendors had the potential to innovate despite the possibilities for opportunism. The opportunism risk had to be mitigated by the contract and other relationship management methods. In Global Geo, Trans Edge and E-Services, the vendor provided either strategically important consulting or was responsible for participation in strategy making. None of the cases show direct strategic partnerships and all the vendors are obligated by contracts to provide strategically important ideas/inputs. Global Geo and E-Services data showed that vendor payments were linked to their strategic contributions. For Global Geo, future opportunities were also linked to their strategic contributions.

In all four cases, the cumulative effects of learning had become one reason for vendor innovations. The cumulative benefits could justify the present costs of innovations. The benefits were not always quantifiable. However, it was possible to analyze the effects of innovation costs, production costs, transaction costs and the benefits of cumulative effects by using abstract terms and transaction cost economics lens. The cumulative learning affected the asset specificity aspects of outsourced activities. Due to the possibility of accumulating values in the vendor organization, even if the vendors created customer specific solutions, they were able to benefit from their innovations. Both administrative and technological innovations will help create other innovations in the future.

Although this paper has discussed the factors beyond just psychological or sociological (as in Feeny, Willcocks and Lacity 2006), there are limitations to this paper. I did not attempt to examine the factors discussed in Fig. 2 at a greater depth. A logical next step will be to see what specific attributes under these factors enable or inhibit innovations and to examine IT functions. The existing innovations research stream in the IT field will be a good basis for examining IT functions. The previous IT research on innovations has to be examined within IT outsourcing, especially in offshore outsourcing contexts.

In summary, as shown earlier using the framework, vendor resources, expertise and leadership are important factors for innovation. We cannot expect vendors to be like 'surf riders' as referred to by Quinn (2000). The services they produce may not be marketable like some other products at the right time. The vendors are not innovators for the sake of innovations; rather they are working within contractual structures. The contracts have to be innovative, too because they have to enable innovations in the vendor organizations and enable effective use of vendor innovations by the clients. Vendors are not limited to providing commodity like common solutions only. However, there are certain risks to both vendors and clients. While risk avoidance is necessary, innovators are faced with a certain degree of uncertainty, which creates the initial explorations. In an outsourcing situation, the contracts and the leadership should provide the necessary structures to create the environment for risk taking and containing the risks within acceptable limitations.

Finally, the focus on innovations must not contradict the efforts to cut costs and the argument based on TCE. Efforts in economics are to factor in the costs of learning as well and same efforts must be taken by the IT outsourcing researchers and practitioners. Opportunism is a behavior and asset specificity is directly related to the technical aspects of the transaction. As seen from the cases discussed here both technical aspects and the behaviors can be organized and managed properly to achieve innovative solutions. This study is limited to identifying the factors enabling innovations and to illustrating the possibility of innovations in outsourcing contexts. However, opportunism and asset specificity are not ignored and the attempt of the future research will be to address the issues of opportunism and asset specificity more explicitly.

References

Amabile, T. M., Conti, R., Coon, H., Lazenby, J., & Herron, M. (1996). Assessing the work environment for creativity. *Academy of Management Journal, 39*(5), 1154–1184.

Anderson, P., & Tushman, M. L. (1991). Managing through cycles of technological change. In M. L Tushman & P. Andersen (eds.), *Managing strategic innovation and change*. New York: Oxford University Press.

Ang, S., & Straub, D. W. (1998). Production and transaction economies and IS outsourcing: A study of the U.S. banking industry. *MIS Quarterly, 22*(4), 535–552.

Apte, U. M., Sobol, M. G., Hanaoka, S., Shimada, T., Saarinen, T., Salmela, T. & Vepsalainen, A. P. J. (1997). IS outsourcing practices in the USA, Japan and Finland: A comparative study. *Journal of Information Technology, 12*, 289–304.

Argyris, C., & Schon, D. (1977). *Organizational learning: A theory of action perspective*. Reading, MA: Addison-Wesley.

Aubert, B. A., Dussault, S., Patry, M., &Rivard, S. (1999). Managing the risk of IT outsourcing. Paper presented at Proceedings of the 32nd Annual Hawaii International Conference on System Sciences, Hawaii.

Cheon, M. J., Grover, V., & Teng, J. T. C. (1995). Theoretical Perspectives on the Outsourcing of Information Systems. *Journal of Information Technology, 10*, 209–210.

Cooper, R., & Jayatilaka, B. (2006) "Group creativity: The effects of extrinsic, intrinsic, and obligation motivations." *Creativity Research Journal, 18*(2), 153–173.

Cooper, R. B., & Zmud, R. W. (1990). Information technology research: A technological diffusion approach. *Management Science, 36*(2), 123–139.

Currie, W. L., & Seltsikas, P. (2001). Exploring the supply-side of IT outsourcing: evaluating the emerging role of application service providers. *European Journal of Information Systems, 10*, 123–134.

Daft, R.L. (1978). A dual-core model of organizational innovation. *Academy of Management Journal, 21*, 193–210.

Dibbern, J., Goles, T., Hirschheim, R., & Jayatilaka, B. (2004). Information systems outsourcing: a survey and analysis of the literature. *Database for Advances in Information Systems, 35*(4), 6–102.

DiRomualdo, A., & Gurbaxani, V. (1998). Strategic intent for IT outsourcing. *Sloan Management Review, Summer*, 67–80.

Dougherty, D., & Hardy C. (1996). Sustained product innovation in large, mature organizations: Overcoming innovation-to-organization problems. *Academy of Management Journal, 39*(5), 1120–1153.

Feeny, D., Lacity, M., & Willcoks, L. (2005) Taking the measure of outsourcing providers, *Sloan Management Review, 46*(3), 41–48.

Globerman, S. (1980). Markets, hierarchies and innovation. *Journal of Economic Issues 14*(4), 977–998.

Grover, V., Cheon, M. J., & Teng, J. T. C. (1996). The effect of service quality and partnership on the outsourcing of information systems functions. *Journal of Management Information Systems, 12*(4), 89–116.

Hancox, M., & Hackney. R. (1999). Information technology outsourcing: conceptualizing practice in the public and private sector. Paper presented in 32nd Annual Hawaii International Conference on System Sciences, Hawaii.

Hirschheim, R. A., & Lacity, M. C. (2000). The myths and realities of information technology insourcing. *Communications of the ACM, 43*(2), 99–107.

Hu, Q., Saunders, C., & Gebelt, M. (1997). Research report: Diffusion of information systems outsourcing: a reevaluation of influence sources. *Information Systems Research, 8*(3), 288–301.

Kaiser, K. M., & Hawk, S. (2004). Evolution of offshore software development: from outsourcing to cosourcing. *MISQ Executive, 3*(2), 69–81.

Kimberly, J.R., & Evanisko, M.J. (1981). Organizational innovation: The influence of individual organizational and contextual factors on hospital adoption of technological and administrative innovation. *Academy of Management Journal, 24*, 689–713.

Lacity, M. C., & Hirschheim, R. A. (1993). Information systems outsourcing: myths, metaphors, and realities. Chichester, New York: Wiley.

Levina, N., & Ross, J. W. (2003). From the vendor's perspective: exploring the value proposition in information technology outsourcing. *MIS Quarterly, 27*(3), 331–364.

Loh, L., & Venkatraman, N. (1992). Diffusion of information technology outsourcing: influence sources and the kodak effect. *Information Systems Research, 3*(4), 334–358.

Lyytinen, K., & Rose, G. M. (2003). The disruptive nature of information technology innovations: the case of internet computing in systems development organizations. *MIS Quarterly, 27*(4), 557–595.

Mahnke, V., & Ozcan, S. (2006). Outsourcing innovation and relational governance. Industry and Innovation, 13(2), 121–125.

McLellan, K. L., Marcolin, B. L., & Beamish, P. W. (1995). Financial and strategic motivations behind IS outsourcing. *Journal of Information Technology, 10*, 299–321.

Miller, D., Kets De Vries, M.F.R., & Toulouse, T. (1982). Top executive locus of control and its relationship to strategy-making, structure, and environment. *Academy of Management of Journal, 25*(2), 237–253.

Monteverde, K., & Teece, D. J. (1982). Appropriable rents and quasi-vertical integration. *The Journal of Law and Economics, 25*, 321–328.

Murmann, J. P., & Tushman, M. L. (2001) From the technology cycle to the entrepreneurship dynamic: The social context of entrepreneurial innovation. In C.B. Schoonhoven & E. Romanelli (eds.), *The entrepreneurship dynamic Origins of entrepreneurship and the evolution of industries* 178–203. Stanford, CA: Stanford University Press

Nadler, D. A., & Tushman, M. L. (1997). A Congruence model for organization problem solving. In M.L Tushman & P. Andersen (eds.), *Managing strategic innovation and change*. New York: Oxford University Press.

Nohria, N., & Gulati, R. (1996). Is slack good or bad for innovation? *Academy of Management Journal, 39*(5), 1245–1264.

O'Reilly III, C. A., Tushman, M. L. (1997). Using culture for strategic advantage: promoting innovation through social control. In M. L Tushman & P. Andersen (eds.), *Managing Strategic Innovation and Change*. New York: Oxford University Press.

Poppo, L. & Zenger, T. (1998) Testing alternative theories of the firm: Transaction cost, knowledge-based, and measurement explanations for make-or-buy decisions in information services, *Strategic Management Journal, 19*(9), 853–877.

Prahalad, C. K., & Krishnan, M. S. (2004). The building blocks of global competitiveness. *Optimize, 3*(9), 30–40.

Quinn, J. B. (1999). Strategic outsourcing: leveraging knowledge capabilities. *Sloan Management Review, Summer*, 9–21.

Quinn, J. B. (2000). Outsourcing innovation: The new engine of growth. *Sloan Management Review, Summer*, 13–28.

Quinn, J., & Hilmer, F. (1994) Startegic outsourcing. *Sloan Management Review, 35*(4), 43–55.

Rogers, E. M. (1983). Diffusion of innovation. New York: Free Press.

Schon, D. (1971) *Beyond the stable state*, New York: Norton.

Sitkin, S. B., & Pablo, A. L. (1992). Re-conceptualizing the determinants of risk behavior. *Academy of Management Review, 17*(1), 9–38.

Slaughter, S. A., & Ang, S. (1996). Employment outsourcing in information systems, *Communications of the ACM, 39*(7), 47–54.

Smith, M. A., Mitra, S. A., & Narasimhan, S. (1998). Information systems outsourcing: A study of pre-event firm characteristics. *Journal of Management Information Systems, 15*(2), 61–93.

Sobol, M. G., & Apte, U. M. (1995). Domestic and global outsourcing practices of America's most effective IS users. *Journal of Information Technology, 10*, 269–280.

Tapon, F. (1989). A transaction costs analysis of innovations in the organization of pharmaceutical R&D. *Journal of Economic Behavior and Organization, 12*, 197–213.

Van de Ven, A. H. (1986). Central problems in the management of innovation. *Management Science, 32*(5), 590–607.

Williamson, O. E. (1985). *The economic institutions of capitalism: Firms, markets, relational contracting*. New York, London: Free Press, Collier Macmillan.

Zaltman, G., Duncan, R. & Holbek, J. (1973). *Innovations and organizations*. Wiley: New York.

Part III
IT Offshoring

Chapter 5
Offshoring Trends

Offshoring and Outsourcing
in the PC Industry: A Historical Perspective

Jason Dedrick and Kenneth L. Kraemer

1 Introduction

Offshoring and outsourcing of manufacturing and knowledge work is a highly visible and controversial issue in the public debate over the impacts of globalization. In their efforts to expand markets and optimize production for competitive advantage, firms distribute their activities around the world through their own offshore subsidiaries, by outsourcing to other firms, or both. This pattern is blamed by many critics for job losses in the U.S., while credited by others with benefiting U.S. firms, shareholders and consumers. In reality the impacts of offshoring and outsourcing are hard to measure as they can be subtle and indirect. For instance, there is no measure for jobs that were never created in the U.S. because new products were sourced from overseas from almost their inception.

However, by observing one industry over time, it is possible to identify patterns in the location of production work and knowledge work, and to qualitatively assess the impacts of offshoring on firms and workers. Production work is operations-oriented and includes activities such as subassembly, final assembly and logistics. Knowledge work is innovation-oriented and includes activities such as R&D, design and development of new products and process engineering. We focus on the PC industry, which offers an important case for understanding the forces that influence U.S. firms to outsource their activities, and for identifying the impacts of those decisions.

Production work was the first to be offshored, but now knowledge work is also being pulled offshore to the locus of production. Although the PC industry was concentrated in the U.S. at the beginning,[1] the industry quickly went global for production. The industry first went offshore to source low cost components from Asia and then moved manufacturing offshore to reduce distribution/logistics costs in overseas markets. As competition in the industry grew more intense, companies outsourced much of their subassembly to contract manufacturers and later also

---

[1] The top ten companies were U.S. firms who did most production themselves, with 50% in the U.S., and who had a 73% share of the global market in 1985 (Dedrick & Kraemer 1998).

R. Hirschheim et al. (eds), *Information Systems Outsourcing,*
© Springer-Verlag Berlin Heidelberg 2009

outsourced much final assembly. Between 1985 and 2005, over 125,000 computer hardware jobs were lost in the U.S., the same time that global computer production more than tripled. So not only have jobs been lost, but new jobs have been created elsewhere as the industry has grown. These jobs in manufacturing, engineering, management and customer service were created in places like Taiwan, Singapore, Malaysia, the Philippines, Mexico, Scotland, France and Ireland, but now those places also are losing jobs as production shifts en masse to China.

Today, this pattern is being repeated in product design and development, especially for notebook computers which are much more design/development intensive than desktops. Notebook development shifted from the U.S. to Taiwan in the 1990s as U.S. firms outsourced development to Taiwanese original design manufacturers (ODMs). Again, more than losing jobs, the U.S. never saw those jobs created, as leading PC makers built their notebook businesses from the ground up using Taiwanese ODMs. As the notebook/laptop segment grew from a very small share of the market to reach over a quarter of all PCs sold in 2005, engineering jobs were created in Taiwan (and to some extent in Japan, where IBM designed most of its notebooks), rather than in the U.S. The knowledge jobs that do exist in the U.S. are mostly in market research, conceptual design, project management and marketing (Dedrick J. & Kraemer K.L. 2008).

Even some of those jobs are now being "pulled" offshore to be closer to the actual engineering development of new products (Dedrick J. & Kraemer K.L. 2006). Branded PC firms such as Apple, Dell and Hewlett–Packard have set up design centers in Taiwan in order to better monitor ongoing contracts and upgrade the capabilities of their suppliers so more design activities can be shifted there (Digitimes 2007). Dell, which had previously done final assembly of notebooks with base units shipped to Malaysia from China, is reported to be considering having the ODMs do full assembly and shipping direct.

At the same time, the Taiwanese manufacturers are moving more engineering activities to China to be close to their manufacturing plants. They also are expanding their design and project management capabilities at home in order to take over more of the design process from the lead PC makers (Yang 2005).

The impact of globalization in the U.S. PC industry is one of continuing job losses, with ever fewer, although higher paying, knowledge jobs retained in the U.S. for new product development, sales and support for large customers, and headquarters operations. On the other hand, U.S. PC companies remain world leaders in market share and U.S. consumers benefit from ever-cheaper hardware. Many U.S. jobs also have been created in complementary industries such as software, IT services and on the Internet, thanks in part to the availability of low cost PCs made offshore. It is beyond the scope of this paper to try to measure all of the economic costs and benefits of offshoring and outsourcing. However, it is possible to distill some lessons from the PC industry by looking at the following issues:

- How have offshoring and outsourcing evolved for operations and innovation activities in the industry?
- What factors have influenced firm decisions?
- What has been the impact of offshoring and outsourcing on the competitiveness of U.S. companies and on U.S. jobs in the industry?

2   Conceptual Framework

2.1   Firm Strategy and Competitive Advantage

Our conceptual approach, which is based in historical analysis similar to Brown and Linden (2005), relies on relating theories of firm strategy to the factors shaping sourcing decisions, and ultimately to the impact of those decisions on jobs and competitiveness (Teece 1986; Porter 1990; Hagel & Singer 1999). Competitive advantage can be built through strategic focus on: (1) differentiation through innovation, and/ or (2) operational excellence through efficiency in production (Porter 1990).

These strategic foci are related to the principal reasons that PC firms keep certain activities in-house and outsource other activities. Innovation in the PC industry is focused mainly on new product development at the system level as component innovation is done upstream by suppliers of chips, software, storage, flat panels, batteries and power supply. It emphasizes developing slightly different products for narrowly defined market niches on short product cycles (Dedrick J. & Kraemer K.L. 2008). Innovation requires access to the lead market and capabilities in market analysis, concept design and product development.

In contrast, operational excellence focuses on production and is related to time and money – rapid product cycles, leveraged procurement, high quality manufacturing, lean supply chains (McMillan et al. 1999; Treacy & Wiersema 1995). As will be seen, the principal reasons for offshoring and outsourcing in the PC industry have been cost and access to specialized capabilities. While operations have been offshored for cost, innovation has been kept in-house for specialized capabilities which are now available offshore too.

2.2   Industry Dynamics

There is a dynamic to industry competition, which may ultimately change industry structure and jobs. When a branded PC company offshores an activity to reduce cost, it potentially improves its competitive position against rivals. In an expanding market, the firm will grow and hire more workers, some of whom will be in the home country and some offshore. If the branded firm is successful, rivals will imitate its actions (Brown & Linden 2005).

Some of the workers in the home country may lose their jobs as the activity is shifted offshore; however the remaining home country workers may benefit if the company grows and is more profitable, and new jobs may be created in other areas (e.g., marketing instead of engineering). Likewise, consumers may benefit from lower prices on products outsourced offshore. The lower prices may expand the home market for the product as well as complementary products, thereby creating jobs in related industry segments (such as software, services, retail). It is difficult to estimate this job creation. In a growing industry, it is also difficult to estimate the number of jobs that would have been created in the U.S. if an activity had not been moved offshore (Brown & Linden 2005).

Competitors and suppliers often follow successful firms in outsourcing offshore, and over time, firm investments in a foreign location may transform that location in a way that changes the industry's structure. A foreign location that initially was little more than a source of low cost labor for production might develop into a specialized industry cluster that becomes a favored location for certain activities for the whole industry (Brown & Linden 2005). In the PC industry, production clusters have emerged in the Taipei/Hsinchu region of Taiwan, in Singapore, in Penang, Malaysia, and in the Shenzhen/Guangdong Province and Shanghai/Suzhou regions of China. These clusters developed extensive supply bases to support manufacturing of PCs, components and peripherals. Some have further developed their capabilities to attract activities farther up the value chain, such as product development and software development, resulting in more outsourcing by branded firms. The knowledge and experience gained in managing these outsourced activities offshore may encourage expanding to other activities such as R&D and design. Within the PC industry, the notebook segment illustrates this dynamic as design, development and manufacturing have become spread across geographic borders, development and manufacturing has been outsourced and the industry increasingly concentrated in the Shanghai/Suzhou area of China.

2.3   Methodology and Data

Within this framework, we describe the historical evolution of operations and innovation activities in the PC industry – analyzing the factors that have shaped the sourcing of these activities over time, assessing the impacts on jobs and competitiveness and drawing industry lessons from the experience. Within operations we focus on manufacturing and within innovation we focus on product design and development (Fig. 1). We also distinguish between desktops and notebooks as their patterns differ.

The data for this analysis is from secondary sources (indicated in tables), news media, our own prior research and over 100 field interviews with PC makers, ODMs

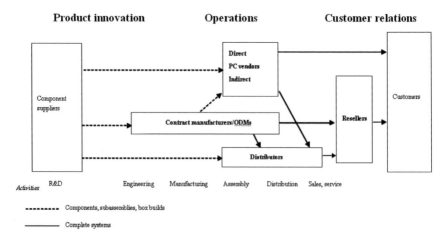

Fig. 1 The PC industry value chain. Adapted from Curry and Kenney, 1999

and component suppliers in the U.S., Japan, Singapore, Malaysia, Ireland, Taiwan and China over the period 1995–2005 (see Dedrick J. & Kraemer K.L. 2005 for list of firms interviewed).

3 The Evolution of Offshoring in the PC Industry

Historically, offshoring in the PC industry occurred in three major phases that map the changes in the industry's key operations and innovation activities. Table 1 provides a detailed timeline and Appendix A summaries key aspects of the industry's evolution for operations and innovation activities.

Table 1 Offshoring evolution in the PC industry

Year	Operations (Manufacturing)	Innovation (Design and development)
Phase 1		
1980	– U.S. assembly of desktops in-house, onshore – Some components sourced offshore from Asia (motherboards, disk drives, cases, power supply)	– U.S. design, development in-house, onshore
1985–1989	– In-house production offshored to major regions – Notebook production begins in U.S., Europe, Asia	– U.S., Japan, Europe (very limited) design, development in-house, onshore
Phase 2		
1990	– Desktop base builds (subassemblies) outsourced to Asia – Desktop final assembly outsourced to contract manufacturers (CMs) in regions – Notebook production outsourced to Japan and Taiwan	– U.S., Europe, Asia design, development in-house, onshore – Notebook design – U.S., Japan in-house, onshore
1995	– Complete desktop systems (low end) outsourced to Taiwan – Notebook production concentrated in Taiwan	– Development outsourced to Taiwan – Taiwan begins notebook development (low end), upgrades capabilities
Phase 3		
2000	– Desktop base builds concentrated in Shenzhen, China – Desktop systems shipped direct from China (low end) – Notebook production moved from Taiwan to Shanghai, China; systems shipped direct from China	 – Design, development outsourced to Taiwan (low end) – Notebook development outsourced to Taiwan
2003		– Vendors establish design centers in Taiwan – ODMs establish R&D centers in Taiwan
2005		– Vendors and ODMs do collaborative design

The first phase is the offshoring of operations from the U.S. and Japan to multiple locations around the world beginning in the early eighties, but accelerating in the late eighties. It coincided with the disaggregation of the computer industry from large vertically integrated companies to a horizontally-segmented structure distributed around the world (Grove 1996; Dedrick J. & Kraemer K.L. 1998). Offshoring started with the sourcing of components from abroad, followed by offshore assembly by U.S. subsidiaries and outsourcing of complete systems to offshore CMs (Contract Manufacturers) and ODMs (Original Design Manufacturers). The second phase is the offshoring of innovation in the form of product design and development in the early 1990s. PC makers first outsourced design of motherboards and other subassemblies, and eventually turned to ODMs to develop complete systems. Most of this activity was concentrated in Taiwan. The third phase in the offshoring of the PC industry is the reconcentration of operations and innovation in China beginning in 2000. This began with operations, and has progressed to the point where nearly all notebook PCs and a large share of desktop PCs are now manufactured in China. The next step is the relocation of innovation activities to China, starting with process engineering for manufacturing and, more recently, some product development activities as well. The next three sections describe this industry evolution in detail.

3.1   Phase 1: Offshoring of Operational Activities

While the PC industry emerged first in the U.S., with most production concentrated there, the industry began to deconcentrate globally early in its history.

3.1.1   Offshoring of Component Production

The first step in the global deconcentration of the industry was the offshore production of many components. Apple and others sourced components from Asian suppliers before 1980, but offshoring of component production expanded dramatically in the early 1980s when IBM sourced components for the original IBM PC from Taiwanese companies (Dedrick J. & Kraemer K.L. 1998). The developers of the IBM PC used outsourcing to bring the PC to market quickly, which required using outside capabilities rather than developing them internally.

There were many small and medium enterprises (SMEs) in Taiwan that had the needed capabilities and therefore the work could be divided among them to provide IBM with flexibility in responding to demand. Taiwan also had low labor costs and skilled workers experienced in electronics assembly (CRTs, cables, connectors) and metalworking (cases). Other components were sourced from Japan and Korea, especially high volume memory chips and displays.

At the same time, the hard disk drive (HDD) industry began moving production to Singapore, led by U.S. companies such as Seagate. Government tax incentives and a skilled, disciplined work force were major factors for the offshore movement of the HDD industry to Singapore. By locating in Singapore, the HDD firms could source labor-intensive parts such as coils and head assemblies from countries with lower labor costs such as Malaysia and Thailand, and do only final assembly in Singapore where labor costs were higher. Like the HDD industry, the semiconductor industry also moved final assembly offshore in the 1980s, also to locations in Southeast Asia such as Penang, Malaysia.

This offshore sourcing of labor intensive components supported final assembly jobs in the U.S. There were few job losses in the U.S. from offshore sourcing of components because most of these manufacturing jobs were created offshore; for instance, Seagate moved HDD production to Singapore only a year after the company was founded (Dedrick J. & Kraemer K.L. 1998). The effect was more a matter of jobs not created in the U.S. rather than a loss of existing jobs. In addition, the rapid growth of the industry enabled by offshore sourcing created many new U.S. jobs in the broader PC industry, including final assembly, distribution (logistics, wholesale, retail) and support (education, training, maintenance). However, this offshore sourcing had a huge impact on future job creation by developing the capabilities of Asian firms that would be eager to move down the supply chain to capture more value added and profits. The most dramatic example is Foxconn (the trade name of Hon Hai Precision Industry), which began as a manufacturer of cables and connectors, and is now the world's largest contract electronics manufacturer with over 200,000 employees and a major producer of PC components and subassemblies as well as PCs, iPods, video games and other final products.

The competitive impact of this initial offshoring was to create a low cost supply base that anyone could use, and more than 200 branded PC makers entered the industry (Langlois 1992). By 1985, IBM was the number one PC maker with 25% of the market, followed by Commodore and Apple with 14% each (Table 2). However, as IBM lost control of the key technology standards to Microsoft and

Table 2 Rank and percent share of world shipments by top 10 PC makers

| 1985 Rank | 1985 | | 1995 | | 2005 | |
	Firm	% share	Firm	% share	Firm	% share
1	IBM	25	Compaq	10	Dell	18
2	Commodore	14	IBM	8	HP/Compaq	16
3	Apple	14	Apple	8	IBM	6
4	Tandy	8	Packard Bell	7	Acer	4
5	Compaq	3	NEC	4	Fujitsu/Siemens	4
6	Atari	3	HP	4	Toshiba	3
7	HP	2	Dell	3	NEC	3
8	ZDS	2	Acer	3	Lenovo	2
9	DEC	1	Fujitsu/ICL	3	Gateway	2
10	NCR	1	Toshiba	3	Apple	2
Top 10 share		73		53		60
U.S. share of Top 10		100		75		78

Source: International Data Corporation: table provided to authors and press releases

Intel, its competitors were able to use the supply base that it created to attack IBM's market share with low cost systems. At the national level, building a supply base in Asia helped U.S. companies to compete with Japanese PC makers who many feared would dominate the PC industry as they had in consumer electronics (Borrus 1997; Dedrick J. & Kraemer K.L. 1998).

3.1.2 Offshoring and Outsourcing of Subassembly and Final Assembly

Beginning in the late 1980s, leading PC makers such as IBM, Compaq, Apple and Dell set up subassembly and final assembly operations for desktops and notebooks offshore. PC makers did assembly in each major world region using their own subsidiaries (including Ireland, Scotland, and France for Europe; Malaysia and Singapore for Asia Pacific; Mexico for the Americas).

Subassemblies such as motherboards and base units were sourced from Asian suppliers or U.S. contract manufacturers who located some production near the major vendors. The motivations for offshore desktop assembly were to reduce logistics cost by producing close to the market, to better understand country requirements, and to utilize local capabilities (suppliers, human resources, language). In addition, PC makers were attracted to Ireland, Malaysia and Singapore by generous tax incentives and a low cost, educated workforce.

3.1.3 Desktops versus Laptops

The form factor of desktops versus laptops has implications for their sourcing. For desktops, their bulk, weight and lower average selling price (ASP) results in concentrated assembly of "base units" in the lowest cost location with shipment by sea to final assembly plants located regionally. Base units include the metal case, motherboard, fan, power supply, and cables and connectors. High value parts such as microprocessor, memory, hard drive, and optical drives are added at final assembly to minimize depreciation. The smaller, lighter form factor, tightly integrated physical design, and higher ASP of laptops leads to full assembly in one location and air shipment to distribution centers and customers.

By 2000, desktop assembly moved in two additional directions. Most PC makers (except Dell) outsourced standard build-to-forecast production completely to CMs or ODMs, who produce in low-cost locations (e.g., Eastern Europe, Mexico, China) for each major region (Europe, Africa and the Middle East; Americas; and Asia–Pacific, respectively). Most build-to-order production was still done by the PC makers themselves in countries with more sophisticated logistics and skilled workers (e.g., Ireland, Scotland, U.S., Malaysia), with base units and components shipped in from Asia. Since 2003, even this pattern has changed, as IBM, HP and Apple all outsourced build-to-order production by selling existing plants to CMs such as Sanmina-SCI who specialize in desktop production.

U.S. PC makers began moving notebook production offshore in the early 1990s. Some turned to Japanese or Korean partners who had developed engineering and fabrication capabilities for small form factors through their consumer electronics businesses. Taiwan developed a homegrown industry focused on notebook PC production, led by a set of ODMs such as Quanta and Compal, who developed specialized technical knowledge in issues critical to notebook performance such as battery life, heat dispersion, rugged mechanicals and electromagnetic interference. The Taiwanese ODMs soon surpassed Korean competitors who specialized in high volume production but lacked flexiblity and system integration skills developed by the Taiwanese. And while one original Apple Powerbook model was manufactured by Sony, Japanese firms generally concentrated on making their own brand name notebooks rather than being contract manufacturers or ODMs.

As vendor pricing pressure increased on the ODMs, the Taiwan government removed restrictions on manufacturing notebooks in China, and the Taiwanese notebook industry moved en masse to the Shanghai/Suzhou area of eastern China.[2] In turn, the PC vendors began sourcing more full systems directly from the ODMs. By 2005, 73% of the world's notebook computers were produced by Taiwanese firms (Table 3), and U.S. PC companies sourced from 40 to 100% of all notebooks from Taiwanese companies (Table 4). In 2007, virtually all notebook production by Taiwanese ODMs is in China. Japanese firms, such as NEC, Toshiba, Sony and Fujitsu, who long touted their manufacturing skills as critical to competitive advantage are increasingly outsourcing notebook production to the Taiwanese firms (Table 4).

Table 3 Taiwanese notebook industry share of global shipments, 1998–2005 (shipments by Taiwan-based firms, including offshore production)

	1998	1999	2000	2001	2002	2003	2004	2005 (f)
Shipments volume[a]	6,088	9,703	12,708	14,161	18,380	25,238	33,340	39,035
Shipments value[b] ($)	8,423	11,073	13,549	12,239	13,847	16,809	21,830	25,177
Average sales prices ($)	1,384	1,141	1,066	864	753	666	655	645
Global market by volume[a]	15,610	19,816	24,437	25,747	30,033	37,857	46,110	53,473
Taiwan's share of global market volume (%)	40	49	52	55	61	66	72	73

Source: MIC (2005);
[a]Units in thousands;
[b]U.S. dollars (millions)

[2] It is significant that knowledgeable experts say that the decision to relocate notebook/laptop production to China was jointly undertaken by Taiwan ODM firms and their brand name partners from the U.S., Japan and Europe. Cited by Merritt T. Cooke (2004) and discussed in an article by Ho and Leng (2004).

Table 4 PC makers outsourcing production to Taiwan firms

Flagship companies	Subsidi-aries in China	Outsourcing, 2003[a] (%)	Outsourcing, 2005[b] (%)	Taiwan ship-ments, 2005[c] (%)	Taiwanese ODM suppliers[a]
Apple		100	100	5.1	Quanta, Asus, Elite
Dell[d]	Xiamen	90	90	21.6	Quanta, Compal, Wistron
HP	Shanghai	90	100	19.1	Quanta, Compal, Wistron, Inventec, Arima
IBM[e]	Shenzhen	40	40	4.2	Wistron, Quanta
Acer		100	100		Quanta, Compal, Wistron
NEC	Shanghai	80	100	5.3	Arima, FIC, Wistron, Mitac
Sharp		50	n.a.	n.a.	Quanta, Mitac, Twinhead
Sony	Wuxi	20	60	4.0	Quanta, Asus, Foxconn
Toshiba	Hangzhou	15	70	9.6	Quanta, Compal, Inventec
Fujitsu-Siemens		15	50	4.0	Wistron, Mitac, Uniwill, Quanta, Compal

[a]Ministry of Economic Affairs (2004);
[b]Digitimes (2005a);
[c]Digitimes (2005b);
[d]Dell's outsourcing figure refers to production of base units. Most of Dell's final configuration is done in its own plants in Penang, Malaysia and Xiamen, China;
[e]IBM's PC business is now part of Lenovo, but this information is for IBM prior to its acquisition. Although IBM had its own notebook factory in Shenzhen, it sourced from Taiwanese firms for lower end products. The number estimated for IBM in the MOEA report for 2003 was 100%; we instead use an estimate of 40% from DigiTimes (2005a), which is consistent with information provided by IBM

3.2 Phase 2: Offshoring and Outsourcing of Innovation – Design and Development

As operations moved offshore, they eventually pulled other activities offshore as well, including new product design and development. Product design involves understanding customer wants and needs, tracking technology trends and translating technological capabilities into products that meet customer needs at the right price. This requires a combination of market intelligence, product planning, financial analysis, high-level technical analysis, and the ability to communicate with both customers and suppliers. Product development is where the actual mechanical, electrical and some software development are done, with prototypes developed and tested. This requires electrical and mechanical engineering skills and experience with small form factor products (for notebook PCs). It also requires expensive physical test facilities.

The branded U.S. PC makers did notebook design/development in-house and onshore in the early years, but fell behind Japanese competitors who had superior skills in miniaturizing components and developing small, light, thin products. For instance, IBM did notebook design/development in the U.S. in the 1980s, but its PC Convertible was a failure and was withdrawn from the market in 1989 (Business Week 1991). IBM reacted by moving notebook design to its IBM Japan subsidiary, which came up with the award-winning Thinkpad design. Compaq worked with Japan's Citizen Watch Co. to engineer its notebooks and produce key subassemblies. Apple contracted with Sony for one of the original Powerbook models.

In time, however, most PC makers turned to Taiwanese ODMs for manufacturing, partly to lower costs and also to avoid dependence on Japanese partners who were competitors. The Taiwanese ODMs developed specialized engineering skills and began to take over product development for companies such as Compaq and Packard Bell. Other companies such as Dell and Gateway were able to enter the notebook market by working with the ODMs on design and development, taking advantage of the capabilities nurtured by their competitors. Currently, the major PC makers keep concept design and product management in-house, while outsourcing product development and process engineering to the ODMs.

A major factor influencing the move to outsourcing development was a "pull" from the ODMs. Taiwanese ODMs often did not charge explicitly for development, but did it in order to win production contracts (interviews in Taiwan and China). In addition, once the ODM had a contract, the relationship created incentives for both sides to continue outsourcing for future upgrades and enhancements to the product. There was a great deal of tacit knowledge created in the development process that was known only by the ODM. In addition, the close linkage of development activities to manufacturing and the feedback to design from manufacturing and sustaining support, created linkages favoring continuing the ODM relationship in order to reduce costs and improve quality (Dedrick J. & Kraemer K.L. 2006).

Some PC makers (Dell and HP) have set up their own design centers in Taiwan in recent years, thus offshoring design while keeping it in-house. The motivations were multiple: lower cost engineers and programmers, faster development by having test facilities nearby, availability of experienced engineers, host government tax incentives and closeness to emerging markets in Asia. However, the primary motivation was proximity. By being close to the ODMs, the design center can send personnel to the ODM for problem solving and use the ODM's testing facilities. If the design team were in the U.S., they would have to duplicate the problem in their own testing facility and try to solve it, which takes time and unnecessarily duplicates testing facilities (PC company design center interview). In addition, by being close to the ODMs, the offshore design center can work on multiple products and with multiple ODMs. Coordination with headquarters marketing people and aligning with other product lines is handled by having a few design center staff located there and establishing common standards and software platforms.

It is significant that the design centers have been located in Taiwan. A design center in Taiwan supports design activities for all the ODMs who might be suppliers to a PC maker. Taiwan has a skilled, experienced pool of moderate cost engineers and software professionals and the Taiwan government provided financial incentives to attract the vendors. It also provided incentives to the Taiwanese ODMs to establish R&D centers in Taiwan to reinforce the linkage.

It is difficult to estimate the impact of this outsourcing on jobs in the U.S., but it is clear that there have been job losses. Dell and HP each employ 300–500 engineers in their Taiwan design centers. More importantly, there has not been new job creation in the U.S. for a growing product line, as there has been a permanent shift of knowledge and skills in notebook development from the U.S. to Taiwan. Dell is now planning to reduce design engineers in the U.S. and Taiwan, relying more on the ODMs for notebook design (Digitimes 2007). In addition, the same ODMs that develop most notebooks have moved into other products such as cell phones, where they are applying their engineering talent to develop new products sold under their own brand names and on an ODM basis to cell phone providers such as Motorola, Siemens, Nokia, Sony Ericsson and Panasonic (Pick 2005).

3.3   Phase 3: Concentration of Operations and Innovation in China

The final stage in the evolution of offshoring appears to be bringing the industry full circle. The U.S. PC industry began with most activities concentrated in the U.S., with some component production in Asia. It then disintegrated, offshored and outsourced activities to various countries. It is now reconcentrating – not in the U.S., but in China. Production and logistics are already operating there, and development is starting to be moved (You-Ren & Hsia 2004). Just as manufacturing has pulled development to China for better time-to-market, flexibility and efficiency, so might development eventually pull design activities, especially as the China market becomes a key market for PCs.

For desktops, the reconcentration is occurring in the Shenzhen area of South China, where nearly all desktop "base builds" are manufactured as well as complete systems for the Asia–Pacific and U.S. markets (at least in build-to-forecast production). For notebooks, the reconcentration is occurring in notebooks as Taiwanese ODMs move development to the Shanghai/Suzhou area. The Taiwanese motivation is described as cost-effective human capital augmentation (Lu & Liu 2004). Accessing capable yet cost effective engineers with the additional benefit of geographical and linguistic proximity is the major motive. Also, Taiwan's supply of engineers does not meet demand, whereas China has a large pool of well-educated local engineers who are about half the cost of their Taiwanese counterparts. China and Taiwan share a common culture and language which facilitates communication. Shanghai/Suzhou and Taiwan are not far apart, which makes managers willing to relocate for several years and also makes it possible for executives in Taipei to supervise operations first hand.

The ODMs' Taiwan design units are responsible for the development of advanced technologies and new products that provide competitive advantage for the parent company. As these products are moved into production in China, development of product variations, incremental improvement and life cycle support has followed. The two major PC makers who continue to manufacture significant amounts of notebooks in-house, Lenovo (including the former IBM PC division) and Toshiba, have concentrated production in China, and also have moved some product development there. By locating development close to production, the manufacturing sites get immediate technical support for the rapid product cycles of notebooks while the designers get immediate feedback from manufacturing and support that enables them to make improvements.

4 Factors Influencing Outsourcing and Offshoring

4.1 Costs

As the foregoing discussion has indicated, offshoring has been shaped primarily by cost and capabilities. Cost has been the major factor pushing production activities offshore in the first instance, while the upgrading of capabilities by offshore firms has been a major factor pulling knowledge activities offshore. Cost pressure is particularly acute in the PC industry because Intel and Microsoft reportedly capture 90% of the industry's profits.[3] Cost has been reduced by locating in lower cost areas, leveraging location for financial incentives from host countries, and outsourcing to CMs and ODMs.

Because the early PCs (desktops and portables) were heavy and bulky, and had to meet different country requirements, production had to be decentralized to major regions rather than concentrated. Most vendors did only final assembly themselves relying on regionally-based CMs and ODMs for base units and suppliers for components. As the industry grew, new entrants located near the first movers in order to achieve agglomeration economies by using their supply base. As competition in the industry increased, vendors sought still lower costs by outsourcing more production to the CMs who could achieve cost savings by large-scale purchasing and assembly for multiple vendors.

---

[3] In the debate over HP's acquisition of Compaq, data presented by Walter Hewlett showed Microsoft and Intel capturing 90% of the industry's profits in 2002. Dell's efficient model enabled it to lower prices, which other vendors have had to match by greater use of outsourcing and continuous pressure on ODMs and suppliers to cut costs. Vendors force the ODMs to compete with one another for business and expect continuous quarterly cost reductions of 5–7% (field interviews with ODMs and suppliers). Suppliers have gone along with these practices in the hopes that lower prices would grow the market and enable them to achieve economies of scale. Low profits on the order of 1–2% have led some ODMs to vertically integrate and to develop their own brand products, while others have moved upstream to produce subassemblies and components. The result for the PC industry has been a continual increase in the volume of units sold, but only a modest increase in the dollar volume of sales, and a continual decline in profits for both PC makers and suppliers.

The PC vendors leveraged their location decisions with government incentives. Tax holidays, land, facilities and work force training attracted vendors to locate in places like Ireland and Scotland in Europe, Tennessee and North Carolina in the U.S., and Singapore and Malaysia in Asia. Usually, the vendors encouraged/required their suppliers and contract manufacturers to locate production or at least supply hubs nearby, which further increased their leverage. As the costs of these places rose over time, the supply bases were moved to lower cost places in Eastern Europe and China. If the government incentives continued, some or all final assembly might be kept in the original location (e.g., Dell in Ireland, Malaysia), or other activities such as regional headquarters, IT services or call centers moved to the old plant location (e.g., Apple in Ireland). Later, even some of these activities were turned over to outsourcers in order to further reduce costs.

4.2 Capabilities

The global production capabilities of large CMs such as Solectron, SCI and Flextronics were also a factor in the move to outsourcing by PC vendors, especially for desktops. The CMs had a global footprint, which enabled them to serve customers anywhere in the world. They built large industrial parks capable of incorporating suppliers, supply hubs and logistics firms for agglomeration economies. Their factories also could run one or many production lines, offering flexibility in responding to the volatile PC demand. As cost pressures increased, the branded vendors decided to also outsource additional activities such as final assembly,[4] logistics and warranty repair to 3–4 global CMs and logistics partners.

For notebook PCs, firm capabilities were also important but the pattern was different as both development and production were outsourced and these capabilities were concentrated in a few ODMs in Taiwan. They had developed skills in small form factor products through work in consumer electronics that they could apply to notebooks. Their lower costs and government assistance enabled the ODMs to invest in new skills (industrial design, engineering design, system integration) and technological upgrading (R&D, prototyping and testing facilities), which they then used to "pull" development activities from the PC vendors. In some cases, the branded PC makers pushed the ODMs to develop greater design skills and even assisted them (Firm interviews). In contrast to desktop computers, where design and development was decentralized due to the high modularity and large form factor, design in notebooks was concentrated because the high level of integration in such a small form factor required design and production engineering to be close to one another and the form factor enabled cost-effective shipment by air to end customers from a centralized production site (Dedrick J. & Kraemer K.L. 2008).

---

[4] Dell outsourced base unit production, but not final assembly because its business strategy and marketing emphasized build-to-order and configure to order production as a differentiator, especially for commercial customers.

5 Impacts of Offshore Sourcing

5.1 Geographical Shift of Activities

The most consequential change from offshore sourcing is the geographical shift of production and development activities from the Americas and Europe to the Asia–Pacific. In 1985, the Americas led in production with a 53% share, with the remainder nearly equally divided between Europe and the Asia–Pacific. By 1990, the Asia–Pacific region surpassed the Americas as the largest producer of computer hardware, even though the largest market was in the Americas and most leading PC vendors were U.S. companies (Table 5). The Asia–Pacific region has continuously gained production at the expense of both the Americas and Europe/Middle East/Africa (EMEA) to the present. The share of production in the Americas was stable from 1990 to 2001 at 31–32%, but has since fallen to 24% (Table 5).

At the country level, the U.S. was the leading computer hardware producer until 2004 when China took over the leading spot with 24.3% of world shipments compared to 17.9% for the U.S. It is likely that the U.S. share will continue to decline as more production is shifted to China. Within the Asia–Pacific region, Japan was the leading producer as late as 2000, with significant production also moving to Taiwan, Malaysia, Thailand and Singapore. Since 2000, China's production has tripled, while Taiwan's production has declined by two–thirds and Japan's has fallen by nearly half (Table 6). This is not a coincidence as most Taiwanese computer manufacturing moved to China, while major Japanese companies have established factories in China as well.

Table 5 Percent share of global computer hardware production by region, 1985–2005

	1985	1990	1995	2000	2005
Americas	53	32	32	31	22
EMEA	24	27	20	17	15
Asia–Pacific	23	41	48	52	63

Source: Reed Electronics Research, *Yearbook of World Electronics Data*, 2006

Table 6 Leading computer producing countries, 1990–2005 (% share global production)

Country	1990	1995	2000	2005	2005 Rank
China	0.4	1.9	7.3	32.4	1
U.S.	27.0	26.5	24.0	17.3	2
Japan	29.2	25.2	17.3	8.7	3
Korea	1.7	2.4	4.0	5.6	4
Singapore	3.9	7.3	5.9	5.4	5
Malaysia	0.2	1.8	4.6	3.0	6
Thailand	0.9	1.9	2.2	2.3	11
Taiwan	3.3	5.	7.2	1.5	13

Source: Reed Electronics Research, *Yearbook of World Electronics Data*, 2005

5.2 Competitiveness of U.S. Firms

U.S. PC companies, particularly Dell and HP with 34% of the market, lead the PC industry in terms of worldwide shipments, and Apple has rebounded since 2005, but other U.S. PC makers are losing money and over the years many have disappeared from the market altogether (Commodore, Tandy, Compaq, Atari, ZDS, AST, DEC, Packard Bell, IBM PC Company) by 2005 (Table 2). Whereas U.S. companies constituted all of the Top 10 in 1985, did most production in-house onshore, and had a 73% share of the market, there were only four U.S. companies in the Top 10 in 2005, most production was outsourced offshore, and they had a 44% share. The competitive fate of many firms in the U.S. PC industry is symbolized by the IBM PC Company, which owned 25% of the market in 1985 and was bought by China's Lenovo in 2005. Still, U.S. firms accounted for a larger share of sales among the top ten countries in 2005 than in earlier years.

In terms of competition in the notebook industry, Taiwanese ODMs largely level the playing field in development and manufacturing, greatly reducing the advantages held by firms such as Lenovo/IBM and Toshiba who have strong internal development and manufacturing capabilities. The ODMs upgrading of capabilities have helped to shift the competitive focus of PC makers away from development to concept design, marketing, branding, distribution and customer service. This plays to the strengths of U.S. companies, and HP and Dell have become the two leading notebook vendors worldwide. The leadership of U.S. companies is even more pronounced in the desktop market, where products are more commoditized and the importance of marketing and service is greater.

5.3 Jobs and Employment[5]

The heavy reliance of U.S. computer makers on offshore production and outsourcing clearly entails a loss of manufacturing jobs in the U.S. For example, the U.S. lost nearly 100,000 jobs in computer hardware between 1998 and 2003, of which 40,000 were production jobs (Table 7).

In PCs, the assembly jobs that remain in the U.S. tend to be in more skill-intensive operations such as configure-to-order assembly. There also is production for corporate customers who require rapid order fulfillment and those that require the PCs to be made in the U.S. for security reasons (such as military, government and their contractors).

---

[5]Comprehensive data on PC production is not available by geography, so we use total computer hardware, for which country data is available. PCs and related peripherals now account for about 65% of total hardware sales. Secondary literature review shows that production of larger systems is distributed among the three regions, but with less dispersion beyond traditional locations—mainly the U.S., Japan, France, Germany and the U.K.

Table 7 U.S. and offshore employment in computer hardware

	1998	2000	2001	2002	2003	2004	2005	2006
Hardware employment in U.S.	322,100	301,900	286,200	250,000	224,000	210,000	205,100	198,800
Production workers	126,100	116,000	103,800	97,700	86,000	87,300	116,900	131,000
Employed by foreign firms	35,600	26,600	24,600	29,800	24,800			
Offshore employment by U.S. MNC's		216,900	205,100	221,700	211,300			

Sources: Dedrick and Kraemer 1998 (for 1985 hardware employment); Bureau of Labor Statistics 2003, Current Employment Statistics Public Data Query (for Hardware employment and Production workers in the U.S. 1990–2003); Mataloni 2000–2005 (for Offshore employment by U.S. MNCs); Mataloni and Fahim-Nader 1996; Zeile 2000–2005 (Hardware employment by foreign firms)
Note: Numbers in italics are after the classification system switch from SIC's Computers and Office Machinery to NAICS/s Computers and Peripheral Equipment

Table 8 U.S. employment in IT services and software

	1985	1990	1995	2000	2004	2005	2006
Information services	600,000	650,900	892,100	1,616,200	1,466,400	1,508,400	1,591,200
Packaged software	Included above	141,500	210,500	324,000	282,200	282,400	284,500

Sources: Dedrick and Kraemer 1998 (for 1985 data); Bureau of Labor Statistics 2003 (for all other years) Website: http://data.bls.gov/PDQ/outside.jsp?survey = ce.

The U.S. has more nonproduction jobs in computer hardware, such as design, marketing, customer service, finance and various headquarters functions. These are better matched to the wage and skill levels of most of the U.S. work force than low-skilled assembly jobs. However, nearly 60,000 of those jobs disappeared from 1998 to 2003 (calculated from Table 7).

It is not possible to measure how many jobs were moved offshore and how many disappeared through automation or for other reasons, but it is clear that the rapid growth of the worldwide PC market, led by U.S. PC makers, was accompanied by a substantial loss of computer hardware jobs in the U.S. The decline of U.S. production from 26.5% of world production in 1995 to 17.3% in 2005 (Table 6) suggests that some of the job loss shown in Table 7 was due to offshoring.

More broadly, offshoring (and increased productivity) in hardware production appears to have been beneficial for the U.S. in the short run—though clearly some sectors, firms and workers lost out. It was likely a factor behind the surge of employment in software and services from 1985 to 2000 (Table 8).

The availability of low cost hardware meant that firms and consumers could afford more computers, creating demand for additional packaged software and information services in the U.S. and around the world. Given that U.S. companies dominated these sectors, their growth led to job creation in the U.S., but now design, software and services jobs are also now going offshore (and in some cases becoming more automated). Since 2000, the U.S. has lost about 220,000 jobs in IT services and another 40,000 in packaged software (Table 8). With the shift of software and services to India and other locations, it is unlikely that these jobs will be recaptured.

6   Conclusion

6.1   Lessons from the PC Industry

Several important lessons can be gleaned from the experience of offshoring in the PC industry. These are generally consistent with findings from the semiconductor industry (Brown & Linden 2005), which suggests that they may be applicable to high-tech industries more generally. *The first lesson is that offshoring was instrumental in the birth and growth of the PC industry, providing affordable products through sourcing components offshore in Asia.* The extension of offshore production through subsidiaries outsourcing to foreign suppliers fueled market growth by reducing production and logistics costs. During the 1980s, there was great concern that Japan would dominate the computer industry as it had earlier with consumer electronics, but it did not happen. Japanese PCs sold well in Japan but were a failure outside because proprietary features made them expensive and incompatible. European champions (ICL, Siemens, Olivetti) also could not compete outside their home markets. U.S. firms' overseas operations helped them to better target global markets, grow the industry, achieve economies of scale and produce profits for reinvestment. For the U.S., offshoring appears to have been an important competitive tool.

The second lesson is that offshoring leads to the redistribution of activities across both organizational and geographical boundaries, thereby changing industry structure. This is most apparent in notebooks where Taiwanese ODMs have taken over product development, manufacturing, and some customer service functions (such as warranty repair), with development in Taiwan and China, assembly in China and services provided in regional markets. Branded PC makers control design, marketing and customer services (sales, technical support). Design is located in the U.S. and in design centers set up in Taiwan close to the ODMs, marketing is mostly in the U.S. and other key markets.

A third lesson is that offshoring can lead to a "sequential hollowing out" of activities from one location to another. Notebook PCs were originally assembled in the U.S., but full assembly migrated to Taiwan and now is in China. The practice of "Taiwan Direct Ship" and now "China Direct Ship" means that logistics is migrating as well, as notebook factories in China ship direct to customers by air. The bulk and weight of desktops means that build-to-order production is done close to the final market, but base units are being sent by sea from China to regional assembly sites with more and more components preinstalled so that only very expensive or custom components are added during final assembly in the local market. Also, build-to-forecast PCs are being built in China and shipped to distributors in the final market.

A fourth lesson is that the loss of manufacturing does not necessarily mean hollowing out of all activity in a particular location. Apple Computer has been in Cork, Ireland for over 20 years, with employment fluctuating between 1,000 and 1,500, but the composition of that work force has changed dramatically since 2000. Apple has outsourced nearly all European production, but its European operations (headquarters, design center, call centers, IT, software localization and some custom assembly) have been consolidated in Cork. Thus, jobs have been lost in several European locations while there has been consolidation of other activities in Cork (Gantly 2003). Likewise, while Quanta has moved all of its notebook production to China, it has built a new R&D center at its Taiwan headquarters, where it expects to employ up to 7,000 scientists and engineers (Quanta interviews). Other ODMs are doing the same.

A fifth lesson is that offshoring can lead to the development of capabilities that "pull" higher level activities to the offshore location. The sourcing of PC components from Asia led to the upgrading of capabilities by local companies; this in turn led to the sourcing of subassemblies and full systems by the PC makers. Local firms in Taiwan became proficient in product development and used those services as a competitive factor for winning production business. Product development in Taiwan is now pulling multinational corporation (MNC) design centers to Taipei, just as manufacturing in China is pulling some development activities from Taiwan to China. Proximity, which enables faster problem resolution and better communication, is a key "pull" factor, reinforced by the availability of lower cost and specialized engineering talent.

A final lesson is that it is unclear whether offshore outsourcing is directly creating new global competitors in the PC industry. For 15 years, most CMs and ODMs have not sought to develop their own brands for global markets. This has been due to lack of marketing and distribution capabilities and fear of losing business from the flagship customers if they are seen as trying to compete with them. Acer, which was both a branded PC company and an ODM, created an independent subsidiary (Wistron) for its ODM business. As the notebook makers have moved to China, they also have not established branded businesses for the China market. Instead, they are suppliers to the Chinese PC makers just as they are to the foreign MNCs. So far there has not been any sign of spin-offs by Chinese entrepreneurs who have worked for U.S. or Taiwanese firms in China.

However, there are signs that some Taiwanese ODMs might become direct competitors in the future. Acer, which separated its ODM business from its own brand business, is now ranked the fourth largest PC maker in the world, and is the leader in Europe. Asustek and Arima are following Acer's example by developing separate companies and promoting their own brands. The huge potential of the China market (and possibly Indian market) and the low profit margins for ODM firms (around 1–2%) are dual motivators for this trend.

6.2   Implications for the PC Industry

In an industry such as PCs, manufacturing and even product development skills are no longer a source of competitive advantage (with the exception of Apple, which charges a premium price for its proprietary PCs, which have distinctive hardware designs), but instead can be purchased in a relatively open global market. Offshoring enables firms to access lower cost knowledge and production workers through their own subsidiaries and through outsourcing to specialists such as CMs and ODMs. The economic advantage of outsourcing is even greater when specialist firms are clustered geographically and serve multiple branded companies, thereby providing economies of scale and specialization that branded firms cannot achieve internally (Hagel & Singer 1999). However, once activities are outsourced offshore, firms need to be aware that they will be giving away current capabilities and need to develop other skills to compete and survive.

The skills that will create competitive advantage for branded technology companies still involve innovation and operations but these are defined differently when activities such as product development and manufacturing can be outsourced to specialists who take advantage of low cost global resources. Today, operational advantage is gained by careful planning and execution in concert with outside manufacturing and logistics partners, so that supply meets demand, quality is maintained and warranty costs minimized—all cost factors. The key activities are demand forecasting, product lifecycle management, and supply chain management.

Innovation-based advantage requires adopting an integrator role (Prencipe 2003), in which the firm creates new products by integrating different mixes of internal and external technologies and capabilities. The skills required include market intelligence, industrial design, product architecture definition, and technology integration. For newer product categories such as the Apple iPod and Microsoft xBox360, successful innovation involves integration of hardware, software and services into a smoothly functioning and attractive entertainment system.

In this environment, firms must develop different skill mixes at home and abroad, and recognize the fact that this can mean eliminating or relocating activities and jobs from the U.S. While more experienced knowledge workers with the "right skills" may get higher paying jobs in the U.S., the less fortunate are replaced by more cost-effective offshore workers. However, those firms who fail to make necessary changes ultimately eliminate the most jobs, as well as destroy shareholder value. The biggest job losses in the PC industry have not come in successful companies, but in the many companies that have disappeared altogether. The best way for executives in the PC industry to sustain employment (including their own) is to learn to succeed in the new global environment, taking advantage of the capabilities that exist beyond their borders while developing new capabilities inside.

Appendix A – Form Factor and Offshore Sourcing

While both desktop and notebook PCs are based on the Wintel standard, there are important differences between these two form factors (Table 9) that affect sourcing.

Desktops are heavy and bulky and too expensive to ship by air so manufacturing is concentrated for scale economies while final assembly is regionalized for closeness to the market. The larger form factor makes two-step assembly easy, and enables using a few chassis upon which multiple models or SKUs can be designed for different markets and with different configurations. On the design side, modularity means that developing a desktop product is primarily a problem of industrial design and system integration, i.e., deciding on the physical design of the product and incorporating new technologies into products and ensuring that they work together.

Most desktop models are based on industry standard form factors, such as the full-tower and mid-tower chassis, and there are standard motherboard layouts available from Intel and various third-party manufacturers that are designed for these chassis. While the design of a new chassis takes around 9 months, a new model based on an existing chassis can be built and tested in as little as 2 weeks. With a configure-to-order model, Dell and others might have thousands of potential hardware and software permutations on a single platform. This complexity creates many opportunities for conflicts and incompatibilities, so testing all of these combinations becomes a major part of the new product development process, which is why design activity is being pulled to development locations.

Notebook PCs have characteristics that create challenges in product development as they must be able to run on batteries, incorporate the display as part of the unit, they must be lightweight yet very sturdy, plus they are more visible so users care about style as well as function. Components must be packaged very tightly into a product that is small, thin, light, portable, durable and energy efficient, and which doesn't become too hot to handle from the heat generated in its operation. Manufacturability is a major issue, as the product must be built in high volumes and at low cost, so final assembly must be a relatively simple process that allows packing components and subassemblies into a very tight space quickly and with a high level of reliability. As a result of these characteristics, notebooks have a longer and more expensive product development process. Even an upgrade of a model based on an

Table 9 Desktop versus notebook form factor

Desktop	Notebook
■ Highly modular design.	■ Highly integrated design.
■ Development = system integration of new parts and software	■ Development = complex mechanical and electrical engineering challenges due to size, heat, ruggedness requirements
■ Mostly standardized parts, e.g., motherboards, drives, chips.	■ Mix of standard and customized parts.
■ Design for easy assembly, repair	■ Design for manufacturability critical
■ Shorter product cycles, more models	■ Longer product cycles, fewer models
■ Mature product	■ Newer, still evolving product

existing platform can take 3–6 months to develop, and a new chassis takes 12–15 months. As with desktops, scale economies require concentration of production, but the small form factor of notebooks enables air shipment. On the other hand, the complexity of notebook development requires close proximity of design teams.

Acknowledgment This research has been supported by grants from the Alfred P. Sloan Foundation (Globalization II) and the U.S. National Science Foundation (SBE-HSD-Agents of Change #0527180) to the Personal Computing Industry Center at The Paul Merage School of Business, University of California, Irvine. Any opinions, findings and conclusions or recommendations expressed in this material are those of the authors and do not necessarily reflect the views of NSF or the Sloan Foundation.

References

Borrus, M. (1997). Left for dead: Asian production networks and the revival of U.S. electronics. In B. Naughton (Ed.), *The China circle*. Washington DC: Brookings Institution.

Brown, C., & Linden, G. (2005). Offshoring in the semiconductor industry: a historical perspective. In S. M. Collins & L. Brainard (Eds.), *Brookings trade forum 2005*. Brookings Institution Press: Washington DC.

Bureau of Labor Statistics (2003). *Current employment statistics public data query*. Washington DC: Department of Labor.

Business Week (1991). Laptops take off. March 18: 118–124.

Cooke, M. T. (2004). The politics of greater China's integration into the global info tech (IT) supply chain. *Journal of Contemporary China, 13*(40): 491–506.

Curry, J., & Kenney, M. (1999). Beating the clock: Corporate responses to rapid change in the PC industry. *California Management Review, 42*(1), 8–36.

Dedrick, J., & Kraemer, K. L. (1998). Asia's computer challenge. New York: Oxford University Press.

Dedrick, J., & Kraemer, K. L. (2005). The impacts of IT on firm and industry structure. *California Management Review, 47*(3), 122–142.

Dedrick, J., & Kraemer, K. L. (2006). Is production pulling knowledge work to China? A study of the notebook PC industry. *IEEE Computer, 39*(7), 36–42.

Dedrick, J., & Kraemer, K. L. (2008). *Personal computing, Innovation in Global Industries*. Washington, DC: National Academy Press.

Dedrick, J., & Kraemer, K. L. (2008). Impacts of globalization and offshoring on engineering employment in the personal computing industry, for NAE Task Force on Offshoring of Engineering. Washington DC: National Academy Press.

DigiTimes (2005a). Taiwan notebook makers to curtail low-price strategy, extend global dominance. Thursday, January 20.

DigiTimes (2005b). Asustek to shift all production line to China by 3Q06. Thursday, July 28.

Digitimes (2007). Dell to rely more on Taiwan-based ODMs for notebook design. Tuesday, March 20.

Gantly, J. (2003). The apple story: moving up the value chain. *Business Ireland, 16*(2), 5.

Grove, A. (1996). *Only the Parnoid survive*. New York: Doubleday.

Hagel III, J., &Singer, M. (1999). Unbundling the corporation. *Harvard Business Review, 77*(2), 133–141.

Ho, S. Y., & Leng, T. K. (2004). Accounting for Taiwan's economic policy toward China. *Journal of Contemporary China, 13*(40), 733–746.

Langlois, R. N. (1992). External economies and economic progress: the case of the microcomputer industry. *Business History Review, 66*, 1–50.

Lu, L. Y. Y., & Liu, J. S. (2004). R&D in China: an empirical study of Taiwanese IT companies. *R&D Management, 34*(4), 453–465.

Mataloni, R. J. (2000–2005). U.S. multinational companies operations in 2002. Washington DC: Survey of current business, U.S. Bureau of Economic Analysis.

Mataloni, R. J., & AMP; Fahim-Nader, M. (1996). Operations of U.S. multinational companies: Preliminary results from the 1994 benchmark survey. Washington DC: Survey of current business, U.S. Bureau of Economic Analysis.

McMillan, M., Pandolfi, S., & Salinger, B.L. (1999). Promoting foreign direct investment in labor-intensive, manufacturing exports in developing countries. CAER II Discussion Paper No. 42, Harvard Institute for International Development.

MIC (2005). *The greater Chinese notebook PC industry, 2004 and beyond.* Taipei, Taiwan: Market Intelligence Center.

Ministry of economic affairs (2004). *Information industry yearbook.* Taipei, Taiwan: Ministry of Economic Affairs, Executive Yuan (in Chinese).

Pick, A. (2005). Mobile phones reshape ODM business. iSuppli Corp., September 20. http://www.emsnow.com/npps/story.cfm?id = 6903

Porter, M. E. (1990). *The competitive advantage of nations.* New York: Free Press.

Prencipe, A. (2003). Corporate strategy and systems integration capabilities: managing networks in complex systems industries. In A. Prencipe, A. Davies, & M. Hobday (Eds.), *The business of systems integration.* Oxford: Oxford University Press.

Reed (2005–2006). *Yearbook of World Electronics Data.* Surrey, U.K.: Reed Electronics Research. Yearbooks and CD-ROM databases.

Teece, D. (1986). Profiting from technological innovation: implications for integration, collaboration, licensing and public policy. *Research Policy, 15,* 285–305.

Treacy, M., & Wiersema, F. (1995). *The discipline of market leaders: Choose your customers, narrow your focus, dominate your market.* Reading, MA: Addison-Wesley.

Yang, Y. K. (2005). *Taiwanese Notebook Computer Production Network in China and Implications for the Upgradings of Chinese Electronics Industry.* Unpublished doctoral dissertation, Manchester Business School, Univeristy of Manchester, Manchester.

You-Ren, Y., & Hsia, C. J. (2004) Local Clustering and Organizational Governance of Transborder Production Networks: a case study of Taiwanese IT companies in the Greater Suzhou area. *Journal of Geographical Science, (36),* 23–54 (Taiwanese).

Zeile, W. J. (2000–2005). *U.S. affiliates of foreign companies operations.* Washington DC: Survey of Current Business, U.S. Bureau of Economic Analysis.

The State of IS Research on Offshoring

William R. King, Reza Torkzadeh, and T. Rachel Chung

1   Introduction

In this chapter we overview the current state of IS research on offshoring by presenting summaries of manuscripts submitted for a Special Issue of the Management Information Systems Quarterly (MISQ) on the topic of IT offshoring, nine of which were eventually published in the special issue in 2008 (King W. R. and Torkzadeh 2008).

In 2005 and until August 2006, papers on the topic of IT offshoring were invited to be submitted for this MISQ Special Issue under the guest editorship of the first two authors. The "call for papers" heavily emphasized a desire for empirical papers, although papers of other varieties were also considered.

Forty-three (43) papers were submitted by the deadline. A number of papers (not included in the 43) were submitted or proposed, but were rejected because they dealt with outsourcing, but not specifically with offshore outsourcing.

Because of the high esteem in which MISQ is held by IS researchers, when we viewed the rather broad range and scope of the 43 papers, we concluded that they might well be a representative sample of the best research that is currently being conducted on the topic by IS researchers. Of course, given the emphasis on empirical work stated in the call, any conclusions that might be drawn from this "sample" are best limited to that domain.

So, in parallel with having the papers reviewed, we conducted our own analysis of the paper topics, research methodologies and other salient descriptors. For each paper, we constructed a profile of these descriptors. The profile did not include attributes of paper quality since the review process was not yet complete at the time of this analysis and because we were, in this activity, not primarily interested in quality, but in the topics studied and the research methods that were used. (Of course, in the review process, we were primarily interested in the quality of each paper). We believe that for purposes of this analysis, we can ignore quality because given the high-quality perception that most IS researchers have of MISQ, there is a significant self-selection bias with regard to quality that exists in any MISQ submission process. The vast majority of IS researchers "self censor" and do not submit papers to MISQ unless they believe them to be of first quality.

R. Hirschheim et al. (eds), *Information Systems Outsourcing,*
© Springer-Verlag Berlin Heidelberg 2009

1.1   The Paper Review Process

Although it is not the focus of this chapter, some aspects of the papers submitted
and the review process may be of interest to researchers in the area.

Authors were asked to nominate two Associate Editors (AEs) from a list of
fourteen and also to nominate six reviewers. We were able to assign about 85% of
the papers to a nominated Associate Editor. The author's nominees for reviewers
were passed along to the AE to whom each paper was assigned with the admoni-
tion that they might use them or not at their own discretion. This resulted in an
average of 1.1 of the nominated reviewers being appointed for each paper by the
AEs. So, about 20% of the reviewers who were actually used were those nominated by the authors. (We did not collect data on how many nominated reviewers
were asked to do a review and declined). The number of nominated reviewers who
were actually used as reviewers varied greatly for different AEs and papers. The
range was 0–5.

1.2   The Dimensions of the Paper Profiles

The 43 papers under consideration are listed in Appendix A by title. Each is given a
number which is for identification purposes only. Table 1 lists each of the papers by
number and provides a succinct version of the profile of each in terms of:

- Research question addressed
- Definition of offshoring (if given)

Table 1 Success/outcome factors

Success/outcome factors
Client factors
■ Vendor management capability
■ Vendor management practices
• Extent of IT application deployment
• Quality-oriented performance measures
■ Task dispersion (−)
Vendor factors
■ Service quality
■ Trust in client
■ Perceived control by clients (ns)
Client–Vendor factors
■ Client–vendor partnership quality
■ Fixed Price Contracts as opposed to Time and Materials Contracts
(−) denotes a negative impact of the variable on outcome factors
(ns) denotes a nonsignificant impact of the variable on outcome factors

- Context of the study
- Theoretical perspective(s) used
- Level of analysis
- Vendor country(ies) considered
- Sample frame
- General research method
- Analysis method
- Findings

2   Applying the Dimensions

Twenty-five papers offer an explicit definition of "offshoring." The most succinct definition is "intercountry outsourcing." Most definitions view offhsoring as a form of outsourcing performed outside the client organization's home country.

The majority of the research concerns the offshoring of software development efforts. However, a few studies examine other kinds of IT projects, including business process outsourcing, automotive engineering work, and help desk services.

2.1   *Level of Analysis*

Most studies examine research issues at the project level (N = 12) and the organizational level (N = 7). The macroeconomic level (N = 3) and the individual level also drew some research interest. Three papers report event studies. Other units of analysis include the offshoring decision (N = 1), the transaction (N = 1), and the task (N = 1). See Fig. 1 for a summary.

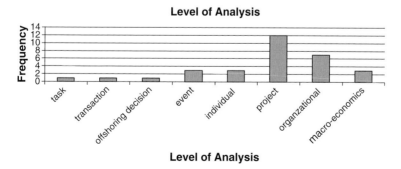

Fig. 1 Level of analysis

2.2   Offshoring Destination

Not all papers explicitly state the country in which the offshoring activities are researched. For those that do, it is not surprising that India is the most frequently cited country of destination (N = 18), with China being the next (N = 6). Other countries discussed explicitly include Jordan, Barbados, Jamaica, Mexico and South Africa. Four papers examine a range of countries that could have included some or all of the countries listed above. See Fig. 2 for a summary.

2.3   Client Location

The client firms studied in these papers are not all based in the US. One is based in Norway, one in Germany, and one in Ireland.

2.4   Theoretical Lens

As is the case in the outsourcing literature, the most commonly applied theoretical lens is transaction cost economics (TCE). However, creative applications of other theories are observed in the submitted papers. These include postcolonial theory, agency theory, social identity theory, knowledge management, national culture, theory of planned behavior, coordination, communication, collaboration, organizational learning, social exchange, relational exchange, psychological contracts, resource based view of the firm, institutional theory, control, and macroeconomics.

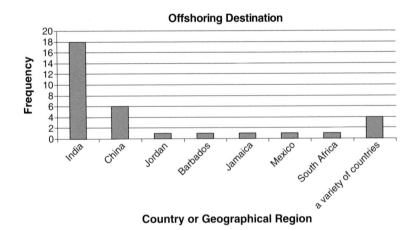

Fig. 2 Offshoring destination

2.5   Research Approach

Most papers take a qualitative approach, examining a small number of cases, often using the interview method (N = 21). Some studies take a more quantitative approach, reporting results from survey studies (N = 8). Four studies report findings based on archival data. Other research methods employed include literature review (N = 3), event study (N = 2), economic modeling (N = 1), and experiment (N = 1). See Fig. 3 for a summary.

2.6   Research Topic

A good number of studies examine factors that contribute to the outcome or success of offshored projects (N = 6). The factors being examined range from vendor and client characteristics, task characteristics, incentive structures, work practice arrangements, the extent of IT deployment, to the extent of knowledge codification.

Other topics that are examined in the submitted papers include risk factors, the role of ICT communication, knowledge management, vendor–client relationship, employee identification, social justice and the concepts of 24-h knowledge factory paradigm and the world-is-flat proposition. See Fig. 4 for a summary.

A group of papers focus on project management issues within the context of offshoring. These issues range from multivendor selection and management, organizational design and practices, internal control mechanisms, to project leader's cultural characteristics.

Another area of intense research interest is the economic value of offshore out-sourcing. In particular, authors have examined the economic value of offshore outsourcing compared to onshore outsourcing, the impact of offshore outsourcing

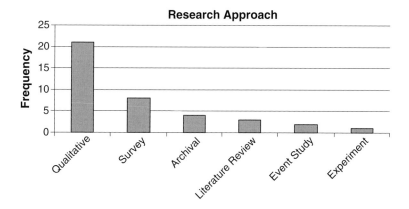

Fig. 3 Research approach

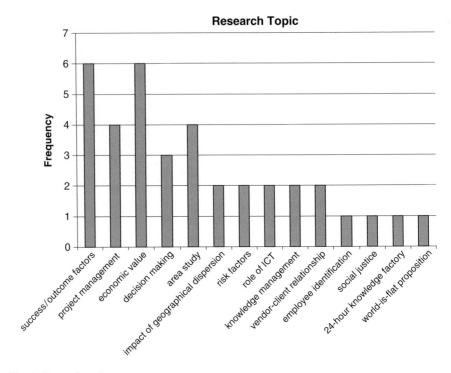

Fig. 4 Research topic

announcement on firm value, determinants of transaction costs in offshore out-sourcing projects, and how IS work may be valued in a global economy.

Authors take a variety of approaches to understand how the decision to offshore outsourcing can be made. One paper proposes an AHP methodology. Another examines the knowledge-based view on the offshoring decision. The behaviorists examine the decision making process using the theory of planned behavior, focusing on factors such as attitude, subjective norm and perceived behavioral control.

A fair distinctive approach is to focus the analyses on a specific geographical location, such as Jordan, Malaysia, Barbados, Jamaica, and India. These analyses examine the strengths and weaknesses of these countries as offshoring locations. A related but distinct approach is to study the impact of geographical dispersion on outsourcing success.

3   Summary of Findings

3.1   Success/Outcome Factors

Studies that examine antecedents to the success or other outcome measures of off-shored projects identify many important factors that are largely under the control of the client firm: Vendor management capability and practices, such as quality-oriented performance measures and IT application deployment, significantly enhance outcome measures such as client–vendor relationship satisfaction. Other factors, such as the extent of task dispersion, negatively impact project outcome. At the same time, factors on the vendor side, such as trust in client and service quality, positively contribute to the success of offshored projects, whereas perceived control by the client bears little relationship to project outcome. Studies that focus on the dynamic relationship between the client and the vendor report that positive client–vendor partnership quality improves project outcome, and that fixed-price contracts as opposed to time-and-materials contracts bring forward more favorable outcome evaluation. Table 1 presents a summary of these findings.

3.2   Project Management

A number of studies have identified the risks and challenges involved in the management of offshored projects, such as those presented by the vendor selection process, and the geographical and cultural differences. One study reports that boundary-spanning practices by middle managers facilitate effective collaboration efforts. Other studies examine team management practices and report that team leaders' cultural characteristics are crucial for project success. Particularly, team selection with client representation from the same nationality as those on the vendor team reduces project cost. These findings are summarized in Table 2.

3.3   Economic Value

As one of the most widely cited assumptions for justifying offshoring initiatives is cost savings, many studies set out to gather empirical evidence that examines the validity of these arguments from an economic perspective. Findings from the papers submitted to the special issue are mixed. On the one hand, a set of studies report that financial markets favor offshoring in general. At the same time, other studies report that, rather than reducing cost, offshoring leads to increases in production and transaction costs. There is also evidence suggesting that financial markets favor onshore outsourcing over offshoring when the firm's motive is to

Table 2 Project management

Project management
• There are various risks involved in multivendor selection and management
• Boundary-spanning practices by middle managers facilitate effective collaboration
• Team selection with client representation from the same nationality reduces cost
• Team leader's cultural characteristics are important

Table 3 Economic value

Economic value
• Financial markets favor offshoring when core IT processes are outsourced
• Global outsourcing is preferred when global processes are outsourced
• Financial markets favor offshoring in general, but when the motive is process quality improvement, onshore is preferred
• Investors usually show no reaction to outsourcing; but offshore outsourcing of business processes with high asset specificity generates sizable cumulative abnormal returns
• Offshoring leads to increased production and transaction costs with high asset specificity, cultural and geographical differences, and vendor characteristics

improve process quality. Another fundamental debate of interest is how the valuation of offshored projects should be conducted. One submitted paper addresses this question by proposing a valuation methodology. These findings are summarized in Table 3.

3.4   The Decision to Offshore

Studies that scrutinize the decision-making process involved in offshore outsourcing have taken diverse approaches. One study illustrates an AHP methodology to formalize the complicated process when firms must decide whether to offshore IT projects. Another study presents a set of propositions about the offshoring decision in relation to factors such as source governance, geographical proximity, the strategic value of offshored knowledge, and the maturity of offshored knowledge. Yet another study examines the offshoring decision using the Theory of Planned Behavior (TPB), and finds that attitude towards offshoring, subjective norm, and perceived behavioral control enhance management's inclination towards offshore outsourcing. These findings are summarized in Table 4.

3.5   Risk Management

Outsourcing IT projects to vendor firms in distant locations with foreign cultures is an intuitively risky endeavor. What can firms do to mitigate the risks involved in offshoring efforts? One study reviews the literature and postulates that task decomposition, explicit articulation and knowledge codification by client firms help reduce risk levels, whereas dependence on offshore vendor and uncertainty and consolidation within the outsourcing industry increase risk levels. Another study observes that, although firms begin with a conservative approach to offshoring, with accumulated experience firms are willing to engage in riskier projects. These findings are summarized in Table 5.

Table 4 Decision to offshore

Decision to offshore
• AHP analysis
• Source governance
• Proximity
• Strategic value of offshored knowledge
• Maturity of offshored knowledge
• Attitude toward offshoring
• Subjective norm
• Perceived behavioral control

Table 5 Risk factors

Risk factors
• Task decomposition, explicit articulation and codification (−)
• Dependence on offshore vendor (+)
• Uncertainty and consolidation within the outsourcing industry (+)
• Firm-specific and industry-wide experience enablers firms to engage in riskier projects

(+) denotes a positive impact of the variable on outcome factors
(−) denotes a negative impact of the variable on outcome factors

3.6   The Role of Information and Communication Technology (ICT)

The management of outsourced projects located in foreign countries cannot be accomplished without the application of ICT. Researchers who set out to examine the role and impact of ICT on offshored projects, however, are surprised to find out that, although the deployment of ICT is extensive, the usage is largely for tacit coordination as opposed to explicit communication. Rich media such as video conferencing are, in reality, rarely used. Instead, ICT is used primarily to ensure seamless coordination and collaboration and as a way to minimize the need for explicit communication. These findings are summarized in Table 6.

3.7   Other Findings

One paper that examines Thomas Friedman's "world-is-flat" thesis discovers that, contrary to the proposition, vendor selection in the contract decision process is based more on prior relationships as opposed to cost or location of labor. The authors also observe that U.S. firms favor offshoring over onshore outsourcing, whereas firms in other countries may do the reverse. Another research team examines the "24-h knowledge factory" concept and argues that geographical dispersion can be viewed as an asset as opposed to a disadvantage. Finally, a study concerned about the social injustice between client and vendor countries discusses mechanisms that can be implemented to balance it. These findings are summarized in Table 7.

Table 6 The role of information and communication technology (ICT)

The role of information and communication technology (ICT)
• Knowledge asymmetry exists between client and vendor countries • Mechanisms must be implemented in order to balance it

Table 7 Other findings

Other findings
• Contract decision is based more on prior relationships as opposed to cost or location of labor • US firms prefer offshoring, whereas non English speaking countries prefer local sourcing; other English speaking countries are in-between • Geographical dispersion can be an asset (the 24-h knowledge factory concept) • Knowledge asymmetry exists between client and vendor countries; mechanisms must be implemented in order to balance it

4   Conclusion

The research topics and findings reviewed in this chapter depict an evolving field which does not yet have an agreed-on framework to guide thinking. Neither is there a clear understanding of the long-term impacts and the measures and criteria that may be appropriately used to judge whether to offshore, to select a vendor, or to evaluate the degree of success of offshoring.

All in all, our review suggests that there is a great deal of work to be done before we feel at all comfortable that we "have a handle" on this hugely important area.

References

King, W. R., & Torkzadeh, G. (2008). Information systems offshoring: Research status and issues. *MIS Quarterly, 32*(2), 205–225.

Appendix A: Assessments of Papers Contributed to the Special Issue

111 Research Question: Develop a theory driven model of the labor supply chain in a generic offshoring vendor in order to study the workforce sizing issue. *Theoretical Perspective*: Systems dynamics. *Level of Analysis*: System. *Method*: Simulation. *Findings*: Contrary to common understanding that unused capacity hurts the bottom line, experiments with the model show that it is indeed necessary to maintain a not-insignificant fraction of workers idle "on the bench" to sustain financial performance. The model also provides insights into barriers to long term growth in offshoring.

112 Research Question: Explore the changing profile of the client-side risks of present and future BPO and to raise the issue whether BPO will likely to increase long-term strategic risks for an outsourcing client. *Theoretical Perspective*: Technology design, market failure, resource dependence, dynamic capabilities, and complementarity in organizational design. *Level of Analysis*: Macro and organizational level. *Method*: Literature review. *Findings*: The outsourcer–client coevolution centers around outsourcers' advantage in developing its competences due to economies of scale and scope in learning, complementarity in organizational design, and modularization and standardization in technology development as well as clients' focus on core activities and knowledge transfer preferences. Clients refer decomposition, explicit articulation and codification of their activity, function and process in order to better leverage outsourcer's expertise. The desire to reduce outsourcing project risks and enhance client's short-term performance sets a positive-feedback loop for the co-evolution, which in turn increases client's dependence on outsourcer, reduces the value of client's strategic assets, shrinks its dynamic capability, weakens its ability to profit from innovation, and stifles its long-term strategy. Uncertainty and consolidation within the outsourcing industry are likely to elevate those strategic risks.

113 Research Questions: (1) How do Jordanian IT companies look at global software outsourcing (GSO)? (2) The strengths of Jordanian IT companies, which enable them to compete in the field of GSO. (3) The weaknesses of Jordanian IT companies, which reduce their ability to compete in the field of GSO. (4) Factors in the local environment, which increase or decrease the ability of Jordanian IT companies competing in GSO. *Definition of Offshoring*: Global software outsourcing (GSO) is the outsourcing of software development to subcontractors outside the client organization's home country. *Context*: Software development, *Offshore Country*: Jordan. *Sample*: IT professionals in Jordan. *Method*: Survey. *Findings*: Various specifics of the Jordanian environment.

114 Research Questions: (1) Examine Malaysia as a destination to outsource call centers. (2) Explain what a call center is in contemporary term. (3) Examine the call center development in Malaysia. (4) Examine the working environment of a typical call center. (5) Describe how to cope with working in a call center environment. *Context*: Call center. *Offshore Country*: Malaysia. *Findings*: Malaysia has distinctive advantages as an offshore outsourcing destination.

115 Research Questions: (1) How do knowledgeable participants view project outcomes? (2) Which project attributes explain differences in participants' ratings of project outcomes? (3) How do contextual issues explain offshore outsourcing experiences? *Definition of Offshoring*: Outsourcing work to a supplier located on a different continent than the client. *Context*: IS projects. *Level of Analysis*: Project and organizational. *Offshore Country*: India. *Sample*: 44 interviews and over 2000 documents from a Fortune 500 biotech firm. *Method*: Case study. *Analysis Method*: Interpretive. *Findings*: At the project level of analysis: (1) Participants rated projects that engaged one large offshore supplier higher than projects that engaged one small offshore supplier or multiple suppliers.(2) Participants rated both development and maintenance/support projects equally. (3) Participants rated projects with some offshore supplier employees onsite higher than projects with all supplier employees offshore. (4) Participants rated projects with greater-valued contracts higher than projects with lesser-valued contracts. (5) Participants rated larger-sized projects higher than smaller-sized projects. (6) Some organizational units had higher participant-rated projects than other organizational units. (7) Participants rated recent projects higher than older projects. At the organizational level of analysis: (1) Strong social networks between biotech IT employees and domestic contractors could not easily be replicated with offshore suppliers. (2) Biotech's "sneaker-net" culture among business users and IT employees.

116 Research Question: Offshoring from vendor perspective, and in historical context. *Definition of Offshoring:* The transfer of IT services from a local company to a foreign country. *Context*: Software development. *Theoretical Perspective*: Postcolonial theory. *Offshore Country*: India. *Sample*: Field observation, collection of documents, e-mails, the Internet, field notes, and other artifacts; interviews. *Method*: Interpretive ethnography. *Analysis Method*: Qualitative. *Findings*: Informants are extremely sensitive to the larger issues of power, control, knowledge ownership and identity, which they believe underpin the IT offshoring phenomenon; the postcolonial theory is helpful in understanding the offshoring phenomenon.

117 Research Question: Whether there is empirical support for the world-is-flat proposition. *Definition of Offshoring*: The proposition that IT providers from low-wage nations can now underbid providers from high-wage nations and win contracts. *Context*: Online programming marketplace. *Theoretical Perspective*: Agency theory; social identity theory. *Level of Analysis*: Transaction. *Offshore Country*: Different countries. *Sample*: Rent-A-Coder marketplace – all transactions from May 2001 for a period of 38 months through July 2004; over 20,000 usable project transactions. *Method*: Statistical analysis of archival data. *Analysis Method*: Stepwise logistic regression. *Findings*: Contract decision is based more on prior relationship as opposed to cost or location of labor; clustering of client provider dyads in terms of their outsourcing preference: US firms prefer offshoring, whereas non English speaking countries prefer local sourcing, and other English speaking countries are in between.

118 Research Question: How AHP can help with the where to outsource decision. *Definition of Offshoring*: The practice among U.S., European, and Japanese companies of migrating business processes overseas to India, China, the Philippines, Mexico, and elsewhere to lower costs without significantly sacrificing quality. *Theoretical Perspective*: Decision making. *Level of Analysis*: Decision. *Method*: Mathematical modeling. *Analysis Method*: AHP and PROMETHEE II. *Findings*: AHP can be useful for analyzing offshoring decision making.

119 Research Question: How the location and accompanying risk profile of country location selection by IS service offshoring firms is determined. *Context*: IS foreign direct projects. *Theoretical Perspective*: International business and multinational management. *Level of Analysis*: IS project. *Offshore Country*: Different countries. *Sample*: More than 860 IT and software offshoring projects in 56 host countries worldwide during the period 2000–2005. *Method*: Analysis of archival panel data. *Analysis Method*: Hierarchical linear modeling. *Findings*: Firm-specific and industry wide experience increases the likelihood of companies investing in progressively riskier markets, but that the core "risk gap" between home and host country dissipates as both types of experience are incorporated into our model.

120 Research Question: How knowledge-based view affects the evaluation of outsourcing decisions. *Definition of Offshoring*: Outsourcing as "outside resource using," subcontracting a part, or all, of an organization's IS work to external vendor(s) to manage on its behalf. *Theoretical Perspective*: Knowledge-based view vs. transaction cost, resource-based theory, institutional theory. *Analysis Method*: Literature review. *Findings*: 16 propositions about outsourcing decisions in terms of source governance, proximity, the strategic value, and maturity of knowledge.

121 Research Question: How resource allocators use information knowledge to wield power in the ISD process, and achieve goals of self interests. *Context*: Software development. *Theoretical Perspective*: Cultural perspective on power issues in ISD, particularly the Chinese Power Game – Face and Favor Theory. *Level of Analysis*: Event. *Sample:* One firm (TaiWire). *Method:* Interview and archival data. *Analysis Method:* Qualitative. *Findings:* Relationship (quanxi) and favor (renqing) play considerable roles in IS politics in a Chinese family firm.

122 Research Question: Selection and management of multivendors in software production. *Definition of Offshoring*: The use of outside vendors, who are physically located in foreign countries, to produce parts or whole of the software. *Context:* Software development. *Theoretical Perspective*: Authors developed their own all-encompassing model of vendor selection, *Sample:* A large multinational telecom company. *Method*: Interview. *Analysis Method*: Qualitative. *Findings*: There are various risks involved in international outsourcing using multivendors.

123 Research Question: Factors influencing vendors' intention to offshore outsourcing. *Definition of Offshoring*: The practice of contracting with third party vendors for the provision of IT services, with the vendors located in countries other than that of the buyers. *Context:* IT decision makers in Fortune 1000 companies. *Theoretical Perspective*: Theory of planned behavior. *Level of Analysis*: Individual. *Sample*: 139 IT decision makers. *Method*: Survey. *Analysis Method*: PLS. *Findings*: IT decision-makers' attitude toward offshore outsourcing, subjective norms, and perceived behavioral control are good predictors of the intention to outsource offshore; the expectation of IT cost savings and competitive benefits influence attitude towards offshore outsourcing while the perception of an offshore vendor's reputation plays a role in influencing perceived behavioral control.

124 Research Question: Whether there is a problem in the IS discipline related to dropping student numbers and what if anything the field can do about it. *Definition of Offshoring*: The migration of all or part of the development, maintenance and delivery of IT services to a vendor who is located in a low cost and different country from that of the client. *Context*: The IS discipline. *Method*: Literature review and macro data summary. *Analysis Method*: Simple descriptive statistics. *Findings*: Organizations will increasingly need "customer-facing" IT personnel which the academic IS community needs to produce. The authors offer guidelines for what students, faculty, and governments can do to preserve and improve the IS field despite the irreversible trend towards offshoring.

125 Research Question: How ICT is used in offshore SD projects. *Definition of Offshoring*: Geographic dispersion of value chains. *Context*: Software Development. *Theoretical Perspective*: Coordination and communicating in distributed work; ICT media richness. *Level of Analysis*: Project. *Offshore Countries*: One U.S. firm and one India firm. *Sample*: 18 collocated and 42 distributed projects in two large software development firms. *Method*: Interview and archival data. *Analysis Method*: Qualitative. *Findings*: Video conferencing rarely used (copresence is required which is hard across time zones); ICT mostly for tacit coordination and for generating common ground, as opposed to supporting communication.

126 Research Question: How ICTs are actually used in distributed software development. *Definition of Offshoring*: Geographic dispersion of value chains. *Context*: Software development. *Theoretical Perspective*: ICT and communication. *Level of Analysis*: Project. *Offshore Country*: India. *Sample*: Qualitative data from 60 distributed and collocated software services delivery projects. *Method*: Interview. *Analysis Method*: Qualitative. *Findings*: ICT based tools are typically not used as channels of direct communication between locations. Instead ICT tools are used to avoid the need for direct communication by creating common ground across locations and thereby enabling tacit coordination.

127 Research Questions: How expertise is institutionalized in different team working settings within software development environments taking into account the increasing internationalization of the ICT Industry. How is expertise synchronized and coordinated among intercultural teams? Which grade of expertise standardization corresponds to differently professionalized occupational fields within the ICT industry? Which is the relation between innovation patterns and expertise requirements? *Context*: Software development. *Theoretical Perspective*: Meuser and Nagel's (1991) theory of experts. *Sample*: (1) Open interviews with 13 female and 17 male software developers; (2) six enterprises. *Method*: Interview and case study. *Findings*: Institutional patterns of expertise and professionalism are embedded in innovation paths that include different transformation rhythms and are marked through national and international regulations.

128 Research Question: What is the economic value of offshoring relative to onshore or global outsourcing? *Definition of Offshoring*: Utilizing skilled labor primarily located in distant foreign nations to supplement or replace in-house resources and activities. *Context*: IT outsourcing announcements. *Theoretical Perspective*: Transaction cost economics, organizational learning, agency, contingency theory. *Level of Analysis*: Event. *Sample*: 133 outsourcing announcements from 111 firms 1996–2004, stock returns of firms in the event windows and financial variables. *Method*: Event study. *Analysis Method*: Econometrics. *Findings*: Financial markets favor offshore vs. global outsourcing when core IT processes are outsourced; global outsourcing is preferred when global processes are outsourced; financial markets respond favorably to offshoring in general; but if the motivation is process quality improvement, onshore and global sourcing is preferred.

129 Research Question: What is the effect of IT outsourcing and offshoring announcements on firm value. *Definition of Offshoring*: Outsourcing is the use of external agents to perform one of more organizational activities; offshoring is a special case of outsourcing. *Context*: IT outsourcing announcements. *Theoretical Perspective*: Transaction cost economics. *Level of Analysis*: Event. *Sample*: 196 announcements from 1998–2004. *Method*: Event study. *Analysis Method*: Econometrics. *Findings*: Not all outsourcing announcements generate a positive market reaction. In many cases, investors had no reaction, indicating that outsourcing is expected and part of normal business operating procedures; the offshore outsourcing of business processes with high asset specificity, however, did result in sizeable cumulative abnormal returns.

130 Research Questions: What are the reasons for relatively higher transaction costs for offshore outsourcing as compared to onshore outsourcing? What can be done to reduce these high transaction costs?. *Context*: IT services. *Theoretical Perspective*: Transaction cost economics. *Offshore Countries*: China and India. *Sample*: China based firms. *Method*: Case study. *Analysis Method*: Qualitative. *Findings*: A number of gaps were identified as the causes of higher transaction costs, and a number of potential solutions were provided.

131 Research Question: Which organizational designs and practices facilitate effective collaboration in offshore settings. *Context*: Software development. *Theoretical Perspective*: Multiparty collaboration, outsourcing; offshoring, global virtual work. *Offshore Countries*: India and Russia. *Sample*: 67 interviews with both onshore and offshore staff. *Method*: interview. *Analysis Method*: Qualitative. *Findings*: Achieving effective collaboration did not depend on whether the project was kept within the firm's boundaries, nor did it depend on choosing a specific offshore location. Instead, effective collaboration was facilitated by specific middle managers who engaged in boundary-spanning practices across country and firm borders.

132 Research Question: Whether the employees may develop dual identification with the vendor and the client, the antecedents and consequences of such dual identification, and the relationship between them. *Definition of Offshoring*: A practice in which an organization (client) contracts all or part of its IS operations to one or more external service providers (vendor) outside its own country. *Context*: Call center. *Theoretical Perspective*: Social and organizational identity theory. *Level of Analysis*: Individual. *Offshore Country*: China. *Sample*: 195 members of an Association of Chinese IT Call Centers through its online forum. *Method*: Survey. *Analysis Method*: PLS. *Findings*: Employees' dual identifications with both the vendor and the client could promote offshored IT service performance.

133 Research Question: Issues in IT offshore outsourcing. *Context*: IT outsourcing. *Offshore Countries*: Australia, China, India, Pakistan, Sri Lanka, United States. *Sample*: 12 "participants" – vendors or clients. *Method*: Interview. *Analysis Method*: Hermeneutics. *Findings*: Most IT outsourcing relationships endure communication problems, cultural differences, and lack of trust. *134 Research Questions*: (1) What additional costs may arise in offshored software projects? (2) How and why do additional costs vary between projects? *Context*: Software Development. *Theoretical Perspective*: Transaction cost economics. *Level of Analysis*: Project. *Offshore Countries*: Germany outsourced to India. *Sample*: Three application and three maintenance projects. *Method*: Case study. *Analysis Method*: Content categorization

(Nvivo). *Findings*: Offshoring can lead to increased effort on client side in terms of production costs and transaction costs; these costs are high when assets are highly specific; cultural and geographic differences and vendor characteristics can lead to additional costs.

135 Research Question: What are the antecedents to vendor performance. *Definition of Offshoring*: Outsourcing outside the boundaries of one's country – near shore, off shore, and far shore. *Context*: IT services. *Theoretical Perspective*: Resource-based view, resource dependency theory, information processing view, agency–cost, social exchange, and power and politics. *Level of Analysis*: Firm. *Offshore Countries*: China and India. *Sample*: 169 vendor firms. *Method*: Survey. *Analysis Method*: LISREL. *Findings*: Vendor management capability, service quality, and client–vendor partnership quality have significant influence on vendor and client satisfaction, vendor market growth and vendor process improvement.

136 Research Question: How different incentive structures inherent in two contract types: time and materials vs. fixed price, influence the quality provided by vendor. *Context*: Software development. *Theoretical Perspective*: Production-based approach? Not very clear what theory is used. *Level of Analysis*: Project. *Offshore Country*: India. *Sample*: 100 projects from a single vendor (60 FP and 40 T&M). *Method*: Survey. *Analysis Method*: Regression. *Findings*: Providing higher quality is associated with higher profit margins for vendors under fixed price contracts as opposed to time and materials contracts.

137 Research Question: What are the critical customer and community obligations in an opensourcing relationship? *Definition of Offshoring*: Outsourcing to a global workforce. *Context*: Opensource development. *Theoretical Perspective*: Psychological contract theory. *Level of Analysis*: Customer–vendor relationship. *Offshore Countries*: Different countries. *Sample*: Three cases and 207 usable responses for the survey. *Method*: An exploratory qualitative multiple case study, followed by a quantitative survey study. *Analysis Method*: Qualitative and principal component factor analysis. *Findings*: Fulfillment of certain customer and community obligations is associated with opensourcing success.

138 Research Question: Implications and opportunities afforded by the bridge role of being both customer and vendor in a two-stage offshoring relationship. *Definition of Offshoring*: Shifting of tasks to low-cost nations often referred to as "developing nations" or "emerging nations." *Context*: Software engineering. *Theoretical Perspective*: Relational exchange theory. *Level of Analysis*: Project. *Offshore Countries*: Irish &clock; India. *Sample*: The Irish sites of two large U.S.-based companies. *Method*: Workshops, meetings, and interviews. *Analysis Method*: Interpretive. *Findings*: The Irish sites hold a dual role of communicating and managing both the U.S. and Asian teams, thus having experience of being both customer and vendor in an IS offshoring relationship; depth of expertise and experience is more important than location for competitiveness.

139 Research Question: What characteristics of a location may make it an effective site for nearshore development? *Definition of Offshoring*: Involves client and vendor companies that are located in different countries. *Context*: Software development. *Theoretical Perspective*: Two opposing views of "place of work" – not very theoretical. firm or country. *Offshore Countries*: Barbados and Jamaica. *Sample*: Two nearshore firms. *Method*: Case study. *Analysis Method*: Content categorization (NUDIST). *Findings:* Many characteristics of a location matter, not just at the region or country level, but at a high level of detail (e.g., size of existing Indian population).

140 Research Question: Antecedents and performance outcomes of onshore and offshore BPO. *Context*: Business process outsourcing (BPO). *Theoretical Perspective*: Transaction cost economics, business process management, strategy and international business. *Level of Analysis*: Firm. *Sample and Method*: Data from the InformationWeek 500 survey and the InformationWeek BPO survey. *Analysis Method*: Regression. *Findings*: (1) A broader IT application deployment is associated w an increased likelihood of both onshore and offshore BPO. (2) BP codification is associated w an increased likelihood of onshore and offshore BPO. (3) No relation between degree of internationalization and offshore BPO. (4) IT application deployment and quality-oriented performance measures and vendor management practices are positively associated with BPO benefits.

141 Research Questions: What legitimacy management strategies are adopted during the institutionalization of offshoring? What role does trust play in the ensuing legitimacy dynamics? *Definition of Offshoring*: Outsourcing of software production globally. *Context*: Software development. *Theoretical Perspective*: legitimacy, institutional theory; trust. *Level of Analysis*: Offshore arrangements? *Offshore Country:* India. *Sample*: Globalco and its Indian vendors. *Method*: Case study. *Analysis Method*: Case analysis. *Findings*: Legitimacy development and trust building are closely connected in offshoring projects.

142 Research Questions: (1) What influence does the global environment have on k transfer? (2) How do organizations manage to develop and retain the evolving knowledge held in the minds of individuals within organizational boundaries? (3) How to organizations manage their learning processes given the participative nature of building knowledge in software development work? *Context*: Software development. *Theoretical Perspective*: Knowledge management. *Level of Analysis*: Firm. *Offshore Country*: India. *Sample*: Six organizations (four medium and two large size). *Method*: Qualitative observations and semistructured interviews. *Analysis Method*: Qualitative. *Findings*: Metalearning is the core to building knowledge in distributed software development processes.

143 Research Questions: (1) How do work practices vary under and evolve within diff org models for offshoring work? (2) To what extent and in what ways do differences in work practice associated with different organizational models affect satisfaction with and performance in offshoring arrangements? *Context*: Automotive engineering work. *Level of Analysis*: Task. *Offshore Countries*: Mexico and India. *Sample*: Offshoring projects. *Method*: Case study and survey. *Analysis Method*: Content categorization. *Findings*: CAE tools enable offshoring, but because the artifacts they produce encapsulate but do not make transparent engineering judgment and assumptions, individuals in both models developed new work practices to compensate for deficiencies associated with CAE.

144 Research Questions: (1) How do informal control mechanisms of team composition, client–vendor interactions and client liaising affect total development costs (TDC)? (2) How do project leaders' cultural characteristics affect the relationship between team composition and TDC? *Definition of Offshoring*: A client organization's outsourcing of a development project to a vendor located in another country. *Context*: Software development. *Theoretical Perspective*: Agency, informal control, national culture. *Level of Analysis*: Project and project leader. *Offshore Country*: India. *Sample*: 131 projects by 22 project leaders from a single firm. *Method*: Survey and archival project data. *Analysis Method*: Hierarchical linear modeling. *Findings*: (1) Team selection with client representation from the same nationality reduces cost; (2) leader's cultural characteristics are important.

145 Research Question: The effects of offshore vendors' sense of trust in their clients and perception of control on performance. *Definition of Offshoring*: The migration of all or part of an organization's IT assets, people, and/or activities to vendors located in a country different from that of the organization. *Context*: Software development. *Theoretical Perspective*: Social exchange theory and trust and control. *Level of Analysis*: Project. *Offshore Countries*: Japan ⊕ China. *Sample*: 110 returned questionnaires from vendor project managers. *Method*: Interview and survey. *Analysis Method*: Hierarchical regression. *Findings*: Trust in the offshore clients was key determinant of project quality, but perceived control by clients is not.

146 Research Question: What are the key capabilities required for a successful offshore outsourcing of IS application development? *Definition of Offshoring*: Outsourcing arrangements, involving cross-border flows and linkages that utilize resources such as technology, know–how, and human capital from IS vendor organizations abroad, for accomplishment of specific goals of the client firm. *Context*: IS projects. *Theoretical Perspective*: Capability thinking. *Level of Analysis*: Firm. *Sample*: Five focus groups, and IS managers from 18 organizations. Method: Focus group and interviews. *Analysis Method*: Qualitative. *Findings*: Dimensions of offshoring capabilities.

147 Research Questions: (1) Analyze conditions and strategies for software development models that imply countries in the South to actively participate and leverage on the potential that offshoring provides. (2) Develop models that can effectively support the implementation of ICT based solutions to address local and pressing national development needs such as in health and education. *Definition of Offshoring*: Making arrangements with an external entity for the provision of goods or services to replace or supplement internal efforts. *Context*: HISP. *Theoretical Perspective*: Socio-political theory. *Offshore Countries*: Norway ⊕ South Africa. *Sample*: HISP software development projects. *Method*: Interpretive research and action research. *Analysis Method*: Interpretive and action research. *Findings*: Knowledge asymmetry exists and mechanisms must be implemented in order to balance it.

148 Research Question: Is India's lead in offshoring sustainable over time. *Definition of Offshoring*: The practice of hiring an external organization to perform some or all business functions in a country other than the one where the product will be sold or consumed. *Context*: IT outsourcing. *Theoretical Perspective*: Macro economics. *Level of Analysis*: Country. *Offshore Country*: India. *Findings*: Offshoring is a win–win situation for most stakeholders; India's cost advantage will erode over time unless they develop advantages in higher level skills.

149 Research Question: How IS work may be valued in a global economy where the sponsor companies and the host companies reside in different countries. *Definition of Offshoring*: Intercountry outsourcing. *Context*: Software valuation. *Theoretical Perspective*: Valuation of intellectual capital. *Level of Analysis*: Software. *Analysis Method*: Theoretical development and analysis of likely scenarios. *Findings*: The proposed valuation makes sense with the examined scenarios.

150 Research Question: Critical success factors for IT outsourcing. *Context*: Helpdesk service. *Sample*: A provider company that provides helpdesk service. *Method*: Case study and survey. *Analysis Method*: Descriptive summary statistics. *Findings*: The authors present a conceptual model which allows companies to homogenize the concepts regarding this area by using an abstract representation.

151 Research Question: Impact of knowledge levels on the trade offs between short-term labor costs and long-term coordination costs. *Theoretical Perspective*: Economic models of learning. *Level of Analysis*: Firm. *Method*: Economic modeling. *Analysis Method*: Economic modeling. *Findings*: Although short-lived offshoring projects may generate substantial cost savings to the domestic firm's long-lived offshoring projects may cause a disruption in the management supply chain, resulting in substantial losses in the later stages of the project.

152 Research Question: Viability of the 24-h knowledge factory paradigm. *Context*: Software development. *Theoretical Perspective*: Group dynamics and tacit knowledge. *Level of Analysis*: Team. *Offshore Country*: India. *Sample*: Two teams from IBM. *Method*: A quasi field experiment. *Analysis Method*: Descriptive comparisons of the two teams. *Findings:* Geographical constitution does not determine team success; geographical distribution can be an asset.

153 Research Questions: (1) How effective are structured, high maturity process platforms deployed by offshore software firms in mitigating risks of distributed work? (2) Why are some offshore improvement initiatives more effective than others? *Context*: Software development. *Theoretical Perspective*: Organizational learning. *Level of Analysis*: Project. *Offshore Country*: India. *Sample*: 42 projects from one offshore software service company with level five CMM. *Method*: Analysis of archival performance data and interviews. *Analysis Method*: Regression. *Findings*: (1) Effect of systems development improvements on offshore projects are mediated through the capability to design and implement learning routines. (2) Task dispersion negatively impacts systems development performance even in high maturity environment.

Chapter 6
Knowledge Sharing in Offshoring

Transactive Memory and the Transfer of Knowledge between Onsite and Offshore IT Outsourcing Teams

Ilan Oshri, Julia Kotlarsky, and Paul van Fenema

1 Introduction

Knowledge transfer has become a key issue for globally distributed work, such as global software development projects (e.g. Kotlarsky & Oshri 2005), global Business Process Outsourcing (e.g. Feeny, Lacity, & Willcocks 2005), and Infrastructure Management (e.g. Beulen, van Fenema, & Currie 2005). In these novel organizational forms, success depends on the rapid transfer of business and technological knowledge from and to offshore facilities. This transfer of knowledge may improve knowledge integration across various sites and products, and may contribute to successfully coordinating complex projects (Grant 1996).

Globally distributed projects, consisting of two or more teams working together from different geographical locations to accomplish project goals, face major challenges in transferring knowledge across remote sites. For example, these teams confront cultural differences that may include, but are not limited to, different languages, national traditions, values and norms of behaviour (Carmel 1999; Carmel & Agarwal 2002). To overcome geographical distances and time–zone differences such teams mainly collaborate through Information and Communication Technologies (ICT), and occasionally meet face-to-face to discuss project matters.

Nonetheless, over the past decade, studies have demonstrated repeatedly that, despite advances in technologies, ICTs do not prevent breakdowns in the transfer of knowledge across distributed sites (e.g. Cramton 2001). While ICTs are critical for knowledge transfer processes in distributed teams, a neighbouring stream of studies within the IS field has considered human-related factors, such as trust (Jarvenpaa & Leidner 1999; Ridings Gefen, & Arinze 2002) and inter-personal ties (Ahuja & Galvin 2003; Kanawattanachai and Yoo 2002), which may act as facilitators for knowledge transfer between remote counterparts.

In line with such advances in the IS field, scholars have increasingly considered the concept of the transactive memory as an enhancer of knowledge transfer (Nevo & Wand 2005). The encoding, storing and retrieving processes involved in a transactive memory system (TMS) (Wegner, Giuliano, & Hertel 1985) could support the transfer of knowledge between individuals (Nevo & Wand 2005). While the concept of transactive memory has been studied in the context of traditional organizational

R. Hirschheim et al. (eds), *Information Systems Outsourcing,*
© Springer-Verlag Berlin Heidelberg 2009

forms and co-located teams, little is known about the process through which a TMS in globally distributed teams could be created and could support knowledge transfer between remote sites. The few studies that have indeed explored the concept of transactive memory in virtual teams have highlighted the importance of it for team performance (e.g. Yoo & Kanawattanachai 2001) without addressing the broader challenge of knowledge transfer.

To contribute to filling this gap, this paper explores how remote counterparts encode, store and retrieve information about the location of knowledge to support knowledge transfer between dispersed sites. In particular, this paper will address the following questions: *how does transactive memory enable knowledge transfer in globally distributed teams?* And *through what mechanisms can a TMS be created and maintained?* In order to understand knowledge transfer in globally distributed teams from a transactive memory perspective, this paper first explores knowledge transfer challenges, and the development and use of a TMS in dispersed teams. This conceptual contribution is followed by an in-depth case study of global software development projects. The paper concludes by providing theoretical and practical implications and suggestions for future research.

2   The Challenges of Knowledge Transfer in Globally Distributed Teams

Globally distributed teams – both within and between organizational boundaries – represent a new organizational form that has emerged in conjunction with the globalization of socio-economic processes. Such teams have replaced the traditional single-site hierarchy and the functional department structure for various reasons. For one, companies in developed nations have outsourced parts of their IT services and business processes to developing nations (Carmel & Agarwal 2002; Currie & Willcocks 1998). Short-cycle development and the launch of new products and software for global markets has required expertise from a range of geographical areas (Desouza & Evaristo 2004). Following this trend, the transfer of knowledge has become a key challenge for global teams attempting to deliver products and services adjusted to local markets and yet aiming to standardize expertise and business and technological operations on an international scale (Sole & Edmondson 2002). Indeed, this growing trend of outsourcing has increased the exchange of information and knowledge between knowledge workers located at offshore and onsite during different stages of product and service lifecycles.

Knowledge transfer is the process through which one organization (or unit) identifies and learns specific knowledge that resides in another organization (or unit), and re-applies this knowledge in other contexts (Hansen, Nohria, & Tierney 1999). On the individual level, Cutler (1989) has previously observed that knowledge transfer is indeed a process by which the knowledge of one actor is acquired and is reapplied by another. While the literature has so far provided various explanations as to how knowledge is transferred between individuals, e.g. through knowledge codification and socialization processes (Nonaka 1994), several studies have expressed concern with regard to the transferability of knowledge between remote counterparts and dispersed teams, prompted by a number of factors.

First, the diversity of local contexts may exacerbate the stickiness of information (von Hippel 1994), hampering the transfer of contextual knowledge between remote sites (Cramton 2001). Second, remote counterparts often adopt unique local routines for working, training and learning (Desouza & Evaristo 2004). These unique routines may obstruct the development of shared understanding of practices and knowledge across remote sites. Third, differences in skills, expertise, technical infrastructure and development tools and methodologies further raise the barriers for knowledge transfer between remote sites. And finally, time–zone differences reduce the window for real time interactions (Boland & Citurs 2001), thus limiting opportunities for remote team members to discuss, debate and explain diverse opinions and perspectives.

Indeed, while co-located teams may develop various memory systems that support knowledge transfer, globally distributed teams often face challenges in developing such memory systems that may provide support for the transfer of contextual and embedded knowledge. The following section discusses the concept of transactive memory and aspects relating to how such a memory system may act as an enabler of knowledge transfer in globally distributed teams.

3   Transactive Memory: The Concept

A TMS has been defined as the combination of individual memory systems and communications (also referred to as 'transactions') between individuals. The group-level TMS is constituted by individuals using each other as a memory source. Transactions between individuals link their memory systems; through a series of processes (i.e. encoding, storing, and retrieving) knowledge is exchanged. Individuals encode information for storing and retrieval, similar to a librarian entering details of a new book in the particular library system before putting it on the shelves. Through encoding, knowledge is categorized (i.e. assigned labels that reflect the subjects of the knowledge) for systematically storing the location of the knowledge, but not the knowledge itself. Then, individuals store this information internally (building their own memory), or externally (storing it in artifacts or indirectly in other people's memories). And lastly, information about the location of the knowledge or expertise is retrieved when someone else asks for it (Nevo & Wand 2005). Retrieval thus consists of two interconnected sub-processes: person A asks person B for information; person B retrieves the information. As Nevo and Wand (2005, p. 551) simply put it, "knowledge is encoded, stored and retrieved through various transactions between individuals" (see Fig. 1).

Wegner (1995) explains that for a TMS to work, three corresponding aspects to encoding, storing and retrieving should be considered. These aspects, which accommodate interactions between multiple actors, are:

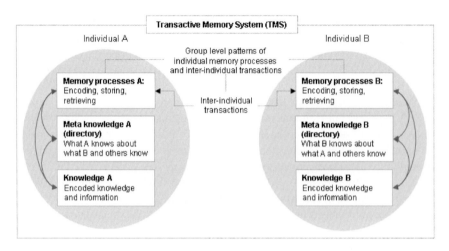

Fig. 1 The concept of a transactive memory system (after Wegner 1987)

1. Directory updating: where actors keep information about "who knows what" up-to-date
2. Information allocation: where actors decide in whose memory to store new information that arrives in the transactive memory system, and
3. Retrieval coordination: where actors use a set of guidelines to determine in which order other actors should be consulted for the missing information

In fact, a common assumption in the knowledge management literature is that the type of knowledge involved in a transaction (i.e. explicit or tacit) matches the type of knowledge management approach to capturing, storing and reapplying it (i.e. codified or personalized). Correspondingly, the literature distinguishes between codified (e.g. Hansen et al. 1999) and personalized memory systems (e.g. Blackler 1995). Similarly, based on Hansen et al.'s (1999) work, Desouza and Evaristo (2004, p. 87) discuss the differences between the codification-based and personalization-based knowledge approaches. With the codification approach, individual knowledge is "made centrally available to members of the organization via databases and data warehouses". The personalization knowledge approach, on the other hand, "recognizes the tacit dimension of knowledge and assumes that knowledge is shared mainly through direct person-to-person contacts" (Desouza & Evaristo 2004, p. 87). Similarly, the directories that point to where knowledge and expertise reside can either be codified (e.g. information systems and technologies) or personalized (e.g. personal memory or other people's memories). In other words, transactions between individuals take place through the use of various codified (e.g. databases) and personalized (e.g. theirs or other people's memory) directories. Such a TMS can be further developed and renewed through a constant update of these codified and personalized directories.

In line with such an approach, the following section addresses the challenges associated with knowledge transfer in globally distributed contexts from a transactive memory perspective.

4   Knowledge Transfer through Transactive Memory: The Challenges

A TMS may offer various benefits to both teams and individuals. Through the development of a TMS and the awareness of "who knows what", the performance of a team can be improved (Faraj & Sproull 2000; Moreland & Myaskovsky 2000). More specifically, a TMS may enhance specialization and division of labour. Teams and individuals could develop expertise in their own areas while being aware of the existence of expertise elsewhere (Majchrzak & Malhotra 2005). In addition, the literature asserts the positive association of a TMS with team learning, speed to market, new product success (Akgun, Byrne, Keskin, Lynn, & Imamoglu 2005), and an efficient coordination of expertise in teams through the development of similar labels and categories for encoding and retrieving information (Faraj & Sproull 2000; Majchrzak & Malhotra 2005; Nevo & Wand 2005).

The development of a TMS can be facilitated through various activities. Past studies have illustrated the development of a TMS by studying the close relationships between couples (Wegner, Raymond, & Erber 1991). More recently, research has proposed that training activities contribute to the development of a TMS (Moreland & Argote 2003). In co-located teams, the development of a TMS within a team seems achievable through sporadic training sessions and continuous problem-solving activities (Majchrzak & Malhotra 2005; Yoo & Kanawattanachai 2001).

However, several studies have raised concerns that developing a TMS may face significant challenges in distributed contexts (e.g. Majchrzak & Malhotra 2005). For one, globally distributed teams often experience changes in membership that negatively affect the long-term development of a TMS (Ancona, Bresman, & Kaeufer 2002). Furthermore, in many distributed settings, team members do not have any prior experience of working together. Their distributed mode of operation decreases communications and increases the possibilities for conflict (Armstrong & Cole 1995), misunderstanding and breakdowns in communication (Chudoba, Wynn, Lu, & Watson-Manheim 2005; Cramton 2001). In teams that do not carry out joint training or arrange face-to-face meetings (Yoo & Kanawattanachai 2001), the development of shared understanding is even more challenging because members of such teams do not stand on "common ground" (Cramton 2001). These challenges faced by distributed teams may hamper individuals' efforts to successfully maintain a system in which personalized directories are created and maintained. Furthermore, developing and updating a codified directory of information may be hampered by the adoption of different routines and methodologies across dispersed teams (Desouza & Evaristo 2004) and by difficulties to standardize work practices across remote locations. This problem results in fewer opportunities to access knowledge by remote counterparts.

Table 1 reviews the meaning of encoding, storing and retrieving processes in the context of codified and personalized directories in globally distributed teams. We have developed these definitions and observations based on the existing literature of globally distributed teams, knowledge management, and transactive memory, as discussed above.

We use transactive memory processes and definitions presented in Table 1 to explore how one software vendor transferred knowledge between onsite and offshore teams.

Table 1 Transactive memory processes, codified and personalized directories in globally distributed teams (based on Wegner 1987)

Memory process in a TMS (Wegner 1987)	Types of Directories in a TMS	
	Codified Directories	Personalized Directories
Encoding Having a shared "cataloging" system	Creating a shared system to categorise information. This can be effectively achieved by developing a set of rules of how to label the subject and location of the expertise.	Creating a shared under standing of context and work-related processes, terminology and language.
Storing The way in which the information is organized in physical locations and in the memories of dispersed team members	Storing information about the subject and location of the knowledge. This can be achieved by creating pointers to the location of knowledge in an expertise directory. Storing capabilities include up-to-date records of available documents and expertise.	Storing information about "who knows what" and "who is doing what" in individuals' memories
Retrieving (1) Knowing where and in what form information is stored in the dispersed team (2) Being able to find required information through determining the location of information, and, sometimes, "the combination or interplay of items coming from multiple locations"	Developing capabilities to find information necessary to coordinate expertise. Includes search capabilities (e.g. keyword-based) for effective and efficient search and retrieval processes.	Developing interpersonal channels through which individuals can search for information about who has expertise and in which areas, and where this expertise resides

5   Research Methods

5.1   Design and Case Selection

In line with past research (Eisenhardt 1989; Yin 1994), a case study method was selected for this research. An in-depth case study of globally distributed software development projects was carried out, and a qualitative, interpretive approach was adopted.

To analyze the role of transactive memory in knowledge transfer between members of dispersed teams our primary case selection criterion was to find globally distributed projects that were actively involved in knowledge transfer. Two projects from TATA Consultancy Services (TCS) were selected and studied in depth in the context of transactive memory. The projects faced complex and challenging knowledge transfer situations, as remote counterparts needed to transfer knowledge while co-developing and implementing the TCS Quartz financial platform for Scandia and Dresdner banks.

5.2   Data Collection

Evidence was collected from interviews, project documentation and observations (Eisenhardt 1989; Yin 1994). Interviews were conducted at two remote sites: in India and Switzerland (for the Scandia bank), and India and USA (for the Dresdner bank). Interviewees were chosen to include (1) counterparts working closely at remote locations, and (2) diverse roles such as managers and developers. In total, 14 interviews were conducted. Interviews lasted on average 1.5 h; they recorded and transcribed in full. A semi-structured interview protocol was applied, to allow the researchers to clarify specific issues and follow up with questions.

5.3   Data Analysis

Data analysis followed several steps. It relied on iterative reading of the data using open-coding techniques (Strauss & Corbin 1998), to sort and refine themes emerging from the data (Miles & Huberman 1994). In particular, six themes that represent the concept of transactive memory were carefully studied: encoding, storing and retrieving processes, each process in relation to codified and personalized directories. Statements that were found to correspond with these six themes were selected, coded and analyzed using Atlas.ti – Qualitative Data Analysis software (Miles & Huberman 1994; Weitzman 2000).

The first step in our data analysis aimed to examine how transactive memory enables knowledge transfer in globally distributed teams (the first part of the research question). It involved reading through the interview transcripts and collected documents, then (1) coding statements that illustrate different elements of a TMS, according to definitions presented in Table 1, and (2) marking evidence of knowledge transfer. During this stage chunks of text (paragraphs or sentences) describing (1) elements of a TMS and (2) evidence of knowledge transfer were coded. Next, statements (i.e. codes) illustrating elements of a TMS were grouped into the six above-mentioned categories that represent the six elements of a TMS.

Then, to address the second part of the research question – through what mechanisms a TMS can be created and maintained – we analyzed statements in each of these six categories to identify specific organizational mechanisms that enabled TCS to develop and maintain a TMS for knowledge transfer in globally distributed teams.

6 The Quartz Project: Knowledge Transfer in a Globally Distributed Team

To understand the complexity involved in transferring knowledge between remote counterparts, we first elaborate on TCS and the challenges they faced in these projects. Following this, the results of the case study will be presented. To explore the role of transactive memory in knowledge transfer the analysis will be organized around knowledge transfer challenges during encoding, storing and retrieving processes and the role that transactive memory has played in overcoming these challenges.

6.1 TCS Background

This study concerns the development and implementation of Quartz, an integrated financial platform aimed at providing solutions for financial institutions such as traditional and internet banks, brokerage/securities houses and asset managers. Quartz consists of a collection of architectural and business components that can be integrated with third party components to provide a solution according to the requirements of a specific customer. The Quartz group (a unit within TCS) is running several Quartz implementations simultaneously, for different clients. A typical Quartz implementation included the integration of Quartz with a customer's system and its customization to suit the needs of a specific customer.

The project organization of a Quartz implementation consists of an onsite team at the customer location and offshore teams at the development centres of TCS for system development and front-end design (Fig. 2). The majority of the Quartz team resided in one location throughout the project, either onsite or offshore, while only a small number of individuals traveled between remote locations for short visits. Teams at each site are headed by project leaders who report back to the project manager and ultimately the Quartz program manager. The following Quartz implementation projects are investigated: (1) Skandia bank in Zurich, and (2) Dresdner bank in San Francisco. Both projects are concerned with the implementation of Quartz, therefore they are analyzed together as one "embedded" case study (Yin 1994): the two projects are sub-units of analysis. In terms of global

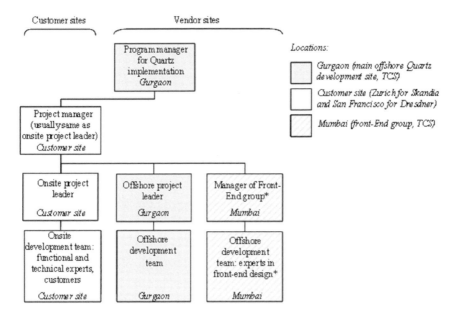

Fig. 2   Organizational structure of the quartz projects

distribution, the Skandia development team was distributed across three geographical locations: two offshore teams in Gurgaon and Bombay (India), and an onsite team at the customer location in Zurich (Switzerland). Furthermore, vendors of third party components were located in different countries (more than 25 vendors in total). The Dresdner development team involved an offshore team in Gurgaon and an onsite team at the customer site in San Francisco (Fig. 2).

6.2   The Need for Knowledge Transfer

The philosophy TCS followed in dividing the work between the onsite and offshore sites was, whenever possible, to send work offshore to take advantage of the cost, quality, and availability of offshore personnel. As one interviewee explained, the onsite team was sending requirements offshore "because the expertise and major source code are here (offshore, in Gurgaon), and mainly because of the expertise, it is quicker and easier to work here". However, the majority of activities required close interactions with customer representatives through the onsite team. Activities during the initial project phases that required direct customer contact and access to the customer's site, such as user requirements and release management, were done onsite. Activities that required involvement of the client and close interactions among the TCS developers were conducted in a mixed onsite-offshore mode. Overall, the majority of the activities required ongoing bi-directional knowledge transfer between onsite and offshore teams. The only activities that were undertaken independently at the offshore location were coding and unit testing. Table 2

Table 2 Knowledge transfer during project phases

Project phases	Knowledge transfer from onsite (Zurich, San Francisco) to offshore (Gurgaon, Bombay)	Knowledge transfer from offshore (Gurgaon, Bombay) to onshore (Zurich, San Francisco)	Knowledge transfer challenges
Requirement definition	Customer requirements		-Onsite team needs to capture all customer requirements (C1) -Offshore team should be able to understand correctly customer requirements as documented by the onsite team, i.e. definition and interpretation of requirements should be consistent between onsite and offshore teams (C2) -Offshore team members need to know who to contact onsite for different requirements if clarifications are required (C3)
Analysis and prototyping	Customer feedback on prototype design	Prototype design	-Onsite team should understand the prototype created offshore and be able to show and explain it to the customer, with minimum guidelines from the offshore team (C4) -Offshore team should be able to understand correctly customer feedback communicated in writing or verbally by the onsite team (C5) -Offshore team members need to know who to contact onsite for different issues that require clarifications (C6)
High-level design	Modified and signed specifications	Specifications	-Onsite team should be able to interpret product specifications created by the offshore team and understand how to address customer requirements (C7) -Offshore team should be able to identify quickly modifications made by the onsite team and interpret them correctly (C8)
Construction (Quartz configuration, coding and unit testing	N.A.	N.A.	-Few challenges as construction is carried out mostly offshore

Phase	Artifacts		Requirements
Integration and system testing	Actual system components and guidelines for integration and testing		- Onsite team should be able to understand functionality of the system components guidelines for system integration, with minimum guidelines for integration and testing (C9) - Members of the onsite team may ask for clarifications and/or help with debugging from the offshore team: they need to know who to contact offshore for different issues (in particular, who wrote codes for different system components) (C10)
		Change requests	- Offshore team members should be notified about new change requests (C11) - Members of the onsite team should be able to track the status of the changes they requested (C12)
	Changes to the system and guidelines for their implementation		- Onsite team members should be notified when change requests have been implemented (C13) - Offshore team members should know who to contact onsite if clarifications are required and/or when changes have been completed (C14) - Onsite team members should be able to understand the essence of the change and what aspects of the system may be affected by the change (C15)
Release management (system roll-out and user training)	Roll-out guidelines and training material		- Onsite team should be able to understand roll-out guidelines and how to use training material, with minimum guidelines and clarifications from the offshore team (C16) - Onsite team members should know who to contact for different issues / system components when they (or customer) have questions (C17)
	Clarifications, modifications	Questions, requests	- Onsite team should be able to quickly identify modifications done by the offshore team and know how to implement them (C18)

illustrates the knowledge transfer flows and challenges per project phase as described by the TCS engineers. Knowledge transfer challenges are identified (C1, C2, etc) for further analysis.

In the next section, we focus on some specific knowledge transfer challenges (from Table 2) to illustrate the way engineers at TCS dealt with these knowledge transfer challenges through the creation, use and updating of codified and personalized directories. We discuss knowledge transfer processes by examining encoding, storing and retrieving processes.

6.3 Knowledge Transfer: Encoding and Updating Codified and Personalized Directories

To overcome knowledge transfer challenges, TCS had developed a memory system that ensured the flow of knowledge between the client, onsite and offshore teams. To achieve effectiveness from this memory system, encoding of the knowledge and updating of directories took place. This was done through a set of rules and standards (for codified directories) and by propagating common terminology, language and concepts that team members use on a daily basis (for personalized directories). The encoding process supported the transfer of knowledge between onsite and offshore by creating a catalog of pointers to knowledge holders and knowledge seekers.

For example, one particular challenge is to transfer knowledge about customer requirements from onsite to offshore team (C2 in Table 2). In overcoming this challenge, onsite team members first codified customer requirements by summarizing them in writing, and following this the onsite team used a template document (e.g. Business Requirement Overview) to describe these requirements. More importantly, this template also encoded the subject and the location of this document. As members of the offshore teams were familiar with these templates and the Quartz terminology, they could locate the document, interpret customer requirements defined onsite (C2), and act upon them. One manager said:

'We have set procedures for defining the requirements. If people follow the procedures, then the things become very easy to interpret or understand.'

Similarly, during high-level design, to transfer knowledge from offshore to onsite about the prototype created offshore (C4), and to enable the onsite team to explain product specifications to the customer (C7), the offshore team encoded the subject and location of this knowledge using Business Requirement Specification templates and High Level Design Document templates. Onsite team members were familiar with these templates (the encoding scheme the templates are based on) and could easily locate the knowledge, understand the specifications created offshore and explain these to the customer. Furthermore, these documents specified the subject, and the name of the expert and his or her location, so that when a remote counterpart needed clarifications about this matter, he or she could easily locate the expert through this codified directory.

The use of standard templates to capture and transfer knowledge from onsite to offshore locations has created a cataloging system that served as a codified directory in which pointers to where information resides have been mapped out. Among the templates that were stored in this cataloging system were (1) procedural standards, such as the Quartz Implementation Methodology for the Quartz system, and (2) documentation standards that include (but are not limited to): the Project Documentation Set (Business Requirements Overview, Business Requirements Specifications, High Level Design Document, DB Design Document, Module Test Specifications, and Product Acceptance Testing Specifications), and the User Documentation Set (Online Help, User's Manual, Installation Manual, Operations Manual). The update of this directory took place each time new information was placed in this directory. For example, when the customer wanted to add new functionality to the prototype design, the onsite team captured this request in Business Requirement Overview template (C5) and created a new entry to the codified directory. This new entry updated the codified directory for both onsite and offshore teams.

Knowledge transfer challenges were also overcome through personalized directories by linking knowledge seekers with knowledge holders. For example, the Requirement Definition stage posed two knowledge transfer challenges (C2 and C3 in Table 2) that the overcoming of which may also depend on the existence of updated personalized directories among members of the onsite and offshore teams. Properly understanding customer requirements (C2) and knowing who to contact at the onsite team with queries (C3) required the offshore team to develop an understanding of the onsite team composition and the respective area of expertise per individual. Personalized directories as such offered an alternative route to the codified directory to transfer knowledge between onsite and offshore teams. Put simply, the constant interactions between onsite and offshore team members created and updated directories that were based on personal memory or other people's memory and that categorised personal experiences (what person A knows) and assigned 'labels' as to what other people know (what A knows about B) and what they know about what other people know (what A knows about what B knows about C). To arrive at such a personalized directory system and to support the development of common patterns for encoding personal knowledge about oneself and other people's knowledge, TCS introduced various activities to encourage interactions between remote counterparts and facilitate shared experiences, shared understanding of the design and the use of common terminology and language. As a first step toward bringing people together and developing a shared understanding of the product, a joint Quartz training program was introduced, compulsory for all employees joining the Quartz group. This program included introductory training during which new employees received an overview session of the Quartz platform and its components, learned about standard Quartz implementation methodologies and were introduced to the terminology used in this project. In addition, newcomers learned the basics of the programming language which was used to develop the Quartz platform. This training provided the basis for common encoding of information in personalized and codified directories that, in turn, improved understanding and created a basis for efficient knowledge transfer between future remote counterparts. For example, as one team leader described it:

"We all speak Quartz language. It is a loss for us if somebody leaves Quartz because for somebody new it will take time to learn Quartz".

Additional training programs were introduced in later stages of the project during which engineers were encouraged to develop their own expertise in one functional area of Quartz. This facilitated the development of mini-teams: though not co-located, each team still shared a specialized functional area and a similar understanding of that particular function. Furthermore, as stated earlier, some team members were rotated between onsite and offshore locations to increase face-to-face interactions between remote counterparts and to promote learning and the development of shared expertise between dispersed teams.

For members of globally distributed teams, updating personalized directories involves updating "what they know" and "what they know about what others know". In terms of updating "what they know", this had mainly relied on individuals encoding new experiences (e.g. about new product functionality) in their memory using 'labels' based on the Quartz terminology, standards and values. Because of the lack of face-to-face and informal interactions between onsite and offshore teams, updating "what they know about what others know" had mainly relied on regular teleconferences and short visits to remote locations by project leaders and some team members.

6.4 Knowledge Transfer: Allocating and Storing Information Through Codified and Personalized Directories

While the encoding process is important to overcome knowledge challenges through the development of a cataloging system, the storing process is imperative for knowledge transfer between onsite and offshore teams because of the risks involved in passing information between onsite and offshore. In such knowledge exchanges there is risk that information will be lost or dispersed in several locations. The storing process, in this regard, ensures the consistent allocation of information according to specific rules (e.g. information organized based on project stages) or according to expertise (information is transferred based on area of expertise). For example, feedback provided by the customer about the prototype design should be captured by the onsite team and transferred to the offshore team (C5 in Table 2). In this process, the TCS onsite team codified the feedback provided by the customer. Indeed, to ensure a consistent storing process, most of the documents used by the Quartz team to capture and codify knowledge were in a digital format and were available from one central location. To transfer this knowledge to the expert off-shore, two storing processes were possible. First, the member of the onsite team relied on his or her personalized directory to allocate the appropriate expert in the offshore team who should receive this information. The second storing process involved a codified directory, in the form of a database (e.g. project repository), which served as an intermediary holder for the knowledge prior to it being retrieved by the offshore expert. The codified knowledge was stored in an intermediary location, labelled according to the subject matter and the location of the expertise involved until the offshore team accessed this object and retrieved this information. Often, the transfer of knowledge was enacted through the use of both personalized and codified directories, i.e. storing the codified knowledge in an intermediary location and placing a call to the offshore expert, so that the effectiveness of the memory system was improved.

To ensure that members of the Quartz project used these documents in a consistent manner, i.e. could access, modify and store documents created by either the offshore or onsite teams, TCS have standardized the tools and methods used across remote locations. One manager explained:

> "In a distributed development environment, we need to clearly identify the quality processes to be followed and ensure commonality in the compliance of such processes. For example, common processes and tools for bug tracking, configuration management, release management, impact analysis, change management".

Indeed, through the standardization of tools and methods, TCS ensured the compatibility and the "integratability" of files, components and applications developed and used at remote locations. Such standardization supported the storing process because understanding "who is the expert" and "whom this knowledge should be allocated to" was commonly communicated and understood. Indeed, when an offshore team transferred knowledge about system components to the onsite team during the integration, the onsite team, we have learned, encountered almost no problems in taking over the integration, with minimum guidelines required from the offshore team (C9). The codified directory was constantly updated since the source code and various project documents were replaced by the new versions, creating new labels and pointers to knowledge holders within the team.

Knowledge transfer also benefited from the application of personalized directories during the storing process. In this regard, members of the onsite and offshore teams enhanced their acquaintance with the pool of expertise available within the project through a division of work based on expertise. One engineer described this process:

> "We [onsite and offshore teams] work in parallel: we send them the source code and they integrate it into the infrastructure before delivering it to the client [...] I'll check out our source code and send the code to the onsite team to work on it. Then they send the changed code back to me and I'll check it in".

One manager reiterated this point:

> "Between us [offshore] and our onsite team we say "we'll do this portion of the job because we have more competent people here who can look at this part, and then you can look at that portion of the job".

Through this systematic approach to the division of work, TCS ensured that knowledge is stored in dedicated storage locations (personal memories of individual team members). Activities generating new knowledge and developing new expertise were allocated to specific team members based on their present expertise or management's attempt to develop new expertise in the particular area. By basing the division of work on expertise, TCS encouraged individuals to interact and establish links with other remote counterparts who shared a similar functional specialization. In addition TCS utilized Centres of Excellence in various functional areas and technologies to disseminate expertise and bring expertise to where and when these were needed. Through such mechanisms, remote counterparts developed an understanding of the area of expertise in each remote location, which in turn assisted them to trace experts during the knowledge transfer process. Indeed, members of a dispersed project contacted remote counterparts to inform them about changes and share with them "experiences" related to the design process. In this regard, members of onsite and offshore teams used their counterparts as "storage" for personalized experiences, in which each member "stored" in his or her memory experiences relating to the area of expertise that the entire team had accumulated during the project. One manager explained:

> "Each and every team member is aware of nearly all the things which are happening, the whole team has a basic knowledge about everything".

Through frequent interactions between onsite and offshore teams, remote counterparts continuously updated information in their personal directories about what others know and what others do, which enabled remote team members to know whom to contact during knowledge transfer processes.

6.5   Knowledge Transfer: Coordinating the Retrieval Process Through Codified and Personalized Directories

To deal with some of the knowledge transfer challenges described in Table 2, the retrieval of knowledge required the application of search mechanisms to locate who held the knowledge and where, using codified and personalized directories. Such a retrieval process can successfully be achieved when the information is previously encoded and stored properly. For example, during integration and system testing, members of the onsite team may need to ask for clarifications and get help from the offshore team. In this specific project, the TCS onsite team needed to know whom to contact (C10). To overcome this knowledge transfer challenge, the onsite team could search the codified directory for experts who were involved in developing this particular code. This information was stored in the codified directory as part of the encoding and storing processes.

In addition, a central project repository was implemented to streamline the retrieval of information between onsite and offshore locations. For example, we have learned that during integration and system testing, an onsite team placed Change Requests into a web-based system (C11). These Change Requests were automatically assigned to the offshore team who notified by email about the additional customer requirements. The offshore team retrieved this information through the Change Request system and implemented the change. Following the completion of the change, the offshore team logged the solution and made the changes implemented accessible to the onsite team (C13). During the critical stages of system integration, this retrieval process allowed the transfer of critical information between onsite and offshore teams, based on the labels created in the encoding and storing processes, during the critical stages of system integration.

Nonetheless, in some situations when help from remote counterparts was urgently needed (e.g. C10: bugs fixing during acceptance testing), remote team members mainly relied on their own knowledge of "who knows what" recorded in their personalized directories to speed up the knowledge transfer process. The utilization of personalized directories for retrieving processes was mainly promoted through the coordination and integration of expertise across the various sites. In addition to familiarizing remote counterparts with the existing expertise in other locations and developing an expertise-based system for the division of labour, TCS invested in various mechanisms such as Centres of Excellence and a computerized-expertise system that allowed for searching for specific expertise among all TCS employees and that brought expertise together when it was needed. In this regard, the retrieval of personalized knowledge and the notion of personalized directories had evolved through expertise coordination and integration activities. Aspects that were critical for coordinating expertise revolved around time–zone differences and the notion of knowing "who is doing what". Indeed, members of the Quartz team indicated that it was common to contact remote counterparts at any time of the day. Flexible working hours even further supported person-to-person interactions for information retrieval despite time–zone differences. For example, one manager illustrated their communication patterns:

> "Within Quartz we can actually call up anybody whom we know at any point in time to get some assistance, even if we don't know somebody, if he's recommended by someone else, then we can call up and get assistance immediately".

Bringing in the needed knowledge to quickly solve problems also relied on the expertise-based division of labour that TCS had implemented across its onsite and offshore locations. Other mechanisms were put in place to coordinate the retrieval of information and to update personalized directories. For example, the management introduced various meetings and review sessions to familiarize and refresh the memory of team members with regard to "who is working on what". One interviewee described the implications of this approach:

> "It's not that only one person can do a job, otherwise, if one person doesn't come in, we won't be able to work without him/her. So we try to overcome this by making each and every team member aware of nearly all the things which are happening".

Lastly, onsite and offshore teams maintained a high degree of communication by phone, up to three or four times a day, which further assisted in keeping updated the notion of "who is working on what". Issues discussed during these conference calls, as observed, revolved around progress updates, handover of work from one team to another when a working day had ended, and clarifications with regard to changes and design problems. One engineer, describing the implications for transferring expertise within the team, explained that:

> "When a project is being established, proper ground work includes that everything should be conveyed and project information is shared among team members. [...] Each and every team member is aware of nearly all the things which are happening, the whole team has a basic knowledge about what others do".

As a result of these communications, interviewees claimed that they developed a better understanding of the team composition in a remote site and the areas of specialties that each member covered. This promoted knowledge transfer at various stages of the project.

7 Discussion

In current IS research, transactive memory is gaining ground as a powerful analytical concept (e.g. Akgun et al. 2005; Yoo & Kanawattanachai 2001). However, the implications for knowledge transfer have hardly been explored, particularly in the context of distributed teams. Therefore, the objective of this paper was to investigate how transactive memory enables knowledge transfer in globally distributed teams, and through what mechanisms a TMS can be created and maintained. Through a transactive memory perspective, we studied knowledge transfer between offshore teams in India and onsite teams in Western Europe and the US.

Indeed, as Table 2 conveys, globally distributed teams involved in offshoring activities face various knowledge transfer challenges. Furthermore, the transfer of knowledge between the customer, onsite and offshore teams almost always involves the codification of the knowledge prior to transferring it. This approach to knowledge, as described in the case above, is an attempt to overcome geographical distances between onsite and offshore teams and to enable the transfer of work from more costly onsite locations to the cost-effective offshore locations. However, such a codification of knowledge may increase the misunderstandings and errors involved in the transfer of knowledge because of local contexts, routines, and different skill and expertise levels between the customer, onsite and offshore teams. The Quartz case suggests that the standardized routines propagated by TCS assisted in creating memory systems that constantly update codified and personalized directories, enabling directory sharing regardless of the physical location of the teams, and offering multiple channels to effectively retrieve information when needed (Wegner 1995). More specifically, standards, guidelines and templates were developed to enable systematic encoding of the subject and location of the information to be exchanged between these teams. This information was allocated to individuals through an intermediary object (e.g. project repository and tools) that, in turn, supported the transfer of codified knowledge between onsite and offshore teams. While common methods for storing enabled compatibility and exchangeability of codified knowledge regardless of the geographical location and local contexts, search capabilities and the use of messaging to inform individuals about the relevant information available in knowledge bases were central in supporting the retrieval of codified knowledge.

The development of personalized directories, on the other hand, relied on individuals' knowledge of who knows what, and their engagement in interpersonal processes disclosing personal knowledge bases to others. Indeed, the Quartz project teams developed patterns for encoding, storing and retrieving knowledge in the sense of a common language (Barinaga 2002) and common patterns of communication. These were initially built through socialization and training. During later phases of the projects, the personalized directories were further developed through the division of work based on expertise, job rotations and regular communications.

From a social constructionist viewpoint (e.g. Lave & Wenger 1991), the Quartz's personalized directories mainly relied on the continuous development, management and coordination of expertise that supported encoding, storing and retrieving processes. Similarly, Orr (1990) has demonstrated how collective expertise could be developed through story-telling in a co-located environment. In this regard, personalized directories, that are "developed communally, over time, in interactions among individuals in the group" and that "exists more or less complete in the head of each group member who has been completely socialized in the group" (Leonard & Sensiper 1998, p. 121), may offer opportunities to remote counterparts to develop, manage and coordinate the collective expertise of the entire team through encoding, storing, and retrieving activities.

First, in the Quartz case, the encoding of project and product knowledge facilitated the development of collective expertise. Indeed, the initial Quartz training program for the entire global team facilitated the development of common terminology and understanding related to product development, project management, and collaborative processes. Through these training activities, members of the Quartz project team negotiated the meanings of various technical and administrative aspects involved in the project, devising a procedure for future engagement (Wegner 1987). In a later stage, short relocations and daily communications between onsite and offshore sites offered new opportunities to renegotiate procedures and redefine the terminology used by the team.

Second, the storing of knowledge enabled the management of collective expertise. This was mainly achieved through an expertise-based division of work. This approach to division of work resulted in the creation of multiple distributed teams consisting of like-minded experts who remotely collaborated on a particular aspect of the project (Evaristo & van Fenema 1999). As part of their personal development and through their participation in problem-solving activities, members of these expertise-based distributed teams relayed stories to remote counterparts (Lave & Wenger 1991). By negotiating the meaning of these stories, an understanding of "what A knows about what B (i.e. a counterpart) knows" emerged for A. This understanding assisted members of the expertise-based distributed teams to locate the most appropriate members, who share the same meaning and context, for future "storing" activities. In this way, members of the distributed team manage their knowledge of the expertise available within the team.

And third, through the retrieval of the knowledge the coordination of collective expertise within the distributed team is made possible. In retrieving knowledge, members of the team coordinated the transfer of knowledge needed for problem-solving. Indeed, retrieving information requires knowing "where expertise lies" (Faraj & Sproull 2000). The development of the meta-knowledge described above supported members of the expertise-based distributed teams when they (re)approached counterparts to "retrieve" knowledge. The retrieval of knowledge was largely enabled by the shared meaning and context that these teams developed throughout the project, supported by virtual and face-to-face meetings, and short visits.

We further argue that the three transactive memory processes, i.e. encoding, storing and retrieving, play different roles in knowledge transfer. First, the development of collective expertise, i.e. encoding, acts as a process for defining the procedure through which knowledge will be transferred. During the encoding, parties negotiate the meaning of knowledge (i.e. the subject and location of the knowledge) following either a codified, standardized approach or by relying on an embedded routine developed within the organization. Second, the management of expertise, i.e. storing, creates a pointer to the location where the knowledge is stored and from which it can later be transferred. In this regard, creating a pointer involves the actual storing activity during which A and B (following Fig. 1) attach particular labels to the knowledge stored within A, B or elsewhere. These labels – including for instance contextual information – make it possible to negotiate and clarify the meaning of this information, and its subsequent retrieval from its place of storage. And third, the coordination of expertise, i.e. retrieval, concerns the integration of knowledge by bringing together experts through search mechanisms and interpersonal contacts. For knowledge transfer to take place, teams rely on the one hand on the procedures and shared meanings established through encoding processes, and on the other hand, on interpretation and the use of labels attached to the transferred knowledge during the storing process. The coordination of expertise – and thus knowledge transfer – can be supported by relying either on the codified or personalized directories or both.

The question that we may pose at this juncture is: to what extent do personalized or codified directories matter to knowledge transfer? We claim that it would be wrong that either of these memory systems would be perceived as 'better' or 'worse' for knowledge transfer. In line with Cook and Brown's (1999) observation on epistemologies of knowledge, we argue that codified and personalized directories are best seen as two complimentary, rather than competing, memory systems (Sorensen & Lundh-Snis 2001). Furthermore, the findings of this study provide insights into how the two types of directories interact. They do not operate in isolation or as substitutes. Absence of the codified directories would deprive the teams of shared methods for encoding, storing and retrieving information, which may strain the personalized directories beyond feasibility. Leaving out the personalized directories, on the other hand, for instance due to high personnel turnover rates, would leave the project with independently working individuals who would find it difficult to agree on collaboration standards (Cramton 2001).

These insights lead to a conceptual question: how to theorize the interplay of codified and personalized directories? We suggest that groups develop meta-routines (Moorman & Miner 1998) that interlink the two types of directories. In this regard, there is a 'generative dance' (Cook & Brown 1999) between these two memory systems that contributes to the transfer of knowledge between A and B. The codified directories depend on interpersonal "norming" processes for defining standards, templates, and procedures. The personalized directories extend the codified system by offering additional avenues in cases when documents provide incomplete knowledge about a task. In these cases, individuals know whom to contact and how to retrieve information. Evidently, the development and use of a

TMS may change over time. During initial phases of the project, rudimentary parameters of transactive memory are defined (e.g. which sites and individuals are responsible for which tasks and knowledge domains). These are extended and refined when people work together over prolonged periods of time, re-negotiating meanings and re-generating learning around the knowledge transfer process.

In terms of the organizational mechanisms that create and maintain a TMS in a distributed context, we claim, based on the case reported above, that a TMS can be developed and maintained in order to support knowledge transfer through the propagation of certain rules and standardized work routines that can overcome differences in local contexts, skill levels and work routines. While such standardization also derives from an increased standardization in software development, evidence from the Quartz case suggests that TCS capitalize on this recent trend to offer remote counterparts a memory system through which knowledge can be exchanged. For example, the standardized templates that were used by the onsite team to capture customer knowledge were designed with the thought in mind that these would also be a pointer to where this knowledge resides. Other organizational mechanisms directed at offering remote counterparts opportunities to expand their personalized directories were also implemented. The rotation of team members, the expertise-based division of work that encouraged interactions between onsite and offshore teams, and frequent teleconferences, are only some of the mechanisms supporting the development of a TMS as an enabler for know-ledge transfer. Table 3 outlines these organizational mechanisms based on the three main processes in a TMS.

Table 3 Organizational mechanisms and processes supporting the development of a tms in globally distributed teams

	Codified directories	Personalized directories
Encoding / updating directories	-standard document templates (for product deliverables and process phases) -'Glossary of terms' to include unique (e.g. product-specific) terminology	-Rotation of onsite and offshore team members -Joint training programs -Team building exercises -Social activities
Storing / allocating information	-Central project repository -Standardization of tools and methods across locations -Centralization of tools on the central server, Web access	-Expertise-based division of work -Creating complementary documentation for software components (includes the name of the developer)
Retrieval coordination	-Standard process procedures (to include pointers to the location of information) -Keywords-based search capabilities -Tools that enable automated notification of changes and requests (e.g. Software Configuration Management and Change Management tools)	-Systematic and frequent communications using email, tele- and video-conferencing -Technologies that enable reachability when on the move and out of working hours (e.g. mobile phones, pagers, PDAs)

8 Implications

What implications does this study have for research and practice? From a theoretical perspective, this study advances understanding of knowledge transfer in distributed contexts and offers linkages to the concept of transactive memory. While the literature on knowledge transfer is extensive, little is known about the challenges involved in transferring knowledge between the customer representatives, onsite and offshore vendor teams. In addressing this gap, this paper outlined specific knowledge transfer challenges involved in the Quartz implementation project and explored through the lens of transactive memory how these teams transferred knowledge and overcame different local contexts, work routines and expertise levels. Indeed, the few studies that had explored the concept of transactive memory in distributed teams provided little insight, if any, into the possibilities to improve knowledge transfer processes through the development of a TMS. In particular, past research paid little attention to the possibility that transactive memory might act as an enabler of knowledge transfer in distributed teams. In addressing this gap, this study has illustrated how transactive memory supports knowledge transfer between onsite and offshore locations. Furthermore, by unpacking the concept of transactive memory and presenting two types of directories, namely, codified and personalized, this study extends the discussion about the elements that constitute a TMS in an organization. For instance, we extend the IS literature, which so far has somewhat downplayed the role of personalized directories and has often focused on codified directories in the context of distributed environments. In exploring the way knowledge was transferred between onsite and offsite locations, an array of processes and mechanisms associated with the personalized directories emerged. Furthermore, by offering a link to the development, management and coordination of collective expertise, this study emphasizes the role that collective expertise plays in knowledge transfer processes.

From a practical viewpoint, we argue that in order to enable the transfer of knowledge between remote sites, organizations should consider the mechanisms reported above that support the development, management and coordination of collective expertise, and enable the transfer of knowledge between onsite and offshore teams. In doing so, managers should consider two key aspects with respect to work division. First, they should attempt to select project members based on their shared histories of collaboration in their respective area of expertise. In doing so, remote counterparts know each other, have already developed a meta-knowledge relating to their counterparts and have established procedures for engagement. Such teams will tend to focus on re-negotiating and (re)clarifying meaning about knowledge transfer procedures and contexts. Such a staffing approach is likely to speed up the development of the TMS, as procedures, codified routines and social ties have already been established. Second, an expertise-based division of work should be considered when members of the team have worked with each other before and have developed shared histories. Teams that do not have shared histories, however, may benefit from a division of work that is based on geographical location for a period of time, which enables this team to establish procedures, standards and templates from the development of its codified directories, before changing to an expertise-based division of work approach.

References

Ahuja, M. K., Galvin, J. E. (2003). Socialization in virtual groups. *Journal of Management, 29*(2), 161–185.

Akgun, A. E., Byrne, J., Keskin, H., Lynn, G. S., & Imamoglu, S. Z. (2005). Knowledge networks in new product development projects: A transactive memory perspective. *Information and Management, 42*(8), 1105–1120.

Ancona, D., Bresman, H., & Kaeufer, K. (2002). The Comparative Advantage of X-Teams. *MIT Sloan Management Review, 43*(3), 33–39.

Armstrong, D. J., & Cole, P. (1995). Managing distances and differences in geographically distributed work groups. In S. E. Jackson & M. N. Ruderman (Eds.), *Diversity in work teams: Research paradigms for a changing workplace*. Washington DC: American Psychological Association.

Barinaga, E. (2002). *Levelling vagueness: A study of cultural diversity in an International Project Group*. Unpublished doctoral dissertation, Stockholm School of Economics, Stockholm, Sweden.

Beulen, E., van Fenema, P. C., & Currie, W. (2005). From application outsourcing to infrastructure management: Extending the offshore outsourcing portfolio. *European Management Journal, 23*(2).

Blackler, F. (1995). Knowledge, knowledge work and organizations: An overview and interpretation. *Organization studies, 16*(6), 1021–1046.

Boland, R. J., & Citurs, A. (2001). Work as the Making of Time and Space. *SPROUTS: Working Papers on Information Environments, Systems and Organizations, 2*, 1–15.

Carmel, E. (1999). *Global software teams: Collaborating across borders and time zones*. Upper Saddle River, NJ: Prentice-Hall.

Carmel, E., & Agarwal, R. (2002). The maturation of offshore sourcing of information technology work. *MIS Quarterly Executive, 1*(2), 65–77.

Chudoba, K. M., Wynn, E., Lu, M., & Watson-Manheim, M. B. (2005). How virtual are we? Measuring virtuality and understanding its impact in a global organization. *Information Systems Journal, 15*(4), 279–306.

Cook, S., & Brown, J. (1999). Bridging epistemologies: The generative dance between organizational knowledge and organization knowing. *Organization Science, 10*(4), 381–400.

Cramton, C. D. (2001). The mutual knowledge problem and its concequences for dispersed collaboration. *Organization Science, 12*(3), 346–371.

Currie, W. L., & Willcocks, L. P. (1998). Analysing four types of IT sourcing decisions in the context of scale, client/supplier interdependency and risk mitigation. *Information Systems Journal, 8*(2), 119–143.

Cutler, R. S. (1989) A comparison of Japanese and U.S. high-technology transfer practices. *IEEE Transactions on Engineering Management, 36*, 17–24.

Desouza, K. C., & Evaristo, J. R. (2004). Managing knowledge in distributed projects. *Communications of the ACM, 47*(4), 87–91.

Eisenhardt, K. M. (1989). Building theories from case study research. *Academy of Management Review, 14*(4), 532–550.

Evaristo, R., & van Fenema, P. C. (1999). A typology of project management: emergence and evolution of new forms. *International Journal of Project Management, 17*(5), 275–281.

Faraj, S., & Sproull, L. (2000). Coordinating expertise in software development teams. *Management Science, 46*(12), 1554–1568.

Feeny, D., Lacity, M., Willcocks, L. P. (2005). Taking the measure of outsourcing providers. *MIT Sloan Management Review, 46*(3), 41–48.

Grant, R. M. (1996). Toward a knowledge-based theory of the firm. *Strategic Management Journal, 17,* 109–122.

Hansen, M. T., Nohria, N., & Tierney, T. (1999). What's your strategy for managing knowledge? *Harvard Business Review, 77*(2), 106–116.

Jarvenpaa, S. L., & Leidner, D. E. (1999). Communication and trust in global virtual teams. *Organization Science, 10*(5), 791–815.

Kanawattanachai, P., & Yoo, Y. (2002). Dynamic nature of trust in virtual teams. *Journal of Strategic Information Systems, 11*(3–4), 187–213.

Kotlarsky, J., & Oshri, I. (2005). Social ties, knowledge sharing and successful collaboration in globally distributed system development projects. *European Journal of Information Systems, 14*(1), 37–48.

Lave, J., & Wenger, E. (1991). *Situated learning legitimate peripheral participation.* Cambridge: Cambridge University Press.

Leonard, D., & Sensiper, S. (1998). The role of tacit knowledge in group innovation. *California Management Review, 40*(3), 112–132.

Majchrzak, A., & Malhotra, A. (2005). Virtual workspace technology use and knowledge-sharing effectiveness in distributed teams: The influence of a team's transactive memory. *Knowledge Management Knowledge Base.*

Miles, M. B., & Huberman A. M. (1994). *Qualitative Data Analysis: An expanded sourcebook.* Thousand Oaks, CA: Sage.

Moorman, C., & Miner, A. (1998). Organizational improvisation and organizational memory. *Academy of Management Review, 23*(4), 698–723.

Moreland, R. L., & Argote, L. (2003). Transactive memory in dynamic organizations. In R. Peterson & E. Mannix (Eds.), *Leading and managing people in the dynamic organization* (pp. 135–162). Mahwah, NJ: Erlbaum.

Moreland, R. L., & Myaskovsky, L. (2000). Exploring the performance benefits of groups training: Transactive memory or improved communication? *Organizational Behavior and Human Decision Processes, 82*(1), 117–133.

Nevo, D., & Wand, Y. (2005). Organizational memory information systems: A transactive memory approach. *Decision Support Systems* 39(4): 549–562.

Nonaka, I. (1994). A dynamic theory of organizational knowledge creation. *Organization Science, 5*(1), 14–37.

Orr, J. (1990). Sharing knowledge celebrating identity: Community memory in a service culture. In D. Middleton & D. Edwards (Eds.), *Collective Remembering.* London, Sage.

Ridings, C., Gefen, D., & Arinze, B. (2002). Some Antecedents and Effects of Trust in Virtual Communities. *Journal of Strategic Information Systems, 11*(3–4), 271–295.

Sole, D., & Edmondson, A. (2002). Situated knowledge and learning in dispersed teams. *British Journal of Management,* 13, S17–S34.

Sorensen, C., & Lundh-Snis, U. (2001). Innovation through knowledge codification. *Journal of Information Technology, 16*(2), 83–97.

Strauss, A. L., Corbin, J. M. (1998). *Basics of qualitative research.* Thousand Oaks, CA: Sage.

von Hippel, E. (1994). "Sticky information" and the locus of problem solving: Implications for innovation. *Management Science, 40*(4), 429–439.

Wegner, D. M. (1987). Transactive memory: A contemporary analysis of the group mind. In G. Mullen & G. Goethals (Eds.), *Theories of group behavior.* New York, Springer.

Wegner, D. M. (1995). A computer network model of human transactive memory. *Social Cognition, 13*(3), 319–339.

Wegner, D. M., Giuliano, T., Hertel, P. (1985). Cognitive interdependence in close relationships. In W. J. Ickes (Eds.), *Compatible and incompatible relationships* (pp. 253–276). New York: Springer.

Wegner, D. M., Raymond, P., & Erber, R. (1991). Transactive memory in close relationships. *Journal of Personality and Social Psychology, 6*(6), 923–929.

Weitzman, E. A. (2000). Software and qualitative research. In N. K. Denzin, & Y. S. Lincoln (Eds.), *Handbook of qualitative research* (pp. 803–820). Thousand Oaks, CA: Sage.

Yin, R. K. (1994). *Case study research: Design and methods.* Newbury Park, CA: Sage.

Yoo, Y., & Kanawattanachai, P. (2001). Developments of transactive memory systems and collective mind in virtual teams. *International Journal of Organizational Analysis, 9*(2), 187–208.

Global Sourcing in a Developing Country Context: Organizing IS Resources to Develop Local Knowledge

Michael Barrett and Eivor Oborn

1 Introduction

With the move towards services in developing countries, firms in the financial sector are using global resources to drive new forms of revenue and growth (Forbath & Brooks 2007). In doing so, they are looking beyond their own national borders for partners to help design, develop, and maintain their information systems (Rao 2004). For these purposes, firms are accessing a growing pool of skilled IT professionals around the world in hot spots like India. Earlier research has focused on outsourcing and offshoring (Hirschheim, Heinzl, & Dibbern 2004; Sahay, Nicholson, & Krishna 2003), with less research on the insourcing of information systems (Hirschheim & Lacity 2000). Insourcing or 'contracting in', involves the delegation of IT within a business to an internal 'stand-alone' entity staffed with specialists, and has significant implications for the organizing of information systems (IS) resources in financial conglomerates.

Our study focused on an insourcing strategy adopted by a Jamaican insurance company, which was forced to redesign their information systems to meet the requirements of reinsurers, who provided them with much needed insurance capacity. Jamaica is a developing country known to be vulnerable to natural disasters, and dependent on global insurance and reinsurance for its economic stability and welfare. Throughout the 1990s, a reinsurance crisis ensued due to heavy underwriting losses, and global reinsurers demanded detailed risk information by type and location before offering insurance cover to local insurers. These actions accentuated local insurers' dependence on global reinsurers, and this also led to a number of sectoral level developments including the use of geographical information systems for hazard mapping to improve risk management.

However, Jamaican firms face a shortage of local information systems (IS) professionals and basic infrastructure (Roche & Blaine 1996), which is typical of developing countries (Austin 1990; Jarvenpaa & Leidner 1998). Acquiring and organising IS resources therefore became a central issue in developing their knowledge capacity for securing reinsurance. In the context of globalization and labour mobility, developing countries like Jamaica are increasingly adopting staff augmentation strategies such as the recruitment of talented Indian IS professionals to

R. Hirschheim et al. (eds), *Information Systems Outsourcing,*
© Springer-Verlag Berlin Heidelberg 2009

provide critical software development skills. This chapter examines how a local Jamaican insurance conglomerate, JAMSURE, sought to develop its local knowledgability through an insourcing arrangement staffed and led by Indian software professionals.

Companies such as JAMSURE, who acquire Indian expatriates as part of their IS strategy, face challenges in working across cultures, an under-explored phenomenon in a South–South context (Barrett, Drummond, & Sahay 1996; Walsham 2002). Recent studies of IS adoption in cross-cultural contexts (Liu & Westrup 2003; Shoib & Nandhakumar 2003) have highlighted a need to go beyond viewing culture as a static, fixed entity (Walsham & Sahay 2005). To understand cross-cultural working inherent in strategizing and (re)organizing IS resources at JAMSURE, we elaborate the organizational becoming perspective as a performative model of change (Tsoukas & Chia 2002) and draw on a knowledge in practice perspective (Orlikowski 2002) to more fully illuminate the microprocesses of change.

2 Theoretical Perspective

Our theoretical perspective examines the formation and development of the insourcing arrangement as a pervasive and emergent process, which both shapes and is shaped by the organizing of IS resources within a financial conglomerate. We also draw on a practice perspective of knowledge to explore the challenges faced by culturally diverse software professionals in accomplishing successful global insourcing. In particular, we draw on Polanyi's (1969) processes of tacit knowing to examine the knowledge sharing on the cross-cultural teams. We also use Wenger's (1998) communities-of-practice perspective, which emphasizes knowledge as acquired and understood through forms of participation in social configurations and continually negotiated and reproduced. This perspective is helpful in understanding changing social configurations when for example insourcing as a for-profit initiative is deployed within a financial conglomerate. Below, we briefly highlight these theoretical directions on radical change as organizational becoming and a practice perspective of knowledge prior to drawing on them in our case analysis.

3 Change as Organizational Becoming

Our starting point was to apply the concept of organizational becoming, a way of rethinking change, to the formation and ongoing development of an insourcing arrangement. Rather than considering change as a property of organization, Tsoukas and Chia (2002) argue that 'change is ontologically prior to organization' (p. 570) – in other words, organization is an emergent property of change. They view change as pervasive and ongoing, and organization as an emerging pattern that is constituted and shaped by change.

The organizational becoming perspective emphasizes change as a radical process theory, which connects to the practitioners' lived experience (Tsoukas & Chia 2002). Consistent with a performative model, IS research on change has recently recognized the role of human agency and enactment in practice (Orlikowski 1996, 2000). This research sees change as an improvisation 'grounded in the ongoing practices of organizations' (Orlikowski 1996) and not simply orchestrated from the top. Tsoukas and Chia (2002) argue that while these accounts are focused on change as 'situated and endemic to the practice of organizing', they tend to be unnecessarily conditional on the technology (e.g., groupware) being introduced and do not go far enough in recognizing the pervasive ongoing nature of change.

In the organizational becoming perspective, an organization is perceived to be both an established generic cognitive category and an emerging pattern drawn on by individuals-in-action. This means that organizations cannot have definitional control over radially structured cognitive categories, which recognize prototypical cases, as well as nonprototypical, peripheral cases. The reflexivity of individuals is critical in developing 'imaginative extensions' away from institutionalized prototypical cases (Tsoukas & Chia 2002) contributing to ongoing change.

Giddens (1991) connects individuals' reflexive thinking to a more collective institutional reflexivity in contemporary organizations at the macro level, which he argues is a consequence of 'chronic revision in the light of new information or knowledge' (p. 20). Recent IS literature on IT-enabled transformation (Barrett & Walsham 1999) has embraced this perspective, as have other researchers studying IS and organizational change in developing countries (e.g., Bada 2002; Barrett, Sahay, & Walsham 2001; Liu & Westrup 2003; Nicholson & Sahay 2001). In the context of a developing country, the dynamism of change involving diverse cultural working (Walsham 2002; Walsham & Sahay 2005) often accentuates reflexivity at multiple levels.

Tsoukas and Chia (2002) also emphasize that organizational becoming involves recognizing individuals' ability to draw new distinctions. Change is the 'reweaving of actors' web of beliefs and habits of action as a result of new experiences obtained through interactions' (p. 570). Tsoukas (2003) suggests that new knowledge 'comes about when our skilled performance is punctuated in new ways through social interaction.' We build on this connection to knowledge in developing organizational becoming as knowing-in-practice.

3.1 Knowledge Perspective of Practice

The knowing-in-practice perspective (Gherardi 2000; Orlikowski 2002) views knowing to be in our actions. In practice, 'knowing' is articulated as partial and indeterminate historical processes. As Orlikowski (2002) suggests, knowledge and practice are closely linked:

> "As people continually reconstitute their knowing over time and across contexts, they also modify their knowing as they change their practices. People improvise new practices as they invent, slip into, or learn new ways of interpreting the world" (p. 253).

Without developing it explicitly, Orlikowski links knowing-in-practice to an improvisational, performative model of change. This view recognizes that there is no objective, explicit knowledge independent of an individual's tacit knowing. Rather, drawing from Polanyi (1968), 'tacit power' supports the deep tacit knowledge held about the world which is the outcome of an individual's active shaping of experience and draws from individual values and dispositions.

As an example, analysts, in the practice of IS development, draw on their tacit understanding of client–user needs for an information system and then explicitly articulate this knowledge by writing a specification (spec). This process is repeated when programmers then code a system from the spec. Those programmers who draw tacitly from different work practices and industry experiences will arrive at different interpretations of the spec's meaning. Thus, a part of a programmer's knowledge is not just in the spec, but also in understanding how to use the spec in practice and involving users in system development. These components of tacit knowing are central to making the explicit knowledge encoded on the spec actionable (Walsham 2001), as tacit knowing lends meaning to explicit knowing and controls its uses (Polanyi 1968, p.156).

Another focus in the practice stream explores the implication that knowing in organizational settings is largely a situated and social phenomenon (Brown & Duguid 2001; Wenger 1998). We draw on Wenger's theoretical developments of communities-in-practice, which emphasize that knowledge is acquired and understood through forms of participation in social configurations and is continually being reproduced and negotiated. We focus on Wenger's concept of identity formation as processes of identification and negotiability. As Giddens has discussed (1990, 1991), the ongoing development of identity formation is integral to reflexivity in contemporary organizations, and characteristic of organizational becoming. Wenger suggests that participation in practice shapes our identification with these practices, and the meaning we give them (Wenger, p. 188). Our ability to negotiate the meaning of a practice helps us to develop ownership of that practice. In contrast, members of a community, whose contributions to a certain practice are never adopted, develop an identity of nonparticipation and are progressively marginalized. Personal goals, intentions and issues of group power dynamics will affect an individual's ability and willingness to negotiate and identify with various practices.

We draw on these interrelated theoretical perspectives of organizational becoming and knowing-in-practice to examine JAMSURE's insourcing strategy as an example of global sourcing in a developing country perspective. The organizational becoming perspective adopts a performative approach to examine the ongoing pervasive change associated with the insourcing arrangement, and the challenges faced in the 'becoming' of this practice within the financial conglomerate. The knowing-in-practice approach recognizes the way individuals' tacit knowing and power affect the ability of analysts and developers to work effectively in cross functional/cross cultural teams. Further, with the organizational becoming of an insourcing arrangement, identity formation as processes of identification and negotiability, is critical within social configurations and communities of practice, as exhibited in the formation of software teams, or in developing IS strategy across the financial conglomerate.

4   Research Methodology

4.1   Data Collection

Case studies are the preferred research strategy for a process study when an in-depth understanding of phenomena in the IS field is needed (Klein & Myers 1999; Walsham 1995). Our longitudinal study was conducted in three phases to examine the question: 'What were the organizing challenges faced by a Jamaican financial conglomerate in building local knowledgability through a global IS (in)sourcing arrangement?'

We adopted a contextualist approach (Pettigrew 1990) to guide the data collection efforts, examining the interrelationships between reinsurers, IT initiatives in the Jamaican insurance sector and IS development at the organizational and individual level, following global changes in the industry. We conducted interviews to examine a range of questions, geared to the participant being interviewed and the issues of importance at a given phase of the study. Questions were organized to examine (1) the content of change around IS and business innovations; (2) macro–micro contexts including global, sectoral, organizational, group levels; (3) exploring processes of human action influencing cross-cultural differences, and (4) political aspects concerning the global sourcing strategy and IS development.

In the first phase of the study, we focused on the macro level context of the global reinsurance crisis and the sectoral initiatives around geographical information systems (GIS) and hazard mapping. We drew on a number of secondary sources collected from sectoral studies, trade journals and local newspapers. In addition, 12 interviews were held with the Insurance College of Jamaica, the regional housing and urban development office, and insurance companies leading sectoral GIS efforts.

> Data collection at the organizational level started at the end of the first phase when access was negotiated through the chairman of JAMSURE. Based on the initial set of interviews, which focused on the adoption and use of IT for business innovation, three initiatives emerged: (1) the insourcing strategy to build knowledge capacity; (2) the ongoing development of heterogeneous IS teams; and (3) centralizing IS resources to enable a group IT strategy. Forty-two interviews were conducted over three phases with a wide range of participants: senior managers of JAMSURE and the software company, GROUPIT; the general insurance company, GENSURE; and the life insurance company, LIFE; project managers and developers at GROUPIT and GENSURE; and users and managers of GENSURE who were the target users of the GENSYS system. Figure 1 is a graphical representation of the different actors and entities and their interrelationships.

Because of the cross-cultural sensitivity that persisted between Indians at GROUPIT and Jamaican staff across JAMSURE, we took detailed notes during interviews rather than recordings. Primary textual data sources supporting the interview data include group strategy, IS strategy, mission statements, newsletters, and annual reports.

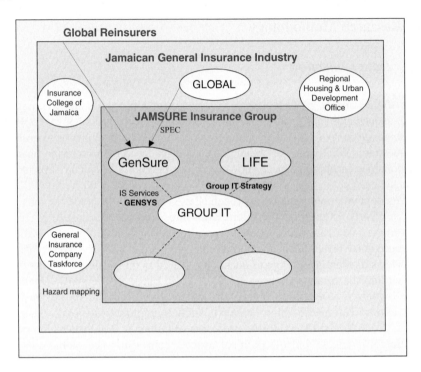

Fig. 1 Key fieldwork entities and their interrelationships

4.2 *Data Analysis*

Open coding was used at the level of analysis of key events and individuals'
responses to the ongoing change process. A 'key categories and issues' document
was written up synthesizing the change processes across macro–micro levels. This
document included descriptions of: macrolevel contextual issues in reinsurance
markets affecting local insurance practices; the challenges and response by key
leaders in the sector; the decisions made by JAMSURE to build local knowledge
capacity through an insourcing arrangement; and the subsequent development of
the software team. Further descriptions of cross-cultural attitudes, and broader
power relations within the team and across this highly decentralized group were
also captured. A further step in the coding analysis was the identification of recurring
themes from across these broad categories. These are presented in Table 1.

Finally, we drew on different theoretical perspectives to think about the information
(Feldman 2000; Langley 1999), specifically, Giddens' theory of change in late
modernity; globalization processes, their application and use in the IS literature;
and the organizational becoming literature. These literature streams enriched our
performative account of the change process and the macro–micro interdependencies,

Table 1 Themes identified in the data

Insourcing strategy to build knowledge capacity
• Coercive influence of changing reinsurer's requirement
• Interactions with GLOBAL led to insourcing as a prototypical strategy
• Labor mobility of IT professionals as opportunity for building knowledge capacity
Knowing in heterogeneous software development teams
• 'Spec' development requires different actors' knowledgeability
• Competing occupational mindsets reifies cross-cultural tensions
• Identification and definitional control a recurring challenge in cross-cultural working
Centralizing IS resources and the development of a group IT strategy
• Definitional control of IS resources by individual firms challenges group IT strategy
• Expatriate leader has difficulty using Kenyan experience in negotiating contracts in the Jamaican context

which were critical to the research setting. We also used theories of knowledge and knowing-in-practice from Polanyi (1968) and Wenger (1998) to deepen our understanding of the microprocesses of the change processes.

5   Case Description

Following Jamaica's independence from Britain in 1962, there were some significant changes in the general insurance industry, including deregulation and the rapid growth of locally owned Jamaican insurance firms. The reinsurance of the 1990s was a wake-up call for reinsurers who now demanded new levels of detailed risk information from local insurers, which were largely nonnegotiable. These actions reinforced the traditional 'heavy parent–child relationship' between reinsurers and Jamaican insurers.

One such local insurance conglomerate, JAMSURE, was well known as an innovative and highly diversified financial group of 27 companies grown through acquisitions, and with revenues of £200 million. This family firm turned financial conglomerate was started by a legendary figure in Jamaican insurance whose entrepreneurial flair and industry knowledge allowed him to take advantage of the business opportunities that followed independence. JAMSURE's vision was 'To become a Fortune 500 Group by 2000, through a team of motivated employees delivering innovative and superior quality service and products to our customers.' Along with his chief financial officer and group human resource (HR) manager, the JAMSURE chairman had been responsible for the genesis of the new general insurance system (GENSYS), which was deemed critical to meet reinsurers' new detailed information requirements.

Following an unsuccessful search for package software, JAMSURE made the decision to develop the software in-house. Instead of involving the MIS department at GENSURE, the top management commissioned the Jamaican office of a Big

Four consultancy firm, GLOBAL. This firm worked closely with top management and a user group at GENSURE to develop the functional specifications and initial design of GENSYS. During this interaction with GLOBAL, JAMSURE took the decision to in-source and establish a for-profit software company, GROUPIT, responsible for software development and coordinating a group IT strategy. Dr Prava and a number of other experienced software developers were hired from software houses in India to form the top management of GROUPIT. Dr Prava, the former president of an Indian software house, had a strong technical background and a PhD in Operations Research from a top US university.

GROUPIT developers were unable to build from the spec and they requested a more detailed design. Short-term help was solicited from GLOBAL to extend the spec as 'details were residing in someone's head there' as a GROUPIT developer noted. However, a further attempt at system development reinforced the need for additional local general insurance expertise in order to build the system. GENSURE's management information system (MIS) manager, together with a select development team from his department, was seconded to join GROUPIT. Despite the circumstances of GENSURE's late involvement and their feelings of being marginalized, there was initially genuine excitement and enthusiasm across this heterogeneous team about state-of-the-art system development and prospects for marketing it internationally. A culture of enthusiasm and knowledge sharing abounded, with weekly awards for the most helpful team member and project champion. A New Zealand insurance company shortlisted GENSYS in an international search for a flexible reinsurance system and a large multinational IT vendor agreed to market the system globally.

Development slowed, however, to the point where Dr Prava called an unsuccessful 'grievance meeting' to resolve team conflict, which centered on interpretations of the spec and the role of users, as well as Dr Prava's authoritative leadership style. Additionally, there was little collaboration between GROUPIT and the rest of the JAMSURE companies, where there were rumors about conflict, time delays and the GENSYS project coming in significantly over-budget.

A change of leadership at GROUPIT occurred shortly after GENSYS was delivered to GENSURE for attempted implementation, a year late. Another Indian, Raj, took over from Dr Prava, who remained as technical director. A computer science graduate from a prestigious UK university, Raj had significant experience running the IT branch of a large Kenyan conglomerate. More adept at social relationships and business development than Dr Prava, Raj's main remit was to develop a group IS strategy and to stimulate business development for JAMSURE, thus meeting the for-profit mandate set for GROUPIT.

However, Raj quickly became frustrated by his lack of progress in establishing the group IS strategy. The CEOs of companies in the conglomerate were unsupportive of his proposals for a centralized IS strategy. GROUPIT was not given any large projects from other JAMSURE companies, instead receiving what Raj called the 'step-brother' treatment. Furthermore, Raj, unable to connect with the Jamaican corporate community, was largely unsuccessful in winning contracts locally. This limited Raj's ability to successfully establish the company's profitability.

6 Case Analysis

Table 1 illustrates three initiatives that unfolded as JAMSURE sought to develop local knowledge capacity and to achieve internal growth strategies to become a Fortune 500 firm. Initiatives are separated out for analytical clarity, and were actually constituted by an ongoing processed of unfolding events, plans and actions. First, JAMSURE decided to build local knowledge capacity by hiring Indian expatriate senior managers to form GROUPIT. Second, the ensuing coding difficulties experienced by GROUPIT led to the addition of local MIS staff to the team. Third, JAMSURE attempted to centralize IS resources and develop a group IT strategy. In the first initiative we highlight macro and micro processes stirring and channeling change at a level of company strategy. The second examines change at a level of ongoing team interactions, while the third highlights the intra organization struggles and redirections in accomplishing change.

6.1 Insourcing Strategy to Build Knowledge Capacity

Obliged to respond to global reinsurer requirements for increased information, the chairman of JAMSURE was faced with the significant challenge of a scarcity of local IT skills. Lack of highly trained and skilled professional workers is a recurring problem in developing countries, which are constrained by access and opportunity costs of training. Despite this, the chairman was able to see positive possibilities. This legendary figure was well known across JAMSURE as someone who was 'always looking for opportunities, always questioning things. He is not adverse to criticism and not autocratic. He takes ideas to incorporate into his vision' (Raj).

For example, his vision for GENSYS was to design a system that would by-pass insurance brokers and allow for new partnerships with reinsurers:

"Reinsurance (in the future) would be seen much more as a partnership, full information allowing for full participation"(Chairman).

JAMSURE's chairman looked beyond the latest requirements from global rein-surers; he did not share the views of others in the industry that they, as insurers, were 'helpless dependent victims'. Instead, he believed that developing knowledge capacity would enable new interactions and facilitate partnerships with reinsurers on commercial ventures. A strategic review identified IT development as a priority for JAMSURE and affirmed the chairman's belief that information technology and a group IT strategy were foremost in this process of becoming:

"Without technology, standards, and quality, we can forget ever attaining our goals and mission" (Chairman).

Before making the decision, top management considered options for software development. The finance director explained:

"The options …were to hire what scarce IT resources were available in Jamaica but it was then difficult to retain them. Another possibility was to use GLOBAL and their consultants to do all the work."

Top management had little faith in GENSURE's MIS group, who had no experience with large- scale state-of-the-art software development, and GLOBAL was given the first phase.

The finance director's interaction with GLOBAL gave him the idea of replicating GLOBAL's acquisition of IT skills by hiring Indian expatriates. He noted:

> "I realized that what GLOBAL was doing was to employ a consultant, mark his wage rate up three times and then charge the client… So I had the idea to bring skilled people in as GLOBAL did from India and replicate GLOBAL in an IT division for the group. India was an appropriate market with a large volume of IT professionals with experience."

This insourcing strategy met with top management's approval. In identifying with GLOBAL as a Fortune 500 company to which they aspired, JAMSURE viewed this as a prototypical case of IS development and a legitimate strategy to mimetically adopt. It also seemed to fit as the 'right' option for strengthening 'local' knowledge capacity within JAMSURE. The software development was put out to tender and GROUPIT went on to underbid GLOBAL and secure the follow on build phase of GENSYS.

Throughout the development of GENSYS, reinsurers' requirements changed. For example, reinsurers changed their treaty structures to include territories as well as products and perils, and later on risk category (e.g., earthquakes) was added to the requirements. Dr Prava explained:

> "Reinsurers have started spelling out different levels of risk based not only on products and perils, but also territories… including different rate structures. This involved a change in the system design to keep track of the territories."

These dynamic shifts in information requirements constantly plagued software development efforts and required design and code modifications. These changes arose less from the improvisational efforts of those involved but more from the darker orchestration of global reinsurers within a dependent 'heavy parent–child' relationship.

The unfolding nature of events and actions in this initiative highlight the pervasive ongoing nature of change. Since its inception JAMSURE had been responding and organizing around the changing context, often through a variety of growth initiatives. Following a wake of natural disasters, the reinsurance crisis was another impetus for reorganizing. Drawing on his vision to build a Fortune 500 company and goals to improve their technological capacity, the CEO responded by hiring a multinational consulting firm. However, after the initial specifications were complete, they redirected plans to insource software professionals from India to build inhouse programming capacity. Though a specification had been set, the requirements from reinsurers in Europe had not. This ongoing pattern of change, redirecting plans, shifting requirements, and imagining new opportunities, develops both within and external to the organization.

6.2   Knowing in Heterogeneous Software Development Teams

GROUPIT professionals drew on their knowledgability of software house practices in their attempts to achieve competent 'delivery' of GENSYS and build a reputation within JAMSURE. Initially, they worked by themselves to code directly from GLOBAL's spec. However, after a few weeks it became obvious that they were unable to code from the spec. The programmers blamed this on the lack of detail in the spec:

> "The GLOBAL specifications from which the reports were written were inadequate. The reports needed to be redesigned incorporating insurance knowledge and customized to GENSURE's operation (GENSURE MIS staff)."

A GLOBAL consultant who had developed the initial spec was hired to clarify it and provide more detailed specifications. Despite this, GROUPIT programmers – who lacked contextual knowledge of the insurance sector, user needs and local industry – were still unable to code the GENSYS system successfully from the revised spec.

GLOBAL, drawing on their past experience, had developed the original spec by consulting users and managers to clarify and understand JAMSURE's needs. The consultants gradually built up a comprehensive understanding of overall system needs according to the numerous and diverse accounts given. They could make a core component of this largely tacit knowledge explicit in the spec. However, the deep tacit knowing that made the spec meaningful and actionable remained inside their heads.

Although the Indian programmers were hired for their expert coding skills, they lacked the tacit contextual knowledge, related to local industry practices, needed to code meaningfully from the spec. Instead, having 'different interpretations' they developed a multiplicity of meanings and were 'unable to develop the detailed design' as a Jamaican developer noted. A group of GENSURE MIS staff were subsequently seconded to work with GROUPIT to improve group knowledge capacity. These people were carefully selected based on their promising technical skills and close involvement with end users. The Indian programmers would share the necessary programming skills and the MIS staff would contribute the unique features of local insurance system requirements to achieve effective integration. This was nicely summarized by a GROUPIT developer:

> "There were delays due to inadequacies of design… GENSURE MIS, who had a better understanding of what functionality was required, along with a few users, played a critical role in quality control and carrying out major reworks."

6.3 Diverse Cultural Practices as Barriers to Sharing Knowledge

At first, morale was high among the Jamaican MIS staff, who were excited and valued this privileged opportunity. However, after a few months, they were having trouble embracing software house practices. They complained that the weekly deadlines were unrealistic. They referred to the 'competitiveness engendered in Indian software houses' and perceived Dr Prava's 'scientific precise, detailed project management' approach as autocratic, 'laying down the law'.

It was initially hoped that the MIS staff would learn programming and project management skills through close collaboration and open sharing with the more experienced Indian programmers. However, missed deadlines put enormous time pressures on both parties, squeezing out opportunities for learning and knowledge sharing. One Jamaican commented:

"Some of them were hard working but others I didn't relate to well at all. On the other hand, they found us too slow."

The Jamaicans' discomfort with team working reflected the independent occupational culture in MIS departments, very different from the world of software development. A Jamaican MIS team leader explained:

"I was not used to the interpersonal relations of the closely knit teams… I was reluctant to fully integrate into the environment …The use of language was different and the official environment was different to what we were used."

MIS developers experienced great difficulty 'entering into the world' of or identifying with the rules of a 'closely knit team' and the strict adherence to deadlines that seemed – at least to them – to be the prototypical case of development in software houses.

Jamaican workers conceived the leader's monitoring and control of activities as inappropriate. As might be expected, this contrasted with Dr Prava, who summarized his experience with Jamaicans as:

"Everybody [Jamaicans] treats everyone as equal… If something is due at the end of the month you are not to intervene as the boss…The attitude is, "I will tell you if the job is done or not done" …They don't want a monitoring system… It is demeaning for the boss to ask about progress of activities in between tasks."
He went on to say how this contrasted with his experience in India:
"If I assign a job in India, as the boss I would ask if there were any problems at the end of the day… The Indian would not feel he is being watched but rather that I am helping him reach his end point."

The MIS staff were unable to adapt swiftly to software house routines, and felt that their knowledgability had been undervalued and largely ignored. Instead of being able to contribute their tacit knowing of user expectations and contextual insurance knowledge to the software team, they felt dominated. A Jamaican developer noted:

"The feeling by most GENSURE staff was that the Indians had been given power over the Jamaicans …The whole project had been taken away from them."

Having had experience with the old system as well as its users, the Jamaicans wanted more control of the development of GENSYS, yet they had little definitional control of work practices. Feelings of perceived injustice surfaced and strengthened as the initial expected benefits of learning started to disappear; the pressures of timelines, and increased competitiveness, led to less knowledge sharing. The feelings of discontent and power asymmetry were heightened when Dr Prava suddenly dismissed the most technically competent Jamaican team leader, who was also the assistant manager of the GENSURE MIS department. The CEO of GENSURE explained:

"There was an atmosphere of mistrust and resentment which resulted in a lack of ownership and political tensions."

One manager commented that the Indian programmers kept changing their stories:

"We couldn't trust them…we had to put everything in writing; they always changed the stories, one thing here, another thing there."

Low levels of identification with the project on the part of the Jamaican MIS workers, and their lack of negotiability, led to decreased participation in the process. The grievance meeting that Dr Prava called highlighted the deep feelings of resentment the MIS staff felt about loss of control and lack of ownership in the project:

> "At the grievance meeting it was largely felt that the top positions were held by Indians, with Jamaicans working for them."

6.4   Knowledge Sharing in Practice

The diverse team, common in development contexts, brought together workers who drew on very different socially defined rules and habits of action, making knowledge sharing more difficult (Nelson & Cooprider 1996). The unequal distribution of power relations among the sub groups within the team led to resistance and disengagement by the Jamaicans, who lacked the ability to influence events (Nelson and Cooprider). There was a general loss of collaboration. Increasingly, GROUPIT became known as a poor performer across the JAMSURE group. The delivery of GENSYS was severely delayed and could not be successfully implemented.

JAMSURE's strategy to improve local knowledge capacity was developed in a context of western rationality. They sought to recontextualize team members with appropriate skills in the hope that knowledge would somehow be shared and combined. Little consideration was given to the process of re embedding established meanings and rules in a new context. As Tsoukas and Chia (2002) highlight, the application of a concept (for example, responding to deadlines), is a normative act presupposing value-laden background assumptions like the priorities of work and proper behavior at work, which are drawn on tacitly.

In the context of this cross-cultural team, diverse socially defined rules and values remained largely undiscussed. The active determination of these rules in practice was being applied to marginal cases: the Indian workers were not working in the programming environment of a software house in India and the MIS staff were not modifying system needs at users' request. Cross-cultural working involves people from multiple contexts, cultures and work backgrounds, and so requires numerous 'imaginative extensions' and increased reflexivity in the redefinition of work practices.

7   Centralizing IS Resources and the Development of a Group IT Strategy

JAMSURE's third initiative for building local knowledge capacity involved centralizing IS resources and developing a group IT strategy to facilitate growth and profitability. Raj was recruited as the new leader of GROUPIT to improve business development. He had had 25 years of IS experience, including the development of a group IS strategy in a Kenyan conglomerate. However, he soon realized that he faced three obstacles in facilitating the change process.

First, 'each company had its own strong MIS department' and 'things had not been properly spelt out' about GROUPIT's role within JAMSURE before his arrival.

"The operating companies are all very anti GROUPIT, protecting their turf, feeling threatened, and wanting control... The very existence of GROUPIT is seen as a threat to the individual companies, especially to their MIS department... They would only offer GROUPIT the dregs of projects."

The local MIS departments were resistant to ceding control of their resources. As an expatriate, Raj found cross-cultural working and negotiating contracts with other Jamaican firms a challenging proposition:

"Being a foreigner makes things more difficult. There are a lot of cliques and networks difficult to break into. Business is very much done by whom you know... I have never worked on such a small island before where everyone knows everyone else."

Second, GROUPIT already had a poor reputation in the conglomerate. Raj experienced these sentiments first hand with the group's life insurance company. LIFE's profitability and leadership role in the Jamaican life insurance industry was attributed to the company's early and successful use of IT for competitive advantage. Raj's proposal to redevelop some of LIFE's strategic systems using state-of-the-art technology fell on deaf ears as the stories of GENSYS's delays, cross-cultural differences, and cost overruns spread quickly across the group. The vice president (VP) at LIFE was quick to highlight GROUPIT's poor reputation:

"The ongoing problems of the implementation of the GENSYS have not injected any confidence that such a system (if undertaken) can be successfully developed and implemented... The relationship has been less ideal, the service has not been good... There has been a lot of turnover at GROUPIT and a number of HR issues."

Third, the conglomerate's fragmented culture presented Raj with a significant challenge. JAMSURE was still trying to integrate a number of recently acquired companies, many of which were highly successful and had strong corporate identities. A senior VP of LIFE noted:

"The group concept is a difficult task with the diversity of operating companies. It is difficult to superimpose a group culture on the individual culture of these acquired firms."

Raj agreed that there was a lack of commitment to the group, pointing to the symbolism of LIFE's letterhead to make his point:

"It has a large logo for LIFE at the top of the paper, with a footnote at the bottom (in fine print) a member of the JAMSURE Group"

As the general manager in charge of finance at GENSURE put it, 'The management team are all moving to the sound of a different drummer.' The vision and strategy formulated by the JAMSURE leadership for improving local knowledge capacity had 'open' interpretations, highlighting that change strategies are precarious and indefinite.

As a result, LIFE and other companies in the group fought to retain definitional control of IS resources, although open challenge was less evident in top management meetings:

"At group meetings the CEOs of firms would not be upfront. Instead, they would agree to everything and then nothing would seem to happen once they were back at their individual companies (GROUPIT leader)."

However, this was not the case at the annual IT strategy retreat. Raj's presentation of possible alternatives for a group IT strategy received open opposition and criticism. He was dejected and felt unsupported by key members of the top management team who did not attend the meeting. He blamed JAMSURE's 'consensus approach' to management and believed the lack of autocratic leadership was severely hampering the implementation of the group's vision for IT:

> "The leadership, including the chairman, accepts a lot more from people than should be tolerated. Unless you are sort of autocratic nothing will happen… However, the attitude in the group is "Don't be too autocratic; if an individual says something don't put him down, let him talk.…The culture is such that each person thinks they know what is good."

For Raj, knowing how to develop a group IT strategy for the conglomerate went well beyond his 25 years' experience, and depended crucially on identification processes as well as negotiability. He was more accustomed to hierarchical working with autocratic leadership and unable to identify with the 'relationally' based way of working on a small island. This was similar to the issue faced by Dr Prava in leading the cross-cultural software team, but Raj's starting point was quite different. From the onset, he was unable to get 'buy in' and his strategies were met with apathy rather than open resistance. Perhaps unsurprisingly, other companies were not interested in giving up resources and power for the common good of meeting top management's goal for the group – becoming a Fortune 500 company.

Raj was unable to extend imaginatively and re embed his knowledge of a prototypical group IT concept from Kenya to Jamaica. An autocratic leadership style was more likely to be supported in Kenyan business, where Indians often hold top management positions. Further, the socio-historical context of politics and power relations in Jamaica affected Raj's negotiability in extending a group IT strategy at JAMSURE, which was for him a nonprototypical case.

The failure of the insourcing arrangement to effectively support the group IT strategy and in software development led top management to be reflexive as to its appropriateness as a strategy. Somewhat ironically, GLOBAL was brought back into the picture for consultation of the matter. They recommended that GROUPIT be disbanded as well as JAMSURE's individual MIS groups, and that a renewed attempt should be made to centralize the group's IS strategy.

8 Implications for Practice

8.1 Building Local Knowledge Capacity through Acquisition of IT Resources

The case of JAMSURE raises implications for developing country firms hiring Indian expatriate IS professionals. First, it highlights the key challenges of adopting an insourcing strategy. Unlike GLOBAL, JAMSURE lacked a supportive infrastructure of software professionals and methodologies. Instead, the company had to rely almost exclusively on local resources across the group's highly decentralized political context. Further, GLOBAL was run by a Jamaican chairman and had senior Indian and Jamaican personnel, experienced in working as a corporate consulting team. A key implication for developing country conglomerates adopting an insourcing arrangement is to go beyond the mere acquisition of IT expatriates. Careful consideration should be given to the appropriate structure, composition, and leadership.

Second, the nature of the skills of recruited expatriates is a crucial part of the decision. Dr Prava, although technically competent, lacked boundary spanning abilities to facilitate knowledge sharing across different vocational and cultural contexts. Later, Raj was unable to identify and to translate his IS group strategy skills from Kenya to Jamaica, and experienced significant difficulty negotiating within the decentralized organization.

The implication is that expatriate leaders need to consider sensitively the political and power contexts, and negotiate ownership and control appropriately, difficult as this may be. This requires leaders not only to have a supportive structure and culture to facilitate their negotiability, but also to cultivate a context of power sharing, and foster participation with locals.

8.2 Organising IS Resources through Cross-Cultural Software Development Teams

Our case provides insights into organizing IS resources through cross-cultural teams composed of members from both functionally and nationally diverse backgrounds. As recently summarized (Milliken & Martins 1996; Williams & O'Reilly 1998), these heterogeneous teams are particularly difficult to develop, experiencing more conflict (Jehn, Northcraft, & Neale 1999) and difficulty with communication (Lovelace, Shapiro, & Weingart 2001; Smith et al. 1994) than homogenous groups. Seminal work on team conflict in IS development (Robey, Farrow, & Franz 1989) has modeled the role of team member influence in creating and resolving conflict, and this has been expanded to highlight the key role of increased participation (Barki & Hartwick 1994; Hartwick & Barki 1994). While conflict in software development teams is frequently encountered (Guinan, Cooprider, & Faraj 1998), teams that work in cross-cultural contexts may be particularly vulnerable to conflict.

Our research goes further, highlighting that in order to gain 'fuller' participation, members need to negotiate meaning and develop identification with common routines of practice. An important implication, then, is for team members to have an early focus on discussing the assumptions and routines of practice. Though Dr Prava did call a grievance meeting, it was too late. An earlier focus on developing respect for others and learning new ways of practice rather than the more immediate task focus on deadlines could have mitigated the blame culture that ensued. Similarly, Ely and Thomas (2001) suggest that showing respect for and valuing culturally divergent priorities, experiences, and perspectives enables multiculturalism to act as a resource for team members rather than as a threat.

A second implication relates to the crucial role of leadership in heterogeneous teams (Lovelace et al. 2001). Williams (2001) suggests that obtaining trust from members of other backgrounds is particularly challenging for team leaders. As the JAMSURE case suggests, it is important for team leaders to heed the fragile and volatile power dynamics and shift them to suit group needs best, rather than assume that previously used leadership styles will suffice (Ely & Thomas 2001).

Our findings also suggest that IS teams in a developing country context should attempt to redress the existing knowledge/power asymmetry (given the low local IS skills) to allow local staff (who are often vulnerable, due to the assumed status of expatriate staff) to contribute more centrally to negotiation of team-based practices. Jamaica's recent socio-political and historical context seems to have heightened general feelings about domination by foreigners and made it more difficult for the leaders to build knowledgability across the diverse team. As we discussed, the dismissal of the most expert Jamaican programmer was viewed as unfortunate, symbolizing a failure to harness effectively the diverse knowledge bases of the members and to balance knowledge/power asymmetries.

9   Implications for Theory

We developed a knowing-in-practice perspective to contribute to a deeper understanding of the microprocesses of organizational becoming, particularly through concepts of tacit knowing, identification, and negotiation. While these theoretical developments were useful in our analysis, our case has also contributed to the further development of this perspective, as highlighted in Table 2. Specifically, our findings emphasize the importance of power and socio-political contexts in the change process, supporting a recent call by Boudreau and Robey (2005) to account for social influences. Our case also highlights that the performative perspective of change would benefit from a mixed analysis, examining how broader contexts interpenetrate the individual level (cf. Markus & Robey 1988). For example, local global interdependencies involved contexts of power whereby global reinsurer demands influenced the ongoing improvisational practices of actors in the local insurance group. These findings support other recent criticisms (Contu & Willmott 2003), which argue that power needs to be more adequately and systematically theorized within situated contexts.

Table 2 highlights that the decision to build knowledge capacity through reorganizing IS resources was a response to demands for information from global reinsurers. These power relations affected the GROUPIT software development process adversely. Instead of being able to code from a fixed spec, typical of Indian software house practices, ongoing changes in system requirements made it difficult for the cross-cultural team to meet deadlines. These coercive interdependencies therefore affected both strategies and work practices in directing the unfolding change. Power relations significantly influenced cross-cultural working and the development of knowledgability throughout the change processes. Additionally,

Table 2 Adapted theoretical perspective with case findings

Organizational becoming	Knowledge perspective in practice	Case findings
Reflexivity enables the ongoing reweaving of actors' webs of beliefs and habits of action as a result of new experiences	Explicit knowledge is made actionable through tacit knowing	• Entrepreneurial beliefs and habits shaped chairman's decision to adopt insourcing strategy • Raj attempted to re embed management practice from Kenyan conglomerate in Jamaican context
Change involving individuals' interaction within diverse social configurations influences definitional control	Knowing involves identity formation as processes of identification and negotiability	• Jamaican MIS staff were unable to identify with the world of software house practice and to negotiate the use of deadlines.
Global context of change involves key Local–Global (Inter-) Dependencies	Power in broader socio-historical structures influences negotiability within and external to social configurations	• Coercive interdependencies of reinsurers affected local strategies and work practices in directing the unfolding change • Socio-historical practices across strong individual companies (local) challenged development of group strategy (global).

broader structural inequities and related socio-political elements influenced negotiability within social configurations.

Table 2 also shows how our case illustrates the way in which historical practices across strong individual corporate identities inhibited both the development of a unified group culture and the formation of a centralized IT strategy. In particular, successful individual companies could resist and subvert the organizational changes being adopted. This situation highlights how institutions as 'deeply embedded practices' (Giddens 1984) influence how 'history' affects our way of knowing and the reweaving of actors' beliefs and actions. The lack of autocratic leadership in directing and channeling the change process towards the desired strategy was particularly challenging in the conglomerate's diverse social configuration of largely acquired companies.

10 Conclusions

Our study examines how a developing country conglomerate acquired and reorganized IS resources through an insourcing arrangement to develop their local knowledge capacity. Theoretically, we draw on a knowing-in-practice perspective to deepen our understanding of microprocesses of organizational becoming. We draw on Polanyi's (1968) understanding of tacit knowing and Wenger's (1998) processes of identification and negotiability to examine organizational change within diverse social configurations, which is particularly characteristic of developing countries (Avgerou 2002). Insights from our case analysis also emphasize how broader power and socio-political structures and interdependencies constrain and enable knowledgability.

We go beyond a 'knowledge transfer' approach to understand processually the challenges JAMSURE faced in their efforts to build knowledge capacity. Case insights suggest that Indian firms should go beyond being a provider of technically skilled resources and implementing strong software methodologies. They should also promote human capital resources such as leadership and managerial skills in their staff to improve knowledge sharing across diverse boundaries (Carlile 2004; Pawlowski & Robey 2004), between expatriates and local staff. Furthermore, expatriates who are sensitized to processes of identification and negotiability may be better able to re embed their knowledgeable practices within new contexts.

Another useful theoretical approach would be to examine trust development in occupationally and nationally diverse communities so as to improve knowledge sharing between diverse programming communities. As pointed out by Nelson and Cooprider (1996), trust and influence are important in sharing knowledge but are hindered where 'shared reality' is limited. In our context, not only were the occupational communities different, but the diversity of national cultures further compounded the problems in the knowledge sharing process by contributing to in-group versus out-group tensions (Ashforth & Mael 1989; Taijfel 1981), constraining the development of trust.

Our findings also resonate with classical debates about IS centralization. Resistance to centralization efforts in large decentralized companies (e.g., Markus 1983) is not unique to a developing country context. Furthermore, some of the software development challenges experienced at JAMSURE also have wider applicability to IS development teams in developed countries with differences in occupational cultures, or within staff augmentation teams made up of developed country professionals and Indian expatriates. However, we suggest that some issues are unique to developing country contexts. First, it is much more common for developing country firms to be in need of expatriate staff because of a lack of locally available skill and knowledgability; they rely heavily on knowledgeable 'others' to secure financial capacity. This compounding of dependence relationships may put developing country staff at greater risk of losing local ownership, and can magnify national differences. Secondly, South–South arrangements are a newer phenomenon with less history of taken-for-granted hierarchies and ways of working. Given these more precarious and uncertain contexts of power relations, heightened sensitivity on both sides is needed, given the diverse practices and cross-cultural routines of working (cf. Walsham 2002).

Finally, we believe our findings are valuable in other contexts. For example, while offshoring has been a growing trend in global sourcing of IS (Sahay et al. 2003), the formation of cross-cultural teams is increasingly common in these

North–South arrangements. Client firms seek to leverage Indian offshoring expertise by forming teams comprised of onsite staff from the offshoring group along with client staff for software development. Future research could explore the development of teams in these North–South contexts as well as the use of offshoring strategies by developing country firms with their own particular issues and needs.

References

Ashforth, B., & Mael, F. (1989). Social identity theory and the organization. *Academy of Management Review, 14*, 20–39.

Austin, J. (1990). *Managing in developing countries*. New York: Free Press.

Avgerou, C. (2002). *Information systems and global diversity*. Oxford: Oxford University Press.

Bada, A. (2002). Local adaptations to global trends: A study of an IT-based organizational change program in a Nigerian bank. *The Information Society, 18*, 77–86.

Barki, H., & Hartwick, J. (1994). User participation, conflict, and conflict resolution: the mediating roles of influence. *Information Systems Research, 5*(4), 422–438.

Barrett, M., Drummond, D., & Sahay, S. (1996). Exploring the impact of cross-cultural differences in international software development teams: Indian expatriates in Jamaica. In J. D. Coelho, W. Konig, H. Krcmar, R. O'Callaghan and M. Saaksjarvi (Eds.), *Proceedings of the Fourth European Conference on Information Systems*, Lisbon, Portugal.

Barrett, M., Sahay, S., & Walsham, G. (2001). Understanding IT and social transformation: GIS for natural resources management in India. *The Information Society, 18*(2), 5–20.

Barrett, M., & Walsham, G. (1999). Electronic trading and work transformation in the london insurance market. *Information Systems Research, 10*(1), 1–22.

Boudreau, M. -C., & Robey, D. (2005). Enacting Integrated Information Technology: A Human Agency Perspective. *Information Systems Research, 16*(1), 3–18.

Brown, J., & Duguid, P. (2001). Knowledge and organization: A socio-practice perspective. *Organization Science, 12*(2), 198–213.

Carlile, P. (2004). Transferring, translating and transforming: An integrative framework for managing knowledge across boundaries. *Organization Science, 15*, 555–568.

Contu, A., & Willmott, H. (2003). The importance of power relations in learning theory. *Organization Science, 14*(3), 283–296.

Ely, R., & Thomas, D. (2001). Cultural diversity at work: The effects of diversity perspectives on work group processes and outcomes. *Administrative Science Quarterly, 46*, 229–273.

Feldman, M. (2000). Organizational routines as a source of continuous change. *Organization Science, 11*(6), 611–629.

Forbath, T., & Brooks, P. (2007). Global service providers: Outsourcing's next wave. *Financial Executive, April*, 21–24.

Gherardi, S. (2000). Practice-based theorizing on learning and knowing in organizations. *Organization, 7*(2), 211–223.

Giddens, A. (1984). *The constitution of society*. Cambridge: Polity

Giddens, A. (1990). *The consequences of modernity*. Cambridge: Polity.

Giddens, A. (1991). *Modernity and self-identity: self and society in the late modern age*. Cambridge: Polity.

Guinan, P., Cooprider, J., & Faraj, S. (1998). Enabling software development team performance during requirements definition: A behavioral versus technical approach. *Information Systems Research, 9*(2), 101–125.

Hartwick, J., & Barki, H. (1994). Explaining the role of user participation in information system use. *Management Science, 40*(4), 440–465.

Hirschheim, R., Heinzl, A., & Dibbern, J. (2004). *Information systems outsourcing*. Berlin: Springer.

Hirschheim, R., & Lacity, M. (2000). The myths and realities of information of information technology insourcing. *Communications of the ACM, 43*(2), 99–107.

Jarvenpaa, S., & Leidner, D. (1998). An information company in mexico: Extending the resource-based view of the firm to a developing country context. *Information Systems Research, 9*(4), 342–361.

Jehn, K., Northcraft, G., & Neale, M. (1999). Why some differences make a difference: a field study of diversity, conflict, and performance in workgroups. *Administrative Science Quarterly, 44*, 741–763.

Klein, H., & Myers, M. (1999). A set of principles for conducting and evaluating interpretive field studies in information systems. *MIS Quarterly, 27*(1), 67–88.

Langley, A. (1999). Strategies for theorizing from process data. *Academy of Management Review, 24*(4), 691–710.

Liu, W., & Westrup, C. (2003). ICT's and organizational control across cultures: The case of a UK multinational operating in China. In M. Korpela, R. Montealegre, & A. Poulymenakou (Eds.), Proceedings in IFIP 9.4 and 8.2 Joint Conference on *Organizational Information Systems in the Context of Globalization* (pp. 155–168), Athens, Greece, June 2003. Dorderecht: Kluwer.

Lovelace, K., Shapiro, D., & Weingart, L. (2001). Maximizing cross-functional new product teams' innovativeness and constraint adherence: A conflict communications perspective. *Academy of Management Journal, 44*(4), 779–793.

Markus, M. (1983). Power, politics, and MIS implementation. *Communication ACM, 26*, 430–444.

Markus, M., & Robey, D. (1998). Information technology and organizational change: causal structure in theory and research. *Management Science, 34*, 583–598.

Milliken, F., & Martins, L. (1996). Searching for common threads: understanding the multiple effects of diversity in organizational groups. *Academy of Management Review, 21*, 402–433.

Nelson, K., & Cooprider, J. (1996). The contribution of shared knowledge to is group performance. *MIS Quarterly, 20*(4), 409–432.

Nicholson, B., & Sahay, S. (2001). Some political and cultural issues in the globalization of software development: Case experience from Britain and India. *Information and Organization, 11*(1), 25–44.

Orlikowski, W. J. (1996). Improving organizational transformation over time: A situated change perspective. *Information Systems Research, 7*, 63–92.

Orlikowski, W. J. (2000). Using technology and constituting structures: a practice lens for studying technology in organizations. *Organization Science, 11*(4), 404–428.

Orlikowski, W. J. (2002). Knowing in practice: Enacting a collective capability in distributed organizing. *Organization Science, 13*(3), 249–273.

Pawlowski, S., & Robey, D. (2004).Bridging user organizations: Knowledge brokering and the work of information technology professionals. *MIS Quarterly, 28*(4), 645–672.

Pettigrew, A. (1990). Longitudinal field research on change: Theory and practice. *Organization Science, 1*(3), 267–292.

Polanyi, M. (1969). *Knowing and being*. London: Routledge and Kegan Paul.

Rao, M. T. (2004). Key issues for global IT sourcing: Country and individual factors. *Information Systems Management, 21*(3), 16–21.

Robey, D., Farrow, D., & Franz, C. (1989). Group process and conflict in systems development. *Management, 35*(10), 1172–1191.

Roche, D., & Blaine, M. (1996). *Information technology, development and policy*. Ashgate, VT: Avebury.

Sahay, S., Nicholson, B., & Krishna, S. (2003). *Global IT outsourcing*. Cambridge: Cambridge University Press.

Shoib, G., & Nandhakumar, J. (2003). Cross-cultural IS adoption in multinational corporations: A study of rationality. In M. Korpela, R. Montealegre, & A. Poulymenakou (Eds.), Proceedings in IFIP 9.4 and 8.2 Joint Conference on *Organizational information systems in the context of globalization* (pp. 435–454). Athens, Greece, June 2003. Boston: Kluwer.

Smith, K. A., Smith, K. G., Olian, J., Sims, H., Obannon, D., & Scully, J. (1994). Top management team demography and process: The role of social integration and communication. *Administrative Science Quarterly, 39*, 412–438.

Taijfel, H. (1981). *Human groups and social categories: Studies in social psychology*. Cambridge, England: Cambridge University Press.

Tsoukas, H. (2003). Do we really understand tacit knowledge? In M. Easterby-Smith & M.A. Lyles (Eds.), *The blackwell handbook of organizational learning and knowledge management* (p. 410). Oxford: Blackwell.

Tsoukas, H., & Chia, R. (2002). On organizational becoming: rethinking organizational change. *Organization Science, 13*(5), 567–582.

Walsham, G. (1995). Interpretive case studies in IS research: Nature and method. *European Journal of Information Systems, 4*(2), 74–81.

Walsham, G. (2001). Knowledge management: The benefits and limitations of computer systems. *European Management Journal, 19*(6), 599–608.

Walsham, G. (2002). Cross-cultural software production and use: A structurational analysis. *MIS Quarterly, 26*(4), 359–380.

Walsham, G., & Sahay, S. (2005). Research on IS in developing countries: Current landscape and future prospects. *Information Technology and Development, 12*, 7–24.

Wenger, E. (1998). *Communities of practice: learning, meaning and identity*. Cambridge: Cambridge University Press.

Williams, K., & O'Reilly, C. (1998). Demography and diversity in organisations. In B. Straw, & R. Sutton (Eds.), *Research in organizational behavior*. Greenwich, VT: JAI.

Williams, M. (2001). In whom we trust: Group membership as an affective context for trust development. *Academy of Management Review, 26*(3), 377–396.

Chapter 7
Dynamics in Offshoring

Pulling Offshore and Staying Onshore: A Framework for Analysis of Offshoring Dynamics

Erran Carmel, Jason Dedrick, and Kenneth L. Kraemer

1 Introduction and Motivation

Given that the force of offshoring is one of the most important economic changes in the early 2000s it is vital to understand what propels it further. The landscape of offshoring is such that firms in the wealthy nations (onshore) have already off-shored, sometimes extensively. As researchers, we need to ask not whether the firm will offshore, but rather how far the firm will go offshore and what are the subtle factors that are driving this offshore decision process. Therefore, in this paper we propose a framework in order to understand the firm-level decisions that are not as well understood and not as well researched.

There are a number of key variables that we already collectively know about offshoring. First, we already know that offshoring is driven by low wages and large labor pools in India, China and elsewhere. Thus, everything else being equal, work will flow to the less expensive offshore locations.

Second, we already know that there are many enabling factors that "level the playing field," enabling the mobility of projects and tasks. These are the factors that make the playing field almost frictionless. Thomas Friedman (2005) titled his well-known book about offshoring, *The World is Flat*. The flatness of the world is enabled by factors such as technology, standards, collaboration tools, task modularity, and interpersonal relationships (Appendix 1).

Third, we also know that offshore migrations tend to begin with lower-level work and proceed over time to higher-level work. This has been the case for many offshore migrations in many manufacturing fields – from steel to consumer electronics. In the software and IT area, there is considerable evidence that some high-level R&D work now is being moved offshore.

Assuming that the world is flat, we ask: what factors tip an activity from onshore to offshore? What is pulling some activities offshore and what is holding others onshore? To shed light on offshoring and possible tipping points, we were inspired by the landscape of computer hardware to examine Pull Factors. Specifically, we were motivated by Dedrick and Kraemer (2006) who show the Pull Factors in

R. Hirschheim et al. (eds), *Information Systems Outsourcing,*
© Springer-Verlag Berlin Heidelberg 2009

Taiwan and China for the notebook PC industry. Taiwan "pulled" new product development activities from the U.S., and now some of those activities are being "pulled" to China. In both cases, engineering activities have followed manufacturing to new locations.

It is useful to examine such Pull factors in the context of software and IT services, and to further examine the factors that tend to keep activities onshore, which we call Stay factors. Thus, we define two kinds of factors that shape offshoring decisions:

- *Offshore PULL factors*: Factors in the offshore location that induce more of the work to be tasked offshore.
- *Onshore STAY factors*: Factors in the onshore location that keep the work from migrating offshore. Some have suggested to call these "sticky" factors.

Views about what can be done offshore are constantly changing. While a decade ago one could argue that many high-level, upstream activities such as R&D, product design and software engineering could not be offshored, this position is increasingly difficult to defend today. There is consensus, however, that there are certain activities that are a better fit at offshore locations while others are better to leave in-house and in-country – "onshore." For example, services that require direct physical contact in their delivery must be performed onshore (assuming the final customer is onshore), while theoretically everything else could migrate offshore.

In this paper, we are painting a picture on a large canvas and include all types of software activities. We do not segregate IT from software. This paper is about *any type of software*-related activity: IT services and IT applications, software products, and embedded software.

2   Methodology

Since our motivation was to examine the more nuanced decisions in offshoring, we move in this paper through three stages: framework creation; exploratory data collection and fit to framework; and synthesis.

Our Pull-Stay Framework is based on primary and secondary data through an iterative process of item surfacing, refinement, and regrouping. The initial primary data we used was culled from our many years of cases and interviews across many countries. We also turned to two subdisciplines: the emerging literature on offshoring/outsourcing; and the more traditional literature on "technology transfer."

We used various recent data to examine the robustness of this framework. The data are from multiple sources, multiple firms, and multiple nations: interviews with 12 firms in India during 2005, seven firms in China during 2006; and five firms in the U.S. from 2006–2007. Since all our data collection are anonymous, we use aliases when discussing the firm names. U.S. firms with aliases include Printco, PDAco, MP3co, StorageCo, US-Tech; Chinese firms with aliases include C-Soft. Some secondary data sources are also used.

3 The Pull/Stay Factors and Framework

We identified nine pull/stay factors from existing literature and research (Table 1). It is important to note that many of the factors can be either Pull or Stay, or simultaneously both. Crown Jewels is the only factor that is unambiguously a STAY factor. There are two unambiguous PULL factors: Freshness and Eagerness.

Each of the factors is defined and discussed in this section.

Tacit Knowledge. Tacit knowledge is that which is difficult to write, document or codify (Carmel & Tija 2005). It is fuzzy knowledge learned from practice, exposure, and experience – the "know–how." It is also the "know–who" of social relations. Much of the tacit knowledge can only be transferred through learning by doing, through "show–how," as when a novice engineer learns on-the-job through mentoring and coaching by a senior engineer.

A specific activity that embodies a great deal of tacit knowledge is that of Software/IT Architects. Software/IT architects are the people who oversee design at the highest level and orchestrate new product development from conceptualization to implementation to maintenance/support. Architects are not specifically trained in universities for their jobs. Rather, they learn on the job following a career path, in the case of software architects, from programmer or systems analyst to project manager to architect of a system or the integration of multiple systems. Through experience, the architect comes to understand how to achieve balance between the system's utility, cost, and risk, and how to ensure that the system meets the requirements of its intended use today while also designing a robust system capable of meeting the needs of tomorrow (ANSI/IEEE Std 1471-2000; Kruchten et al. 2006). Consequently, the literature identifies the IT architect function as one of the least likely or last to be offshored (Zwieg et al. 2006). IT architects work upstream in the new product development process and are closely tied to design innovation, which might also make their work strategic.

Because tacit knowledge is difficult to transfer it is typically a Stay factor. However, we hypothesize that once tacit knowledge is present in an offshore location, it will begin to pull similar knowledge work offshore.

Table 1 The Pull and Stay factors introduced and discussed in this paper

Factor	Is it an	
	Offshore PULL Factor?	Onshore STAY Factor?
1. Tacit knowledge	Yes	Yes
2. Technology transfer policy	Yes	Yes
3. Control of standards	Yes	Yes
4. Critical mass of activities	Yes	Yes
5. Proximity to clients and to lead clients	Yes	Yes
6. Synergistic operations	Yes	Yes
7. Eagerness	Yes	–
8. Freshness	Yes	–
9. Crown jewels	–	Yes

Technology Transfer Policy. Some nations require foreign firms to transfer technology in exchange for market access. Such transfer might occur through licensing, joint ventures or joint R&D. Usually this is only a factor for countries with big emerging markets such as China and India, or lead user markets such as Japan and Korea, who are in a good bargaining position to set formal or informal requirements of foreign firms in exchange for market access.

One of the major factors in the award of a joint venture with China's Shanghai Automotive Industry Corp (SAIC) to General Motors was its agreement to advanced and continuous technology transfers through state-of-the-art technology, joint R&D projects and training (DFI International 1997; The Economist 1999). More subtle pressures are used in other industries. For instance, Microsoft provided access to its source code to several governments, including China, in response to security concerns (CNET 2003). It also set up an R&D center in Beijing, at least in part to improve relations with the Chinese government (although the Chinese government has failed to prevent large-scale software piracy and continues to support open source alternatives to Microsoft products).

By contrast, home countries also can restrict technology transfer. For instance, Taiwan has prohibited its companies from moving their most advanced chip manufacturing processes to China. The U.S. restricts transfer of many technologies to various countries including China for national security reasons. In these cases, government policy inhibits the offshoring of sophisticated activities.

Thus, in summary, technology transfer policy is a Pull and a Stay factor.

Control of Standards. Standards represent any kind of codified technical specification or methodology that are used in IT/software. These include, for example, the CMM, ISO and SOX standards for IT/software development processes. Standards are generally an enabler, allowing work flows to move around the globe more easily since less of the knowledge is tacit or proprietary. However, in some cases, a firm or a country exerts control over a standard, thus altering its neutral enabling characteristics.

Another type of standard is a product standard, which can be a source of competitive advantage for software companies (Shapiro & Varian 1998). For example, Microsoft controls the key software standards for PC operating systems, and has tried with varying success to extend its control to servers, PDAs, media players, smart phones and the Internet. Those who create and control standards for an industry are in a position to reap huge financial benefits as shown by Microsoft's profit margins and market capitalization, or the performance of other standard setters such as Oracle, Adobe and Cisco. Such companies tend to keep development and upgrading of standard-setting technologies in-house and onshore in order to maintain tight control.

Control of Standards is generally a Stay factor.

However, there are some areas where it is becoming a Pull factor. China has focused on several standards around which it has also built or attracted expertise. For example, the TD-SCDMA (Time Division-Synchronous Code Division Multiple Access) technology, developed by China in conjunction with Western companies, is an official standard for 3G mobile telephony in China. Firms that wish to develop 3G products and services for this market will likely have to locate R&D in China.[1] In a different domain, Indian firms have been faster than U.S. companies to adopt process standards such as ISO and CMM, a factor which has certainly helped pull more software development offshore by signaling high quality to the marketplace. Moreover, in recent years, Indian organizations have begun to exert increasing influence on these standards setting bodies.

Critical Mass of Activities. When activities are highly interrelated it is better to colocate them and to decouple them from other activities that are only loosely related. The colocated activities sometimes become a critical mass of activities that draw new tasks to that location like a magnet. We see two layers of such critical mass: the first is internal to the firm; the second is in the firm's technological cluster.

Certain activities are colocated because they are highly interrelated and require proximity for effective performance. Product design is such an activity as it requires the frequent interaction of specialists from marketing, market analysis, industrial design, engineering and product management. A critical mass of such specialists are colocated because proximity matters, especially for such complex tasks involving multiple disciplines. However, many units perform focused and isolated tasks that require relatively little interaction and can function effectively in distributed offshore locations. This is called decoupling.

For example, some activities in offshore development centers (ODCs) are easier to do independently once they reach a steady-state. Once the work is shifted there, it is unlikely to be moved again and unlikely to be shared with other locations. Thus, once there is a critical mass around some activity, it develops its own force of attraction in pulling similar activities to the same location. Of course, this notion is common to many forms of work. In IT and BPO (Business Process Outsourcing), we see this manifestation of critical mass with the acceptance of the "Shared Services" concept. Shared Services often involves the centralization of services enabling some economies of scale. Firms now accept that centralization of services is better and cheaper than the decentralized model of yester-year.

The other tier of critical mass is known as "Cluster Effects," best illustrated by Silicon Valley (Porter 1998; Saxenian 1994). Bangalore is now a software and services cluster. Beijing's Haidian district has now developed cluster characteristics in software. Clustering of firms together means that there is an agglomeration of suppliers of inputs or complementary services such as legal, financial and marketing services. The firm actually benefits by being next to other firms that are similar to it. Thus, location is determined by other firms in the region in order to tap human resources, supplier firms, and infrastructure.

---

[1] It is worth noting that Motorola has established large R&D and engineering activities in China, partly to develop products for the world's largest mobile market – whatever the standards may be, so such standard setting efforts by the Chinese government might not have much of an additional pull effect on Motorola.

Critical mass of task activities is a Stay factor, however once a critical mass does move offshore, it becomes a Pull factor.

Proximity to Clients and to Lead Clients. Clients demand proximity, face-to-face interaction, and relationships. Providers need to be close to the clients to meet, shake hands, have lunch and work together. Lead clients are the most innovative clients and those from which the firm learns the most (von Hippel 1994). These are the clients that help make the technology firm successful.

Proximity to Clients–and to Lead Clients – is a Stay Factor because until just a few years ago there were few clients of significance in many of the offshore markets. The lead clients – the most innovative – were onshore in developed countries (mainly the G7 nations). Offshore nations (developing/emerging) did not have sophisticated/discerning consumers; they had little middle class buying power; their corporations were relatively rudimentary in their use of technology, their ability to integrate technology, their size, and their resources.

Given this context, foreign software firms had to go abroad to reach lead clients. Indian firms grew by serving clients in the U.S. while Israeli software startups succeeded by entering the American markets with their product innovations.

However, the context is different now. The largest global firms are dispersed around the world with a very large presence in India and China. Also, there are large local companies in both India and China, as well as in some other emerging countries. These lead clients are now a *Pull factor* in the developing world as well as in the developed world.

Synergistic Operations. Many firms have some kind of operations already located in one or more places around the world. These may be sales, distribution, manufacturing or even design and R&D. As a result of such operations, the organization develops knowledge of the location's human capital, work culture, infrastructure and government policy.

The location draws other activities especially when there are synergies between activities. Thus, an onshore manufacturing site which has been very successful in recruiting local staff for its own IT shop, might become attractive as a place for performing the corporate IT function. *This is a Stay factor.*

Conversely, an engineering design center established to collaborate more closely with its manufacturing outsourcer, might develop a cost-effective talent pool of CAD software engineers. In this case, there is a *Pull* of software activities from headquarters to the offshore location. In some cases, the captive offshore operations may be totally managed by locals who also have personal connections (family, schoolmates) and deep understanding of the local culture and institutions that uncover additional opportunities. The local managers may develop an affinity to the offshore location and lobby for expanding activities there. Further, some of the local managers might have advanced to high-level positions in the headquarters location where they become advocates for moving work to their home country based on its comparative advantage. The movement of manufacturing to the Asia–Pacific region and China, as well as the movement of software to India, is credited in part to their large diasporas which functions in this manner.

Thus, existing synergistic operations can be either a Pull factor or a Stay factor.

Eagerness. Once you expose an elite set of engineers to the action and excitement and challenge of the global leading edge in software, they will not be content to settle for mundane tasks. They will demand more. They will "pull." *Eagerness is a Pull factor.* The young engineers have the confidence of working with global firms; they will demand the most challenging tasks that they now feel entitled to (Saxenian 2006). Also, local managers of MNC subsidiaries desire to increase the size and scope of their own operations, and will begin to compete within the company to host different activities.

Freshness. Companies seek fresh perspectives in design: in creativity, in innovation, in ideas. For example in the auto industry, several Japanese companies sought fresh perspectives by setting up design centers in trendy Southern California (Honda in Torrance, Isuzu in Cerritos, Mazda in Irvine, Subaru in Cyprus, Toyota in Gardena). The trendy clients are there, but so are the trendy designers. By 2006 there were 3,600 employed in Japanese automakers' design centers in the U.S. (Moavenzadeh 2006).

Another approach to freshness is to rely on acquiring innovation offshore. Israel is an incubator for innovative new software technologies in its hundreds of start-ups. These are then acquired and absorbed by foreign multinationals (De Fontenay & Carmel 2004). Cisco, Intel, and IBM have each acquired several Israeli start-ups in recent years.

Almost all software has to be localized to local language and culture. Situating localization in the target market allows firms to better customize products to the local markets, particularly the large and more promising markets, such as India and China. This is the case with Microsoft's significant presence in China, with its development centers in Shanghai and Beijing which devote significant resources to Chinese language scripts and other local needs.

Thus, the quest for freshness is a Pull factor.

Crown Jewels. Companies tend to keep "high-end" tasks at home (onshore) as well as in-house to maintain their competitiveness. These "high-end" tasks have many labels, such as core activities, proprietary activities, sensitive activities, and leading product design. Regardless of label, they usually are key to the company's competitive edge. Companies are reluctant to let the crown jewels from under their immediate watch whether these jewels are outsourced onshore or outsourced offshore or even in-housed (in a "captive" center) offshore. The lack of effective legal protection of IP in many offshore nations.is a major concern to firms with significant IP. *Thus, the crown jewels is a Stay factor.*

The crown jewels might involve tasks that are easy to copy or emulate if made public, but they might also be creative, innovative, and research-oriented, or require very broad knowledge and experience. For a software product company such as Microsoft, Oracle or SAP, its software code base is its "crown jewel." Some large user corporations also have some IT which is in this category (e.g., Amazon), but most IT applications at end user firms (e.g., banks, insurance firms) involve relatively few activities which are proprietary. Such companies are not hesitant to offshore as these applications are not the firms' crown jewels.

There are few companies that have not sourced some innovation or crown jewels offshore. But there are dangers, as pointed out by Engardio and Einhorn (2005):

> "Start with the danger of fostering new competitors. Motorola hired Taiwan's BenQ Corp. to design and manufacture millions of mobile phones. But then BenQ began selling phones last year in the prized China market under its own brand. That prompted Motorola to pull its contract. Another risk is that brand-name companies will lose the incentive to keep investing in new technology. "It is a slippery slope," says Boston Consulting Group Senior Vice-President Jim Andrew. "If the innovation starts residing in the suppliers, you could incrementalize yourself to the point where there isn't much left."

Even companies where software is a crown jewel exhibit apparently contradictory behavior. For example, there is significant offshoring of R&D among independent software vendors. It is quite difficult to estimate the magnitude of this phenomenon, but it was estimated that 5–15% of American software product R&D was offshored in 2003 and such offshoring was forecast to rise to 25–30% by 2007/2008 (Martin 2003). Some of the companies which are offshoring software product R&D are the largest U.S. technology firms. This may not be so contradictory however, as significant amounts of software development may not involve the crown jewels. Also, just moving development offshore does not necessarily put core technologies at risk if it is kept in-house and steps are taken to prevent IP leakage.

3.1 Pull/Stay Factors in the Life Cycle

One method for analyzing which activities are suitable for offshoring is to use the software development life-cycle (see Table 2). Recall that the economic *Pull Factor* – low costs – tends to first pull lower-value activities such as coding and testing offshore.

Table 2 Importance of factors (*pull/stay*) to selected life cycle stages

	Requirements and architecture	Design	Coding and testing	Integration
Typical positions involved→ ↓Pull/Stay factor	IT architect; Systems analyst	Database designer	Programmer; QA engineer	Programmer; QA engineer
1. Tacit knowledge	High	High	Low	High
2. Technology transfer policy			N/A	
3. Control of standards	High	High	High	Medium
4. Critical mass of activities	Low	Low	High	Low
5. Proximity to clients and lead clients	High	High	Low	High
6. Synergistic operations	High	Medium	High	High
7. Eagerness	High	High	Medium	Low
8. Freshness	High	High	Low	Low
9. Crown jewels	High	High	High	High

Yet, most *Pull/Stay* factors are strongest at the early stages of the value chain – *upstream*. The important exception is one *downstream* activity – the integration stage.

In general, the life-cycle phases and offshoring are driven by two factors: proximity and location of knowledge. Proximity means the proximity to activities, to operations, to clients, and to resources. Knowledge refers to tacit knowledge, IP knowledge, and trade secrets.

The integration stage is interesting in its effect on *pull/stay*. This stage usually requires all the IT/software components to come together at one location in order to build and debug. The one location is at the hub of activity – usually in the company's home country or at the site of a major client. Hence, we see the Indian-based firms send key personnel to the client site at the end of the development cycle.

3.2   Examination of the Pull/Stay Framework with Exploratory Data

Here we use our exploratory field data to illustrate the framework. (The data sources were described in the methodology section). For each of the nine *Pull/Stay* factors we present data. Some of the data are supportive, some unsupportive, and sometimes they are contradictory.

Tacit Knowledge (TK). In our software interviews in China, we heard conflicting claims about the transfer of TK. Using IT architects as an example, some sources argued that architects are still coming from the U.S., that the work is still specified abroad and that the Chinese generally don't have such experienced people. Others point out that the Chinese are developing such TK. Part of the discrepancy may be definitional. As with many titles in IT, there is no IT architect title per se, the definition is fuzzy and the function does not require a particular license or degree.

At the Chinese R&D site of a giant American tech firm our source stated that TK is still in the USA; that the "big picture" is not here [in China] and that "they're still quite young [in China]." Another source at a different firm argued that there were no software architects in China because engineering education was theoretical and software engineers came without practical skills from universities–as opposed to the more practice-minded IITs[2] in India. At another firm we heard that Chinese software engineers don't know about business or business processes because they are not trained in business and that, anyway, Chinese business is all based on *guanxi* (interpersonal connections and relationships, particularly with people close to the party and the government).

Technology Transfer Policy. Interestingly, we have no data about this factor pulling software development offshore in our exploratory dataset. However, IBM and other leading PC companies were required to engage in joint ventures with local Chinese computer firms in the early 1990s, and Microsoft was required to engage

---

[2] IIT – Indian Institute of Technology, the top-tier technical universities in India.

a domestic firm to create the Chinese version of Windows for sale in the PRC. We suspect that this *Pull* factor surfaces in narrow cases at particular times, and is becoming more subtle as blatant requirements are likely to be challenged in the WTO or draw retaliation from other governments.

Prohibitions on technology transfer are becoming less effective as well, as they are seen to put national companies at a disadvantage with foreign competitors whose governments do not have similar restrictions. For example, if the U.S. government prevents U.S. companies from transferring technology to China, Japanese or European companies may do so.

Control of Standards. It appears that this factor surfaces only in particular technologies. For example, China required US-Tech's embedded software to use the Chinese crypto standard. As a result, US-Tech had to contract with a local Chinese company to write the crypto code.

Firms that control product standards may be hesitant to move development offshore for IP protection reasons. On the other hand, if they wish to establish their standards in other countries, they may need to do development in those countries in order to create products that will succeed in those countries, or work with local partners who will do so. So for instance, Qualcomm worked closely with Korean cell phone makers to establish its CDMA standard in that country, and Cisco worked with Japanese hardware manufacturers to establish its proprietary operating system in Japan.

Critical Mass of Activities. Our interviews with Chinese IT Services firms that manage offshore development centers (ODCs) reveal that, as with the Indian ODCs, once tasks migrate into those centers, the task managers become independent and tasks are unlikely to be moved again and unlikely to be shared with other locations. At that point, due to cost advantages, similar tasks tend to follow offshore.

At US-Tech, which develops some of the world's most complex computer chips, our interviewee emphasized that such tasks required complicated collaborations and multiple owners. These characteristics drive colocation in the U.S. Hence, this is a *Stay factor.* More specifically, US-Tech likes to colocate the (embedded) software with the silicon designers. Why keep/move software close to hardware design? This does not hold for all hardware activities, but, in the words of our interviewee: "[the firm is….] really focused on collocating software that directly controls the hardware, such as device drivers as being coresident with the silicon team, creates better communication, results in innovations on the silicon/software boundary, and makes initial bring up and debug go faster."

US-Tech has significant software development in India. In the case of India, there seems to be some shifting in critical mass. It used to be that all new system on chip (SOC) designs were done in the U.S. but not anymore. The India design center now has hundreds of software engineers. And now there is colocation of silicon engineers and software engineers.

Also, for US-Tech, India now offers cluster effects – agglomeration effects of supplier networks: "[We have…] ability to engage with subcontractors to augment our team to handle new projects, and [we have an] abundance of third party software partners that can provide middleware, etc. on top of our products."

We heard a contradictory piece of evidence in China. One of the interesting developments, globally, is the production of mobile telephone handsets. For these handsets, companies tend to disperse the production of the three main components: the hardware, the embedded software, and the user interface. Our source in China, for example, developed embedded software for mobile phones and was emphatic that there were no advantages to colocating hardware and software.

Proximity to Clients and to Lead Clients. As expected, this is becoming evident in India and China. For China-based providers, many of the clients are not offshoring to them, as in the India model. Rather the clients are MNCs in China: these are the foreign firms (e.g., American) that require local support for their large presence in China – in Beijing, Shanghai, Hong Kong, Shenzhen, and elsewhere. Restated – all the most advanced firms in the world are operating in the country.

Two examples support this point. First, there are now many Indian firms in China. Our interviewee at one of these companies noted that the firm sees China as a pilot roll-out site for many clients. Second, Microsoft China increasingly works not with Redmond or other American firms, but with Chinese startups.

On the subject of lead clients, we hear some confirmation from US-Tech in embedded software, that lead clients are now in Japan and China, and more recently, also in India. We note that a precedent in hardware may soon apply to software: In hardware, U.S. suppliers of manufacturing and measuring equipment such as Tectronics have moved some R&D to China to be close to their clients, which are Taiwanese firms doing original design manufacturing for U.S. PC companies. So who then is the real client? The U.S. or Taiwanese firms? These supplier firms have moved to China because they need to work closely with the Taiwanese ODMs to design new equipment that might be needed 9–12 months down the line.

Synergistic Operations. In our interviews and the literature, we found examples of existing offshore operations pulling other related activities. Dell provides an interesting Pull chronology in Brazil and Taiwan, that we describe here. We have early indications that similar pulling is now happening in India.

Dell established a production facility in Brazil in 1999. This allowed Dell to compete in this market due to cost savings obtained from tax incentives, tariffs savings, and local economic benefits. Three years later, Dell opened its Global [Software] Development Center (GDC) in Brazil, which is responsible for supporting corporate software development that is used in-house. Rather quickly the GDC began to lead in some activities. For example, the Brazil GDC was the first of Dell's offshore facilities to attain the SW-CMM Level 2 standard (Bothelo 2003). In 2004, Dell announced it would be expanding its services in Brazil to offer specialized consultancy in migration, in infrastructure and in consolidation of server and storage, training and certification.

Similarly, Dell established a design center in Taiwan in 2003 to work with its ODM contractors on engineering problems related to notebook development and manufacturing (Digitimes 2003). The reason was to be closer to where the problems occurred, to be able to see the problems and resolve them faster, and to be able to use the ODM's testing facilities rather than duplicate them in Austin. In addition, being close to the ODM enabled Dell to build deep relationships between engineers.

Perhaps more important, the offshore location enabled Dell to combine lower labor costs with distinctive skills. Low wages allowed Dell to hire more middle managers who could then devote more time to building the skills of their employees and to improving their processes that would be economical in the U.S. These greater capabilities have enabled Dell's design center to pull more work from Austin to Taiwan and move up to server design. A recent news article indicates that the design center has grown from about 100 engineers in 2003 to over 500 in 2005 and is slated to increase further (Digitimes 2005).

Eagerness. Our interviews in India and China indicate that another *Pull factor* results from the upgrading of individual capabilities through experience working on multiple projects with multinational firms. As their capabilities increase, software engineers become eager to take on higher level activities and they proactively seek them, either inside the firm or outside in their own enterprises.

In our interviews in India with engineers in ISVs we encountered this type of behavior, though still in its early stages. One lead Indian engineer working at a major American firm in Bangalore declared again and again that he and his colleagues wanted more of the firm's leading tasks, which were currently being conducted onshore in the U.S. They were confident in their abilities, felt entitled to take on more complex projects and lobbied higher level management to transfer the work.

Another Indian software engineering manager from another well-known American firm in Bangalore quit his job because he was not given enough challenges. Given his contacts and experience, and the liberal availability of venture capital, he was able to start his own firm in India. Thus, some of this *Pull* happens inside the existing chain, as with the first engineer, while some happens outside the chain as with the second engineer.

Finally, we interviewed managers in one MNC subsidiary in Australia that was competing aggressively with the company's Singapore subsidiary to run a new data center, and with a Hong Kong subsidiary for a customer support center. In this case, the eagerness of managers in each country to expand the scale and scope of activities, and the confidence they could do so, was a *Pull factor*.

Freshness. We have no data about this factor pulling offshore in our exploratory dataset. We suspected that this factor surfaces in narrow cases.

Crown Jewels. Our field interviews indicate that a firm's crown jewels might be in hardware, software or both, as in the case of embedded software on a chip. At US-Tech, the hardware division is concerned with protecting the firm's technology secrets. Hence the leading fabs and design centers are kept in the U.S. At StorageCo the core technology is not only the tiny recording head for the hard drive, but also the software for firmware. R&D, design, development of the hardware and software, are all kept in-house onshore, but manufacturing is done in-house offshore at low cost locations.

At other American-based hardware technology firms (i.e., Printco, PDAco, MP3co), the crown jewels are increasingly in software. The software controls not only the operation of the hardware but also its interface with other technologies where these controls operate as part of a complete system. Software is also a core technology because it allows the hardware products to be customized for different uses and markets without the need to build separate products for each use or market. Thus, the entire software development process is kept in the U.S. to protect IP and corporate knowledge while hardware production is outsourced offshore to low cost locations.

Thus, there is clear support in all of the interviews for the hypothesis that Crown Jewels are a *Stay factor.*

3.3 Application of the Framework to Life Cycle Stages

Although the integration phase is downstream in the software development life cycle, it is affected by most of our *Stay factors.* Integration requires some of the highest skills, proximity of lead designers, and proximity to the client. Integration seems to continue to have strong *Stay factors.*

At US-Tech the integration stage usually requires all the software components to come together at one location in order to build and debug (including "bring-up"). While some integration, for some products, is conducted in all four offshore locations, India is most interesting. The senior executive at US-Tech said: "Software bring-up is done where the silicon team exists. For certain product lines, that is in India. It's [now] more a function of having a senior team in place in India [whereas before we did not]."

Another example of integration is in the following Japanese (onshore)/Chinese (offshore) relationship in which integration comes together onshore. C-Soft is one the major Chinese software firms. A number of firms, including Japanese firms, outsource mobile telephony software to C-Soft. C-Soft found that it could not test the telephony software that it developed in China. Rather, it had to send its engineers to Japan for final test for networks not available in China.

Our field observations about the integration phase and offshoring are a modification to Khan et al's (2003) notion that downstream activities are most likely to be offshored. It appears that rather than activities representing a clear progression with downstream activities offshored and upstream activities kept onshore, the distribution is U-shaped with some activities at both ends of the life cycle needing to be done onshore. This is closer to Stan Shih's "smiling curve" which shows that higher value activities are upstream and downstream, with lower value activities in the middle (Dedrick & Kraemer 1998).

4 Synthesis and Summary

Our exploratory analysis through case studies and interviews supports the premise that noneconomic factors are important influences in decisions about the offshoring of software development activities. The analysis also provides preliminary support for the hypothesized relationships. Specifically, the findings provide support for

Crown Jewels as a clear STAY factor whereas two other factors are clearly only PULL factors: Freshness; and Eagerness. The other factors show a mixed picture. While they tend to Pull activities offshore, once the activity is offshore they may work to keep the activity offshore (a new "Stay Offshore" factor).

When one looks at the offshoring of software development activities over time, there is a clear evolutionary pattern towards more higher-value activities being offshored (Fig. 1).

Whereas in 1995 only some maintenance was offshored, by 2005 more coding and maintenance activities were offshored, with some design and testing also being offshored.

We cautiously speculate that, given some of the trends we describe in this paper, by 2010, requirements, architecture and system integration activities will remain onshore at the clients' or software vendors' location. Although not shown in the figure, it is also the case that once moved offshore, these activities seldom return to the home country; they stay or migrate to another location.

This pattern in software development is worth comparing to new product development (NPD) in PC hardware (Dedrick & Kraemer 2006), which is shown in Fig. 2. The pattern of gradual movement of more and more activities offshore over time is the same, but offshoring is generally more advanced in PC hardware than in software. All NPD activities but design were offshored by 2005 and it is likely that architecture design and product planning will be done jointly with the outsourcing firms by 2010, if not completely outsourced. Then only product concept design would be performed onshore as it must be located close to the lead market (the U.S.).

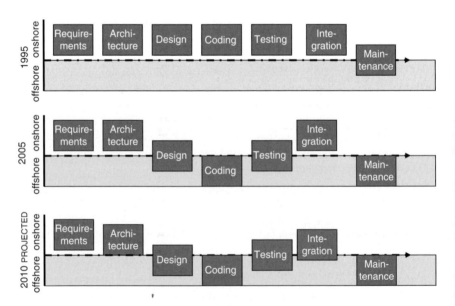

Fig. 1 Information systems and services. Adapted from Carmel and Tija 2005

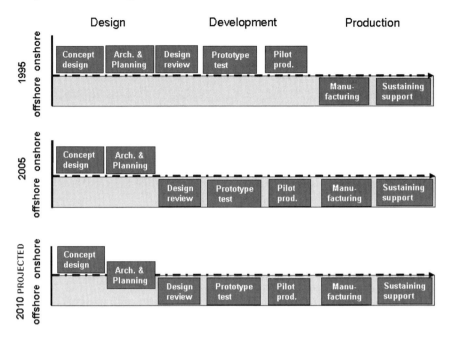

Fig. 2 New product development in PC hardware. Adapted from Dedrick and Kraemer 2006

In sum, the influence of various factors on offshoring decisions is complex, with some going both ways – acting as a staying force in one instance and pulling activities offshore in another. The dynamics or evolution of offshoring is clearer, with things seeming to move mainly in one direction from lower-level to ever higher-level activities.

Acknowledgment This material is based upon work supported by the U.S. National Science Foundation under grant number SES-0527180. Any opinions, findings, and conclusions or recommendations expressed in this material are those of the authors and do not necessarily reflect the views of the National Science Foundation.

References

ANSI/IEEE Std 1471-2000 (2000). Recommended practice for architectural description of software-intensive systems. accessed from http://standards.ieee.org/reading/ieee/std_public/description/se/1471-2000_desc.html

Bothelo, A. J. (2003). *The Brazilian software industry*. Working paper Instituto Gênesis, PUC – Rio de Janeiro e, Brasil. Giancarlo Stefanuto.

Carmel, E., & Tija, P. (2005). Offshoring information technology: Sourcing and outsourcing to a global workforce. Cambridge: Cambridge University Press.

Cnet (2003). China looks into Windows code. CNET News.com, September 29, 2003. http://news.com.com/China+looks+into+Windows+code/2100-1016_3-5083458.html. Last accessed March 6, 2007.

Dedrick, J., & Kraemer, K. L. (1998). *Asia's computer challenge*. New York: Oxford University Press.

Dedrick, J., & Kraemer, K. L. (2006). Is production pulling knowledge work to China? A study of the notebook PC industry. *IEEE Computer, 39*(7), 36–42.

DeFontenay, C., & Carmel, E. (2004). Israel's Silicon Wadi: The forces behind cluster formation. In T. Bresnahan, A. Gambardella, & A. Saxenian (Eds.), *Building High Tech Clusters*. Cambridge: Cambridge University Press.

DFI International (1997). *U.S. commercial technology transfers to the people's republic of China*, Part 2 (pp. 45–75). Washington DC: DFI International.

Digitimes (2003). HP, Dell expanding R&D offices in Taiwan. *Digitimes.com*, May 1.

Digitimes (2005) Dell: Procurement budget in Taiwan to surpass US$10 billion this year. *Digitimes.com*, April 20.

Economist (1999). General Motors finally won the license to establish a joint R&D centre in Shanghai, May 1.

Engardio, P., & Einhorn, B. (2005). Outsourcing innovation. *Business Week*, March 21, 2005.

Friedman, T. L. (2005). *The world is flat: A brief history of the twenty-first century*. New York, NY: Farrar, Straus and Giroux.

Greenstein, S. (2005). Outsourcing and climbing a value chain. *IEEE Micro, 25*(5), 83–84.

Khan, N., Currie, W. L., Weerakkody, V., & Desai, B. (2003). *Evaluating offshore IT outsourcing in India: Supplier and customer scenarios*. Paper presented at 36th Hawaii International Conference on Systems Sciences (HICSS), January 6–9, Big Island, USA.

Martin, K. (2003). *Research and development goes offshore*. META Group News Analysis, September 12. Corporate report.

Moavenzadeh, J. (2006). *Offshore automotive engineering: Globalization and footprint strategy in the motor vehicle industry*. Paper presented at the National Academy of Engineering workshop on the offshoring of engineering, Washington D.C.

Kruchten, P., Obbink, H., & Stafford, J. (2006). (Guest Eds.), The past, present, and future of software architecture. *IEEE Software, 23*(2), 22–30.

Porter, M. E. (1998). Clusters and the new economics of competition. *Harvard Business Review, 76*(6), 77–90.

Saxenian, A. (1994) *Regional advantage: Culture and competition in Silicon valley and Route 128*. Cambridge, MA: Harvard University Press.

Saxenian, A. (2006). *The new argonauts: Regional advantage in a global economy*. Cambridge, MA: Harvard University Press.

Shapiro, C., & Varian, H. R. (1998). *Information rules: A strategic guide to the network economy*. Boston: Harvard Business School Press.

Von Hippel, E. (1994). *The sources of innovation*. Oxford: Oxford University Press.

Zwieg, P., Kaiser, K. M., Beath, C., Bullen, C., Gallagher, K., Goles, T. et al. (2006). The information technology workforce trends and implications 2005–2008. *MIS Quarterly, 5*(2), 47–54.

Appendix 1: Enabling Factors

Enabling factors are those that enable the frictionless mobility of projects and tasks to different locations around the world. Several key factors are listed here.
* *Technology*. The range of communication and collaboration technologies from e-mail to project-ware, and many more. These are now cheap and ubiquitous.
* *Standards*. Standards allow codified knowledge to flow easily to offshore locations. The standard creates such a level playing field that there is no advantage to the traditional bastions of knowledge in the USA. One can see the enabling impact of standards in the field of hardware. Taiwan was able to move from CM to

CDM in the 1980s because basic components became standardized (Engardio and Einhorn 2005).

- Global Collaboration *Methodologies*. These ease task hand-offs with distant collaboration. For example the Indian IT firms have their GDM, the Global Delivery Model, which codifies such work.
- Professional *providers and intermediaries* have emerged to oil, smooth and otherwise help in moving tasks offshore, e.g., the offshore provider Ness runs centers called Build Operate Transfer (BOT) in India for its clients. Such a structure, now increasingly common, eases the complexity of offshoring and reduce risks.
- *Ease of doing business*. Increased number of joint ventures and alliances into the new offshore locations.
- *Relationships*. Relationships formed between people and firms help smooth the transitions. Legal arrangements are easier. Now, more than a decade in the new globalization era, a network of relationships of global managers and ex-pats have been formed.

Appendix 2: Moving up the Value Chain

Moving up the value chain is a topic that has received a great deal of attention. We know that this topic is an important one because there are many terms to describe it: moving up the value chain, moving up the food chain, moving upstream. We present two such value chains in Table 3.

Table 3   Examples of moving up the value chain

Greenstein (2005)	1. CM – Contract Manufacturing
For *computer hardware* value chain	2. CDM – Contract and Design Manufacturing
	3. ODM – Original Design and Manufacturing
Khan et al (2003)	1. Body shopping
For *IT services firms in India*	2. Offshore development and project execution
	3. Establishing standards
	4. Consultancy and designing the IT architecture
	5. Design and product development

Turnover Intentions of Indian IS Professionals[*]

Mary C. Lacity, Vidya V. Iyer, and Prasad S. Rudramuniyaiah

1 Introduction

In India, the turnover rates have been reported as high as 80% in the IT services sector (Gupta 2001) and as high as 100% for Indian call centers (Mitchell 2005, 2007). For example, Wipro announced that it replaced 90% of its call enter and BPO workers in 2004 (McCue 2005). The lowest rates we found reported on turnover in Indian software services was 30% (Mitchell 2004). No matter which turnover number one considers – the low estimate of 30% or the high estimate of 100%, there is no denying that turnover is a major issue to Indian suppliers and their global clients. Supplier staff turnover delays the clients' projects, reduces quality, and increases costs (Jiang & Klein 2002). Clearly, both clients and suppliers share the objective of high retention of the supplier's most qualified workers.

One contribution academics can make is to develop and test a model of Turnover that is applicable to the Indian IS context. Although there are nearly 50 studies on Western IS professionals (Joseph, Ng, Koh, & Ang 2007), we are not aware of any research specifically addressing turnover among Indian IS professionals. The purposes of this paper are to propose a model of turnover based on interviews with Indian IS professionals and to identify implications for practice. Our hope is that by better understanding why Indian IS professionals want to leave or stay with their current organizations, suppliers (and perhaps clients) will be able to target practices to increase retention. We initially developed a model based on extensive research from the organizational behavior and information systems literatures and identified six hypotheses (see Sect. 2). We then interviewed 25 Indian IS professionals working for 13 different suppliers (see Sect. 3). We tested the initial hypotheses using nonparametric statistics and interpret these findings based on the interview data (see Sect. 4). Based on the results the hypothesis tests and the additional constructs

---

[*] This paper previously appeared as: Lacity, M. C., Iyer, V. V. and Rudramuniyaiah, P. S. "Turnover intentions of Indian IS professionals", Information Systems Frontiers (10) 2008, pp. 225–241. The current version appears with permission of Springer, the publisher of ISF.

that emerged from the interviews, we significantly revised the model (see Sect. 5). The revised model must be empirically assessed, but we believe we have made important progress towards understanding turnover intentions of Indian IS professionals. We discuss four implications for practice in Sect. 6.

2   Identifying an Initial Model of Turnover Intentions

Although researchers want to ideally understand turnover *behavior,* in reality, it is often difficult to empirically examine the behavior. Instead, researchers more typically survey current employees and ask them their turnover *intentions.* Turnover intentions are a reliable predictor of turnover behaviors (Ajzen & Fishbein 1980). Substantial empirical evidence supports the theory that attitude affects behavior more than behavior affects attitude. For example, a time sequenced meta-analysis of 49 studies on job attitudes (including Job Satisfaction[1] and Organizational Commitment) and work behavior (including Turnover) comprising over 10,000 individuals found that predictive correlations between attitude-to-behavior were stronger than predictive correlations between behavior-to-attitude (Harrison, Newman, & Roth 2006). They conclude: *"The combined evidence from dozens of time-lagged studies tends to favor the attitude–behavior mechanism"* (Harrison et al. p. 318).

2.1   Models of Turnover/Turnover Intentions
    from Organizational Behavior Literature

Within the Organizational Behavior literature, there are many well-tested models of Turnover Intention based on the following theories:

- The Two Factor Theory (motivation and hygiene factors) suggests that when factors are fulfilled, Turnover is lower (Herzberg 1968).
- Theory of Needs (affiliation, achievement and power needs) suggests that when an individual's needs are met at an organization, Turnover is lower (McClelland 1961).
- Turnover Theory posits that Job Satisfaction, Organizational Alternatives, and Search Intention are antecedents to Quit Intention (Hom, Caranikas-Walker, & Prussia 1992; Mobley, Horner, & Hollingsworth 1978).
- Person-to-Organization Fit Theory posits that high compatibility between an individual and an organization is negatively related to Turnover (Argyris 1957; Arthur, Bell, Villado, & Doverspike 2006; Hoffman & Woehr 2006; Pervin 1989).

---

[1] From here forward, formal constructs are indicated through the use of capitalization.

- Turnover models suggest that job characteristics (Skill Variety, Task Significance, Task Identity, Autonomy, and Feedback) determine Job Satisfaction which in turn determines Turnover (Hackman & Oldham 1976, 1980).
- The Job Investment Model posits that Job Rewards and Job Costs determine Job Satisfaction, that Organizational Alternatives and Investment in the organization determine Organizational Commitment, and that both Job Satisfaction and Organizational Commitment determine turnover (Farrell & Rusbult 1981).

We found *thousands* of tests of these models within the organizational behavior literature. The rich research base from organizational behavior has significantly informed the IS turnover research.

2.2 Models of Turnover/Turnover Intentions from Information Systems Literature

Within the IS literature, the basic model of Turnover Intentions shows that Job Satisfaction and Organizational Commitment directly affect Turnover Intentions among Western (mostly US) IS professionals (see Fig. 1). Joseph et al. (2007) conducted a meta analysis of IS turnover research among IS professionals and found that Job Satisfaction was the most frequently studied determinant of Turnover. In the 16 IS studies that used this construct, all 16 found a negative relationship between Job Satisfaction and Turnover. The second most frequently studied construct was Organizational Commitment. Eleven IS studies found a negative relationship between Organizational Commitment and Turnover among IS professionals (Ahuja, Chudoba, Kacmar, McKnight, & George 2007; Baroudi 1985; Igbaria & Greenhaus 1992).

IS academics have also extended the basic model in Fig. 1 by testing many antecedents of Job Satisfaction and/or Organizational Commitment for IS professionals. These constructs have included Boundary Spanning Activities, Burnout, Career Expectations, Career Orientation, Career Satisfaction, Gender, Internal Labor Market Strategies, IT Human Resource Management configurations, Job Autonomy, Job Involvement, Job Tasks, Management Policy, Role Ambiguity, Role Conflict, Salary, Shocks, Turnover Culture, Work Exhaustion, Work Experiences, and Work Family Conflict (Ahuja et al. 2007; Baroudi 1985; Ferrat et al. 2005; Gupta &

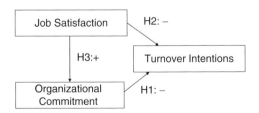

Fig. 1 Basic turnover model found among western IS professionals

Gupta 1990; Igbaria & Greenhaus 1992; Igbaria, Parasuraman, & Bawawy 1994; McMurtrey, Grover, Teng, & Lightner 2002; Moore 2000; Moore & Burke 2002; Niederman & Sumner 2004; Rouse 2001; Sethi, Barrier, & King 1999). Furthermore, many of these higher level constructs have multiple dimensions, such as the five dimensions of HR configuration (1) work environment, (2) community building, (3) incentives, (4) employment and security, and (5) nontechnical skill recruitment (Ferrat et al. 2005).

2.3   Our Initial Model of Turnover Intentions

Because we did not know a priori which antecedents of Job Satisfaction and Organizational Commitment from the study of Western IS professionals might be the most relevant to Indian IS professionals, we sought a general but comprehensive model that would allow the Indian IS professionals to suggest the most important antecedents. We selected the investment model initially proposed by Kelly and Thibaut (1978) and applied to Turnover Intentions by Farrell and Rusbult (1981) and Van Dam (2005). This model is comprehensive because it includes job factors (Job Satisfaction and Job Attraction), organizational factors (Organizational Commitment and Investment in Current Organization), and environmental factors (Organizational Alternatives). This model also appealed to us because it generically defines the determinants of Job Satisfaction as the individual's overall subjective estimation of job rewards versus job costs. Thus, we could ask Indian IS Professionals generic questions about the rewards and costs of the current job without limiting the scope to a few specific constructs. We were very interested in specifically including Organizational Alternatives because the vibrant job market in India is likely to be a driving force behind high turnover. Our initial research model is thus found in Fig. 2.

The initial research model includes six constructs. These constructs are defined in Table 1 based on the literature.

The most widely cited theorists of Organizational Commitment include Porter, Steers, Mowday, and Boulian (1974), Steers (1977), Meyer and Allen (1997). Over

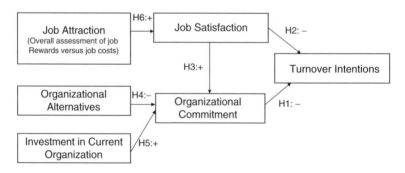

Fig. 2 Initial research model

Table 1 Construct definitions used in the initial research model

Construct	Definition used for the interviews	References
Turnover intention	The extent to which an employee plans to leave the organization	Igbaria and Greenhaus (1992); Kim Price, Mueller, & Watson (1996); Sujdak (2002)
Organizational commitment	The extent to which an employee feels emotionally attached to his/her organization	Within the IS literature, the 11 studies that included Organizational Commitment adopted the Affective Commitment component of the Meyer and Allen (1997) definition (Joseph et al. 2007)
Job satisfaction	The extent to which an employee likes his/her current job	Carsten and Spector (1987); Spector (1996)
Organizational alternatives	The employee's perceived availability of equal or better jobs in other organizations	Allen and Meyer (1990); Mitchell Holtom, Lee, Sablynski, & Erez (2001); Van Dam (2005)
Investment in current organization	The nonportable resources invested in or by the employee	Farrell and Rusbult (1981)
Job attraction	The employee's overall perception of job rewards versus job costs	Farrell and Rusbult (1981); Kelly and Thibault (1978); Rusbult and Farrell (1983); Van Dam (2005)

300 studies have used the construct Organizational Commitment as defined by these scholars. As evident by several meta analyses, a strong general finding is that Organizational Commitment is negatively correlated with Turnover (Mathieu & Zajac 1990; Tett & Meyer 1993). As previously indicated by the basic model of Turnover Intentions among IS professionals, Organizational Commitment has been found to be a major determinant of Turnover Intentions among Western IS professionals (Gallivan 2004; Joseph et al. 2007). Based on this vast empirical support, the first hypothesis is:

H1: Organizational Commitment is negatively related to Turnover Intentions

Job Satisfaction has been extensively studied since the 1930s, with more than 12,400 studies published on the topic by 1991. Substantial evidence from several meta analyses found that Job Satisfaction is negatively related to Turnover Intentions (Cotton & Tuttle 1986; Hom et al. 1992; Tett & Meyer 1993). As previously indicated by the basic model of Turnover Intentions among IS professionals (Gallivan 2004; Joseph et al. 2007) Job Satisfaction is negatively related to Turnover Intentions among Western IS professionals. Our second hypothesis is:

H2: Job Satisfaction is negatively related to Turnover Intentions

Job Satisfaction has also been found to have a direct relationship with Organizational Commitment. In the Job Investment Model of Intentions to Leave,

Job Satisfaction is one of the three major determinants of Organizational Commitment, along with Organizational Alternatives and Investment (Farrell & Rusbult 1981). Empirical research supports this model. Two studies tested all three antecedents to Organizational Commitment. In Rusbult and Farrell's 1983 test of the Investment model with 88 employees in professional service organizations, they found that Organizational Commitment was determined by high Job Satisfaction, poor Alternative quality, and large Investment size. Van Dam (2005) tested these relationships with a survey of 953 employees from three hospitals. She found that Job Satisfaction was positively related to Organizational Commitment, Organizational Alternatives were negatively related to Organizational Commitment, and Investments were positively related to Organizational Commitment. Several other meta-analyses also support that Job Satisfaction is an antecedent to Organizational Commitment (Mathieu & Zajac's 1990; Tett & Meyer 1993). Because Organizational Commitment takes longer to develop and is more stable than Job Satisfaction, turnover models suggest Job Satisfaction directly affects Organizational Commitment rather than the other way around (Tett & Meyer). Based on this research, we hypothesize:

H3: Job Satisfaction is positively related to Organizational Commitment

In Rusbult and Farrell's 1983 test of the Job Investment Model, they found that Organizational Commitment was significantly determined by poor Organizational Alternatives. Van Dam (2005) found that Organizational Alternatives were negatively related to Organizational Commitment. In addition to these studies, a meta-analysis of seven empirical studies comprising 2,657 individuals found that Perceived Job Alternatives was negatively related to Organizational Commitment (Mathieu & Zajac's 1990). It is also interesting that a meta-analysis of 21 studies found that Organizational Alternatives is only weakly directly related to Turnover Intentions (Steel & Griffeth 1989). Thus, the evidence suggests that Organizational Alternatives affects Turnover Intentions through the mediating variable, Organizational Commitment. Based on this research, we hypothesize:

H4: Organizational Alternatives is negatively related to Organizational Commitment

Investment in Current Organization includes acquisition of nonportable skills, nontransferable retirement programs, and length of service. Although early research suggests that Organizational Investment is what the individual puts into the organization, it is clear that organizations also invest in the individual. Expensive training programs, for example, may make the employee feel obligated to the organization and thus increase their Organizational Commitment (Cole & Bruch 2006). Previously cited research has empirically found a significant relationship between Organizational Investment and Organizational Commitment (Rusbult & Farrell 1983; Van Dam 2005). Our hypothesis is:

H5: Investment in Current Organization is positively related to Organizational Commitment

Job Attraction is derived from the Job Investment Model of Intentions to Leave. In this model, Job Attraction comprises the overall assessment of job rewards and job costs. Job rewards and costs may include *compensation* such as salary, bonuses, benefits and *job characteristics* such as task variety, task identity, task significance, task autonomy, role ambiguity, role complexity, and job stress (Kelly & Thibault 1978; Farrell & Rusbult 1981; Rusbult & Farrell 1983; Van Dam 2005). Job rewards and job costs are considered isomorphic. Any of the components may either be a job reward or a job cost, depending on the individual's perception. For example, if an individual is highly satisfied with their salary, salary would be considered a job reward. Conversely, if an individual was highly dissatisfied with their salary, salary would be considered a job cost.

In Rusbult and Farrell's 1983 test of the Investment model, they found that greater Job Satisfaction resulted from higher job rewards and lower job costs. They conclude: *"The results of this study provide good support for the investment model predictions. In general, greater job rewards and lower job costs induce greater employee satisfaction."* (p. 436). Van Dam (2005) found the overall assessment of Job Attraction (Job Rewards versus Job Costs) was positively related to Job Satisfaction. In her study, Job Attraction captures Job Rewards versus Job Costs by asking respondents to assess nine job reward items. She followed Rusbult and Farrell's argument that the absence of a reward implies the presence of a cost. She concludes: *"Consistent with predictions, employees who perceived a more favorable jobs rewards–costs ratio reported great satisfaction"* (p. 265). Based on this research, our hypothesis is:

H6: Job Attraction is positively related to Job Satisfaction

3   Research Method

3.1   The Interview Method

To assess to the applicability of our initial model, we used interviews. The primary purpose for the interviews was to assess whether the initial model, which was developed primarily by Western academics and tested with Western workers, is applicable to the context of Indian IS professionals. Interviews are an appropriate method when researchers:

(a) Seek to understand themes of the lived daily world from the subject's own perspectives (Kvale 1996)
(b) Do not want to limit the study to predefined constructs or predefined categories within constructs (Glaser & Strauss 1999)
(c) Seek participation from *busy* or *high-status* respondents (Mahoney 1997)
(d) Seek answers to questions in which the subject matter is *sensitive* (Mahoney 1997)
(e) Are concerned with the *quality*, not quantity of responses (Fontana & Frey 1994)
(f) Are concerned with the participants' *values* (Bourne & Jenkins 2005; Gummesson 2000)
(g) Seek to answer a why or how questions about contemporary events over which the researcher has little or no control (Fontana & Frey 1994; Yin 2003)

We believe that interviews were the best research method to assess the applicability of our initial model and hypotheses. First, we wanted a method that would allow additional constructs beyond the initial model to emerge from the interviews (and indeed they did). The interview method, therefore, allowed us to expand the research model. Second, we believed that *busy* IS professionals, who hold a significant position of *status* within the Indian culture, would be more likely to respond to a personal interview than to an anonymous survey. Third, many people would likely perceive intentions to leave an organization as a *sensitive* subject. Thus, we selected an interview method because it allows researchers to clearly communicate the purpose of the research, to ensure confidentiality, and to build trust during a personal interview. Once trust is established, research participants would be more likely to answer sensitive questions about their current job satisfaction, job commitment, and turnover intentions (and indeed they did).

We selected *semistructured* interviews because we wanted to leave the method fluid enough to explore constructs that may be missing from the model, but rigid enough to assess whether the six constructs were applicable. Interviews were conducted by telephone because the authors are located in the US and Indian IS professionals are located in India.

The Interview Guide. The Interview Guide (see Appendix A) is designed to capture the six constructs in the initial model, to allow participants to freely explain their reasoning and values, and to explore uncharted constructs. Concerning the six constructs, the interview guide clearly prompted participants to respond to the model's constructs so that we could later code their answers. This proved an effective method because we were able to code the constructs and identify new constructs, except for our initial questions to capture Organizational Commitment. Our first set of questions were: *"How do you feel about your company?"* and *"Does the organization mean a lot to you?"* These questions did not prompt participants to discuss their emotional bond to the organization. After interview seven, we added the question *"Do you feel emotionally attached to your company?"* As we later discuss, this additional question yielded some fascinating results.

The open-ended questions gave the participants the latitude to explain their responses and to identify constructs that were not previously identified in the model. Indeed, we added three new constructs to the model based on the interviews.

Research Participants. Twenty-five Indian IS professionals were interviewed. The interviews were conducted by the two Indian coauthors. We believed that they would elicit more trust than the American coauthor due to higher homophile with Indian participants (Rogers 2006). In addition, the IS professionals were selected based on mutual acquaintances of the Indian coauthors, which further served to elicit trust from the respondents. Although the sample is opportunistic, we believe it is better to ensure the trust and cooperation from an opportunistic sample than to attempt to solicit cooperation from an anonymous random sample because the topic is sensitive.

The interviews were conducted between November 2006 and March 2007. The demographic information of the 25 Indian IS professionals is summarized in

Table 2 Demographics of 25 participants

Sex:	Females: 7	Males: 18
Age:	Range: 26–36 years	Average: 29.7 years
Years in current job:	Range: 5 months to 6.5 years	Average: 23 months
Years work experience:	Range: 1.5–10 years	Average: 5.38

Table 2. The 25 Indian IS professionals worked for 13 different supplier firms. (In embedded quotes, the 13 supplier names have been replaced with S1 through S13) Nineteen participants work in Bangalore, three in Pune, one in Hyderabad, and one in Delhi. The sample contained 13 different job titles, including senior software engineer, assistant project manager, project manager, analyst, developer, team lead, process lead, quality engineer, and quality lead.

3.2   Coding the Transcriptions

The 25 interviews were transcribed. Each participant was assigned an identifier labeled P1–P25. For each participant, the three authors coded the six constructs independently as "high," "moderate" or "low." Table 3 shows examples of how five of the six constructs were coded from interview extracts.

We independently agreed on the coding for Turnover Intentions, Job Satisfaction, Organizational Alternatives, and Job Attraction for all 25 participants. We initially could not code Organizational Commitment (discussed above) until we added another question after interview seven. We did not independently code three "Organizational Alternatives" and six "Investment in Current Organization" the same. Because responses were ambiguous in these cases, we left these as "unable to code." Job Attraction required more consideration to code because we had to consider the participants' responses to 12 questions on compensation and job characteristics. Responses to these questions could consume three pages of transcription, but we were easily able to code Job Attraction. Three patterns were readily evident:

- The participant was satisfied with nearly all their compensation and job characteristics (high Job Attraction)
- The participant reported satisfaction with some of the compensation and job characteristics and dissatisfaction with other compensation and job characteristics (moderate Job Attraction)
- The participant was dissatisfied with nearly all their compensation and job characteristics (low Job Attraction)

Table 4 summarizes the coding for all six constructs.

Table 3 Examples of coding five constructs based on participants' responses

	Low	Moderate	High
Turnover intention:	Author: *"Are you thinking of leaving this company?"* P3: *"No, not right now."* Author: *"Where do you see yourself in 1 year?"* P3: *"Hopefully in this company."*	Author: *"Where do you see yourself 1 year from now?"* P6: *"There is a possibility I will be here or gone. As I said, in the next 6 months, if I don't get a position suitable inside S2, then I will have to look outside S2."*	Author: *"Where do you see yourself 1 year from now?"* P16: *"I have already resigned from the current organization. I will be moving shortly to the other organization."*
Job satisfaction	Author: *"Are you satisfied with your job?"* P10: *"No I am not happy with my job. I am dissatisfied...I mean I am feeling bad [about my job]"*	Author: *"Are you satisfied with your job?"* P12: *"Sort of yes and no, kind of 50:50."*	Author: *"Are you satisfied with your job?"* P14: *"Yes, I'm satisfied... I'm very much enthusiastic [about my job]"*
Organizational commitment:	Author: *"Do you feel emotionally attached to your company?"* P15: *"No, no emotional bond between me and my company."*	Author: *"How do you feel about S2?"* P22: *"It's good. The brand name is good."* Author: *"Do you feel emotionally attached to your company?"* P22: *"Not exactly."*	Author: *"Do you feel emotionally attached to your company?"* P18: *"The company means a lot to me and I have attachment to it."*
Organizational alternatives:	Author: *"If you wanted to change organizations tomorrow, how difficult would it be?"* P7: *"In my case, I'm still having 1 year experience, so it may be difficult because in the present situation in Bangalore, all companies want 2 years experience. Maybe some companies will treat me just as a fresher."*	Author: *"Can you get another job easily if you want to?"* P4: *"I don't say that's it difficult. I don't say that it's very easy. It's kind of in between difficult and easy."*	Author: *"Can you get another job easily of you want to?"* P21: *"Yes, of course. If I want to change today, I get at least 100 calls per day. Even before joining the company I used to get 20 to 30 calls per day."*

(continued)

Table 3 (continued)

	Low	Moderate	High
Investment in current organization:	Author: *"Is your training and work experience portable to other organizations?"*	Author: *"Is your training and work experience portable to other organizations?"*	Author: *"Is your training and work experience portable to other organizations?"*
	P1: *"Yes, if you have experience, then it is not difficult to start working on a new project [for a new company.] If you are in India, you know the kind of work Indians get across the IT industry is almost the same. If you change a project or even a company, then you can handle it."*	P12: *"Whatever training we get is product related. It won't be of any use outside the company. Other things, you know my skill set is valid across companies."*	P3: *"What happens is that when you go to a new company, you have to establish yourself. That takes 2–8 months. I would not like to go to a new one because I would have to prove myself again. Because you are new, they don't recognize your talents. You need to establish yourself all over again."*
	Author: *"So your tenure in a company doesn't matter?"*		
	P1: *"Doesn't matter."*		

Table 4 Code summaries

Construct	Low	Moderate	High	Unable to code
Turnover intention	13	5	7	0
Job satisfaction	5	6	14	0
Job attraction	3	9	13	0
Organizational commitment	7	6	6	6
Organizational alternatives	1	4	17	3
Investment in current organization	4	12	3	6

4 Findings from the Interviews

To investigate the hypotheses, we created a series of tables that mapped independent variables to dependent variables (Tables 5 through 10) and ran two nonparametric statistical tests. The tables illustrate the hypothesized relationships with dark gray shading. The light gray shading indicates somewhat of a relationship. The clear cells indicate observations that are counter to hypotheses. The clear cells, which are anomalies, provide important clues for modifying the model.

Table 5 H1: Organizational commitment versus turnover intentions (n = 19[a])

Organizational commitment	Turnover intentions		
	Low	Moderate	High
Low	3	2	2
Moderate	2	1	3
High	4		2

Kendall's tau-c = −0.066, Approximate significance = 0.742
Somers' d: = −0.067, Approximate significance = 0.742

[a]n = 19 because 6 uncodable observations for Organizational Commitment were not included in the analysis

Because the sample data is ordinal, small, and opportunistic, we ran two non parametric tests. Kendall's tau-c is a symmetrical test of association between X and Y. Somers' d is asymmetrical, testing the directional association of X on Y. Both tests generate values ranging from −1 for a perfectly negative relationship to +1 for a perfectly positive relationship. For the six tests, we applied $p < .01$ as the required level of significance.

4.1 H1 Not Supported

Table 5 maps Turnover Intentions to Organizational Commitment.

We hypothesized that Organizational Commitment is negatively related to Turnover Intentions. The evidence does not support the hypothesis as evidenced by the two statistical tests. Twenty-six percent of the observations fall within the clear cells, representing five anomalies.

Three participants (P15, P19, and P25) had low Turnover Intentions and low Organizational Commitment. P15 is a male who wants to stay in his current organization because of the career opportunities, but reports no emotional bond with the company. P19 has only been working for S9 for 5 months, so he reports that he does not have an emotional bond to the company even though he intends to remain with the organization. P25 is a female who wants to stay with the current organization because of the career development opportunities and because her organization is close to her family. But she does not feel emotionally attached to her organization.

Two participants (P20 and P24) had high Turnover Intentions and high Organizational Commitment. P20 is a male who has high Turnover Intentions for the primary reason of locating closer to his family, even though he reports high Organizational Commitment. He states, *"I do feel part of the company. I do feel a sense of belongingness. I feel proud to be working for S4, which has 80% market share in semiconductors. The only reason I want to leave is to make sure I spend some time with my family."*

P24 is a female who intends to leave the organization to pursue an MBA even though she currently reports high Organizational Commitment. These anomalies suggest that emotional attachment to an organization is not a significant determinant of Turnover Intention for these participants.

4.2 H2 Supported

We hypothesized that Job Satisfaction is negatively related to Turnover Intentions. Table 6 maps Turnover Intentions to Job Satisfaction. The evidence supports the hypothesis as evidenced by the two statistical tests. There are no anomalies within the clear cells to examine. We keep this hypothesis unaltered in the final model.

4.3 H3 Not Supported

We hypothesized that Job Satisfaction is positively related to Organizational Commitment. Table 7 maps Job Satisfaction to Organizational Commitment.

The evidence does not support the hypothesis. Twenty-one percent of the observations, representing four participants (P15, P19, P25, and P24), fall within the clear cells.

Table 6 H2: Job satisfaction versus turnover intentions (n = 25)

	Turnover intentions		
Job satisfaction	Low	Moderate	High
Low		2	3
Moderate	1	1	4
High	12	2	

Kendall's tau-c = −0.634, Approximate significance = 0.000
Somers' d: = −0.717, Approximate significance = 0.000

Table 7 H3: Job satisfaction versus organizational commitment (n = 19)

	Organizational commitment		
Job satisfaction	Low	Moderate	High
Low	1	2	1
Moderate	3	2	1
High	3	2	4

Kendall's tau-c = 0.100, Approximate significance = 0.611
Somers' d: = 0.105, Approximate significance = 0.611

Three participants (P15, P19, and P25) report low Organizational Commitment but high Job Satisfaction. These anomalies were previously discussed in conjunction with H1. They like the work they do, but they do not feel emotionally attached to their organizations. One participant, P24 again, reported high Organizational Commitment but low Job Satisfaction. She is female who intends to leave the organization to pursue an MBA. Her main issue with her current job is that she does not like IT work, even though she likes her current company.

4.4 H4 Not Supported

Hypothesis 4 posited that Organizational Alternatives is negatively related to Organizational Commitment. Table 8 maps Organizational Alternatives to Organizational Commitment. The evidence does not support the hypothesis as evidenced by the two statistical tests. Five participants (29% of observations) fall within the clear cells. One issue may be the fact that there is not much variability in Organizational Alternatives. Sixteen of the 25 IS professionals perceived a high availability of equal or better jobs in the market.

Five participants (P8, P9, P18, P21, and P24) perceived high Organizational Alternatives and high Organizational Commitment. P8, P9, P18, and P21 all had many positive things to say about their organizations. Although these four all perceived that Organizational Alternatives were plentiful, the opportunities do not tempt them to leave. P24 again surfaces as an anomaly – she is the one leaving to pursue her MBA.

4.5 H5 Not Supported

We hypothesized that Investment in the Current Organization is positively related to Organizational Commitment. Table 9 maps Investment to Organizational Commitment. The evidence does not support the hypothesis as evidenced by the two statistical tests.

Table 8 H4: Organizational alternatives versus organizational commitment (n = 17)

Organizational alternatives	Organizational commitment		
	Low	Moderate	High
Low			
Moderate		1	
High	7	4	5

Kendall's tau-c = −0.055, Approximate significance = 0.580
Somers' d: = −0.133, Approximate significance = 0.580

Table 9 H5: Investment versus organizational commitment (n = 15)

Investment	Organizational commitment		
	Low	Moderate	High
Low	1	2	1
Moderate	5	3	3
High			

Kendall's tau-c = −0.107, Approximate significance = 0.646
Somers' d: = −0.136, Approximate significance = 0.646

Table 10 H6: Job attraction versus job satisfaction (n = 25)

Job attraction	Job satisfaction		
	Low	Moderate	High
Low	2	1	
Moderate	3	5	1
High			13

Kendall's tau-c = 0.734, Approximate significance = 0.000
Somers' d: = 0.836, Approximate significance = 0.000

There are a couple of noteworthy issues from this analysis. First, the only anomaly in the clear cell is once again P24. Second, there are no observations in which Investment in Current Organization is perceived as high. As a group, the participants thought that their IT skills were highly portable. The participants with moderate investments stated that although their IT skills were highly portable, other investments were not. Nonportable investments included benefits from tenure in the organization such as becoming vested, establishing a good reputation within the current organization, and understanding the organization's idiosyncratic processes or domain-specific knowledge.

4.6 H6 Supported

We hypothesized that Job Attraction is positively related to Job Satisfaction. Table 10 maps Job Attraction to Job Satisfaction. The evidence strongly support the hypothesis as evidenced by the two statistical tests. There are no anomalies within the clear cells to examine. Thus, we keep this hypothesis unaltered in the final model.

5   Revised Model Based on Interview Data

Based on the 25 interviews, there is reasonable evidence to support H2 and H6. However, the other hypotheses are not supported. In this section, we discuss three changes to the turnover model suggested by the interview data. The revised model is found in Fig. 3.

5.1   Replace Organizational Commitment with Organizational Satisfaction

Organizational Commitment was the one variable common in the four hypotheses that were not supported. A closer examination of this variable is warranted.

One possible explanation is a problem with the definition of Organizational Commitment, which IS academics define as emotional attachment to the organization. It was very difficult to get participants to discuss their emotional attachment to an organization. This construct resulted in the highest number of uncodable responses (n = 6) during our initial interviews when we only asked how they feel about the organization and whether the organization means a lot to them. Participants did not naturally reply to these questions by expressing emotional attachment to the organization.

After P7, we added the specific question, *"Do you feel emotionally attached to the organization?"* Responses were interesting because many hesitated and some even laughed at the notion that a human is bonded to an organization. For example, when we asked P13 how he feels about the organization he said, *"Company as such is great. It is a number two company in the world. If I see the company on the whole, definitely one of the best companies to have every existed."* The follow-up question, "Do you feel emotionally attached to your company?" resulted in *"No, no, no!"*

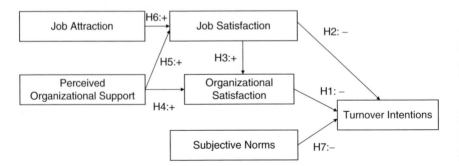

Fig. 3 Revised model of turnover intentions among Indian IS professionals

For another example, consider the following dialog with P11:

Author: *"How do you feel about your company?"*
P11: "General feeling is satisfactory, not good."
Author: "Does the organization mean a lot to you?"
P11: "Yeah, as I have worked here all these years, I must be loyal."
Author: "Do you feel emotionally attached to your company?"
P11: "No, not at all…My responsibility is my personal life."

P25 provides a third example of positive feelings about the organization, yet not feeling emotionally attached:

Author: *"How do you feel about your company? What is the general feeling that you have?"*
P25: "In general it is a good company where we can learn a lot of knowledge in the semi-conductor industry and we get lot of opportunities to grow. Good for growth also."
Author: "Do you feel emotionally attached to your company?"
P25: "Emotionally, not so."

In some other interviews, individuals reported that they did not feel emotionally connected to the organization, but they did feel emotionally connected to their colleagues. When asked, *"Do you feel emotionally attached to your company?"* P10 said no, but clarified with: *"But they are very good group. We are very close. I think if I leave this company, I will miss those people."* P23 had a similar response: *"Not really. Not the company, but maybe with the people I work with."*

Thus, many Indian IS professionals we spoke to could not relate to the concept of emotional attachments to an organization. We highly suspect, based on the responses to the Organizational Commitment questions, that Organizational Satisfaction will better capture the sentiments of Indian IS professionals towards their organizations.

Organizational Satisfaction. Organizational Satisfaction is defined as "the extent to which an employee is satisfied with their current organization." We found that when we initially asked participants how they felt about their organizations, they frequently responded with the extent to which they were satisfied or dissatisfied with their organizations. Organizational Satisfaction is clearly different than Organizational Commitment (affectual). Indian IS professionals could be satisfied with their organization but not feel emotionally attached to it. In addition, Organizational Satisfaction is clearly a separate construct from Job Satisfaction, in that some participants were happy with their current jobs (job characteristics and compensation), yet dissatisfied with the overall organization. Conversely, a number of participants were dissatisfied with their current jobs, but were satisfied with their organizations. In these circumstances, the employees were seeking job changes within their organizations.

Within the OB literature, Organizational Satisfaction has been linked to Turnover Intention (Shore & Tetrick 1991; Kittiruengcharn 1997; Szamosi 2006). For example, Kittiruengcharn (1997) administered a survey to 408 public sector engineers in Thailand and found a significant negative correlation between Organizational Satisfaction and Turnover Intention. Therefore, one hypothesis developed from this replacement construct is:

H1: Organizational Satisfaction is negatively related to Turnover Intention

Kittiruengcharm's path analysis of the survey data found that Job Satisfaction contributed to Organizational Satisfaction, and visa versa. However, the path was stronger from Job Satisfaction to Organizational Satisfaction than from Organizational Satisfaction to Job Satisfaction. The findings are consistent with the view that attitudes about jobs are formed quicker than attitudes about organizations (Tett & Meyer 1993). We therefore hypothesize:

H3: Job Satisfaction is positively related to Organizational Satisfaction

5.2 Include Perceived Organizational Support as a Determinant of Organizational Satisfaction and Job Satisfaction

When we asked participants how they felt about the organization, we noted they frequently expressed their level of satisfaction with the organization. They also justified the *reasons* for their level of satisfaction by discussing management support, supervisor support, career development opportunities, organizational culture, and company policies. Table 11 summaries the number of participants who mentioned these reasons. The three authors coded these responses as "participants spoke only unfavorably," "participant spoke unfavorably and favorably," and "participant spoke only favorably."

Management Support. Twenty participants discussed Management Support as a justification for their feelings about the organization. Fourteen participants spoke only favorably about their managers. Participants discussed that they could bring problems to their managers, ask for help, seek resources, and talk about career opportunities. Only three participants spoke only unfavorably about Management Support. Below are representative quotes of the three classifications of Management Support:

> P8 *(favorably):* "Managers are very nice. They give enough time to the people who are not up to the work by trying to bring them up to the mark. It's a very good, friendly company."

Table 11 Participants' reasons for explaining organizational satisfaction

Construct	# of participants who spoke only unfavorably	# of participants who spoke unfavorably and favorably	# of participants who spoke only favorably	Total # of participants who mentioned this as a reason
Management support	3	3	14	20 (80%)
Organizational culture	4	1	13	18 (72%)
Career development	6	3	8	17 (68%)
Supervisor support	4	0	12	16 (64%)
Company policies	4	0	5	9 (36%)

P13 (favorably/unfavorably): "Management is supportive of our endeavors but management does not have proper control of the people sitting in the US and Europe."
P11 (unfavorably): "Management is not supportive."

Organizational Culture. Eighteen participants discussed Organizational Culture as a justification for their feelings about the organization. Thirteen spoke only positively about the culture. Some examples of favorable descriptions include:

P11 (favorably): "The company culture is very good."
P21 (favorably): "The work culture is good. Every individual shares his or her knowledge with everyone else in the company."
P24 (favorably): "The work culture is amongst the best that I have seen. It's a great place to work in."

Only four participants spoke only unfavorably about the Organizational Culture. For example, P13 did not like the relaxed culture in his company. He said, *"What does not give you fulfillment is the kind of environment that we have in the business. People not applying proper processes, people not working in a structured format that is disappointing with the organization."*

Career Development. Seventeen participants discussed Career Development as a justification for their feelings about the organization. Eight spoke only favorably about Career Development. For example, P9 discussed the career paths as a clear "roadmap" at his company. Six participants spoke only unfavorably about Career Development. For example, P1 believes management placates employees with the rhetoric of Career Development, but that in reality they assign employees where the company needs them. She stated, *"To be very frank they talk a lot about career development. They call you and ask you what your career objectives are, but they want you to adjust according to their requirements. That's how it happens. They try to pacify you."*

Supervisor Support. Sixteen participants discussed Supervisor Support as a justification for their feelings about the organization. These responses were bipolar. Like Management Support, most participants spoke favorably about their direct supervisors:

P18 (favorably):"My manager [direct supervisor] is like a guide to me. I go to him for guidance."
P7 (favorably): "He is encouraging actually."

Four spoke only unfavorably about their direct supervisor. For example, P1 stated,

"My manager [direct supervisor] is very bossy and sometimes I feel like quitting the job just because of him."

Company Policies. Nine participants discussed company policies as a justification for their feelings about the organization. These responses were also bipolar. Five spoke only favorably about company policies such as the company's "open door policy" and the policy at one supplier that allows employees to request a new position every 18 months. Four participants talked only unfavorably about company policies. P3, for example, was very frustrated with her company's HR recruiting policies. She felt that the company hired "freshers" and assigned them to projects without proper training. She said:

> "Sometimes we end up with really dumb recruits. They don't have any aptitude for the kind of job they have to do...sometimes you end up doing their work."

To summarize, five constructs emerged from the interviews concerning participants' feelings about their organizations: Management Support, Organizational Culture, Career Development, Supervisor Support, and Company Policies. Rather than add five new constructs to the model, we searched the literature to identify a construct rich enough to encompass all these factors. We selected Perceived Organizational Support as the umbrella construct.

Perceived Organizational Support. This construct is formally defined in the literature (Rhodes & Eisenberger 2002) as follows:

> *Perceived Organizational Support:* The employees' beliefs concerning the extent to which the organization values their contributions and cares about their well-being and socioemotional needs.

Whereas Organizational Commitment is about the employees' commitment to the organization, Perceived Organizational Support is about the employee's perceptions about the organization's commitment, support, and care to the employee. A meta-analysis of 70 empirical studies of Perceived Organizational Support found that the major antecedents included supervisor support, fair policies, and organizational rewards (Rhodes & Eisenberger 2002). Joiner and Bakalis (2006) also found that supervisor support is a major antecedent of Organizational Commitment. Perceived Organizational Support thus captures much of what our participants cited as reasons for their feelings about the organization. The meta-analysis also looked at the consequences of Perceived Organizational Support. The authors found that Perceived Organizational Support had a *large*, positive, overall effect on Organizational Commitment (aggregate) and Job Satisfaction. Our resulting hypotheses are:

H4: *Perceived Organizational Support is positively related to Organizational Satisfaction*

H5: *Perceived Organizational Support is positively related to Job Satisfaction*

5.3   Include Social Norms as a Determinant of Turnover Intentions

One construct that was missing from the initial model but may be important is Social Norms. Ajzen and Fishbein (1980) define norms as *"an individual's perceptions of the social pressures put on him to perform or not to perform the behavior in question."* Among our interviews, nine Indian IS professionals mentioned pressure to reside in the same city as the family. We did not ask this question directly, yet it became a prominent theme during these nine interviews. This frequently trumped all other reasons for intending to stay or leave an organization. Four participants mentioned the importance of family/work life balance. Both types of family pressures are discussed below.

Family pressure to reside in the same city as the family. The participants did not claim that their family pressured them to remain or leave a particular *organization*, only to remain or leave a particular *location*. If the current organization was located near the family, the pressure was to remain. If the current organization was remotely located, the pressure was to relocate to the family. Below are some excerpts from the interviews to illustrate family location pressures:

- P2 (male) feels pressured to remain in Bangalore. While his family does not care which organization he works for, he states, "I am not willing to relocate to any other city. We generally live with our parents and it would be generally difficult to relocate to another part of the country."
- P3 (female, married) does not like living in Delhi, but she moved back to Delhi to be near her husband's family. "I have adjusted here but it was not my choice of place."
- P10 (male) said, "My parents are dependent upon me. So I can't go long distance because I have to go home every 15–20 days."
- P20 (male) is working in Bangalore. Despite his high Organizational Commitment and medium Job Satisfaction, he intends to leave his organization within 6 months to move back home to Belgaum. He stated, "On a personal front, I am not happy. I want to spend more time with my friends and family in Belgaum… The only reason I want to leave is to make sure I spend more time with my family."

Family pressure to balance work and family life. Four participants said that family pressures to better balance work and family life affected their turnover intentions. For example, P23 is a married female. She likes most aspects of her job, but the commute across Bangalore consumes too much time and she feels work/family conflict: *"The days when your family needs you, I mean, lots of times, both [work and family] need you at the same time and it's difficult to balance the two – work life and professional life. You can't guarantee that you can leave work at 5:00. You could be late, it could extend for long hours."*

Given the strong family orientation of Indian culture, we believe that the inclusion of Social Norms is important to our study of Turnover Intentions among Indian IS professionals. In addition, Social Norms may include peer pressure in addition to family pressure. For example, P8 said: *"When I talk to my friends and excolleagues they are saying S2 is a wonderful place to work, the culture, the atmosphere, the facilities and all these kind of things, we can't match with any other company."* For the revised model, the construct is defined as follows:

Social Norms: The employee's beliefs that family and peers think that he/she should remain with their current employer

And we hypothesize:

H7: Social Norms is negatively related to Turnover Intention

6 Additional Findings: Implications for Practice

What do our participants' 25 voices suggest for offshore outsourcing? For offshore outsourcing suppliers, the interviews reveal a number of interesting findings about the factors that affect intentions to leave an organization. For offshore clients, the interviews reveal some serious concerns.

1. *Offer Indian IS professionals more interesting work rather than more money to increase Job Satisfaction and to reduce Turnover.* Given the rising salaries among Indian IS professionals, we were interested to know how their perceptions of their current compensation affected their Job Satisfaction and ultimately Turnover Intentions. We asked four compensation questions pertaining to base salary, egalitarian bonuses (bonuses distributed equally among employees), performance based bonuses, and benefits such as healthcare. Among the 25 participants, seven felt they were underpaid, but only two of these seven had low Job Satisfaction. *Fifteen participants were satisfied with their salaries even though they said they could increase their base salary if they left their current organization.* Furthermore, all but one participant said they could easily get a job in another organization because of the strong demand for IS talent. It is clear that salary is not the main reason for changing organizations among our interviewees.

Beyond compensation, a strong theme throughout the interviews was that Indian IS professionals want challenging jobs, just like their US/Western counterparts. Among the five professionals who were very dissatisfied with their jobs, four were mostly upset about the lack of task variety and low skill set utilization. For example, P1 complained:

> *"I have been put into testing and coding and now it is kind of maintenance phase. Now I am not able to use my skill set much. I am not satisfied with the kind of work I am doing. Every alternate day I go to my manager and I tell him that I am not satisfied with the kind of work I am getting and I need more challenging work so I can improve my skills."*

P2 complained about merely maintaining a client's application. He says he just,

> *"fixes errors in the application and monitors the jobs...I utilize only 20% of my knowledge."*

Among the 14 professionals who were highly satisfied with their jobs, 12 mentioned task variety or skill set utilization as the major reasons for their satisfaction. In contrast to the previous participants, these participants talked enthusiastically about their jobs. For example, P15 reported high Job Satisfaction and mentioned direct contact with customers as a reason for his satisfaction:

> "Every software release or every major target, we are getting feedback from the customer as well as our managers."

P21 is a male working as software engineer. He stated:

> "My job is completely fulfilling. The challenges they throw at me. The challenges I get in my job. Like the technology with which I am working is really good and you get so many challenges each day. I do get a lot of variety. Like I send the proposal document, talk to the clients, and I even do development and testing."

Thus, while compensation matters, the type of work was a more important component of Job Attraction. *Indian IS professionals preferred client-facing activities, design, and development work over application maintenance and support. This finding is troubling because many US clients justify offshore outsourcing by arguing that their internal IS staff should do more challenging work while offshore supplier employees can do more routine work.* Clients might experience higher supplier turnover if they only offshore routine tasks such as monitoring and maintenance of existing systems or just outsource the coding or testing phases of new development.

2. *Rotate Indian IS professionals from routine jobs within 18 months.* What can suppliers do if routine tasks are the bulk of their clients' work? Most of our Indian respondents were willing to tolerate routine work provided the supplier had a *reliable* career path that promised more interesting work in the future. We stress *reliable* because some respondents indicated that their managers made false promises about career opportunities. In contrast, employees from one major global supplier were very happy with an HR policy that allowed employees to get a job transfer every 18 months. They were more willing to execute routine tasks because they knew it was a stepping stone to more challenging jobs. Clients might also investigate supplier's HR policies to determine the extent to which the supplier can motivate and retain their IS staff.

3. *Caring HR policies can increase Job Satisfaction and Organizational Satisfaction among Indian IS professionals.* While Indian IS professionals did not feel emotionally attached to their organizations, the extent to which they were satisfied with their organizations determined their Turnover Intentions. The good news is that suppliers have much control over the practices that affect employee Turnover Intentions. Indian IS employees want to remain with organizations that have supportive senior managers, supportive direct supervisors, fun and open cultures, and company policies such as flextime and the ability to occasionally work from home. This latter policy was particularly stressed by six participants who suffered long work commutes.

Within the US IS literature, there are two important studies that suggest that *collections* of HR IS practices influence IS employee turnover (Agarwal, Brown, Ferratt, & Moore, 2006; Agarwal, Ferratt, & De 2007; Ang & Slaughter 2004; Ferratt, Agarwal, Brown, & Moore 2005; Igbaria et al. 1994). Two studies identified five different IS HR configurations and found that the "Human Capital Focused Profile" was associated with the lowest turnover rates (10.3%) and that the "Incented Technician Profile" was associated with the highest IS turnover rates (19.9%) (Agarwal et al. 2006; Ferratt et al.). Organizations with a Human Capital Focused Profile implemented the most number of HR practices for work environment, career development, community-building initiatives, monetary incentives, and employment incentives.

4. *Involve the family.* Concerning Social Norms, what emerged from these interviews was a strong sense of family obligations. Primarily, Indian IS employees are obliged to live near their parents. This may suggest that suppliers are better

off recruiting talent locally or relocating entire families for exceptional talent that currently resides afar. One small supplier moves entire families to his corporate campus in Hyderabad. While this practice is costly, the CEO said that family pressure to remain at his company is so strong, he can offer lower than market salaries and still retain most of his employees (Willcocks & Lacity M.C. 2006). Another Indian supplier involves the family in all corporate social functions such as bowling night and parties.

Within the US literature, there has been some evidence that "family friendly HR policies" reduce turnover (Kopelman, Prottas, Thompsom, & White Jahn 2006). Although these HR practices have not been tested in the Indian context, they might be of interest. These 21 practices are sick child days off, part time work, family leaves, flexible benefits, flexible time, flexible spending account, compensatory time, family picnic, family resource center, childcare subsidy, sick/emergency childcare, flexible place, compressed work week, work/family seminars, job sharing, onsite childcare, work/family support group, caregiver fair, after school program, summer camp, and adoption assistance (Mesmer-Magnus & Viswesvaran 2006).

7 Conclusions

Our research suggests a model of Turnover Intentions for Indian IS Professionals that differs from models that have been developed and tested on Western workers in general, and on Western IS professionals specifically. Models of Western IS professionals have generally found that Job Satisfaction, Organizational Commitment, and Work Exhaustion are the main determinants of Turnover Intentions. Among our Indian IS professionals, the concept of Organizational Commitment was troublesome. Many did not relate to the idea of an emotional bond with an organization. Instead, what emerged from these interviews was a strong sense of Social Norms from families and feelings of Organizational Satisfaction rather than Organizational Commitment. Some of these differences may be cultural. Prior research has shown, for example, that the Indian culture has much greater power distance and long term orientation and much lower individualism than say, the United States and Great Britain (Hofstede 2001). Although we are naturally cautious to extrapolate too much based on 25 interviews, we believe we have identified a solid model of turnover intentions of Indian IS professionals. Our ambition is to test our model with a large sample survey in the near future.

References

Agarwal, R., Brown, C., Ferratt, T., & Moore, J. E. (2006). Five mindsets for retaining IT staff. *MIS Quarterly Executive, 5*(3), 137–150.
Agarwal, R., Ferratt, T., & De, P. (2007). An experimental investigation of turnover intentions among new entrants in IT. *Database for Advances in Information Systems,* 8–28.

Ahuja, M., Chudoba, K., Kacmar, C., McKnight, D., & George, J. (2007). IT road warriors: Balancing work-family conflict, job autonomy, and work overload to mitigate turnover intentions. *MIS Quarterly, 31*(1), 1–17.

Ajzen, I., & Fishbein, M. (1980). *Understanding attitudes and predicting social behavior.* Englewood Cliffs, NJ: Prentice-Hall.

Allen, N., & Meyer, J. (1990). The measurement and antecedents of affective, continuance, and normative commitment to the organization. *Journal of Occupational Psychology, 63,* 1–18.

Ang, S., & Slaughter, S. (2004). Turnover of IT professionals: The effects of internal labor market strategies. *Database for Advances in Information Systems, 35*(3), 11–27.

Argyris, C. (1957). The individual and organization: some problems of mutual adjustment. *Administrative Science Quarterly, 2,* 1–24.

Arthur, W., Bell, S., Villado, A., & Doverspike, D. (2006). The use of person-organizational fit in employment decision-making: An assessment of its criterion-related validity. *Journal of Applied Psychology, 91*(4), 786–801.

Baroudi, J. (1985). The impact of role variables on IS personnel work attitudes and intentions. *MIS Quarterly, 9*(4), 341–356.

Bourne, H., & Jenkins, M. (2005). Eliciting manager's personal values: an adaptation of the laddering interview method. *Organizational Research Methods, 8*(4), 410–428.

Carsten, J., & Spector, P. (1987). Unemployment, job satisfaction, and employee turnover: A meta-analytic test of the Munchinsky model. *Journal of Applied Psychology, 73*(3), 374–381.

Cole, M., & Bruch, H. (2006). Organizational identity strength, identification, and commitment and their relationships to turnover intention: Does organizational hierarchy matter? *Journal of Organizational Behavior, 27,* 586–605.

Cotton, J., & Tuttle, J. (1986). Employee turnover: A meta-analysis and review with implications for research. *The Academy of Management Review, 11*(1), 55–70.

Farrell, D., & Rusbult, C. (1981). Exchange variables as predictors of job satisfaction, job commitment, and turnover: The impact of rewards, costs, alternatives, and investments. *Organizational Behavior and Human Performance, 28*(1), 78–96.

Ferratt, T., Agarwal, R., Brown, C., & Moore, J. E. (2005). IT human resource management configurations and IT turnover: Theoretical synthesis and empirical analysis. *Information Systems Research, 16*(3), 237–255.

Fontana, A., & Frey, J. (1994). Interviewing: The art of science. In Denzin & Lincoln (Eds.), *Handbook of qualitative research* (pp. 361–376). Thousand Oaks: Sage.

Gallivan, M. (2004). Examining IT professionals' adaptation to technological change: The influence of gender and personal attributes. *Database for Advances in Information Systems, 35*(3), 28–49.

Glaser, B., & Strauss, A. (1967). *The discovery of grounded theory: strategies for qualitative research.* Chicago: Aldine, reprinted 1999.

Gummesson, E. (2000). *Qualitative methods in management research.* Thousand Oaks: Sage.

Gupta, P. (2001). Growth scenario of IT industries in India. *Communications of the ACM, 44*(7), 40–41.

Gupta, Y., & Gupta, M. (1990). A process model to study the impact of role variables on turnover intentions of IS personnel. *Computers in Industry, 15*(3), 211–239.

Hackman, J., & Oldham, G. (1976). Motivation through the Design of Work: Test of a Theory. *Organizational Behavior and Human Performance, 16,* 250–279.

Hackman, J., & Oldham, G. (1980). *Work redesign.* London: Addison-Wesley.

Harrison, D., Newman, D., & Roth, P. (2006). How important are job attitudes? Metal-analytic comparisons of integrative behavioral outcomes and time sequences. *Academy of Management Journal, 49*(2), 305–325.

Herzberg, F. (1968). One more time: how do you motivate employees? *Harvard Business Review, 46*(1), 53–62.

Hoffman, B., & Woehr, D. (2006). A quantitative review of the relationship between person-organization fit and behavioral outcomes. *Journal of Vocational Behavior, 68,* 389–399.

Hofstede, G. (2001). *Cultural consequences: Comparing values, behaviors, institutions, and organizations across nations,* 2nd Edn. Thousand Oaks: Sage.

Hom, P., Caranikas-Walker, F., & Prussia, G. (1992). A meta-analytical structural equations analysis of a model of employee turnover. *Journal of Applied Psychology, 77*(6), 890–909.

Igbaria, M., & Greenhaus, J. (1992). Determinants of MIS employees' turnover intentions: A structural equation model. *Communications of the ACM, 35*(2), 34–49.

Igbaria, M., Parasuraman, S., & Bawawy, M. (1994). Work experiences, job involvement, and quality of work life among IS personnel. *MIS Quarterly, 18*(2), 175–201.

Jiang, J., & Klein, G. (2002). A discrepancy model of information systems personnel turnover. *Journal of Management Information Systems, 19*(2), 249–272.

Joseph, D., Ng, K., Koh, C., & Ang, S. (2007). Turnover of IT professionals: A narrative review, meta-analytic structural equation modeling, and model development. *MIS Quarterly, 31*(3), 1–31.

Joiner, T., & Bakalis, S. (2006). The antecedents of organizational commitment: The case of Australian casual academics. *International Journal of Educational Management, 20*(6), 439–452.

Kelly, H., & Thibaut, J. (1978). *Interpersonal relations: A theory of Interdependence.* New York: Wiley.

Kim, S., Price, J., Mueller, C., & Watson, T. (1996). The determination of career intent among physicians at a US air force hospital. *Human Relations, 49,* 947–976.

Kittiruengcharn, N. (1997). Impacts of job and organizational satisfaction, and organizational commitment on turnover intentions in Thai public sector engineers, Unpublished doctoral thesis, Concordia University, Quebec, Canada.

Kopelman, R., Prottas, D., Thompsom, C., & White Jahn, E. (2006). A multi-level examination of work-life practices: Is more always better? *Journal of Managerial Issues, 18,* 232–254

Kvale, S. (1996). *Interviews: An introduction to qualitative research interviewing.* Thousand Oaks: Sage.

Mahoney, C. (1997). Common qualitative techniques. In *User-Friendly Handbook for Mixed Method Evaluations* (pp. 1–17). Arlington: Division of Research, Evaluation and Communication for the National Science Foundation, publication number NSF97–153.

Mathieu, J., & Zajac, D. (1990). A review and meta-analysis of antecedents, correlates, and consequences of Organizational Commitment. *Psychological Bulletin, 108*(2), 171–194.

McClelland, D. (1961). *The achieving society.* Princeton: Van Nostrand.

McCue, A. (2005). High staff turnover hits India offshore firms. *Silicon Research,* January 2005, available on: http://www.silicon.com/research/specialreports/offshoring/0,3800003026,39127243,00.htm/

McMurtrey, M., Grover, V., Teng, J., & Lightner, N. (2002). Job satisfaction of information technology workers: The impact of career orientation and task automation in a CASE environment. *Journal of Management Information Systems, 19*(2), 273–302.

Mesmer-Magnus, J., & Viswesvaran, C. (2006). How family-friendly work environments affect family/work conflict: A meta-analytical examination. *Journal of Labor Research, 28*(4), 555–574.

Meyer, J., & Allen, N. (1997). *Commitment in the workplace: Theory, research, and application.* California: Sage.

Mitchell, A. (2005). India maintains outsourcing advantage. *E-commerce Times,* May 3, 2005, available on http://crmbuyer.com/story/42781.html.

Mitchell, A. (2004). Offshore labor markets impact IT outsourcing. Technewsworld, September 28, 2004 available online at http://www.technewsworld.com/story/36949.html.

Mitchell, A. (2007). Pakistan now a hot spot for IT outsourcing. Medialinkers, available on http://www.medialinkers.com/itoutsourcingpakistan.html.

Mitchell, T., Holtom, B., Lee, T., Sablynski, C., & Erez, M. (2001). Why people stay: Using job embeddedness to predict voluntary turnover. *Academy of Management Journal, 44*(6), 1102–1121.

Mobley, W., Horner, S., & Hollingsworth, A. (1978). An evaluation of precursors of hospital employee turnover. *Journal of Applied Psychology, 63*, 408–424.

Moore, J. E. (2000). One road to turnover: An examination of work exhaustion in technology professionals. *MIS Quarterly, 24*(1), 141–148.

Moore, J. E., & Burke, L. (2002). How to turn around 'turnaround culture" in IT. *Communications of the ACM, 45*(2), 73–78.

Neiderman, F., & Sumner, M. (2004). Effects of tasks, salaries, and shocks on job satisfaction among IS professionals. *Information Resources Management Journal, 17*(4), 49–72.

Pervin, L. (1989). Persons, situations, interactions: The history of a controversy and a discussion of theoretical models. *Academy of Management Review, 14*(3), 350–360.

Porter, L., Steers, R., Mowday, R., & Boulian, P. (1974). Organizational commitment, job satisfaction, and turnover among psychiatric technicians. *Journal of Applied Psychology, 59*, 603–609.

Rhodes, L., & Eisenberger, R. (2002). Perceived organizational support: A review of the literature. *Journal of Applied Psychology, 87*(4), 698–714.

Rogers, E. M. (2006). *Diffusion of innovations.* New York: Free.

Rouse, P. (2001). Voluntary turnover related to information technology professionals: A Review of rational and instinctual models. *International Journal of Organizational Analysis, 9*(3), 281–291.

Rusbult, C., & Farrell, D. (1983). A longitudinal test of the investment model: The impact on job satisfaction, job commitment, and turnover variations in rewards, costs, alternatives, and investments. *Journal of Applied Psychology, 68*(3), 429–438.

Sethi, V., Barrier, T., & King, R. (1999). An examination of the correlates of burnout in IS professionals. *Information Resources Management Journal, 12*(3), 5–13.

Shore, L., & Tetrick, L. (1991). A construct validity study of the survey of perceived organizational support. *Journal of Applied Psychology, 76*, 637–643.

Spector, P. (1996). *Industrial and organizational psychology: Research and practice.* New York: Wiley.

Steel, R., & Griffeth, R. (1989). The elusive relationship between perceived employment opportunity and turnover behavior: A methodological or conceptual artifact? *Journal of Applied Psychology, 74*(6), 846–854.

Steers, R. M. (1977). Antecedents and outcomes of organizational commitment. *Administrative Science Quarterly, 22*(1), 46–56.

Sujdak, E. (2002). *An investigation of the correlation of job satisfaction, organizational commitment, perceived job opportunity, organizational communications, job search behavior, and the intent to turnover in IT professionals.* Unpublished doctoral dissertation, Wayne Huizenga School of Business and Entrepreneurship, Nova Southeastern University, Florida.

Szamosi, L. (2006). Just what are tomorrow's SME employees looking for? *Education and Training, 48*(8/9), 654–665.

Tett, R., & Meyer, J. (1993). Job satisfaction, organizational commitment, turnover intention, and turnover: Path analyses based on meta analytic findings. *Personnel Psychology, 46*(2), 259–293.

Van Dam, K. (2005). Employee attitudes toward job changes: An application and extension of Rusbult and Farrell's investment model. *Journal of Occupational and Organizational Psychology, 78*(2), 253–273.

Willcocks, L., & Lacity, M. (2006). *Global sourcing of business and IT services.* United Kingdom: Palgrave.

Yin, R. (2003). Case study research: Design and methods, 3rd Edn. Thousand Oaks: Sage.

Appendix A: Interview Guide

Confidentiality Policy

We are working on a research paper as part of our doctoral studies. We are interested in understanding the reasons why Indian IS professionals intend to stay or leave their current employers. Specifically we are looking at IS professionals located at the supplier side (India) with 2–7 years of experience. We will highly appreciate your cooperation. The interview will be tape-recorded, but only the researchers will have access to the full transcriptions. Your name and company will be kept anonymous. Thank you for your participation.

Demographic Questions

> How long have you worked in IT?
> What is your current position in the organization?
> What responsibilities does your job entail?
> How long have you worked in this company?

Job Satisfaction

> Are you satisfied with your job?
> What parts of your job make you happy/unhappy?
> Do you feel enthusiastic about your job?
> Does your job give you fulfillment?

Rewards/Costs

> Are you generally satisfied with your compensation?
> Concerning your current job, what do you like about the work you do?
> Concerning your current job, what do you not like about the work you do?

Follow up prompts as needed

> Are you paid enough for the work you do?
> Is it according to the industry norms- what others in the industry are getting for the same work?
> Is there a lot of variety in your job?
> Are you free to decide how you perform your tasks? Or is it controlled by your manager?

Do you receive adequate feedback at work?
Do you get any other benefits- flextime, bonus, or performance based rewards?
Are you happy with it?
Do you feel your job is monotonous?
Do you experience a lot of stress and burnout in your job?
Is your role clearly defined or is it ambiguous?

Organizational Commitment

How do you feel about your company?
Does the organization mean a lot to you?
Added after P7 interview: Do you feel emotionally attached to your company?

Investment

Is your training and work experience portable to other organizations?
If you left this organization, would you lose any particular benefits?

Organizational Alternatives

Are equal or better jobs readily available to you in other organizations?
Can you get another job easily of you want to?

Turnover Intentions

Where do you see yourself in another year–in this organization or another?
Would you prefer to keep working in this current organization?
Are you thinking of leaving this company? Why?
Do you regularly check if there are suitable jobs for you elsewhere?
Are you actively looking out for alternatives/other job avenues?
Have you updated your resume recently?
Finally, is there anything that we haven't covered that is important to your overall satisfaction with your current job or current employer?

Relocating Routines: The Role of Improvisation in Offshore Implementation of Software Processes

S. Krishna and Jayarama Holla

1 Introduction

Offshored Software and IT-enabled Services have grown spectacularly over the last decade, particularly from India (McKinsey & Nasscom, 2005; Nasscom, 2007). In western economies, while domestic outsourcing won acceptance from 1980s, offshored outsourcing has assumed increasing importance since the late nineties (Hirschheim, Heinzl, & Dibbern, 2006). Global outsourcing could be regarded as a component of the ongoing phenomenon of globalization (Friedman, 2005). Global outsourcing or offshoring involves transfer of work from its original locale within organizational boundaries or at a domestic firm, to a location at a considerable distance. In a general sense, such transfers are a core component of Globalization. The well known sociologist Anthony Giddens, for example, considers time–space distantiation and disembedding mechanisms as the major features modernity and globalization (Giddens, 1990). Such process transfers however, need to confront significant complexities since they involve work transfers across differences or gaps in five dimensions – geographical distance, time zone differences, governance differences, cultural differences and infrastructural differences (van Fenema, 2002). Because of these complexities, disembedding processes from locales where they have earlier been performed to new locations is not in itself an uncomplicated and routine process. There could be considerable risk of failures. We argue in this paper however, that a creative and effective use of resources of the new environment provides scope for major improvements and gains. High levels of quality and productivity reported from India (McKinsey & Nasscom; Nasscom, 2005) point to the fact such gains have been obtained in many cases. We consider Improvisation, which may be defined as creative problem solving that is grounded in the realities at hand, as essential for successful work relocation. In this paper we present two cases of global companies setting up centers in India. While creativity as a value is prized by both organizations, in confronting a new context, organizational approach to improvisation differs leading to different outcomes.

We review the literature on Improvisation in Sect. 2. Research approach is outlined in Sect. 3. We present two cases – one of a British and the second of an American multinational commencing work in their Indian software subsidiary in

R. Hirschheim et al. (eds), *Information Systems Outsourcing,*
© Springer-Verlag Berlin Heidelberg 2009

Sect. 4. Of these, while one succeeds in the venture and its subsidiary goes on to achieve outstanding performance amongst global centers of the firm, the Indian subsidiary of the other firm fails to meet expectations of the parent and had to fold up. In the final section we contrast the two approaches and consider key organizational factors that facilitated appropriate improvisation and contributed to the outcomes.

2 Improvisation

Organizational improvisation is a topic that has been studied quite extensively (Barrett, 1998; Bastien & Hostager, 1988; Eisenberg, 1990; Hatch, 1999; Kamoche & Cunha, 2001; Meyer, Frost, & Weick, 1998; Peplowski, 1998; Weick, 1998). Organizational improvisation can be carried out by an individual or by a collective (groups, departments or the whole organization), as a result of the joint action by a set of individuals and is defined as the degree to which composition and execution of an action converge in time (Moorman & Miner, 1998b). Improvisation has been defined in varying, but broadly compatible ways, with many of the early approaches drawing inspiration from Jazz (Barrett; Bastien & Hostager; Eisenberg; Hatch; Kamoche & Cunha; Meyer et al.; Weick). Weick for example adopts an earlier definition by Berliner:

> Improvisation involves reworking precomposed material and designs in relation to unantici-
> pated ideas conceived, shaped, and transformed under the special conditions of performance,
> thereby adding unique features to every creation.

Organizational improvisation would need to focus on organizational setting as the domain of interest. By combining various definitions of improvisations available in the literature, Cunha, Cunha, and Kamoche (1999) have the following definition for organizational improvisation:

> Organizational *improvisation* is the conception of action as it unfolds, by an organization
> and/or its members, drawing on available material, cognitive, affective and social resources.

While there is broad agreement on the concept of improvisation, authors vary on emphasis with respect to factors like spontaneity, intentionality and originality.

The concept of improvisation in organizations may be related to the notions of emergence (Truex & Klein, 1991). In contrast to the structuration theory of Giddens, the emergence theory theorizes that the human activities are dominated by change or de-structure and that the organizational phenomenon tends to continually move towards structure without actually reaching a steady state (Truex, Baskerville, & Travis, 2000). Mintzberg and Waters (1985) contrast the emergent strategy from deliberate strategy and called it emergent change. It is the action taking place in the absence of an a priori intention and planning and cannot be anticipated. Improvisation is similar in nature to reinvention (Rice & Rogers, 1980) in the sense that the latter redefines the generalized innovation to the local or preexisting organizational conditions, such that a matching of the different abilities, resources and needs takes place. Improvisation can be deliberate(Moorman & Miner, 1998a). It can not be planned for, but can be purposefully triggered and it occurs during action. Ciborra highlights the spontaneous character of improvisation. Improvisation is intentional and purposeful, ruled by intuition, competence, design, chance and happens almost unexpectedly (Ciborra, 1999). Improvisation could be a situated change enacted by the members of an organization, and is an ongoing process, not deliberate, subtle with unintended outcome (Orlikowski, 1996). Improvisation can result in learning and lessons drawn from an improvisation episode become a part of organizational memory which in turn can influence improvisation (Moorman & Miner, 1998b). In emergencies, improvisation could be crucial for the survival of an organization by reducing panic and the collapse of the teams. Similarly entering a new market requires an organization to adapt to the local conditions. Improvisation does occur at workplaces having well defined work practices and routine jobs (Ciborra). Improvisation is usually done on material resources (resources that lie outside the individual and organizational social system), cognitive resources (set of explicit or tacit mental models held by the individual members of the organization), affective resources (improvisers' experience and emotional interconnectedness among the group), social resources (the social structures like formal and informal relationships, explicit and implicit rules present among members performing improvisation) (Cunha et al., 1999).

The outcome of improvisation can be measured in several ways. Moorman and Miner (1998a) suggested measuring the degree of improvisation in terms of Novelty (The degree of deviation from the existing routine), Degree of coherence (The extent of internal and external fit) and Speed (Time to plan and execute an action). Similarly Weick (1998) refers to a continuum ranging from Interpretation (Plans are strictly followed), Embellishment (The plan is rephrased to an extent but still recognizable), Variation (Unplanned actions are inserted along with the original plan) and Improvisation (Radical departure from the plan are observed).

As per Kamoche, Cunha, and Cunha (2003) the quality and the degree of improvisation is affected by the Leadership Style, Individual characteristics (Creativity, skills, mutual trust, not resting on the past successes and the ability to handle stress), Organizational Culture (Encourages risk taking and tolerates mistakes, promotes action and a sense of urgency), Organizational Memory and Group Size (Larger groups tend to have lower improvisation due to poor communication). Moorman and Miner (1998b) list environmental turbulence and real time organizational informational flows as having a positive impact on the incidence and effectiveness of improvisation. Organizational memory has a negative impact on the incidence of improvisation but has an opposite effect on the effectiveness of the improvisation produced. Moorman and Miner (1998b) also talk about the effect of procedural and declarative memory on the organizational improvisation and classify improvisation in terms of Collective Vs Individual, Product Vs Process, Behavioral Vs Cognitive.

2.1   Constructs Associated with Improvisation

Constructs like creativity, adaptation and innovation are often associated with improvisation. The time between planning and execution is the key aspect of improvisation. The usual urgency and the temporal necessity to act quickly are missing in these constructs (Cunha et al., 1999). Although creativity may not involve any improvisation, it still might represent the organizational capability to improvise. Similarly, while all improvisation involves innovation to some degree, it is the time to plan, which differentiates improvisation from innovation. Adaptation is adjustment to external stimulus and all improvisation might not result in an adaptation (Moorman & Miner, 1998a).

Bricolage is one construct, which is used very frequently in the context of improvisation, but is different. It is defined as the ability to build non-optimal solutions from available resources. Formal definition of bricolage presented by Thayer (1988) states that it means "making things work by ingeniously using whatever is at hand, being unconcerned about the 'proper' tools and resources." Bricolage is something that can occur while improvising if the availability of right resources is an issue (Moorman & Miner, 1998b).

Similarly the Indian word 'Jugaad' implying alternatives, substitutes, improvisations and make-dos, is spurred by a native inventiveness steeped in a culture of scarcity and survival (Talukdar, 2005). The origin of the word seems to be from the makeshift vehicle made by assembling the parts of different vehicles such as jeeps, tractors etc. and powered by a water pump, used by the farmers of Punjab and Western U. P. provinces in India.

Jazz and Indian music models both require that the performers should be highly skilled and be familiar with the instruments (Barrett, 1998; Kamoche et al., 2003; Weick, 1998). In an organization managers should foster skills development, expertise in tools and techniques along with creativity. Improvisation, like any tacit skill can only be learned through practice (Cunha & Cunha, 2001). Although there is a large variation in the creative capability of individuals, it has been observed that certain cultures, places and historic periods, termed cultural configurations have been fertile for creative personalities (Simonton, 1999). These so called golden periods have numerous creative minds, where as there would be hardly any during the periods of the dark ages, suggesting that there are special political, cultural, economic, and societal circumstances that may serve either to encourage or repress the development and manifestation of the individual capacity to generate variations (Simonton). So it is important for the organizations to create a kind of environment, which encourages non conformity, independence, appreciation of diverse perspective and a variety of interests which foster creativity.

In a study of the effect of cultural diversity in new product development setting in a mold industry, the authors conclude that the right level of cultural diversity has a positive impact on improvisation (Cunha & Cunha, 2001). Larger the number of variations in improvisation, greater is the likelihood of the solution being suitable for the situation at hand and higher the chances of success of the solution. This is quite relevant to organizations which operate in multi-country and multi-cultural distributed work settings.

2.2 Planning and Improvisation

Traditionally, plans precede action and are facilitated by shared knowledge of typical situations and appropriate actions. Advanced planning requires prior knowledge of the environment and any unanticipated event calls for re-planning. This view, called the planning view, requires that planning be done prior to action. As per the alternative view proposed by Suchman (1987), every course of action is dependent in some ways on the material and social circumstances of the actor and the local interactions. In this view, although plans are an important resource for situated action, they would not determine the course of situated action. Plans, presupposing embodied practices, provide the details for action, but fall short of providing concrete details for every changing circumstance during the action. Since it is difficult to anticipate the alternative courses of action, the implementer ends up doing some improvisation during the course of action based on the present situation. The plan is then reconstructed backwards from the results of the situated action as a post hoc analysis (Suchman). Planning complements improvisation by outlining general strategy and the direction for the firm and by providing employees with a tool to measure their actions (McKnight & Bontis, 2002). An alternative stance taken by Vera and Simon (1993) is that plans, rather than being a fixed sequence of actions, are strategies which determine the course of action based on current information. They emphasize that proper planning is crucial for the success of a task.

2.3 Improvisation in IT

In IT industry, software engineering practices have always insisted on planned and deliberate activities systematically carried out and to be completed on time (Bansler & Havn, 2003). The initiatives of Software Engineering Institute (SEI), such as the Capability Maturity Model (CMM) aim to introduce discipline and order into the software development process. Models such as these, popularized by SEI, have been used by agencies such as the US Department of Defense (DoD) to assess the software capability of the vendors and reduce the risk associated with the complex task of software development. CMM helps to standardize the software processes. Similarly the outsourcing capability of the vendors is indicated by eSCM-SP (eSourcing Capability Model for Service Providers) and the readiness of the clients can be assessed by eSouricng-CL (Hyder, Heston, & Paulk, 2004). The time required for the standardized tasks reduce, and the variances in the performance decrease, improving reliability (Dyba, 2000).

A longitudinal study of a web based groupware application implementation in a multinational corporation shows that improvisation happens outside the standard system methodologies and processes (Bansler & Havn, 2003). The users of the system are also an important source of innovation and the teams who respond to these unanticipated problems in a creative way will have successful implementations. This is due to the difficulty in capturing the complex, not stable and not very well understood requirements of the users or the business systems. Similarly Dyba (2000) points out that the standard software methodologies are not conducive for small software firms to maintain the level of innovation. In this study of 55 Norwegian software firms, it was found that firms using improvement models as CMM can institutionalize the routines, there by effectively blocking the exploration of new alternative routines, becoming obstacles to improvement. In a paper published in 1995, Eisenhardt and Tabrizi establish, using an empirical analysis of global computer industry that the experiential model accelerates product development in comparison to a model that has predefined processes. In the experiential model processes are not laid out in the beginning and it relies on improvisation, real time experience and flexibility (Eisenhardt & Tabrizi, 1995).

There are no empirical studies on improvisation taking place in IT firms in India. The rapid, extensive growth and global prominence of these however point to the possibility of improvisation at various levels. For example, the captive offshore centers of the multi-national corporations which have development centers in India have a special challenge of implementing the processes which have been developed and perfected in a different country, cultural setting and employee maturity state. Managers need to improvise to suit them to the local conditions. Some of these practices go on to become the organization wide best practices. This is similar in nature to the phenomenon reported in a study by Orlikowski (1996) who discusses the implementation of a new technology solution at a call center of a software company where over a period of 2 years the organizational actors, through a series of improvisations and local changes, adopt the system for their use. She points out that rather than a single big change in the organization, there was a sequence of five stages during which changes were effected by the organizational players. Similarly Indian IT services firms have shown tremendous creativity in hiring and ramping up manpower strength very quickly and in large numbers. Many of these firms have setup their own in house training centers to train the personnel as per their needs and thus do not depend very much on the Indian education system to provide them with trained manpower. Improvisation can take place even in so called low end jobs such as bug fixing, as each bug is unique and the situatedness forces the programmer to improvise a solution without going in for a major change in the code.

3   Research Setting and Methodology

For this paper we have selected two cases from our research on IT firms who opened offshore development centers in India. The data for analysis developed here was obtained from earlier research projects undertaken at Bangalore. Data for first of these cases is from research undertaken by a team of which one of the authors was a part and reported elsewhere as part of an overall study of Global software Work (Sahay, Nicholson, & Krishna S., 2003). It is briefly summarized and reanalyzed here to aid comparative analysis. Data for the second case is from doctoral research for which one of the present authors was the advisor and reported in a different framework and in part in an unpublished doctoral dissertation (Sharma, 2004). The first is an account of a UK company called WebCo and the second that of a US multinational, Orion Microsystems. WebCo was not successful in this venture and had to fold up its development center in India largely due to the failure of the Indian manager at WebCo in setting right expectations with the WebCo team at the UK and in understanding the ground realities in India. Orion had a different experience and its India development center went on to become one of the most productive centers worldwide for Orion. We contrast the contexts surrounding the success of Orion and the failure of WebCo and analyze as to how the management team at Orion was able to improvise to adapt to local context and in doing so improved and enhanced work at a global level.

3.1 Data Collection and Analysis

The research approach taken for both the studies can be classified as interpretive case studies (Walsham, 1995). Longitudinal study of WebCo extended over a period of 2 years between 1998 and 2000. The method was mainly semi-structured interviews, 14 in number at the Bangalore office and 7 at the UK offices in London. Both managers and programmers were interviewed at both the locations.

At Orion, a total of 15 people, at all levels in the organizational hierarchy from senior engineers to group heads, were interviewed. The interviews, with an average length of an hour, were conducted at the project sites. After the transcription of each interview, the researchers would review data and refine questions, where relevant, before subsequent interviews. Grounded theory approach was adopted to select significant aspects of the case and structure the case study (Sharma, 2004).

4 Two Cases

4.1 WebCo: Freedom to Conform

The first case concerns a U.K. company called WebCo (a pseudonym) which sought to avail of programming talent available in India to supplement its growing operations. In 1998 they had offices in London, Brighton, New York and California. WebCo was a small company with a staff of around 100 persons and a turnover of around $15 million at the time of the interviews. The company specialized in executing short lifecycle, customized software projects for clients in a wide range of domains. Their projects were on client server and subsequently in e-commerce applications. They had particular strengths in visual interface design. The company faced increasing difficulty in recruiting good quality development personnel in the U.K. The salaries for skilled and qualified staff in the U.K. were also rapidly escalating. The decision to set up a development center in Bangalore was intended to address these problems. Accounts of plentiful and inexpensive software talent in India set high expectations. In the words of a manager:

> We thought streets in Bangalore were paved with programmers.

The company did not undertake a detailed evaluation of issues involved and left the responsibilities with a senior executive of Indian ethnic origin who they felt would be familiar with the local environment. The executive however was an immigrant from the African continent and a U.K. resident since childhood and was quite unfamiliar with the Indian context.

WebCo in the U.K. had a young, tech-savvy leadership. The culture was an informal and interactive one which prized creativity and open discussion of technical and other issues. They were very upbeat about their values and work styles and the vision, in the words of a manager, was to develop "*a little bit of WebCo in India*." It was envisaged that unlike many companies who were undertaking support function in India, WebCo would execute entire project – "the full lifecycle" from its Bangalore center. The Indian staff would interact with clients in the U.K. directly by telephone, email and video conferencing. WebCo style of development in the U.K. involved very close liaison with clients. Regular face to face client meetings, every 10 days or less, with client executives was the usual practice. It was felt that with high bandwidth telecom infrastructure these could be carried out from Bangalore also. The company leased telephone and video links so that customers would not have to incur additional costs and thereby encourage good communication. The view thus was that video conferencing equipment would transcend distance and replace face to face contact.

The Bangalore office commenced work in 1998. As processes of implementation commenced, a host of problems unfolded. The video conferencing with clients didn't work well in practice. Setting up video links was delayed as the WebCo manager was unfamiliar with the ways of Indian bureaucracy. After it was put into operation, it was discovered that clients were not eager to travel to WebCo's London office to avail of charge free video-conferencing to India. So the equipment was little used.

WebCo, being a small and little known company, was not able to attract and recruit the best in class Indian programmers. Though Indian developers spoke English, many spoke English with an accent with which the client executives were not always comfortable. The Indians were "encouraged" to be more sensitive to the issue of accents and were enrolled in training courses in the evenings. In a successful project cited to us, the developer had traveled to the U.K. and had met the client at his office and then continued interaction over video. This was necessary to capture fully the client's requirements which were broadly envisaged and needed close sustained discussion for many clarifications. Thus the hopes for complete offshore development including the early lifecycle work were found to be more problematic than originally hoped.

The manager of the Indian center also had problems with manners and work culture of Indian programmers. They had adequate technical abilities but could not fit in easily with WebCo's work style. For example, at WebCo, technical issues were intensely and openly discussed. Senior mangers would mix well with the juniors both during work and after hours. However the Indian developers would maintain a polite distance from their seniors even while discussing technical matters. The following quotes from WebCo India Manager illustrate some typical situations:

> In meetings the staff will often stay quiet and I get a lengthy email maybe an hour later when the meeting is over. I have to start the thing all over again and I think.. Well, why not bring all that up in the meeting? It ends up taking twice the time. They will not confront me in meetings
>
> In London when someone joins us we open a bottle of champagne. People casually mill around, say "hi" and move on. Here most people don't drink. We have to get some soft drinks. I am expected to make a speech. People don't loosen up. It feels very different.

Misunderstandings occurred in project execution also. In the UK, total time logged on a project was considered the measure of performance. Focus on work during official work hours was the norm and non-professional concerns were strictly kept out of work hours. In India, work-life conditions demanded a different mix. Close-knit families and infrastructure difficulties meant that a developer may take time off during work hours to attend to domestic priority tasks. However, he/she would make up by working longer hours and over weekends. The developers primarily focused on project deadlines. As long as project deadlines were met, they felt work was satisfactory. This particular interpretation suited work-life conditions in India. WebCo, with their original metrics would notice a 25% or higher "leakage" on Indian projects –a metric Indian staff found very perplexing. They would be disappointed when told there were project leakages despite extra effort they had put in through longer hours and work over weekends and after they had met specified deadlines.

As Web applications exploded, WebCo started getting many more development projects than they could handle. Also given the novelty of the applications and being concerned with faster time to market, clients preferred developers to keep in touch closely or even stay and work on their premises as against working remotely and out of sight. For many projects it contracted in the U.S., WebCo had to flow in programmers from Bangalore to locations in the U.S. The processes of remote work, which were weak to start with, collapsed under these conditions.

Due to these and similar other issues, WebCo was unable continue to work satisfactorily from India. In the year 2000, WebCo transferred all its Indian employees to its New York office and closed its Bangalore operations. It was a clear admission that while Indian programming talent was acceptable, the company was unable to establish satisfactory structures and processes for remote work.

4.2   Orion: Enacting and Enhancing Processes

Since its inception in 1982, a singular vision – Network is the Computer – has propelled the Silicon Valley based firm Orion Ltd. (a pseudonym) to its position as a leading provider of industrial – strength hardware, software, and services that make the "Net" work. At the time our research was initiated, Orion's World wide revenues were around $13 billion. Orion entered India in 1987, through Wipro, its sole distributor. Orion India was established in 1995. Soon after, the company established a 100 percent subsidiary, the first such subsidiary of any MNC in the country. Orion's India Engineering Center (IEC) commenced operations towards the end of 1998 and was formally launched in May 1999.

IEC in Bangalore has now become a key site for technology development for the company worldwide. Each of Orion's six divisions (Enterprise Services, OrionOne, Network Service Provider, Network Storage and Systems Products and Software Systems Group) has teams working at IEC. Products and technologies at IEC include mission-critical Stern Operating Environment, and OrionOne product line including E-commerce infrastructure and application products; security products and advanced network storage solutions. The IEC is slated to grow to a core engineering site with 3,000–5,000 employees, with all worldwide projects being done partly or fully from India.

The IEC follows a business model of 'virtual teams' where all teams at India IEC are part of worldwide teams that operate across geographies. Team in each geography decides which part of the project will be tackled in their region. It then approaches teams in other geographies; if it makes sense to the other teams then they may choose to participate or not.

At the time Orion commenced operations in India it had well established centers in the U.S. and the U.K. Many of the processes were standardized and documented. For example, Orion had a standardized process called Orion Global Resolution process which every sustenance group followed and every engineer was trained in the same. Orion had a well documented code review and approval process in place to review the code delivered by any engineer. The task envisaged was to transfer and implement these in the new setting of the Indian center. Orion also had a good number of senior personnel of Indian origin in U.S. offices, some of whom looked forward to returning to India.

Building a new high performance center in India however, as the WebCo case revealed, is not a simple task. Orion Management carefully assembled a set of senior managers. They included Indian managers who had 8–10 years work background in the U.S. as well as U.S. managers who came across as culturally sensitive and mature. A developer told us his (American) manager carefully evolved a working team. During early stages…

> She got some people from there (U.S.) to come here and work with the team in the initial stages…so that the rapport is built and stuff like that…and initially we had people traveling either way quite frequently to get to know each other.…these things really helped…otherwise if it was only a team sitting here and working over emails and phone calls it wouldn't have come to this level.

The Indian group started with a disadvantage that most of the people they hired had very little experience. The sustenance team in India commenced with some of the processes that were in place at the US and the UK centers and augmented these with new processes intended to increase productivity under local conditions. A team head in Bangalore told us:

> In fact when we started the group…ours was the third group in the whole company…we had a disadvantage that most of these people came straight from colleges. They were not only new to Orion, they were also new to this group, and they were also new to this job. … there was a very big need for training to tell them how things are done…so we kind of used that opportunity to put processes in place which was not there in UK or US before…..

Once the advantages of starting fresh were recognized, Orion managers went ahead to design new structures, artifacts and tools in to addition training programs specifically oriented towards local resources and talent. We indicate these in the following paragraphs:

4.2.1 Write a New Bible

One of the key artifacts envisaged to assist quick training was the "process bible." The manager involved in the development of process bible said,

> We realized we needed something………a solid process and bunch of documents to guide the young graduates. I was the one who actually started the initiative…we used to call it then and we still call it as the process bible for our group…so we have a thick web based book called as bible…ever evolving book…which defines all the processes that our engineers need to know to work here…so when I wanted to do that …………took a lot of my effort to do that because I had also lot of other responsibilities along with that…so I picked up lot of guys from the team here…seven or eight guys…and all of us together did that thing.…once it was done………we took it to the global team and said we did that as part of ramping up the team here and obviously all these processes are applicable to the whole global team who are working on this…and it was totally accepted in the global team……so now that book is sustained by voluntary effort from all over the globe and not just the team here.……

4.2.2 Customize Training

The managers realized that while local inductees had generic programming skills, more specific competencies were needed to fit them for tasks at Orion. Training for this consisted of two parts – some Global Orion training modules and others specific to local assignments.

> We get fresh hires from the college most of the time… we wanted to come up with a training program… they go through the Orion induction program but that is relevant for whole of Orion but we need to train them for our group. So we designed a fifteen-day intensive training program for our group. It is conducted by various team members here… the idea is that when you teach others you naturally learn more… so we make them teach the fresh hires all the technical and process stuff… so people become expert in that… so lot of it was technical also… so when they come here they are trained in that… the idea is that after our group induction training they should straight away start working on the job without any lag period. They may not be able to work on the most complex issues but at least they get productive right from day one, this we achieved.

4.2.3 Restructure Processes

In order to ensure good performance even while accommodating limited experience of new hires, new structures and roles were created. Some of these were Gates, Gate Keepers and Advocates for code repositories. More frequent builds were also introduced internally.

A senior manager explains the problem and the designed solution:

> ...... previously the central repository of source code... any body can go in check-in check-out... there was no real control over the quality or the time when it could be done... there were no real processes well defined when a person can check-in and check-out... what are the exit and entry criteria for this... so we defined those..... that there has to be a code review... code review has to be done by so many people then the test report has to be attached... then we said... these are the processes that we took directly from the Stern processes... so there is something more... we introduced a concept of a gatekeeper and then an advocate... so gatekeeper has to say ok... there is a form we call RTI... RTI is actually Request To Integrate... integrate with the main repository... if you give this information and then the gatekeeper will decide whether it is right or not... you have to convince the gatekeeper that you have good quality code to be checked in... the other thing we did was we do a nightly build...

4.2.4 Retool for Performance

A particularly notable fact was the large number of new tools which had been put in place in Bangalore. Some of these were developed locally. Few others were adapted from open source software.

> So we use some tool... web based tool which sits on top of Scopus (database of reported problems) and which actually finds out from Scopus what are all escalations that need an update today... so engineers have a web based tool to go and have a look at that to say I have twelve escalations... of those twelve escalations six of them the deadline to update is today... or deadline to update is tomorrow or day after tomorrow... we have come up with these tools to help engineers in meeting the deadlines and make sure that they don't miss them... so we have such kind of proactive tools...... but if there is a process breakdown then we don't penalize the engineers for them.

Other tools we came across were an FAQ database developed specifically to answer questions raised locally and a Web based message board style tool to help suggestions and new ideas.

4.2.5 Manage People in the Local Context

Indian software Industry, particularly in Bangalore suffers from high staff attrition rates largely due high growth rates in the Industry. Young software professionals, as soon as they acquire new competencies look for higher rewards and change jobs if required. Attrition is a problem which many companies find difficult to address. Orion was sensitive to this issue. One of the approaches to address this was to have a slightly different set of job levels in India. This is revealed in responses of a manager:

Typically... we have... with engineers there are four levels right... we start with what the designation is called MTS... MTS1... Member of a Technical Staff 1 and then there is 2, 3, 4 and then there is a staff engineer who is more like a Tech Lead, and then there is a senior staff, but in India we have a IEC specific level which came in about February 2002, this is something which we have done here and it is still under a kind of debate. So we have levels that are not exactly the same that our peers in UK and US have.

In MTS 2 we have sublevels... we have MTS 2a and 2b and then MTS 3a and 3b... this was initiated by local HR... it said that if you look at local HR practices then more levels give people more opportunity to rise high... so that is the rationale behind that... we have more levels here as compared to our peers... other than that there are first level and second level managers.

4.2.6 Set High Goals

The Indian groups had set themselves high performance benchmarks. The sustenance group for example had set itself the objective to be the "BOSS" (Best of Stern Sustaining). These were spelled out in detail for all members of the group.

Question: Did this group have any mission?

Answer: "Yeah, we do... starting at my director's level... she has a mission and vision for her organization right... and... so we are basically the Stern sustenance team so her vision was to be "exactly right just in time every time everywhere" so basically responsive, accuracy and quality those were the things that she wanted to convey... last year in 2002 our vision was to be the BOSS... it is "Best of (Stern) Sustaining"... so basically among the three teams we wanted to be the best... we identified what are the things that we want to do best... so we participated a lot in global technical discussions and do quality work... basically all your escalations... so that is what built the team spirit ... having one single team goal ... as a team we need to achieve this ... that helped a lot ...so I said these are the few things that we should be doing so then we developed objectives in those areas for each of the engineers and their teams ... and went towards that ... I wouldn't say we completed all of those 100% ... but still we made significant progress."

4.2.7 Acknowledge Good Performance

In a span of 3 years the Indian center was able to perform remarkably well in comparison with other centers of Orion. IEC scored higher in quite a few parameters of performance, with many local groups emerging as the best globally.

Question: Has it also reduced the time taken by the Indian teams to come up with solutions; Are they faster than their counterparts in the UK or the US?

Answer: "Yes ... yes ...earlier we had all fresh grads with no work experience ... or some people had some work experience but very little and from that to 2 to 3 years of solid work experience ... there has to be a difference right ... what we consciously focused on all around was on increasing the technical competence... that is one thing that has really helped us in delivering faster solutions ...we diagnose a problem faster and come up with a fix faster."

> If you measure the cost in engineering days then yes... we had a graph which we have stopped showing now because it has become an old news now ... but when we completed two years we kind of charted out the quarterly graph of what we call time to release to time to resolve metric ... so we had a linear line which came down for seven to eight consecutive quarters ... so that was a huge amount ... so I would say if you use engineer time as cost metric then we reduced the cost also ... and right now our work load is the highest ......we are pretty much one-third the strength of the global team but we are handling more than forty percent of global defects ... so we are delivering more.

Three years from inception, the Bangalore center had scored consistently higher on all metrics on productivity, speed as well as technical competence, ahead of Orion's other centers in the U.S. and the U.K. Many of the artifacts developed by them like the process bible, process changes like Gatekeepers and new tools were recommended and adopted at other centers.

The groups had set themselves new goal of "Onward and upward"-

> ... in fact in the performance review time the director came back and said ... I am absolutely thrilled at the way the things are happening in India ... so having reached that stage ... we said that is done now lets look at what our mission is going to be this time ... so we have changed our mission to "onward and upward" ... so we do go through these team exercise where we sit together and we ask our team members to brainstorm and come up with vision and mission and stuff like that.

5   Discussion

The striking aspects of these two cases is that while Orion seems to have had little difficulty in making the Indian operation measure up to and even exceed their expectations in terms of the productivity and the quality of work delivered, WebCo struggled to make its offshore team take off. Both firms had a vision and a plan for their entry into India. WebCo had relatively fixed ideas in terms of patterns of work into which it wanted to fit Indian resources. Orion on the other hand assessed realities of the local context and could recombine knowledge, processes and structure in the course of its execution. We consider basis of this ability to improvise (or lack of it) in the respective organizations in terms of Culture (Organizational and local context), Leadership Style and balance between Planned Vs Situated action.

Culture: The culture at WebCo was an informal and interactive one which prized creativity. They encouraged and expected open discussion without being held up by hierarchical considerations. This open culture should have encouraged novel approaches and improvisation at the Indian center. However WebCo valued western ideals in the domain of culture. They were not responsive local cultural ethos, as revealed by the remarks on social drinking and drinking at work not being a part of the Indian culture. WebCo, being a small company, was not able to attract and retain talent from the top Indian universities, due to which the candidates that they hired were not equipped with language skills to interact directly with the clients in the western countries. Although WebCo did send their programmers for accent correction training, it was a delayed reaction than a planned action. WebCo was not flexible in terms of accommodating alternative work cultures. This was further accentuated due to the expatriate "Indian" manager who was not tuned to Indian work realities.

Orion facing a similar situation did not directly expose their Indian developers to complex systems in the initial stages. Orion had managers of Indian origin who had Indian culture embedded in them as well as American managers who were culturally sensitive. Orion encouraged the team in India to improvise on the processes to suit the local context and further recognized their efforts by implementing the same at other global locations around the world. We can see that the Orion managers trusted their Indian counter parts and their confidence paid off. The Indian managers generated novel ideas such as the process bible which the global teams recognized as valuable and accepted for their groups.

The early effort by the US manager to get Indian and US staff to travel and work together may also be interpreted as attempts to bridge perceptual gaps which arise due to differing cultural backgrounds. A breakdown is any interruption in the flow of action. Breakdowns can occur when the language is not interpreted in the same way due to cultural differences and contexts (Flores, Graves, Hartfield, & Winograd, 1988). It is important to develop shared meanings and contexts for social coordination of action. The initial face to face formal interaction helped the later transfer of knowledge using other channels like e-mail and telephone (Heeks, Krishna S., Nicholsen, & Sahay, 2001; Maznevski & Chudoba, 2000). WebCo hoped to achieve the same by setting up the Video conferencing facility, but it is clear that this facility could not be a substitute for proximate interaction. There was also initial problem with setting up the conference facility and the delayed recognition of the reluctance of the clients to travel to the WebCo office in the UK for video conference.

Leadership: Much of the improvisation literature, reviewed earlier, emphasizes the importance of leadership for successful improvisation. At WebCo we can see that the expatriate Indian manager was not accustomed to the ground realities regarding setting up and doing business in India. He was an Indian brought up in Kenya and later worked in the UK and had no personal stake in the success of the Indian center. He would get back to the UK where his home was, irrespective of success or failure of the center. His remarks reveal an outsider's perspective on local context and cultural issues. A close understanding of context, which alone could have facilitated improvisation and positive achievement, eluded him.

Orion had relocated several managers who had come over to US from India. They had personal stake in making this center work as these managers had relocated to India voluntarily. They were better tuned to the realities of the Indian work culture. The top management emphasized the development of team spirit by encouraging team work and incorporating the soft skills into performance reviews. The management promoted action by having vision and mission statements such as – to be the BOSS: "Best of Stern Sustaining." The project statistics and team performance on various parameters were well disseminated. They conducted mission and vision exercises to develop shared objectives. The management also adapted the organization structure to the local needs by introducing more levels in the hierarchy in India to motivate the employees in India.

Tools and Expertise: Improvisation literature (Barrett, 1998; Kamoche et al., 2003; Weick, 1998) emphasizes the need for building expertise in the tools used by the organization to facilitate improvisation. WebCo was not able to recruit developers who had specialized and advanced skills. Without exploring Indian technical pool adequately, they recruited programmers and expected them to perform effectively. Further WebCo did not train the programmers proactively in the business domains and soft skills. WebCo struggled to put the technical infrastructure in place; however it expected its Indian team to deliver.

Orion had a standardized process called Orion Global Resolution process which every group followed and every engineer was trained in the same. Well documented processes and technological infrastructure were put in place to bridge the time–space gap. Orion had a well documented code review and approval process in place to review the code delivered by any engineer. When Orion setup the product development team, the new team was asked understand the source code of an existing product and work on bugs reported in the product. Only six months later they were asked to work on a new version of the product. Orion thus focused on tools and building competence in a systematic manner while WebCo expected its engineers in India to start delivering too early in the game.

Planning and Situated Action: Advocates of situated action perspective point out that organizations can not plan for every eventuality and there is situatedness involved in decision and action particularly in novel circumstances (Suchman, 1987). In case of WebCo, we see little improvisation which could be termed reinvention – matching of the different abilities and resources to accommodate local context (Rice & Rogers, 1980). We can relate this to the whitewater rafting example provided by Suchman (1987) where, however good the initial planning may be, there is a need to respond based on the actual events that happen during the downstream journey. Orion on the other hand anticipated many issues and had planned for cultural differences, training gaps and a gradual buildup in transferring responsibilities to the Indian team. The team in India, when faced with the challenge of global processses being not suitable for the local needs, made significant improvements to the existing practices.

WebCo had a top down approach to dealing with issues, setting the expectation in terms of what is acceptable whether in performance metrics or in terms of behavior (drinking Champagne, interaction in the meetings). Orion had a bottom up approach to dealing with the issues at the Indian center. Orion management was open to the changes in the processes done by their Indian counterparts.

WebCo also failed to distinguish between global and local processes. Global processes are generic in nature and need to be adapted to the local circumstances. In Gidden's terms, globalization involves disembedding processes before they could be implemented in new geographies (Giddens, 1986, 1990; Giddens & Dallmayr, 1982). Reembedding in new contexts, as we have argued, can be effective only with improvisation. WebCo could not disembed their processes from British local context. They attempted to carry them out with all their local (British) cultural inscriptions in the new context of India with its own cultural moorings. Nor could any improvisation be possible by WebCo managers with their poor awareness of local resources and context.

6 Conclusion: Valuing Diversity

We conclude with an insightful comment by an Orion staff member concerning his U.S. based manager who set up his group in India.

> … I think she is a person by nature who values diversity and so she was able to spread that culture and thought among the team

Geoff Walsham in his book on IS in a Global setting calls upon IS practitioners and academics to help create a "World of Difference" (Walsham, 2001). Our study points to the possibility that the World of Difference may also be a World of greater achievements.

References

Bansler, J. P., & Havn, E. C. (2003). Improvisation in action: Making sense of IS development in organizations. Unpublished Manuscript, 51–63.

Barrett, F. J. (1998). Coda: Creativity and improvisation in Jazz and organizations: Implications for organizational learning. *Organization Science, 9*(5), 605–622.

Bastien, D. T., & Hostager, T. J. (1988). Jazz as a process of organizational innovation. *Communication Research, 15*(5), 582.

Ciborra, C. U. (1999). Notes on improvisation and time in organizations. *Accounting, Management and Information Technologies, 9*(2), 77–94.

Cunha, M. P., & Cunha, J. V. (2001). Managing improvisation in cross cultural virtual teams. *International Journal of Cross Cultural Management, 1*(2), 187–208.

Cunha, M. P., Cunha, J. V., & Kamoche, K. (1999). Organizational improvisation: What, when, how and why. *International Journal of Management Reviews, 1*(3), 299–341.

Dyba, T. (2000). Improvisation in small software organizations. *Software, IEEE, 17*(5), 82–87.

Eisenberg, E. M. (1990). Jamming: Transcendence through organizing. *Communication Research, 17*(2), 139–164.

Eisenhardt, K., & Tabrizi, B. N. (1995). Accelerating adaptive processes: Product innovation in the global computer industry. *Administrative Science Quarterly, 40*(1), 84–110.

Flores, F., Graves, M., Hartfield, B., & Winograd, T. (1988). Computer systems and the design of organizational interaction. *ACM Transactions on Office Information Systems, 6*(2), 153–172.

Friedman, T. L. (2005). *The world is flat a brief history of the 21st century*. London: Penguin.

Giddens, A. (1986). *The constitution of society: Outline of theory of structuration*. Berkeley: University of California Press.

Giddens, A. (1990). *The consequences of modernity*. Cambridge: Polity Press.

Giddens, A., & Dallmayr, F. R. (1982). *Profiles and critiques in social theory*. London: Macmillan.

Hatch, M. J. (1999). Exploring the empty spaces of organizing: How improvisational Jazz helps redescribe organizational structure. *Organization Studies, 20*(1), 75–100.

Heeks, R., Krishna, S., Nicholsen, B., & Sahay, S. (2001). Synching or sinking: Global software outsourcing relationships. *IEEE Software, 18*(2), 54–60.

Hirschheim, R., Heinzl, A., & Dibbern, J. (2006). *Information systems outsourcing: Enduring themes, new perspectives and global challenges*. New York: Springer.

Hyder, E. B., Heston, K. M., & Paulk, M. C. (2004). *The eSourcing capability model for service providers (eSCM-SP) v2, Part 1: Model Overview, CMU-ISRI-04-113*. Pittsburgh, PA: Carnegie Mellon University.

Kamoche, K., & Cunha, M. P. (2001). Minimal structures: From Jazz improvisation to product innovation. *Organization Studies, 22*(5), 733–64.

Kamoche, K., Cunha, M. P., & Cunha, J. V. (2003). Towards a theory of organizational improvisation: Looking beyond the Jazz metaphor. *Journal of Management Studies, 40*(8), 2023–2051.

Maznevski, M. L., & Chudoba, K. M. (2000). Bridging space over time: Global virtual team dynamics and effectiveness. *Organization Science, 11*(5), 473–492.

McKinsey and Nasscom. (2005). Nasscom-McKinsey Report 2005. www.nasscom.org.

McKnight, B., & Bontis, N. (2002). E-improvisation: collaborative groupware technology expands the reach and effectiveness of organizational improvisation. *Knowledge and Process Management, 9*(4), 219–227.

Meyer, A., Frost, P. J., Weick, K. E. (1998). The organization science Jazz festival: Improvisation as a metaphor for organizing: Overture. *Organization Science, 9*(5), 540–542.

Mintzberg, H., & Waters, J. A. (1985). Of strategies, deliberate and emergent. *Strategic Management Journal, 6*(3), 257–272.

Moorman, C., & Miner, A. S. (1998a). Organizational improvisation and organizational memory. *The Academy of Management Review, 23*(4), 698–723.

Moorman, C., & Miner, A. S. (1998b). The convergence of planning and execution: Improvisation in new product development. *Journal of Marketing, 62*(3), 1–20.

Nasscom. (2005). Quality milestones. *NASSCOM News Line, 43*, 1–4.

Nasscom. (2007). Strategic Review 2007. www.nasscom.org.

Orlikowski, W. J. (1996). Improvising organizational transformation over time: A situated change perspective. *Information Systems Research, 7*(1), 63–92.

Peplowski, K. (1998). The process of improvisation. *Organization Science, 9*(5), 560–561.

Rice, R. E., & Rogers, E. M. (1980). Reinvention in the innovation process. *Science Communication, 1*(4), 499–514.

Sahay, S., Nicholson, B., & Krishna, S. (2003). *Global IT outsourcing: Software development across borders*. Cambridge: Cambridge University Press.

Sharma, R. (2004). *Control and coordination of global software projects: An empirical study*. Bangalore: Indian Institute of Management Bangalore.

Simonton, D. K. (1999). Creativity as blind variation and selective retention: Is the creative process Darwinian?" *Psychological Inquiry, 10*(4), 309–328.

Suchman, L. A. (1987). *Plans and situated actions: the problem of human–machine communication*. Cambridge: Cambridge University Press

Talukdar, S. (2005). *Makeshift miracles: The Indian genius for Jugaad*. India: The Times of India.

Thayer, L. (1988). Leadership/communication: A critical review and a modest proposal. *Handbook of Organizational Communication*, 231–263.

Truex, D., Baskerville, R., & Travis, J. (2000). Amethodical systems development: The deferred meaning of systems development methods. *Accounting, Management and Information Technologies, 10*(1), 53–79.

Truex, D. P., & Klein, H. K. (1991). A rejection of structure as a basis for information systems development. *Collaborative Work, Social Communications and Information Systems*, 213–236.

van Fenema, P. C. (2002). Coordination and control of globally distributed software projects. *Erasmus Research Institute of Management*, 572.

Vera, A. H., & Simon, H. A. (1993). Situated action: A symbolic interpretation. *Cognitive Science, 17*(1), 7–48.

Walsham, G. (1995). Interpretive case studies in IS research: nature and method. *European Journal of Information Systems, 4*(2), 74–81.

Walsham, G. (2001). *Making a world of difference: It in a global context*. New York: Wiley.

Weick, K. E. (1998). Introductory essay: Improvisation as a mindset for organizational analysis. *Organization Science, 9*(5), 543–555.

Chapter 8
Determinants of Offshoring Success

A US Client's Learning from Outsourcing IT Work Offshore[*]

Joseph W. Rottman and Mary C. Lacity

1 Introduction

Offshore outsourcing is the outsourcing of information technology (IT) work to a 3rd party supplier located on a different continent than the client.[1] Although client organizations have outsourced manufacturing services offshore for decades, the practice of offshore outsourcing IT services is still maturing. The offshore IT outsourcing (ITO) market (primarily India) will conservatively represent about 25% of the global $56 billion ITO market by 2008 (E-business Strategies, 2006). Forrester, McKinsey and NASSCOM predict that India alone could grab $142 billion of the ITO market by 2009 (E-business Strategies; Ross, 2004). Although there have been recent reports that India is struggling with high turnover, wage increases, and infrastructure issues associated with rapid growth (McCue, 2005; Srivastava, 2005), evidence suggests that India will continue to be a dominant player in the global ITO market (Carmel & Tjia, 2005; Engardio, 2006; Minevich & Richter, 2005).

Western clients, particularly in the US, are attracted to offshore outsourcing to India (and other destinations) because of the promised benefits of lower IT costs, faster delivery speed, the ability to focus in-house IT staff on more higher-value work, access to supplier resources and capabilities, and process improvement (Carmel & Tjia, 2005). But juxtaposed to the promised benefits of offshore outsourcing, many IT executives we interviewed struggle to realize its full potential. Although offshore outsourcing is technically possible because any work that can be digitized can be moved, there are many managerial challenges. One common complaint was that overall cost savings was less than anticipated due to the high transaction costs associated with finding suppliers, coordinating, and monitoring

---

[*] This paper previously appeared as: Rottman, J., & Lacity, M. (2008). A US Client's Learning from Outsourcing IT Work Offshore. *Information Systems Frontiers, Special Issue on Outsourcing of IT Services, 10*, 259–275.

[1] Offshore outsourcing is different than "offshoring." "Offshoring" occurs when an organization moves work from one location to another location on a different continent.

R. Hirschheim et al. (eds), *Information Systems Outsourcing*,
© Springer-Verlag Berlin Heidelberg 2009

work done offshore. Other common complaints were that quality was initially poor, delivery was slow, and personnel issues such as high supplier turnover interfered with success (Lacity M.C. & Rottman J.W., 2008).

Western clients have a significant learning curve to conquer. Several academic researchers found that Western clients initially engage offshore suppliers to lower IT costs (Carmel & Agarwal, 2002; Kaiser & Hawk, 2004). Clients are frequently shocked at the lack of in-house capabilities they have to ensure offshore outsourcing expectations are realized. Frequently, Western clients have to re-launch their offshore outsourcing efforts to be successful (Rottman J.W., 2006). In this paper, we present a highly realistic picture of a client's experiences with offshore outsourcing of IT work for the first time and how best and worst practices quickly emerge from experience. In telling this story, we hope that other clients may apply insights to accelerate their own path on the learning curve.

The client company, assigned the pseudonym Biotech, employs approximately 15,000 employees spread across 400 locations in more than 40 countries. Our research, based on 45 interviews and over 2000 documents, focuses on the IT group at US headquarters. This group engaged six Indian offshore suppliers on 21 IT projects during 2003–2005. The official documents from the Program Management Office (PMO) report that offshore outsourcing was successful in reducing Biotech's IT costs. But interviews with knowledgeable participants suggest that many projects were not successful in meeting cost, quality, and productivity objectives. Thus, different stakeholders within Biotech often had drastically different views on the success of offshore outsourcing. This case study is important because it suggests that merely surveying CIOs on offshore outsourcing practices and outcomes may not reveal a very realistic or rich picture.

The paper is organized as follows. We briefly summarize the growing body of academic research on offshore outsourcing of IT work, describe the research method, and tell Biotech's offshore outsourcing story. We then explain Biotech's mixed results with offshore outsourcing at two levels of analysis. At the organizational level of analysis, we found evidence that Biotech's offshore strategy to simply replace domestic contractors with cheaper, offshore suppliers was a poor fit with Biotech's social and cultural contexts. At the project level of analysis, we analyzed seven project attributes to differentiate highly-rated projects from poorly-rated projects. We conclude the paper with four overall insights for clients and suppliers.

2   Prior Research on IT Outsourcing

Academics have been studying domestic outsourcing[2] since the early 1990s. The first published outputs from academic research appeared in 1991, which documented companies pursuing large-scale *domestic* ITO (Applegate & Montealegre, 1991;

---

[2] We define "domestic outsourcing" as outsourcing to a supplier located in the same country as the client.

Huber, 1993). More quantitative research and multiple-case studies followed, focusing on why firms outsource (Loh & Venkatraman, 1992) and how firms benefit (or do not benefit) from ITO (Lacity M.C. & Hirschheim, 1993; Whang, 1992). Between 1994 and 2000, at least 79 other academic studies were published (Dibbern, Goles, Hirschheim, & Bandula, 2004).

Overall, we learned *why* firms outsource (mostly to reduce costs, access resources, focus internal resources on more strategic work[3]), *what* firms outsource (mostly a portion of their overall IT portfolio), *how* firms outsource (mostly by formal processes), and ITO *outcomes* as measured by realization of expectations, satisfaction, and performance (Dibbern et al., 2004). Overall, we know that client readiness, good strategy, good processes, sound contracts, and good relationship management are key success factors (Cullen, Seddon, & Willcocks, 2005; Feeny & Willcocks, 1998; Teng, Cheon, & Grover, 1995; Willcocks & Lacity M.C., 2006).

In the area of offshore outsourcing of IT work, academics are trying to understand how offshore outsourcing differs from domestic outsourcing. So far, researchers have found that offshore outsourcing poses additional challenges than domestic outsourcing (Rottman J.W. & Lacity M.C., 2006). For example, offshore outsourcing is more challenging because of time zone differences (Carmel, 2006), the need for more controls (Choudhury & Sabherwal, 2003), cultural differences (Carmel & Tjia, 2005), defining requirements more rigorously (Gopal, Sivaramakrishnan, Krishnan, & Mukhopadhyay, 2003), and difficulties in managing dispersed teams (Oshri et al., 2007). Researchers are also looking at offshore outsourcing at both the decision and relationship levels (Rivard & Aubert, 2007). There are also several special issues forthcoming in *MIS Quarterly* and the *Journal of Information Technology* that should be available in 2008, as well as a collection of current academic research forthcoming from the *Third International Conference on Outsourcing of Information Systems*.[4]

Our case study contributes to this body of knowledge by showing how emerging "best" practices need to be compatible with an organization's social context or the practices will likely be ineffective. However, the possibility for managers to change a social context always exists. In practice, we see this in the form of CIOs and other IT leaders who re-launch offshore outsourcing initiatives more successfully the second time. We hope that other agents will benefit from Biotech's lessons.

3   Research Method

This case study emerged over a two-year period that involved cycles of data collection, interpretation of data, and participant feedback on data interpretation. As will be shown, different stakeholders have different views on offshore outsourcing. They did not uniformly share a clear, consistent, objective "reality." The analysis was

---

[3] Besides these rational reasons, some studies find personal agendas dominating large-scale outsourcing decisions (Hall and Liedtka, 2005; Lacity M.C. & Hirschheim, 1993).

[4] Hirschheim, Heinzl, & Dibbern (Eds.). (2008). *Information systems outsourcing*. Berlin: Springer.

mostly an iterative process of letting the data drive the story, searching for patterns across the interviews, looking for documents to shed light on the interviews, and re-reading interviews to shed light on the documents. We used prior empirical research on project management and outsourcing to help us look for clues in the data. Thus, although our findings are organized and clearly presented, the process of inquiry was mostly iterative and emergent.

The project consisted of three distinct phases. Data was collected in the first two phases and the findings reviewed and data analyzed in phase three.

Phase I: Five interviews conducted with senior IT managers. During Phase I, we approached Biotech to participate in a study that examined the best practices for managing offshore outsourcing. (See Rottman J.W. & Lacity M.C., 2004 for a full description of this project.) In February of 2004, we interviewed five people from Biotech—the then CIO (since promoted and replaced by a direct report), three IT Leads who report directly to the CIO, and the Head of the PMO who managed all offshore outsourcing activities.

Phase II: Forty interviews conducted and over 2000 documents gathered. In spring of 2005, the Head of the PMO asked us to systematically assess IT employees' perceptions of offshore outsourcing. He felt that the IT employees would be more honest if they were interviewed by academics and if their identities would not be revealed. He also wanted us to identify the practices that contributed to project outcomes. He said he would allow us access to any people we wanted for interviews. Additionally, he offered us access to all documents pertaining to offshore.

The authors developed the interview guide (see Appendix) and the interview questions were designed to create a project rating, to investigate potentially important attributes that may contribute to project outcome based on prior research, and to explore new ideas, practices, and experiences with offshore outsourcing.

The lead author then interviewed 40 Biotech employees (including the new CIO who was appointed in February, 2005) and re-interviewed the Head of the PMO. Participants held various titles including Project Manager, Project Lead, Team Lead, and Architect. All interviews were conducted face-to-face, tape-recorded, and lasted approximately 90 minutes. Over 1,000 pages of transcription were generated.

In addition to the interviews, we had access to documents Biotech generated related to their offshore efforts. We examined over 200 statements of work (SOW), over 400 spreadsheets tracking various projects, and all the PMO's presentations relaying the status of offshore projects. We also examined the PMO's extensive database of all offshore contractors, invoices, requisitions, timesheets and disbursements. Additionally, individual participants provided project timelines, supplier correspondence, and code samples.

Phase III: Participant feedback and data analysis. In September 2005, the Head of the PMO and CIO were independently debriefed on the research findings. Despite our criticisms of the PMO office and senior management's role in implementing offshore, both accepted the report as accurate. Most of their questions centered on "How can we do this better?"

Using the transcripts of the interviews, internal documents and the feedback of participants, project ratings and project characteristics were analyzed. Besides assessing participants' views on project outcomes, we assessed which attributes differentiated highly-rated projects from poorly-rated projects. We coded the documents and transcribed interviews into data categories and mapped these categories against the project rating. The data categories were selected based on prior research as well as data categories that emerged from the interviews. We examined the following data categories:

1. Size and number of offshore supplier(s) engaged on the project
2. Supplier engagement model used on the project as indicated by the physical location of offshore supplier managers and developers
3. Contract value in terms of dollars paid to the supplier on a project
4. Project size in terms of duration in number of days
5. Organizational unit within IT managing the project
6. Project type as either development of new applications or maintenance/support of existing applications
7. Year the project was started

These categories and the relationship to project ratings are examined in the project analysis section.

Section 4 describes Biotech's offshore journey. We wrote this case description based on the socially constructed "facts" from the interviews and documents.

4   Biotech's Journey Offshore

As stated above, Biotech is a Fortune 500 company and a leading provider of bio-technology-based products. According to 10-K (annual) reports, Biotech experienced flat revenues yet increasingly positive net income from 1999 to 2001. According to the CIO, in 2001, senior management was beginning to feel the financial pains of a major litigation, increased competition, and rising costs of inputs. Predicting losses for 2002, senior management sought to cut the budgets of overhead departments. For 2002, the CIO's IT budget was reduced by five percent. *"Doing more with less"* became the CIO's major challenge for 2002.

Senior IT Leads explore offshore outsourcing as a means to reduce IT costs. In spring 2002, the CIO tasked the senior IT Leadership Team, comprised of 12 senior IT managers (called IT Leads), to develop a strategy to cope with the tighter IT budget. One of their proposals was to possibly move some IT work offshore.

The CIO and IT Leads intend to replace domestic contractors with cheaper offshore IT workers. The participants were in agreement pertaining to reasoning behind the projected cost savings. Most of Biotech's IT workforce resides in the corporate IT department on the headquarters campus. The corporate IT department comprises about 600 people, including 200 domestic contractors. The domestic contractors earn hourly wages of about $65. If domestic contractors were replaced with offshore workers who typically earn $25 per hour, then the CIO and IT Leads reasoned they would save at least $40 per hour. Thus, their number one objective was to reduce IT costs, primarily by replacing some of the domestic contractors with cheaper offshore equivalents. (There was no evidence that the CIO or IT Leads intended to use offshore outsourcing to replace any Biotech IT employees.) According to the CIO:

> One was simply looking at how much work do we give India? And if you make the assumption that we would be doing that work anyway, it's pretty easy to calculate the cost if you [would] have done it in the US versus doing it in India. It becomes a pretty straightforward calculation.

The CIO mandates offshore outsourcing. Because offshore outsourcing would likely meet with resistance from the internal IT staff, and to reach what the CIO called "a critical mass of projects and people," the CIO implemented the strategy as a mandate: New projects would require that at least 15% of the budget be outsourced offshore. In total, the CIO budgeted $6.2 million for offshore outsourcing during 2003–2005.

The Head of the PMO and IT Leads select suppliers. The offshore consultant helped the IT Leads and Head of the PMO identify potential suppliers. The IT Leads and PMO Head were interested in engaging suppliers with significant science domain knowledge as well as the willingness to participate in small projects during the start-up stage. Ultimately, Biotech engaged six Indian suppliers. Two suppliers were large, earning more than $1 billion in revenues in 2005. Four suppliers were small, the largest of which earned less than $150 million in 2005.

Biotech launches 21 projects offshore in 2003–2005. To kick off the offshore initiative, the CIO and the IT Leads held a town hall meeting for all IT employees. During this meeting, the offshore strategy and the role of the PMO were introduced. IT employees were told that no Biotech employee would lose their job as a consequence of offshore outsourcing.

IT Leads started bringing projects to the PMO in early 2003. The PMO was tasked with coordinating project selection, project management, tactical duties (bringing supplier employees on-site, facilitating system account creation, interfacing with Biotech IT security for login IDs, etc.) and tracking all SOWs, invoices, and timesheets. During 2003 and 2004, the PMO and IT Leads met to discuss successes and failures in the offshore initiative and to assess supplier performance. Two small suppliers were identified as poor performers and when the engagements expired, contracts were not renewed.

In all, 14 projects were launched in 2003, six projects in 2004, and one project in 2005. The number of offshore supplier workers peaked in October, 2004 at 68 and as of June, 2005, Biotech engaged 35 offshore workers. As of summer, 2005, a total of $4.1 million dollars had been paid to offshore suppliers.

The official word from the PMO: offshore outsourcing is realizing projected cost savings. During the 2003–2005 timeframe, the PMO was in charge of reporting on the project status of offshore projects. The PMO created monthly and yearly reports on the total costs of offshore outsourcing. Every document reports a total cost savings. For example, the document titled "2004 IT Offshore Accomplishments," states that as of July 23, 2004, Biotech saved $560,000 with offshore outsourcing. According to the Head of the PMO and the Offshore Project Coordinator, the number is based on multiplying the costs of the offshore hours and comparing this number with what it would have cost had they used domestic contractors. The number does not consider transaction costs, productivity, or quality. Thus, month after month, the PMO documents report that offshore outsourcing is successful in meeting Biotech's cost savings targets.

The burning question: is offshore outsourcing really worthwhile? The Head of the PMO questioned whether these cost savings were realistic. During our first interview with him, he said:

> It is clear that we saved money on a per hour basis, there is no way to argue about that, but did [the offshore supplier] do it as fast as we would do it? The other big complaint came from the project managers: 'Managing offshore projects is really hard. ...' If I had to count up how hard this is, then we lost money. That is clearly anecdotal since they don't keep track of how much they spend on domestic project in terms of project management.

However, two other IT Leads seemed to think offshore outsourcing, in general, was successful. The first quote by an IT Lead claimed that overall economic benefits were met:

> They all delivered on the date. They all delivered at the economic level we expected. And when I say, pretty much on the dates, we probably had one or two that missed a little bit, but I wouldn't call those significant. – IT Lead

The CIO concludes:

> Our offshore experiences have certainly been mixed. I am working with the IT Leads now to do a kind of 'good, bad and ugly' analysis to see where we are and what worked and how we can utilize the offshore model. I think that some of the setbacks were due to the suppliers' shortcomings and some of them were due to how we do business at [Biotech]. We need to understand which were which and go from there.

Thus, there were different opinions as to whether Biotech actually met their offshore objective to reduce IT costs. To move beyond random anecdotes, the Head of the PMO wanted to capture the opinions of all the IT employees involved in offshore outsourcing. We assessed their opinions at a project level so that we could find attributes to help explain differences in project outcomes. The next sections explain the project outcome *indicator* we used, the attributes we measured, and the overall project level findings.

5   Participants' Project Ratings

Traditionally, practitioners define project success[5] as a project being delivered on time, on budget, with promised functionality (Nelson, 2005; Standish Group International, 2003). At Biotech, there were no formal metrics to uniformly assess project success across the 21 projects, other than to compare offshore expenses with what those hours would have cost if Biotech had used domestic contractors.

---

[5] Academics frequently use system use, system adoption, and system diffusion as indicators of success (Jeyaraj, Rottman, & Lacity M.C., 2006), but these measures are more appropriate to assess from users (Nelson, 2005).

We created a project indicator of success based on subjective evaluations of the people knowledgeable of the project.

Subjective evaluations are the most common form of IT project evaluation for projects of less than one year duration. For example, researchers found that most small and medium-sized IT projects (less than 1 year to complete) are subjectively evaluated by people involved in the project in a technical, business, or managerial capacity (Gudea, 2005; Willcocks & Lester, 1999). In comparison, they also found that most large projects (more than 1 year to complete) are evaluated using hard numbers such as return on investment, payback period, and net present value (Gudea). This difference in evaluation methods is likely due to the fact that small projects are expensed, whereas large projects typically pass through a capital budgeting process.

We asked the 44 participants:

> Considering the degree to which project objectives were met, budgets and schedules were met, and the quality of the delivered product, what letter grade would you assign the project?

For each specific project discussed by a participant, the participant assigned a standard US letter grade (A, B, C, D, or F). We used the standard US grading system because it is a common frame of reference for the US participants. Based on the interviews, it was clear that all participants could clearly articulate and defend a letter grade.

Among the 21 projects for which participants graded the project outcome, 17 projects had at least two participants independently assign a grade. For four projects, one participant assigned a grade. To calculate the average grade for each project, we converted letter grades reported by participants to numbers. We assigned A = 4, A–/B+ = 3.5, B = 3, B–/C+ = 2.5, C = 2, C–/D+ = 1.5, D = 1, D– = .5, and F = 0. In Table 1, we show the 21 projects (labeled A through U), the number of participants that graded the project, the letter grades assigned, the average project rating after converting letters to numbers, and the standard deviation. The overall mean project rating was 1.73 and the median was 1.75 (indicating a grade of between a C and a C–).

In some instances, participants had a shared view of project outcome as evidenced by the similar grades for a project. For example, all five participants independently graded Project D as an "F." Project D entailed Database Administration (DBA) support tasks. The project was managed in the US and delivered by Biotech's captive center in Bangalore. The project deliverables were late and frequently wrong. According to one DBA Team Lead:

> The project was bloody awful! I had business users demanding, 'Don't send it to Bangalore – they will just screw it up and we will have to redo all the work and it will take five times as long!'

In other instances, participants had different perceptions of project outcome. Project C provides an example. Project C entailed the visual mapping of DNA to help scientists manage the lineage of traits. Project C was graded by three participants: an IT Team Lead graded the project a D, a Software Architect graded

Table 1 Participants' ratings of project outcomes

Project	Number of Participants who assigned a grade	Letter grades assigned by participants	Average project rating using A = 4, A–/B+ = 3.5, B = 3, B–/C+ = 2.5, C = 2, C–,D+ = 1.5, D = 1, D–,F+ = 0.5 and F = 0	Standard deviation of average project rating
A	3	C+, D, F	1.17	1.26
B	1	C–	1.50	n/a
C	3	D+, D, A–	2.00	1.32
D	5	F, F, F, F,F	0.00	0.00
E	3	F, C, B	1.67	1.53
F	4	C, B, B, D	2.25	0.96
G	5	A, A, A, B, B	3.60	0.55
H	4	F, F, F, D	0.25	0.50
I	1	D	1.00	n/a
J	2	B, C–	2.25	1.06
K	2	F, D,	0.50	0.71
L	3	A, A, C	3.33	1.15
M	4	C, D, C–, B	1.88	0.85
N	4	C, F, F, F	0.50	1.00
O	3	B+, B+,B+	3.50	0.00
P	3	B, C+, D+	2.33	0.76
Q	9	D, C, D, D, B, B, F, B, B	1.89	1.17
R	2	C+, D	1.75	1.06
S	1	C–	1.50	n/a
T	1	D	1.00	n/a
U	3	C–, B, B	2.50	0.87
Overall			1.73 (mean) 1.75 (median)	1.02

the project a D+, and a Project Lead graded the project an A–. One explanation for the divergent views may be that participants viewed different outputs. The IT Team Lead and Software Architect viewed the project outputs directly from the supplier. They defended their grades as follows:

> [The offshore supplier] would send me code that would not compile! I would have to fix the code, submit it to the code repository and then run it. That is the code that feeds the status: the vendor's bad code that we fixed. – Software Architect

In contrast, the Project Lead viewed the outputs only after the IT Team Lead and Software Architect fixed the supplier's errors. This may explain his higher grade:

> I never talked with the supplier's developers, just the Project Lead for the offshore team…I think it went OK, some issues with code, but in general, I think it went well. – Project Lead

It is quite clear from our interviews that the projects sourced offshore were not as uniformly successful as the official PMO reports. Whereas the PMO reports focused only on the cost part of the services, the participants focused on cost, quality, and speed. The participants' assessments are much richer and less uniformly enthusiastic than the PMO reports. What was really going on at Biotech? To answer this question, we conducted two levels of analysis. At the organizational level, we found evidence that Biotech's offshore strategy to simply replace domestic contractors with cheaper, offshore suppliers was a poor fit with Biotech's social and cultural contexts. At the project level of analysis, we found that different project attributes explained differences in project outcomes.

6   Organizational Level Analysis: Offshore Outsourcing was a Poor Fit

From the case description section, it is clear that the official word in PMO documents was that offshore outsourcing was meeting Biotech's objective to reduce IT costs. Based on the project ratings from knowledgeable participants, results were obviously mixed, and generally less positive than the "official word." This section focuses on the broader contextual issues to explain why offshore sourcing of IT work resulted in mixed results at Biotech.

Initially, the CIO and IT Leads' strategy was to replace, person-for-person, domestic contractors with offshore IT workers. Three findings suggest why this strategy was a poor fit with Biotech's social and cultural contexts.

1. Strong social networks between Biotech IT employees and domestic contractors were not easily replicated with offshore suppliers. Although prior research suggests significant differences between contractors and permanent employees (Ang & Slaughter, 2001), this was not evident at Biotech. At Biotech, we learned that domestic IT contractors are treated like Biotech IT employees. They are housed in the same types of cubicles with permanent workers, wear the same identification badges, attend the same meetings, and are tightly integrated into project teams. One reason for the lack of distinction is that Biotech often uses domestic contractor positions as a precursor to fulltime positions. Indeed, among the 44 people we interviewed, 10 were previously domestic contractors before becoming fulltime Biotech employees. The following quotation describes the close integration of domestic contractors and Biotech employees:

> Our culture is totally different from a contract resource point of view. I came from some other companies. I was shocked when I came into [Biotech] to see how the contractors were actually integrated into the scene. I mean, I couldn't tell [who was a contractor and who was a fulltime employee]. Same meetings, you have as many responsibilities as some of the senior managers have here. Some [contractors] have been around sometimes for over a decade. This is a totally different paradigm. – IT Lead

In contrast, the Indian offshore IT workers were treated differently. Despite efforts to integrate the offshore workers into the teams, internal Biotech employees never felt a sense of connection with them. According to an IT Team Lead,

> We even tried bringing over some people from India for team building, and it worked when they were here, but when they went back, the team aspect fell apart.

In addition to the social disconnection, there were technical barriers as well. Due to security concerns and bandwidth constraints, offshore workers were not allowed to access production data or Biotech's internal systems such as the code repository. This hampered development and created obstacles for the offshore workers.

2. Biotech's "sneaker-net" culture among business users, IT employees and domestic contractors were not easily replicated with offshore suppliers. At Biotech, we learned that requirements analysis is an informal process. Because IT workers reside on the same campus as business users, Biotech's IT employees and domestic contractors typically walk over to meet business users to seek or clarify functional requirements. Thus, the process was called "sneaker-net" by some participants. Like the social networks that facilitate knowledge transfer between IT employees and domestic contractors, there are also social networks that facilitate knowledge transfer among IT employees, domestic contractors, and business users. According to the CIO,

> Here at [Biotech], we have always worked very closely with our contractors and our business sponsors. Tight collaboration is part of our DNA. That makes this offshoring pretty tough.

Furthermore, the CIO said that requirements are not only informally *gathered*, requirements are also informally *documented*. He said requirements are typically "documented" on white boards or in personal notebooks. A Web Developer corroborated the CIO's statement:

> A lot of times in our environment, the developers will be involved in requirements, meaning taking their own notes and gathering that understanding. And that's not something that happened with offshore. We had to retranslate what he had on paper and then translate it to them, and it doesn't work very well. I think in a development environment, it's important that the developers be part of requirements gathering, so that they can understand what it is and why it is.

Biotech's "sneaker-net" culture did not fit well with offshore. Indian-based IT workers did not have access to users to establish the social networks needed to facilitate knowledge transfer. A Project Manager in R&D said:

> We had no way to get requirements from the user and get them to the offshore team. We could have easily done this project onshore because we know how to go back and forth with the user, but the offshore team just couldn't do it.

In hindsight, an IT Lead acknowledged that Biotech had not thought through the knowledge transfer process:

> We didn't have anything in place that was really allowing us to transfer the knowledge. There was, like, a huge leak.

3. Biotech's project management processes and expectations were often incompatible with offshore suppliers. Despite the cultural awareness training, many participants were unprepared for the cultural differences between US IT workers and Indian IT workers. In the US, domestic contractors are trusted to speak up when deadlines slip or when they do not understand requirements or processes. An Application Architect describes the trust he has in his domestic contractor to communicate with him:

> And I make it clear to my contractors, if you don't understand something, you're in my office, every day. I mean, I got one contractor who is reasonable, $54 bucks an hour, really reasonable guy. He basically comes in my cube, probably 15 times a day, and that's what

we have to do. We've got a couple other guys that are very similar to him and, basically come in all the time for clarification.

In contrast, we heard from many participants that the offshore IT workers could not be relied upon to report that the project was behind schedule or that they did not understand the requirements. The following quotes serve as evidence about not reporting project delays:

> When the project was going so far off course, they never really told us that they were behind on deadlines. They always said everything was going well. – Offshore Project Coordinator

> They didn't feel like they could tell us if they were going to miss a deadline. This seems to be the modus operandi, dig and dig and spade and spade to get anybody to tell you that things are wrong. Because they just simply won't. They will tell you it is great. – Head of the PMO

One IT Lead summed it up by saying,

> The place could be on fire and they would say, 'Oh it's great, a little warm, but it is great!

During an offshore outsourcing class the second author attended, Biotech's offshore consultant talked about the cultural challenges at Biotech. According to him, Biotech's Indian suppliers view time more fluidly than Westerners. He said,

> If an Indian IT worker knows how to complete a task even though he knows it will be late, then he would view it as unnecessary to contact the customer. He is the expert and the customer should trust that he is professionally completing the task.

7   Project Level Analysis: For Biotech, Bigger was Better

Since the project ratings are numeric, there are several ways to divide the data into categories of "success." We divided the data into two. We categorized individual projects that rated above the mean project rating of 1.73 as the "more successful projects" and projects that rated below the project mean as the "less successful projects." Given the sample contains 21 projects, dividing the data into two categories by mean seemed the most reasonable criterion. (We note that the mean and median are nearly identical and selecting the median would not change results.) Our analysis yields seven project level findings.

1. Overall, participants rated projects that engaged one large offshore supplier higher than projects that engaged one small offshore supplier or multiple suppliers. Prior research has found that outsourcing to a single supplier, particularly under circumstances of high asset specificity, is riskier than using multiple suppliers (Aubert, Dussault, Patry, & Rivard, 1999; Currie & Willcocks, 1998; Gallivan & Oh, 1999; Williamson, 1991). However, multi-sourcing creates higher transaction costs than outsourcing to a single supplier (Lacity M.C. & Willcocks, 2001). Prior research has used the client as the unit of analysis (Chaudhury, Nam, & Rao, 1995; Cross, 1995; Gallivan & Oh). Thus, these studies addressed the question, "Did/ Should the *client* engage more than one supplier?" At the client level, Biotech multi-sourced by engaging six offshore suppliers. But we viewed this research as an opportunity to ask the question at a project level: "Does the number of suppliers on a *project* matter?"

In addition to single versus multi-sourcing, we also examined the size of the supplier (large versus small). Practitioners and researchers have found that supplier size affects their capabilities (Levina & Ross, 2003; Martorelli, Moore, McCarthy, & Brown, 2004) which, we reason, would affect a project's outcome. On the one hand, large suppliers would likely have better sourcing capabilities, economies of scale, and economies of scope to help them deliver successful projects (Feeny, Lacity M.C., & Willcocks, 2005; Levina & Ross). On the other hand, small suppliers may pay more attention to the client because the client represents a larger portion of their revenues (Feeny et al.). We did not conjecture whether large or small suppliers would have higher success rates, but instead viewed this research as an opportunity to investigate the effect of supplier size on project outcome.

Among the 21 projects, Biotech engaged one small Indian supplier on 12 projects, one large Indian supplier on five projects, and multiple suppliers on three projects. In addition, one project used Biotech's captive center in Bangalore. When mapping suppliers to project outcomes in Table 2, the two most definitive findings based on this analysis are:

1. Participants rated four out of five projects (80%) that engaged one *large* supplier above the mean project rating
2. Participants only rated five of the 12 projects (42%) that engaged one *small* supplier above the mean project rating

The participants provide insights to these findings. According to the participants, a major advantage of the larger suppliers was that they had greater access to experienced IT personnel. An IT Lead with over 25 years with Biotech said:

> [The small vendors] would take forever to find resources with the skills and levels of experience we were needing. The small vendors did not seem to be able to attract and retain good people. That really hurt our projects – it took longer to ramp up and if there was unplanned turnover – we were dead. The larger vendors seemed to have a much deeper bench and turnover seemed much less of an issue with the larger vendors.

Table 2 Project rating vs. size and number of offshore suppliers

	Project rating		
Offshore supplier size	Number of more successful projects	Number of less successful projects	Percentage of more successful projects
One large supplier (greater than $1 billion in annual revenues)	4	1	80
Multi-sourced	2	1	67
One small supplier (less than $150 million annual revenue	5	7	42
Captive center	0	1	0

One Program Lead expressed dissatisfaction with the smaller suppliers. In his experiences, the smaller suppliers lacked the experience to accurately bid and manage projects. He said:

> [The small supplier] just didn't get it. We estimated internally (using offshore rates) that a project we had pegged for offshore should cost about $80,000 and take about six to nine months. The supplier's bid was $40,000 and they estimated it would take four months. I wanted an accurate estimate of the effort and time it would take more so than just trying to get the lowest dollar I could on the project. So I told the supplier they were significantly off in their bid and asked them to resubmit. The second bid came in at $60,000 with a time frame of six months. By this time, we were already running behind schedule and needing to pursue offshore, so we accepted the bid. The supplier ended up spending an additional six months and we ended up fixing a lot of the code and doing the testing ourselves.

Table 2 also shows that participants rated two of the three multi-sourced projects above the mean project rating. Because only three projects were multi-sourced, we must be very cautious in deriving conclusions based on this data. However, the Team Lead SAP provided insight into the efficacy of using multiple suppliers on a project:

> You have to understand what the supplier wants and what the supplier brings to the table and how your project fits in. For example, [a large supplier] should bring in process expertise and great talent, but they aren't interested in my $5000 little project. However, small suppliers are often hungry for business and can bring in specific skills.

2. Overall, participants rated projects with some offshore supplier employees onsite higher than projects with all supplier employees offshore. We defined the supplier engagement model as the physical location of offshore supplier managers and developers. Biotech used three supplier engagement models to organize the 21 projects. The cheapest model in terms of hourly wages entailed having all the offshore supplier employees (managers and developers) in India. This model was used on 12 projects. The most expensive model had some offshore supplier managers and developers onsite. This model was used on five projects. The middle model had some offshore developers onsite, but no offshore supplier manager onsite. This model was used on four projects.

We cross-tabulated the supplier engagement model with project rating. Table 3 shows that participants rated seven of the nine projects (78%) that had some

Table 3 Project rating vs. supplier engagement model

Offshore Supplier engagement model	Project rating		
	Number of more successful projects	Number of less successful projects	Percentage of more successful projects
Some supplier managers and developers onsite	4	1	80
Some supplier developers onsite but no supplier managers onsite	3	1	75
No supplier managers or developers onsite	4	8	33

supplier managers and/or developers onsite higher than the mean project rating. In contrast, participants rated four of the twelve projects (33%) that located all the supplier employees offshore higher than the mean project rating.

According to multiple participants, project managers at Biotech were under extreme pressure to keep projects costs low. Because any offshore supplier employee onsite is paid onshore rates (about $65 per hour versus about $25 per hour offshore), project managers were pressured to keep as much of the supplier headcount offshore as possible. However, some participants said that quality suffered when all of a supplier's employees were offshore because they did not understand Biotech's requirements and could not easily communicate with Biotech's IT staff and business users. Several participants concluded that an onsite engagement manager (OEM) and some onsite developers were needed to better understand and communicate requirements and thus ensure quality. According to a Program Lead:

> We priced in an OEM to interface between the business sponsors and the two offshore developers. We realized that all project cost savings was lost, but the OEM helped us improve our processes, interviewed and managed the developers and was responsible for status updates.

According to the Team Lead HR Services,

> Even though the OEM is expensive, they are worth it. They interface between our analysts and the offshore developers and save a lot of time and rework. They help to protect our environment.

3. Overall, participants rated projects with greater-valued contracts higher than projects with lesser-valued contracts. Practitioners have frequently told us that the more strategic a client account, the more attention the supplier will pay to the account. The two most important determinants of a supplier's perception of a strategic account are current revenues generated from the account and the potential for future revenues generated from the account (Feeny, 2006). We wondered: Does value of the contract matter?

We used actual dollars spent as the indicator of contract value because Biotech closely tracked these figures for each project. Using dollars spent, the contract values ranged between $4,300 and $1,363,098, with a mean contract value of $193,000 and a median contract value of $64,473.

For this analysis, we cross-tabulated contract value with project rating. Because the mean contract value ($193,000) is substantially different than the median contract value ($64,473), we analyzed both. Tables 5 and 6 show the results.

Table 4 is based on the *mean* spend as dividing line between greater and lesser-valued contracts. It shows that participants rated 71% of the greater-valued contracts above the mean project rating, compared to 43% of the lesser-valued contracts. Table 5 is based on the *median* spend as dividing line between greater and lesser-valued contracts. It shows that participants rated 70% of the greater-valued contracts above the mean project rating, compared to 30% of the lesser-valued contracts. Thus, contract value mattered.

Because contract value only captured the offshore part of the project, we also examined an indicator of overall project size in terms of duration of the project.

Table 4 Project rating vs. contract value using mean

	Project rating		
Contract value	Number of more successful projects	Number of less successful projects	Percentage of more successful projects
Greater-value (greater than $193,000 mean spent)	5	2	71
Lesser-value (less than the $193,000 mean spent)	6	8	43

Table 5 Project rating vs. contract value using median

	Project rating		
Contract value	Number of more successful projects	Number of less successful projects	Percentage of more successful projects
Greater-value (greater than $64,473 median spent)	7	3	70
Lesser-value (less than the $64,473 median spent)	3	7	30

4. Overall, participants rated longer projects higher than shorter projects. For over 25 years, IT researchers have recognized the relationship between project size, risk, and outcome (Gopal et al., 2003; Keil & Montealegre, 2000; Keil, Rai, Mann, & Zhang, 2003; McFarlan, 1981; Wallace, Keil, & Rai, 2004). In general, prior research has found that longer projects are riskier and have lower success rates than shorter projects (Jones, 1994). For example, Carroll (2005) found that shorter projects (less than 6 months) had a success rate of 50%, medium-length projects (6–9 months) had a 40% success rate, and none of the projects in the sample (n = 22) over nine months were successful. Aladwani (2002) in a study of 42 IT projects found that project duration negatively affects project planning, which negatively impacts project success. Practitioners and researchers suggest that large projects should be transformed into smaller projects through phased functionality, prototyping, or pilot testing to reduce risk and increase success (Jones; Standish Group International, 2003; Willcocks, Feeny, & Islei, 1997).

We were able to use duration of the project in days because Biotech's PMO closely tracked this number. (Biotech did not track total costs of the project, only the costs directly invoiced by the offshore suppliers.) Using duration, the project sizes ranged from 11 days long to 1,030 days long. The average project was 350 days long and the median project was 272 days long.

For this analysis, we cross-tabulated project duration with project rating. We initially used three rules to categorize projects as "longer" versus "shorter." The rules were (1) Gudea's (2005) cut-off of over/under one year in duration, (2) over/under the mean duration of 350 days, and (3) over/under the median duration of 272 days. However, rules (1) and (2) are coincidentally equivalent with our data. Tables 6 and 7 show the results.

Table 6 Project rating vs. project duration (mean)

	Project rating		
Project duration	Number of more successful projects	Number of less successful projects	Percentage of more successful projects
Longer (more than one year)	5	3	63
Shorter (less than one year)	6	7	46

Table 7 Project rating vs. project duration (median)

	Project rating		
Project duration	Number of more successful projects	Number of less successful projects	Percentage of more successful projects
Longer (longer than 272 year)	7	3	70
Shorter (less than 272 days)	3	7	30

Table 6 is based on the *mean* and *one-year cut-off* as the dividing line between longer and shorter projects. It shows that participants rated 63% of the longer projects above the mean project rating, compared to 46% of the shorter projects. Table 7 is based on the *median* duration as dividing line between longer and shorter projects. It shows that participants rated 70% of the longer projects above the mean project rating, compared to 30% of the shorter projects.

Some of the participants claimed that shorter projects could not meet financial objectives because the transaction costs of dealing with the offshore suppliers swallowed the projected cost savings. Below are some of the quotes supporting this interpretation:

> On the smaller projects, the overhead costs of documenting some of the projects exceeded the value of the deliverables. – IT Lead

> A lot of our projects were too small. We had one, maybe one and a half, resources working offshore and the overhead was killing us trying to keep track of what was going on offshore. – Program Lead

Conversely, one IT Team Lead explained that longer projects allowed Biotech to recover overhead by benefiting from mounting experience:

> The larger projects I did seemed to work a little better. It took quite some time to figure things out, and with the smaller projects, they would end at that point. With the larger ones, we could use the learning and relationships we built for longer periods of time and improve as we went along.

5. Overall, some organizational units had higher participant-rated projects than other organizational units. During the interviews, it became apparent that some groups seemed to be experiencing more success with offshore outsourcing than others. Six units report directly to the CIO. Five of these units engaged offshore suppliers for at least one project: Enterprise Architecture, ERP, R&D, Marketing, and Web.

Table 8 Project rating vs. organizational unit

Organizational unit within biotech	Project rating		
	Number of more successful projects	Number of less successful projects	Percentage of more successful projects
Web	5	0	100
ERP	2	0	100
Marketing	3	2	60
R&D	3	7	30
Enterprise Architecture	0	1	0

Participants from five of the six units that report directly to the CIO managed at least one offshore project. Table 8 cross-tabulates these five units against project rating. Projects managed by the Web and ERP units all scored above the mean project rating. The most interesting finding, however, is that the R&D unit did the most offshore projects, yet participants rated only 30% of projects above the mean project rating.

The level of domain specific knowledge required by these different units may explain the results. Some participants noted that projects within the R&D area required the supplier to have very specific scientific knowledge, whereas the Web and ERP units required more common knowledge. According to an IT Lead in the R&D area:

> What makes some of this [offshore outsourcing] hard is that we are making up the questions at the same time we are asking the supplier to come up with answers. We are inventing new products with highly scientific processes and foundations. In our area, we are really 'out there' in regards to the kinds of things we are creating.

Conversely, all of the projects in the less scientifically-intense areas of Web and ERP were rated above the mean. A Team Lead SAP explained:

> A lot of what we do in our area is more generic than in the [R&D] area. The bulk of our work is change requests to our SAP systems. The suppliers are well equipped in the SAP tools like ABAP. Once we accurately explain the specifications and modifications needed to fulfill the change request, the ABAP part is fairly straight forward.

6. Contrary to expectations, participants rated both development and maintenance/ support projects equally. Prior ITO research has examined the types of IT work that clients outsource (Ang & Straub, 1998; Grover, Cheon, & Teng, 1996): applications development and maintenance, systems operations, telecommunications, end user support, and systems planning and management. In a survey of 188 IT executives, Grover et al. found that type of IT work affected outcomes. Specifically, outsourcing of systems operations and telecommunications led to increased client satisfaction. They also found that outsourcing applications development and maintenance, end user support, and systems management did not lead to increased client satisfaction. Poppo & Zenger (1998) hypothesized a negative relationship between technological uncertainty and outsourcing satisfaction based on transaction cost economics (TCE). Based on all this research, we conjectured that the new software development projects would entail more uncertainty, and would thus contribute to lower project ratings, as predicted by TCE (Williamson, 1991).

For this analysis, we cross-tabulated project type with project rating (See Table 9). Based on prior research, we speculated that new development projects would have more risk and thus lower project ratings than projects involving maintenance or support of existing systems. However, evidence did not support this speculation. Overall, participants rated both development (53%) and maintenance/support (50%) above the mean project rating nearly equally. According to an interview with a Software Architect, it was evident that the type of project did not matter because all the work was new to the suppliers. He said:

> It really didn't matter the types of work we gave to the supplier. Even for what we considered to be routine, like maintenance, they had to learn the system, the tools and how we worked. Even though it was old to us, it was like new development to the supplier. For example, we have a Lotus Notes database to maintain, it was very difficulty to find Notes experts. They had to learn the system from scratch.

7. Overall, participants rated recent projects higher than older projects. Based on prior research, we thought that earlier projects would have lower ratings than later projects. For example, researchers (Lacity M.C. & Willcocks, 1998) found that more recent contracts had higher frequencies of success than older contracts. They attributed this finding to learning curve effects. Three research studies on offshore outsourcing also found learning curve effects (Carmel & Agarwal, 2002; Kaiser & Hawk, 2004; Rottman J.W. & Lacity M.C., 2006). All three studies found that clients use offshore outsourcing more strategically over time.

For this analysis, we compared the project ratings for earlier projects that were launched in 2003 against projects that were launched after 2003. Table 10 shows that participants rated 43% of the earlier projects above the mean project rating, compared to 71% of the later projects, indicating that organizational learning did occur.

Several participants stated that as projects and engagements matured, the quality of the deliverables improved.

Table 9 Project rating vs. project type

	Project rating		
Project type	Number of more successful projects	Number of less successful projects	Percentage of more successful projects
New software development	8	7	53
Support and or maintenance of existing software	3	3	50

Table 10 Project rating vs. project start year

	Project rating		
Project start year	Number of more successful projects	Number of less successful projects	Percentage of more successful projects
During 2003	6	8	43
During 2004 or 2005	5	2	71

Thus far, we have explained Biotech's experiences with offshore outsourcing at the organizational and project levels. The next section points to learning from Biotech that may be valuable to other practitioners.

8 Four Insights for Clients and Suppliers

1. An offshore strategy must either fit with the client's norms and practices, or the client may have to change norms and practices to achieve offshore success. Offshore suppliers often rely heavily on Capability Maturity Model (CMM) or Capability Maturity Model Integrated (CMMI) processes to ensure that business requirements are properly documented (Adler, McGarry, Talbot, & Binney, 2005) However, if their clients are operating at CMM/CMMI levels of two or below, the relationship may struggle with the issues experienced at Biotech. Suppliers may have to help clients improve their CMM/CMMI processes, or be flexible by finding ways to fit into the client's requirements analysis processes.

At Biotech, the "sneaker-net" culture and close social networks between business users, IT employees, and domestic contractors were a poor fit with offshore outsourcing. Within some project teams, Biotech participants changed the practices. Some Biotech project managers abandoned the "sneaker-net" process in favor of formal documentation of business, technical, and procedural requirements. Participants pursuing this option generally agreed that it facilitated knowledge transfer. According to a Technical Architect:

> They [the offshore supplier] improved our internal processes. They all have been documenting procedures and processes. Now, we've got it so proceduralized that we've anticipated 90% of the questions.

But participants also complained that it significantly increased their project overhead. As previously noted, one IT Lead said:

> On the smaller projects, the overhead costs of documenting some of the projects exceeded the value of the deliverables.

2. Clients and suppliers should invest in social capital to facilitate knowledge transfer. Although the first insight indicates the importance of process, a corollary to that insight is that the people who perform the processes matter. Nahapiet & Ghosal (1998) argue that social capital (such as social networks) helps to create intellectual capital (such as understanding user requirements). They also posit that organizations have an advantage over markets in creating and sharing intellectual capital. Researchers have begun to apply social capital theory to the ITO context, concluding that this perspective richly enhances our view of outsourcing (Chou, Chen, & Pan, 2006; George, 2006; Miranda & Kavan, 2005; Rottman J.W., 2007) Thus, maybe domestic contractors at Biotech performed better than offshore IT workers because domestic contractors are essentially insiders. We have one anecdote that suggests that offshore IT workers can essentially become "insiders" over time. A quote from an Indian Project Lead who has been a fulltime Biotech employee for 4 years sums up the need for a greater understanding of the social networks in knowledge transfer:

> Communication was a real issue – even for me and I am from Mumbai. I found it hard during the conference calls to understand what they were saying, especially during the interviews and code reviews. And when we would send emails back and forth, I thought, 'What are they trying to say, I don't understand where they are coming from.' It would take two or three extra emails, just to make sure we were talking about the same things.

One good way to build social capital is to let the project team members meet face-to-face. It is much easier to switch to lower cost media such as teleconferences and email after meeting people face-to-face. Some project managers at Biotech bore the cost of bringing the Indian developers onshore to meet Biotech employees face-to-face:

> Once you get good at specking out what you need face-to-face, then an awful lot of the work happens by e-mail and it's just follow up questions and lots of that happens by e-mail.
> – Global Leadership Team member

The downside of course, is the increased expense associated with face-to-face meetings. We do note, however, that one IT Team Lead stated that meeting face-to-face solidified the team at first, but that "*the team aspect fell apart*" after the Indian workers returned to India. This suggests that social capital requires an ongoing investment to sustain benefits.

One of the best mechanisms for building sustainable social capital is to invest in OEMs. Biotech experienced significant challenges in transferring knowledge to the suppliers. The best solution to this challenge was to keep some supplier managers and developers onsite to build social networks. Unlike the "face-to-face" meetings suggested above, OEMs entail a long-term investment in social capital. Among the 21 projects, Biotech brought offshore supplier employees onsite for nine projects, of which seven scored above the mean project rating. Again, the benefit of this practice is that it facilitates knowledge transfer from user to offshore IT worker. Participants said it was worth the extra cost. The drawback of this practice is that it also increases costs.

Offshore suppliers must also protect knowledge after it is transferred. Because of increasing employee turnover rates (McCue, 2005; Srivastava, 2005), Indian suppliers in particular must have good knowledge management processes. Some participants at Biotech said that supplier turnover was a problem because when supplier employees left, they took the hard-earned, client-specific knowledge with them. An IT Lead said:

> And the other thing, too, is their turnover rates. So those five-year guys on the offshore team, they're already looking to move. They're looking to move to a technical lead or architect or programming. And the opportunity is there. So, personally for them, it's a great opportunity, they could move at five years. And, so we can't even keep them on the offshore team.

Suppliers must find innovative ways to capture tacit knowledge by using, for example, video repositories, interactive training modules, mentoring and shadowing to groom replacements (Rottman J.W., 2006).

3. Clients and suppliers may achieve greater success with bigger commitments.
At Biotech, we found that the larger projects in terms of number of days and contract value had higher frequencies of success. We believe that this finding is attrib-
utable to (1) transaction costs and (2) supplier attention. Concerning transaction
costs, offshore outsourcing has higher transaction costs associated with coordination, management, communication, and travel compared with insourcing or domestic outsourcing. In order to achieve total cost savings, the volume of work has to be
large enough to compensate for the additional transaction costs. Of course, large
commitments to offshore suppliers must be made cautiously, but the lesson may be
that client managers should not expect significant cost savings while they are still
conducting pilot projects and getting to know their offshore suppliers. It is only
after progressing along the learning curve that service can be improved in terms of
cost savings, quality, and speed.

Concerning supplier attention, it is no surprise that suppliers are motivated to
allocate their top resources to their most prestigious clients. Prestigious clients
commit large volumes of work over a long period time. Thus, the larger-sized
projects and contracts at Biotech may have commanded more attention from their
suppliers than smaller-sized projects and contracts.

*4. Clients need robust measures and independent audits to manage and assess
offshore outsourcing programs.* Biotech's simple formula for calculating cost savings
(cost of hours offshore versus what the hours would have cost onshore) disseminated
the message that offshore outsourcing was successful. Metrics that capture productivity,
quality, process improvement, supplier compatibility, and organizational learning are
needed to carefully manage offshore outsourcing. Furthermore, CIOs are advised to
occasionally engage an independent third party to assess the effectiveness of offshore
strategy. We found that lower level IT employees were less likely to honestly report
on sourcing issues. Our favorite quote comes from a Biotech informant was:

> You didn't want to tell them [senior management] the bad news too much. Because, this
> was their baby and you didn't want to say, "You have a terribly ugly baby!" – Software
> Architect, biotechnology company

While a CIO's strong commitment to success is a key enabler, the commitment
cannot come at the price of lost learning. Independent assessments of an offshore
initiative will more objectively gather learning across projects without compromis-
ing the IT staff's confidentiality.

Appendix: Interview Guide

Participant Data:
- Job title
- Length of time in current position
- Where are you in the organizational chart?
- Previous positions and organizations

Please begin by telling us your offshore outsourcing story – why did your organizational unit initiate an offshore project, who was involved, what process did you go through, how did your internal organization react, how did you manage the supplier, who was the business sponsor, and what was the outcome?

Expected Benefits of Offshore Outsourcing *per project*: (lower costs, better service, meet short term IT demand, experience gained with offshore outsourcing, etc.)

Actual Benefits of Offshore Outsourcing *per project*: (lower costs, better service, meet short term IT demand, experience gained with offshore outsourcing, etc.)

For each offshore project you worked on, please describe:

Project Characteristics
- Describe the business function of the project
- Describe the technical platform
- New development/Support/Maintenance
- Name of suppliers on project
- Supplier headcount including on/offshore ratio

Quality of Offshore Outsourcing:
How did you analyze and protect the quality of the deliverables (code, test scripts, documentation etc.)?

What mechanisms in the contract or processes did you use to protect quality?

Compare the quality of individual projects with the quality of domestically sourced projects.

Did you witness quality differences from the different suppliers?

Project Metrics:
What metrics were in place for quality control of offshore project deliverables/milestones? SLAs? Defect rates? Submission rates? Unit/IT Acceptance/User Acceptance Tests?

Project Outcome of Offshore Outsourcing:
Perceptions of Success/Failure
How measured
Considering the degree to which project objectives were met, budgets and schedules were met, and the quality of the delivered product, what letter grade would you assign the project? (A – F):

Costs of Offshore Outsourcing:
Contract:
- What are the contract terms as far as baseline services, service level requirements, and penalties for non-performance?
- What do you perceive as the strengths and weaknesses of the contract?
- How many pages is the contract?
- What differences did you see in the projects from various contract models and sizes?

Infrastructure: Organizational Structure, Tools, and Processes:
- Which supplier employees were onsite and which were offsite?
- Did you use an onsite engagement manager?

- How do you govern the supplier's activities?
- Project Scheduling and Tracking
- Did you have to create special tools, such as data repository, to coordinate supplier activities?
- Configuration Management (keeping track of modules and sections of code)
- Work Flow automation system
- What differences did you see in the projects from various engagement models?

Problem Recognition and Resolution:
- How would you characterize your relationship with the supplier?
- What is going well?
- Have you had any disputes with the supplier? How were they resolved?
- Have you ever been charged for services you assumed were covered in the contract?

Extent to Which You Encountered Problems with:
- Cultural differences
- Time Zone differences
- Language differences
- Strange Foreign Work-Hour Regulations
- High Employee Turnover in Supplier organization
- Difficulties in Arranging Visas
- Other legal/government difficulties
- An offshore unit's lack of domain knowledge
- Unreliable Telecommunications Infrastructure

Evaluation Process of Offshore Outsourcing:
- Who in your organizational unit became the most avid champion of offshore outsourcing?
- Offshore outsourcing can be a threat to domestic employees. What organizational members were opponents of offshore outsourcing and how were their oppositions addressed?
- What was senior management's perception of offshore?
- What is the general atmosphere at Biotech concerning offshoring?
- What is the plan for future projects and offshore?

Supplier Selection:
- What was included in the RFP?
- Which suppliers were invited to respond? Why were they selected?
- What was your organization's selection criteria?
- Which suppliers worked on the projects you are familiar with?

Practices and Capabilities Needed for Offshore Outsourcing Success
- You now have some experience under your belt concerning offshore outsourcing. If you had it to do all over again, what would you do differently?

Practices and Capabilities Needed for Offshore Outsourcing Success
- You now have some experience under your belt concerning offshore outsourcing. If you had it to do all over again, what would you do differently?

- What are the lessons you learned concerning the best and worst practices for offshore outsourcing?
- What capabilities do you need in-house to make sure offshore outsourcing is a success?

References

Adler, P., McGarry, F., Talbot, W., & Binney, D. (2005). Enabling process discipline: lessons from the journey to CMM level 5. *MIS Quarterly Executive, 4*(1), 215–227.

Aladwani, A. (2002). IT project uncertainty, planning, and success. *Information Technology & People, 15*(3), 210–237.

Ang, S., & Slaughter, S. (2001). Work outcomes and job design for contract versus permanent information systems professionals on software development teams. *MIS Quarterly, 25*(3), 321–350.

Ang, S., & Straub, D. (1998). Production and transaction economies and information systems outsourcing – A study of the U.S. banking industry. *MIS Quarterly, 22*(4), 535–552.

Applegate, L., & Montealegre, R. (1991). *Eastman kodak organization: Managing IS through strategic alliances*. Boston: Harvard Business School Case 9-192-030.

Aubert, B., Dussault, S., Patry, M., & Rivard, S. (1999). Managing risk in IT outsourcing. *Proceedings of the 32nd annual Hawaii international conference on system sciences* (pp. 685–691).

Carmel, E. (2006). Building your information systems from the other side of the world: How infosys manages time zone differences. *MIS Quarterly Executive, 5*(1), 43–53.

Carmel, E., & Agarwal, R. (2002). The maturation of offshore sourcing of information technology work. *MIS Quarterly Executive, 1*(2), 65–77.

Carmel, E., & Tjia, P. (2005). *Offshoring information technology: sourcing and outsourcing to a global workforce*. Cambridge: Cambridge University Press.

Carroll, J. (2005). The John Carroll research survey results. Project Management Institute. Available on: http://www.pmi.org/Prod2/groups/public/documents/info/pp_carroll.pdf.

Chaudhury, A., Nam, K., & Rao, H. (1995). Management of information systems outsourcing: A bidding perspective. *Journal of Management Information Systems, 12*(2), 131–159.

Chou, T., Chen, J., & Pan, S. (2006). The impacts of social capital on information technology outsourcing decisions: A case study of Taiwanese high-tech firms. *International Journal of Information Management, 26*, 249–256.

Choudhury, V., & Sabherwal, R. (2003). Portfolios of control in outsourced software development projects. *Information Systems Research, 14*(3), 291–314.

Cross, J. (1995). IT outsourcing at British petroleum. *Harvard Business Review, 73*(3), 94–102.

Cullen, S., Seddon, P., & Willcocks, L. (2005). Managing outsourcing: The life cycle imperative. *MIS Quarterly Executive, 4*(1), 229–246.

Currie, W., & Willcocks, L. (1998). Analyzing four types of IT sourcing decisions in the context of scale, client/supplier interdependency, and risk mitigation. *Information Systems Journal, 8*(2), 119–144.

Dibbern, J., Goles, T., Hirschheim, R., & Bandula J. (2004). Information systems outsourcing: A survey and analysis of the literature. *Database for Advances in Information Systems, 34*(4), 6–102.

E-business strategies (2006). Offshoring statistics: Dollar size, job loss, and market potential. http://www.ebstrategy.com/Outsourcing/trends/statistics.htm.

Engardio, P. (2006). The future of outsourcing. *BusinessWeek, 3969*, January 30, 50–58.

Feeny, D. (2006). *Managing IT suppliers, presentation to UK cabinet office representatives*. United Kingdom: Said Business School, Oxford University.

Feeny, D., Lacity, M., & Willcocks, L. (2005). Taking the measure of outsourcing providers. *Sloan Management Review, 46*(3), 41–48.

Feeny, D., & Willcocks, L. (1998). Core IS capabilities for exploiting information technology. *Sloan Management Review, 39*(3), 9–21.

Gallivan, M., & Oh, W. (1999). Analyzing IT outsourcing relationships as alliances among multiple clients and customers. *Proceedings of the 32 annual Hawaii international conference on systems sciences* (pp. 1–15).

George, B. (2006). *Exploring information systems outsourcing: The role of social capital.* Unpublished Ph.D. thesis, University of Houston.

Gopal, A., Sivaramakrishnan, K., Krishnan, M., & Mukhopadhyay, T. (2003). Contracts in offshore software development: An empirical analysis. *Management Science, 49*(12), 1671–1683.

Grover, V., Cheon, M., & Teng, J. (1996). The effect of service quality and partnership on the outsourcing of information systems functions. *Journal of Management Information Systems, 12*(4), 89–119.

Gudea, S. (2005). IT project valuation survey. Posted on the Project Management Institute Web Ssite, http://www.pmi.org/prod/groups/public/documents/info/pp_soringudea.pdf viewed 6/1/06.

Hall, J., & Liedtka, S. (2005). Financial performance, CEO compensation, and large-scale information technology outsourcing decisions. *Journal of Management Information Systems, 22*(1), 193–222.

Huber, R. (1993). How continental bank outsourced its crown jewels. *Harvard Business Review, 71*(1), 121–129.

Jeyaraj, A., Rottman, J., & Lacity, M. (2006). A review of the predictors, linkages, and biases in IT innovation adoption research. *Journal of Information Technology, 21*(1), 1–23.

Jones, C. (1994). *Assessment and control of software risks.* Englewood Cliffs, NJ: Prentice-Hall.

Kaiser, K., & Hawk, S. (2004). Evolution of offshore software development: From outsourcing to co-sourcing. *MIS Quarterly Executive, 3*(2), 69–81.

Keil, M., & Montealegre, R. (2000). Cutting your losses: Extricating your organization when a big project goes awry. *Sloan Management Review, 41*(3), 55–68.

Keil, M., Rai, A., Mann, J., & Zhang, G. (2003). Why software projects escalate: The importance of project management constructs. *IEEE Transactions on Engineering Management, 50*(3), 251–261.

Lacity, M., & Hirschheim, R. (1993). *Information systems outsourcing: Myths, metaphors and realities.* Chichester: Wiley.

Lacity, M., & Rottman, J. (2008). *Offshore outsourcing of IT work.* United Kingdom: Palgrave.

Lacity, M., & Willcocks, L. (1998). An empirical investigation of information technology sourcing practices: Lessons from experience. *MIS Quarterly, 22*(3), 363–408.

Lacity, M., & Willcocks, L. (2001). *Global information technology outsourcing: Search for business advantage.* Chichester: Wiley.

Levina, N., & Ross, J. (2003). From the vendor's perspective: Exploring the value proposition in information technology outsourcing. *MIS Quarterly, 27*(3), 331–364.

Loh, L., & Venkatraman, N. (1992). Determinants of IT outsourcing: A cross-sectional analysis. *Journal of Management Information Systems, 9*(1), 7–24.

Martorelli, W., Moore, S., McCarthy, J., & Brown, A. (2004). Indian offshore suppliers: The second tier, forrester research report, July 14. Available on: http://www.forrester.com/Research/Document/Excerpt/0,7211,34847,00.html.

McCue, A. (2005). Outsourcing flops blamed on tunnel vision, Silicon.com, published on ZDNet News: June 22. Available on: http://news.zdnet.com/2100-9589_22-5757832.html

McFarlan, F. W. (1981). Portfolio approach to information systems. *Harvard Business Review, 59*(5), 142–150.

Minevich, M., & Richter, F. (2005). Top spots for global outsourcing. *CIO Insight, 1*(51), 55–57.

Miranda, S., & Kavan, B. (2005). Moments of governance in IS outsourcing: Conceptualizing effects of contracts on value capture and creation. *Journal of Information Technology, 20*(3), 152–169.

Nahapiet, J., & Ghosal, S. (1998). Social capital, intellectual capital, and the organizational advantage. *Academy of Management Review, 23*(2), 242–265.

Nelson, R. (2005). Project retrospectives: Evaluating success, failure and everything in between. *MIS Quarterly Executive, 4*(3), 361–372.

Oshri, I., Kotlarsky J., & Willcocks L. P. (2007). Managing dispersed expertise in IT offshore outsourcing: lessons from Tata consultancy services, *MISQ Executive, 6*(2), 53–65.

Poppo, L., & Zenger, T. (1998). Testing alternative theories of the firm: Transaction cost, knowledge-based, and measurement explanations for make-or-buy decisions in information services. *Strategic Management Journal, 19*, 853–877.

Rivard, S., & Aubert, B. (Eds.). (2007). *Information technology outsourcing.* New York: M.E. Sharpe.

Ross, C. (2004). Services market sizing update: 2003 to 2008. Forrester research report, April 27.

Rottman, J. (2006). Successfully outsourcing embedded software development. *IEEE Computer, 39*(1), 55–61.

Rottman, J. (2007). Successful knowledge transfer within offshore supplier networks: A case study exploring social capital in strategic alliances, the first information systems workshop on global sourcing: services, knowledge and innovation, Val d'Isère, France.

Rottman, J., & Lacity, M. (2004). Twenty practices for offshore sourcing. *MIS Quarterly Executive, 3*(3), 117–130.

Rottman, J., & Lacity, M. (2006). Proven practices for effectively offshoring IT work. *Sloan Management Review, 47*(3), 56–63.

Srivastava, S. (2005). Could rising wages diminish India's outsourcing edge? News Report, Siliconeer, Jan 21. Available on: http://news.pacificnews.org/news/view_article.html?article_id=167d1c86c1d28e7607c942fd9891938e.

Standish Group International. (2003). CHAOS chronicles V3.0. Available on: http://www.standishgroup.com/chaos/toc.php.

Teng, J., Cheon, M., & Grover, V. (1995). Decisions to outsource IS functions: Testing a strategy-theoretic discrepancy model. *Decision Sciences, 26*(1), 75–103.

Wallace, L., Keil, M., & Rai, A. (2004). How software project risk affects project performance: An investigation of the dimensions of risk and an exploratory model. *Decision Sciences, 35*(2), 289–121.

Whang, S. (1992). Contracting for software development. *Management Science, 38*(3), 307–324.

Willcocks, L., & Lacity, M. (2006). *Global sourcing of business and IT services.* United Kingdom: Palgrave.

Willcocks, L., & Lester, S. (Eds.). (1999). *Beyond the IT productivity paradox: Assessment issues.* Chichester: Wiley.

Willcocks, L., Feeny, D., & Islei, G. (Eds). (1997). *Managing IT as a strategic resource.* London: McGraw Hill.

Williamson, O. (1991). Comparative economic organization: The analysis of discrete structural alternatives. *Administrative Science Quarterly, 36*(2), 269–296.

The Impact of Cultural Differences in Offshore Outsourcing: Case Study Results from German–Indian Application Development Projects

Jessica K. Winkler, Jens Dibbern, and Armin Heinzl

1 Introduction

In the early 1990s, offshoring of software work to development centers in low wage countries pertained to large Western companies such as IBM and SAP who systematically attempted to take a hold of wage differences and resources of a global market. With the rise of the new millennium, former development countries such as India and emerging nations in Eastern Europe began to establish themselves as outsourcing vendors in the global market of IT services, drawing from a growing pool of qualified IS resources (Bode & Mertens, 2006; Hirschheim, George, & Wong, 2004). Given this global supply, offshore outsourcing of IT services has become a widely adopted part of many global organizations' sourcing strategies, especially in the labor-intensive domain of application services. Similar to domestic outsourcing, however, offshore outsourcing is associated with the typical market-based frictions. These frictions pertain to the very nature of systems development and maintenance as services that require a lot of communication and cooperation between the client (e.g., users, business managers, as well as systems analysts and architects) and the vendor (e.g., solutions architects, systems designers and programmers). It is therefore of little surprise that studies on domestic outsourcing have shown that effective relationship management that is aimed at reducing frictions is one of the key challenges and success factors of IS outsourcing (Goles, 2001; Grover, Cheon, & Teng, 1996; Kern, 1997; Lee & Kim, 1999).

Offshore outsouring, however, brings about yet another challenge to relationship management: the cultural differences between client and vendor. Existing literature on IS offshoring frequently mentions cultural differences and associated problems (Heeks, Krishna, Nicholson, & Sahay, 2001; Krishna, Sahay, & Walsham, 2004; Nicholson & Sahay, 2001; Rao, 2004; Vogel, 2005). However, the actual effect of cultural differences on offshore outsourcing success has not been analyzed in a

---

*This paper previously appeared as: Winker, J. K., Dibbern, J., & Heinzl, A. (2008). The impact of cultural differences in offshore outsourcing – Case study results from German–Indian application development projects. *Information Systems Frontiers, 10*(2), 243–258. The current version appears with permission of Springer, the publisher of ISF.

systematic way. When examining the emergent literature, it is striking that little attempt has been made to draw on existing research on outsourcing success factors (for an overview see Dibbern J., Goles, Hirschheim, & Jayatilaka, 2004) and to analyze the influence of offshore-specific factors. Existing studies have mostly discussed offshore outsourcing as a separate phenomenon, either on a conceptual basis (Carmel & Agarwal, 2001; Kliem, 2004; Krishna et al.; Rao) or by developing "best practices" based on case studies (Heeks et al.; Kaiser & Hawk, 2004; Nicholson & Sahay; Rottman & Lacity, 2004). However, when looking closer, there is considerable overlap between the arguments pertaining to IS outsourcing success in general and IS offshore outsourcing success in particular.

Accordingly, the main goal of this paper is to draw a link between general outsourcing success factors and offshore-specific factors. From the range of offshore-specific factors (Carmel & Agarwal, 2001; Gopal, Sivaramakrishnan, Krishnan, & Mukhopadhyay, 2003; Heeks et al., 2001; Kliem, 2004; Krishna et al.; Nicholson & Sahay, 2001), the focus is set on cultural differences in offshore outsourcing of application development. The following research questions will be addressed:

1. How can cultural differences in offshore outsourcing be characterized?
2. How do cultural differences affect the success of offshore application development projects?

Specifically, offshore development projects involving German customer organizations and Indian vendor organizations are considered. By focusing on offshoring projects to India, the results of this study may be compared to other, mostly U.S. and U.K. based studies that also analyzed offshore outsourcing to India (such as Heeks et al., 2001; Kaiser & Hawk, 2004; Nicholson & Sahay, 2001; Rottman & Lacity, 2004). Our study takes an exploratory approach, thereby attempting to identify relevant cultural differences in German–Indian software development projects and to analyze the influence of those differences on established determinants and measures of outsourcing success from studies on domestic outsourcing.

2 Research Framework

This work starts with an a priori development of a theoretical, heuristic framework (Eisenhardt, 1989), thereby allowing for a focused analysis of the role of cultural differences in offshore outsourcing. It will serve as a guide for gathering qualitative data, ensuring that those factors that turned out to be relevant in previous (offshore) outsourcing studies will be considered. The research framework is shown in Fig. 1.

The influence of relationship quality on offshore outsourcing success essentially reflects previous findings about success factors of outsourcing relationships. The focus of this study will be to analyze how those factors are influenced by cultural differences. It is important to note that the framework serves as a *conceptual framework* that guides our research (Eisenhardt, 1989; Kubicek, 1977); we do not intend to test specific relationships between selected variables. The framework

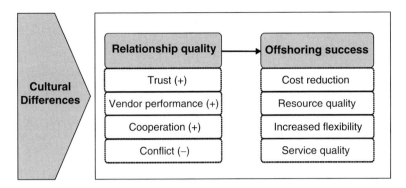

Fig. 1 Research framework

shall foster our understanding of the factors that may be influenced by cultural differences. In the spirit of Eisenhardt's (1989) process of building theory from case study research, we specified our dependent variable based on existing outsourcing literature, which is the relation between relationship quality and offshoring success. Moreover, we outline our preliminary thoughts about potential cultural differences; however, we do not a priori specify specific relationships between cultural differences and our dependent variable. Instead, the influence of cultural differences will be examined in an exploratory fashion by the means of case study analysis.

In the following, the constructs will be presented in detail. Furthermore, based on literature on cross-cultural issues and offshore outsourcing, cultural dimensions will be selected which lend themselves to explain cultural differences between clients and vendors in IS offshore outsourcing arrangements.

2.1 Success Measures in IS Outsourcing Literature

Two ways of measuring success have commonly been applied in the literature on IS outsourcing (see Dibbern J. et al., 2004, pp. 69 ff.): (1) the realization of initial expectations and (2) the level of overall satisfaction. As existing studies indicate, the reasons for offshore outsourcing center around saving costs, getting access to skilled and qualified resources, increasing flexibility, and receiving a good quality of services (Bartenschlager et al., 2005; Carmel & Agarwal, 2001). In contrast to domestic outsourcing (Teng, Cheon, & Grover, 1995), strategic considerations play a less significant role for the offshore outsourcing decision and only become relevant in later stages (Carmel & Agarwal, 2002). Therefore, this study will use four measures of offshore outsourcing success, that is, cost reduction, resource quality, increased flexibility, and service quality (Grover et al., 1996; Lee & Kim, 1999; Saunders, Gebelt, & Hu, 1997) (Fig. 1). In aggregate, these four success indicators amount for a higher level of overall satisfaction with an outsourcing arrangement (Goles, 2001; Grover et al.).

2.2 Success Factors in IS Outsourcing Literature

In various empirical studies, the quality of the relationship between the client and the vendor was found to have a key influence on outsourcing success (Goles, 2001; Grover et al., 1996; Lee & Kim, 1999). The concept of a client–vendor "relationship" is related to Social Exchange Theory (Blau, 1964) which explicitly considers social processes between two parties. This client–vendor relationship becomes highly relevant in offshore outsourcing of application services, since such tasks require an ongoing exchange of information between the parties involved (Ramarapu & Parzinger, 1997).

In our study, *relationship quality* will be defined as the degree of connectedness between a client and a vendor in an aim to achieve specified goals. It is indicated by four attributes, that is, trust, vendor performance, cooperation and conflict (Grover et al., 1996; Lee & Kim, 1999). The level of *trust*, that is, the confidence in the other's benevolence (Ring and Van de Ven, 1994) was found to be a major attribute of outsourcing relationships (Grover et al.; Heinzl A. & Sinß, 1993; Lee & Kim; Sabherwal, 1999; Willcocks & Kern, 1998). Existing findings suggest that higher levels of trust positively affect the quality of the relationship between the client and the vendor (Grover et al.; Lee & Kim). The *performance of the vendor's employees*, that is, the results which they achieve, was also found to have a positive effect on the quality of the relationship (Grover et al.). Furthermore, the *cooperation* between the client and the vendor, that is, the common pursuit to perform (Kern, 1997), was found to have a positive effect on their partnership (Grover et al.; Kern, 1997). Finally, Lee and Kim suggest that *conflict*, that is, the incompatibility of activities and goals, has a negative effect on the partnership.

2.3 Cultural Differences in IS Offshore Outsourcing

The concept of "*cultural differences*" or "*cultural distance*" is a common concept which has been applied in a variety of cross-cultural research in order to assess differences between two national cultures (Shenkar, 2001, p. 519). Cultural differences refer to the extent to which the members of two distinct groups differ on one or more *cultural dimensions*, that is, their shared values, norms, beliefs and assumptions that help them organize and structure the world (based on Roberts & Wasti, 2002, p. 545).

From the variety of cultural dimensions which have been identified and analyzed in the literature (Lytle, Brett, Barsness, Tinsley, & Janssens, 1995), five dimensions are selected which will be included in the IS offshore outsourcing research framework. The dimensions are evaluated in terms of their suitability to explain cultural variations that may affect the success factors identified in domestic outsourcing. Two dimensions – individualism and power distance – are selected based on findings from existing cross-cultural studies (Hofstede, 1980) which showed differences between Germany and India. In addition, three dimensions are selected based on cross-cultural studies (Doney, Cannon, & Mullen, 1998; Earley, 1993; Kumar & Bjorn-Andersen,

1990; Lytle et al.; Triandis, 1982) and existing IS offshoring literature (Carmel & Agarwal, 2002; Heeks et al., 2001; Hirschheim et al., 2004; Nicholson & Sahay, 2001; Rao, 2004; Vogel, 2005). In the following, the selected dimensions will be illustrated and exemplified in a comparison between India and Germany.

2.3.1 Individualism Versus Collectivism

In one of the most influential cross-cultural studies which was conducted by Hofstede in the 1970s, Hofstede (1980) identified four dimensions to describe national cultures. *Individualism*, that is, "the degree to which people in a country prefer to act as individuals rather than as members of groups," was found to be one of those characteristic dimensions (Hofstede, 1993, p. 89). In Hofstede's study (1983), Germany was found to be more individualist, whereas India was found to be more collectivist. In recent studies, the Indian culture is also described as collectivist (Sahay & Walsham, 1997; Sinha & Sinha, 1990). Differences in individualism/collectivism are likely to have some influence on the cooperation. In a study on collectivistic and individualistic work groups, Earley (1993) found that collectivist individuals show lower *performance* when working by themselves or as part of an outgroup, that is, a group they do not identify with, as compared to collectivist individuals that work in an ingroup, that is, a group they identify with and feel they belong to. In contrast, individualistic people were found to perform better when working alone (Earley, p. 335). The results suggest that individualists and collectivists perform differently in different group settings. If a group is made up of employees from different cultures, differences in individualism may result in different levels of performance in a given group setting. In another study, Doney et al. (1998) propose that the degree of individualism has an influence on the way how *trust* is built. They argue that individualists are more likely to develop trust through calculative and capability processes, that is, through a control of behavior and through an assessment of competencies and abilities, whereas collectivists rather develop trust through prediction, intentionality and transference processes, that is, through an observation of consistency, through shared values and beliefs, and through connections that are perceived to be strong and reliable (Doney et al., p. 610ff.). As Doney et al. point out, differences in the degree of individualism or collectivism may hinder the process of building trust.

2.3.2 Power Distance

On the dimension of *power distance*, that is, the extent to which unequal distribution of power is accepted within a society (Hofstede, 1993, p. 89), Germany and India showed the highest discrepancy in Hofstede's study (1983). In Germany, power distance was found to be quite low, suggesting a rather equal distribution of power between superiors and subordinates, whereas in India power distance was found to be rather high. Social relationships in India have been described as hierarchical

(Sahay & Walsham, 1997). Those findings are consistent with what has been observed in several studies on IS offshore outsourcing. Indian professionals were described as submissive and hierarchically oriented, or sometimes as "always saying yes" (Heeks et al., 2001, p. 57; Nicholson & Sahay, 2001, p. 36). The less hierarchical client organizations were not used to the Indian organizations' rigid hierarchies, which frequently led to *conflicts* (Vogel, 2005, p. 14). Furthermore, Doney et al. (1998) propose that the degree of power distance – similarly to individualism – influences the way how *trust* is developed. They argue that in high power distance cultures, trust is developed through calculative, prediction and capability processes, whereas in low power distance cultures, trust is more likely to be developed through intentionality, transference and calculative processes. Just as in the case of individualism–collectivism, differences in the degree of power distance may hinder the process of building trust.

2.3.3 Activity Versus Passivity

In offshore outsourcing arrangements between German clients and Indian vendors, some German clients have observed that Indian co-workers tend to keep to specifications, often unreflectedly, rather than actively contributing their own ideas. Furthermore, some German clients have complained about lacking communication on behalf of their Indian vendors (Vogel, 2005, p. 14). In cross-cultural literature, such behaviors are described by the degree of *activity or passivity*, that is, the "extent to which individuals in a culture see themselves as doers (active shapers of the world) or beers (passive reactors to the world)" (Lytle et al., 1995, p. 178). Depending on the degree of activity, different management styles are more or less effective. Participatory forms of management are likely to be more effective in active cultures, whereas directive methods of management are considered more effective in passive cultures (Triandis, 1982, p. 148). Managers may have certain expectations about the level of activity, and they will choose their management style accordingly. However, if they do not account for cultural differences in activity, *conflicts* may arise or the *performance* my not be as expected.

2.3.4 Communication Styles

In offshore outsourcing arrangements between German and Indian organizations, English is usually the common language in which the two parties communicate. Since English is not a native language for either of the countries, differences in language skills and language usage can cause difficulties in communication and misunderstandings (Carmel & Agarwal, 2002; Hirschheim et al., 2004; Rao, 2004). The way in which language is used frequently interplays with the way in which a culture communicates. In *abstractive cultures*, only that information which is considered significant and relevant is communicated in an explicit and precise way. In contrast, *associative cultures* also communicate many other – seemingly irrelevant

– things which are associated with an issue (Triandis, 1982, p. 150). In *high context cultures*, information which is communicated usually carries some sort of symbolic or embedded meaning. Communication in *low context cultures*, in contrast, occurs very directly without implicit or hidden meaning (Lytle et al., 1995, p. 183). Communication can also occur with greater or lesser reference to the context of an issue. *Holistic cultures* take a more systemic view on issues, that is, all aspects that may be affected by a decision are discussed in its context. In contrast, *linear cultures* look at issues in a more isolated way, that is, aspects associated with a decision are looked at separately (Lytle et al., p. 182). Differences in communication styles can lead to misunderstandings and thus hamper the *cooperation* or even cause *conflicts* in offshoring arrangements.

2.3.5 IS Designer Values

Kumar and Bjorn-Andersen (1990) found that the process of IS development is influenced by the underlying values of the IS designers. These values were found to differ between countries. IS designer values are shaped by the developer's individual background, that is, socialization and education, her or his personal context, that is, organizational and societal environment, the chosen IS development methodology, that is, prescribed development guidelines and standards, and the control and reward structure of an organization (Kumar & Bjorn-Andersen, pp. 529 ff.). These values can be technical, economical, or socio-political in nature. In the case described by Nicholson and Sahay, the Indian developers used a methodology that placed emphasis on a structured and disciplined development approach that followed international standards. The client's UK employees used different methodologies, however, the client's management pursued the goal of intendedly imposing the vendor's methodology onto their own organization. The UK client successfully adapted to the new methodology (Nicholson & Sahay, 2001). The case provides an example how differences in IS designer values can be successfully addressed. However, differences in IS designer values may also cause disruption or affect performance when expectations towards certain standards are not met.

It should be noted that the cultural dimensions "power distance" and "activity" are not completely disjunctive. Activity may be a result of power distance. That is, if power distance is high, a lower level of activity should be expected. However, in order to grasp different aspects of power distance and activity, different dimensions will be used.

3 Empirical Exploration

In order to gain empirical insights into the field of offshore application development, multiple case studies were conducted between August and October 2005. The case study method was chosen as it is especially applicable for the purpose of theory building (Eisenhardt, 1989). Personal interviews with key informants enabled us to find out about how the offshore outsourcing relationships evolved over time and to identify causal relationships (Benbasat, Goldstein, & Mead, 1987; Yin, 2003). Moreover, due to a rather limited amount of existing cross-cultural studies in the context of offshore outsourcing, a qualitative research method was deemed to be appropriate.

For the purpose of data gathering, a total of nine project managers and senior IS managers from five German companies were interviewed to describe their experiences with six specific offshore development projects with Indian vendors. Two of the six cases (BANK1a and BANK1b) were conducted at the same company. The respective company representatives were interviewed in an open one-hour interview. The interview language was German. All interviews were face-to-face, except for one interview which took place via conference call. The interviews were based on a semi-structured interview guideline that included several questions about each phase of the offshore outsourcing process (decision and implementation). The participants were also requested to describe issues and situations in which they had to handle cultural differences. In addition, the interviewees were asked to evaluate the offshore outsourcing projects with regard to the different success measures on a scale between 0 and 100%. The interview guideline is included in Appendix.

All interviews were tape-recorded and transcribed. The transcripts from the interviews were aggregated into a case protocol which comprised 54,449 words and 108 pages of text. In order to become familiar with the individual cases, the interview data was processed for each case. Based on the transcripts and some general information from the companies' websites, case write-ups and case profiles containing the qualitative data were made. A brief overview of the cases is given in Table 1

The projects were encoded and structured using the software NVivo. The coding involved the identification of cultural themes. Based on the interviewees' descriptions of situations in which they had to handle issues related to cultural differences, those text passages were assigned codes that best described the issues and cultural themes (Stake, 2006). Furthermore, text passages with statements relating to the pre-specified relationship dimensions of the theoretical framework (i.e., trust, vendor performance, cooperation, and conflict) were selected during this part of the coding procedure. Finally, management reactions to address issues and cultural differences were identified. The coding procedure to identify cultural themes and relationship dimensions is illustrated in Table 2.

Building on the individual case findings, a cross-case analysis was conducted (Miles & Huberman, 1994; Stake, 2006; Yin, 2003). Patterns were searched throughout the cases and similarities and differences were discussed based on the constructs of the research framework and the pre-selected cultural dimensions. Based on the coding of cultural themes, "grand themes" were identified, that is, themes that recurred across several cases. Thereafter, relationships between the extracted cultural themes and the pre-specified cross-cultural dimensions as well as the success factors

Table 1 Case overview

Case	LOGIS1	TELE1	INSUR1	BANK1a	BANK1b	FINANCE1
Sector	Transportation	Tele-communication	Financial services	Financial services	Financial services	Financial services
Interviewees	Project manager	Senior IS manager	Project manager	Project manager, Senior IS manager	Project manager, Senior IS manager	Two senior IS managers
Application to be developed offshore	Handling system	System landscape for B2B	E-business solution for re-insurance	Payment systems	Payment system	Sales cooperation platform
Offshore outsourcing arrangement	Onsite-offshore model	Onsite-offshore model	Offshore model	Onsite-offshore model	Offshore model	Onsite-offshore model
Number of personnel (onsite: offshore)	Onsite-offshore model (4:5)	Onsite-offshore model (40:40)	Offshore model (0:10)	Onsite-offshore model (2:7)	Offshore model (0:14)	Onsite-offshore model (8:42)

Table 2 Coding of cultural themes and relationship dimensions

Case	Quote	Theme (code)	Relationship dimension
INSUR1	"It turned out to be a real problem in the course of the project that the Indian professionals like to nod – which doesn't necessarily imply 'yes'." (Project manager)	Difficulty in saying no	N/A
LOGIS1	"They have difficulty in saying no, they have a hard time saying 'I haven't understood' or 'I want to ask further questions'. This is getting better. In the beginning, it was more difficult. They simply accepted and said 'Yes, I will do so'. At some point, this comes up and I say 'Gee, if we had only talked about this for two minutes. Then this [inappropriate software quality] could have been prevented'." (Project manager)	Difficulty in saying no	Vendor performance (*software quality*)
BANK1a	"They have a different way of addressing problems. While I prefer to work in a very analytical and structured way, Indian professionals are often pragmatic and prefer short and straight ways to reach their objectives." (Project manager)	Different development approaches (*structural versus pragmatic*)	N/A
BANK1b	"I didn't expect that we would have to define the processes and templates ourselves. That we would have to say four or five times, 'this is plain text', or 'you have to use content from this document'." (Project manager)	Different development approaches (*broad versus narrow specification*)	N/A
TELE1	"The Indian professionals also need more time [to complete a task], for example because they design their program in a less structured way [...] because they are not able to relate to the whole. [...] They are less inclined to anticipate future changes." (Project manager)	Different development approaches (*systemic versus pragmatic*)	Vendor performance (*software quality/ project delay*)

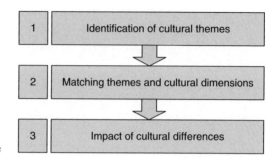

Fig. 2 Analysis procedure

and success measures were examined across the cases (Stake, 2006). The analysis procedure is outlined in Fig. 2. The findings are presented in Sect. 4.

4   Findings

4.1   Success

At the time when the interviews were conducted, the offshore development projects were perceived as successful in the majority of the cases. Initial expectations about cost improvement, increased flexibility and service quality were also fulfilled to a large extent (80–100%). This is also reflected by a rather high level of perceived overall satisfaction (80–100%). However, the projects had not been successful from the start, as challenges occurred in all projects that the managers needed to cope with. Accordingly, the perception of certain success factors varied within the cases in the course of time. As it will be shown in the following section, cultural differences between the clients and the vendors caused some recurring problems in the relationship between the client and the vendor that had to be dealt with as the projects proceeded in order to ensure a successful cooperation.

4.2   Cultural Analysis

4.2.1   Matching Themes and Cultural Dimensions

All of the companies studied observed some cultural differences during the cooperation with their offshore vendors. In the following, several cultural themes will be presented. Grand themes, that is, themes which appeared throughout a number of cases, as well as individual themes, that is, themes which were identified only in one individual case, will be pointed out. The cultural themes will be linked to the cultural dimensions identified in Sect. 2.3.

Grand theme 1: The Indian professionals have difficulty in saying no
One theme which appeared in the majority of the cases is that the Indian team members were perceived to have difficulty in saying no. When asked if they had fully understood a problem or instructions they were given, the Indian staff showed a tendency of simply saying yes, as illustrated by the following quotes.

> They have difficulty in saying no, they have a hard time saying 'I haven't understood' or 'I want to ask further questions'." (LOGIS1, project manager)
> In India, people have a certain service attitude, they have a very hard time to say no, they have a hard time delivering bad news. This can be fatal in a software development environment. (FINANCE1, senior IS manager)

Nicholson and Sahay made similar observations in the case of a British software company outsourcing to India (2001, p. 36).

Cultural interpretation: Apparently, the Indian team members had a hard time to communicate whenever they had not fully understood a given task towards superiors from both the Indian vendor and the German client company. This behavior may be interpreted as a consequence of the high level of *power distance* between the Indian team members and their superiors.

Grand theme 2: Indian and German IS professionals pursue different development approaches
In four cases (LOGIS1, TELE1, INSUR1, BANK1b), we were able to observe that the perception of what makes up software quality differed between the German and the Indian team members. While German team members placed a high emphasis on modular and structured programming, the Indian team members preferred a much more pragmatic approach towards software development.

> What I really perceive as a problem is that they have a different understanding of quality. [...] We were certainly aware of the fact that, at a price of €120,000, €130,000, we wouldn't get a product that can be enhanced or further developed. But they were not so sure about this. [...] They said, 'yes, we can easily build upon this software, it is clustered, we have classes' and whatsoever. And then we had the source code checked by our own IT people, and they said 'this is the famous spaghetti code, you cannot re-use any of this. (INSUR1, project manager)

Moreover, the Indian developers appeared to prefer to develop software based on precisely described specification, while in the German firms it was more common to develop systems based on loose specification where the system is developed through gaining a joint understanding of the solution between the business side and the IS professionals. The result was that the business side and the clients' IS groups had to invest much more time in systems analysis and specification. The desire for detailed specification has also been a result of a lack of business understanding by the offshore personnel, which had to be compensated for by the client through detailed specifications. However, there was a general tendency among Indian IS professionals to work from detailed specifications.

> On the working level – development, testing, etc. – you have to give very precise specifications. And they will do exactly as prescribed. But if you don't say 'you should also consider this or that', if you don't specify in a clear way – that's why you encounter a lot of problems in software development projects, because they are not able to relate to the whole. (TELE1, senior IS manager)

Cultural interpretation: The differences in the development approaches described above may be interpreted as differences in (a) IS designer values, (b) activity versus passivity, and (c) power distance. Apparently, the German IS employees – compared to their Indian co-workers – placed a different emphasis on certain development approaches, for example, the employment of flexible development standards which can be associated with agile methods and the importance of relating to the business context. In this context, differences in *IS designer values* become apparent. Moreover, the Indian employees had a different way of applying their skills and knowledge to the given tasks. While in the majority of the cases studied the German employees were perceived to be more *active*, the Indian team members were described as rather passive reactors to pre-specified tasks and methodologies. Furthermore, the higher level of *power distance* among Indian professionals may explain their preference for working from clearly defined instructions, such as detailed specifications.

Grand theme 3: Indian and German IS employees differ in criticism behavior

From the cases studied, another common theme concerning the cooperation with Indian vendors can be identified. In three cases (INSUR1, BANK1a, BANK1b), management found that the Indian team members, in contrast to the German staff, were much more sensitive towards criticism.

> How to criticize Indian team members is definitely an issue. When I say something, it often involves personal criticism. For example, if I reprimand my German team or if I address an issue that didn't work out the way it should have, then I am very direct in telling the team members in order to show them what went wrong. And I think that's the way you have to do it in Germany, so they will understand for sure. You cannot act like this to somebody from Asia. You can't, you must not simply blame someone from Asia and tell him it was his mistake. You have to advise him in a very polite way and explain the mistake to him, but you also have to give him a chance to keep his face. […] You have to find a way to convey criticism. (BANK1a, project manager)

Cultural interpretation: The attitude towards criticism may also be explained by different levels of *power distance*. While in Western countries with a low level of power distance voicing criticism is an integral part of the discourse between superiors and subordinates, in countries with a high level of power distance a less open way of holding discourse and resolving issues is preferred. As Sinha and Sinha (1990, p. 709) have observed, Indian professionals place high value in personal relationships and rather accommodate than confront each other.

4.2.2 Individual Themes

In INSUR1, the Indian professionals showed the tendency to repeat statements throughout hierarchical levels. A plausible explanation for this behavior is that a high degree of *power distance* prevailed in the vendor organization in INSUR1. The client, in contrast, was not used to such behavior, since at the client organization the level of power distance was rather low. In INSUR1, the Indian professionals also provided an excessive amount of documentation, which was not appreciated by the German client. This differing perception of good documentation can be associated with differences in the underlying *IS designer values*.

Table 3 Matching cultural themes and dimensions

Cases	Themes	Cultural dimensions
LOGIS1, TELE1, INSUR1, BANK1b, FINANCE1	Difficulty in saying no	Power distance
LOGIS1, TELE1, INSUR1, BANK1b	Different development approaches	IS designer values; Activity; Power distance
INSUR1, BANK1a, BANK1b	Different criticism behavior	Power distance
INSUR1	Repeat statements through hierarchy	Power distance
INSUR1	Excessive documentation	IS designer values
BANK1a	Open team meetings not appreciated	Activity; Power distance

In BANK1a, the German project manager had to realize that the open team meetings which he intended were not appreciated by the Indian team members. The differing preferences can be explained by the different levels of *activity* which prevailed in the client and in the vendor organization, that is, the client's employees were more active and the vendor's employees were perceived as more passive. Another explanation is that the Indian team members were comfortable with a higher level of *power distance* and thus preferred to get instructions from their superiors.

As shown above, the cultural themes we identified from the cases related to three of the cultural dimensions presented in Sect. 2.3: *power distance, IS designer values, and activity*. The matching of cultural themes with those cultural dimensions is summarized in Table 3. For the remaining dimensions (individualism and communication styles) we were not able to find strong evidence of cultural differences in the cases.

4.2.3 The Influence of Cultural Differences on Offshore Outsourcing Success

The German client and the Indian vendor organizations showed general differences on the cultural dimensions which were attributed to the grand and individual themes described above (power distance, IS designer values, and activity). From the case situations, it can be inferred that cultural differences can affect the factors preliminary to offshore outsourcing success, that is, relationship quality (trust, vendor performance, cooperation, and conflict). Examples from the cases will be used to illustrate this point.

- Differences in power distance and IS designer values can affect the performance in IS offshore outsourcing arrangements.

We saw performance influenced by two cultural dimensions: (1) power distance and (2) IS designer values. The tendency to say yes (cf. *power distance*) can cause misunderstandings between Indian and German team members, for example, if the Indian team members develop a software solution without having fully understood the specifications and the underlying business processes. This can necessitate adaptations that may cause a project delay.

We realized rather late that the Indian professionals do indeed have difficulty in saying no. They tend to take things and believe they will succeed, and they try really hard to achieve. But sometimes they fail. And such problems come up relatively late. (Example (power distance) from TELE1, senior IS manager)

Differences in *IS designer values* may result in the client's perception of poor software quality and inadequate development methods.

What I learned during the past years is that the Indian colleagues—or at least what I know from our vendor—the company may have a lot of know-how, they may have a CMM certificate, they may be a big company with processes in place. However, they are not always able to apply their know-how to a specific project, for that the Indian team benefits from this know-how. I would have expected them to bring in a methodology of how to test software, to have processes, documentation, and templates. But what we got was plain text documents, and the methodology they used was really chaotic in the beginning. (Example (IS designer values) from BANK1b, project manager)

- Differences in power distance and activity can affect the cooperation between the client and the vendor.

This is illustrated by a situation in the case of BANK1a, where open team meetings as intended by the project manager were not appreciated by all of the Indian team members.

Once a week, we have a team meeting with all team members – onsite coordinators, offshore project managers, and the entire team. In fact, they don't like this that much, they don't like things to be that open. With the Indian professionals, structures are very hierarchical, which means that the project manager passes on information to the team. I do not want this, I want all the members of the development team to be equally informed. (Example (power distance and activity) from BANK1a, project manager)

- Differences in power distance can lead to conflicts and decrease trust.

Two situations from the cases BANK1b and INSUR1 will be used to illustrate this point. In the case of BANK1b, the Indian team members were criticized by their German colleagues for repeatedly asking the same questions. This led to a decrease of trust, since, after this situation had occurred, the Indian team members refrained from asking questions at all.

We had two members in our team who were very experienced and also very direct. It occurred that colleagues from our vendor asked the same questions two or three times. Our people got tired of giving the same answers again and again, and they were a bit harsh in telling the Indian colleagues. The Indian team members saw this as an insult. This wouldn't have been a problem, but as a result, the Indian team members hardly asked questions, which was really a problem. (Example (criticism behavior) from BANK1b, project manager)

In the case of INSUR1, the German team members criticized their Indian colleagues for repeating statements throughout the hierarchy. This led to a conflict and a decrease of trust, as communication between the cultures stopped for a while.

At one point, a conflict occurred and even escalated – as I said, the hierarchical structure, which implied that they repeated everything their subordinate had just said – when they started doing this on the phone. Which made us tell them 'you can talk to yourselves, it is enough if one of you talks to us', because time really was too precious to keep listening to those repetitions. Then they were a bit insulted, and we had no telephone conferences for a while. (Example (power distance) from INSUR1, project manager)

4.2.4   Management Practices Addressing Cultural Differences

Despite some problems and conflicts in the cooperation between the client and the vendor, the companies in the cases studied were able to conduct successful offshore outsourcing projects, as the success ratings indicate (see Sect. 4.1). Three major management themes appeared in the cases which enabled the companies to successfully increase performance and address cultural differences in the cooperation: (a) a clear definition of roles and mechanisms, (b) strong leadership, and (c) managing culture. Those management practices were successfully implemented in the cases.

(a) *Clear definition of roles and mechanisms.* A structured management approach seems very important for the coordination of the offshore outsourcing arrangement. All of the companies in the cases studied had certain roles (e.g., project manager) and mechanisms (e.g., telephone conferences) in place which coordinated the day-to-day cooperation and accounted for incidents, that is, conflicts.

> What we have learned is that you need clear contact persons on different organizational levels and with different functions. […] This evolved over time. It wasn't clear from the beginning which roles we would have to establish. (TELE1, senior IS manager)

The establishment of management mechanisms ensures close cooperation between the client and the vendor and facilitates control. As the head of international accounts in FINANCE1 points out:

> We have been fostering a very close cooperation, and we do alike in other projects. We have regular meetings on different organizational levels, on a project and on a management level, and we have steering committees where we constantly work with our partner.

An important issue in establishing management mechanisms is to consider the offshoring arrangement as part of the entire organizational structure, especially when different organizational units or even different organizations are involved. The project manager in BANK1a emphasizes this point.

> If you have many interfaces, specifying those interfaces is a critical issue. […] You need clear interfaces and dedicated contact persons.

(b) *Strong leadership and coordination.* Based on the case findings, strong leadership seems to be a key element in managing the offshore outsourcing arrangement. The case of BANK1b provides an example in which the client tried to manage the offshore outsourcing arrangement in a more independent way. However, the project manager soon came to realize that strong management and guidance of the Indian team members was essential for the project to succeed. As the project manager explains:

> I had to lead them – contrary to my initial expectation that they would have the know-how, that I would be more of an observer to the project. […] Eventually, we decided to adopt more control and tell them what we expected. A lot more than we had thought initially.

One central aspect about leadership which was found in the cases was the provision of detailed documentation. This guided the vendor in the development activities and ensured better performance. As the senior IS manager of TELE1 points out:

At the level of work you have to provide very detailed specifications for the developers, testers, etc. And they will perform very accurately. But if you don't say 'please do this and that' and if you don't specify this clearly, then you will encounter problems in software development, because they are not able to relate to the project as a whole.

Another central aspect about leadership was to manage the Indian offshore employees as a team. The project manager in BANK1a explains this team approach.

The colleagues who are onsite, I see them as a team. For me, this is not a mere supplier-buyer relationship, but a team.

The case findings suggest that personal leadership is important in the management of offshore outsourcing arrangements. Especially in the cases LOGIS1 and BANK1a the project managers adopted key roles in managing the development teams. The project manager in LOGIS1 explains his way of leadership:

I don't expect more from my team than I would expect from myself. If I expect them to be here in the middle of the night, then I will also be here by no doubt. I think this is a matter of leadership.

Providing leadership for the team also proved to be an effective way to increase performance. The project manager in BANK1a explains how the team setup encouraged the Indian team members to make contributions:

As a matter of fact, we were able to realize that people are willing to speak out on things, for example when innovations are concerned. Or if you ask a question about improving a certain issue, someone from way behind […], someone who is usually very quiet, tries to make a contribution, really shows the courage to communicate within the team. I think this is great. You have to see, we have a very young team, and we have a good cooperation, we also get along personally. The team lead was not top-down, simply giving instructions, but has been very open.

(c) *Managing culture.* An active management of cultural issues that usually caused some problems was found to be a successful way of addressing cultural differences. This helped the companies to dampen the negative effects of cultural differences and thus improve performance, cooperation, and trust, and reduce conflicts between the client and the vendor. Cultural differences were successfully addressed in two different ways:

Adaptation to the client's culture: One way of addressing cultural differences which was pursued in one of the cases was to actively manage the team through setting clear rules for the cooperation. For example, the project manager in LOGIS1 highly emphasized that the Indian team members asked questions instead of simply saying yes. The project manager made clear what his expectations were, and the team members learned how he expected them to behave.

Once they have been here for about a month, they should know how to behave. I really emphasize on this. You have to talk to the people a lot. (LOGIS1, project manager)

Adaptation to the vendor's culture: Another way of addressing cultural differences which was pursued in two of the cases was to recognize cultural differences and to adjust management styles accordingly. For example, the project manager in BANK1a came to realize that the Indian team members preferred to be instructed by their superiors rather than participating in open team meetings. As a result, the project manager agreed on less open team meetings.

> Now I leave it to the Indian colleagues. Previously, I insisted that everyone participated in the meeting. But I have come to accept that when a colleague says that it does not make sense to involve everyone because half of the team members are not interested, then I agree that they resolve things within the team. (BANK1a, project manager)

In FINANCE1, IT management tried to address cultural differences by adopting a mediating role between the business units and the Indian team members. As the head of international accounts explains:

> I think what it all comes down to is that IT adopts more of a mediating role between what the business units say and what the Indian vendor says on the other hand. […] This implies that we pay attention to whether our partner over-commits. This would be great because we can get very cheap services. On the other hand, if I know from my experience, if our organization knows that this implies that in the end the project is at risk because our partner has over-committed himself and cannot provide the service at the suggested cost and time, […] then we will intervene and say 'wait, this is not right', and then we will mediate.

In the cases studied, getting to know and learning about the Indian co-workers' cultural traits and working behaviors proved essential to be able to successfully manage the offshore outsourcing arrangement. Most of those issues were relatively subtle and required dedicated managers to get personally involved. Learning about cultural differences involves a lot of personal interaction and communication with the Indian team members. Yet, just as cultural management, cultural learning is something which should be actively promoted by the company.

> If you have no experience in working with Indian colleagues, then you easily 'put your foot in your mouth'. That's the way it is, you simply don't have the experience. This is why intercultural training is very, very important. I think the Indian colleagues did have inter-cultural training, they take this very seriously. I think we underestimate this. We might be an international company – but not everyone gets along with Indian colleagues. There are really huge differences. That's why you simply have to know how they are and how they think. Then you are able to get along. (BANK1a, project manager)

Learning about cultural differences involves a lot of personal interaction and communication with the Indian team members. In the cases, this was described to be an ongoing process, as the head of international accounts in FINANCE1 explains:

> I think we didn't really deal with this in a conscious way. This is something we learned from talking to the people, having a glass of wine with our partner, to create an understanding of what is happening. But we didn't address this in a conscious way, no, I couldn't say so.

4.3   Refinement of the Research Framework

Now that cultural constructs and relationships between cultural differences and offshore outsourcing success factors have been identified based on the case findings, the IS offshore outsourcing framework can be refined to include cultural differences

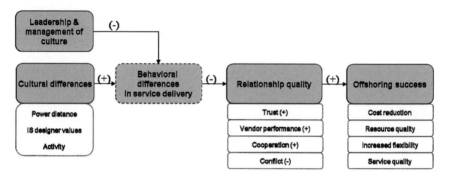

Fig. 3 Refined research framework including the effects of culture

(Fig. 3). The cultural constructs which have been found to play a role in offshore outsourcing – power distance, IS designer values, and activity – are subsumed as *persistent* 'cultural differences' between nations. In the framework, the relationships between cultural differences and offshore outsourcing success factors are portrayed according to the findings in Sect. 4.2: persistent cultural differences (e.g., in power distance) can translate into *behavioral* differences between Indian and German team members (e.g., differences in criticism behavior). In this study, persistent cultural differences between the German and the Indian culture were identified as drivers of behavioral differences. As illustrated in Table 3 in Sect. 4.2.1, recurring themes or behaviors are associated with cultural dimensions. That is, cultural differences (as classified by the cultural dimensions power distance, IS designer values, and activity) manifest themselves in terms of behavioral differences between team members from different cultures. As shown in the cases (Sect. 4.2.2), these behavioral differences in service delivery can negatively affect relationship quality (e.g., if conflicts occur), which in turn has a negative influence on offshoring success (e.g., reduced service quality or project delays). However, as shown by the case evidence (Sect. 4.2.3), those culturally induced behavioral differences may be addressed by effective management techniques. In the cases studied, a clear definition of roles and mechanisms, providing strong leadership and an active management of culture were identified as effective management reactions to cultural differences in order to ensure a successful cooperation. The case findings suggest that dedicated leadership, for example by a project manager who is personally committed to the team, helps to improve the cooperation and hence the team performance by avoiding frictions due to behavioral differences (e.g., differences in criticism behavior). Corresponding with findings of Tripathi (1990, p. 719) Indian workers prefer personal leadership, since they consider it highly important to know who they are working for. In this respect, an active management of culture proves to be essential. On the one hand, culturally induced behavioral differences may be addressed by fostering an adaptation of behaviors to the client's culture (e.g., by encouraging criticism or "saying no"). On the other hand, the client may choose to address culturally induced behavioral differences by adapting project management and leadership styles to the vendor's culture (e.g., by pursuing a more hierarchical project management). It is important to note that leadership and management techniques do not influence the cultural differences directly. That is, they do not change the culturally grown norms and values of the project members. Rather, they influence the specific culturally induced behaviors that project members show within a project.

5 Discussion

5.1 Limitations

Before delving into the discussion of the study results, it is important to point out its major limitations in order to put these findings into perspective. First of all, the results of this study have been derived from six cases, four of which took place in the financial services industry. Therefore, this study can by no means be considered representative for a larger population; it is rather an attempt to explore the impact of cultural differences in real world offshore outsourcing settings, thereby identifying relationships that subsequently can be substantiated and tested with other case studies or surveys.

Second, this study addresses offshore outsourcing arrangements between two specific countries (Germany and India). Although India holds a dominant position in the IS offshore outsourcing market, differences on the cultural dimensions which have been identified in this study may be specific for offshoring arrangements between Germany and India. Furthermore, India should be recognized as a continent with 14 languages, thus being subject to cultural variation. Still, an important finding of this study is that cultural differences do matter in IS offshoring arrangements. The way in which those differences were identified and analyzed may be transferred to other offshoring arrangements.

Finally, it must be recognized that this study analyzes offshore outsourcing arrangements solely from a client perspective. The offshore vendors may perceive cultural differences differently.

5.2 Theoretical Implications

Despite these limitations, this paper makes a dual contribution from a theoretical point of view. First of all, as shown in Sect. 4.3, the existing framework of success factors of an outsourcing relationship (Goles, 2001; Grover et al., 1994; Lee & Kim) can be extended by two offshore-specific constructs: (1) differences in the country-specific cultural profile between client and vendor reflected by differences in selected cross-cultural dimensions and (2) the resulting culturally induced behavioral differences. As the case findings demonstrate, *culture does matter* in IS offshore outsourcing arrangements (compare to Moczadlo, 2002). Cultural differences between the client and the vendor are observable on a number of dimensions, for example, power distance, IS designer values, and activity versus passivity. Such differences can result in behavioral differences between client and vendor personnel that negatively affect attributes of relationship quality, such as trust, performance, cooperation, and conflict, which are important antecedents of offshore outsourcing success. This paper's contribution is unique in a sense that (1) it outlines a method of linking behaviors (i.e., themes) to cultural dimensions and (2) reveals the relationship between cultural differences and preliminary success factors of offshore outsourcing projects.

Another important finding with regard to culture is that cultural differences in IS offshore outsourcing arrangements can be *successfully managed*, that is, certain managerial practices play a moderating role by alleviating the negative effects of cultural differences. It is important to note that such management practices do not change the cultural norms and values of either the client or vendor personnel directly, but rather have an influence on the actual behavior of the persons involved in a particular offshore outsourcing project. Persistent changes of behavior patterns that sustain beyond the end of a particular project may only be achieved over a very long time.

Thus, active management should be an integral part of a successful offshore outsourcing venture. The managerial practices which have successfully addressed cultural differences center around the provision of strong leadership and an active management of culture. Thereby, this study illustrates the interplay of managerial practices, culture and relationship factors that is necessary to move up the learning curve. Thus, this paper offers yet another theoretical contribution, as existing outsourcing literature has omitted to thoroughly analyze the interplay of management practices and relationship factors (Dibbern J. et al., 2004).

Furthermore, the case findings indicate that a lot of managerial effort, that is, an establishment of roles and mechanisms, providing personal leadership and documentation, is necessary for IS offshore outsourcing arrangements to succeed. From a theoretical point of view, this managerial effort may be seen as extra transaction costs for the client (Carmel & Tija, 2005; Dibbern J. et al., 2008), for example, costs for conflict resolution and team coordination. These costs need to be explicitly accounted for when calculating and controlling the cost savings from offshore outsourcing.

The results of this study and its limitations provide interesting opportunities for future research. The case study results show that managerial perceptions of offshore outsourcing success of particular projects are subject to changes over time. The successful implementation of management practices led to an improved perception of success by the managers. Future research may analyze project dynamics and the effects of specific management practices (e.g., control and coordination (Sabherwal & Choudhury, 2006)) in the light of cultural differences. Moreover, the study of the costs of such management practices provides another fruitful avenue for future research.

5.3 Implications for Practice

The role of management was found to be essential for conducting successful off-shore outsourcing projects. From the case findings, a number of best practices emerged of how to successfully manage IS offshore outsourcing arrangements. It should be kept in mind, however, that these findings pertain to German–Indian offshoring projects which were the focus of our case studies.

(1) *Establish a structure including roles and mechanisms for the management of the offshoring arrangement.* Good organization provides the basis for successful management of offshore outsourcing arrangements. Clear roles and dedicated contact persons, for example, project managers and coordinators, should be selected, and management mechanisms, such as steering committees and regular meetings, should be implemented for coordination and control.

(2) *Nominate a dedicated project manager who provides strong leadership within the project team.* A dedicated project manager is able to integrate team members from different countries. As a central person of contact, a dedicated project manager gets deep insights into the working processes and gets to know the team members' capabilities. If necessary, he or she can exercise direct coordination and control.

(3) *Learn about the specific cultural traits of the offshore vendor's team members.* Creating an understanding for specific cultural traits of the offshore vendor's team members is important in offshore outsourcing arrangements, since such an awareness can prevent misunderstandings in the cooperation between the different cultures. An awareness of specific cultural traits can be raised by a lot of communication with the offshore vendor's team members. Another way to actively spur cultural awareness is to provide cultural training for employees.

(4) *Recognize cultural differences and actively balance them.* Companies should aim at recognizing cultural differences early in the cooperation with an offshore vendor. If not actively managed, culturally induced behavioral differences can decrease performance, hamper cooperation, decrease trust, and lead to conflicts. Management, however, can balance those culturally induced differences by tactics of adapting to either the client's or the vendor's culture.

6 Conclusion

As in the face of internationalization the IS offshore outsourcing trend is likely to continue (Schaaf & Weber, 2005), it will become increasingly important to recognize, understand and manage cultural differences between client and vendor organizations. This study has identified relevant cultural differences, and it has presented a framework which illustrates how cultural differences influence the success of IS offshore outsourcing arrangements. As such, the framework provides an important contribution to the incorporation of the construct of culture into IS research. Furthermore, this study has identified best practices which can guide companies to successfully manage cultural differences. Future research is encouraged to further investigate cultural differences in various forms of IS offshore outsourcing arrangements. There is clearly a need to enhance the understanding of unique features in offshore outsourcing.

Appendix

Interview Guideline

I   General project information

    1. Please give a short description of your offshore development project:
       i   Type of project
       ii Project timeframe
       iii Offshore provider and country
       iv Project size (man days, % of total IS budget, number of people involved)

II. Decision to offshore

    1. What were your reasons for outsourcing application development to an offshore vendor?
    2. What were the main drawbacks associated with offshoring during the decision process?
    3. Who was involved in the decision process to offshore?
    4. Who was most influential in the decision to offshore?
    5. Have you had previous experience with
       i   Domestic outsourcing?
       ii Offshore outsourcing?

III. Implementation

    1. How did you evaluate and compare potential offshore vendors?
    2. How did you select your particular offshore vendor?
    3. Please provide some information about your offshore development contract:
    4. What arrangements did you make prior to the project launch during the transition phase?
       i   Meetings for top management to get to know each other
       ii Meetings for team members to get to know each other
       iii Meetings to make clear each other's goals
       iv On-site visits
       v   Cultural training for staff
       vi …

5. How did the transfer of knowledge take place?
6. What coordination and control mechanisms do you have in place? Please describe the role of each mechanism you use.
7. Please describe conflict situations you encountered in cooperating with your vendor. Why did those conflicts arise? How did you address those conflicts? Were you able to resolve those conflicts?
8. Please describe situations in which, during the project, you had to cope with cultural differences.

IV. Evaluation

1. Has the project met your expectations? Please indicate to what extent (0–100%) your expectations were met with regard to:
   i   Cost savings
   ii Quality of the vendor's resources
   iii Increased flexibility
   iv Quality of service delivered

2. Overall, how satisfied (0–100%) are you with:
   i   The resulting application?
   ii The relationship with your offshore vendor?
   iii The performance of the vendor's employees?
   iv The project as a whole?

3. Are you planning to have follow-up projects with this vendor?

References

Bartenschlager, J., Giza, H., Heinzl, A. H., Herrmann, N., Heym, M., Horstmann, A.-J., et al. (2005). *Marktsituation und handlungsoptionen zum near- und offshoring* (pp. 1–43). Process Alliance Institute.

Benbasat, I., Goldstein, D. K., & Mead, M. (1987). The case research strategy in studies of information systems. *MIS Quarterly, 11*(3), 369–386.

Blau, P. (1964). *Exchange and power in social life*. New York: Wiley.

Bode, A., & Mertens, P. (2006). Globalization and offshoring of software. *Informatik Spektrum, 29*(3), 171–173.

Carmel, E., & Agarwal, R. (2001). Tactical approaches for alleviating distance in global software development. *IEEE Software, 18*, 22–29.

Carmel, E., & Agarwal, R. (2002). The maturation of offshore sourcing of information technology work. *MIS Quarterly Executive, 1*(2), 65–77.

Carmel, E., & Tija, P. (2005). *Offshoring information technology – sourcing and outsourcing to a global workforce*. Cambridge: Cambridge University Press.

Dibbern, J., Goles, T., Hirschheim, R., & Jayatilaka, B. (2004). Information systems outsourcing: a survey and analysis of the literature. *The DATA BASE for Advances in Information Systems, 35*(4), 6–102.

Dibbern, J., Winkler, J., & Heinzl, A. (2008). Explaining variations in client extra costs between software projects offshored to India. *MIS Quarterly, 32*(2), 333–366.

Doney, P. M., Cannon, J. P., & Mullen, M. R. (1998). Understanding the influence of national culture on the development of trust. *Academy of Management Review, 23*(3), 601–620.

Earley, P. C. (1993). East meets West meets Mideast: Further explorations of collectivistic and individualistic work groups. *Academy of Management Journal, 36*(2), 319–348.

Eisenhardt, K. M. (1989). Building theories from case study research. *Academy of Management Review, 14*(4), 532–550.

Goles, T. (2001). *The impact of the client/vendor relationship on outsourcing success.* Houston: Department of Decision and Information Sciences, University of Houston.

Gopal, A., Sivaramakrishnan, K., Krishnan, M. S., & Mukhopadhyay, T. (2003). Contracts in offshore software development: An empirical analysis. *Management Science, 49*(12), 1671–1683.

Grover, V., Cheon, M. J., & Teng, J. T. C. (1994). A descriptive study on the outsourcing of information systems functions. *Information & Management, 27*(1), 33–44.

Grover, V., Cheon, M. J., & Teng, J. T. C. (1996). The effect of service quality and partnership on the outsourcing of information systems functions. *Journal of Management Information Systems, 12*(4), 89–116.

Heeks, R., Krishna, S., Nicholson, B., & Sahay, S. (2001). Synching or sinking: Global software outsourcing relationships. *IEEE Software, 18*, 54–60.

Heinzl, A., & Sinß, M. (1993). Kooperationen zur zwischenbetrieblichen Entwicklung von Anwendungssystemen. *Information Management, 2*, 60–67.

Hirschheim, R., George, B., & Wong, S. F. (2004). Information technology outsourcing: The move towards offshoring. *Indian Journal of Economics and Business, Fall*(Special Issue), 103–124.

Hofstede, G. (1980). *Culture's consequences: International differences in work-related values.* Beverly Hills, CA: Sage.

Hofstede, G. (1983). National culture in four dimensions. *International Studies of Management and Organization, 13*(2), 46–74.

Hofstede, G. (1993). Cultural constraints in management theories. *Academy of Management Executive, 7*(1), 81–94.

Kaiser, K. M., & Hawk, S. (2004). Evolution of offshore software development: From outsourcing to cosourcing. *MIS Quarterly Executive, 3*(2), 69–81.

Kern, T. (1997). *The gestalt of an information technology outsourcing relationship: An exploratory analysis* (pp. 37–57). Atlanta, GA: International Conference on Information Systems.

Kliem, R. (2004). Managing the risks of offshore IT development projects. *Information Systems Management, 21*(3), 22–27.

Krishna, S., Sahay, S., & Walsham, G. (2004). Managing cross-cultural issues in global software outsourcing. *Communication of the ACM, 47*(4), 62–66.

Kubicek, H. (1977). Heuristische Bezugsrahmen und heuristisch angelegte Forschungsdesigns als Elemente einer Konstruktiosstrategie empirischer Forschung. In R. Köhler (Ed.), *Empirische und handlungsorientierte Forschungskonzeptionen* (pp. 3–36). Stuttgart.

Kumar, K., & Bjorn-Andersen, N. (1990). A cross-cultural comparison of IS designer values. *Communication of the ACM, 33*(5), 528–538.

Lee, J.-N., & Kim, Y.-G. (1999). Effect of partnership quality on IS outsourcing success: Conceptual framework and empirical validation. *Journal of Management Information Systems, 15*(4), 29–61.

Lytle, A. L., Brett, J. M., Barsness, Z. I., Tinsley, C. H., & Janssens, M. (1995). A paradigm for confirmatory cross-cultural research in organizational behavior. In B. M. Staw & L. L. Cummings (Eds.), *Research in organizational behavior* (Vol. 17, pp 167–214). Greenwich, CT: JAI Press.

Miles, M. B., & Huberman, A. M. (1994). *Qualitative data analysis: An expanded sourcebook.* Thousand Oaks, CA: Sage.

Moczadlo, R. (2002). Chancen und Risiken des Offshore-Development, pp. 1–16.

Nicholson, B., & Sahay, S. (2001). Some political and cultural issues in the globalisation of software development: Case experience from Britain and India, *Information and Organization, 11*, 25–43.

Ramarapu, N., & Parzinger, M. J. (1997). Issues in Foreign outsourcing. *Information Systems Management, 14*(2), 27–31.

Rao, M. T. (2004). Key issues for global IT sourcing: Country and individual factors. *Information Systems Management, 21*(3), 16–21.

Ring, P. S., & Van de Ven, A. H. v.d. (1994). Developmental processes of cooperative interorganizational relationships. *Academy of Management Review, 19*(1), 90–118.

Roberts, C., & Wasti, S. A. (2002). Organizational individualism and collectivism: Theoretical development and an empirical test of a measure. *Journal of Management, 28*(4), 544–566.

Rottman, J. W., & Lacity, M. C. (2004). Twenty practices for offshore sourcing. *MIS Quarterly Executive, 3*(3), 117–130.

Sabherwal, R. (1999). The role of trust in outsourced IS development projects. *Communications of the ACM, 42*(2), 80–86.

Sabherwal, R., & Choudhury, V. (2006). Governance of remotely outsourced software development: A comparison of client and vendor perspectives. In R. Hirschheim, A. Heinzl, & J. Dibbern, et al. (Eds.), *Information systems outsourcing: Enduring themes, new perspectives, and global challenges* (pp. 187–222). Berlin: Springer.

Sahay, S., & Walsham, G. (1997). Social structure and managerial agency in India, *Organization Studies, 18*(3), 415–444.

Saunders, C., Gebelt, M., & Hu, Q. (1997). Achieving success in information systems outsourcing. *California Management Review, 39*(2), 63–79.

Schaaf, J., & Weber, M. (2005). Offshoring report 2005 ready for take-off. *Deutsche Bank Research Economics, 52*, 1–23.

Shenkar, O. (2001). Cultural distance revisited: towards a more rigorous conceptualization and measurement of cultural differences. *Journal of International Business Studies, 32*(3), 519–535.

Sinha, J. B. P., & Sinha, D. (1990). Role of social values in Indian organizations. *International Journal of Psychology, 25*, 705–714.

Stake, R. E. (2006). *Multiple case study analysis*. New York: Guilford Press.

Teng, J. T. C., Cheon, M. J., & Grover, V. (1995). Decisions to outsource information systems functions: Testing a strategy-theoretic discrepancy model. *Decision Sciences, 26*(1), 75–103.

Triandis, H. C. (1982). Dimensions of cultural variations as parameters of organizational theories. *International Studies of Management and Organization, 12*(4), 139–169.

Tripathi, R. C. (1990). Interplay of values in the functioning of Indian organizations. *International Journal of Psychology, 25*, 715–734.

Vogel, M. (2005). Einmal Indien und zurück. *CIO*.

Willcocks, L. P., & Kern, T. (1998). IT outsourcing as strategic partnering: The case of the UK. *European Journal of Information Systems, 7*(1), 29.

Yin, R. K. (2003). *Case study research – Design and method* (3rd edn.). Thousand Oaks: Sage.

Determinants of Service Quality in Offshore Software Development Outsourcing

Anandasivam Gopal and Balaji R. Koka

1 Introduction

Offshore outsourcing has assumed great importance as a strategic option for many firms over the past few years. Primarily driven by cost considerations, increasing number of software projects have been outsourced by organizations in the US and Europe to firms in countries such as India and China. In recent times, managers of both outsourcing and vendor firms have realized that cost considerations, generally assumed to be the primary reason for offshore outsourcing, need to be balanced with the need to maintain quality. For instance, mixed experiences with respect to quality forced firms like Valicert and Dell to significantly rethink their offshoring strategies (Thurm, 2004). In addition, as the offshore industry in locations such as India mature, vendor firms have to look beyond being the low-cost option and understand the dynamics in providing high-quality services to their clients as a source of competitive advantage (Carmel & Agarwal, 2002).

There is currently little work that has explicitly studied the antecedents of quality in offshore software projects. Much of the previous research in studying software quality has focused on projects that were conducted in-house. The presence of relative homogeneity amongst platforms and applications in in-house development made it easier to model the quality of software produced as the result of a "production process" (Russell & Chatterjee, 2003). Offshore outsourcing differs from these contexts in some significant ways. First, outsourcing involves operating across organizational boundaries significantly reduce the ability of client managers to directly control the software development process. Second, offshoring such work compounds the difficulty inherent in such issues because of factors such as geographical distance, culture and language. Both these reasons lower the ability of client managers to control quality compared to in-house IT services, where the risks of mismatch between the incentives of the IT group and user community are reduced due to the presence of administrative hierarchy within the firm. In the offshoring context, however, incentive alignment and monitoring may play a larger role in affecting quality. In such contexts, in addition to traditional drivers of quality, we need to examine the role of factors such as the contract type governing the relationship and client MIS experience in determining the quality of the project. In this

R. Hirschheim et al. (eds), *Information Systems Outsourcing,*
© Springer-Verlag Berlin Heidelberg 2009

study, we address these issues by developing and testing hypotheses on the drivers of quality in the offshore outsourcing context.

We empirically test our hypotheses by analyzing data collected on 100 offshore projects completed by a leading Indian offshore developer. We formulate models for project quality and estimate them using regression analysis. There are three primary contributions of our analysis. *First*, there is no published research, to the best of our knowledge, on quality in the offshore software development context. We contribute to this literature by providing an analysis of vendor-provided quality in this domain. *Second*, we explicitly study the moderating influence of the contract type on quality. There is again little empirical research in the outsourcing or off-shoring literature that has addressed the role of the contract on determining quality; our work is the first to provide some evidence of this relationship. *Third*, we add to the small but growing literature on offshore software development, specifically the Indian offshore industry. In Sect. 2, we review the background literature in order to motivate the research hypotheses.

2 Theory and Research Hypotheses

Offshoring is commonly defined as the relocation or provision of business proc-esses and services to lower cost locations in other countries (Erber & Sayed-Ahmed, 2005). Although the term has been broadly accepted as encompassing several distinct types of services ranging from programming and software mainte-nance to high-end services such as financial analysis and pathological research (Davis, Ein-Dor, King, & Torkzadeh, 2006), in our study we focus on the offshore outsourcing of *software development projects*. The basis for offshoring software development activities is still predicated on the cost differential argument, i.e., Indian programmers cost one-sixth as much as American programmers for equiva-lent skills (Shah, 2004), although these cost advantages are expected to disappear over time. Scholars studying offshoring have indicated that in the face of declining cost advantages, Indian offshore vendors have to change focus from cost to the quality and effectiveness of the software services provided (Carmel & Agarwal, 2002; Davis et al.). Indeed, for the offshore vendor, developing the ability to pro-vide higher quality software services and thus move up the value chain is a strategic necessity (Ethiraj, Kale, Krishnan, & Singh, 2005). Understanding the drivers of service quality is thus important in the evolving strategy for both offshore vendors and clients.

There has been little empirical research examining the antecedents of quality in the IS literature, particularly in the offshoring outsourcing context. Much of the published research in offshoring has largely been theoretical analyses and reviews of the phenomenon. For instance, Davis et al.'s review of current thinking in off-shoring and Carmel and Agarwal's (2002) exposition on potential changes in the offshoring market provide insightful albeit theoretical analyses of the dynamics underlying this phenomenon. Other researchers have provided process/project management guidelines on managing offshoring activities based on case studies (Cullen, Seldon, & Willcocks, 2005; Rottman & Lacity, 2004). Anecdotal evidence about offshoring abounds in the practitioner press (for instance, Hayes 2003; Thurm 2004) while prescriptive models of offshoring have been offered by Aron and Singh (2005) and Gottfredson, Puryear, and Phillips (2005). Of the few studies that have examined offshoring empirically, Ethiraj et al. focused on the impact of repeated ties between the vendor and client on project performance using primary data from an Indian vendor. Gopal A., Sivaramakrishnan, Krishnan, and Mukhopadhyay (2003) and Banerjee and Dulfo (2000) studied the role of contracts in offshore projects while Krishna, Sahay, and Walsham (2004) studied the impact of cross-cultural issues in managing outsourcing projects. To the best of our knowledge, there has thus been little published quantitative, empirical work on offshore relationships that tests the analytical models that have been proposed by scholars in the field thus far. Given that vendor provided service quality plays a central role in the offshoring strategies of vendors and clients alike, we address this gap by examining the drivers of quality in this study.

A second motivation for this study is related to the issues surrounding the nature of the offshoring phenomenon itself. Part of the reason for the paucity of empirical research, apart from data availability and confidentiality considerations, is that there is considerable debate on how transformational and different offshoring is. Current thinking in the literature is in two minds about whether the offshore domain is significantly different in its operational details or merely an extension of an outsourcing model (Bhagwati, Panagariya, & Srinivasan, 2004; Davis et al., 2006). While we do not address this debate directly, we hope to shed some light on it by drawing on arguments from current research on quality drivers in software development and testing them on data drawn from offshore projects. Empirical evidence from this study would thus provide a base to address the question of whether, and how, offshore outsourcing is different from other outsourcing contexts or indeed any global sourcing activities.

2.1   Vendor Provided Quality in Offshore Outsourcing

Prior research on the drivers of quality has largely been driven by two distinct yet complementary themes. First, the focus has largely been on understanding quality in an in-house development context. More specifically, this literature has examined the linkages between quality and the costs of development in-house. Second, such research has adopted a production-based approach to software development that conceived of quality in terms of the number of defects per lines of code (Harter, Krishnan, & Slaughter, 2000; Westland, 2004) in order to identify variables that affect the final defect rates in the software developed. Concurrent research focusing on the development of *software products*, rather than turnkey software projects, has also used this production-based approach in understanding the drivers of quality (Krishnan, Kriebel, Kekre, & Mukhopadhyay, 2000; Westland, 2004).

However, characterizing quality in software development activities primarily through defect rates provides for an inadequate and often misleading assessment of quality for three main reasons. *First*, a large part of such activities are now being carried out through outsourcing arrangements (Carmel & Agarwal, 2002). Defect rates may not be a useful measure since projects are executed by vendors on a multitude of platforms, programming languages and applications. Moreover, many projects involve not only software development but also software services along with other value-added activities that are not always captured in code.

Second, testing software for defects occurs typically at the tail end of the development process. Typical software development processes follow a "waterfall" model, starting with requirement gathering and analysis, high level design, low level design, followed by coding and testing (Arora & Asundi, 1999). As several researchers have noted, poor quality often results due to inadequate attention to critical parameters at the *requirements analysis and design* stage (Krishnan et al., 2000; Ravichandran & Rai, 2000). A defect count from the testing phase based on test plans arising from faulty design or inadequate requirements will not reflect the true quality of the developed software or service rendered to the client.

Third, while defect-free coding is important, it is apparent in the outsourcing context that broader measures of quality such as ease of use, functionality, reliability, robustness and cost of its operations (Rao, 1998) are also critical. For instance, the *cost of operating* software in the context of this project depends on intrinsic design parameters of the software as well as its integration with other systems, the quality of these application interfaces and the total cost of ownership of the systems. *Reliability* ensures that the software performs its functions consistently in different system environments by across different user loads and stresses. Here again, adequately incorporating user specifications and requirements earlier in the design leads to more reliable systems. Simpler production-based metrics such as defect rates may not accurately reflect the presence of other such desirable quality parameters in offshore projects. It is also true that aspects of quality such as reliability, robustness and cost of operations are observable only in the final operating environment ex post (Lacity & Hirschheim, 1993) and may not even be observed or measured during acceptance testing (Gopalakrishnan, Kochikar, & Yegneshwar, 1996) by the client.

The above three reasons encourage a shift from the technical aspects of software development to the organizational and behavioral issues that affect quality. As Ravichandran and Rai (2000) note, conceptualizing the software development process as a *technical* process with emphasis on precision and technical accuracy has only had a marginal effect on overall quality. The software development process is similar to new product development since both activities involve unique and often unstructured work (Ravichandran & Rai, 2000), reflecting the fact that there is no one best way to design, develop and manage projects and that variation at each of these stages affect the quality of the project. In addition, quality in such environments depends more on how the project members work together, how they draw on resources within the organization, and the nature of their incentive and control

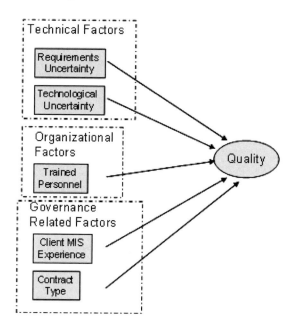

Fig. 1 Theoretical framework

systems (Sawyer, 2001) rather than just on the technical skills and abilities at the individual and group level.

An implication of this line of reasoning is that in the offshore context, vendors have greater discretion with respect to the choices they make with respect to structuring, staffing and planning their projects and consequently, the extent of quality they provide in the project. Many of these decisions are made on a day-to-day basis, without the client necessarily being privy to many of them. In addition, this discussion indicates that we need a broader framework that includes not just technical factors but also *organizational* and *governance* related factors in order to develop a more complete understanding of the antecedents of project quality. We propose such a model of offshore development quality, shown in Fig. 1 as a diagram, and discuss the key antecedents of quality next.

2.2   Drivers of Quality: Technical Drivers of Project Quality

As we noted above, much of the work in in-house software development has focused on the technical nature of the project in determining quality. Typically, such research has identified requirements uncertainty and technological uncertainty of the project as key factors influencing quality in the software development process (Harter et al., 2000; Pressman, 2005). While these variables reflect the arguments underlying quality in the in-house development environment, we draw on them to develop a more comprehensive model of quality drivers in the offshore context.

2.2.1 Requirements Uncertainty

Requirements uncertainty has been hypothesized to be an important source of poor quality in software development (Barki, Rivard, & Talbot, 1993; Harter et al., 2000; Nidumolu, 1995) and emerges from an inability to apply a standardized process to converting requirements into functional specifications (Pressman, 2005). Unstable requirements typically result in sub-optimal design during the initial phases of the project. As requirements keep changing throughout the life cycle of the project, subsequent changes to the design and the need for rework creates disruptions in the organization's processes for managing requirements and produces significant scope for defects (Pressman, 2005). A second source of uncertainty arises when there is user diversity in requirements that requires the vendor firm to reconcile the differences (Nidumolu, 1995). Such differences are likely to lead to poor perceived quality because most users are unlikely to be satisfied with the final product given that it is a compromise between conflicting requirements. Finally, requirements uncertainty allows for ambiguous interpretations increasing again the likelihood that the final solution falls short of client expectations. While most studies have hypothesized the effects of requirements uncertainty in in-house projects, its effects are exacerbated in the offshore domain because of geographical and organizational boundaries between the client and vendor. Therefore, we propose

Hypothesis 1: Requirements Uncertainty is associated with lower vendor-provided quality.

2.2.2 Technological Uncertainty

A significant challenge in managing offshore development is the need to replicate, for purposes of development, to a reasonable extent the technology platforms existing in the client organization (Gopalakrishnan et al., 1996). Vendors face technological uncertainty when there is unpredictability in aspects of software development technologies and techniques such as hardware platform; software platform; programming languages; database technologies; coding and testing techniques. Unpredictability arises due to the rise in unexpected or novel problems that occur in the use of these technologies (Nidumolu, 1995). As technology platforms increase in complexity, there is significant risk in the ability of the vendor to effectively replicate that platform and use the replicated environment in development activities. Moreover, newer and more sophisticated systems increase the need for training and experienced personnel while concurrently increasing the risk of failure (Pressman, 2005).

Hypothesis 2: Technological uncertainty is associated with lower vendor-provided quality.

2.3 Drivers of Quality: Organizational Factors

Several researchers (Gosain, Gopal A., Darcy, & Lichtenstein, 2003; Nidumolu, 1995; Ravichandran & Rai, 2000) have highlighted the role of organizational processes and factors in affecting quality. Given the single vendor context in our study and our focus in examining project-level variations, we argue that such factors are manifested in the staffing of these projects. Staffing is a key organizational decision variable in software development as these activities are entirely dependent on the presence of trained and competent personnel unlike other service and manufacturing contexts (Pressman, 2005).

2.3.1 Presence of Trained Personnel

Accordingly, the availability of trained personnel for each project is a key determinant of project quality. This is a critical factor particularly in the off-shoring environment because software development is personnel-intensive and one of the reasons cited for the rise of the offshore industry in India has been the apparent ready availability of engineers. However, one of the more significant risks faced by offshore vendors is the increasing difficult in attracting and retaining trained personnel. For instance, NASSCOM, the premier software trade association in India, reports that by 2009 demand for technically qualified personnel will exceed supply by at least half a million programmers (Doraisamy, 2006). Trained programmers use better design techniques, are more aware of the link between requirements and systems parameters and are able to write better code (Pressman, 2005). Experienced personnel are also more capable in testing and defect prevention activities, thereby leading to better quality and more productive use of resources (Krishnan et al., 2000). Prior research has emphasized the importance of personnel capabilities in providing high-quality software. This effect should be particularly true in the offshore market since there is clearly a supply-demand imbalance with respect to trained professionals (Shah, 2004). In offshoring projects, the availability (or lack thereof) of trained personnel is further reflected in the lack of continuity in the staffing of projects. Frequent staffing changes further affect quality because different personnel, at different points in times, make changes to the project that may have little relation to earlier choices and specifications. More importantly, it leads to poor design and development of the project, resulting in poor quality. Thus, the lack of trained personnel affects quality of offshore projects in two ways: first, by the staffing of inexperienced and untrained personnel and second, by frequently shifting personnel between projects as managers seek to manage multiple projects with insufficient numbers of trained personnel. Therefore, we propose

Hypothesis 3: Lack of trained personnel for the project is associated with lower vendor-provided quality.

2.4 Drivers of Quality: Governance Related Factors

2.4.1 Client MIS Experience

Governance of in-house software development projects has largely been a function of administrative hierarchy, given that the IS department and the users belong to same organization. Issues such as opportunism and moral hazard are controlled by administrative fiat and oversight. However, in offshore outsourcing, monitoring becomes important if the client is to reduce opportunism, particularly given that there is lesser face-to-face interaction between client and the vendor due to geographical distance (Lacity & Hirschheim, 1993). Typically, offshoring introduces several points of potential conflict between the vendor and client. Davis et al. (2006) identify monitoring of the vendor progress, managing accuracy and completion risks associated with offshoring, and managing the knowledge required for systems development and delivery as three key responsibilities that the client has in offshoring. Prior research has also indicated that clients in outsourcing relationships that are able to efficiently use control portfolios in motivating vendor teams are able to obtain successful projects (Kirsch, Sambamurthy, Ko, & Purvis, 2002). In effect, clients that are able to use formal and informal modes of control over the vendor team are able to incentivize the vendor team appropriately and thus lead to favorable project outcomes. Therefore, the onus is on the client to establish and manage processes and controls by which timely feedback on various project-related decisions is provided to the vendor team.

More experienced clients are able to manage the risks inherent in offshore development better as they are able to establish the appropriate control mechanisms, incentivize the vendor team appropriately and manage the development risks that commonly emerge. The presence of an experienced and capable MIS department at the client side, which typically plays the role of liaison between the client and the vendor (Gopal A., Mukhopadhyay, & Krishnan, 2002), is thus a critical and strategic resource in managing offshoring (Mata, Fuerst, & Barney, 1995). Technical and managerial expertise even on the client side, constitute important resources in ensuring that quality and productivity metrics are met within the project. An experienced MIS department is instrumental in establishing the right communication mechanisms, clearing up open issues that might arise during software development and providing timely feedback on interim project deliverables (Gopal A. et al.). In addition, an experienced MIS department is also able to operate as a check on agent shirking and opportunism by virtue of its own expertise (Banerjee & Duflo, 2000). Finally, experienced MIS departments are repositories of vast amounts of tacit knowledge about project and vendor management within organizations (Mata et al.). This tacit knowledge is particularly useful in managing software development projects. The offshore context enhances the uncertainty and thus makes the role of the client MIS department even more critical. Therefore, we propose

Hypothesis 4: An experienced client MIS department is associated with higher vendor-provided quality.

2.4.2 Contract Type

A final governance mechanism that could affect quality in offshore software development is the type of contract governing the project. The role of offshore outsourcing contracts has received some attention in the literature as contract types have been shown to affect profitability (Gopal A. et al., 2003) and over-runs (Banerjee & Duflo, 2000) in offshore projects. However, no extant research has addressed the role of contract in influencing the quality of the software delivered. There are primarily two kinds of contracts used in the offshore domain – fixed price (FP) and time and materials (T&M). FP contracts specify a fixed amount to be paid to the vendor in exchange for completion of a specified task and are thus riskier for the vendor who has to bear the risk of all cost and schedule over-runs in the project (Banerjee & Duflo, 2000). It thus incentivizes the vendor to be more efficient and effective in its software development processes, since the premium is on managing costs incurred in the project (Bajari & Tadelis, 2001). T&M contracts, on the other hand, are cost plus contracts where the services of the vendor are bought at a specified billing rate. They protect the vendor from most of the risk while transferring the cost of monitoring and control to the client. The final price (revenue) for the project is broadly decided in an FP contract ex ante, while the effective billing rate is agreed upon in T&M contracts. T&M contracts thus provide weaker incentives for managing process efficiency and effectiveness because all costs are passed on to the client. Relative to FP contracts, the vendor's incentives to effectively manage the development process are thus weaker.

In a complete contracting environment where it is possible to clearly specify the quality requirements, it would be reasonable to expect no significant difference in quality between FP and T&M contracts. The vendor would follow the same processes and activities to ensure similar quality in different projects. However, in incomplete contracting environments, all future contingencies cannot be predicted and hence, it is considerably hard to explicitly capture, ex ante, specific quality requirements in the contract (Lacity & Hirschheim, 1993). Therefore, the impact of incentives and the risks of opportunism that exist in incomplete contracting environments become key factors to consider. Specifically, these factors will influence the manner in which the project is executed within the vendor organization. Since the incentive structure and the risk of opportunism systematically vary between FP and T&M contracts, we argue that contract types systematically affect the quality in a project by affecting the way vendor project managers *manage* the software development process on a day-to-day basis.

Typically, project managers at any point of time are responsible for a set of projects for different clients with different requirements, schedules and project goals (Lacity & Hirscheim, 1993). Successful completion of these projects depends upon how the project managers manage logistics, develop and implement schedules, staff them with appropriate skilled personnel and appropriately monitor progress (Pressman, 2005). In an ideal situation, one would expect all projects to receive the same managerial and technical resources and follow similar processes, resulting in similar levels of quality. However, managers operate in an environment that has many constraints resulting from aggressive deadlines, scarce resources and complex projects, which force them to make resource allocation choices between projects. We argue that such choices are, to an extent, driven by the different incentive structure of FP and T&M contracts.

Consider the example of trained personnel on the project, which is a critical factor affecting output quality (Krishnan et al., 2000). In a resource-scarce environment, project managers have to decide how to allocate these key resources between the different projects. Given the risk exposure in FP contracts to the vendor, the vendor manager is liable to staff FP projects first with the most appropriately skilled personnel, as suggested by anecdotal evidence (Arora & Asundi, 1999), which leads to higher quality. Moreover, in many cases, project managers move personnel between projects depending on the urgency and requirements of different projects. Such moves affect the effectiveness of the team as a whole as the newcomer needs to come up to speed on the new project. More importantly, the newcomers have little understanding of the overall project requirements and design specifications, resulting in a greater possibility of errors (Nidumolu, 1995). Thus, projects that face greater turnover are likely to end up with lower quality. Given the cap on revenues in FP projects, it is in the interest of the project managers to ensure that these projects are completed on schedule and in time. They are, therefore, unlikely to make frequent changes in the staffing of such projects. For T&M projects, on the other hand, project managers can afford to move personnel away from the project to other projects unless clearly specified in the contract. The aggregate effect of these factors leads to stronger incentives for staffing, process management and risk management in FP than in T&M contracts (Bajari & Tadelis, 2001; Banerjee & Duflo, 2000).

In addition, project quality depends on ensuring that requirement analysis and design are conducted well at the beginning of the project itself, as discussed earlier. Here again, we argue that project managers are likely to focus more on FP contracts to ensure that earlier stages of the project are carried out thoroughly. Any errors at the requirements and design stages could result in significant rework, leading to cost and schedule over-runs, with disastrous consequences in FP contracts. In T&M contracts, these project dynamics are relatively less likely to happen since the cost of not fixing possible requirements at the outset is borne by the client. There is, in fact, a perverse incentive for project managers to not anticipate and fix the problems at the early stages because of the potential for higher revenues through quality problems and rework at the latter stages of the project (Bajari & Tadelis, 2001). But, rework and the emergence of quality-related problems later in the project lead to lower overall quality (Harter et al., 2000).

Finally, the level of monitoring by the client exerted in a project could also have a positive impact on quality. In FP contracts, there is a marginally lesser need for the clients to monitor and control the project. The stronger incentives inherent in FP contracts compensate for the reduced need for monitoring. However, in T&M contracts, the burden of monitoring shifts to the client (Banerjee & Duflo, 2000). The question, therefore, is the extent to which clients are able to and are *effective* in monitoring the vendor. Evidence suggests that the effectiveness of monitoring depends on the transparency of the software development process, especially given the organizational and geographical boundaries inherent in the offshoring domain (Banerjee & Duflo, 2000; Gosain et al., 2003). Thus, adherence to schedules, costs and budgets are easier to monitor since they are observable and measurable (Kirsch et al., 2002). However, factors such as reliability, robustness and cost of operations are observable only in the final operating environment ex post (Lacity & Hirschheim, 1993) and may not even be observed or measured during acceptance testing (Gopalakrishnan et al., 1996). Therefore, in most offshore projects, the relationship between monitoring and quality is uncertain, given the difficulty of effectively monitoring the vendor. In T&M contracts, this indicates that there will be considerable variance in the level and effectiveness of monitoring performed by the client (Lacity & Hirschheim, 1993). It is highly probable that monitoring may not occur systematically across all T&M projects. However, in FP contracts, the need to monitor is reduced marginally due to the presence of strong vendor incentives to be efficient (Bajari & Tadelis, 2001).

In sum, we argue that on the margin, FP projects are more likely to receive more resources from top management resulting in better monitoring and control; are more likely to be staffed consistently with higher skilled personnel and are more likely to be better managed in terms of requirements analysis and design. In addition, although client monitoring on T&M projects may be high on some projects, these may not be able to systematically mitigate the adverse effects of weaker incentives on internal efficiencies. Thus:

Hypothesis 5: FP contracts will be associated with higher vendor-provided quality than T&M contracts, all else being equal.

Since the contract type chosen for the project drives the risk-sharing and incentives in the project between the vendor and client, we argue that the contract type also moderates the effect of the quality drivers discussed earlier on perceived quality. In other words, the marginal effects of quality drivers on quality differ between FP and T&M contracts. As we noted earlier, in software development projects, requirements uncertainty leads to significant rework and redesign that, in conditions where the development environment is stressed, leads to inadequate quality. It would seem that the nature of the FP contract ensures that requirements uncertainty is reduced because of the need to specify parameters at the beginning of the project. Prior research shows that FP contracts are generally chosen when the requirements are relatively well-understood and the ambiguity in the project is lower (Bajari & Tadelis, 2001). Therefore it is likely that FP contracts should lead to higher quality since the up-front work in determining a stable set of requirements has been completed. Since T&M projects are preferred for development projects that are poorly specified because of high uncertainty arising out of user diversity in requirements as well as poorly understood technologies, opportunities for poorer quality increases. Further, the ability to change requirements is higher in T&M contracts creating more opportunities to lower quality.

Similar arguments can be made for technological uncertainty and the lack of trained personnel and how contract type moderates their effect on quality. Since vendors poorly understand new technologies, it is difficult for them to ex ante anticipate the technological problems. The fixed nature of the contract forces them to bear the risks of developing poorly understood technologies. Vendors absorb that risk by acting opportunistically and lowering quality. Alternatively, contract safe-guards put in place by the client could reduce avenues for such opportunism such that vendors respond to such situations by moving their most talented and experi-enced personnel to these FP projects, thereby enabling higher quality. For T&M contracts on the other hand, vendors could address issues arising out of technological uncertainty by enabling their personnel to learn on the job. Since there are relatively less constraints on costs in such contracts, vendors are in effect paid by the buyers to learn the new technologies. Anecdotal evidence from the offshore market indi-cates that vendors use T&M projects to train newer employees at highly subsidized costs. On the one hand, the ability to learn at the client's cost may ensure that quality is not affected in technologically uncertain T&M projects. On the other hand, the fact that such projects are likely to use untrained and inexperienced personnel who are learning on the job, may actually result in lower quality. Here again, while these arguments make clear that contract type moderates the effect of technological uncertainty and trained personnel on quality, the direction of the effect depends on the contract specifics that determine the nature of risks, incentives and opportunism. Thus, we propose the following:

Hypothesis 6: The contract type moderates the effect of quality drivers on vendor-provided quality.

3   Research Methodology and Data Collection

3.1   Research Site

We collected data for this study on projects completed by a leading offshore soft-ware developer in Bangalore, India. The firm employed around 5,000 people at the time of data collection. Its primary area of expertise is software development and maintenance of business systems, which consists of one of the five primary areas of offshoring as described by Davis et al. (2006). Focusing on a single vendor not only enabled us to control for vendor capabilities that could affect quality, it helped us control for geographical and cultural variations between projects which has been hypothesized to affect the dynamics between vendor and clients in the offshoring context. The use of micro-level firm-specific data is useful in helping us tease out effects of project characteristics on project performance that might not be clear in larger industry-wide samples and is also consistent with other studies (Ethiraj et al., 2005; Kalnins & Mayer, 2004) in the field. A random sample of 120 projects from the projects completed by the firm over a 2-year period was identified for data col-lection, i.e., the data collected was cross-sectional. We sought two sources of data for each project. The *project manager* in charge of development provided informa-tion pertaining to the technical variables from the project while the *business unit manager* was the source for market and client-related information on the project.

From the 120 projects identified, we could collect data on 100 projects because of the unavailability of project personnel or business unit managers due to travel and attrition. Of the final sample of 100 projects, 60 were FP contracts and 40 were T&M contracts. The ratio of FP to T&M projects in our sample was obtained through the random project selection process and is similar to other published work on contracts in the offshore area (Banerjee & Duflo, 2000; Ethiraj et al., 2005). Summary statistics for the two sub-samples are shown in Table 1, with the correlation matrix shown in Table 2.

Primary data was collected through two questionnaires that were developed after discussions with the senior management at the research site. The questionnaires were pre-tested at the research site by members of the quality assurance group before they were administered to project and business unit managers. One questionnaire included project-level information and was completed by the project manager. The second questionnaire included the quality measures and information about the business environment around the project, completed by the business unit manager. Finally, we collected objective project-level data such as effort from company databases.

The measurement of *service quality* is an important component of our research methodology and we discuss this in some detail. We define quality as the extent to which the software services (*software* as well as *services* around the software)

Table 1 Summary statistics

Variable	Mean	Std. Dev.	Minimum	Maximum
For FP Contracts, N = 60				
Effort	1,149.90	1,605.33	31.00	8,100.00
Req_Unc	2.25	1.17	1.00	5.00
Tech_Unc	2.03	0.78	1.00	4.20
Trained Pers	2.38	0.89	1.00	4.67
MIS experience	2.93	0.84	1.00	5.00
Project type	1.33	0.57	0.00	2.00
Prior client	10.43	15.79	0.00	75.00
Duration	349.03	274.42	60.00	824.00
Team size	10.75	10.66	3.00	50.00
Quality	3.93	0.41	3.00	5.00
For T&M contracts, N = 40				
Effort	754.48	784.54	31.00	3,100.00
Req_Unc	2.13	0.79	1.00	4.00
Tech_Unc	2.00	0.70	1.00	3.60
Trained Pers	2.84	1.02	1.33	5.00
MIS experience	2.79	0.85	1.00	5.00
Project type	1.10	0.67	0.00	2.00
Prior client	4.20	6.01	0.00	30.00
Duration	345.55	280.51	27.00	882.00
Team size	7.18	4.64	1.00	20.00
Quality	3.62	0.49	2.60	4.60

Table 2 Correlation table, N = 100

Variables	(1)	(2)	(3)	(4)	(5)	(6)	(7)	(8)	(9)	(10)
(1) Effort	1.00									
(2) Req_Unc	−0.01	1.00								
(3) Tech_Unc	0.13	0.32*	1.00							
(4) Trained Pers	0.08	0.24*	0.38*	1.00						
(5) MIS Exp	−0.11	0.30	0.11	0.48**	1.00					
(6) Proj Type	−0.01	0.07	−0.10	0.041	0.19	1.00				
(7) Prior Client	−0.02	0.01	−0.02	−0.30*	−0.20	−0.31*	1.00			
(8) Duration	0.53*	−0.08	0.03	0.07	−0.24	−0.18	−0.05	1.00		
(9) Team size	0.35*	0.01	0.07	0.05	0.38*	0.09	−0.20*	0.30*	1.00	
(10) Quality	0.02	−0.28*	−0.61*	−0.61*	−0.38*	−0.06	0.34*	0.10	0.03	1.00

$^*p < 0.05$

provided by the vendor address the requirements of the client's business practice (Pressman, 2005). Prior research in software development quality has used metrics such as defect rates per line of code to capture quality, as discussed before. However, given the limitations of such an approach in the outsourcing domain, it was not seen as a feasible manner to accurately capture the quality of the services provided. In addition, such clear-cut measures of software quality were not easily available at our research site. Alternatively, customer satisfaction from clients could be used to gauge the quality of software. Prior research indicates, however, that customer satisfaction and quality are two distinct though related constructs (Taylor & Baker, 1994). In addition, a significant intermediating variable in the link between the two constructs is the ease of evaluating ex post quality (Anderson & Sullivan, 1993). In the outsourcing domain, it is often hard to establish ex ante quality parameters than can then be evaluated ex post with accuracy (Pressman, 2005). In addition, it is not clear how knowledgeable the client is about the exact quality parameters of the final project until after considerable time has elapsed after acceptance testing (Gopalakrishnan et al., 1996; Krishnan et al., 2000). Therefore, it would be difficult to use customer satisfaction data as representative of quality without confounding fundamentally distinct entities.

A third option is then to elicit quality information from the vendor manager who is the most closely associated with quality. We therefore use the business unit manager as our source of quality data for the project. S/he is responsible financially for the project and is also usually the executive liaison between the vendor firm and the client (Gopalakrishnan et al., 1996). More importantly, as the person responsible for the project, s/he understands the consequences of organizational choices made with respect to staffing, designing and managing the project. Thus, using the business unit managers' perceptions of vendor-provided quality is consistent with our objectives. Prior research in the services operations and management literature has also indicated that clients and vendors tend to share reasonably similar opinions on service quality (Anderson & Narus, 1990; Heide & John, 1992). Thus, eliciting quality data from the vendor side is consistent with prior research on software development (Nidumolu, 1995; Tiwana, 2004). Since we obtain project information from the project manager and quality data from the business unit manager, we are able to avoid common method bias in our analysis.

However, we also validated our measure of quality by comparing it to more objective quality and defect rate data that is available for a subset (46) of the projects in our sample. Specifically, we had access to two sources of objective data for the projects in our sample. The first quality metric is the number of reported defects during acceptance testing of the project at the client site. This is a commonly used metric of software quality in the existing literature on software quality (Krishnan et al., 2000; Pressman, 2005). The second metric is the number of modification requests issued during vendor testing of the completed software. Modification requests are generally issued before delivery of the final system and are meant to address bugs that emerge during testing (Pressman, 2005). This metric also has been used in prior research in evaluating software projects (Herbsleb & Mockus, 2003). Our quality measures are significantly and negatively correlated (high quality–low defects) with these objective metrics of quality, providing support for the validity of our quality measure.

3.2   Variable Operationalization

The variables for this study were operationalized based on prior work in software development that had established scales for these constructs. Some variable items were modified to suit the offshore context. All variables were measured on a 5-point Likert scale. The individual constructs for the five independent variables are described briefly below and the questionnaire items used are shown in the Appendix.

3.2.1   Technical Factors

1. Requirements Uncertainty (Req Unc): This variable was measured using four questionnaire items used by Nidumolu (1995). Cronbach's alpha = 0.90.
2. Technological Uncertainty (Tech Unc): This variable measured the extent to which five technical aspects of the project's technologies were risky and was adapted from Nidumolu (1995). Cronbach's alpha = 0.84.

3.2.2   Organizational Factors

1. Presence of Trained Personnel (Trained Pers): This variable measured the extent to which trained people were available in the project and is adapted from Lacity and Hirshheim (1993). Three questionnaire items were used in measurement. Cronbach's alpha = 0.77.

3.2.3   Governance Related Factors

1. Client MIS Experience (MIS Experience): We operationalize this construct using four questionnaire items adapted from Lacity and Hirschheim's (1993) discussion of the importance of the client. Cronbach's alpha = 0.77.

2. Contract type: We operationalized contract type as dichotomous variable with FP contracts coded as 1 and T&M contracts coded as 0.

3.2.4   Control Variables

In addition, to these independent variables, we also controlled for several project related variables that have been studied in this context.

1. Prior Interactions with client (Prior Client): Research on inter-organizational relationships has focused on the role of prior ties in fostering trust between the contracting partners. It consequently reduces costs of shirking and renegotiations costs (Kalnins & Mayer, 2004). While prior ties have been hypothesized to affect choice of contracts and project profitability, there has been little work on examining its role in affecting service quality. This variable is measured by the number of previous projects completed by the vendor for the same client.
2. Project type (Proj Type): This variable is categorical and captures whether the project was a development, re-engineering or maintenance project. Development projects involve new requirements and platforms while re-engineering projects involve existing requirements but new platforms. Maintenance projects are usually associated with existing requirements on existing platforms but with minor modifications and enhancements. Development projects are coded 1, re-engineering projects 2 and maintenance projects 3.
3. Effort (Effort): We measured this variable in person-days to capture the total effort expended on the project. Consistent with prior work, we used the log of effort as a control variable for the size of the project (Harter et al., 2000).
4. Duration (Duration): We measured the duration of the project in calendar days, from the time the project was opened to the time it was signed off by the client. Consistent with prior work, we use the log of this variable in our analysis (Harter et al., 2000).
5. Team size (Team Size): This variable measures the number of personnel on the core team of the project. Although the size of the team might fluctuate at times, particularly during testing, the core team typically stays with the project throughout the duration of the project. This has been a significant control variable in prior research (Guzzo & Dickson, 1996).

3.2.5   Dependent Variable

1. Quality (Quality): This variable was measured using five items pertaining to characteristics of the final software delivered to the client. We adapt the Operational Effectiveness dimension used by Nidumolu (1995) to measure quality. Cronbach's alpha = 0.76.

As a first step, we establish that our perceptual measures have construct and discriminant validity. The questionnaire items pertaining to the independent variables were subjected to a factor analysis with principal components and

Table 3 Confirmatory factor analysis of quality drivers (principal components with varimax rotation, N = 100)

Questionnaire Items	Factor 1	Factor 2	Factor 3	Factor 4
REQ_UN1	0.715	0.086	0.126	−0.064
REQ_UN2	0.712	−0.089	0.206	−0.202
REQ_UN3	0.689	−0.272	−0.062	0.317
REQ_UN4	0.869	0.125	0.033	0.097
TRAINEDPER1	0.047	0.631	0.121	−0.464
TRAINEDPER2	−0.402	0.699	−0.194	0.121
TRAINEDPER3	0.113	0.898	−0.033	−0.055
MISEXP1	0.270	−0.046	0.783	0.018
MISEXP2	0.088	−0.024	0.783	0.065
MISEXP3	−0.061	−0.077	0.785	0.202
MISEXP4	0.141	−0.272	0.749	−0.007
TECH_UN1	0.059	−0.083	0.165	0.864
TECH_UN2	−0.216	0.068	0.157	0.852
TECH_UN3	0.136	−0.147	−0.064	0.792
TECH_UN4	0.031	−0.257	0.134	0.665
TECH_UN5	−0.027	−0.440	0.205	0.701
% Variance	25	19	14	11

varimax rotation. The items loaded well on individual factors, supporting the hypothesized four-factor structure, as seen in Table 3.

Each of the factor loadings was above 0.6 with cross-loadings of less than 0.35, indicating good construct and discriminant validity. In addition, as shown above, each of the constructs showed good reliability measured by Cronbach's alpha. The factor scores were created by averaging the individual items pertaining to each construct for use in subsequent analysis.

3.3 Data Analysis

In order to test our first five hypotheses we estimate the following equation for quality:

$$Quality = f(\textit{Effort, ProjType, Prior Client, Req Unc, Tech Unc,} \\ \textit{Trained Per, MIS Experience, Control}) \qquad (1)$$

Testing Hypothesis 6, which suggests a moderating effect of the contract type on the quality drivers, requires the use of further testing. Under the standard statistical techniques for testing moderation effects, an interaction of the *moderating* variable with the *moderated* variable is introduced into the OLS estimation. The coefficient of the interaction term as well as the differences in the model's F-statistic form appropriate tests for moderation. However, in the present case, this is rendered ineffective by the fact that the contract is endogenously determined, necessitating a different statistical approach.

We account for the endogeneity that arises from contract choice by using the Heckman two-stage model (Greene, 1997). The Heckman procedure essentially instruments for the contract choice model by estimating the predicted probability of the contract being either FP or T&M and introducing this instrument (called the Inverse Mills Ratio) as an additional independent variable in the quality and profit equations. The procedure accounts for any effects of the endogeneity from the contract choice model and renders the resulting OLS coefficients unbiased and consistent (Maddala, 1983) and is referred to as the *treatment effects* model. The mechanics of the two-stage procedure are as follows. We first estimate a contract choice probit model in the first stage. The estimated probit equation is then used to calculate the Inverse Mills Ratios for inclusion into the second stage, which in essence accounts for all factors that may affect contract choice. The Inverse Mills Ratio, referred to as lambda, is introduced into the quality equation as an independent variable and the resulting form of (1) is estimated using OLS. We use the contract choice model from Gopal A. et al. (2003) to estimate the Inverse Mills Ratios for inclusion in the quality equation. The results of the probit contract model are shown in Table 4[1]. We do not discuss these results in the interest of space; these results are available in detail in Gopal A. et al.

In order to test moderation, we extend the above methodology by using the *sample selection* procedure (Maddala, 1983). Specifically, we first estimate the Inverse Mills Ratios from the contract choice model. Subsequently, we enter the appropriate set of Inverse Mills Ratios into the quality equation that is estimated for individual contract sub-samples only (Maddala). In other words, we estimate two separate

Table 4 Probit results for contract choice, N = 100 (adapted from Gopal A. et al. (2003))

Variable	Coefficient	Std Error	t-Ratio	p-Value
Requirements uncertainty	−0.07	0.16	−0.46	0.65
Effort	−0.17	0.19	−0.87	0.38
Trained personnel	−0.48	0.18	−2.65	0.01
Client MIS experience	0.28	0.28	1.01	0.31
Client experience	0.10	0.21	0.45	0.65
Client reputation	0.11	0.16	0.66	0.51
Future business potential	0.12	0.14	0.84	0.40
Client SIZE	0.58	0.26	2.23	0.02
Project importance	−0.39	0.20	−2.00	0.05
Competition (vendor)	−0.53	0.19	−2.83	0.00
Competition (client)	0.43	0.21	2.04	0.04
Prior client	−0.03	0.02	−1.63	0.10
Project type	−0.55	0.27	−2.05	0.04

Log-likelihood Function = −51.59. Chi-Square = 31.40, 12 degrees of freedom, p = 0.0017

[1] While there are some differences in the estimated probit model here and shown in Table 4 and the model reported in Gopal A. et al (2003) due to some differences in the sample, the individual coefficients are consistent with those in Gopal A. et al (2003).

equations for the FP and T&M subsamples. The presence of moderation can then
be examined by studying the difference in the coefficient parameters for the quality
drivers across the two contractual regimes.

Before performing the OLS regressions in the second stage of the Heckman
procedure, we tested for assumptions of the OLS model in both the quality and
margin equations. We tested for autocorrelation using the Durbin–Watson statistic,
which was close to 2 in the quality equation, indicating the absence of autocorrelation in the residuals (Greene, 1997). The normality of the residuals was tested using
the Shapiro–Wilks test which indicated no violation of the normality assumption
(Greene). We tested for heteroskedasticity in each equation through the Breusch–
Pagan test which failed to reject the null of homoskedasticity in each regression. No
significant outliers were identified through the use of Cook's distance measures
(Belsley et al., 1980). We also tested for multi-collinearity in the full sample quality
model. The variance inflation factors in our analysis were under 2 and the condition
indices were much lower than the threshold value of 15 identified by Belsley et al.
In addition, most of the correlations (Table 2) are below 0.5 confirming that multicollinearity is not a problem.

The results of for the quality equation are shown in Table 5. The first column
provides the endogeneity-corrected regression coefficients for the full sample while

Table 5 Regression analysis of vendor-provided quality model

Variables	Full model Heckman OLS	Full model OLS	T&M Heckman OLS	FP Heckman OLS
	N = 100	N = 100	N = 40	N = 60
Constant	4.30**	4.17**	3.94**	3.87**
	(0.33)	(0.27)	(0.44)	(0.43)
Effort	−0.003	−0.002	−0.003	0.002
	(0.032)	(0.031)	(0.051)	(0.039)
Prior client	0.007**	0.007**	0.010	0.007**
	(0.003)	(0.003)	(0.011)	(0.003)
Project type	−0.11*	−0.09	−0.090	−0.059
	(0.059)	(0.066)	(0.11)	(0.090)
Requirements uncertainty	−0.071**	−0.068*	−0.147**	−0.048*
	(0.032)	(0.039)	(0.071)	(0.028)
Technological uncertainty	−0.029	−0.019	−0.021	−0.121*
	(0.059)	(0.059)	(0.098)	(0.073)
Trained personnel	−0.127**	−0.146**	−0.187**	−0.080*
	(0.055)	(0.048)	(0.091)	(0.055)
Client MIS experience	0.086**	0.080*	0.092*	0.051
	(0.038)	(0.045)	(0.056)	(0.064)
Contract type	0.348**	0.240**	–	–
	(0.171)	(0.082)		
Lambda	0.076	–	0.162	−0.031
	(0.126)		(0.179)	(0.180)
R-Squared	0.42	0.41	0.31	0.23
F-Statistic	7.25**	8.18	3.27**	3.25**
Rho	0.215	–	0.43	−0.094

Heckman-corrected model and OLS, (standard errors in parenthesis)

the second column provides the OLS estimates. It is useful to provide both the endogeneity-corrected and uncorrected estimates as a test of the robustness of the model (Shaver, 1998). The subsample regression results using the sample selection methodology are shown in the third and fourth columns of Table 5. In the subsample analysis, the direct effect of the contract variable is omitted. We discuss the regression results in Sect. 3.4.

3.4   Results and Discussion

Table 5 provides the regression results for the drivers of quality equation. We first examined the control variables. Project type was marginally significant in affecting quality (-0.11; $p < 0.1$). As expected, prior interactions with client had a positive effect on quality (0.007; $p < 0.05$), indicating that there are beneficial impacts of repeated interactions between the client and the vendor, possibly through enhanced learning. Effort on the other hand had no significant effect on quality.

We next examined the results of our analysis vis-à-vis our hypotheses. In our first four hypotheses, we had argued for the effects of requirements uncertainty, technological uncertainty, presence of trained personnel and client MIS experience on quality. We found significant support for three of our four hypotheses. Higher requirements uncertainty lowered vendor provided quality significantly (-0.071; $p < 0.05$) providing support for Hypothesis 1. Technology uncertainty was not significant in affecting quality indicating that Hypothesis 2 was not supported. We thus found mixed support for the effect of technical factors on project quality. We found significant support for Hypothesis 3, showing that the lack of trained personnel lowered quality (-0.127; $p < 0.05$; reverse-scored). Finally, client MIS experience also significantly increased quality (0.086; $p < 0.05$) providing support for Hypothesis 4. Hypothesis 5 argued that contract type would affect quality. Specifically, we argued that FP contracts are more likely to be associated with higher quality than T&M contracts. We found strong support for this hypothesis as well (0.348; $p < 0.05$). The complete direct effects model explained 42% of the variance and was significant at $p < 0.05$. We thus found strong support for the role of organizational and governance factors in determining the extent of vendor-provided quality.

The broad support for a variety of variables suggest that quality in the offshore domain is a function of multiple and possibly inter-related factors. For instance, our findings suggest that the presence of trained personnel and an experienced client MIS department have a direct effect on quality. In addition, we had argued that these factors may have an indirect effect on quality because of the differential deployment under the different contract regimes. Evidence from this study for the effect of contracts type on quality provides some support for this argument. In line with prior research, we also found that requirements uncertainty affected project quality even in the offshore outsourcing context. While conventional wisdom has established that offshoring should only be undertaken for projects where there is a high level of process and requirements definition (Farrell, 2005; Hayes, 2003), it is interesting to note that requirements uncertainty continues to affect quality even in this domain. However, surprisingly, technological uncertainty had little effect on quality. One possible reason could be that the technological capabilities of vendor may be broader (given that providing software services is their main line of business) relative to in-house software development departments. Vendor expertise in a diverse range of technological platforms may make this a less important factor in determining quality in the offshore outsourcing context. Alternatively, it is possible that, consistent with prescriptive models of offshoring, clients only offshore projects with low technological risk, preferring to keep the riskier projects in-house (Gottfredson et al., 2005). More research is needed to accurately tease out these effects.

A significant contribution of our work in this paper is to highlight the impact of governance-related factors on project quality. The variables we study, the contract and client MIS experience, have not been studied in the context of quality before. Our results indicate that in the offshore outsourcing context, governance-related factors have as much of a role to play in ensuring quality as organizational and technical factors. At a broader level, our results suggest that project quality is not as simple as merely controlling requirements and choosing stable technologies. It also involves choosing the right vendor, the right contract and managing the vendor through a competent MIS department.

Hypothesis 6 postulates a moderation effect of the contract type on the quality drivers, based on differential effects that the incentives and risks inherent in FP and T&M contracts might have on the management of the project. The third and fourth column of Table 5 show the results for the split-sample analysis. There are two primary points that arise from the results. First, although the individual coefficients differ in magnitude between the FP and T&M samples, the direction of the effect is consistent across the two contract types, indicating a certain stability in the effects of quality drivers on service quality. Indeed, this provides some support for the underlying hypotheses regarding the direct effects of these quality drivers.

The second point pertains to the differences in statistical significance across the two contract types, leading to some support for Hypothesis 6 with respect to the quality drivers in our study. The negative effects of requirements uncertainty are more pronounced in T&M contracts than in FP contracts. Conventional wisdom indicates that requirements tend to be more unstable in T&M contracts (Kalnins & Mayer, 2004). In addition, the effects of changing requirements are possibly exacerbated in the T&M case due to the resource allocation decisions made by the vendor manager, as discussed before (Arora & Asundi, 1999). Thus, we see a stronger negative effect in T&M contracts. Consistent results are also seen with respect to access to trained personnel. The effect of this factor are also pronounced in T&M projects than in FP projects, suggesting that when resources are scarce, the vendor's incentives would compel him to allocate these resources to the FP contract than the T&M contract. The effect of these decisions results in a marginal higher impact of this variable on service quality.

We observe a weak but surprising result with respect to technological uncertainty, which appears to be marginally significant in the case of FP contracts but not significant in T&M contracts. Extant literature provides a possible explanation for this effect. It is sometimes hypothesized that vendors use T&M contracts to learn about newer technologies and domains, at relatively lower risk (Arora & Asundi, 1999). The presence of significant technological risk also incentivizes the client to opt for a T&M contract as a means of controlling and monitoring the progress on the project (Gopal A. et al., 2003). Therefore, it would appear that any technological risk would be resolved by allowing the vendor to learn, adapt and thereby provide higher quality. In the FP case, the vendor is limited in his ability to resolve all technological issues that arise in the project and is also prone to opportunism, i.e., the vendor can deliver marginally lower quality service in the face of technical difficulties. The option of improving quality by extending the life of the project is limited in the FP case. Thus, we see a marginally stronger effect in FP contracts. While this reasoning is exploratory at this point, we believe these dynamics need to be explored more thoroughly in future research.

Finally, our analysis indicates that the presence of an experienced MIS department has a beneficial impact in the T&M contract but not so in the FP contract. This effect would follow directly from an analysis of the risk exposure and incentives faced by the client in a typical T&M contract. Since the T&M contract pushes the larger share of risk onto the client, there is greater monitoring and control exercised by the client in such situations (Bajari & Tadelis, 2001). Specifically, knowledge sharing between the client and vendor as well as client monitoring and control will lead to better quality outcomes, as expected. In the case of the FP contract, the presence of strong incentives reduces the need and indeed, the value, of client monitoring. Monitoring thus may not have a significant effect on quality in FP projects. We see results consistent with this reasoning in our subsample analysis.

While we are confident about the robustness and validity of our findings, we highlight some of the limitations of our study. First, our results are based on data from one single company, thereby raising questions about the generalizability of our findings. However, as was pointed out earlier, controlling for variations in firm capabilities, cultural distance and reputation enables us to tease out the effects of various quality drivers on quality and the effect of quality on margins. But clearly, more industry level studies are needed to establish the generalizability of our findings. Second, the sub-samples for T&M and FP contracts were not of the same size. While this, in itself, may not be a problem, the fact there were only 40 T&M projects may be an issue that could affect validity. While we recognize this limitation, we believe that a sample size of 40 is well above the minimum size necessary to get significant power for our results. In addition, we are well within the sample size parameters established within extant IS research (Banker & Slaughter, 2000; Harter et al., 2000; Krishnan et al., 2000). Our results have to be interpreted with these limitations in mind.

4   Conclusion

Our analysis in this paper was predicated on a significant gap in the offshoring and outsourcing literature. Specifically, there is little existing work examining the drivers of service quality. In this study, we propose and empirically test a model of quality based on prior research in IS outsourcing, software development and economics. We find significant support for our theoretical framework and arguments regarding the antecedents of vendor provided quality in the offshore outsourcing environment. In addition, we find some evidence for the moderation of the effects of quality drivers on quality by the contract type used in governing the project. As we noted earlier, understanding quality and its drivers are important given the growing debate about the importance and role of offshore outsourcing. Our study is thus, one of the first studies to provide an empirical understanding of these important relationships in the offshoring context.

Findings from our study provide some clear managerial implications. Recall that our analysis controls for endogeneity in contract choice. In a sense, our focus has been on understanding the drivers of quality after controlling for factors affecting contract choice. In other words, given a particular contract type, what should vendors and clients do to enhance quality? First, our results suggest that it is in the client's best interest to finalize their organizational requirements as much as possible before contracting with a vendor. Uncertain requirements continue to affect quality even in the offshore domain. Second, even when clients decide on FP contracts, they need to examine the staffing and personnel capabilities of the vendor. Most clients choose vendors based on prior interactions and vendor reputation (Banerjee & Duflo, 2000; Kalnins & Mayer, 2004). However, the vendor's specific personnel availabilities, in terms of the availability of trained personnel to staff projects, are possibly as important for project success as either prior interaction or reputation. Third, clients need to enhance their monitoring capabilities if they are to ensure high quality for their projects. In addition, cost, distance, transparency and sometimes culture may have played a role in the exacerbating the situation. All these issues highlight the need for a broad research agenda in order to enhance our understanding of the vital role of client monitoring.

More generally, the above discussion highlights some implications for the considerable debate on offshore outsourcing quality. Common wisdom on offshore outsourcing quality seems to accept as inevitable that cost advantages of offshore outsourcing are almost always accompanied by problems with quality. Our results suggest that firms can address their quality issues not only by controlling the project's technical environment but also by choosing the appropriate contract, better client monitoring and better interactions with vendor teams. As the offshore industry matures in India and other parts of the world, it is not necessary that low cost has to be associated with lower relative quality (Carmel & Agarwal 2002).

Our study also addresses, albeit indirectly, the debate about how different offshoring outsourcing is from domestic outsourcing. One of the biggest differences that researchers have highlighted is the fact that offshore outsourcing introduces cultural issues as a critical factor affecting the relationship between vendor and client. In our study, there is little variation on cultural distance *between projects* since our data is based on projects completed by one vendor for clients in the USA and Western Europe. We have, therefore, ignored this variable in our analysis since it is constant. Not surprisingly, our results support arguments and hypotheses that are drawn from traditional outsourcing literature. However, even though there is little variation between projects, the cultural distance between the vendor and clients in our study's context is high. The vendor is from India and the clients are from the West, unlike domestic outsourcing where the vendor and client typically come from the same cultural background. The fact that the results in this study are not very different from traditional outsourcing would seem to indicate that the difference between offshore outsourcing and domestic outsourcing may be one of *degree* rather than of *kind*. What this suggests is that we perhaps do not need a different "theory" of offshore outsourcing. We recognize, however, that this conclusion is limited by the fact that it is based on evidence from one vendor and that we have no comparative data from domestic outsourcing. We believe more work is needed to resolve this debate one way or the other.

Appendix: Questionnaire Items

Requirements Uncertainty: To What Extent was the Following True for This Project?

Req_un1 There was a clearly known way to convert client needs into requirements specification.

Req_un2 Established processes could be relied upon to convert client needs into requirements specifications.

Req_un3 There was a clearly known way to develop software that would meet these functional requirements.

Req_un4 There were established procedures and practices that could be relied upon to develop software to meet these requirements.

Technological Uncertainty: To What Extent were the Following were Complex for This Project?

Tech_un1 Systems software

    Tech_un2 Programming languages/application

    Tech_un3 Database technology

    Tech_un4 Coding and testing aspects

    Tech_un5 Installation techniques

Trained Personnel: To What Extent was the Following True for This Project?

TrainedPer1 It was difficult to hire trained people for this project from the market
   TrainedPer2 There was a shortage of trained people for this project in our company
   TrainedPer3 It was difficult to provide training to employees in skills required for this project

Client MIS Experience: To What Extent do You Agree with the Following Statements?

MISExp1 The client company had a very capable MIS department
   MISExp2 The client's MIS department was very experienced with handling outsourcing projects
   MISExp3 The client MIS department was technically capable of managing outsourced projects like <roject name>
   MISExp4 The project could have been as successfully executed by the MIS department in the client's organization

Perceived Quality: Please Rate the Project on the Following Criteria on the Scale Provided

Quality1 Reliability of final software
   Quality2 Cost of software operations
   Quality3 Response time performance of final software
   Quality4 Ease of use of final software
   Quality5 Ability to customize outputs to various user needs

References

Anderson, J. C., & Narus, J. A. (1990). A model of distributor and manufacturer firm working relationships. *Journal of Marketing, 54*(1), 42–58.
Anderson, E. W., & Sullivan, M. W. (1993). The antecedents and consequences of customer satisfaction for firms. *Marketing Science, 12*(2), 125.
Aron, R., & Singh, J. V. (2005). Getting offshoring right. *Harvard Business Review, 83*(12), 135–143.
Arora, A., & Asundi, J. (1999). Quality certification and the economics of contract software development: A study of the Indian software service companies, presented at the NBER conference on 'Organizational Change and Performance', Santa Rosa, CA.

Bajari, P., & Tadelis, S. (2001). Incentives versus transaction costs: A theory of procurement contracts. *Rand Journal of Economics, 32*(3), 387–407.

Banerjee, A. V., & Duflo, E. (2000). Reputation effects and the limits of contracting: A study of the indian software industry. *Quarterly Journal of Economics, 115*(3), 989–1017.

Banker, R. D., & Slaughter, S. (2000). The moderating effects of structure on volatility and complexity in software enhancement. *Information Systems Research, 11*(3), 219–240.

Barki, H., Rivard, S., & Talbot, J. (1993). Toward an assessment of software development risk. *Journal of Management Information Systems, 10*(2), 203–225.

Belsley, D. A., Kuh, E., & Welsch, R. E. (1980). *Regression Diagnostics*. New York, NY: Wiley.

Bhagwati, J., Panagariya, A., & Srinivasan, T. N. (2004). The muddles over outsourcing. *Journal of Economic Perspectives, 18*(4), 93–114.

Carmel, E., & Agarwal, R. (2002). The maturation of offshore sourcing of information technology work. *MIS Quarterly Executive, 1*(2), 65–78.

Cullen, S., Seldon, P., & Willcocks, L. (2005). Managing outsourcing: The lifecycle imperative. *MIS Quarterly Executive, 4*(1), 229–246.

Davis, G. B., Ein-Dor, P., King, W. R., & Torkzadeh, R. (2006). IT offshoring: History, prospects, challenges. *Journal of the AIS, 7*(11), 770–795.

Doraisamy, V. (2006). Talent Crunch Likely in IT Industry: NASSCOM. *The Hindu, 2*nd February 2006. Chennai, India.

Erber, G., & Sayed-Ahmed, A. (2005). Offshore outsourcing. *Intereconomics, 40*(2), 100–112.

Ethiraj, S. K., Kale, P., Krishnan, M. S., & Singh, J. V. (2005). Where do capabilities come from and how do they matter? A study in the software services industry. *Strategic Management Journal, 26*(1), 25–45.

Farrell, D. (2005). Offshoring: Value creation through economic change. *Journal of Management Studies, 42*(3), 675–683.

Gopal, A., Mukhopadhyay, T., & Krishnan, M. S. (2002). The role of software processes and communication in offshore software development. *Communications of the ACM, 45*(4), 193–200.

Gopal, A., Sivaramakrishnan, K., Krishnan, M. S., & Mukhopadhyay, T. (2003). Contracts in offshore software development: An empirical analysis. *Management Science, 49*(12), 1671–1683.

Gopalakrishnan, S., Kochikar, V. P., & Yegneshwar, S. (1996). The offshore model for software development: The infosys experience. *Proceedings of the ACM SIGCPR Conference on the Virtual Workplace: The Impact on Individuals, Organizations and Societies, Denver, Colorado*.

Gosain, S., Gopal, A., Darcy, D., & Lichtenstein, Y. (2003). Organizational control systems and software quality: A cross national study. *Proceedings of the International Conference in Information Systems, Seattle WA. December 2003*.

Gottfredson, M., Puryear, R., & Phillips, S. (2005). Strategic sourcing: From the periphery to the core. *Harvard Business Review, 83*(2), 132–139.

Greene, W. (1997). *Econometric analysis*, 3rd edn. New Jersey: Prentice-Hall.

Guzzo, R. A., & Dickson, M. W. (1996). Teams in organizations: Recent research on performance effectiveness. *Annual Review of Psychology, 47*, 307–338.

Harter, D. E., Krishnan, M. S., & Slaughter, S. A. (2000). Effects of process maturity on quality, cycle time, and effort in software product development. *Management Science, 46*(4), 461–475.

Hayes, M. (2003). Precious connection. *InformationWeek, 34*–50.

Heide, J.B, & John, G. (1992). Do norms matter in marketing relationships. *Journal of Marketing, 56*(2), 32–45.

Herbsleb, J. D., & Mockus, A. (2003). An empirical study of speed and communication in globally distributed software development. *IEEE Transactions on Software Engineering, 29*(2), 481–494.

Kalnins, A., & Mayer, K. J. (2004). Relationships and hybrid contracts: An analysis of contract choice in information technology. *Journal of Law, Economics and Organization, 20*(1), 207–229.

Kirsch, L. J., Sambamurthy, V., Ko, D-G., & Purvis, R. L. (2002). Controlling information systems development projects: The view from the client. *Information Systems Research, 48*(4), 484 –498.

Krishna, S., Sahay, S., & Walsham, G. (2004). Managing cross-cultural issues in global software outsourcing. *Communications of the ACM, 47*(4), 62–66.

Krishnan, M. S., Kriebel, C. H., Kekre, S., & Mukhopadhyay, T. (2000). An empirical analysis of productivity and quality in software products. *Management Science, 46*(6), 745–759.

Lacity, M. C., & Hirschheim, R. A. (1993). *Information systems outsourcing: Myths, metaphors and realities.* New York: Wiley.

Maddala, G. S. (1983). *Limited-dependent and qualitative variables in econometrics.* Cambridge, UK: Cambridge University Press

Mata, F. J., Fuerst, W. L., & Barney, J. B. (1995). Information technology and sustained competitive advantage: A resource-based analysis. *MIS Quarterly, 19*(4), 487–505.

Nidumolu, S. (1995). The effect of coordination and uncertainty on software project performance: Residual performance risk as an intervening variable. *Information Systems Research, 6*(3), 191–219.

Pressman, R. S. (2005). *Software engineering: A practitioner's approach.* New York: McGraw-Hill.

Rao, S. K. (1998). Financial implications of inculcating quality in software development: A call for "Value-Based Quality Budgeting". *Journal of Financial Management and Analysis, 11*(1):15–19.

Ravichandran, T., & Rai, A. (2000). Quality management in systems development: An organizational system perspective. *MIS Quarterly, 24*(3),381–415.

Rottman, J. W., & Lacity, M. C. (2004). Twenty practices for offshore outsourcing. *MIS Quarterly Executive, 3*(3), 117–130.

Russell, B., & Chatterjee, S. (2003). Relationship quality: The undervalued dimension of software quality. *Communications of the ACM, 46*(8), 85–89.

Sawyer, S. (2001). Effects of intra-group conflict on packaged software development team performance. *Information Systems Journal, 11*, 155–178.

Shah, S. (2004). Dwindling labor. *Optimize,* September, 66–71.

Shaver, J. M. (1998). Accounting for endogeneity when assessing strategy performance: Does entry mode choice affect FDI survival? *Management Science, 44*(4), 571–585.

Taylor, S. A., & Baker, T. L. (1994). An Assessment of the relationship between service quality and customer satisfaction in the formation of consumers' purchase intentions. *Journal of Retailing, 70*(2), 163–178.

Thurm, S. (2004). Tough shift – Lesson in India. Wall Street Journal, Eastern Edition. 3rd March, A1.

Tiwana, A. (2004). An empirical study of the effect of knowledge integration on software development performance. *Information and Software Technology, 46*(13), 899–906.

Westland, J. C. (2004). The cost behavior of software defects. *Decision Support Systems, 37*, 229–238.

Part IV
Business Process Outsourcing

The Impact of Process Standardization on Business Process Outsourcing Success[*]

Kim Wuellenweber, Wolfgang Koenig,
Daniel Beimborn, and Tim Weitzel

1 Introduction

It seems a safe bet to say that process standardization is desirable (Lee & Kim, 1997; Manrodt & Vitasek, 2004) and, particularly in service industries, offers technical interchangeability, compliance with regulations, and improved customer confidence (de Vries, 1999). Also, many expect that standardized business processes are better to outsource and there are empirical indications that business process standardization reduces the risks of BPO (Wüllenweber & Weitzel, 2007). Yet, despite the importance of both areas – process standards and outsourcing – neither the outsourcing nor standardization literature has so far offered a conclusive picture of the value of process standardization to business process outsourcing (BPO). In this paper, our overall research question thus is: *What is the impact of business process standardization on BPO success?*

We argue that process standardization has a direct and positive production cost effect on BPO success, since economies of scale and skill can be achieved more easily. Further, we expect an indirect and positive effect via improved contractual and relational governance means: process standardization allows defining clear and precise process output objectives to be met by the service provider. On the other side, uniformity of process activities facilitates communication and coordination between exchange partners. Our results provide strong evidence that process characteristics – such as the degree of standardization – are an important prerequisite for BPO ventures.

For the purpose of this paper, BPO is defined as the delegation of one or more entire business processes to third party providers, including all related resources, such as IT and HR (Dayasindhu, 2004; Halvey & Melby, 1996). The provider takes over the complete business function and is free to choose the implementation; the outsourcer receives only the process result (Braun, 2004). A business process, as

---

[*]This paper previously appeared as: Wuellenweber, K., Koenig, W., Beimborn, D., and Weitzel, T. (2008). The impact of process standardization on business process. *Information Systems Frontiers,* *10*, 211–224. The current version appears with permission of Springer, the publisher of ISF.

the outsourcing object, is defined as a "set of logically related tasks performed to achieve a defined business outcome" (Davenport & Short, 1990).

BPO has been said to offer unique potentials as business processes can – in contrast to IT operations – be much closer to the outsourcer's core business and even to the outsourcer's customers (Willcocks, Hindle, Feeny, & Lacity, 2004). Thus, the domain knowledge or expertise the outsourcer brings in to the BPO venture is usually much higher than in IT outsourcing arrangements. This enables the creation of new, unique capabilities by leveraging the competencies of both the outsourcer and the service provider. BPO is therefore expected to not only offer greater efficiency but to also enable strategic advantages in the form of business innovation (Borman, 2006; Feeny, Willcocks, & Lacity, 2003; Gottfredson, Puryear, & Phillips, 2005; Mani, Barua, & Whinston, 2006; Willcocks et al.). However, the upside potential comes at the cost of additional risks that have limited the growth of BPO (Aron, Clemons, & Reddi, 2005; Gewald et al., 2006). In particular, the complexity of business processes, the high degree of interdependence with other processes, and the lack of BPO governance experience have been identified as main inhibitors (Aron et al.; Mani et al.). As high complexity and high interdependency are typical characteristics of less standardized processes (see Sect. 2), the impact of standardization on outsourcing is particularly relevant for BPO ventures. That is the reason for choosing BPO as context of analysis in this paper.

2   Theoretical Foundation and Research Model

Our main goal is to explore whether process standardization positively impacts outsourcing success. Researchers and practitioners alike seem increasingly interested in the value of business process standardization, and it seems common to strive for process standardization for at least two reasons: the first reason is the proposition that standardized processes will show better performance (Fomin & Lyytinen, 2000; Ramakumar & Cooper, 2004; Swaminathan, 2001). The second reason is that standardization is sometimes considered to be a prerequisite for outsourcing and can reduce the risks associated with BPO (Wüllenweber & Weitzel, 2007). While the outsourcing literature offers mature perspectives on many facets of outsourcing, the consideration of the standardization argument seems worthwhile to explore further. A business process view and the corresponding focus on BPO, instead of ITO, have been chosen as the complexity of and high interdependence among business processes are widely considered to be major inhibitors of BPO (Aron et al., 2005; Mani et al., 2006).

Figure 1 gives an overview of our research model which, in essence, hypothesizes a positive relationship between business process standardization and BPO success. We propose three different theoretical arguments in order to explain this relationship: (1) a direct relation based on production cost economics (PCE), (2) an indirect effect, mediated by increased contractual governance abilities, based on transaction cost economics, and (3) a further indirect effect, mediated by increased relational governance, based on relational exchange theory (RET).

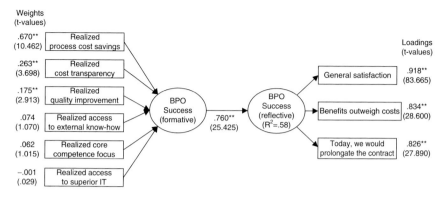

Fig. 1 Research model

2.1   Direct Effect of Process Standardization on BPO Success

As we can learn from production and supply chain literature (de Toni & Panizzolo, 1993; Manrodt & Vitasek, 2004; Phelps, 2006; Ramakumar & Cooper, 2004) standardization of business processes aims at improving operational performance and reducing costs by decreasing process errors, facilitating communication, or just profiting from expert knowledge which has, among others, been used to develop process standards to achieve those goals. A certain degree of process standardization is considered a necessary precondition for successful BPO since a vendor needs to bundle similar business processes from different clients in order to be able to achieve economies of scale (Lancellotti, Schein, Spang, & Stadler, 2003; Ramakumar & Cooper, 2004; Rouse & Corbitt, 2004). The objective of standardization is to make process activities transparent and achieve uniformity of process activities across the value chain and across firm boundaries.

The proposition that the more standardized the business process the more likely the vendor can achieve economies of scale and skill from producing services for different clients draws on the main PCE argument in the outsourcing literature. PCE is the part of production economics which addresses the cost side of production. Production costs include any direct and indirect costs for producing a service or product as well as the delivery and service costs. From a PCE perspective, firms treat outsourcing (or make-or-buy considerations in general) as a decision that compares production costs of internal operations with the price offered on the market (Ford & Farmer, 1986). Firms therefore outsource activities in order to achieve the production cost advantages appearing on the vendor side (Ang & Straub, 1998; Loh & Venkatraman, 1992). This theory has probably received more empirical support in explaining outsourcing decisions than any other theory. Differences in production costs between different firms result from a different scale and scope of operations as well as from different production resources and skills (Baumol, Panzar, & Willig, 1982; Poppo & Zenger, 1998). *Economies of scale* arise from the ability to perform activities more efficiently at larger volumes (Porter, 1985). They can result both from fixed cost digression and from a declining shape of the cost function (Baumol et al.; Murray & White, 1983). Economies of scale are often considered to be one of the main reasons for outsourcing, and we expect standardization to potentially increase scale benefits. The service provider is expected to provide services at lower costs by bundling similar – ideally standardized – processes of several firms, thereby reducing average costs per unit (Cachon & Harker, 2002; Gurbaxani, 1996).

Beside econmies of scale, cost advantages from outsourcing can result from economies of skill. *Economies of skill* can be distinguished into ex ante and ex post. *Ex ante economies of skill* determine the form and the position of the cost function (Auguste, Hao, Singer, & Wiegand, 2002). If a firm's cost function leads to lower average costs compared to other firms, this implies comparatively higher skill economies, representing a certain core competence of the firm (Langlois, 1995; Prahalad & Hamel, 1990) and thus a potential insourcer firm. Comparatively higher economies of skill can result from, for example, technology leadership and/or superior resource bundles. As process standards can encompass experiences or "good practice" from other firms and projects, they can be positively related to process performance and thus BPO success.

As multiple standardized processes of different clients can be processed by a single vendor we thus expect standardization to positively affect BPO success due to economies of scale (higher transaction volumes) and skill (process standards capture the aggregate knowledge and experience of many persons, and, further, enable stronger learning effects on the vendor side). Hence, in order to be able to realize economies of scale in a BPO context, the vendor firm has to establish and to provide a standardized business process to all of its clients (Rouse & Corbitt, 2004) which some even see as a precondition for outsourcing in general (Ramakumar & Cooper, 2004).

Hypothesis D1: Process standardization is positively and directly associated with BPO success.

2.2 Effect of Standardization on BPO Success Mediated by Contractual Governance

In addition to the direct effect of business process standardization on BPO success, we propose a mediated effect resulting from governance advantages due to higher transparency and better monitoring possibilities (Davenport, 2005).

Modern theories of the firm argue that environmental uncertainty or complexity lead to imperfect or incomplete contracts where the contracting parties are not able to specify or observe all contingencies that may affect the outcome of their relationship (Milgrom & Roberts, 1992). As a consequence, the *first-best* effort levels cannot necessarily be obtained (Feenstra & Hanson, 2003; Hart & Moore, 1990). Complete contracts are considered infeasible or at least associated with extensively high transaction costs (Williamson, 1975).

Yet, the so-called "theory of incomplete contracts" (TIC) has not received much attention in empirical outsourcing research. Nam, Rajagopalan, Rao, and Chaudhurry (1996) based their study on TIC and "transaction cost economies" (TCE) and found a significant relationship between uncertainty and the degree of outsourcing. Multiple outsourcing studies have examined contractual governance, thereby focusing on the degree of contract completeness on the degree of outsourcing or outsourcing success. For example, Aubert, Houde, Patry, & Rivard (2003) investigate factors influencing the completeness of IT outsourcing contracts and find that, among others, less measurability in the outsourced activities leads to less complete contracts and, as a consequence, to less successful outsourcing. Poppo & Zenger (2002) show that managers are less satisfied with the cost performance of outsourced IT services when they could not easily measure its performance.

Aubert et al. (2003) show that the design of outsourcing contracts follows a trade-off between the marginal benefits and costs of contractual completeness. For standardized and transparent processes this implies a higher degree of completeness (Nam et al., 1996) since performance parameters are easier to specify and agreement on them can be better achieved due to a common understanding (Ramakumar & Cooper, 2004). Therefore, we hypothesize that process standardization leads to higher contract completeness. In this regard, we further argue that process standardization leads to higher measurability. Measurability refers to the outsourcer's ability to measure the provider's performance in executing the delegated business process. This includes measuring output criteria as well as establishing control points during the workflow which are required to adequately monitor the vendor.

Hypothesis C1: Process standardization is positively associated with process measurability.

Hypothesis C2: Process standardization is positively associated with contract completeness.

To complete the mediation effect, drawing on organizational theories like transaction cost economics, agency theory, and incomplete contract theory and on the outsourcing literature (Aubert et al., 2003; Loh & Venkatraman, 1995; Nam et al., 1996; Poppo & Zenger, 2002) we expect a positive impact of measurability on contract completeness and in turn that a more complete contract leads to higher outsourcing success.

Hypothesis C3: Process measurability is positively associated with contract completeness.

Hypothesis C4: Contract completeness is positively associated with BPO success.

2.3   Effect of Standardization on BPO Success Mediated by Relational Governance

The increase in transparency and process uniformity even across firm boundaries that results from standardization not only improves controllability but also facilitates collaboration (Aubert, Patry, & Rivard, 1998; Aubert, Patry, Rivard, & Smith, 2001;

Earl, 1996; Willcocks, Lacity, & Kern, 1999). Thus, we also hypothesize an indirect effect of process standardization on BPO success via relationship factors explained by "RET".

RET has been used as the most appropriate theory to explain inter-organizational behavior (Blau, 1964; Emerson, 1972). It focuses on dyadic exchange relations involving the transfer of resources for mutual benefit of the involved actors. It is based on the notion that the exchanging parties are in mutual agreement about expecting better outcomes from their collaboration than from other forms of exchange (Goles & Chin, 2002). This dyadic focus accentuates collaboration activities between parties that are particularly governed by informally negotiated rules of exchange (Goles & Chin, 2005; Macaulay, 1963).

In the outsourcing literature, RET has been used to analyze different factors to explain relationship aspects. For the purpose of this paper, we adopt the distinction suggested by Goles and Chin (2005) who present a detailed and systematic concep- tualization of relational factors, distinguishing between *attributes* and *processes* of an outsourcing relationship. Attributes are the inherent characteristics or key properties that establish the relationship and contribute to its sustainability and functionality. By contrast, processes are ongoing actions that affect the operational performance of the partnership and also form the attributes. As processes focus on the operational aspects of an outsourcing relationship they can be regarded as the "key factors that create the day-to-day working relationship" (Henderson, 1990).

The most fundamental process in this context is considered to be communication. It enables other dimensions of relationship quality such as conflict resolution, coor- dination, cooperation, or consensus. We adopt the understanding of communication which is most common in outsourcing relationship research and "focuses on the efficacy of information exchange, rather than quantity or amount" (Goles & Chin, 2005). Process standardization facilitates communication about how the business operates (Davenport, 2005; Ramakumar & Cooper, 2004). The positive effect of process standardization on communication particularly applies to business processes across firm boundaries since otherwise the vendor has to learn the process particularities first of all. If standards are used within the business process, the process can be more easily understood by both parties and, thus, facilitate communication about process execu- tion, changes, and improvements. Process standardization therefore gives the BPO venture a common ground for mutual understanding and facilitates information sharing.

Hypothesis R1: Process   standardization   is   positively   associated   with
communication.

Process standardization includes common definitions of metrics, common languages that maintain the integrity of business rules, process logic and data, and flexibility (Ramakumar & Cooper, 2004). By referring to those standard-related process char- acteristics, disparate goals and actions can be better re-aligned to solve day-to-day problems. In other words, standards are an effective instrument to resolve conflicts and ensure consensus (Davenport, 2005; Mohr & Spekman, 1994).

Hypothesis R2: Process standardization is positively associated with consensus.

Exchange partners are facing changing business and technology environments during a BPO venture. Thus, the client and the vendor have to manage the interdependencies between the two entities on an ongoing basis (Mohr & Spekman, 1994). If there are only a few interdependencies or if these interdependencies are of less complexity, coordination between exchange partners is facilitated (Narus & Anderson, 1987; Pfeffer & Salancik, 1978). Using process standards reduces complexity (Davenport, 2005; de Toni & Panizzolo, 1993; Ramakumar & Cooper, 2004) and therefore allows better coordination. Exchange partners can refer to standards to create a mutual understanding and agree on a way forward.

Hypothesis R3: Process standardization is positively associated with coordination.

Since communication is the foundation for any interaction and thus represents the fundament for relational governance, we propose that the effect of process standardization on coordination and consensus is at least partially mediated by the efficacy of communication patterns between the outsourcer firm and the vendor. Several sources showed the close relation between communication quality and consensus (e.g., Kern & Willcocks, 2000; Ring & Van de Ven, 1994) as well as coordination (e.g., Goles & Chin, 2005; Mohr & Spekman, 1994) in B2B relationships.

Hypothesis R4: Communication is positively associated with coordination.
Hypothesis R5: Communication is positively associated with consensus.

Environmental dynamism and complexity require continuous change of structures and processes. If multiple parties are involved in providing a service, a high degree of coordination of activities is necessary to enable a successful B2B relationship (Mohr & Spekman, 1994; Narus & Anderson, 1987; Pfeffer & Salancik, 1978). Therefore, coordination has also been adopted by outsourcing relationship research (Goles & Chin, 2005; Lee & Kim, 1999) in order to identify the elements of relational governance and their impact on outsourcing success.

Hypothesis R6: Coordination is positively associated with BPO success.

Sooner or later, conflicts arise in B2B relationships (Dwyer, Schurr, & Oh, 1987). The way in which conflicts are settled has great implications for future collaboration (Anderson & Narus, 1990; Lee & Kim, 1999; Mohr & Spekman, 1994). Given the complexity and interdependence of business processes, conflict resolution is of particular importance in BPO ventures. Well-defined procedures to resolve conflict enable BPO partners to communicate more effectively, solve problems, and learn from experience. Thus, when both exchange partners often reach consensus, this particularly contributes to the success of the entire BPO venture.

Hypothesis R7: Consensus is positively associated with BPO success.

3   Analysis

The theoretical framework in Fig. 1 has been operationalized and transferred into a structural equation model. Each construct is represented by a set of indicators which were measured on a 7-point Likert scale (from "strongly disagree" to "strongly agree"). Whenever possible, existing measures from prior empirical studies were adopted and sometimes adapted to the application context of this research (i.e., BPO of banking processes). The questionnaire was pre-tested several times with different managers from various banks which were not included in the final sample. This procedure helped to reduce semantic ambiguities and to customize it to the target audience before it was sent out.

In 2005, 2,344 banks were registered for conducting business in Germany, comprising 1,500 savings banks (64%), 445 cooperative banks (19%), and 399 private banks (17%). For the analysis, the 500 largest banks in Germany were chosen, based on their total assets as reported in their balance sheets of the year 2005 (latest available figures at the time of preparing the survey). Four back-office processes were selected as unit of analysis: (1) settlement of securities, (2) processing of consumer credits, (3) credit card settlement, and (4) processing of domestic payments. In 2006, the questionnaire was sent to the banking managers in charge of (one of) these business processes. All banks were first contacted by phone to personally identify the managers responsible for the processes mentioned above. The time period for sending back the completed questionnaires was six weeks from October 30th to December 15th 2006. Managers who had not returned the questionnaire by December 15th were called again and asked whether they needed assistance. This action resulted in an increased quota of responses.

As some banks do not offer all of the four products (processes) to their clients, following the procedure described above 1,931 questionnaires were sent out. Also, as not all processes in all of these banks are outsourced, we asked managers via phone to indicate if the particular business process is externally provided. We received information that processes were outsourced in 761 cases and were not outsourced in 904 cases. The outsourcing status of the remaining 266 remained unknown to us. Overall, 335 usable questionnaires from 215 banks were returned. This represents a response rate of 44.0% among processes and 68.2% among banks given the unknown processes are not outsourced (or else 32.6% among processes and 48.8% among banks).

3.1   Descriptive Data

The cumulated assets of the responses accounted for more than 90% of the total cumulated German banking balance sheet. This is only a rough estimate, as the questionnaire asked for the sum of assets on an interval scale to ensure anonymity. The response rate amongst large banks (assets > EUR 20 bn) was exceptionally high (60.4%). The outsourcing duration ranges from early ventures starting in the 1960s to late adopters in 2006 (median = 2001). The distribution of the banking groups (savings banks, cooperative banks and private banks) in the sample nearly matches the distribution in the market.

3.2 Measurement

The assessment and estimation of the research model was done using Partial Least Squares (PLS) (Chin, 1998; Wold, 1985). PLS is particularly suitable if a more exploratory analysis close to the empirical data is preferred. All PLS calculations were carried out using SmartPLS Version 2 M3 (http://www.smartpls.de).

3.2.1 Measurement Model

Most of the model elements (all but "BPO success") have been measured in a reflective way; the indicators can be found in Appendix as well as the test results of the measurement models. Only BPO success has been measured formatively, consisting of five different aspects of BPO success.

The quality of the reflective measurement models is determined by the following criteria (Bagozzi, 1979; Bagozzi & Phillips, 1982; Churchill, 1979; Peter, 1981):

- *Reliability* is analyzed by indicator reliability and construct reliability (Peter, 1981). Indicator reliability was examined by looking at the construct loadings. In the model tested, all loadings are significant at the 0.01 level and above the recommended 0.7 parameter value (significance tests were conducted using bootstrapping (Chin, 1998) with 1,000 re-samples).
- *Convergent Validity* was tested using two indices: (1) the composite reliability (CR) and (2) the average variance extracted (AVE). All estimated indices are above the threshold of 0.6 for CR (Bagozzi & Yi, 1988) and 0.5 for AVE (Chin, 1998) (cf. Appendix).
- *Discriminant Validity* of the construct items is analyzed by comparing the cross-loadings. They are obtained by correlating the component scores of each latent variable with both their respective blocks of indicators and all other items that are included in the model (Chin, 1998). As depicted in Appendix, the loading of each indicator is higher for its respective construct than for any other construct. In addition, it is confirmed that each construct loads highest with its own items. Therefore, the indicators of different constructs are not interchangeable, resembling discriminant validity. Moreover, the square roots of AVE are higher than the respective inter-construct correlations (cf. Appendix).

BPO success was measured using a formative measurement model. Formative measurement models risk disregarding substantial elements forming BPO success. To meet this peril, we measured BPO success both in a formative and in a reflective way, trying to capture all relevant arguments for BPO as formative indicators (like process cost savings, cost transparency, quality improvement, access to external know-how, core competence focus etc.). Linking the formatively measured BPO success construct to the reflectively measured one showed that the formative measurement model has high external validity (i.e., very strong and highly significant relationship, Fig. 2).

In the research model, we shortened the measurement model of BPO success to those success arguments which still showed weights larger than 0.05. (cf. Appendix

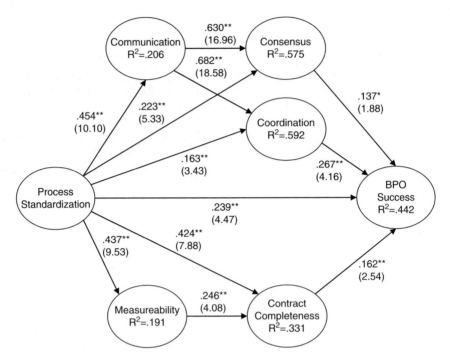

Fig. 2 Development of measurement model for BPO success

for the complete list of indicators and measurement results). Nevertheless, using all formative indicators in the main model did not lead to major changes. Moreover, using the reflective measurement model in the main model yielded structurally identical test results (but higher R^2 and more significant path coefficients).

3.3 Structural Model

After validating the measurement model, the hypothesized relationships between the constructs can be tested. A bootstrapping with 1,000 samples has been conducted which showed that most of the hypotheses are supported with an error probability of less than 0.01 (all but R7: consensus → BPO success). As shown in Fig. 3, the standardized path coefficients range from 0.137 to 0.682 while the R^2 is moderate (between 0.191 and 0.592) (Chin, 1998) for all endogenous constructs.

Analyzing the individual effect size (f^2) (Chin, 1998; Cohen, Cohen, West, & Aiken, 2003) revealed that all independent variables have a moderate effect on their dependent variables. Overall, the key construct of our research, process standardization shows a total effect of 0.522 on BPO success.

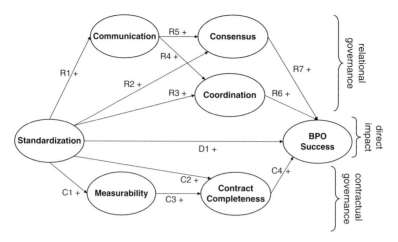

Fig. 3   Research model results ($^{**}p \leq 0.01$, $^{*}p \leq 0.1$, *t*-values in brackets)

3.4   Effect of Control Variables

In order to control for the influence of distinctive characteristics within the sample, we considered several control variables like business process type, size of the bank (total assets), contract duration, and deal volume. Almost all of the results remained unaffected. Subgroup analyses on different process types revealed that the test results on the hypotheses derived from RET are weaker and can become insignificant in case of testing on particular business processes (process standardization → consensus (R2), process standardization → coordination (R3), consensus → BPO success (R7)). Nevertheless, non-significance of R2 and R3 can be explained by the strong mediator effect of communication on the relationship between process standardization and consensus or coordination, respectively.

3.5   Common Method Bias Assessment

We evaluated possible common method bias following the procedure recommended by Podsakoff, MacKenzie, Lee, and Podsakoff (2003). This procedure specifies, besides theoretical constructs, a common method construct whose indicators include all the indicators used in the empirical research model. We then assessed the variance explained by the common method construct relative to that explained by the substantive constructs. As shown in Table 7 in Appendix, the average explained variance by the substantive constructs is 0.72 while the average variance explained by the common method construct is 0.03. This analysis supports the conclusion that common methods bias did not significantly affect our results, although one has always to be aware that no statistical analysis procedure can guarantee the absence of common method bias.

Table 1 Explanatory power of different theoretical lenses (cumulated effects)

PCE perspective	Direct effect of process standardization on BPO success	0.239
TCE perspective	Effect of process standardization on BPO success is mediated by contractual governance	0.086
RET perspective	Effect of process standardization on BPO success is mediatedby relational governance	0.228
	Total effect (sum):	0.522

3.6 Differential Impact of Theoretical Arguments

After testing the overall model, we tested alternative reduced models for capturing the mediating effects. First, a very basic model was tested, just consisting of the direct link between process standardization and BPO success (D1). In this case, the R^2 of BPO success drops down to 0.291, driven by a quite high path coefficient of 0.54.

In a second step, we tested a model which considers the direct effect and the mediation by contractual governance (i.e., D1, C1–C4). As a result, the R^2 increased to 0.368 (compared to 0.442 in the total model), but nevertheless shows a strong explanation of BPO success via the direct link (D1).

Looking at the total effects of process standardization on BPO success through different theoretical lenses leads to the results in Table 1.

The basic PCE argument as well as the RET perspective both provide a substantial degree of explanation on the relation between process standardization and BPO success, with the contractual perspective showing a weaker but still significant impact.

4 Key Findings and Limitations

The results show that process standardization has a significant impact both directly and indirectly on outsourcing success. The direct impact can be explained from the PCE perspective by arguing that the vendor will only be able to achieve an efficient cost basis by generating economies of scale if it can provide one standardized process to all clients. Therefore, process standardization is a critical requirement from the vendor's perspective and in turn for the outsourcing organization. As there are very few standards for business processes available (Davenport, 2005), unification of process activities is a challenge of particular importance in BPO environments.

There are two indirect effects of process standardization on outsourcing success. First, process standardization is mediated by relational governance. Specifically, communication, coordination, and consensus are positively affected by process standardization. Using process standards allows a better understanding about how the business operates and can be improved. This facilitates communication and coordination between exchange partners and allows re-aligning disparate goals and actions to solve day-to-day problems. These findings show that process standardization increases the effectiveness of relational governance. Standardized business processes are therefore of special importance in outsourcing ventures where the outsourcer relies on relational governance mechanisms. This particularly applies for outsourcing ventures with high business and/or technological uncertainty where contractual provisions can hardly be designed. This has been identified as main characteristic and thereby major challenge of BPO ventures (Aron et al., 2005).

The second indirect effect can be explained using a TCE perspective. Process standardization implies better process documentation and transparency and thus leads to higher measurability of process output and to an easier implementation of performance control points throughout the business process. Thus, more complete contracts can be designed and negotiated between the exchange partners.

Considering our findings for indirect effects of process standardization on outsourcing success, we conclude that process standardization can be regarded as a driver of both effective contractual and relational governance. There might be different reasons why organizations rely on both or on just one of these governance approaches but process standardization plays an important role in either way. Moreover, the results contribute to the understanding that governance arrangements should consider certain contingency factors (Sambamurthy & Zmud, 1999) as different approaches are required in different situations (Donaldson, 2001). Specifically, the degree of process standardization should be considered when governance approaches are designed.

There are several limitations. For one, literature regarding the impact of process standardization is almost nonexistent. In standardization research (that has largely focused on data and compatibility standards), determining the value of a standard has remained an open issue for decades. Looking at process standards, things seem to be even worse as there is no clear understanding of what constitutes a process standard. In this paper, we use an operationalization of "process standardization" that unfortunately cannot build on earlier work too much. We are also not able to foster the operationalization of process standardization by analyzing how standardization has or has not been achieved as we do not have sufficient data on causes or drivers of standardization. In addition and as always the case with cross-sectional survey data, statements about causality are limited as we have measured the exogenous and endogenous variables simultaneously. Apart from the difficulties in explicating the advantages of standardization, we neglected possible disadvantages like a loss of individuality and its potential business impact.

An interesting theoretical path for further research is to strengthen hypotheses C1–4 by adapting arguments from organizational control theory (e.g., Ouchi, 1979) to outsourcing: the appropriate use of three control mechanisms – input, behavior and output oriented – is seen as a function of two contextual characteristics, outcome measurability and task programmability. Task programmability – or in our context the control part of the standardization impact – refers to transparent definitions of behaviors to be performed (Govindarajan & Fisher, 1990). Therefore and with respect to transparency, task programmability is very similar to process standardization. Programmable activities can be monitored more easily and corrective action can be taken if necessary when task programmability is high. Thus, high programmability allows behavior-based control including process rules and procedural norms, e.g., development methodologies, job descriptions and organizational hierarchies. If programmable tasks go along with measurable outcomes, output controls can be applied as well: performance measures – such as target dates, budgets, milestones and expected levels of performance – are developed in order to determine service excellence. As outsourcing contracts may contain behavior and output-related control mechanisms (Macneil, 1974) one could argue that this study has successfully applied organizational control theory to a BPO context and expanded it with respect to the relations among contingencies, i.e., that process standardization/task programmability increases the measurement ability and measurability serves as mediator for the impact of process standardization/task programmability on contract completeness.

5 Conclusion

Our analysis suggests that process standardization is quite solidly related to BPO success. Using PCE arguments, our data support the expected direct influence as a vendor needs to standardize insourced business processes in order to reap scale economies. Adding a TCE and RET view we can also show indirect effects from process standardization via relational and contractual governance to BPO success. Thus, the main contribution of this paper is an empirically validated model revealing the threefold impact of process standardization on BPO success.

Encouraged by the results and by recent discussions on the topic with academics and practitioners alike, we expect the issue of standardization and BPO to gain substantial momentum as the debate on modularization and service orientation gathers pace and opens interesting future research questions: what is the interplay between process modularity and process standardization? How can, then, process standardization be measured when the process parts get increasingly encapsulated and develop towards granular (standardized) and quality checked business functions or "services" in a true service-oriented paradigm? Davenport expects this to "lead to commoditization and outsourcing on a massive scale" (Davenport, 2005, p. 100). We thus expect contributions aligning arguments from the literature on standards, services and outsourcing focusing on the business impact of standards and distributed service delivery to be more relevant than ever.

Acknowledgments We are greatly indebted to Jens Dibbern for his thoughtful comments and suggestions that helped us to substantially improve this paper. Also, we would kike to thank Rudy Hirschheim, Armin Heinzl, and the participants of the ICOIS 2007 conference for their valuable support. We are also grateful for the financial support of the E-Finance Lab.

Appendix

Tables 2–7

Table 2 Used indicators

Construct	Label	Indicator (fully disagree (1).... fully agree (7))	Selected references
Degree of process standardization	stan1	The activities of the process are transparent and comprehensible	Davenport (2005), Phelps (2006), and Ramakumar and Cooper (2004), Weitzel, Beimborn, and König (2005), and Wüllenweber and Weitzel (2007)
	stan2	Process can easily be learned via documentation and trainings	
	stan3	The outsourced process is highly standardized	
BPO success	suc1	We achieved the BPO goal of reducing processing costs	Gewald (2006), Goles (2001), Grover, Cheon, and Teng (1996), Lee and Kim (1999), Lee,Miranda, and Kim (2004), and Saunders, Gebelt, & Hu (1997)
	suc2	We achieved the BPO goal of increasing cost transparency	
	suc3	We achieved the BPO goal of improving quality	
	suc4	We achieved the BPO goal of utilizing externl know-how	
	suc5	We achieved the BPO goal of focusing on our core competencies	
Measurability	mea1	Appropriate SLAs can be defined	Govindarajan and Fisher (1990), Kirsch (1996), and Ouchi (1979)
	mea2	Process execution can be easily controlled	
	mea3	Control of process output is easily possible	
Contract completeness	cc1	The outsourcing contract covers all our requirements and expectations	Aubert et al. (2003), Goo, Kim, & Cho (2006), and Poppo and Zenger (2002)
	cc2	The contract regulates all tasks and responsibilities within the outsourcing project	
	cc3	The outsourcing contract is very detailed and precisely defined	
	cc4	The outsourcing contract is complete, extensions are not necessary	
Communication	com1	Our vendor and we provide each other with sufficient information to perform the process	Anderson and Narus (1990), Dyer and Singh (1998), Hansen (2002), Heide and John (1992), Uzzi (1997), and Goles (2001)

(continued)

Table 2 (continued)

Construct	Label	Indicator (fully disagree (1)....fully agree (7))	Selected references
	com2	Our vendor and we effectively exchange information with each other	
	com3	Our vendor and we communicate well with each other and discuss at eye level	
Coordination	coord1	Activities are aligned between both parties	Goles (2001), Kern and Willcocks (2000, 2002), Lee and Kim (1999), and Mohr and Spekman (1994)
	coord2	We cooperate well with each other	
	coord3	There are periodical meetings for adjusting expected and actual service	
Consensus	cons1	The provider and we are able to find solutions for any problem which are satisfying from both partners' perspectives	Goles (2001), Kanter (1994), and Ring and Van de Ven (1994)
	cons2	Critical situations get discussed in an open and solution-oriented manner	
	cons3	Conflicts get solved in consensually	

Table 3 Indicator and construct reliability of reflectively measured constructs

Construct	CR	AVE	Indicator	Loading	t-Value
Process standardization	0.853	0.660	stan1	0.853	50.273
			stan2	0.755	22.089
			stan3	0.826	33.931
Measureability	0.941	0.843	mea1	0.849	30.874
			mea2	0.949	106.454
			mea3	0.953	160.083
Contract completeness	0.914	0.728	cc1	0.891	66.916
			cc2	0.924	55.598
			cc3	0.724	16.296
			cc4	0.860	39.238
Communication	0.953	0.871	com1	0.930	97.949
			com2	0.962	178.340
			com3	0.908	75.592
Coordination	0.932	0.872	coord1	0.923	89.092
			coord2	0.945	135.364
Consensus	0.946	0.855	cons1	0.907	74.953
			cons2	0.917	63.238
			cons3	0.950	149.525

Table 4 Indicator and construct reliability of formatively measured construct

Construct	Indicator	Weight	t-Value
BPO success	suc1	0.649	6.564
	suc2	0.403	4.143
	suc3	0.079	1.003
	suc4	0.065	0.715
	suc5	0.126	1.618

Table 5 Inter-construct correlations (diagonal shows square root of AVE)

	Process stan.	Measure-ability	Contract comp.	Communi-cation	Coordination	Consensus
Process standardization	0.812					
Measureability	0.437	0.918				
Contract completeness	0.532	0.433	0.853			
Communication	0.454	0.440	0.563	0.933		
Coordination	0.473	0.430	0.603	0.756	0.934	
Consensus	0.509	0.472	0.649	0.732	0.749	0.924

Table 6 Cross-loadings of reflectively measured construct

	Contract completeness	Measure-ability	Process standardization	Communi-cation	Consensus	Coordination
Cc1	**0.891397**	0.465489	0.496210	0.560958	0.675283	0.637138
Cc2	**0.923650**	0.418426	0.520090	0.518580	0.589260	0.565489
Cc3	**0.724437**	0.223945	0.325325	0.302573	0.327773	0.310900
Cc4	**0.859949**	0.304813	0.433824	0.481511	0.542308	0.463302
mea1	0.313249	**0.849059**	0.331902	0.331030	0.384677	0.348790
mea2	0.420823	**0.948667**	0.405711	0.418692	0.444602	0.402102
mea3	0.441538	**0.952681**	0.451910	0.449111	0.463450	0.426622
stan1	0.472801	0.415562	**0.852784**	0.459238	0.501969	0.474566
stan2	0.360606	0.302647	**0.754549**	0.303383	0.365748	0.328355
stan3	0.450172	0.330736	**0.826067**	0.319350	0.352616	0.327533
com1	0.520361	0.401394	0.393227	**0.929810**	0.627867	0.685737
com2	0.551335	0.403665	0.444794	**0.961545**	0.687479	0.710741
com3	0.504312	0.425819	0.429246	**0.907730**	0.728355	0.718848
cons1	0.625988	0.442902	0.489688	0.670003	**0.906766**	0.732971
cons2	0.561044	0.427471	0.465680	0.646520	**0.916576**	0.630784
con3	0.611888	0.437813	0.456221	0.711831	**0.949576**	0.710760
coord1	0.542152	0.392915	0.403091	0.660014	0.619078	**0.922923**
coord2	0.581909	0.409583	0.474966	0.747221	0.768662	**0.945055**

K. Wuellenweber et al.

Table 7 Common method bias assessment

		construct	(construct)²	CMB	(CMB)²
Communication	commu1	0.92	0.85	−0.10	0.01
	commu2	0.98	0.96	−0.01	0.00
	commu3	0.8	0.64	**0.12**	0.01
Consensus	cons1	0.81	0.66	**0.11**	0.01
	cons2	0.91	0.83	−0.11	0.01
	cons3	0.95	0.90	0.00	0.00
BPO success	bporea1	0.52	0.27	**0.31**	0.10
	bporea2	0.56	0.31	**0.23**	0.05
	bporea3	0.88	0.77	−0.14	0.02
	bporea4	0.92	0.85	−0.28	0.08
	bporea5	0.75	0.56	−0.13	0.02
Contract Completeness	cc19	0.61	0.37	**0.32**	0.10
	cc20	0.84	0.71	**0.10**	0.01
	cc21	0.959	0.92	−0.36	0.13
	cc22	0.94	0.88	−0.09	0.01
Measurability	mea1	0.92	0.85	0.09	0.01
	mea2	0.94	0.88	0.01	0.00
	mea3	0.9	0.81	0.07	0.00
Standardization	standar1	0.71	0.50	**0.16**	0.03
	standar2	0.88	0.77	**0.12**	0.01
	standar3	0.86	0.74	−0.04	0.00
Coordination	coord1	0.95	0.90	−0.14	0.02
	coord2	0.82	0.67	**0.14**	0.02
	Average		0.72		0.03

References

Anderson, J., & Narus, J. (1990). A model of distributor firm and manufacturer firm working partnerships. *Journal of Marketing, 54*(1), 42–58.

Ang, S., & Straub, D. (1998). Production and transaction economies and IS outsourcing: A study of the U.S. Banking Industry. *MIS Quarterly, 4*, 535–552.

Aron, R., Clemons, E. K., & Reddi, S. (2005). Just right outsourcing: Understanding and managing risk. *Journal of Management Information Systems, 22*(2), 37–55.

Aubert, B. A., Houde, J.-F., Patry, M., & Rivard, S. (2003). Characteristics of IT outsourcing contracts. *36th Hawaii International Conference on System Sciences, Hawaii, 2003.*

Aubert, B. A., Patry, M., & Rivard, S. (1998). Assessing the risk of IT outsourcing. *31st Hawaii International Conference on System Sciences, 1998.*

Aubert, B. A., Patry, M., Rivard, S., & Smith, H. (2001). IT outsourcing risk management at British petroleum. *34th Hawaii International Conference on System Sciences, 2001.*

Auguste, B. G., Hao, Y., Singer, M., & Wiegand, M. (2002). The other side of outsourcing. *McKinsey Quarterly, 1*, 52–63.

Bagozzi, R. P. (1979). The role of measurement in theory construction and hypothesis testing: Toward a holistic model. In O. C. Ferrell, S. W. Brown, & C. W. Lamb (Eds.), *Conceptual and theoretical developments in marketing* (pp. 15–32). Chicago: American Marketing Association.

Bagozzi, R. P., & Phillips, L. (1982). Representing and testing organizational theories: A holistic construal. *Administrative Science Quarterly, 27*(September), 459–489.

Bagozzi, R. P., & Yi, Y. (1988). On the evaluation of structural equation models. *Journal of the Academy of Marketing Science, 16*, 74–94.

Baumol, W. J., Panzar, J. C., & Willig, R. D. (1982). *Contestable market and the theory of industry*. New York: Structure Harcourt Brace Jovanovich, Inc.

Blau, P. M. (1964). *Exchange and power in social life*. New York: Wiley.

Borman, M. (2006). Applying multiple perspectives to the BPO decision: A case study of call centres in Australia. *Journal of Information Technology, 21*, 99–115.

Braun, M. (2004). Vom IT- zum business process outsourcing. *Bankmagazin, 53*(2), 22.

Cachon, G., & Harker, P. (2002). Competition and outsourcing with scale economies. *Management Science, 48*(10), 1314–1333.

Chin, W. W. (1998). The partial least squares approach to structural equation modeling. In G. A. Marcoluides (Ed.), *Modern methods for business research* (pp. 295–336). London: Lawrence Erlbaum Associates.

Churchill, G. (1979). A paradigm for developing better measures of marketing constructs. *Journal of Marketing, 16*(February), 64–73.

Cohen, J., Cohen, P., West, S. G., & Aiken, L. S. (2003). Applied multiple regression/correlation analysis for the behavioral sciences. London: Lawrence Erlbaum Associates.

Davenport, T. (2005). The coming commoditization of processes. *Harvard Business Review,* June, 100–108.

Davenport, T. H., & Short, J. E. (1990). The new industrial engineering: Information technology and business process redesign. *Sloan Management Review, 31*(4), 11–27.

Dayasindhu, N. (2004). *Information technology enabled process outsourcing and reengineering: Case study of a mortgage bank*. New York: Proceedings of the Americas Conference on Information Systems.

De Toni, A., & Panizzolo, R. (1993). Product and process standardization in intermittent and repetitive production. *Journal of Production Research, 31*(6), 12–32.

De Vries, H. (1999). *Standardization*. Boston: Kluwer Academic.

Donaldson, L. (2001). *The contingency theory of organizations*. Thousand Oaks, CA: Sage.

Dwyer, F. R., Schurr, P. H., & Oh, S. (1987). Developing Buyer–Seller relationships. *Journal of Marketing, 51*(2), 11–27.

Dyer, J. H., Singh, H. (1998). The relational view: Cooperative strategy and sources of interorganizational competitive advantage. *Academy of Management Review, 23*(4), 660–679.

Earl, M. J. (1996). The risks of outsourcing IT. *Sloan Management Review*, Spring, 26–32.

Emerson, R. M. (1972). Exchange theory part I and II. In J. Berger, M. Zelditch, & B. Anderson (Eds.), *Sociological theories in progress* (pp. 38–87).

Feenstra, R.C., & Hanson, G. H. (2003). Ownership and control in outsourcing to China: Estimating the property rights theory of the firm. *The Quarterly Journal of Economics, 120*(2), 729–761.

Feeny, D. F., Willcocks, L. P., & Lacity, M. C. (2003). *Business process outsourcing: The promise of the 'Enterprise Partnership' model*. Oxford: Templeton Executive Briefing, Templeton College, University of Oxford.

Fomin, V., & Lyytinen, K. (2000). How to distribute a cake before cutting it into pieces: Alice in Wonderland or radio engineers' gang in the Nordic countries? In K. Jakobs (Ed.), *Information technology standards and standardization: A global perspective* (pp. 222–239). Hershey, PA: IGI Publishing.

Ford, D., & Farmer, D. (1986). Make or buy – A key strategic issue. *Long Range Planning, 19*(5), 54–62.

Gewald, H. (2006). *Assessing the benefits and risks of business process outsourcing in the German banking industry*. Frankfurt am Main.

Gewald, H., Wüllenweber, K., & Weitzel, T. (2006). The influence of perceived risks on banking managers' intention to outsource business processes – A study of the German banking and finance industry. *Journal of Electronic Commerce Research, 7*(2), 78–96.

Goles, T. (2001). *The impact of the client–vendor relationship on information systems outsourcing success* (p. 230). Houston: University of Houston.

Goles, T., & Chin, W. W. (2002). Relational exchange theory and IS outsourcing: Developing a scale to measure relationship factors. In R. Hirschheim, A. Heinzl, J. Dibbern (Eds.), *Information systems outsourcing* (pp. 221–250). Berlin: Springer.

Goles, T., & Chin, W. W. (2005). Information systems outsourcing relationship factors: Detailed conceptualization and initial evidence. *The Data Base for Advances in Information Systems, 36*(4), 47–67.

Goo, J., Kim, D. J., & Cho, B. (2006). Structure of service level agreements (SLA) in IT outsourcing: The construct and its measurement. *Twelfth Americas Conference on Information Systems, Acapulco, Mexico, 2006.*

Gottfredson, R., Puryear, R., & Phillips, S. (2005). Strategic sourcing from periphery to the core. *Harvard Business Review, 83*(2), 132–139.

Govindarajan, V., & Fisher, J. (1990). Strategy, control systems, and resource sharing: Effects on business-unit performance. *Academy of Management Journal, 33*(2), 259–285.

Grover, V., Cheon, M., & Teng, J. (1996). The effect of service quality and partnership on the outsourcing of information systems functions. *Journal of Management Information Systems, 12*(4), 89–116.

Gurbaxani, V. (1996). The new world of information technology outsourcing. *Communications of the ACM, 39*(7 July), 45–46.

Halvey, J. K., & Melby, B. M. (1996). Information technology outsourcing transactions: Processes, strategies, and contracts. New York: Wiley.

Hansen, M. T. (2002). Knowledge networks: Explaining effective knowledge sharing in multiunit companies. *Organization Science, 13*(3), 232–248.

Hart, O., & Moore, J. E. (1990). Property rights and the nature of the firm. *Journal of Political Economy, 98*(6), 1119–1158.

Heide, J. B., & John, G. (1992). Do norms matter in marketing relationships? *Journal of Marketing, 56*(2), 32–44.

Henderson, J. C. (1990). Plugging into strategic partnerships: The critical IS connection. *Sloan Management Review, 31*(3), 7–18.

Kanter, R. (1994). Collaborative advantage: The art of alliances. *Harvard Business Review, 72*(4), 96–108.

Kern, T., & Willcocks, L. (2002). Exploring relationships in information technology outsourcing: The interaction approach. *European Journal of Information Systems, 11*, 3–19.

Kern, T., & Willcocks, L. P. (2000). Exploring information technology outsourcing relationships: Theory and practice. *Journal of Strategic Information Systems, 9*, 321–350.

Kirsch, L. J. (1996). The management of complex tasks in organizations: Controlling the systems development process. *Organization Science, 7*(1), 1–21.

Lancellotti, R., Schein, O., Spang, S., & Stadler, V. (2003). ICT and operations outsourcing in banking. *Wirtschaftsinformatik, 45*(2), 131–141.

Langlois, R. (1995). Capabilities and coherence in firms and markets. In C. A. Montgomery (Ed.), *Resource-based and evolutionary theories of the firm: Towards a synthesis* (pp. 71–100). Boston, MA: Kluwer.

Lee, J.-N., & Kim, Y.-G. (1997). Information systems outsourcing strategies for affiliated firms of the Korean Conglomerate Groups. *Journal of Strategic Information Systems, 6*(3), 203–229.

Lee, J.-N., & Kim, Y.-G. (1999). Effect of partnership quality on IS outsourcing success: Conceptual framework and empirical validation. *Journal of Management Information Systems, 15*(4), 29–61.

Lee, J. N., Miranda, S., & Kim, Y.-M. (2004). IT outsourcing strategies: Universalistic, contingency, and configurational explanations of success. *Information Systems Research, 15*(2), 110–131.

Loh, L., & Venkatraman, N. (1992). Determinants of information technology outsourcing: A cross-sectional analysis. *Journal of Management Information Systems, 9*(1), 7–24.

Loh, L., & Venkatraman, N. (1995). An empirical study of information technology outsourcing: Benefits, risk and performance implications. *Sixteenth International Conference on Information Systems, Amsterdam, 1995* (pp. 277–288).

Macaulay, S. (1963). Non-contractual relations in business: A preliminary study. *American Sociological Review, 28*(1), 55–67.

MacNeil, I. R. (1974). The many futures of contracts. *Southern California Law Review, 47*(3), 691–816.

Mani, D., Barua, A., & Whinston, A. B. (2006). Successfully governing business process outsourcing relationships. *MIS Quarterly Executive, 5*(1), 15–29.

Manrodt, K. B., & Vitasek, K. (2004). Global process standardization: A case study. *Journal of Business Logistics, 25*(1), 1–23.

Milgrom, P., & Roberts, J. (1992). *Economics, organization and management.* Englewood Cliffs, NJ: Prentice-Hall.

Mohr, J., & Spekman, R. (1994). Characteristics of partnership success: Partnership attributes, communication behavior, and conflict resolution techniques. *Strategic Management Journal, 15*(2), 135–152.

Murray, J. D., & White, R. W. (1983). Economies of scale and economies of scope in multiproduct financial institutions: A study of British Columbia Credit Unions. *Journal of Finance, 38*, 887–902.

Nam, K., Rajagopalan, S., Rao, H. R., & Chaudhurry, A. (1996). A two-level investigation of information systems outsourcing. *Communications of the ACM, 39*(7), 37–44.

Narus, J., & Anderson, J. (1987). Distribution contributions to partnerships with manufacturers. *Business Horizons, 30*, 34–42.

Ouchi, W. G. (1979). A conceptual framework for the design of organizational control mechanisms. *Management Science, 25*(9), 833–848.

Peter, J. (1981). Reliability: A review of psychometric basics and recent marketing practices. *Journal of Marketing Research, 16*(February), 6–17.

Pfeffer, J., & Salancik, G. R. (1978). The external control of organizations. Boston: Pittman.

Phelps, R. (2006). Process standards: Pursuing best practices. *Controlling Engineering, 53*, 69–74.

Podsakoff, P. M., MacKenzie, S. B., Lee, J.-Y., & Podsakoff, N. P. (2003). Common method biases in behavioral research: A critical review of the literature and recommended remedies. *Journal of Applied Psychology, 88*(5), 879–903.

Poppo, L., & Zenger, T. (1998). Testing alternative theories of the firm: Transaction cost, knowledge-based, and measurement explanation for make-or-buy decisions in information services. *Strategic Management Journal, 19*(9), 853–877.

Poppo, L., & Zenger, T. (2002). Do formal contracts and relational governance function as substitutes or complements? *Strategic Management Journal, 23*(8), 707–725.

Porter, M. E. (1985). Competitive advantage. New York: The Free Press.

Prahalad, C. K., & Hamel, G. (1990). The core competence of the corporation. *Harvard Business Review, 68*, May–June, 79–91.

Ramakumar, A., & Cooper, B. (2004). Process standardization proves profitable. *Quality, 43*(2), 42–45.

Ring, P., & Van De Ven, A. H. (1994). Developmental processes of cooperative interorganizational relationships. *Academy of Management Review, 19*(1), 90–118.

Rouse, A. C., & Corbitt, B. (2004). IT-supported business process outsourcing (BPO): The good, the bad and the ugly. *Eight Pacific Asia Conference on Information Systems, Shanghai, China, 2004.*

Sambamurthy, V., & Zmud, R. W. (1999). Arrangements for information technology governance: A theory of multiple contingencies. *MIS Quarterly, 23*(2), 261–290.

Saunders, C., Gebelt, M., & Hu, Q. (1997). Achieving success in information systems qutsourcing. *California Management Review, 39*(2), 63–80.

Swaminathan, J.M. (2001). Enabling customization using standardized operations. California Management Review 43 (3), 125–135.

Uzzi, B. (1997). *Social structure and competition in interfirm networks: The paradox of embeddedness. Administrative Science Quarterly, 42*(1), 35–67.

Weitzel, T., Beimborn, D., & König, W. (2005). A unified economic model of standard diffusion: The impact of standardization cost, network effects, and network topology. *MIS Quarterly, 30*, 489–514.

Willcocks, L., Hindle, J., Feeny, D. F., & Lacity, M. C. (2004). IT and business process outsourcing: The knowledge potential. *Information Systems Management, 21*, 7–15.

Willcocks, L. P., Lacity, M. C., & Kern, T. (1999). Risk mitigation in IT outsourcing strategy revisited: Longitudinal case research at LISA. *Journal of Strategic Information Systems, 8*(3), 285–314.

Williamson, O. E. (1975). Markets and hierarchies: Analysis and antitrust implications. A study in the economics of internal organization. London: Free Press.

Wold, H. (1985). *Partial least squares*. New York: Wiley.

Wüllenweber, K., & Weitzel, T. (2007). An empirical exploration of how process standardization reduces outsourcing risk. *Proceedings of the 40th Hawaii International Conference on System Sciences (HICSS40), Hawaii, USA, 2007*.

Offshore Business Process Outsourcing to India: Two Australian SME Case Studies

Kevan Penter and Graham Pervan

1 Introduction

The Australian economy currently faces labour and skill shortages and an aging work force, a legacy of ineffective education and training practices plus a strong economy. As a result, Australian medium and large firms require a global sourcing strategy in order to continue to grow and create value for shareholders. A significant source of expert labour is India and offshore business process outsourcing (BPO) by Australian firms to India increasingly requires systematic analysis by Australian managers (Barrett, 2007). In this paper we present a brief history of BPO in India and discuss two case studies of small to medium sized Australian organizations which have chosen to offshore significant parts of their operation to Bangalore, India. The research results may be of interest to Australian managers, government policy makers, academics in business and information systems management and their counterparts in India.

2 Business Process Outsourcing

BPO is defined as handing over to a third party responsibility for performing certain business processes that are required for an organization to carry out its mission. In defining BPO, some researchers view IT outsourcing (ITO) as a subset (Willcocks, Lacity, & Cullen, 2006; Robinson & Kalakota, 2004), so for the purposes of this research, BPO is defined as the outsourcing of any knowledge-intensive business process, including ITO. BPO can apply to various 'back office' functions, which can include human resources, finance and accounting, processing of insurance and credit transactions, procurement, and IT services (Grant, 2005; Davies 2004; Feeny, Lacity, & Willcocks, 2003, 2005). Common to many of these back office processes is that they are IT-intensive. In the past fifteen years, academic research on ITO has expanded significantly (Dibbern, Goles, Hirschheim, & Jayatilaka, 2004; Willcocks et al.), but published research on both offshore ITO and BPO is limited, particularly on Australian organizations.

R. Hirschheim et al. (eds), *Information Systems Outsourcing,*
© Springer-Verlag Berlin Heidelberg 2009

Offshoring originally referred to a business decision to employ workers in another country to do the work once done by locals. It is a global expression of 'outsourcing' as companies in western countries increasingly consider outsourcing business processes that do not contribute to competitive advantage, or are not regarded as a fundamental part of their value chain (Davies, 2004; Grant, 2005). Increasingly the 'Offshoring' model is moving up the value chain – to more core business functions - as businesses become more confident and knowledgeable and India becomes more capable at providing skilled, competent and motivated labour (Bhargava & Bhatia, 2005).

A key business driver for offshore outsourcing is the ability to arbitrage lower cost, skilled labour in countries such as India (Davies, 2004; Grant, 2005). Other reasons include:

- Access to a pool of highly skilled professionals
- Access to special expertise not easily obtained in the home country
- Relieving resource constraints
- Focus on core competencies
- Cycle time reduction in both processes and projects (which deliver market entry advantage)
- Using time zones to advantage

India currently dominates as the country that is the destination for most offshore BPO (Carmel & Agarwal, 2002; Davies, 2004; Friedman, 2006; Grant, 2005). Carmel and Agarwal conclude that India dominates offshore ITO because of the following advantages:

- Low-cost skilled labour
- Large supply of skilled professionals
- English-speaking workforce
- High quality work processes
- ITO industry structure in India
- Effective support from both Union and State Governments
- Scalability

For Australian companies, offshore outsourcing of business processes to service providers in India is a controversial practice (Hughes, 2007). There is evidence that successful management of BPO to Indian service providers can have a transformational impact on the growth prospects and performance of Australian firms. On the other hand, BPO by Australian firms to Indian service providers is claimed to result in the transfer of Australian jobs overseas (Grant, 2005).

3 A Brief History of the BPO Industry in India

India has been recognized for almost two decades as a source of expertise and capability in information technology outsourcing. BPO draws upon similar skills and capabilities from the deep Indian talent pool of highly qualified, well-trained,

IT-literate, English-speaking professionals. The genesis of the BPO industry in India appears to have been decisions in the mid-1990s by global multinationals such as McKinsey, American Express, British Airways and GE to utilize India as a centre for their 'back office' processes. From 1995 onwards, American Express (Amex) established a significant BPO operation in India at its Global Infrastructure Operation at Gurgaon just outside the capital Delhi.

British Airways (BA) was also an early participant in both IT and BPO in India, commencing in 1996. Building upon its decades-long presence and substantial operational experience in India, BA steadily increased its involvement in both ITO and BPO from 1997 onwards. BA outsourced IT activity to NIIT Technologies through 'arm's length contracts' and conducted BPO through a captive operation in Mumbai (Eddington, 2006; Marshall, 2005). Initially, the offshore ITO by BA had three objectives:

- Augment UK-based IT development teams with skilled Indian resources
- Reduce the costs of major software development projects
- Address staffing shortages resulting from a lack of programmers with skills in the legacy airline software protocol Transaction Processing Facility

BA was able to leverage the training and education capabilities within the NIIT Group to increase rapidly the pool of IT and BPO professionals in India with in-depth understanding of the airline business and of the specific requirements of BA. With India 4.5h ahead of UK time, BA was also able to hand problems off from UK at the close of business and receive a solution back from India at the start of the next business day (Eddington, 2006).

Two business drivers for offshore BPO were the strong growth in the US economy in the late 1990s which, together with demographic trends, meant that firms such as GE Capital had difficulty finding enough skilled workers to perform back office transaction processing, and the potential for significant reductions in operating costs through labour arbitrage. These trends are considered by some analysts to have generated critical mass in the BPO industry in India from 1997 onwards when GE Financial Assurance decided to shift their back office operations to GE Capital International Services (GECIS), based in Gurgaon near Delhi in India. In 1998, GECIS had 800 employees and revenues of $4 million USD. The numbers increased to 5,000 and $85 million in 2000 and 17,500 and $426 million in 2004, by which time GECIS was handling insurance, finance and accounting, treasury management and document and content management for most of the 35 business making up the global operations of the GE conglomerate (Sengupta, Gupta, & Singh, 2004).

When it commenced business operations as GECIS, the company was a 'captive' operation of GE (a wholly-owned subsidiary of GE and providing BPO services only to the parent company). On 31 December 2004, GECIS concluded a transaction that saw GE sell 60% of its equity to General Atlantic Partners and Oak Hill Capital Partners. Subsequently, Wachovia Bank acquired from GE an equity stake of 7% in Genpact when it signed a seven-year BPO contract (Singh, 2006). Now Genpact employs 20,000 people in six countries and services over 80 customers through 16 operating centres. The core of its operations continue to be in India where Genpact employs 17,500 people across the cities of Gurgaon, Bangalore, Mumbai-Pune, Kolkata, Hyderabad and Jaipur. The company also plans to expand in second tier Indian cities, and reflecting the growth potential of the global BPO industry, Genpact plans to open a 1,000-seat Call Centre and BPO facility every four months, and expects this rate of expansion to continue for the next five years. With revenues growing at 25–28% per annum, Genpact plans to hire an additional 8,000–10,000 staff per annum (The Economic Times India, 19 April 2006).

The demand for skilled programming staff to address potential software problems associated with the handling of the transition to Y2K created opportunity and generated critical mass (Friedman, 2006). According to 'Jerry' Rao, foundation CEO of MphasiS, quoted in Friedman:

> The Indian IT industry got is footprint across the globe because of Y2K. Y2K became our engine of growth, our engine of being known around the world. We never looked back after Y2K.

The international consulting firm McKinsey initiated a project in 1995 led by Anil Kumar (Bhargava & Bhatia, 2005) to exploit reductions in global telecommunications rates that would create opportunities for 'remote business services' whereby providers in locations such as China and India could work for customers located in economies such as the US, UK and Australia. This led McKinsey to establish a Knowledge Centre in Delhi whereby staff and researchers would develop models and analyse trends for McKinsey consultants worldwide (McKinsey, 2004).

Having seen at first hand the value creation potential of BPO, McKinsey consultants and GECIS alumni were quick to spread the gospel of BPO (Business Week, 2006). Neeraj Bhargava left McKinsey to play a major role in the development of WNS Global Services, now the second largest BPO service provider in India. Started as a 'captive' transaction processing centre for British Airways, WNS Global made the transition to a third-party BPO provider when Warburg Pincus, a leading global private equity firm took a majority stake in 2002 with Bhargava as group CEO. Head of Knowledge Services at WNS is Amit Bhatia who conceived, co-founded and led the McKinsey Knowledge Centre in Delhi (Bhargava & Bhatia, 2005; Business Week). The alumni of GECIS and McKinsey share a number of common characteristics. They view outsourcing as a tool to increase growth and efficiency and not just as a pure cost savings exercise. Firms founded and led by the alumni have attracted top performers in management ranks, have acquired global scale and are comfortable with multiple cultures and languages.

Just as the BPO industry has grown at a phenomenal rate, so have Indian operators increased in sophistication. Indian BPO brands, such as Genpact, WNS Global Services Wipro BPO, Infosys, NIIT Technologies, and MphasiS are becoming major global players. They have experienced and highly qualified management with strong track records, and have received benefits from investments by major US and global private equity firms. Both Genpact and WNS Global services have made a common journey from 'captive' operation based in India for a global multinational company (MNC), to a globalizing service provider with operations in multiple jurisdictions, to a third-party service provider with the introduction of private equity and a consequent 'sell down' by the original parent MNC (Shukla, 2006).

The BPO industry in India generated around $5 billion USD in revenue and employed 400,000 people in 2005 (Bhargava, 2006). The industry creates 5–10 times more jobs in areas such as Transportation, Construction, Catering, Telecommunications, Accommodation, etc. Because BPO jobs are high paying by Indian standards, the industry also drives domestic economic activity in retail, financial services, hotels, restaurants, and real estate. New townships like Gurgaon near Delhi have arisen because of the BPO phenomenon, and 50% of new commercial real estate occupied in India in the last 3 years has been taken up by BPO companies. Bhargava reported that the BPO industry adds 1–2% per annum to India's economic growth. It also seems clear that the BPO growth story appears far from over. According to estimates contained in a joint report prepared by McKinsey and the Indian National Association for Software and Service Companies (NASSCOM), India's IT software and BPO services exports will generate revenues of $50 billion USD by 2008 (McKinsey, 2004).

Table 1 below summarizes the major BPO service providers, and provides some indication of the scale and scope of the BPO industry in India.

For firms located in Europe, Australia or North America that make the decision to outsource business processes to service providers located in India, there are a variety of ownership and relationship structures that are possible with Indian service providers (Ramachandran & Voleti, 2004). A fundamental decision is whether to establish a 'captive' operation in India (i.e. wholly owned subsidiary) or to enter into some form of contracting relationship with an established Indian service provider. Key factors that should be considered include:

- Direct costs of establishing operations in India, and possibility of economies of scale
- Long-term assessment of India as a low-cost operating centre with a deep pool of high quality staff
- Cost-benefit analysis of 'owning' versus 'renting'
- Possible loss of control over their transactions and confidentiality and security of their data if an 'arms length' contractor handles them
- Brand implications of perceived loss of control or drop in quality
- Robustness of existing systems and procedures

To date, there has been limited academic research published on the nature and extent of offshore BPO by Australian firms. Grant (2005) reports that offshoring by

Table 1 Major BPO service providers headquartered in India

Company	Revenue (USD)	Employees	Major clients
Genpact	$493 million	20,000	GE, GSK, Wachovia, Linde, Nissan, Air Canada
WNS Global Services	$224 million	9,000	British Airways, Air Canada
Wipro BPO	$200 million	14,000	Amex, Dell, GSK
HCL BPO	$156 million	11,200	Deutsche Bank, British Telecom
IBM Daksh	$120 million	15,000	Lloyds TSB, Barclays, Allstate

Source: India Today International, 8 May 2006

Australian firms commenced in 1989 with ANZ Bank's decision to open a software development and maintenance facility in Bangalore, and that momentum has grown significantly in the past two to three years. Australian companies engaged in the industry sectors of Information and Communications Technologies (ICT), banking and insurance appear to be the most actively engaged in offshore BPO to Indian service providers. Telstra is Australia's most prolific offshoring company, having announced four major offshoring decisions. Offshore BPO activity by other Australian firms has accelerated in the past 2–3 years with Hutchison Telecommunications, Optus, Axa, DC, NAB, Westpac and Hewlett Packard providing examples of Australian firms either engaging Indian service providers or developing 'captive' BPO operations in India (Grant).

4   Research Methodology and Data Collection

The methodology being used in this research project involves an initial exploratory field survey, followed by in-depth case studies of Australian firms engaged in offshore BPO and their Indian service providers. Initial theoretical frameworks developed from the case study findings will be validated by a survey and quantitative analysis of data collected from a larger sample of Australian firms engaged in offshore BPO. The case study method appears well suited to the current situation where there has been little published research into offshore BPO by Australian firms. As pointed out by Borman (2006) the case study method is well established in information systems research, especially where research and theory are at a formative stage and the phenomenon is not well understood.

Two cases are reported here and, for confidentiality, the organizations will be hereafter referred to as the Debt Collector (DC) and the Asset Manager (AM). For both cases, a detailed interview protocol was developed which contained a mix of specific literature-based questions to test existing knowledge and open-ended questions to explore new knowledge. The protocol was provided beforehand to interviewees. At DC interviews were conducted with the managing director, CIO, CFO, management staff, and some floor staff while at AM the two Australian principals and the Indian COO were interviewed. Further data was collected via focus groups and participant observation of daily staff debriefings. The interviews were recorded and transcribed and transcripts were returned to interviewees for correction and/or confirmation. Preliminary analysis has been to synthesize interviews (and other documentation) into descriptive papers about the organization and feed papers back to interviewees for further correction and additional information.

The information gathered in this research may be of significance to Australian firms and managers that are considering or participating in offshore outsourcing, and also to Government policy makers and academic staff involved in business and information systems management. The research also has value for researchers and practitioners outside Australia in its focus on small to medium enterprises (SMEs) that have chosen a captive operation as their organizational model for India.

The bulk of ITO and BPO published research has focused (a) on large US and European corporations, and (b) often in partnership with the large Indian service provides such as Infosys, Tata Consulting Services, and Wipro. This research aims to address that gap.

5 The Case of Debt Collector

DC was formed in 1973 as a privately owned company providing various debt collection and management services. By 1996 it had grown to the point where it was turning over approximately $4 million per annum, but growth potential of the business was limited because director's guarantees were required in order to secure debt and working capital. In 2001, the owners of DC received an unsolicited takeover offer that valued the firm at $3 million. Formal advice was sought on the offer to purchase the business, and DC was advised that it needed either to change corporate structure and raise expansion capital, or exit the Australian debt services industry because it lacked adequate scale. DC took the decision to convert to a public company structure and list on the Australian Stock Exchange (ASX). This goal of ASX listing was achieved in May 2002. At the time of the Initial Public Offer, DC had a market capitalization of about $5 million (all dollar amounts are Australian with current A$1.00 = US$0.95 approximately) and about 50 people in the office in Perth with small representative offices in Sydney and Melbourne. At the time Australia was in its tenth year of continuous economic growth, and the business strategy was based on fairly rapid expansion of the existing business model, with additional staff to be hired for the Australian operations.

Experience after listing demonstrated that there were a number of opportunities to expand DC's business (for example, by purchasing debt from providers of credit), but DC began to experience difficulty in finding and retaining enough qualified and experienced staff in Australia. The business drivers for DC's offshore BPO strategy were to address the skill shortages facing the Australian business, to continue the process of rapid business growth and to lower transaction costs associated with performing certain high-volume business processes.

DC's initial approach was to conduct research into the capabilities of BPO suppliers in India. GE Capital was a major client of DC, and the Managing Director of DC had become aware of the IT and BPO capabilities that were available in India. In January 2003, a visit was arranged to Chennai, Hyderabad and Bangalore, for a team from DC to look at Technology Parks, Call Centre solutions and BPO service providers. Having satisfied themselves that the capabilities and infrastructure in India were adequate to meet DC's requirements, within a month the team recommended to the DC Board of Directors that a presence be established in Bangalore. The Board approved an initial investment of $500,000 to establish a Business Processing office in Bangalore. The operation in Bangalore was to be wholly-owned by DC. The 'captive' route was taken because of the non-scripted nature of DC's main processes and a concern about corruption. DC relocated a senior manager to

Bangalore to commission the facility which was operational within four months. After some initial teething problems, DC's Bangalore facility was expanded to 180 staff and was generating $1 million AUD in revenue within 18 months.

By 2004 the Indian operation consisted of these 180 Indian staff in one call centre in Bangalore (which was chosen because it was growing with BPO and ITO, had a pool of well-qualified labour, and had an international airport). DC had set up their own captive operation but the MD had a close working relationship with an Indian Singaporean whose family came from the Bangalore region whom he appointed as GM of the Bangalore operation and he was able to understand and handle local customs, regulations, national government restrictions, and web of contacts. By 2007 they have expanded the Indian operation to their own building and now have 400 staff in Bangalore with 70–80 staff in Australia. Their business includes collecting on their own consumer debt 'assets' plus doing fee-for-service debt collection for other companies. Their debt-collection process includes inbound and outbound calls, a team approach, and opportunity for promotion. They claim to adopt a professional, constructive approach to debt collection via collaborative problem solving. Calls utilize a VOIP service provided by a major telco and their processes incorporate various software including CRM, searching/tracing database queries, and whitepages.

They operate on two shifts (10.30 a.m. – 6.30 p.m., 6.30 p.m. – 2.30 a.m.), staff are bussed door-to-door, provided with meals, and are trained in-house. Staff all have degrees (usually Business/Commerce) and some have Masters, about 50% are female, about 50% are Muslim, and they are paid about one-sixth of Australian rates (but good pay by Indian standards).

DC sees India as a strategic initiative, not just cost, providing opportunity for growth into other markets not possible from Australia and with staff numbers not possible in Australia. Offshore outsourcing to Bangalore was only way that DC could achieve their business plan objective to increase scale and scope of its operations because they could not obtain sufficient skilled Australian staff – debt collection is not seen as a desirable career choice in Australia whereas working for an international company is attractive to Indians. DC reports greater than 60% labour cost saving for complex, value adding activity conducted in India and deducting costs associated with establishing in Bangalore and on-going overheads for co-ordination and management this still generates a 40% cost reduction overall. Staff in Bangalore are well qualified (e.g. MBAs), highly motivated, and some already have multinational company experience. Most Indian staff had never spoken to Australians before and they had to be taught to handle the relationship with the clients in a very different power relationship to most other call centre operations. Staff turnover was 32.5% for 2006 whereas other Indian centres it varies from 60 to 130% while in Australia the rate is about 25%. The MD is very culturally aware but still has had some problems.

DC provides a case study on the business benefits of offshore BPO. Offshore BPO has enabled DC to grow revenue and profit five-fold in a five-year period from 2001 to 2006. Important success factors appear to be that senior management at DC has embraced the concept of transformational outsourcing, has immersed in key cultural factors and has mastered the skills required to co-ordinate offshore BPO. In terms of the model of CEO behaviour described by Feeny et al. (2003), the MD of DC has demonstrated that he is a 'believer' in offshore and DC's success with offshore BPO appears to be based on more than just arbitraging lower labour costs in Bangalore.

6   The Case of Asset Manager

AM commenced operation in March 2006 with a view to developing a new business as a boutique funds manager that would focus on establishing an Australian Smaller Companies Fund. The principals were already familiar with an offshore BPO model as a result of a previous successful investment that they had made in an Australian small cap stock that had succeeded in establishing an operation in Bangalore.

With an established track record in identifying value by bringing process and science to under researched market sectors, the principals of AM view offshore BPO not simply as an opportunity for cost reduction, but primarily as a means to achieve faster reaction times by analysing more companies and more ideas. The basic value proposition is that Australian portfolio managers will be supported by equity analysts based in Bangalore to focus on overlooked market sectors, with a view to finding undiscovered value within the Australian small caps, ultimately leading to better performance and increased funds under management. The straight labour cost arbitrage argument for offshore BPO to India is that suitably skilled equity analysts can be recruited in Bangalore for about 25% of the personnel costs associated with an Australian analyst. However, the additional costs of coordinating activities of equity analysts conducting research and modelling from Bangalore must also be factored into the equation. The Australian principals of AM each spend about 15% of their time in Bangalore driving and developing the business, and during the recruitment and establishment phase, more than 50% of their time was spent in India. Strong local management, effective use of technology and frequent 'virtual' contact will be the keys to remotely managing the Bangalore operation.

Other costs of coordination include travel, management time, accommodation and telecommunications. Generally, these costs are not onerous for Australian companies considering BPO to service providers located in Bangalore. Travel links are excellent, and high-performance broadband telecommunications connections are available at reasonable cost.

According to one of the principals:

> Historically, the Australian small cap sector has been under-researched because analysts are time poor with too many companies to follow up. Experienced Australian analysts become slaves to financial model maintenance rather than being able to get out and investigate smaller companies, talking to management, searching for value.

Electronic upload of financial data from annual reports and ASX stock market releases provides a base financial model for each company. AM equity analysts based in Bangalore perform financial analysis of Australian small cap stocks, including the following tasks:

- The creation of financial models in MS Excel to forecast key company metrics, including Price Earnings Ratio, Earnings Per Share, Net Profit After Tax, etc.
- The tailoring of these financial models to provide ready manipulation of key value drivers and 'what if' scenario analysis based upon Investment Manager feedback from company visits in Australia
- Identification of any sustainable and responsible investment (SRI) issues
- Monitoring stock for updates and changes (e.g. new information, quarterly and half yearly earnings reports) and keep all models up to date
- Response to requests for reports and analysis on Australian companies being tracked via database of models
- The mining of the models database in order to identify potential value investment opportunities

Equity analysts employed by AM in Bangalore generally have an MBA and a first degree in a quantitative discipline (including Engineering, Accounting, Commerce, Science, Biochemistry), and some have post-graduate Finance qualifications (for example, actuarial). Typically, they will have a background as a financial equities analyst for a stock broker, mutual fund or investment bank, and some have experience of the US equities market. Analysts are organized around market sectors such as Oil & Gas, Pharmaceuticals, Financial Services, IT and Engineering. Within AM Bangalore, career progression is generally from analyst to senior analysts/team leader (covering multiple sectors), with the ultimate possibility of progressing to portfolio manager and then fund manager.

While AM sees that the relatively deep pool of experienced and qualified equity analysts is the major part of the model, also important is the Internet and broadband telecommunications technology that now allows for collaboration, communication and control in ways not previously possible. Experience with offshore BPO also demonstrates that the activity has the effect of forcing improvements in process design and control, leading to higher quality outcomes. Hence, AM aims to transform small cap equity analysis from a 'cottage industry' to an industrial strength process that can be replicated. As part of this transformation, it aims to increase the number of stocks that can be analysed in detail and to shorten the cycle time associated with successful small cap stock selection. In addition, AM aims to increase the frequency with which new ideas can be generated, and also aims to free up senior, experienced investment professionals in Australia to be out visiting companies and talking with management of these companies. The principals believe that better research will result in better returns.

Likely challenges will be similar to those facing the broader industry in India. The success of the offshore BPO model is likely to mean that costs will escalate dramatically in the so-called Tier One BPO cities in India (which include Mumbai, Bangalore, Chennai, Pune, Delhi (Gurgaon) and Hyderabad). The BPO industry in

India is faced with growth-related infrastructure bottlenecks, high rates of staff turnover (30% p.a.), rising salaries and soaring real estate prices in the key locations for BPO activity. For AM, recruitment and retention of skilled quantitative analysts is likely to be the most significant challenge. There will also be subtle cultural issues to be managed, including training Bangalore staff to become familiar with the Australian business and investment environment. The firm is addressing staff turnover risks by offering staff a share in the performance fees generated by its funds. This approach of treating Indian BPO staff as full partners in the success of the firm is relatively new in an industry that is still less than 10 years old

However, this research has demonstrated that Bangalore continues to enjoy significant location advantages over other possible BPO sites in India. Bangalore continues to demonstrate advantages in terms of world class educational institutions, a deep pool of talented and highly motivated staff, and the presence of a cluster of sophisticated and successful BPO firms. Located in southern India, Bangalore is relatively accessible via airline connections with the major Australian cities. It is regarded by Australian managers as a convivial destination for re-location. Bangalore enjoys a temperate climate, is less adversely impacted by the monsoon (which can cause Mumbai to shutdown) and poverty is less evident.

7   Conclusions and Future Work

In this paper we have provided a descriptive analysis of two cases where business processes have been offshored to India. While most academic published BPO and ITO research has focused on large North American and European corporations (banks, telcos, consulting firms, IT firms) entering into third-party arrangements with large Indian BPO and ITO providers such as Infosys, MphasIS, Tata Consulting Services, and many others (see Table 1), little research has been conducted on smaller organizations offshoring BPO. Little attention has also been paid to different forms of offshoring, particularly to a captive operation. While it can be argued that such offshoring is technically not outsourcing, Indian customs and rules mean these captives are separate corporate entities and so they are effectively outsourced operations with their own staff, procedures and processes. This research addresses both the lack of studies on captive operations and smaller firms. Table 2 below provides a summary of the factors that have led to this small-firm captive offshore BPO model.

Comparison of these two cases indicates a lack of skilled labour (at a reasonable cost) in Australia can be compensated by an availability in India for non-scripted higher level processes which support a strategic move, either to expand operations or fill a gap in the market (or both). Offshoring therefore applies not just to lower-level heavily scripted processes but to higher level processes too. For smaller organizations that desire greater control over the offshored processes, the captive model may be appropriate.

Australian companies appear under-represented compared to North American and European counterparts in taking advantage of the capabilities of BPO service

Table 2 Identifying factors in the two case studies

Factor	DC	AM
Cost of transactions (necessary but not sufficient)	Yes	Yes
Availability of skilled, trainable labour in Australia	No	No (not at a feasible price)
Availability of skilled, trainable labour in India	Yes	Yes
Non-standard skill set (not scripted)	Yes	Yes
Need for operational control	Yes	Yes
Identified a gap in the market	No	Yes
Strategic move – expansion	Yes	No
Company relatively small	Yes	Yes

providers in India. Australian companies (including SMEs) can obtain business benefits from offshore BPO to service providers located in India. A key business benefit is derived from access to a well educated, motivated and skilled work force. Labour unit cost reductions approaching 40% can be obtained from this skilled workforce. The largest business benefits will be derived from BPO activities classified as Knowledge Services, although gains can also be achieved in voice services and transaction processing.

Establishing a 'captive' operation in India will be the preferred engagement option for Australian companies. Successful 'captive' operations require intense senior management commitment, and effective leadership of staff from different cultural backgrounds. Managing staff turnover rates (e.g. 25%–30% per annum) and salary and cost increases will be risk factors for 'captive' BPO operations. Relationship quality (especially both parties demonstrating trustworthiness) will be a key success factor in 3P BPO. Whether using a 'captive' operation or 3P provider, a lag of 12–18 months in delivering productivity gains from offshore BPO is likely. Australian firms can learn from the experience of other firms to reduce risks and avoid operational difficulties with offshore BPO, and to maximize productivity gains from cost reductions, quality and service. In order to succeed with offshore BPO, Australian managers will need increased knowledge of cultural factors ('cultural intelligence') but India will remain the preferred location for offshore BPO.

A limitation in this research is that it is focused on two Australian firms that are operating one particular BPO model (i.e. 'captive' operation) in one location, Bangalore. In addition, it is confined to two industry sectors and is based primarily on qualitative data. Furthermore, the data has been gathered over a relatively limited time span of just over six months. However, published case studies on the participation of Australian firms in offshore BPO are scarce, and the case studies are intended to add to the literature on this currently under-researched area.

Future research will track the evolution of both cases' BPO model through longitudinal case studies. Other case studies that are currently underway will gather data across a broader range of Australian and multinational firms that participate in offshore BPO to service providers located in India. Data is being collected on a wider range of industry sectors, and on several different BPO models, which will enable cross-case comparisons and results obtained from a range of case studies.

Following an exploratory field survey phase, the in-depth case studies will be constructed on a sample of Australian and multinational firms, together with Indian service providers. The data collected will be used to develop a model that will assist Australian managers to make decisions about whether their organizations should participate in offshore BPO, and to maximize the benefits to Australian firms and the Australian economy from the global BPO phenomenon.

References

Barrett, J. (2007). Numbers point to India. *The Australian Financial Review*, 18 April, 60–61.

Bhargava, N. (2006). Redefining BPO. http://www.wnsgs.com. Accessed 17 May 2006.

Bhargava, N., & Bhatia, A. (2005). Knowledge services: Painless offshoring. http://www.wnsgs. com. Accessed 17 May 2006.

Borman, M. (2006). Applying multiple perspectives to the BPO decision: A case study of call centres in Australia. *Journal of Information Technology, 21*, 99–115.

Business Week (2006). Offshoring: Spread the Gospel. http://www.businessweek.com. Accessed 27 February 2006.

Carmel, E., & Agarwal, R. (2002). The Maturation of offshore sourcing of information technology work. *MIS Quarterly Executive, 1*, 65–79.

Davies, P. (2004). *What's this India business? Offshoring, outsourcing and the global services revolution*. London: Nicholas Brearley.

Dibbern, J., Goles, T., Hirschheim, R., & Jayatilaka, B. (2004). Information systems Outsourcing: A survey and analysis of the literature. *Data Base, 35*, 6–102.

Eddington, R. (2006). Personal telephone conversation conducted on 18 May 2006.

Feeny, D., Lacity, M., & Willcocks, L. (2003). Business process outsourcing: The promise of the "enterprise partnership" model. http://www.templeton.ox.ac.uk/oxiim/bpo.htm. Accessed 28 July 2006.

Feeny, D., Lacity, M., & Willcocks, L. P. (2005). Taking the measure of outsourcing providers. *Sloan Management Review, 46*, 41–48.

Friedman, T. L. (2006). *The world is flat: The globalised world in the twenty-first century*. London: Penguin.

Grant, R. (2005). *Offshoring jobs: US and Australian debates*. Parliament of Australia, Canberra: Parliamentary Library Research Brief.

Hughes, A. (2007). Credit corp wary of doing offshore jobs. *The Australian Financial Review*, 23 April, 2007.

Marshall, R. (2005). British airways goes to India in 1996. http://www.ciol.com. Accessed 22 May 2006.

Mckinsey & Co. (2004). Extending India's leadership of the global IT and BPO industries. http://www.mckinsey.com. Accessed 22 May 2006.

Ramachandran, K., & Voleti, S. (2004). Business process outsourcing (BPO): Emerging scenario and strategic options for IT-enabled services. Vikalpa, p. 29.

Robinson, M., & Kalakota, R. (2004). Offshore outsourcing business models ROI and best practice. Alpharetta: Mivar Press, Inc.

Sengupta, S., Gupta, I., & Singh, S. (2004). The house Jack built… and Jeffrey is about to sell. Business World India, 11 October 2004. http://www.businessworldindia.com. Accessed 21 May 2006.

Singh, H. (2006). To GE or not to GE. The financial express, 1 April 2005. http://www.financial-express.com. Accessed 22 May 2006.

Shukla, A. (2006). Genpact's gems. *India Today International*, 8 May 2006, 29–33.

The Economic Times India (2006). Genpact to set up shop in Poland, Philippines, China. *Times News Network*, 19 April 2006, http://www.economictimes.indiatimes.com. Accessed 22 May 2006.

Willcocks, L., Lacity, M., & Cullen, S. (2006). Information technology sourcing: Fifteen years of learning. Working Paper Series, Department of Information Systems, London School of Economics and Political Science, April.

From Professional Dominance to Market Mechanisms: Deinstitutionalization in the Organizational Field of Health Care

Wendy L. Currie

1 Introduction

The concept of deinstitutionalization is central to institutional theory. It represents the process by which the legitimacy of an established or institutionalized organizational practice becomes eroded or discontinued (Oliver, 1992, p. 564). Deinstitutionalization witnesses the delegitimization of institutionalized organizational practices as political, functional and societal forces conspire to destabilize and reproduce previously legitimated or taken-for-granted organizational action and behaviour (Oliver). Research studies on the processes of deinstitutionalization remain relatively few, despite the vast interest in how and why institutionalized practices atrophy and change (Greenwood, Suddaby, & Hinings, 2002; Tolbert & Zucker, 1996).

This paper is a five-year study on the processes of deinstitutionalization in the UK health care sector, where the National Health Service (NHS) was established in 1948 to offer free health care at the point of delivery to all citizens. Over the past six decades, the NHS has been subjected to numerous government interventions ranging from radical change programs to incremental tinkering around the edges (Webster, 2002). Observations over a 50-year period show that the organizational field of health care has moved from one of professional dominance by clinicians from the 1950s to early 1980s, to one where institutional logics supporting the virtues of market mechanisms have been encouraged by politicians ever since (Bloomfield, 1991; Burgoyne, Brown, Hindle, & Mumford, 1997; Currie W.L. & Guah, 2006). Part of this move is to create a market for elective health care provision, where patients are given greater powers to make choices about competing health care options (Laing & Hogg, 2002; Raey & Hinings, 2005).

Our research centres on a major innovation designed to deinstitutionalize existing institutionalized procedures and practices introduced in 2002. Following the publication of the Wanless (2002), the UK government launched the largest civil IT program worldwide in the form of the National Program for IT (NPfIT), under the control of an agency named Connecting for Health. Despite NHS spending comprising the largest public expenditure after social security at around £90 bn and rising, the report suggests that information technology is a key element in public

R. Hirschheim et al. (eds), *Information Systems Outsourcing,*
© Springer-Verlag Berlin Heidelberg 2009

sector reform to enable the delivery of more efficient health care services to citizens. Between 1999 and the early part of the twenty-first century, the annual UK government spend on computer systems and services doubled to reach a figure of £14 bn. This amounted to the highest IT spend in Europe, with UK public sector IT relying on the private sector to deliver 55% of its IT work through large-scale outsourcing contracts with major IT service providers. NPfIT would vastly increase this spend, with a pledge from the UK government to invest $6.2 bn on connecting IT across the NHS over a 10 year program.

Our investigation of IT in health care is fuelled by two reasons. First, health care is a highly institutionalized environment that regularly receives government directives to change existing procedures and practices. There are many studies in the information systems and management literature that examine specific change programs targeted towards health care, such as re-engineering in the 1990s (McNulty & Ferlie, 2004) and, more recently, knowledge management. But most of them do not consider the historical context that conspires to inhibit or encourage deep rooted change, as they often only consider case-based examples of specific organizational settings. However, secondary source material in the form of government reports and white papers provide a rich source of data to enable us to capture, organize and understand past and present institutional logics that prevail in the health care organizational field.

Second, the introduction of the NPfIT, which began in 2002 and runs for 10 years, will exert pressures on the institutionalized processes and practices of clinicians, NHS managers and administrators to impose change, or become deinstitutionalized. This is because the vision, design and implementation of the various initiatives under the NPfIT umbrella will inevitably change the working practices of these groups. While this will pose a major challenge for politicians and NHS managers, institutional logics from a past era of professional dominance may conflict and collide with more recent logics that advocate market forces as a way to achieve enhanced productivity and efficiency in health care organizations. By tracking the development of one of the more controversial elements of NPfIT (the *Choose & Book* system) over a five year period, this research study exposes some of the key challenges and contradictions in the health care environment and raises important questions about the difficulty of pursuing change programs where deinstitutionalization is critical to their implementation.

This paper is structured as follows. First we present the key theoretical concepts that underpin this study. These include deinstitutionalization, institutional logics and isomorphic change. We frame this discussion around the organizational field of health care. Second, we present our research methods and four propositions developed from the institutional theory literature. Multiple methods of data collection are used in this study: primary interviews with NHS clinicians, managers and administrators, and secondary sources including government documents, media sources and annual reports from hospitals. Third, we present our analysis and discussion of introducing a large-scale IT innovation into the field of health care. Finally, we introduce a non-linear model that shows the tensions that arise from introducing large-scale innovations to deinstitutionalize working practices. This study contributes to our theoretical understanding of the relationship between institutionalization and deinstitutionalization through unbundling some of the factors that encourage and inhibit isomorphic change in health care.

2   Theoretical Context

2.1   Deinstitutionalization

Many studies in the institutional theory literature are concerned with processes of institutionalization which emphasize cultural persistence and stability (Zucker, 1977, 1983) with fewer studies on deinstitutionalization and change (Greenwood et al., 2002). This paper is informed by three important contributions on the pressures and processes of institutionalization and deinstitutionalization. First, deinstitutionalization is described as the 'process by which the legitimacy of an established or institutionalized organizational practice erodes or discontinues' (Oliver, 1992, p. 564). It involves the delegitimization of an institutionalized 'organizational practice or procedure as a result of organizational challenges to, or the failure of, organizations to reproduce previously legitimated or taken-for-granted organizational actions' (Oliver, p. 564).

The antecedents of deinstitutionalization are identified by three distinct political, functional and social pressures divided into organizational and environmental levels of analysis. Political pressures arise from an emerging performance crisis, conflicting internal interests, increasing innovation pressures, and changing external dependencies. Functional pressures comprise changing economic utility, increasing technical specificity and competition for resources and also from emerging events and data. Social pressures involve increasing social fragmentation, decreasing historical continuity, changing institutional rules and increasing structural disaggregation. Although the antecedents of deinstitutionalization of an organizational practice may be state-driven, normatively encouraged, politically motivated or functionally based, it may also result from 'changes to the structure and patterns of interaction within an organization or in an organization's field. These disaggregating changes, which include diversification, geographic dispersion and parochial differentiation, apply to deinstitutionalizing changes both within and across organizations that occupy the same organizational field' (Oliver, 1992, p. 577).

The second contribution develops a model of the component processes of institutionalization (Tolbert & Zucker, 1996). It considers how a new innovation proceeds through three distinct stages: habitualization, objectification, and sedimentation. Habitualization involves the generation of new structural arrangements in response to a specific organizational problem or set of problems, and the formalization of such arrangements in the policies and procedures of a given organization, or set of organizations that experience the same or similar problems. These processes result in structures that can be classified as being at the pre-institutional stage.

Habitualized action encapsulates behaviours that have been developed empirically, and adopted by an actor or collection of actors to solve ongoing or recurring problems. These behaviours are habitualized because they are 'evoked with minimal decision-making effort by actors in response to particular stimuli' (Tolbert & Zucker, p. 182). The values and norms that are attributed to habitualized behaviour have therefore become generalized in day-to-day society, and are independent of the specific individuals who carry out the action.

The next stage of the process is where the generalization of the meaning of action is described as *objectification* (Zucker, 1977). This is a key component of the process of institutionalization, which occurs in conjunction with the diffusion of structure. Described as objectification, this process involves the 'development of some degree of social consensus among organizational decision-makers concerning the value of a structure, and the increasing adoption by organizations on the basis of that consensus'. The final stage in the model is referred to as sedimentation, where organizational practices and procedures become institutionalized. This is where structures reproduce themselves and become taken-for-granted in the wider society and at the level of the organizational field and by individuals themselves. Sedimentation is a process that 'rests on the historical continuity of structure, and especially on its survival across generations of organizational members'. It is achieved by the almost complete diffusion of structures across a group of actors who may be likely adopters, and by the reinforcement of structures over a significant time period.

Implicit in this model is that some patterns of social behaviour are subject to more critical evaluation, modification, and even elimination than others. Such patterned behaviours are claimed by Tolbert and Zucker (1996, p. 181) to, 'vary in terms of the degree to which they are deeply embedded in a social system (more objective, more exterior), and thus vary in terms of their stability and their power to determine behavior'. This processual model offers a useful conceptual framework for understanding the different degrees to which, attitudes, values, norms and behavioural patterns become institutionalized over time.

The third contribution builds on the previous work and develops a six stage model of institutional change (Greenwood et al., 2002). The first stage occurs when precipitating jolts, which may arise from social, technological and regulatory pressures, set of a process of deinstitutionalization. At this stage, emerging new players, the ascendance of different actors, and institutional entrepreneurship all play a part. Following this, preinstitutionalization occurs, in which organizations embark on a process of innovation to seek technically viable solutions to locally perceived problems.

The next stage is theorization which enables new practices to become widely adopted. 'Theorization is the development and specification of abstract categories and the elaboration of chains of cause and effect. Such theoretical accounts simplify and distill the properties of new practices and explain the outcomes they produce (Greenwood et al., 2002, p. 60). It is a process that sees localized deviations from prevailing conventions become abstracted and thus made available in simplified form for wider adoption. Successful theorization is followed by diffusion. Diffusion occurs if new ideas are compellingly presented as more appropriate than existing practices. As innovations diffuse, they become 'objectified' where they gain social consensus concerning their pragmatic value, leading to their further diffusion. From their conceptualization of institutional change, the authors question how new ideas become justified and legitimized in highly normative settings (Greenwood et al., p. 61).

2.2   Institutional Logics

In conjunction with the above process models, it is important to observe and understand the role played by institutional logics in delineating, shaping and influencing institutional change. In highly institutionalized organizational fields like health care, organizations and actors are constantly receiving and responding to competing political, functional and social pressures to change existing practices and procedures. Institutional logics are 'sets of material practices and symbolic constructions which constitute a field's organizing principles and which are available to organizations and individuals to elaborate' (Friedland & Alford, 1991, p. 248). They 'provide the formal and informal rules of action, interaction, and interpretation that guide and constrain decision makers in accomplishing the organization's tasks and in obtaining social status, credits, penalties and rewards in the process' (Ocasio, 1997). They are the cognitive maps or belief systems that are carried by individuals within an organizational field to ascribe 'meaning to their activities' (Scott, Ruef, Mendel, & Caronna, 2000, p. 20). The health care system is infused with institutional logics that are the organizing principles underpinning how field participants carry out their work. Yet the dimensions of systems of logics vary according to 'content, penetration, linkage, and exclusiveness'. It therefore follows that the content of institutional logics should be examined observing the specific belief systems understood and interpreted by field members (Scott, 2001, p. 139).

In the field of health care, institutional logics have emanated from an era which we describe as professional dominance, beginning with the launch of the NHS in 1948 to one which is now characterized by market dynamics (Pollack, 2005). We assert, however, that unlike institutional models that observe innovations passing through several stages of a process, institutional logics are more likely to prevail with varying degrees of influence at any given time. They may ebb and flow across decades of political, social and economic change, sometimes gaining ground, and at other times becoming obscured by competing logics.

So by examining the content of institutional logics over a protracted period, the distinctive categories, beliefs, and motives created by a specific logic will provide a conceptual basis for understanding and explaining the nature and types of social relations existing between organizations and individuals (Friedland & Alford, 1991, p. 252). Two critical issues – addressed in this chapter – therefore concern, (1) how past and present institutional logics are justified and legitimized in the highly institutionalized environment of health care, and (2) how they become discredited or abandoned to enable deinstitutionalization and change.

2.3 Isomorphic Change

The concept of isomorphic change is relevant to our study of innovation within the health care organizational field. As an innovation spreads, a threshold is reached beyond which adoption provides legitimacy rather than improve performance (Meyer & Rowan, 1977). Strategies considered rational for some organizations may not be rational if adopted by others. But the very fact they are normatively sanctioned increases the likelihood of their adoption. So where organizations try to impose constant change, beyond a certain point in the structuration of an organizational field, the aggregate effect of change within specific organizations may be to constrain or weaken the extent of diversity within the field (Dimaggio & Powell, 1983). This concept captures the process of homogenization. Isomorphism is thus a constraining process that forces one unit in a population to resemble other units that face the same set of environmental conditions.

Three mechanisms of institutional isomorphic change are identified (Dimaggio & Powell, 1983). Coercive isomorphism results from both formal and informal pressures exerted on organizations by other organizations upon which they are dependent and by cultural expectations in the society within which organizations function. Mimetic processes show how uncertainty is also a powerful force that encourages imitation. So when organizational technologies are poorly understood, when goals are ambiguous, or when the environment creates symbolic uncertainty, organizations may model themselves on other organizations. The advantages of mimetic behaviour in the economy of human action are considerable; when an organization faces a problem with ambiguous causes or unlikely solutions, problemistic search may yield a viable solution with little expense. Normative pressure is where isomorphic organizational change is normative and stems primarily from professionalism. Professionalism is the collective struggle of members of an occupation to define the conditions and methods of their work, to control 'the production of producers' and to establish a cognitive base and legitimation for their occupational autonomy. The professional project is rarely achieved with complete success. Professionals must compromise with non-professional clients, bosses, or regulators. The recent growth in the professions has been among organizational professionals, particularly managers and specialised staff of large organizations. It follows from our discussion of the mechanisms by which isomorphic change occurs that we may be able to predict from historical and empirical data sources how and why the organizational field of health care comprises elements which are homogeneous in structure, processes and behaviour, while also experiencing pressures for greater heterogeneity.

3 Methods

Since it is difficult to define and explain, a priori, the forces of deinstitutionalization within an organizational field (Dimaggio & Powell, 1983) our research combines empirical investigation to observe how the field of health care is institutionally defined, with historical sources which shed light on past and prevailing institutional logics. This combined research method enables us to gain a rich picture of how and why the field of health care has changed over past decades, in addition to gaining deeper insights into the institutional logics that enable and inhibit the implementation of the NPfIT, which is the largest innovation and change program in the NHS to date (NAO, 2006).

3.1 The Organizational Field of Health care

The organizational field of health care offers a rich and diverse context for undertaking longitudinal case-based research into a large-scale government supported innovation (Scott et al., 2000). Institutional theorists have suggested that, 'in the initial stages of their life cycle, organizational fields display considerable diversity in approach and form. Once a field becomes well established.....there is an inexorable push towards homogenization', (Dimaggio & Powell, 1983, p. 148). Examples of coercive, mimetic and normative isomorphism in health care are, government pressures which enforce strict regulatory and legal requirements on health care organizations, requiring them to conform to contemporary standards; teaching hospitals imparting 'best practice' solutions on other hospitals across the field to encourage imitation; and professional bodies which govern their clinical members through a strict code of conduct, where failure to adhere to the rules and regulations and standards of practice may lead to a clinician being 'struck-off' the medical register.

Despite strong pressures for isomorphism, health care has become a more complex environment over the past two decades, as new entrants in the form of external service providers, and changing roles of health care consumers (i.e. patients) all conspire to alter a previously stable institutional setting. For several decades from the post-war period, the field of health care was dominated by professional groups, governed by powerful regulatory and professional bodies (Meyer, Brooks, & Goes, 1990; Scott et al., 2000). But from the 1980s, government imposed market logics on health care for the purpose of improving efficiency and performance (Laing & Hogg, 2002). These varying pressures for institutionalization and deinstitutionalization produce a complex scenario, where coercive pressures to change working practices are likely to be inhibited by the normative embeddedness of an organization within its institutional context.

Recognizing that coercive, mimetic and normative pressures have led to organizational practices and procedures in the NHS to become institutionalized over several decades, new pressures to deinstitutionalize working practices, particularly from external forces, are likely to produce disruptive change (Scott et al., 2000), environmental jolts or even industry revolutions (Meyer et al., 1990). Prior research suggests that, government regulations and policies are most likely 'to deinstitutionalize past practices, given the strength of coercion that underpins the legal enforcement of government mandates' (Dimaggio & Powell, 1991; Scott, 2001), unlike more locally-based change management practices which may be abandoned by a new management regime (McNulty & Ferlie, 2004).

Over past decades, the NHS has experienced multiple directives from government agencies to reduce the power of clinicians by working with external service providers to drive through targets for efficiency and performance improvement. From the 1980s onwards, there was a growing trend to adapt private sector methods and practices for public sector settings. Management consultancies were eager to develop new business in the health care sector, as innovation and change panaceas and 'fads' (Abrahamson, 1996) were adopted in health care organizations (McNulty & Ferlie, 2004). Although the outcome of many of these government-led initiatives has been disappointing (Wyatt, 1998), sometimes leading to unexpected outcomes, as private sector logics do not sit easily with the dominant logics in health care organizations.

3.2 The National Program for IT

In the late 1990s, the NHS Executive embarked upon an ambitious scheme to transform IT-enabled health care services by establishing a target for all NHS hospitals to have electronic patient records (EPR) implemented by 2005 (Department of Health, 2002). By the spring of 2002, only 3% of participating hospitals were set up to meet this target. The Treasury's Wanless Report suggested two main reasons for this. The first was that budgets for information technology, allocated locally, were being used to relieve financial pressures. The second was the inadequate setting of central IT standards. The report recommended ring fencing and doubling the IT budget (Hendy, Reeves, Fulop, Huchings, & Masseria, 2005). The UK government responded with £2.3 bn for a new national program for information technology in the NHS, later rising to £6.2 bn (Connecting for Health, 2004, p. 33). The NPfIT was designed as part of a broader task of modernizing public sector services, to 'to put in place through the use of new technology, information systems that give patients more choice and health professionals more efficient access to information and thereby ensure delivery of better patient care' (Connecting for Health, p. 2). NPfIT would comprise four major elements: (1) an electronic transfer of prescriptions, (2) Picture Archiving Communications System (PACS), (3) a care records service, and (4) the 'Choose and Book' patient electronic appointments system.

But against a background of past disappointments from public sector innovation and change programs (NAO, 2004), the UK health care industry continues to recognize that change is difficult in a sector that values its traditions and practices. Attempts to legitimize the NPfIT are expected to deliver 'a better NHS that gives public and patients services that fit the 21st century' (NAO, p. 2). Rather than being yet another large-scale public sector IT project, NPfIT is planned as a major long-term, root and branch change program to transform clinical working practices across the national health care system. But rapid change is not usually a characteristic attributed to health care, as hospitals display highly institutionalized structures and practices, which, by definition, are more amenable to incremental rather than discontinuous change (Scott et al., 2000). Although when existing structures and beliefs are undermined or severely challenged, profound change may occur rapidly, producing mixed results, sometimes with unintended consequences (Greenwood & Hinings, 1996).

Further, if the technologies produce disruptive change, organizations may seek to replicate the policies and practices of others that leads to greater homogeneity within the organizational field (Dimaggio & Powell, 1983). Given that NPfIT is a combination of several large-scale innovations, this study isolated only one system – Choose and Book – for empirical investigation.

3.3   *Choose and Book*

The *Choose and Book* system was initially designed to be an electronic booking system at an initial cost of around £65 m arising to an estimated £200 m 4 years later. The rationale for the system aimed 'to give patients a greater say in how they are treated. This includes giving them access to a wider range of primary care services and increasing choice of where and how to get medicines, treatment and care'. A government report gave political justification for the system by stating that, 'Several surveys have indicated that patients want to be more involved in taking decisions and making choices about their health care. They want services shaped to fit with their lives' (Connecting for Health, 2004, p. 15). As one element of the NPfIT, Choose and Book would allow patients to choose the hospital where they are to be treated and to book appointments based on their convenience. It would combine electronic booking and choice of time, date and place for the first outpatient appointments. Primary care trusts would commission a range of services to give patients the choice of four for five hospitals, or other appropriate services from which to choose. In conjunction, information would be provided to patients to enable them to make an informed choice of hospital. Choose and Book was designed to transform patients' experience of the NHS in three ways: (1) Patients will have greater opportunity to influence the way they are treated by the NHS, (2) Patients will be able to discuss their treatment options and experience a more personalized health service, (3) Patients will experience greater convenience and certainty, which will enable them to fit their treatment in with their life, not the other way around

Benefit to clinicians and NHS staff would include: (1) General practitioners and their practice staff will have much greater access to their patients' care management plans, ensuring that the correct appointments are made, (2) General practitioners and practice staff will see a reduction in the amount of time spent on the paper chase and bureaucracy associated with existing referral processes, (3) Consultants and booking staff will see a reduction in the administration burden of chasing hospital appointments on behalf of patients, (4) The volume of Did Not Attends (DNAs) will reduce, because patients will agree their date, and consultants will have a more secure referral audit trail.

3.4   Data Collection

The research study began in late 2001, prior to the publication of the Wanless (2002) which, presented the UK government with a review of the long term trends affecting the health service. Our initial interest was to conduct an exploratory-descriptive study in ten NHS hospitals to explore why, 'historically, the NHS has not used or developed IT as a strategic asset in delivering and managing health care' (Department of Health, 2002). The literature suggested two reasons for the low maturity of IT in health care. First, past governments had under-invested in IT which had resulted in pockets of excellence in specific clinical or administrative settings (i.e. radiology systems and patient administration systems) rather than across the NHS as a whole (NAO, 2006 Second, the more recent tendency of NHS management to jump on management bandwagons (Willcocks & Currie W.L., 1997) had produced mixed results with many examples of failure and disappointment (Heathfield, Pitty, & Hanka, 1998).

Our reading of the IS and general management literature on health care unveiled few longitudinal studies, which systematically and rigorously examined how IT systems were introduced and changed over time. There were no studies that examined inter-organizational relationships between different constituents in the adoption and diffusion of IT systems (i.e. government agencies, NHS executives, hospital trusts, IT suppliers and patients). Most of the studies were descriptive and lacked an historical dimension. The existing literature on IS in health care was largely a-theoretical, with most contributions reporting the findings of a specific IT project implementation using simple success and failure criteria.

One of the most significant contributions was Scott et al.'s (2000) study on institutional change within health care organizations, conducted in the US. These authors suggest that, 'the field of health care services...presents a marvellous opportunity to examine an institutional arena undergoing rapid, even 'profound' change' (Scott et al., 2000, p. xvii). This empirical work tracks the changes occurring over half a century in the health care delivery system of one metropolitan area, the San Francisco Bay Area. Although this investigation is limited to explaining the developments in a single, large, but geographically limited region, the authors' claim the effects of institutional environments are not restricted to local arenas, but have repercussions for other regions.

Using this relevant and wide-ranging study as a backdrop for our own research into the UK health care system, we recognized that it was important to extend our empirical enquiry for two reasons. First, exploratory-descriptive case studies on a single organization or site (i.e. an NHS hospital) would not elicit in-depth and rich data to develop any meaningful analysis and conclusions on how IT was being deployed and managed. Second, the introduction of a large-scale IT-enabled change program needed to be researched at the wider societal, organizational field and individual levels, covering an extended period of time, to understand the component processes of institutionalization (Tolbert & Zucker, 1996).

Three methods of data collection were adopted. First, the researchers assembled a range of academic, government and industry studies on the health care sector.

These studies were not restricted to the UK only, but included articles and reports on health care services in many countries, regions and locations. This material proved invaluable for eliciting and understanding how institutional logics surrounding UK health care have changed over several decades. Second, we attended various trade fairs, conference, workshops and exhibitions on health care. Some of these events were focused on general topics (i.e. IT in health care, patient services, hospital management and professional best practice), with others more focused upon specific activities (i.e. the NPfIT, presentation of the Wanless Report, IT strategy). These events generated many useful research contacts. Third, we engaged in primary data collection, where 125 interviews were conducted with a range of constituents (i.e. health service professionals and administrators, clinicians, doctors, patients, IT service providers, and politicians). The majority of interviews were with health service professionals (i.e. NHS hospital executives, managers, administrators) engaged in the implementation of the NPfIT.

Ten UK NHS hospitals were selected for case studies. A semi-structured interview schedule was used to enable interviewees to expand on their answers. This method of data collection was critical for allowing interviewees to raise additional themes, issues and concerns that they felt were important to the research study. Interviews with respondents took place over a four-year period. Most of the interviews lasted around two hours. The interviews at the NHS hospitals were tape-recorded and the tapes were transcribed. Respondents were sent a transcript of the interview to verify it was a true account of what was discussed. Any errors were corrected. Since some of the interview content is politically contentious, the interviewees asked for themselves and their NHS hospitals to retain their anonymity (Table 1).

The open-ended and semi-structured interviews were conducted during the first four years of the NPfIT project implementation, part of which was the negotiation of contracts to the service providers. Multiple informants were interviewed both

Table 1 Primary and secondary data collection

Method	Type of data	Data source	Number
Primary Sources	Interview Schedule (February 2002-May 2006)	Open-ended and semi-structured interviews carried out in the UK with 10 NHS hospitals with clinicians, managers and administrators	125 interviews
Secondary Sources	Government Reports/ websites	Department of Health, Connecting for Health, Hospital sites	35
	Newspaper articles	Financial Times, Other 'Broadsheet' daily newspapers, Local newspapers, NHS news	630
	Hospital Reports	Annual Reports	10

within the ten NHS hospitals and with other constituents. During the first year of interviews, the scope of the study was extended as it was important to elicit data and information from a wider range of respondents engaged in the implementation of the NPfIT. These included, IT service firms bidding for public sector IT contracts and doctors in general practice (external to the NHS hospitals). Respondents from IT service firms offered critical insights into the political and procurement processes within the NHS and public sector more generally. GPs offered useful insights about the communication channels underpinning the NPfIT.

3.5 *Data Analysis*

The three methods of data collection required an organized and methodical approach to data analysis. NPfIT, as a high profile innovation in health care, fuelled prolific media coverage with both positive and negative reports giving contradictory and mixed messages about the innovation at different periods. We therefore concur with others that not less than three years is required to gain some indication of how an innovation brings about organizational change (Greenwood & Hinings, 1996; Nadler & Tushman, 1989).

The data were analysed as follows: First we read the government reports about the NHS in chronological order. The key policy aims and objectives of these reports were recorded on a database. By organizing the data in chronological order, it was possible to pinpoint key policy changes and initiatives to introduce IT. For example, the internal market of the late 1980s saw an increase in outsourcing contracts in the NHS, moving from traditional, 'blue-collar' work like cleaning and refuse disposal to 'white-collar' IT work. A comparative analysis of government reports further showed that contemporary ideas about 'patient choice' were 'borrowed' and adapted from previous policy documents such as 'patients first' in 1979. The same process was followed with the hospital annual reports and other secondary-source material on the history of the NHS covering the four-year period of the study.

Second, we organized the transcripts from the interviews under specific categories or themes. For example, where respondents talked about the history of technical change in the NHS, we included this material under the category of 'IT history'. This data extended beyond a technical discussion of IT to include how government and NHS policy-making for IT had changed over the years. Our analysis of this data suggested that technology was increasingly becoming politicised as government saw it as both a vehicle to drive through change, as well as a vote winner. Since new sources of material were increasingly available, we noted any changes in policy statements from government and NHS organizations in relation to their information systems strategy. In addition, we recorded the key events over the four-year period in relation to the progress of the NPfIT and more specifically, the Choose and Book system. This provided critical insights into how the rationale and rhetoric underwent significant changes within the period, as politicians changed the functional and technical specification of the system (NAO, 2006).

4 Analysis and Discussion

The NHS in England is responsible for health care delivery and serves around 50 million citizens, and is cost-free at the point of delivery. It was created in the post-war period by a parliamentary act initiated by the Labour government following a national health care review. The past six decades have witnessed periods of some stability, as well as profound change in the NHS. Successive governments have introduced numerous policies designed to regulate and monitor all aspects of NHS care and service provision. From the early 1950s, policy makers were concerned to improve administration largely through a command and control system of organization. But as the NHS continued to consume large resources, successive governments focused their attention on policies designed to make the NHS more efficient and effective. This has seen many new players entering the organizational field of health care, as attempts have been made to adopt and adapt the methods of the private sector for the public services. New institutional logics have accompanied these changes, although our research suggests that while some represent new and untested visions, ideas and beliefs, others are merely re-interpretations of past logics. Described as a 'monolithic organization' (Mohan, 2002) the NHS routinely experiences tensions between government, hospital managers, health care professionals, external contractors and patients. Conflicting stories fuel the media with endless negative interpretations about policy issues, performance, service delivery and occasionally, patient deaths in hospitals caused by human error. A core finding from our study of the NPfIT shows that tensions emanating from the collision of contradictory institutional logics conspire to make introducing large-scale innovation and change difficult and challenging.

4.1 From Professional Dominance to Market Mechanisms

The creation of the NHS was founded upon an institutional logic to provide socialized medicine to all citizens (see Table 2). From its inception, the NHS was funded by the taxpayer where clinicians were predominantly concerned with providing a professional service to their patients. The role of patients was inherently passive, as they deferred to the expert role and judgment of clinicians (Fennel, 1980). Clinicians were guided by normative logics of medical professionalism where the doctor–patient relationship was the most important component in the system (Reay & Hinings, 2005). Between 1960 and 1975 expenditure on health care increased in OECD countries to around 8%, although it was around 4% in the UK. This period was described as the 'golden age of social expenditure in western economies' (Webster, 2002, p. 70).

Over a period of four decades up till the late 1970s, an era of professional dominance prevailed in the NHS. Government decisions about policy, practice and procedures in health care were negotiated with professional bodies, with structure and

Table 2 Major healthcare policy initiatives and their dominant institutional logics

Time period	Healthcare policy initiatives	Dominant institutional logics
1945–1959	The National Health Service Bill and White Paper (1945)	Creation of socialised medicine. Nationalization and Regionalization of the hospital service. Free healthcare at the point of delivery. The NHS is the 'most civilised achievement of modern government'. Structure of NHS seen as centralised command and control systems. Clinicians focusing upon clinical rather than administrative and managerial concerns
1960–1975	In OECD group of countries, average rate of expansion in social expenditure was 8%. In UK it was below 4%	'The Golden age of social expenditure in Western economies' (Webster, 2002, p. 70)
1976	'Priorities for Health and Social Services'	Consultation paper which called for a shift away from hospital treatment to primary care
1979–1991	Conservative Govt.	
1979	'Patients First' (White Paper)	Need for radical management reform in the NHS. Looked at structure and management with emphasis on devolving responsibility to local units of management. Claimed 'too much administration and not enough management'. Advocated 'cutting red tape' and developing consensus management
1982–1985	New Public Management	Era of Management Reforms. Apply methods and practices of the private sector to the public services
1982	Financial Management Initiative	Focus upon performance measurement, cost control and efficiency. Greater auditing of NHS expenditure
1983	The Griffiths Report	Reconstitute healthcare management. Replace consensus management with a system of general management applying at regional, district and unit levels within the NHS. Develop a management board. GPs to become more involved in budgets and commissioning services to enable care to be built around community services
1986	Resource Management Initiative	Involve clinicians and nurses in the efficiency drive
1987	Promoting Better Health	Advocates GPs, nurses and dentists to be given more control of funds to set up their own services
1989	Working for Patients	Unveiled proposals for the internal market. Increased competition would engender greater efficiency and consumer satisfaction. Separate the running of hospitals from their financing. Introduction of purchaser/provider split and self governing NHS Hospital Trusts. 'The most far reaching reform of the NHS in its forty year history' (Webster, 2002, p. 190)
1990–1995		'Business process-reengineering'
1996	Choice and Opportunity	Called for alternative providers to become involved in primary care and end GP monopoly. More involvement of private sector firms in NHS community services
1997	Labour Govt.	

(continued)

Table 2 (continued)

Time period	Healthcare policy initiatives	Dominant institutional logics
1997	The New NHS	Advocate integrated care. Abolish GP fund-holding. Set up primary care groups (to be called Trusts) to build up care around community services. Replace the internal market with one that is partnership and performance driven. Increase in admin costs from 5% to 12% of the NHS budget, with some managers aiming for 17% (Webster, 2002, p. 203). Need to create 'a modern and dependable NHS'; 'a third-way of running the NHS', and to 'renew and improve the NHS through evolutionary change rather than organizational upheaval'
1998–2002	Information for Health (Sept 1998)	"The challenge for the NHS is to harness the information revolution and use it to benefit patients." (UK Prime Minister, July 1998)
	Building the Information Core: Implementing the NHS Plan (Jan 2001)	
		"To put in place over the next seven years the people, the resources, the culture and the processes necessary to ensure" (Information for Health, 1998)
	Delivering 21st Century IT support for the NHS (June 2002)	
		"To improve patient choice and the quality and convenience of care by ensuring that those who give and receive care have the right information at the right time" (Wanless, 2002)
	Securing our future health: taking a long-term view (Wanless, 2002) National Program for IT	
2005–2006	Patient Choice 'Choose and Book' system	Choice of provider at the point of referral.
		Patients value having a choice of provider. Choice does not mean any reduction in the importance of clinical advice and judgement. The choices that patients will be offered will be in the bounds of what is clinically appropriate

systems remaining largely in place. Clinicians practiced under relative autonomy and freedom. A dominant logic during this era was about quality of care, as determined by clinicians not government or patients. The medical profession was centrally committed to the quality of care, using this logic as an important justification to resist any attempts by some to impose 'corporate' or market values on health care.

Quality of service and how services were administered were under the direction of clinicians as gatekeeper to the system (Reay & Hinings, 2005). Another important logic concerned a *public service ethos,* as NHS staff offered served their patients for the public good rather than as an exercise for profit-maximisation.

Against a background of relative stability for three decades, the end of the 1970s saw some major changes in health care policy. First, the conservative government came to power and introduced some radical reforms for the NHS. A White Paper, entitled, 'Working for Patients' looked at the structure and management of the NHS. The report suggested 'too much administration in the NHS and not enough management'. It advocated the development of 'consensus management' where responsibility would be devolved to local units of management.

Second, a more fundamental institutional logic was emerging in the form of the 'New Public Management'. Health care was witnessing some fundamental changes to ideology, policy and practice. Continuing the policies of a previous conservative government in the early 1970s, the Thatcher government (1979–1991) introduced the ethos of private sector economics and control to govern the health care system. The Financial Management Initiative (1982) called for greater auditing of NHS expenditure, with the objective of improving performance measurement and monitoring. The following year saw the publication of the Griffiths Report (1983) which aimed to 'reconstitute health care management'. This report argued that 'consensus management' should be replaced with a system of general management at regional, district and unit levels within the NHS. The Resource Management Initiative (1986) developed the ideas espoused in the previous report by suggesting clinicians and other NHS staff, i.e. nurses, should become involved in the government's efficiency drive. Promoting Better Health (1987) further developed the theme that GPs, nurses and dentists be given more control of funds to set up their own services.

Against a background of logics that suggested moving from a centralized to a decentralized organization structure for the NHS, Working for Patients (1989) unveiled proposals to establish what has now become controversially known as the 'internal market'. Under this system, the NHS would be exposed to increased competition with the purpose of increasing efficiency and patient satisfaction. By separating the running of hospitals from their financing by introducing the purchaser/provider split, hospitals would become more accountable for their performance. These changes represented some of the most far reaching reforms of the NHS in its history (Webster, 2002).

Throughout the 1980s and 1990s, a proliferation of 'management methods and practices' were introduced by increasing numbers of management consultants and advisors hired to reform the NHS (Asoh, Rivers, McCleary, & Sarvela, 2005). Management fads and panaceas were adopted in the form of 'business process re-engineering' and 'change management' (McNulty & Ferlie, 2004; Willcocks & Currie W.L., 1997). In conjunction with some hospitals adopting radical as opposed to evolutionary change, the government published a paper on 'Choice and Opportunity in 1996 calling for alternative providers to become involved in primary care with the aim of ending the GP monopoly in this area. Again, more private sector involvement was encouraged to work with the NHS to develop a range of community services.

Following the change to a Labour government in 1997, 'the New NHS' was swiftly published which aimed to develop integrated care. It was proposed to replace the internal market with one that was 'partnership and performance driven'. This 'third-way' approach was intended to create a 'modern and dependable NHS'. But like the previous government, the use of private sector firms to spearhead this change was equally sought, with the continuing use of external management consultants and advisors.

As government built on the era of managerialism which began in the early 1980s, the move from professional dominance to market mechanisms increasingly fragmented the delivery of health care (Pollack, 2005). The growing popularly and practice of outsourcing (referred to as contracting-out in the 1980s) was transferred from the private sector into the public sector (Burgoyne et al., 1997). This policy was extended to the role of IT in the NHS. In the mid-1990s, the governance structure for IT was decentralized or division-based, although decisions about organizational-wide IT projects remained centralized at the level of government and the NHS Executive. IT divisions were spread across several regional authorities, with medical functions centrally controlled. This precluded many small IT service firms from gaining a foothold in the NHS, as their larger counterparts had the political, organizational and technical capacity to deliver large-scale IT work.

4.2   Extending Market Logics to the Delivery of Information Technology

In the late 1990s, the government recognized the opportunity to use IT to improve the delivery of service within the NHS. After a series of reviews of NHS IT, a more integrated and seamless IT organization was recommended. The NHS Information Authority (NHSIA) embarked on the Integrated Care Report Service (ICRS) project to provide, among other services, a nationwide electronic patient database. A document called 'Information for Health' (1998) advocated a strategic approach for the use of IT in the NHS and specified the need for the complete automation and integration of various patient information databases in the country. Such a system would be commissioned to selected IT service providers at a combined price of $10 billion. Introducing the concept of a national program for IT, a report four years later placed IT at the centre stage in achieving government policy to modernize the NHS.

The report discussed the transformational attributes of IT and conveyed the 'vision', 'strategy', 'delivery' and 'risk analysis and management' for delivering '21st Century IT Support for the NHS' (Department of Health, 2002). Thus, 'It is widely accepted that the NHS Plan to improve care and services in the NHS depends on a number of transformations in quality, speed and capacity of the organization. Information technology and the electronically stored information it handles are key enablers of some of this transformation. With modern IT, information can be captured once and used many times, working practices can be modernized and communications speeded up' (DoH, p. 3).

Institutional logics to fuel the market oriented approach to transforming the NHS through IT depended on extending the number of suppliers which would transact with government agencies. While this may increase the degree of isomorphism in the field of health care, our findings unveil a complex scenario. From historical data and interviews with a range of clinicians and IT staff, it was apparent that IT had developed in the NHS as a decentralized and fragmented activity over several decades. While the large teaching hospitals had invested in patient administration systems, radiology systems and other forms of technology, less financially well-endowed hospitals operated with less sophisticated technology.

NPfIT was designed to change this by creating 'ruthless standardization' in health care technology across the NHS. Yet the structural design of how IT would be procured under NPfIT was complex. England was divided into five regional clusters, each of which would invite IT suppliers to bid for large-scale contracts. Since only a small number of major IT suppliers were able to bid for the work, the result was that these suppliers won the contracts in the five regions. Paradoxically, the desire to move from the logics of the 'internal market' to an external market to fuel competition between NHS suppliers produced regional monopolies, as firms like BT, IBM and Accenture won enormous contracts to undertake IT work in some, rather than all of the clusters.

Since these large firms would have a significant influence on the regional clusters they serve, our findings point to a possible outcome of regional isomorphism in health care delivery. This is because hospitals within a cluster would adopt the technology introduced by the key suppliers to that region, which would be different from that supplied in other regions. Interviews with clinicians, managers and administers confirmed that pressures were imposed by suppliers to change their working practices by adapting to the requirements of new IT systems. This had led to some resistance, particularly as respondents criticized the lack of 'user engagement' policies under NPfIT. In the case of 'Choose & Book', resistance was in the form of GPs refusing to adopt the system.

4.3   Deinstitutionalizing Working Practices Using IT-Enabled Innovation

As new entrants into the health care field generated new institutional logics, the task of fulfilling government objectives from NPfIT was highly complex and controversial. Alongside an institutional logic advocating the virtues of innovation and change, the checkered history of introducing large-scale IT-enabled projects into the public services did not bode well for the outcome of NPfIT. Prior research suggests IT project delivery failure rates in the public sector between 60 and 80% (Brown, 2001). Even a recent government report admitted, 'there is a history of failure of major IT-enabled projects, characterized by delay, overspend, poor performance and abandonment' (NAO, 2004, p. 3). The report recommended the solution to these failures was to introduce 'Gateway Reviews' to monitor the progress of IT projects at various stages in the project life-cycle. Such a measure was intended to improve the performance from an annual public sector IT spend of around £2.3bn and rising. While the repercussions from poorly performing IT projects reflect unfavourably on IT staff, a wider analysis of NHS IT projects suggests the explanation for disappointing results extends beyond IT responsibilities. Past case studies indicate that the term 'IT failure' is misguided as the problems which contribute to poor performance are more likely to be explained at the societal and organizational levels (Currie W.L., 1997).

Against a background of perceived and real failure of public sector IT projects, our research into the NPfIT unveiled a wide gap between the strategic intentions of policy-makers and the implementation by managers and staff. Since NPfIT comprised several interlinked large-scale IT systems, our focus was to isolate and track the progress of the Choose and Book system over an extended period of time. Our findings reveal this innovation was originally conceptualized as an electronic booking system. A government report (Department of Health, 2002, p. 12), stated that one element of NPfIT was to provide a 'bookings service', and gave advice and guidance on how this innovation would proceed. Thus, 'The Booked Appointments programme will shortly commence (in 2002) procurement activities to provide a national specification for information brokering, and to provide local sites with a list of accredited suppliers from whom to choose solutions. These suppliers will have been selected on the basis of meeting both the functional requirements and conformance with NHS standards. A small number of 'Enterprise Communities' are about to commence electronic booking to provide experience to support rapid implementation of the proposed framework for Electronic Booking. An accredited list of suppliers will be available by the end of 2002, with implementation and roll-out to follow in 2003 and 2004' (p. 12).

This report paid lip service to the patient's role in the referral and appointment booking procedures since the innovation was originally designed as a 'Choice at Referral' and the 'Electronic Booking Service (EBS)'. But as the government increasingly promoted the logic of patient choice, EBS was changed to 'Choose and Book', with the intention that the patient would become actively involved in the referral and appointment booking process. There are around 10m GP referrals each year.

As the new logics surrounding Choose and Book changed the remit of the NPfIT, the increased scope of the technical and functional specification posed additional challenges to NHS IT staff and clinicians. Unlike the more narrow electronic booking system, Choose and Book now planned to give patients the 'choice of 4–5 services' or appointment options. This would include the choice of hospital, consultant, date and time of the referral appointment. Choose and Book was described as 'a big step in giving patients greater involvement in the choices and decisions about their treatment' and the 'first step towards an NHS where everyone is connected electronically' (http://www.chooseandbook.nhs.uk).

Documents taken from the government website claimed that research found that patients demanded 'more choice' and wanted the 'certainty of having an appointment immediately rather than waiting for a letter'. The traditional system of being referred by a letter from a GP, only to wait for several weeks for an appointment at a potentially inconvenient time which was difficult to change was considered out of date. Choose and Book would eliminate these problems and shorten the referral process. The outcome of changing from an electronic booking system to one which emphasized patient involvement in the referral process was significant, since it would demand a redesign of the software.

As well as revising the EBS to Choose and Book, the NPfIT came under the jurisdiction of a government agency called 'Connecting for Health'. Given the scale and scope of NPfIT, it was not just another public sector IT project, but a large-scale innovation and change program designed to alter the working practices of clinicians, managers and other NHS staff. The report, 'Delivering 21st Century IT Support for the NHS' (2002, p. 9) claimed that, 'a critical element in the strategy to change working practices and encourage adoption of the IT must be changes in the measures used at PCT (primary care trust)/hospital level on the use of IT systems'. The report further noted that, 'We will work with the Modernization Agency to consider a series of pragmatic measures that could be applied to identify those practices/hospitals that are grasping the IT opportunity, and those who are falling behind. We will also consider rewards and sanctions that could be applied to encourage adoption, including 'Best Practice' and 'Early Adopter' rewards that could have tangible financial benefit'.

As our interviews with NHS clinicians, managers and administrators progressed over a four year period, a core finding was that Choose and Book became one of the most controversial elements of NPfIT. Whilst the government tended to under-play the problems of the system, using institutional logics which emphasized the benefits from technological change (see http://www.chooseandbook.nhs.uk), inter-views with GPs confirmed serious problems in the conceptualization of the system. The fundamental issue was that the system architecture had been developed 'top-down' with insufficient user engagement. Many clinicians were also concerned about the financial cost of Choose and Book, particularly as many hospitals were experiencing serious shortfalls in their annual financial budgets. One GP at County Hospital summed up many of the concerns raised in the media about the shortcom-ings of Choose and Book,

> GPs are sometimes accused of not wanting to embrace new technology, but this is untrue. Many GPs are extremely proficient in using IT. The trouble with Choose and Book is that it has been imposed by government and IT suppliers without a real understanding of how GPs work. In my experience, the patient wants their GP to advise them on referral choices – they trust the GP to make the right decision. I have no problem with patients wanting to get involved in this process but the average GP cannot spend large amounts of time in an advisory role. Also, we tend to suggest hospitals and consultants that we know – rather than selecting them from a long list of possibilities. This has never been a problem in my 30 years experience until now!.

For Choose and Book to become a practical reality, the existing working practices of GPs would need to become deinstitutionalized. Whereas the original electronic appointment booking system was uncontroversial, the extended scope of Choose and Book with the involvement of patients was not embraced by many GPs as well as patients. The traditional 'passive' role of patients had become institutionalized. To deinstitutionalize the existing doctor/patient relationship could not be achieved simply by imposing an IT system, despite government policies to encourage 'patient choice'.

4.4   Isomorphic Change from Disruptive Technology

By introducing technologies that could produce disruptive change, the government hoped that hospitals would seek to replicate the policies and practices of other, more successful hospitals. An evaluation scheme had been implemented to score the performance of hospitals on a 1–3 point scale. Replication would engender greater homogeneity within the organizational field (Dimaggio & Powell, 1983). However, our findings reveal that Choose and Book constituted a technology surrounded by uncertainty and ambiguity within the field of health care, where the rate of isomorphic change was reduced. Coercive pressures from government for hospitals to implement Choose and Book through either incentives or sanctions represented new institutional logics that were in direct conflict with past logics that valued professional dominance.

Mimetic pressures where uncertainty is a powerful force that encourages imitation was met with counter-productive actions and behaviour as clinicians and hospital managers questioned the value of technology over expenditure on other key areas, notably, front-line patient services. This was demonstrated in cases where Primary Care Trusts (PCTs), having initially refused drug treatments to patients, responded to negative media coverage by imitating the behaviour of other PCTs which gave their patients the same drug. No examples were found where imitative behaviour extended to Choose and Book or other technologies, especially since technology was perceived as a comparatively low priority by NHS managers. In fact, a PCT in one area found that GPs were vehemently opposed to Choose and Book, preferring instead to explore a referral management centre as one option.

Normative pressures to adopt technology were further weakened by the conflicts between past and present institutional logics which emphasised medical professionalism and market mechanisms respectively. At one level, clinicians were deeply critical of the centrist approach to introducing new technology under the remit of NPfIT. Between 2004 and 2006, media coverage on Choose and Book became more critical as the opinions and views of clinicians were increasingly sought. At another level, government agencies and websites were keen to promote NPfIT and its various components in a positive light, attempting to eclipse negative stories with the latest statistics on performance targets. Whilst the polarity of views about Choose and Book continued to circulate throughout the media, the government was forced to admit in May 2006 that NPfIT was over budget and two years behind schedule (Financial Times, 30 May, 2006).

4.5   Theorizing the Institutionalization and Deinstitutionalization of Health care Delivery

From our historical and empirical data, we are able to generate new insights into the processes and logics underpinning the institutionalization and deinstitutionalization of health care delivery. Our study builds on prior theoretical models on the processes of institutionalization which follow a linear path of how innovations progress through distinct stages of habitualization, objectification and sedimentation (Tolbert & Zucker, 1996) or begin by precipitating jolts before entering stages of deinstitutionalization, preinstitutionalization, theorization, diffusion and reinstitutionalization (Greenwood et al., 2002). In this section, we unbundle some of the pressures arising from attempts to deinstitutionalize existing institutionalized practices. From our data analysis, we develop a model that contains a range of factors which may constrain or prevent institutionalized practices becoming deinstitutionalized over time.

Our model depicts the tensions which exist when coercive, mimetic and normative pressures which lead to isomorphic change come into conflict with political, functional and social pressures for deinstitutionalization. While pressures for institutionalization and deinstitutionalization are two sides of the same coin, our analytical model conceptualizes these processes as highly challenging, as competing and contradictory pressures conspire to make the outcome from innovative change difficult to predict (Fig. 1).

As a highly institutionalized field, health care has witnessed isomorphic change where coercive, mimetic and normative pressures (Dimaggio & Powell, 1983) have resulted in stable and persistent working practices with clinicians experiencing relative autonomy and control over the running of the NHS between the 1950s and late 1980s. In parallel, we observe that political, functional and social pressures (Oliver, 1992) comprise the antecedents to deinstitutionalization. Our historical and empirical data

Fig. 1 Institutionalization and deinstitutionalization of working practices within health care

show that successive government initiatives over the past three decades have promoted the logic of market forces to replace the command and control structure of the earlier health care era. But past and present institutional logics come into direct conflict, leading to structural and cultural tensions, as different stakeholders compete in what is described as a 'battlefield' within an organizational field (Dimaggio, 1983).

Our model depicts these tensions as contradictory or incompatible manifestations, as institutional logics are introduced and even re-introduced into health care by a growing number of stakeholders, all of whom serve their own political and professional agenda. Reinforcing other institutionalist accounts, our data suggest that an organization may respond to the imposition of a new innovation with either isomorphic actions (i.e. actions that are consistent with those of other legitimate actors in the institutional environment) or non-isomorphic actions (i.e. actions that depart from what is considered legitimate in the institutional environment) (George, Chattopadhyay, Sitkin, & Barden, 2006, p. 348).

On one hand, top-down, government-led innovation was an attempt to deinstitutionalize the entrenched working practices of clinicians. But this was strongly resisted. The lack of clinical engagement between politicians and NHS staff about the Choose and Book system, for example, produced a counter-productive response, as clinicians became more critical about the financial and practical implications of technical change. As a powerful institutional group, clinicians could appeal to a past era where professional dominance, infused with logics which preserve the doctor–patient relationship, were more important than the 'market-driven' agenda of short-term politicians.

On the other hand, the perceived poor performance of the public services over several decades, gave legitimacy and support to the logic that 'something must be done' to improve the NHS. With a history of disappointing results from IT investment, with many cases of 'IT disasters', politicians, together with the IT industry, were keen to show that large-scale investment was a key factor in 'modernizing' the public services. As the proliferation of new entrants (i.e. IT suppliers) resulted in further fragmenting the field of health care, the views of clinicians, managers and administrators were joined by many more stakeholders (i.e. the media and patients). This produced a much more complex picture, as the structural and cultural homogeneity of an earlier health care era, where clinicians and NHS managers, as the gatekeepers of the system, was replaced by greater heterogeneity. This was shown by an increase in competing logics about health care delivery where politicians stepped up their use of external service providers to fulfil their policy agenda (i.e. more outsourcing of health care services) and also by encouraging the public to become more involved in decisions about their health.

However, competing institutional logics did little to ease the path of innovation. As prior work from institutional theory demonstrates, innovations are subject to a process of theorization before they are either accepted or rejected in the wider community (Currie W.L., 2004; Swanson & Ramiller, 1997). The theorization of NPfIT was influenced by both past and present institutional logics that contained mutually exclusive and contradictory messages. Logics emanating from the late 1980s about creating an internal market for health care and more recent logics about patient choice were contradicted by past logics which emphasized the dominant role of the clinician and the passive role of the patient (Fennel, 1980). The difficulties of changing this historical relationship by imposing an IT system was underestimated by the designers and implementers of the system as they came to realize that coercive pressures on GPs to adopt Choose and Book were met with strong resistance, not only by the GPs themselves, but by the powerful professional bodies to which they belong. This suggested that the isomorphic changes that led to stability and persistence in the working practices of clinicians could only be deinstitutionalized through non-isomorphic change which extended beyond coercive measures.

But despite attempts by government to provide financial incentives for clinicians to adopt IT systems, this was not sufficient to win their political support. This is because clinicians had to reconcile competing logics. For example, if presented with the choice of purchasing an IT system or front-line patient services, clinicians were likely to choose the latter, as politically-driven directives (i.e. NPfIT) came into conflict with social pressures (i.e. public perception about the availability of health care services, such as treatment and drugs). New technology was therefore a secondary consideration and one which could not gain priority over other, more traditional aspects of health care delivery.

Our study on introducing large-scale innovation into health care extends the literature on institutional theory by unveiling the tensions in the theorization process between different stakeholders. A core finding shows that, as an organizational field becomes increasingly fragmented, conflicting logics conspire to derail the legitimation of a new innovation. Powerful normative logics that stress the professional role of clinicians collide with equally powerful coercive logics from politicians that emphasize the need to introduce performance measurement into health care. This was further complicated where government invites patients to increase their participation through a logic of 'patient choice'. Our conceptual model thus suggests a more iterative approach to adoption and diffusion of large-scale IT innovation, rather than a more linear, stage model, where IT innovations follow a pathway leading to full institutionalization. Also, institutionalization and deinstitutionalization were not final stages since logics that supported persistence and stability within health care were constantly challenged by competing logics that supported change and disruption.

5   Conclusion

The aim of this study was to investigate the introduction of a large-scale IT innovation in the highly institutionalized field of health care over a four year period. NPfIT provides a rich source of primary and secondary data to gain an understanding of how potentially disruptive technology requires the deinstitutionalization of institutionalized working practices, if politically-driven innovation is to succeed. Our findings reinforce prior research which shows how institutional logics in health care have shifted from a previous era which emphasized professional dominance

(Scott et al., 2000) or medical professionalism (Reay & Hinings, 2005) to the more recent emphasis upon market mechanisms, where the methods and practices of the private sector are imposed on health care sector to achieve greater efficiency and effectiveness (Pollack, 2005). However, we find that dominant logics from the past era continue to influence and shape current thinking within health care, particularly as clinicians and other health care workers challenge government attempts to 'modernize' health care through introducing market reforms.

Illustrating this point, our data that tracked the highly controversial Choose and Book system found that past and present institutional logics conspired to produce contradictory forces in the field of health care. Recent attempts to treat the patient as 'consumer' were in direct conflict with the patient as a 'passive' recipient of health care services, particularly as 'physicians and hospital administrators are the actual consumers' (Fennel, 1980). Policies to use innovation as a tool to change the relationship between doctor and patient were therefore misguided, as politically-driven was resisted by clinically-driven institutionalized agendas.

In developing our model to unbundle some of the pressures for institutionalization and deinstitutionalization, we concur with previous work that suggests that radical innovation is the 'product of processes that are oscillatory and iterative', rather than following a sequential and linear pattern (Greenwood & Hinings, 1996, p. 1047). Further, we concur that, although institutional arrangements are unlikely to change abruptly, any sudden change or environmental jolts (Meyer et al., 1990) are likely to stem from pressure from a previous era (Scott et al., 2000). While our study found little evidence of past institutional logics acting as an enabler of innovation and change, logics emanating from an era of professional dominance were in stark contrast to the 'market' agenda. The dynamics of imposing top-down innovation on the NHS was, in turn, met with some resistance by NHS staff, as witnessed by the many obstacles and problems which beset the implementation of the NPfIT.

In response, government agencies produced optimistic accounts of the progress of NPfIT, which resulted in mixed messages and increased confusion. This was further exacerbated by additional inputs from the media and the public, particularly as expenditure on IT was seen as a lower priority than other frontline health care services. In summary, we suggest that to understand the inter-organizational dynamics of a large-scale innovation in a highly institutionalized setting such as health care, future research may consider the conflicting forces that produce isomorphic and non-isomorphic change. As the NHS example shows, while there were significant coercive pressures to force through IT-enabled change, there were equally strong normative pressures to resist and even circumvent the change process. IS researchers studying market driven reforms more generally in the not-for-profit sectors, need therefore to understand how historical influences and policy initiatives exert pressures on fields, organizations and individuals in interpreting, legitimating and mobilizing IT innovation. This becomes even more relevant since much of the outsourcing literature, more specifically, shows that IT outcomes often produce unintended consequences when compared with explicit organizational and managerial strategies.

References

Abrahamson, E. (1996). Management fashion. *Academy of Management Review, 21*(1), 254–285.

Asoh, D. A., Rivers, P. A., McCleary, K. J., & Sarvela, P. (2005). Entrepreneurial propensity in health care: Models and propositions for empirical research. *Health Care Management Review, 30*, 212–219.

Bloomfield, B. P. (1991). The role of information systems in the UK National Health Service: Action at a distance and the fetish of calculation. *Social Studies of Science, 21*, 701–734.

Brown, T. (2001). Modernization or failure? IT development projects in the UK public sector. *Financial Accountability and Management, 17*(4), 363–381.

Burgoyne, J. G., Brown, D. H., Hindle, A., & Mumford, M. J. (1997). Multi-disciplinary identification of issues associated with 'contracting' in market-orientated health service reforms. *British Journal of Management, 8*, 39–49.

Connecting for Health. Business Plan. (2004). Available form: http://www.connectingforhealth.nhs.uk.

Currie, W. (1997). Computerising the stock exchange: A comparison of two information systems. *New Technology, Work and Employment, 12*(2), 75–83.

Currie, W. L. (2004). The organizing vision of application service provision: A process-oriented analysis. *Journal of Information and Organization, 14*, 237–267.

Currie, W. L., & Guah, M. (2006). IT-enabled healthcare delivery: The UK National Health Service. *Information Systems Management, 23*, 7–21.

Department of Health. (2002). *Delivering 21st century IT support for the NHS*. London: Department of Health, NHS.

Dimaggio, P. (1983). State expansion and organizational fields. In R. H. Hall & R. E. Quinn (Eds.), *Organizational theory and public policy* (pp. 147–161). Beverley Hills, CA: Sage.

DiMaggio, P. J., & Powell, W. W. (1983). The iron cage revisited: Institutional isomorphism and collective rationality in organizational fields. *American Sociological Review, 48*(2), 147–160.

DiMaggio, P. J., & Powell, W. W. (1991). Introduction. In W. W. Powell & P. J. DiMaggio (Eds.), *The new institutionalism in organizational analysis*. Chicago: University of Chicago Press.

Fennel, M. L. (1980). The effects of environmental characteristics on the structure of clusters. *Administrative Science Quarterly, 25*, 485–510.

Friedland, R., & Alford, R. R. (1991). Bringing society back in: Symbols, practices, and institutional contradictions. In W. W. Powell & P. J. Dimaggio (Eds.), *The new institutionalism in organizational analysis* (pp. 232–263). Chicago: University of Chicago Press.

George, E., Chattopadhyay, P., Sitkin, S. B., & Barden, J. (2006). Cognitive underpinnings of institutional persistence and change: A framing perspective. *Academy of Management Review, 31*(2), 347–365.

Greenwood, R., & Hinnings, C. R. (1996). Understanding radical organizational change: Bringing together the old and new institutionalism. *Academy of Management Review, 21*, 1022–1054.

Greenwood, R., Suddaby, R., & Hinings, C. R. (2002). Theorizing change: The role of professional associations in the transformation of institutionalized fields. *Academy of Management Journal, 45*(1), 58–80.

Heathfield, H., Pitty, D., & Hanka, R. (1998). Evaluating information technology in health-care: Barriers and challenges. *British Medical Journal, 316*, 1959–1961.

Hendy, J., Reeves, B. C., Fulop, N., Huchings, A., & Masseria, C. (2005). Challenges to implementing the national program for information technology: A qualitiative study. *British Medical Journal, 331*:1–6.

Laing, A., & Hogg, G. (2002). Political exhortation, patient expectation and professional execution: Perspectives on the consumerization of health-care. *British Journal of Management, 13*, 173–188.

McNulty, T., & Ferlie, E. (2004). Process transformation: Limitations to radical organizational change within public service. *Organization Studies, 25*(8), 1389–1412.

Meyer, A. D., Brooks, G. R., & Goes, J. B. (1990). Environmental jolts and industry revolutions: Organizational responses to discontinuous change. *Strategic Management Journal, 11*(Special Issue), 93–110.

Meyer, J. W., & Rowan, B. (1977). Institutionalized organizations: Formal structure as myth and ceremony. *American Journal of Sociology, 83*(2), 340–363.

Mohan, J. (2002). *Planning, markets and hospitals.* London: Routledge.

Nadler, D. A., & Tushman, M. L. (1989). Organizational frame bending: Principles for managing reorientation. *Academy of Management Executive, 3*(33), 194–203.

National Audit Office. (2004). Improving IT procurement. Report by the comptroller and auditor general, HC 877 Session 2003–4: 5 November. London: The Stationary Office.

National Audit Office. (2006). *The national programme for IT in the NHS.* London: The Stationary Office.

Ocasio, W. (1997). Towards an attention-based view of the firm. *Strategic Management Journal, 18*, 187–206.

Oliver, C. (1992). The antecedents of deinstitutionalization. *Organization Studies, 13* (4), 563–588.

Pollock, A. (2005). *NHS plc: The privatisation of our health-care.* London: Verso.

Reay, T., & Hinings, C. R. (2005). Recomposition of an organizational field: Healthcare in alberta. *Organization Studies, 26*(3), 351–384.

Scott, W. R. (2001). *Institutions and organizations.* USA: Sage.

Scott, W. R., Ruef, M., Mendel, P. J., & Caronna, C. A. (2000). *Institutional change and health-care organizations.* Chicago: University of Chicago Press.

Swanson, E. B., & Ramiller, N. C. (1997). The organizing vision in information systems innovation. *Organization Science, 8*(5), 458–474.

Tolbert, P. S., & Zucker, L. G. (1996). The institutionalization of institutional theory. In S. R. Clegg, C. Hardy, & W. R. Nord (Eds.), *Handbook of organization studies* (pp. 175–190). London: Sage.

Wanless, D. (2002). Securing our future health: Taking a long-term view. Final report of an independent review of the long-term resource requirement for the NHS. April. London. http://www.hm-treasury.gov.uk/Consultations_and_Legislation /wanless/consult/wanless_final.cfm.

Webster, C. (2002). *The NHS: A political history.* Oxford: Oxford University Press.

Willcocks, L., & Currie, W. L. (1997). Pursuing the re-engineering agenda in public administration. *Public Administration, 75*(4), 617–650.

Wyatt, J. F. (1998). Four barriers to realising the information revolution in health-care. In J. Lenaghan (Ed.), *Rethinking IT & Health* (pp. 100–122). London: Institute for Public Policy Research.

Zucker, L. G. (1977). The role of institutionalization in cultural persistence, *American Sociological Review, 42*(5), 726–743.

Zucker, L. G. (1983). Organizations as institutions. In S. B. Bacharach (Ed.), *Research in the sociology of organizations* (pp. 1–42). Greenwich, CT: JAI Press.

Index

Printing: Krips bv, Meppel, The Netherlands
Binding: Stürtz, Würzburg, Germany